Documents in World History

Volume II: Since 1500

PEARSON

Prentice
Hall

Upper Saddle River, New Jersey 07458

Copyright 2005 by PEARSON EDUCATION, INC.

Upper Saddle River, New Jersey 07458

ISBN 0-13-177323-2

CONTENTS

PART 14
European Explorations and Expansion

14.1 Kilwa, Mombasa, and the Portuguese: Realities of Empire

The heroic depiction of Portuguese exploration in the "Lusiads" is countered by accounts of the acquisitive brutality which became part-and-parcel of all colonial enterprises. It did not take the Portuguese long to realize their superiority in military technology, and to employ this to their advantage. The prosperous Swahili cities were obvious targets, and moreover held the key to the linkage of Portugal to its commercial concessions in India. The colonial soldier-administrator followed closely on the heels of the merchant-explorer and the missionary, in this instance, in the person of Francisco d'Almeida. D'Almeida's no-nonsense approach included brute force, and in 1505 the cities of Kilwa and Mombasa were sacked. The following account is believed to have been written by Hans Mayr, a German seaman in the service of the Portuguese.

Source: E. Axelson, "South East Africa," 1940; pp. 231–238. Quoted in G.S.P. Freeman-Grenville, *The East African Coast: Selected Documents* (London: Rex Collings, 1974), pp. 105–112.

The Voyage and Acts of Dom Francisco, Viceroy of India, written in the ship *Sam Rafael* of Oporto, captained by Fernan Suarez.

In the year 1505, on 25 March, Tuesday, the feast of the Annunciation of Our Lady, Dom Francisco d'Almeida sailed with a fleet of twenty vessels. There were fourteen large men-of-war and six caravels.

They rounded the Cape of Good Hope on 20 June and were driven away from it seventy leagues. On 2 July there were great storms with thunder, and two men from the flagship and one from the *Lyomarda* fell overboard. On 18 July they sighted land for the first time, 369 leagues beyond the Cape of Good Hope, near the Ylhas Darradeiras, which are thirty leagues from the island of Mozambique. On 19 July they were in sight of Mozambique, and on 2I July they were crossing the shallow waters of Sam Rafael, which are thirty leagues from Kilwa.

On Tuesday, 22 July, they entered the harbour of Kilwa at noon, with a total of eight ships. Immediately on their arrival the Grand-Captain, Dom Francisco d'Almeida, sent Bona Ajuta Veneziano to summon the king. He excused himself from coming, but sent the Grand-Captain gifts instead; They were five goats, a small cow and a large number of coconuts and other fruit.

Next flay the Grand-Captain ordered the ships to have their artillery in readiness. Then the captains, each in his best clothes, and full armour, went in his own boat to lie off the town in the hope that the king would decide to come out. The sheikh, however, sent a message to say that he could not come since he had guests, but, if required, he would send the tribute due to the King of Portugal. This message was brought by a party of five Moors, who were immediately seized.

At dawn on Thursday, 24 July, the vigil of the feast of St. James the Apostle, all went in their boats to the shore. The first to land was the Grand-Captain, and he was followed by the others. They went straight to the royal palace, and on the way only those Moors who did not fight were granted their lives. At the palace there was a Moor leaning out of the window with a Portuguese flag in his hand, shouting: 'Portugal! Portugal!' This flag had been left behind by the admiral [Vasco da Gama] when he had arranged for Kilwa to pay a tribute of 1,500 ounces of gold a year. The Moor was asked to open the door, and, when he did not do so, the door was broken down with axes. They found neither the Moor nor anyone else in the Palace, which was deserted.

In Kilwa there are many strong houses several storeys high. They are built of stone and mortar and plastered with various designs. As soon as the town had been taken without opposition, the Vicar-General and some of the Franciscan fathers came ashore carrying two crosses in procession and singing the Te Deum. They went to the palace, and there the cross was put down and the Grand-Captain prayed. Then everyone started to plunder the town of all its merchandise and provisions.

The town of Kilwa lies on an island around which ships of 500 tons can sail. The island and town have a population of 4,000 people. It is very fertile and produces maize similar to that of Guinea, butter, honey, and wax. On the trees hang beehives like jars of three *almudes* capacity, each closed with woven palm leaves. There are holes through which the bees go in and come out.

There are many trees and palms here and on the mainland, some of them different from those of Portugal. From the island to the mainland the distance is in some places two leagues and in others one.

There are sweet oranges, lemons, vegetables, small onions, and aromatic herbs. They are grown in gardens and watered with water from the wells. Here also grows betel which has leaves like ivy and is grown like peas with sticks at the root for support. The leaf is used by the wealthy Arabs for chewing together with specially prepared limes which look like an ointment. They keep the leaves as if they were to be put on wounds. These leaves make the mouth and teeth very red, but are said to be most refreshing.

There are more black slaves than white Moors here: they are engaged on farms growing maize and other things. There are various types of peas which are produced by plants as high as large pepper trees; when they are ripe, they are gathered and stored. The soil is red, the top layer being sandy; the grass is always green. There are many fat beasts, oxen, cows, sheep, and goats and also plenty of fish; there are also whales which swim round the ships. There is no running drinking water on the island. Near the island there are other small islands which are inhabited. There are many boats as large as a caravel of fifty tons and other smaller ones. The large ones lie aground on the shore and are dragged down to the sea when the people wish to sail them. They are built without nails: the planks are sewn together with rope made from knotted coir from the coconut palm. The same kind of rope is used for the rudder. The boats are caulked with black pitch made from crude incense and resin. They sail from here to Sofala, 255 leagues away.

The palms here do not produce dates but from some of them wine and vinegar are obtained. These come from the palm trees which do not produce coconuts. The coconuts are the size of large melons, and from the fibres inside the shell all kinds of rope are made. Inside the shell is a fruit the size of a large pineapple. It contains half a pint of milk which is very pleasant to drink. When the milk has been drunk the nut is broken and eaten; the kernel tastes like a walnut which is not fully ripe. They dry it and it yields a large quantity of oil.

People here sleep raised above the ground in hammocks made of palm leaves in which only one person can lie.

The Portuguese found here a large quantity of pure drinking water. Flasks of very good perfume are exported from here and a large quantity of glass of all types and all kinds of cotton piece-goods, incense, resin, gold, silver, and pearls. The Grand-Captain ordered the loot to be deposited under seal in a house.

The fortress of Kilwa was built out of the best house there was there. All the other houses round it were pulled down. It was fortified and guns were set in place with everything else a fort needs. Pero Ferreira was left in command of it with eighty men.

The country is not very hot. The men are armed with bows and large arrows, strong shields of palm leaves bound with cotton, and pikes better than those of Guinea. Few swords were seen. They have four catapults for hurling stones but do not yet know the use of gunpowder.

The sea laps the entrance of the fortress at high water near where the ships enter.

When the king fled from Kilwa, the Grand-Captain appointed another, a local Moor beloved by all, whom they took in procession on horseback through the town.

Lime is prepared here in this manner: large logs of wood are piled in a circle and inside them coral limestone is placed; then the wood is burnt. The process after that is the same as in Portugal.

Cotton is found in abundance. It is of good quality and is planted and grows well in the island. The sheep have wool no better than goats. The slaves wear a cotton cloth round the waist and down to the knees; the rest of the body is naked. The white Arabs and slave owners wear two pieces of cotton cloth, one round the waist down to the feet and the other thrown over the shoulders and reaching down as far as where the first cloth is tied.

They have copper coins like our *ceptis,* four being equal to one *real;* Portuguese coins have the same value there as at home. There are no gold coins but the weight of their *mitical* is equal to 460 *reis* in Portugal.

The winter season in Kilwa is from April to September. It is not cold and for this reason the people wear scanty clothes.

The Grand-Captain twice went from one side of the town to the other. Once he saw twenty-five gazelle which had been let loose on the island. There are also many wild cats in the bush.

There are many vaulted mosques, one of which is like that of Cordova. All the upper-class Moors carry a rosary.

MOMBASA

On 9 August the ships left Kilwa for Mombasa, sixty leagues up the coast. The ship Sam Rafael reached there on 14 August, but the Grand-Captain arrived with the other ten ships a day earlier.

The Moors of Mombasa had built a strongpoint with many guns at the entrance of the harbour, which is very narrow. When we entered, the first ship, which was under the command of Gonzalo de Paiva, who was going in front to explore the channel, was fired on by the Moors from both sides. We promptly replied to the fire, and with such intensity that the gunpowder in their strongpoint caught fire. It started burning and the Moors fled, thus allowing the whole fleet to enter and lie at anchor in front of the town. And on that day, the vigil of the feast of the Assumption, the town was bombarded with all the guns on the ships, while the guns of the town replied to our fire.

When the Grand-Captain went ashore he seized a Moor who happened to be a member of the royal household. The Portuguese obtained good information from him.

The first night the fleet arrived in Mombasa there came out on the shore a Spanish Christian who was living there, a gunner by profession and a convert to Islam. He told the Christians to go away and that Mombasa was not like

Kilwa: they would not find people with hearts that could be eaten like chickens as they had done in Kilwa, but that if they were keen to come ashore the people were ready to set about them for their supper. The Grand-Captain, however, offered him his protection and pardon, but he refused.

Mombasa is a very large town and lies on an island from one and a half to two leagues round. The town is built on rocks on the higher part of the island and has no walls on the side of the sea; but on the land side it is protected by a wall as high as the fortress. The houses are of the same type as those of Kilwa: some of them are three storeyed and all are plastered with lime. The streets are very narrow, so that two people cannot walk abreast in them: all the houses have stone seats in front of them, which makes the streets yet narrower.

The Grand-Captain met with the other captains and decided to bum the town that evening and to enter it the following morning. But when they went to burn the town they were received by the Moors with a shower of arrows and stones. The town has more than 600 houses which are thatched with palm leaves: these are collected green for this purpose. In between the stone dwelling-houses there are wooden houses with porches and stables for cattle. There are very few dwelling houses which have not these wooden houses attached.

Once the fire was started it raged all night long, and many houses collapsed and a large quantity of goods was destroyed. For from this town trade is carried on with Sofala and with Cambay by sea. There were three ships from Cambay and even these did not escape the fury of the attack. It was a moonless night.

On Friday 25 August, the feast of the Assumption of Our Lady, the Grand-Captain drew up eight ships on one side of Mombasa. On the other side was his son, Dom Lourenço d'Almeida, with three ships. Early in the morning they all prepared their arms and had breakfast. The Grand-Captain had ordered that all should land as soon as a shot from a big gun was fired. Thus all the boats were waiting ready on the water: when the shot was fired all got quickly on to the shore in very good order. The archers and gunners went ahead of everyone else, all going up the steep ascent into the town. When they entered, they found that some of the houses had been deserted as a result of the fire of the previous night. Further on they found three storeyed houses from which stones were thrown at them. But the stones which were thrown fell against the walls of the very narrow streets, so that much of the force of their fall was lost. There were also many balconies projecting over the streets under which one could shelter.

The Grand-Captain went straight to the royal palace: he was led by the Moor who had been captured on the previous day. He had ordered that no one should enter any of the houses, and that anyone who did so should die. When the Grand-Captain arrived at the palace, Captain Verraudez immediately climbed up the wall and hoisted our flag, shouting: Portugal, Portugal. And there were many Moors killed on the way there.

They saw from there some sixty Moors leaving the town, all dressed in gowns and turbans; they were going towards a palm grove and did not seem in any hurry. Some said that the king was among them. The Christians, however, did not follow them. All the people of the town were taken to this palm grove, and the entrance to it was guarded by more than 500 archers. These archers were all negro slaves of the white Moors, and obedient to their masters in their captivity like those of Kilwa.

The Grand-Captain ordered that the town should be sacked and that each man should carry off to his ship whatever he found: so that at the end there would be a division of the spoil, each man to receive a twentieth of what he found. The same rule was made for gold, silver, and pearls. Then everyone started to plunder the town and to search the houses, forcing open the doors with axes and iron bars. There was a large quantity of cotton cloth for Sofala in the town, for the whole coast gets its cotton cloth from here. So the Grand-Captain got a good share of the trade of Sofala for himself. A large quantity of rich silk and gold embroidered clothes was seized, and carpets also; one of these, which was without equal for beauty, was sent to the King of Portugal together with many other valuables.

When night came the Grand-Captain ordered all the men to a field which lay between the town and the sea. A section of it was allotted to each captain and a watch was set for the night. They were at a distance of a gun shot from the palm grove where the Moors were with their king. On the morning of the 16th they again plundered the town, but because the men were tired from fighting and from lack of sleep, much wealth was left behind apart from what each man took for himself. They also carried away provisions, rice, honey, butter, maize, countless camels and a large number of cattle, and even two elephants. They paraded these elephants in front of the people of the town before they took it, in order to frighten them. There were many prisoners, and white women among them and children, and also some merchants from Cambay.

On Saturday evening the Grand-Captain ordered that all should return to the ships in a disciplined manner, keeping a watch for the Moors as they went on their way. And as the Christians left by one way, so the Moors entered by the other to see what destruction had been done. For the streets and houses were full of dead, who were estimated to be about 1,500.

Dom Fernando de Sà was wounded with an arrow which did not have an iron point. Some of their arrows are made of wood with iron points, others of burnt wood soaked in an unknown poison. Some say the wood itself is poisonous. The arrows with iron points have herbs at the tip, but these are not dangerous, as was evident from those wounded by them.

According to the Moors this town is the most famous of all the coast of Abyssinia. The island is very fertile, and produces a large quantity of sweet oranges, pomegranates, lemons, and sugar cane; all these things are more abundant here than at Kilwa.

All the guns belonging to the town were taken to the ships. They found one old cannon lying in the street which five men could not lift. It was said to have belonged to a ship called *Rey* which had been lost nearby. They also found an anchor which had been stolen from the Admiral Vasco da Gama. Because the Portuguese could not take it the Arabs pointed it out to each other. There were only five Portuguese dead in the battle and many wounded—more by the grace of God than by any act of man.

After returning to the ships they weighed anchor and moved inshore so that the anchors were exposed on dry land at low water. They remained there for ten days. It was very difficult to go out through the narrow entrance and also because there were strong contrary winds blowing. The ship *Lyomarda* lost its rudder and they could not find it again. So they were obliged to make a new one, for which each ship had to give up one of its hooks.

The ship *San Gabriel* arrived on 20 August with its mainmast broken, but the whereabouts of the supply ships was still not known.

Now the King of Mombasa and the King of Malindi were at war, and many of their people had been killed on both sides, the cause of the war being the friendship of the King of Malindi with the King of Portugal. Eventually the King of Mombasa had been defeated by the King of Malindi, and for the present they were friends. So the King of Mombasa wrote the following letter to the King of Malindi:

May God's blessing be upon you, Sayyid Ali! This is to inform you that a great lord has passed through the town, burning it and laying it waste. He came to the town in such strength and was of such cruelty, that he spared neither man nor woman, old nor young, nay, not even the smallest child. Not even those who fled escaped from his fury. He not only killed and burnt men but even the birds of the heavens were shot down. The stench of the corpses is so great in the town that I dare not go there; nor can I ascertain nor estimate what wealth they have taken from the town. I give you these sad news for your own safety.

There were more than 10,000 people in Mombasa, of whom 3,700 were men of military age.

MALINDI

Thence they sailed to Malindi, twenty-five leagues further north. Five leagues outside Malindi they were halted by strong currents and there they met the caravel of Johan Homere, which had captured two islands for Portugal. One of them was 450 leagues beyond the Cape of Good Hope and was uninhabited. They took in firewood and water there.

The other island lies between Kilwa and Mombasa and is known as Zanzibar. As the Moors of this island already knew of the destruction of Kilwa, they presented the captain with provisions and said they were at the service of the King of Portugal. The ship had arrived there on 24 August, and they had taken in water, firewood and meat.

Mogadishu lies on this coast and is 100 leagues from Malindi. It is a large town with plenty of horses....

Questions:
1. *What was the apparent reason for the attack on Kilwa? What were the results? How did d'Almeida change Kilwa's government?*
2. *How did the situation at Mombasa differ from that at Kilwa?*
3. *What orders did d'Almeida give at Mombasa?*
4. *What was Malindi's decision?*

14.2   Vasco da Gama, Journey to India

Vasco da Gama (1460?–1524) was one of the great mariners who helped Portugal take the lead in the era of explorations. In 1497, with four ships and 168 men, da Gama sailed down the west coast of Africa, rounded the Cape of Good Hope, fought Muslims along the way, and reached India. He did not return to Lisbon until 1499, after a voyage of two years and two months, but he brought back pepper, cloves, nutmeg, cinnamon, and precious stones. Shortly after da Gama's return, another explorer, Pedro Cabral, assembled a fleet and set out for India. According to the official account, his ships were blown far off their course and on April 22, 1500, they sighted the coast of Brazil. Although with this discovery the Portuguese Crown could then boast of an empire and stake out its claim in America, Portugal devoted far more interest and attention to its growing empire in the East. The following reading is an excerpt from da Gama's journal of his voyage to India in 1497–1499.

Source: From *Portuguese Voyages*, 1498–1663, ed. Charles David Ley (London: J. M. Dent & Sons Ltd; New York: E. P. Dutton & Co., 1947), pp. 27–38, passim. Reprinted by permission.

The city of Calicut is inhabited by Christians. They are of tawny complexion. Some of them have big beards and long hair, whilst others clip their hair short or shave the head, merely allowing a tuft to remain on the crown as a sign that they are Christians. They also wear moustaches. They pierce the ears and wear much gold in them. They go naked down to the waist, covering their lower extremities with very fine cotton stuffs. But it is only the most respectable who do this, for the others manage as best they are able.[1]

The women of this country, as a rule, are ugly and of small stature. They wear many jewels of gold around the neck, numerous bracelets on their arms, and rings set with precious stones on their toes. All these people are well disposed and apparently of mild temper. At first sight they seem covetous and ignorant.

When we arrived at Calicut, the captain-major sent two men to the King with a message, informing him that an ambassador had arrived from the King of Portugal with letters.

The king presented the bearers of this message with much fine cloth. He sent word to the captain bidding him welcome.

A pilot accompanied our two men, with orders to take us to a place called Pandarani, below the place [Capua] where we anchored at first. At this time we were actually in front of the city of Calicut. We were told that the anchorage at the place to which we were to go was good, whilst at the place we were then it was bad, with a stony bottom, which was quite true; and, moreover, that it was customary for the ships which came to this country to anchor there for the sake of safety. We ourselves did not feel comfortable, and the captain-major had no sooner received this royal message than he ordered the sails to be set, and we departed. We did not, however, anchor as near the shore as the king's pilot desired.

When we were at anchor, a message arrived informing the captain-major that the king was already in the city. At the same time the king sent a bale [governor], with other men of distinction, to Pandarani, to conduct the captain-major to where the king awaited him. This bale is always attended by two hundred men armed with swords and bucklers. As it was late when this message arrived, the captain-major deferred going.

On the following morning, they took us to a large church, and this is what we saw:

The body of the church is as large as the monastery, all built of hewn stone and covered with tiles. At the main entrance rises a pillar of bronze as high as a mast, on the top of which was perched a bird, apparently a cock. In addition to this, there was another pillar as high as a man, and very stout. In the center of the body of the church rose a chapel, all built of hewn stone, with a bronze door sufficiently wide for a man to pass, and stone steps leading up to it. Within this sanctuary stood a small image which they said represented Our Lady. Along the walls, by the main entrance, hung seven small bells. In this church the captain-major said his prayers, and we with him.

We did not go within the chapel, for it is custom that only certain servants of the church should enter. These men wore some threads passing over the left shoulder and under the right arm, in the same manner as our deacons wear the stole. They threw holy water over us, and gave us some white earth, which the Christians of this country are in the habit of putting on their foreheads, breasts, around the neck, and on the forearms. They threw holy water upon the captain-major and gave him some of the earth, which he gave in charge of someone, giving them to understand that he would put it on later.

Many other saints were painted on the walls of the church, wearing crowns. They were painted variously, with teeth protruding an inch from the mouth, and four or five arms.

The captain, on entering, saluted in the manner of the country: by putting the hands together, then raising them towards Heaven, as is done by Christians when addressing God, and immediately afterwards opening them and shutting the fists quickly.

And the captain told the king that he was the ambassador of a king of Portugal, who was lord of many countries and the possessor of great wealth of every description, exceeding that of any king of these parts; that for a period of sixty years his ancestors had annually sent out vessels to make discoveries in the direction of India, as they knew that there were Christians kings there like themselves. This, he said, was the reason which induced them to order this country to be discovered, not because they sought for gold or silver, for of this they had such abundance that they needed not what was to be found in this country. He further stated that the captains sent out traveled for a year or two, until their provisions were exhausted, and then returned to Portugal, without having succeeded in making the desired discovery. There reigned a king now whose name was Dom Manuel, who ordered him not to return to Portugal until he should have discovered the king of the Christians, on pain of having his head cut off. That a letter had been entrusted to him to be presented in case he succeeded in discovering him, and, finally, he had been instructed to say by word of mouth that he [the king of Portugal] desired to be his friend and brother.

In reply to this the king said that he was welcome; that, on his part, he held him as a friend and brother, and would send ambassadors with him to Portugal. This latter had been asked as a favor, the captain pretending that he would not dare to present himself before his king and master unless he was able to present, at the same time, some men of this country.

On Tuesday the captain got ready the following things to be sent to the king: twelve pieces of lambel, four scarlet hoods, six hats, four strings of coral, a case containing six washstand basins, a case of sugar, two casks of oil, and two of honey. And as it is the custom not to send anything to the king without the knowledge of the Moor [who advised him on commercial matters], and of the bale, the captain informed them of his intention. They came, and when they saw the present they laughed at it, saying that it was not a thing to offer to a king, that the poorest merchant from Mecca, or any other part of India, gave more, and that if he wanted to make a present it should be in gold, as the king would not accept such things. When the captain heard this he grew sad, and said he had brought no gold, that, moreover, he was no merchant, but an ambassador; that he gave of that which he had, which was his own [private gift] and not the king's; that if the King of Portugal ordered him to return he would entrust him with far richer presents; and that if King Samolin would not accept these things he would send them back to the ships. Upon this they declared that they would not forward his presents, nor consent to his forwarding them himself. When they had gone there came certain Moorish merchants, and they all depreciated the present which the captain desired to be sent to the king.

When the captain saw that they were determined not to forward his present, he said that he would go to speak to the king, and would then return to the ships. They approved of this, and told him that if he would wait a short time they would return and accompany him to the palace. And the captain waited all day, but they never came back. The captain was very wroth at being among so phlegmatic and unreliable a people, and intended, at first, to go to the palace without them. On further consideration, however, he thought it best to wait until the following day. As to us others, we diverted ourselves, singing and dancing to the sound of trumpets, and enjoyed ourselves much.

On Wednesday morning the Moors returned, and took the captain to the palace. The palace was crowded with armed men. Our captain was kept waiting for fully four long hours, outside a door, which was only opened when the king sent word to admit him, attended by two men only, whom he might select. It seemed to him, as it did to us, that this separation portended no good.

When he had entered, the king said that he had expected him on Tuesday. The captain said that the long road had tired him, and that for this reason he had not come to see him. The king then said that he had told him that he came from a very rich kingdom, and yet had brought him nothing; that he had also told him that he was the bearer of a letter, which had not yet been delivered. To this the captain rejoined that he had brought nothing, because the object of his voyage was merely to make discoveries, but that when other ships came he would then see what they brought him; as to the latter, it was true that he had brought one, and would deliver it immediately.

The king then asked what kind of merchandise was to be found in his country. The captain said that there was much corn, cloth, iron, bronze, and many other things. The king asked whether he had any merchandise with him. The captain replied that he had a little of each sort, as samples, and that if permitted to return to the ships he would order it to be landed, and that meantime four or five men would remain at the lodgings assigned them. The king said no. He might take all his people with him, securely moor his ships, land his merchandise, and sell it to the best advantage. Having taken leave of the king the captain returned to his lodgings, and we with him. As it was already late no attempt was made to depart that night.

The next morning the captain asked for boats to take him to his ships. They began to whisper among themselves, and said that we should have them if we would order our vessels to come nearer to the shore. The captain said that if he ordered his vessels to approach his brother would think that he was being held a prisoner, and that he gave this order on compulsion, and would hoist the sails to return to Portugal. They said that if we refused to order the ships to come nearer we should not be permitted to embark. The captain said that King Samolin had sent him back to his ships, and that as they would not let him go, as ordered by the king, he should return to the king, who was a Christian like himself. If the king would not let him go, and wanted him to remain in his country, he would do so with much pleasure. They agreed that he should be permitted to go, but afforded him no opportunity for doing so, for they immediately closed all the doors, and many armed men entered to guard us, none of us being allowed to go outside without being accompanied by several of these guards.

On the following day, these gentlemen [i.e., the bale and others] came back, and this time they "wore better faces." They told the captain that as he had informed the king that he intended to land his merchandise, he should now give orders to have this done. The captain consented, and said that he would write to his brother to see it being done. They said this was well, and that immediately after the arrival of the merchandise he would be permitted to return to his ship. The captain at once wrote to his brother to send certain things, and he did so at once. On their receipt the captain was allowed to go on board, two men remaining behind with the things that had been landed.

At this we rejoiced greatly, and rendered thanks to God for having extricated us from the hands of the people who had no more sense than beasts, for we knew well that once the captain was on board those who had been landed would have nothing to fear. When the captain reached his ship he ordered that no more merchandise should be sent.

Questions:
1. Describe the Portuguese impressions of the inhabitants of Calicut.
2. Compare and contrast da Gama's historic voyage with that of the other explorers in this section.
3. Do you sense some deception or self-deception in the reporting of strong Christian influences in Calicut (modern Kozhihode)?
4. What were the consequences of the discovery of an ocean route to India at the close of the fifteenth century?

14.3   The Portuguese in Africa and India: Duarte Barbosa

In the following selection the establishment of these commercial colonies came at a distinct price for the inhabitants of those regions. In the following selection, Duarte Barbosa (ca. 1480–1521), an agent of the Portuguese government who helped establish commercial contacts along the east African coast, gives a description of the people and products of the area and of Portuguese methods for controlling trade.

Source: "The East Coast of Africa" is from *The Book of Duarte Barbosa: An Account of the Countries Bordering the Indian Ocean*, 2 vols. (London: Hakluyt Society, 1918, 1921).

THE EAST COAST OF AFRICA
DUARTE BARBOSA

Sofala

Going forward in the direction of India there is a river of no great size upon which up the stream is a town of the Moors [African Muslims] which they call Sofala, close to which the King our Lord [Portuguese King Manuel I] possesses a fort. These Moors have dwelt there a long time by reason of the great traffic which they carried on with the heathen of the mainland. The Moors of this place speak Arabic and have a king over them who is subject to the King our Lord.

And the manner of their traffic was this: they came in small vessels named zambucos from the kingdoms of Kilwa, Mombasa, and Malindi, bringing many cotton cloths, some spotted and others white and blue; also some of silk, and many small beads, grey, red, and yellow, which things come to the said kingdoms from the great kingdom of Cambay [on the coast of northwest India] in other greater ships. And these wares the said Moors who came from Malindi and Mombasa paid for in gold at such a price that those merchants departed well pleased. . . .

Kilwa

Going along the coast from the town of Mozambique, there is an island hard by the mainland which is called Kilwa, in which is a Moorish town with many fair houses of stone and mortar, with many windows after our fashion, very well arranged in streets, with many flat roofs. The doors are of wood, well carved, with excellent joinery. Around it are streams and orchards and fruit-gardens with many channels of sweet water. It has a Moorish king over it. . . . Before the King our Lord sent out his expedition to discover India, the Moors of Sofala, Cuama, Angoya and Mozambique were all subject to the King of Kilwa, who was the most mighty king among them. And in this town was great plenty of gold, as no ships passed toward Sofala without first coming to this island. . . .

This town was taken by force from its king by the Portuguese, as, moved by arrogance, he refused to obey the King our Lord. There took many prisoners and the king fled from the island, and His Highness ordered that a fort should be built there, and kept it under his rule and governance. . . .

Mombasa

Further on, an advance along the coast toward India, there is an isle hard by the mainland, on which is a town called Mombasa. . . . This Mombasa is a land very full of food. Here are found many very fine sheep with round tails, cows and other cattle in great plenty, and many fowls, all of which are exceedingly fat. There is much millet and rice, sweet and bitter oranges, lemons, pomegranates, Indian figs, vegetables of diverse kinds, and much sweet water. The men are often times at war . . . but at peace with those of the mainland, and they carry on trade with them, obtaining great amounts of honey, wax, and ivory.

The king of this city refused to obey the commands of the King our Lord, and through this arrogance he lost it, and our Portuguese took it from him by force. He fled away, and they slew many of his people and also took captive many, both men and women, in such sort that it was left ruined and plundered and burned. Of gold and silver great booty was taken here, bangles, bracelets, earrings and gold beads, also great store of copper with other rich wares in great quantity, and the town was left in ruins.

The City of Brava

Yet further along the coast, beyond these places, is a great town of Moors, of very fine stone and mortar houses, called Brava. It has no king, but is ruled by elders, and ancients of the land, who are the persons held in the highest esteem, and who have the chief dealings in merchandise of diverse kinds. And this place was destroyed by the Portuguese, who slew many of its people and carried many into captivity, and took great spoil of gold and silver and goods. Thenceforth many

285

of them fled away toward the inland country, forsaking the town; yet after had been destroyed the Portuguese again settled and peopled it, so that now it is as prosperous as it was before.

Questions:
1. What does Barbosa find most important and impressive about the east coast of Africa?
2. How does he justify the destruction of African cities?

14.4 "Cut Off Their Ears, Hands and Noses!": Gaspar Correa

The following selection is an excerpt from the journals of Gaspar Correa, who sailed with Vasco da Gama in 1502. This incident occurred after a group of Portuguese had been killed in the trading station of Calcutta. Vasco da Gama sought to control the situation by exacting a bloody vengeance.

Source: "Cut Off Their Ears, Hands and Noses!" is from H.E.J. Stanley, ed., *The Three Voyages of Vasco da Gama* (London: The Hakluyt Society, 1869), pp. 328-332.

The captain-major [Vasco da Gama], on arriving at Calecut, was in the passion because he found the port cleared, and in it there was nothing to which he could do harm, because the Moors, knowing of his coming, had all fled, and hid their vessels and sambuks in the rivers. . . . The King of Calecut thought that he might gain time, so that the captain-major should not do him harm; and when his fleet arrived he sent him a Brahman [religious official] of his in a boat with a white cloth fastened to a pole, as a sign of peace. This Brahman came dressed in the habit of a friar, one of those who had been killed in the country; and on reaching the ship, he asked for a safe conduct to enter. When it was known that he was not a friar—for the captain-major and everyone had been joyful, thinking that he was one of our friars—seeing that he was not, the captain-major gave him a safe conduct, and bade him enter the ship. . . . He then ordered all the fleet to draw in close to the shore, and all day, till night, he bombarded the city, by which he made a great destruction. . . .

While they were doing this business, there came in from the offing two large ships and twenty-two sambuks and Malabar vessels, which came from Coromandel laden with rice, which the Moors of Calecut had ordered to be laden there; . . . but our fleet having sighted them, the [Portuguese] caravels went to them, and the Moors could not fly, as they were laden, and the caravels brought them to the captain-major, and all struck their sails. . . .

Then, the captain-major commanded them to cut off the hands and ears and noses of all the crews, and put all that into one of the small vessels, into which he ordered them to put the friar, also without ears, or nose, or hands, which he ordered to be strung round his neck, with a palm-leaf for the King, on which he told him to have a curry made to eat of what his friar brought him. When all the Indians had been thus executed, he ordered their feet to be tied together, as they had no hands with which to untie them: and in order that they should not untie them with their teeth he ordered them to strike upon their teeth with staves, and they knocked them down their throats; and they were thus put on board, heaped up upon the top of each other, mixed up with the blood which streamed from them; and he ordered mats and dry leaves to be spread over them, and the sails to be set for the shore, and the vessel set on fire; and there were more than eight hundred Moors; and the small vessel with the friar, with all the hands and ears, was also sent on shore under sail, without being fired. These vessels went at once on shore, where many people flocked together to put out the fire, and draw out those whom they found alive, upon which they made great lamentations.

Question:
1. What does this selection say about how control was maintained over Portuguese colonies?

14.5 Christopher Columbus

It is easily forgotten that when Christopher Columbus (1451-1506) set sail across the "Western Ocean" with his three tiny ships on August 3, 1492, he was bound not for a new world but for "the Indies" (India, China, and the islands of East Asia). His venture was a prosaic even though a hazardous one. He hoped to discover a sea route that would make trade with the East-with its highly desired silks, rugs, jewelry, drugs, and spices-easier than the long and arduous caravan treks across Asia. According to Columbus's (mis)calculations, his destination could be reached by sailing some three thousand miles due west around the world. As it turned out, this was the distance to the islands of the Western Hemisphere that he encountered.

In 1484 Columbus had submitted his proposal of reaching the East by sailing west to the king of Portugal, hoping to receive financial support for the project. But the Portuguese were already deeply committed to an attempt to reach the same destination by sailing south around Africa and thence east to India and beyond, so Columbus's appeal was rejected. From there he went to Spain and after two years of effort he gained an audience with King Ferdinand and Queen Isabella. After six more years in negotiations, the monarchs finally agreed to underwrite the venture, and Columbus set off on his epochal voyage. The crossing of the Atlantic, from the Canary Islands (the last port of call on the European side) to an island in the Bahamas group (northeast of Cuba), where Columbus landed on October 12 and took possession in the name of Ferdinand and Isabella, took thirty-six days.

Over a period of twelve years Columbus made four voyages, exploring many of the Caribbean islands and establishing several colonies. His voyages took him to the mainland of South and Central America as well. And although he heard tales of a great ocean farther to the west, he never realized that the lands he had reached belonged not to the Orient but to another continent.

The two selections that follow consist of the initial entry in a journal Columbus kept of his first voyage and a letter he wrote as he neared the end of that voyage, describing some of what he had seen and done. Of special interest is his description of the people who lived on the Caribbean islands, particularly his account of their character, style of life, and reception of the Europeans.

Source: Trans. J. B. Thacher

JOURNAL AND LETTER

Prologue

Because, most Christian and very exalted and very excellent and very powerful Princes, King and Queen of the Spains and of the Islands of the Sea, our Lords, in this present year of 1492 after your Highnesses had made an end to the war of the Moors, who were reigning in Europe, and having finished the war in the very great city of Granada, where in this present year on the 2nd day of the month of January, I saw the Royal banners of your Highnesses placed by force of arms on the towers of the Alhambra, which is the fortress of the said City: and I saw the Moorish King come out to the gates of the City and kiss the Royal hands of your Highnesses, and the hands of the Prince, my Lord: and then in that present month, because of the information which I had given your Highnesses about the lands of India, and about a Prince who is called Great Khan, which means in our Romance language, King of Kings,- how he and his predecessors had many times sent to Rome to beg for men learned in our Holy Faith that they might be instructed therein, and that the Holy Father had never furnished them, and so, many people believing in idolatries and receiving among themselves sects of perdition, were lost:-your Highnesses, as Catholic Christians and Princes, loving the Holy Christian faith and the spreading of it, and enemies of the sect of Mahomet and of all idolatries and heresies, decided to send me, Christopher Columbus, to the said regions of India, to see the said Princes and the peoples and lands, and learn of their disposition, and of everything, and the measures which could be taken for their conversion to our Holy Faith: and you ordered that I should not go to the east by land, by which it is customary to go, but by way of the west, whence until to-day we do not know certainly that any one has gone. So that, after having banished all the Jews from all your Kingdoms and realms, in the same month of January, your Highnesses ordered me to go with a sufficient fleet to the said regions of India: and for that purpose granted me great favours and ennobled me, that from then hence-forward I might entitle myself Don and should be High Admiral of the Ocean-Sea [Atlantic—*Ed.*] and Viceroy and perpetual Governor of all the islands and continental land which I might discover and acquire, and which from now henceforward might be discovered and acquired in the Ocean-Sea, and that my eldest son should succeed in the same manner, and thus from generation to generation for ever after: and I started from the city of Granada on Saturday, the 12th day of the month of May in the same year 1492: I came to the village of Palos, which is a seaport, where I fitted out three vessels, very suitable for a similar undertaking: and I left the said port, well supplied with a large quantity of provisions and with many seamen, on the 3rd day of the month of August in the said year on a Friday at the half hour before sunrise, and took my way to the Canary Islands of your Highnesses, which are in the said Ocean-Sea, in order to set out on my voyage from there and sail until I arrived at the Indies, and make known the message of your Highnesses to those Princes, and fulfil the commands which had thus been given me: and for this purpose, I decided to write everything I might do and see and which might take place on this voyage, very punctually from day to day, as will be seen henceforth. Also, Lords and Princes, besides describing each night what takes place during the day, and during the day, the sailings of the night, I propose to make a new chart for navigation, on which I will locate all the sea and the lands of the Ocean-Sea, in their proper places, under their winds; and further, to compose a book and show everything by means of drawing, by the latitude from the equator and by longitude from the west, and above all, it is fitting that I forget sleep, and study the navigation diligently, in order to thus fulfil these duties, which will be a great labour.

LETTER

Sir:

As I know that you will have pleasure of the great victory which our Lord hath given me in my voyage, I write you this, by which you shall know that, in twenty days I passed over to the Indies with the fleet which the most illustrious King and Queen, our Lords, gave me: where I found very many islands peopled with inhabitants beyond number. And, of them all, I have taken possession for their Highnesses, with proclamation and the royal standard displayed; and I was not gainsaid. On the first which I found, I put the name San Salvador, in commemoration of His high Majesty, who marvellously hath given all this: the Indians call it Guanahani. The second I named the Island of Santa Maria de Concepcion, the third Ferrandina, the fourth Isabella, the fifth La Isla Juana [Cuba]; and so for each one a new name. When I reached Juana, I followed its coast west-wardly, and found it so large that I thought it might be the mainland province of Cathay. And as I did not thus find any towns and villages on the sea-coast, save small hamlets with the people whereof I could not get speech, because they all fled away forthwith, I went on farther in the same direction, thinking I should not miss of great cities or towns. And at the end of many leagues, seeing that there was no change, and that the coast was bearing me northwards, whereunto my desire was contrary since the winter was already confronting us, I formed the purpose of making from thence to the South, and as the wind also blew against me, I determined not to wait for other weather and turned back as far as a port agreed upon; from which I sent two men into the country to learn if there were a king, or any great cities. They travelled for three days, and found interminable small villages and a numberless population, but nought of ruling authority; wherefore they returned. I understood sufficiently from other Indians whom I had already taken, that this land, in its continuousness, was an island; and so I followed its coast eastwardly for a hundred and seven leagues as far as where it terminated; from which headland I saw another island to the east, ten or eight leagues distant from this, to which I at once gave the name La Spañola. And I proceeded thither, and followed the northern coast, as with La Juana, eastwardly for a hundred and seventy-eight great leagues in a direct easterly course, as with La Juana. The which, and all the others, are very large to an excessive degree, and this extremely so. In it, there are many havens on the seacoast, incomparable with any others that I know in Christendom, and plenty of rivers so good and great that it is a marvel. The lands thereof are high, and in it are very many ranges of hills, and most lofty mountains incomparably beyond the Island of Centrefrei; all most beautiful in a thousand shapes, and all accessible, and full of trees of a thousand kinds, so lofty that they seem to reach the sky. And I am assured that they never lose their foliage; as may be imagined, since I saw them as green and as beautiful as they are in Spain during May. And some of them were in flower, some in fruit, some in another stage according to their kind. And the nightingale was singing, and other birds of a thousand sorts, in the month of November, round about the way that I was going. There are palm-trees of six or eight species, wondrous to see for their beautiful variety; but so are the other trees, and fruits, and plants therein. There are wonderful pine-groves, and very large plains of verdure, and there is honey, and many kinds of birds, and many various fruits. In the earth there are many mines of metals; and there is a population of incalculable number. Spañola is a marvel; the mountains and hills, and plains and fields, and land, so beautiful and rich for planting and sowing, for breeding cattle of all sorts, for building of towns and villages. There could be no believing, without seeing, such harbours as are here, as well as the many and great rivers, and excellent waters, most of which contain gold. In the trees and fruits and plants, there are great differences from those of Juana. In this, there are many spiceries, and great mines of gold and other metals. The people of this island, and of all the others that I have found and seen or not seen, all go naked, men and women, just as their mothers bring them forth; although some women cover a single place with the leaf of a plant, or a cotton something which they make for that purpose. They have no iron or steel, nor any weapons; nor are they fit there-unto; not because they be not a well-formed people and of fair stature, but that they are most wondrously timorous. They have no other weapons than the stems of reeds in their seeding state, on the end of which they fix little sharpened stakes. Even these, they dare not use; for many times has it happened that I sent two or three men ashore to some village to parley, and countless numbers of them sallied forth, but as soon as they saw those approach, they fled away in such wise that even a father would not wait for his son. And this was not because any hurt had ever been done to any of them:-on the contrary, at every headland where I have gone and been able to hold speech with them, I gave them of everything which I had, as well cloth as many other things, without accepting aught therefor; but such they are, incurably timid. It is true that since they have become more assured, and are losing that terror, they are artless and generous with what they have, to such a degree as no one would believe but he who had seen it. Of anything they have, if it be asked for, they never say no, but do rather invite the person to accept it, and show as much lovingness as though they would give their hearts. And whether it be a thing of value, or one of little worth, they are straightways content with whatsoever trifle of whatsoever kind may be given them in return for it. I forbade that anything so worthless as fragments of broken platters, and pieces of broken glass, and strap-buckles, should be given them; although when they were able to get such things they seemed to think they had the best jewel in the world, for it was the hap of a sailor to get, in exchange for a strap, gold to the weight of two and a half castellanos, and others much more for other things of far less value; while for new blancas they gave every thing they had, even though it were the worth of two or three gold castellanos, or one or two arrobas of spun cotton. They took even pieces of broken barrelhoops, and gave whatever they had, like senseless brutes; insomuch that it seemed to me ill. I forbade it, and I gave gratuitously a thousand useful things that I carried, in order that they may conceive affection, and furthermore may be made Christians; for they are inclined to the love and service of their Highnesses and of all the Castilian nation, and they strive to combine in giving us things which they have in abundance, and of which we are in need. And they know no sect, or idolatry; save that they all believe that power and goodness are in the sky, and they believed very firmly that I, with these ships and crew, came from the sky; and in such opinion, they received me at every place where I landed, after they had lost their terror. And this comes not because they are ignorant; on the contrary, they are men of very subtle wit, who navigate all those seas, and who give a marvellously good account of everything-but because they never saw men wearing clothes or the like of our ships. And as soon as I arrived in the Indies, in the first island that I found, I took some of them by force, to the intent that they should learn our speech and give me information of what there was in those parts. And so it was, that very soon they understood us and we them, what by speech or what by signs; and those Indians have been of much service. To this day I carry them with me who are still of the opinion that I come from heaven, as appears from much conversation which they have had with me. And they were the first to proclaim it wherever I arrived; and the others went running from house to house and to the neighbouring villages, with loud cries of "Come! come to see the people from heaven!" Then, as soon as their minds were reassured about us, every one came, men as well as women, so that there remained none behind, big or little; and they all brought something to eat and drink, which they gave with wondrous lovingness. They have in all the islands very many canoes, after the manner of rowing-galleys, some larger, some smaller; and a good many are larger than a galley of eighteen benches. They are not so wide, because they are made of a single log of timber, but a galley could not keep up with them in rowing, for their motion is a thing beyond belief. And with these, they navigate through all those islands which are numberless, and ply their traffic. I have seen some of those canoes with seventy and eighty men in them, each one with his oar. In all those islands, I saw not much diversity in the looks of the people, or in their manners and language; but they all understand each other, which is a thing of singular towardness for what I hope their Highnesses will determine, as to making them conversant with our holy faith, unto which they are well disposed. I have already told how I had gone a hundred and seven leagues, in a straight line from West to East, along the seacoast of the Island of Juana; according to which itinerary, I can declare that that island is larger than England and Scotland combined; as, over and above those hundred and seven leagues, there remains for me, on the western side, two provinces whereto I did not go-one of which they call Anan, where the people are born with tails-which provinces cannot be less in length than fifty or sixty leagues, according to what may be understood from the Indians with me, who know all the islands. This other, Española, has a greater circumference than the whole of Spain from Colibre in Catalunya, by the seacoast, as far as Fuente Ravia in Biscay; since, along one of its four sides, I went for a hundred and eighty-eight great leagues in a straight line from West to East. This is a land to be desired,-and once seen, never to be relinquished-in which-although, indeed, I have taken possession of them all for their Highnesses, and all are more richly endowed than I have skill and power to say, and I hold them all in the name of their Highnesses who can dispose thereof as much and as completely as of the kingdoms of Castile-in this Española, in the place most suitable and best for its proximity to the gold mines, and for traffic with the continent, as well on this side as on the further side of the Great Can, where there will be great commerce and profit, I took possession of a large town which I named the city of Navidad. And I have made fortifications there, and a fort which by this time will have been completely finished and I have left therein men enough for such a purpose, with arms and artillery, and provisions for more than a year, and a boat, and a man who is master of all sea-craft for making others; and great friendship with the King of that land, to such a degree that he prided himself on calling and holding me as his brother. And even though his mind might change towards attacking those men, neither he nor his people know what arms are, and go naked. As I have already said, they are the most timorous creatures there are in the world, so that the men who remain there are alone sufficient to destroy all that land, and the island is without personal danger for them if they know how to behave themselves. It seems to me that in all those islands, the men are all content with a single wife; and to their chief or king they give as many as twenty. The women, it appears to me, do more work than the men. Nor have I been able to learn whether they held personal property, for it seemed to me that whatever one had, they all took shares of, especially of eatable things. Down to the present, I have not found in those islands any monstrous men, as many expected, but on the contrary all the people are very comely; nor are they black like those in Guinea, but have flowing hair; and they are not begotten where there is an excessive violence of the rays of the sun. It is true that the sun is there very strong, notwithstanding that it is twenty-six degrees distant from the equinoctial line. In those islands, where there are lofty mountains, the cold was very keen there, this winter; but they endure it by being accustomed thereto, and by the help of the meats which they eat with many and inordinately hot spices. Thus I have not found, nor had any information of monsters, except of an island which is here the second in the approach to the Indies, which is inhabited by a people whom, in all the islands, they regard as very ferocious, who eat human flesh. These have many canoes with which they run through all the islands of India, and plunder and take as much as they can. They are no more illshapen than the others, but have the custom of wearing their hair long, like women; and they use bows and arrows of the same reedstems, with a point of wood at the top, for lack of iron which they have not. Amongst those other tribes who are excessively cowardly, these are ferocious; but I hold them as nothing more than the others. These are they who have to do with the women of Matremonio-which is the first island that is encountered in the passage from

Spain to the Indies-in which there are no men. Those women practise no female usages, but have bows and arrows of reeds such as above mentioned; and they arm and cover themselves with plates of copper of which they have much. In another island, which they assure me is larger than Española, the people have no hair. In this, there is incalculable gold; and concerning these and the rest I bring Indians with me as witnesses. And in conclusion, to speak only of what has been done in this voyage, which has been so hastily performed, their Highnesses may see that I shall give them as much gold as they may need, with very little aid which their Highnesses will give me; spices and cotton at once, as much as their Highnesses will order to be shipped, and as much as they shall order to be shipped of mastic-which till now has never been found except in Greece, in the island of Xio, and the Seignory sells it for what it likes; and aloe-wood as much as they shall order to be shipped; and slaves as many as they shall order to be shipped-and these shall be from idolaters. And I believe that I have discovered rhubarb and cinnamon, and I shall find that the men whom I am leaving there will have discovered a thousand other things of value; as I made no delay at any point, so long as the wind gave me an opportunity of sailing, except only in the town of Navidad till I had left things safely arranged and well established. And in truth I should have done much more if the ships had served me as well as might reasonably have been expected. This is enough; and thanks to eternal God our Lord who gives to all those who walk His way, victory over things which seem impossible; and this was signally one such, for although men have talked or written of those lands, it was all by conjecture, without confirmation from eyesight, importing just so much that the hearers for the most part listened and judged that there was more fable in it than anything actual, however trifling. Since thus our Redeemer has given to our most illustrious King and Queen, and to their famous kingdoms, this victory in so high a matter, Christendom should take gladness therein and make great festivals, and give solemn thanks to the Holy Trinity for the great exaltation they shall have by the conversion of so many peoples to our Holy faith; and next for the temporal benefit which will bring hither refreshment and profit, not only to Spain, but to all Christians. This briefly, in accordance with the facts. Dated on the caravel, off the Canary Islands, the 15 February of the year 1493.

At your command,

The Admiral

Questions:
1. Which aspects of the land and people most interested Columbus?
2. Describe Columbus' attitude towards the Native Americans he encountered.

14.6   Bernal Díaz del Castillo

Bernal Díaz del Castillo, the author of the selection that follows, was born in the Spanish town of Medina del Campo in the year of Columbus's epochal voyage, 1492. Like many of his contemporaries, he was excited by the tales that soon began to circulate through Spain of the gold to be had in the lands recently discovered beyond the great "Western Ocean," so he decided to seek his fortune there. He left his home in 1514, crossing first to Cuba, where he spent about three years, before going on two exploratory trips farther west. In 1519 he joined the historic expedition of the conquistador Hernando Cortés (1485-1547) that was to lead to the subjugation of Mexico and part of Central America and the annexation of these lands to the Spanish crown. Except for two trips he made back to his native land in later years Bernal Díaz remained in the Western Hemisphere for the remainder of his long life, dying in Guatemala around the year 1581. He wrote his book, which he called The True History of the Conquest of New Spain, in his old age, many years after the events he describes in it.

According to Bernal Díaz's account, Cortés, after landing on the east coast of what is now Mexico and burning his ships (so he could not retreat), marched with a small band of soldiers, fighting his way inland and arriving at the capital city of the Aztec civilization, Tenochtitlán (or Mexico City), in November 1519. There he was received by the great cacique (king) Montezuma. The selection that follows begins with the meeting between these two warriors. Its central figure, however, is the Aztec, Montezuma. Bernal Díaz describes his person at some length, as well as his family and court. He gives a detailed account of the personal and physical environment in which the Aztec chief lived, from the architecture of his palaces to the contents of his storehouses to the ritual surrounding his meals. The selection ends with a more general description of the society and commerce of Mexico City, in particular its great marketplace. It is obvious from his comments that Bernal Díaz was greatly impressed by many of the sights he beheld in this strange land and realized that in some ways its civilization equaled or even surpassed that of his native Spain.

Source: Trans. A. P. Maudslay.

THE CONQUEST OF NEW SPAIN

About the Great and Solemn Reception which the Great Montezuma Gave Cortés and all of us at the Entering of the Great City of Mexico.

EARLY next day we left Iztapalapa with a large escort of those great Caciques whom I have already mentioned. We proceeded along the Causeway which is here eight paces in width and runs so straight to the City of Mexico that it does not seem to me to turn either much or little, but, broad as it is, it was so crowded with people that there was hardly room for them all, some of them going to and others returning from Mexico, besides those who had come out to see us, so that we were hardly able to pass by the crowds of them that came; and the towers and cues were full of people as well as the canoes from all parts of the lake. It was not to be wondered at, for they had never before seen horses or men such as we are.

Gazing on such wonderful sights, we did not know what to say, or whether what appeared before us was real, for on one side, on the land, there were great cities, and in the lake ever so many more, and the lake itself was crowded with canoes, and in the Causeway were many bridges at intervals, and in front of us stood the great City of Mexico, and we,- we did not even number four hundred soldiers! and we well remembered the words and warnings given us by the people of Huexotzingo and Tlaxcala and Tlamanalco, and the many other warnings that had been given that we should beware of entering Mexico, where they would kill us, as soon as they had us inside.

Let the curious readers consider whether there is not much to ponder over in this that I am writing. What men have there been in the world who have shown such daring? But let us get on, and march along the Causeway. When we arrived where another small causeway branches off (leading to Coyoacan, which is another city) where there were some buildings like towers, which are their oratories, many more chieftains and Caciques approached clad in very rich mantles, the brilliant liveries of one chieftain differing from those of another, and the causeways were crowded with them. The Great Montezuma had sent these great Caciques in advance to receive us, and when they came before Cortés they bade us welcome in their language, and as a sign of peace, they touched their hands against the ground, and kissed the ground with the hand.

There we halted for a good while, and Cacamatzin, the Lord of Texcoco, and the Lord of Iztapalapa and the Lord of Tacuba and the Lord of Coyoacan went on in advance to meet the Great Montezuma, who was approaching in a rich litter accompanied by other great Lords and Caciques, who owned vassals. When we arrived near to Mexico, where there were some other small towers, the Great Montezuma got down from his litter, and those great Caciques supported him with their arms beneath a marvellously rich canopy of green coloured feathers with much gold and silver embroidery and with pearls and chalchihuites suspended from a sort of bordering, which was wonderful to look at. The Great Montezuma was richly attired according to his usage, and he was shod with sandals. For so they call what they wear on their feet, the soles were of gold and the upper part adorned with precious stones. The four Chieftains who supported his arms were also richly clothed according to their usage, in garments which were apparently held ready for them on the road to enable them to accompany their prince, for they did not appear in such attire when they came to receive us. Besides these four Chieftains, there were four other great Caciques, who supported the canopy over their heads, and many other Lords who walked before the Great Montezuma, sweeping the ground where he would tread and spreading cloths on it, so that he should not tread on the earth. Not one of these chieftains dared even to think of looking him in the face, but kept their eyes lowered with great reverence, except those four relations, his nephews, who supported him with their arms.

When Cortés was told that the Great Montezuma was approaching, and he saw him coming, he dismounted from his horse, and when he was near Montezuma, they simultaneously paid great reverence to one another. Montezuma bade him welcome and our Cortés replied through Doña Marina wishing him very good health. And it seems to me that Cortés, through Doña Marina, offered him his right hand, and Montezuma did not wish to take it, but he did give his hand to Cortés and then Cortés brought out a necklace which he had ready at hand, made of glass stones, which I have already said are called Margaritas, which have within them many patterns of diverse colours, these were strung on a cord of gold and with musk so that it should have a sweet scent, and he placed it round the neck of the Great Montezuma and when he had so placed it he was going to embrace him, and those great Princes who accompanied Montezuma held back Cortés by the arm so that he should not embrace him, for they considered it an indignity.

Then Cortés through the mouth of Doña Marina told him that now his heart rejoiced at having seen such a great Prince, and that he took it as a great honour that he had come in person to meet him and had frequently shown him such favour.

Then Montezuma spoke other words of politeness to him, and told two of his nephews who supported his arms, the Lord of Texcoco and the Lord of Coyoacan, to go with us and show us to our quarters, and Montezuma with his other two relations, the Lord of Cuitlahuac and the Lord of Tacuba who accompanied him, returned to the city, and all those grand companies of Caciques and chieftains who had come with him returned in his train. As they turned back after their Prince we stood watching them and observed how they all marched with their eyes fixed on the ground without looking at him, keeping close to the wall, following him with great reverence. Thus space was made for us to enter the streets of

291

Mexico, without being so much crowded. But who could now count the multitude of men and women and boys who were in the streets and on the azoteas, and in canoes on the canals, who had come out to see us.

. . .

They took us to lodge in some large houses, where there were apartments for all of us, for they had belonged to the father qf the Great Montezuma, who was named Axayaca, and at that time Montezuma kept there the great oratories for his idols, and a secret chamber where he kept bars and jewels of gold, which was the treasure that he had inherited from his father Axayaca, and he never disturbed it. They took us to lodge in that house, because they called us Teules, and took us for such, so that we should be with the Idols or Teules which were kept there. However, for one reason or another, it was there they took us, where there were great halls and chambers canopied with the cloth of the country for our Captain, and for every one of us beds of matting with canopies above, and no better bed is given, however great the chief may be, for they are not used. And all these palaces were coated with shining cement and swept and garlanded.

As soon as we arrived and entered into the great court, the Great Montezuma took our Captain by the hand, for he was there awaiting him, and led him to the apartment and saloon where he was to lodge, which was very richly adorned according to their usage, and he had at hand a very rich necklace made of golden crabs, a marvellous piece of work, and Montezuma himself placed it round the neck of our Captain Cort6s, and greatly astonished his own Captains by the great honour that he was bestowing on him. When the necklace had been fastened, Cortés thanked Montezuma through our interpreters, and Montezuma replied-"Malinche you and your brethren are in your own house, rest awhile," and then he went to his palaces which were not far away, and we divided our lodgings by companies, and placed the artillery pointing in a convenient direction, and the order which we had to keep was clearly explained to us, and that we were to be much on the alert, both the cavalry and all of us soldiers. A sumptuous dinner was provided for us according to their use and custom, and we ate it at once. So this was our lucky and daring entry into the great city of Tenochtitlan Mexico on the 8th day of November the year of our Savior Jesus Christ 1519.

. . .

How on the Following Day our Captain Cortés went to See the Great Montezuma, and About a certain Conversation that Took Place

THE next day Cortés decided to go to Montezuma's palace, and he first sent to find out what he intended doing and to let him know that we were coming. He took with him four captains, namely Pedro de Alvarado, Juan Velásquez de Leon, Diego de Ordás, and Gonzalo de Sandoval, and five of us soldiers also went with him.

When Montezuma knew of our coming he advanced to the middle of the hall to receive us, accompanied by many of his nephews, for no other chiefs were permitted to enter or hold communication with Montezuma where he then was, unless it were on important business. Cortés and he paid the greatest reverence to each other and then they took one another by the hand and Montezuma made him sit down on his couch on his right hand, and he also bade all of us to be seated on seats which he ordered to be brought.

Then Cortés began to make an explanation through our interpreters Doña Marina and Aguilar, and said that he and all of us were rested, and that in coming to see and converse with such a great Prince as he was, we had completed the journey and fulfilled the command which our great King and Prince had laid on us. But what he chiefly came to say on behalf of our Lord God had already been brought to his [Montezuma's] knowledge through his ambassadors, Tendile, Pitalpitoque and Quintalbor, at the time when he did us the favour to send the golden sun and moon to the sand dunes; for we told them then that we were Christians and worshipped one true and only God, named Jesus Christ, who suffered death and passion to save us, and we told them that a cross (when they asked us why we worshipped it) was a sign of the other Cross on which our Lord God was crucified for our salvation, and that the death and passion which He suffered was for the salvation of the whole human race, which was lost, and that this our God rose on the third day and is now in heaven, and it is He who made the heavens and the earth, the sea and the sands, and created all the things there are in the world, and He sends the rain and the dew, and nothing happens in the world without His holy will. That we believe in Him and worship Him, but that those whom they look upon as gods are not so, but are devils, which are evil things, and if their looks are bad their deeds are worse, and they could see that they were evil and of little worth, for where we had set up crosses such as those his ambassadors had seen, they dared not appear before them, through fear of them, and that as time went on they would notice this.

The favour he now begged of him was his attention to the words that he now wished to tell him; then he explained to him very clearly about the creation of the world, and how we are all brothers, sons of one father and one mother who were called Adam and Eve, and how such a brother as our great Emperor, grieving for the perdition of so many souls, such as those which their idols were leading to Hell, where they burn in living flames, had sent us, so that after what he [Montezuma] had now heard he would put a stop to it and they would no longer adore these Idols or sacrifice Indian men and women to them, for we were all brethren, nor should they commit sodomy or thefts. He also told them that, in course of time, our Lord and King would send some men who among us lead very holy lives, much better than we do, who will explain to them all about it, for at present we merely came to give them due warning, and so he prayed him to do what he was asked and carry it into effect.

As Montezuma appeared to wish to reply, Cortés broke off his argument, and to all of us who were with him he said: "with this we have done our duty considering it is the first attempt."

Montezuma replied-"Señor Malinche, I have understood your words and arguments very well before now, from what you said to my servants at the sand dunes, this about three Gods and the Cross, and all those things that you have preached in the towns through which you have come. We have not made any answer to it because here throughout all time we have worshipped our own gods, and thought they were good, as no doubt yours are, so do not trouble to speak to us any more about them at present. Regarding the creation of the world, we have held the same belief for ages past, and for this reason we take it for certain that you are those whom our ancestors predicted would come from the direction of the sunrise. As for your great King, I feel that I am indebted to him, and I will give him of what I possess."

. . .

While this conversation was going on, Montezuma secretly sent a great Cacique, one of his nephews who was in his company, to order his stewards to bring certain pieces of gold, which it seems must have been put apart to give to Cortés, and ten loads of fine cloth, which he apportioned, the gold and mantles between Cortés and the four captains, and to each of us soldiers he gave two golden necklaces, each necklace being worth ten pesos, and two loads of mantles. The gold that he then gave us was worth in all more than a thousand pesos and he gave it all cheerfully and with the air of a great and valiant prince. As it was now past midday, so as not to appear importunate, Cort6s said to him: "Señor Montezuma, you always have the habit of heaping load upon load in every day conferring favours on us, and it is already your dinner time." Montezuma replied that he thanked us for coming to see him, and then we took our leave with the greatest courtesy and we went to our lodgings.

And as we went along we spoke of the good manners and breeding which he showed in everything, and that we should show him in all ways the greatest respect, doffing our quilted caps when we passed before him, and this we always did, but let us leave this subject here, and pass on.

Of the Manner and Appearance of the Great Montezuma and What a Great Prince He Was

THE Great Montezuma was about forty years old, of good height and well proportioned, slender, and spare of flesh, not very swarthy, but of the natural colour and shade of an Indian. He did not wear his hair long, but so as just to cover his ears, his scanty black beard was well shaped and thin. His face was somewhat long, but cheerful, and he had good eyes and showed in his appearance and manner both tenderness and, when necessary, gravity. He was very neat and clean and bathed once every day in the afternoon. He had many women as mistresses, daughters of Chieftains, and he had two great Cacicas as his legitimate wives, and when he had intercourse with them it was so secretly that no one knew anything about it, except some of his servants. He was free from unnatural offences. The clothes that he wore one day, he did not put on again until four days later. He had over two hundred chieftains in his guard, in other rooms close to his own, not that all were meant to converse with him, but only one or another, and when they went to speak to him they were obliged to take off their rich mantles and put on others of little worth, but they had to be clean, and they had to enter barefoot with their eyes lowered to the ground, and not to look up in his face. And they made him three obeisances, and said: "Lord, my Lord, my Great Lord," before they came up to him, and then they made their report and with a few words he dismissed them, and on taking leave they did not turn their backs, but kept their faces toward him with their eyes to the ground, and they did not turn their backs until they left the room. I noticed another thing, that when other great chiefs came from distant lands about disputes or business, when they reached the apartments of the Great Montezuma, they had to come barefoot and with poor mantles, and they might not enter directly into the Palace, but had to loiter about a little on one side of the Palace door, for to enter hurriedly was considered to be disrespectful.

For each meal, over thirty different dishes were prepared by his cooks according to their ways and usage, and they placed small pottery brasiers beneath the dishes so that they should not get cold. They prepared more than three hundred plates of the food that Montezuma was going to eat, and more than a thousand for the guard. When he was going to eat, Montezuma would sometimes go out with his chiefs and stewards, and they would point out to him which dish was best, and of what birds and other things it was composed, and as they advised him, so he would eat, but it was not often that he would go out to see the food, and then merely as a pastime.

I have heard it said that they were wont to cook for him the flesh of young boys, but as he had such a variety of dishes, made of so many things, we could not succeed in seeing if they were of human flesh or of other things, for they daily cooked fowls, turkeys, pheasants, native partridges, quail, tame and wild ducks, venison, wild boar, reed birds, pigeons, hares and rabbits, and many sorts of birds and other things which are bred in this country, and they are so numerous that I cannot finish naming them in a hurry; so we had no insight into it, but I know for certain that after our Captain censured the sacrifice of human beings, and the eating of their flesh, he ordered that such food should not be prepared for him thenceforth.

Let us cease speaking of this and return to the way things were served to him at meal times. It was in this way: if it was cold they made up a large fire of live coals of a firewood made from the bark of trees which did not give off any smoke, and the scent of the bark from which the fire was made was very fragrant, and so that it should not give off more heat than he required, they placed in front of it a sort of screen adorned with figures of idols worked in gold. He was seated on a low stool, soft and richly worked, and the table, which was also low, was made in the same style as the seats, and on it they placed the table cloths of white cloth and some rather long napkins of the same material. Four very beautiful cleanly women brought water for his hands in a sort of deep basin which they call "xicales," and they held others like plates below to catch the water, and they brought him towels. And two other women brought him tortilla bread, and as soon as he began to eat they placed before him a sort of wooden screen painted over with gold, so that no one should watch him eating. Then the four women stood aside, and four great chieftains who were old men came and stood beside them, and with these Montezuma now and then conversed, and asked them questions, and as a great favour he would give to each of these elders a dish of what to him tasted best. They say that these elders were his near relations, and were his counsellors and judges of law suits, and the dishes and food which Montezuma gave them they ate standing up with much reverence and without looking at his face. He was served on Cholula earthenware either red or black. While he was at his meal the men of his guard who were in the rooms near to that of Montezuma, never dreamed of making any noise or speaking aloud. They brought him fruit of all the different kinds that the land produced, but he ate very little of it. From time to time they brought him, in cupshaped vessels of pure gold, a certain drink made from cacao which they said he took when he was going to visit his wives, and at the time he took no heed of it, but what I did see was that they brought over fifty great jugs of good cacao frothed up, and he drank of that, and the women served this drink to him with great reverence.

Sometimes at meal-times there were present some very ugly hump-backs, very small of stature and their bodies almost broken in half, who are their jesters, and other Indians, who must have been buffoons, who told him witty sayings, and others who sang and danced, for Montezuma was fond of pleasure and song, and to these he ordered to be given what was left of the food and the jugs of cacao. Then the same four women removed the table cloths, and with much ceremony they brought water for his hands. And Montezuma talked with those four old chieftains about things that interested him, and they took leave of him with the great reverence in which they held him, and he remained to repose.

As soon as the Great Montezuma had dined, all the men of the Guard had their meal and as many more of the other house servants, and it seems to me that they brought out over a thousand dishes of the food of which I have spoken, and then over two thousand jugs of cacao all frothed up, as they make it in Mexico, and a limitless quantity of fruit, so that with his women and female servants and bread makers and cacao makers his expenses must have been very great.

Let us cease talking about the expenses and the food for his household and let us speak of the Stewards and the Treasurers and the stores and pantries and of those who had charge of the houses where the maize was stored. I say that there would be so much to write about, each thing by itself, that I should not know where to begin, but we stood astonished at the excellent arrangements and the great abundance of provisions that he had in all, but I must add what I had forgotten, for it is as well to go back and relate it, and that is, that while Montezuma was at table eating as I have described, there were waiting on him two other graceful women to bring him tortillas, kneaded with eggs and other sustaining ingredients, and these tortillas were very white, and they were brought on plates covered with clean napkins, and they also brought him another kind of bread, like long balls kneaded with other kinds of sustaining food, and "pan pachol" for so they call it in this country, which is a sort of wafer. There were also placed on the table three tubes much painted and gilded, which held liquidambar mixed with certain herbs which they call tabaco, and when he had finished eating, after they had danced before him and sung and the table was removed, he inhaled the smoke from one of those tubes, but he took very little of it and with that he fell asleep.

• • •

Montezuma had two houses full of every sort of arms, many of them richly adorned with gold and precious stones. There were shields great and small, and a sort of broadswords, and others like two handed swords set with stone knives which cut much better than our swords, and lances longer than ours are, with a fathom of blade with many knives set in it, which even when they are driven into a buckler or shield do not come out, in fact they cut like razors so that they can shave their heads with them. There were very good bows and arrows and double-pointed lances and others with one point, as well as their throwing sticks, and many slings and round stones shaped by hand, and some sort of artful shields which are so made that they can be rolled up, so as not to be in the way when they are not fighting, and when they are needed for fighting they let them fall down, and they cover the body from top to toe. There was also much quilted cotton armour, richly ornamented on the outside with many coloured feathers, used as devices and distinguishing marks, and there were casques or helmets made of wood and bone, also highly decorated with feathers on the outside, and there were other arms of other makes which, so as to avoid prolixity, I will not describe, and there were artizans who were skilled in such things and worked at them, and stewards who had charge of the arms.

Let us leave this and go on to another great house, where they keep many Idols, and they say that they are their fierce gods, and with them many kinds of carnivorous beasts of prey, tigers and two kinds of lions, and animals something like wolves which in this country they call jackals and foxes, and other smaller carnivorous animals, and all these carnivores they feed with flesh, and the greater number of them breed in the house. They give them as food deer and fowls, dogs and other things which they are used to hunt, and I have heard it said that they feed them on the bodies of the Indians who have been sacrificed. It is in this way: you have already heard me say that when they sacrifice a wretched Indian they saw open the chest with stone knives and hasten to tear out the palpitating heart and blood, and offer it to their Idols in whose name the sacrifice is made. Then they cut off the thighs, arms and head and eat the former at feasts and banquets, and the head they hang up on some beams, and the body of the man sacrificed is not eaten but given to these fierce animals. They also have in that cursed house many vipers and poisonous snakes which carry on their tails things that sound like bells. These are the worst vipers of all, and they keep them in jars and great pottery vessels with many feathers, and there they lay their eggs and rear their young, and they give them to eat the bodies of the Indians who have been sacrificed, and the flesh of dogs which they are in the habit of breeding.

. . .

Let us go on and speak of the skilled workmen he [Montezuma] employed in every craft that was practised among them. We will begin with lapidaries and workers in gold and silver and all the hollow work, which even the great goldsmiths in Spain were forced to admire, and of these there were a great number of the best in a town named Atzcapotzalco, a league from Mexico. Then for working precious stones and chalchihuites, which are like emeralds, there were other great artists. Let us go on to the great craftsmen in feather work, and painters and sculptors who were most refined; from what we see of their work to-day we can form a judgment of what they did then, for there are three Indians to-day in the City of Mexico named Marcos de Aquino, Juan de la Cruz and El Crespillo, so skilful in their work as sculptors and painters, that had they lived in the days of the ancient and famous Apelles, or of Michael Angelo Buonarotti, in our times, they would be placed in the same company. Let us go on to the Indian women who did the weaving and the washing, who made such an immense quantity of fine fabrics with wonderful feather work designs; the greater part of it was brought daily from some towns of the province on the north coast near Vera Cruz called Cotaxtla, close by San Juan de Ulua, where we disembarked when we came with Cortés.

In the house of the Great Montezuma himself, all the daughters of chieftains whom he had as mistresses always wore beautiful things, and there were many daughters of Mexican citizens who lived in retirement and wished to appear to be like nuns, who also did weaving but it was wholly of feather work. These nuns had their houses near the great Cue of Huichilobos and out of devotion to it, or to another idol, that of a woman who was said to be their mediatrix in the matter of marriage, their fathers placed them in that religious retirement until they married, and they were [only] taken out thence to be married.

Let us go on and tell about the great number of dancers kept by the Great Montezuma for his amusement, and others who used stilts on their feet, and others who flew when they danced up in the air, and others like Merry-Andrews, and I may say that there was a district full of these people who had no other occupation. Let us go on and speak of the workmen that he had as stone cutters, masons and carpenters, all of whom attended to the work of his houses, I say that he had as many as he wished for. We must not forget the gardens of flowers and sweet-scented trees, and the many kinds that there were of them, and the arrangement of them and the walks, and the ponds and tanks of fresh water where the water entered at one end and flowed out at the other; and the baths which he had there, and the variety of small birds that nested in the branches, and the medicinal and useful herbs that were in the gardens. It was a wonder to see, and to take care of it there were many gardeners. Everything was made in masonry and well cemented, baths and walks and closets, and apartments like summer houses where they danced and sang. There was as much to be seen in these gardens as there was everywhere else, and we could not tire of witnessing his great power. Thus as a consequence of so many crafts being practised among them, a large number of skilled Indians were employed.

. . .

How our Captain went out to See the City of Mexico and Tlaltelolco, Which is the Great Market Place and the Great Cue of Huichilobos, and What else Happened

As we had already been four days in Mexico and neither the Captain nor any of us had left our lodgings except to go to the houses and gardens, Cortés said to us that it would be well to go to the great Plaza and see the great Temple of

Huichilobos, and that he wished to consult the Great Montezuma and have his approval. For this purpose he sent Jerónimo de Aguilar and the Doña Marina as messengers, and with them went our Captain's small page named Orteguilla, who already understood something of the language. When Montezuma knew his wishes he sent to say that we were welcome to go; on the other hand, as he was afraid that we might do some dishonour to his Idols, he determined to go with us himself with many of his chieftains. He came out from his Palace in his rich litter, but when half the distance had been traversed and he was near some oratories, he stepped out of the litter, for he thought it a great affront to his idols to go to their house and temple in that manner. Some of the great chieftains supported him with their arms, and the tribal lords went in front of him carrying two staves like sceptres held on high, which was the sign that the Great Montezuma was coming. (When he went in his litter he carried a wand half of gold and half of wood, which was held up like a wand of justice). So he went on and ascended the great Cue accompanied by many priests, and he began to burn incense and perform other ceremonies to Huichilobos.

Let us leave Montezuma, who had gone ahead as I have said, and return to Cortés and our captains and soldiers, who according to our custom both night and day were armed, and as Montezuma was used to see us so armed when we went to visit him, he did not look upon it as anything new. I say this because our Captain and all those who had horses went to Tlaltelolco on horseback, and nearly all of us soldiers were fully equipped, and many Caciques whom Montezuma had sent for that purpose went in our company. When we arrived at the great market place, called Tlaltelolco, we were astounded at the number of people and the quantity of merchandise that it contained, and at the good order and control that was maintained, for we had never seen such a thing before. The chieftains who accompanied us acted as guides. Each kind of merchandise was kept by itself and had its fixed place marked out. Let us begin with the dealers in gold, silver, and precious stones, feathers, mantles, and embroidered goods. Then there were other wares consisting of Indian slaves both men and women; and I say that they bring as many of them to that great market for sale as the Portuguese bring negroes from Guinea; and they brought them along tied to long poles, with collars round their necks so that they could not escape, and others they left free. Next there were other traders who sold great pieces of cloth and cotton, and articles of twisted thread, and there were cacahuateros who sold cacao. In this way one could see every sort of merchandise that is to be found in the whole of New Spain, placed in arrangement in the same manner as they do in my own country, which is Medina del Campo, where they hold the fairs, where each line of booths has its particular kind of merchandise, and so it is in this great market. There were those who sold cloths of henequen and ropes and the cotaras with which they are shod, which are made from the same plant, and sweet cooked roots, and other tubers which they get from this plant, all were kept in one part of the market in the place assigned to them. In another part there were skins of tigers and lions, of otters and jackals, deer and other animals and badgers and mountain cats, some tanned and others untanned, and other classes of merchandise.

Let us go on and speak of those who sold beans and sage and other vegetables and herbs in another part, and to those who sold fowls, cocks with wattles, rabbits, hares, deer, mallards, young dogs and other things of that sort in their part of the market, and let us also mention the fruiterers, and the women who sold cooked food, dough and tripe in their own part of the market; then every sort of pottery made in a thousand different forms from great water jars to little jugs, these also had a place to themselves; then those who sold honey and honey paste and other dainties like nut paste, and those who sold lumber, boards, cradles, beams, blocks and benches, each article by itself, and the vendors of ocote firewood, and other things of a similar nature. I must furthermore mention, asking your pardon, that they also sold many canoes full of human excrement, and these were kept in the creeks near the market, and this they use to make salt or for tanning skins, for without it they say that they cannot be well prepared. I know well that some gentlemen laugh at this, but I say that it is so, and I may add that on all the roads it is a usual thing to have places made of reeds or straw or grass, so that they may be screened from the passers by, into these they retire when they wish to purge their bowels so that even that filth should not be lost. But why do I waste so many words in recounting what they sell in that great market, for I shall never finish if I tell it all in detail. Paper, which in this country is called Amal, and reeds scented with liquidambar, and full of tobacco, and yellow ointments and things of that sort are sold by themselves, and much cochineal is sold under the arcades which are in that great market place, and there are many vendors of herbs and other sorts of trades. There are also buildings where three magistrates sit in judgment, and there are executive officers like Alguacils who inspect the merchandise. I am forgetting those who sell salt, and those who make the stone knives, and how they split them off the stone itself; and the fisherwomen and others who sell some small cakes made from a sort of ooze which they get out of the great lake, which curdles, and from this they make a bread having a flavour something like cheese. There are for sale axes of brass and copper and tin, and gourds and gaily painted jars made of wood. I could wish that I had finished telling of all the things which are sold there, but they are so numerous and of such different quality and the great market place with its surrounding arcades was so crowded with people, that one would not have been able to see and inquire about it all in two days.

Then we went to the great Cue, and when we were already approaching its great courts, before leaving the market place itself, there were many more merchants, who, as I was told, brought gold for sale in grains, just as it is taken from the mines. The gold is placed in thin quills of the geese of the country, white quills, so that the gold can be seen through, and according to the length and thickness of the quills they arrange their accounts with one another, how much so many mantles or so many gourds full of cacao were worth, or how many slaves, or whatever other thing they were exchanging.

Questions:
1. What impresses Díaz most about Aztec civilization? What is he most critical of?
2. How are the Aztecs different from the Caribbean people Columbus encountered?

14.7 Bartolome De Las Casas: Persecutor Turns Protector

The Spaniard who was to ultimately be awarded the title "Apostle to the Indies," Bartolome De Las Casas (1474–1566), first sailed to the Americas in Christopher Columbus' third expedition. He soon settled in the Caribbean and, for the first few years, became a planter/slave-owner. In 1510, appalled by what he had seen and perhaps done, he released his Indian slaves and became a Catholic priest, and later, Bishop of Chiapas in Mexico (1644–47). Las Casas became an indefatigable advocate of Indian rights and freedom. His "The Devastation of the Indies: A Brief Account" is considered the most hard-hitting and accurate indictment of the murderous treatment of Caribbean natives in the aftermath of the Columbian voyages.

Source: Herma Briffault, trans., *Batolome De Las Casas: The Devastation of the Indies: A Brief Account* (Baltimore: Johns Hopkins University Press, 1992), pp. 27–33, 48–53, 128–132.

THE INDIES were discovered in the year one thousand four hundred and ninety-two. In the following year a great many Spaniards went there with the intention of settling the land. Thus, forty-nine years have passed since the first settlers penetrated the land, the first so-claimed being the large and most happy isle called Hispaniola, which is six hundred leagues in circumference. Around it in all directions are many other islands, some very big, others very small, and all of them were, as we saw with our own eyes, densely populated with native people called Indians. This large island was perhaps the most densely populated place in the world. There must be close to two hundred leagues of land on this island, and the seacoast has been explored for more than ten thousand leagues, and each day more of it is being explored. And all the land so far discovered is a beehive of people; it is as though God had crowded into these lands the great majority of mankind.

And of all the infinite universe of humanity, these people are the most guileless, the most devoid of wickedness and duplicity, the most obedient and faithful to their native masters and to the Spanish Christians whom they serve. They are by nature the most humble, patient, and peaceable, holding no grudges, free from embroilments, neither excitable nor quarrelsome. These people are the most devoid of rancors, hatreds, or desire for vengeance of any people in the world. And because they are so weak and complaisant, they are less able to endure heavy labor and soon die of no matter what malady. The sons of nobles among us, brought up in the enjoyments of life's refinements, are no more delicate than are these Indians, even those among them who are of the lowest rank of laborers. They are also poor people, for they not only possess little but have no desire to possess worldly goods. For this reason they are not arrogant, embittered, or greedy. Their repasts are such that the food of the holy fathers in the desert can scarcely be more parsimonious, scanty, and poor. As to their dress, they are generally naked, with only their pudenda covered somewhat. And when they cover their shoulders it is with a square cloth no more than two varas in size. They have no beds, but sleep on a kind of matting or else in a kind of suspended net called *hamacas*. They are very clean in their persons, with alert, intelligent minds, docile and open to doctrine, very apt to receive our holy Catholic faith, to be endowed with virtuous custom: and to behave in a godly fashion. And once they begin to hear the tidings of the Faith, they are so insistent on knowing more and on taking the sacraments of the Church and on observing the divine cult that, truly, the missionaries who are here need to be endowed by God with great patience in order to cope with such eagerness. Some of the secular Spaniards who have been here for many years say that the goodness of the Indians is undeniable and that if this gifted people could be brought to know the one true God they would be the most fortunate people in the world.

Yet into this sheepfold, into this land of meek outcast there came some Spaniards who immediately behaved like ravening wild beasts, wolves, tigers, or lions that had been starved for many days. And Spaniards have behaved in no other way during the past forty years, down to the present time, for they are still acting like ravening beasts, killing, terrorizing, afflicting, torturing, and destroying the native peoples, doing all this with the strangest and most varied new methods of cruelty, never seen or heard of before, and to such a degree that this Island of Hispaniola, once so populous (having a population that I estimated to be more than three millions), has now a population of barely two hundred persons.

The island of Cuba is nearly as long as the distance between Valladolid and Rome; it is now almost completely depopulated. San Juan and Jamaica are two of the largest, most productive and attractive islands; both are now deserted and devastated. On the northern side Cuba and Hispaniola lie the neighboring Lucayos comprising more than sixty islands including those called *Gigantes,* beside numerous other islands, some small some large. The least felicitous of them were more fertile and beautiful than the gardens of the King of Seville. They have the healthiest lands in the world, where lived more than five hundred thousand souls; they are now deserted, inhabited by not a single living creature. All the people were slain or died after being taken into captivity and brought to the Island of Hispaniola to be sold as slaves. When the Spaniards saw that some of these had escaped, they sent a ship to find them, and it voyaged for three years among the islands searching for those who had escaped being slaughtered, for a good Christian had helped them escape, taking pity on them and had won them over to Christ; of these there were eleven persons and these I saw.

More than thirty other islands in the vicinity of Juan are for the most part and for the same reason depopulated, and the land laid waste. On these islands I estimate there are 2,100 leagues of land that have been ruined and depopulated, empty of people.

As for the vast mainland, which is ten times larger than all Spain, even including Aragon and Portugal, containing more land than the distance between Seville and Jerusalem, or more than two thousand leagues, we are sure that our Spaniards, with their cruel and abominable acts, have devastated the land and exterminated the rational people who fully inhabited it. We can estimate very surely and truthfully that in the forty years that have passed, with the infernal actions of the Christians, there have been unjustly slain more than twelve million men, women, and children. In truth, I believe without trying to deceive myself that the number of the slain is more like fifteen million.

The common ways mainly employed by the Spaniards who call themselves Christian and who have gone there to extirpate those pitiful nations and wipe them off the earth is by unjustly waging cruel and bloody wars. Then, when they have slain all those who fought for their lives or to escape the tortures they would have to endure, that is to say, when they have slain all the native rulers and young men (since the Spaniards usually spare only the women and children, who are subjected to the hardest and bitterest servitude ever suffered by man or beast), they enslave any survivors. With these infernal methods of tyranny they debase and weaken countless numbers of those pitiful Indian nations.

Their reason for killing and destroying such an infinite number of souls is that the Christians have an ultimate aim, which is to acquire gold, and to swell themselves with riches in a very brief time and thus rise to a high estate disproportionate to their merits. It should be kept in mind that their insatiable greed and ambition, the greatest ever seen in the world, is the cause of their villainies. And also, those lands are so rich and felicitous, the native peoples so meek and patient, so easy to subject, that our Spaniards have no more consideration for them than beasts. And I say this from my own knowledge of the acts I witnessed. But I should not say "than beasts" for, thanks be to God, they have treated beasts with some respect; I should say instead like excrement on the public squares. And thus they have deprived the Indians of their lives and souls, for the millions I mentioned have died without the Faith and without the benefit of the sacraments. This is a well-known and proven fact which even the tyrant Governors, themselves killers, know and admit. And never have the Indians in all the Indies committed any act against the Spanish Christians, until those Christians have first a many times committed countless cruel aggressions against them or against neighboring nations. For in the beginni the Indians regarded the Spaniards as angels from Heaven. Only after the Spaniards had used violence against them, killing, robbing, torturing, did the Indians ever rise up against them.

HISPANIOLA

On the Island Hispaniola was where the Spaniards first landed, as I have said. Here those Christians perpetrated their first ravages and oppressions against the native peoples. This was the first land in the New World to destroyed and depopulated by the Christians, and here they began their subjection of the women and children, taking them away from the Indians to use them and ill use them, eating the food they provided with their sweat and toil. The Spaniards did not content themselves with what the Indians gave them of their own free will, according to their ability, which was always too little to satisfy enormous appetites, for a Christian eats and consumes in one day an amount of food that would suffice to feed three houses inhabited by ten Indians for one month. And they committed other acts of force and violence and oppression which made the Indians realize that these men had not come from Heaven. And some of the Indians concealed their foods while others concealed their wives and children and still others fled to the mountains to avoid the terrible transactions of the Christians....

...This tyrant-Governor who had gone to the mainland along with a large company of Spaniards invented new cruelties, new methods of torture to force the Indians to reveal and hand over their stores of gold. One captain, at the orders of the Governor, slew in a single attack more than forty thousand Indians. This massacre was witnessed by a Franciscan religious who was with him, by name Fray Francisco de San Romàn. The people were killed by the sword, by fire, by being torn to pieces by the fierce dogs kept by the Spaniards, and by being tortured to death in various ways.

And because of the pernicious blindness that has always afflicted those who have ruled in the Indies, nothing was done to *incline* the Indians to embrace the one true Faith, they were rounded up and in large numbers *forced* to do so. Inasmuch as the conversion of the Indians to Christianity was stated to be the principal aim of the Spanish conquerors, they have dissimulated the fact that only with blood and fire have the Indians been brought to embrace the Faith and to swear obedience to the kings of Castile, or by threats of being slain or taken into captivity. As if the Son of God who died for each one of them would have countenanced such a thing! For He commanded His Apostles: "Go ye to all the people" (*Euntes docete omnes gentes*). Christ Jesus would have made no such demands of these peaceable infidels who cultivate the soil of their native lands. Yet they are told they must embrace the Christian Faith immediately, without hearing any sermon preached and without any indoctrination. They are told to subject themselves to a King they have never heard of nor seen and are told this by the King's messengers who are such despicable and cruel tyrants that deprive them of their liberty, their possessions, their wives and children. This is not only absurd but worthy of scorn.

This wretch of a Governor thus gave such instructions in order to justify his and their presence in the Indies, they themselves being absurd, irrational, and unjust when he sent the thieves under his command to attack and rob a settlement of Indians where he had heard there was a store of gold, telling them to go at night when the inhabitants were securely in their houses and that, when half a league away from the settlement, they should read in a loud voice his order: "Caciques and Indians of this land, hark ye! We notify you that there is but one God and one Pope and one King of Castile who is the lord of these lands. Give heed and show obedience!" Etcetera, etcetera. "And if not, be warned that we will wage war against you and will slay you or take you into captivity." Etc., etc.

Then, in the early dawn, when these innocents are asleep with their wives and children, the Spaniards attack and enter the town and set fire to the houses, which, being commonly made of straw, burn rapidly with all who are within them.

Thus they proceeded, killing as many as they liked, and torturing those they took alive, because they had been told of other settlements where there was gold, more than there was in this one, and then they took a number of survivors in chains to sell them as slaves.

They always searched for gold in the ruins of the towns they burned. In this manner and with such acts, that Godforsaken Governor busied himself and his company from the year fourteen until the year twenty-one or twenty-two, sending into those actions five or six of his officers, giving each of them such and such an amount of the booty. The major part of the gold, the pearls, the enslaved Indians falling to himself as their captain-general. The representatives of the King acted in the same way, each one sending out as many underlings as they could, and the first Bishop of that kingdom also sent out his underlings so as to have his share of the treasure-trove. I believe I underestimate when I say they robbed more gold in that time and in that kingdom than was worth one million castellanos, of which amount they sent to the King only three thousand castellanos. And during these actions they killed some eight hundred thousand souls.

The other tyrant who succeeded this one on the mainland until the year one thousand five hundred and twenty-three, killed and allowed to be killed by his henchmen in the wars that followed all the native peoples that survived.

That wretch of a Governor who first penetrated the mainland committed countless vile deeds, of which I shall mention a few. A cacique (as a native ruler was called) had given the tyrant, either of his own accord or impelled by fear, gold worth nine thousand castellanos. Not content with this amount, the Governor had the cacique bound to a stake in a sitting posture, his legs extended, and set a fire to burn the soles of his feet, demanding more gold. The cacique sent to his house for more gold and the servant brought back three thousand castellanos' worth. Not content with this, more gold was demanded of the cacique. And, either because there was no more or else he was unwilling to give more, he continued to be tortured until the bone marrow came out of the soles of his feet and he died. Such things were done to the Indians countless times, always with the aim of getting as much gold as possible from them.

Another instance of such cruelty was when a company of Spaniards made an attack on a mountain refuge where some Indians were hiding from the pestilential acts of the Christians. Falling upon this numerous band, the Spaniards captured some women and maidens, sixty or eighty of them, holding them captive while they killed most of the men. Next day, some of the surviving Indians, anxious about the captive women, came upon the Christians from the rear and attacked them. Seeing they were hard-pressed, the Christians, who hesitated to bring up their cavalry, set their swords against the bodies of the women and maids, leaving not one of them alive. At sight of this, the Indians screamed in an access of grief and horror: "Oh, vile men! Oh, cruel Christians! So you kill women? (In their language their word for women is *iras,* meaning wrath, or vengeance.)

At a distance of ten or fifteen leagues from Panama was a great chief named Paris, who was very rich in gold. The Spaniards went there and he received them as if they were brothers, presenting the captain with gold worth fifty thousand castellanos, giving this of his own free will. It seemed to the captain of the Christian troops that anyone who could give that amount freely must possess a very great quantity (and discovering such treasures of gold was their sole aim and consolation). They dissimulated and made as if to depart. But in the early dawn they turned back and fell upon the town, setting fire to it, killing and burning many people. When the fires died down, they found and took away gold worth fifty or sixty thousand castellanos.

The cacique managed to escape, was neither killed nor captured, and very quickly he assembled as many surviving Indians as he could, and by the end of two or three days caught up with the Christians who were carrying away his gold, and valiantly attacked them, killing fifty Christians and taking the gold from them. The others, badly wounded, fled. But later on they marched against that cacique with a large company and killed him, along with a great many of his troops, taking captives and subjecting them to slavery in the usual way. In short, at the present time there remains no vestige of the large town where once ruled a great chieftain. And this does not take into account the killings and destructions that wretch of a Governor carried out which resulted in the extinction of those kingdoms....

***

...I will finish at this point and shall write no more until more news comes of still more egregious wickedness (if that is possible) or until we return to the Indies and see these things with our own eyes as we constantly did for twenty-two years, constantly protesting before God and my conscience. For I believe, no, I am sure that what I have said about such perditions, injuries, and horrible cruelties and all kinds of ugliness, violence, injustice, thefts, and massacres that those men have perpetrated in these parts of the Indies (and are still perpetrating), I am sure that what I have described is only the ten-thousandth part of what has been done, in quality and quantity, by the Spaniards in the Indies, from the beginning until today.

And so that any Christian may have more compassion for those innocent and ruined nations and their plight, so they may feel the pain of guilt and detest still more the greed and ambition and cruelty of the Spaniards in the Indies, let all that I have said be taken for the real truth, along with what I have affirmed, which is that from the discovery of the Indies until today, never in any part of that New World have the Indians done wrong to the Christians without first having been hurt and robbed and betrayed by them. For in the beginning they thought the Christians were immortals who had come down from Heaven, and they welcomed them, until they saw by their works what these Christians were and what they wanted.

Another thing must be added: from the beginning to the present time the Spaniards have taken no more care to have the Faith of Jesus Christ preached to those nations than they would to have it preached to dogs or other beasts. Instead, they have prohibited the religious from carrying out this intention, and have afflicted them and persecuted them in many ways, because such preaching would, they deemed, have hindered them from acquiring gold and other wealth they coveted. And today in all the Indies there is no more knowledge of God, whether He be of wood or sky, or earth, and this after one hundred years in the New World, except in New Spain, where some religious have gone, and which is but a very small part of the Indies. And thus all the nations have perished and are perishing without the sacraments of the Faith.

I, Fray Bartolomé de Las Casas (or Casaus), a Dominican friar, through the mercy of God, was induced to come to this court of Spain to bring about the ending of that inferno in the Indies and the irremediable destruction of souls that were redeemed by the blood of Jesus Christ; and to set up a work that would bring those souls to know their Creator and Savior. I am also here because of the compassion I have for my native land, Castile, that it not be destroyed by God as punishment for the great sins committed by Spaniards devoid of faith. I am also here because there reside in this court certain persons who are zealous for the honor of God and have compassion for the afflictions of their fellow men.

Finished in Valencia this eighth day of December, one thousand five hundred and forty-two, when actually all the force and violence are at their peak, when conditions in the Indies are at their worst, with all the anguish and disasters, all the massacres, looting, and destruction, outrages, and exterminations I have described. They are the lot of the native peoples in every part of the Indies where there are Christian conquerors. Although in some parts the Christian Spaniards are more ferocious and abominable in their behavior, they are a little less so in Mexico, or at least there they dare not commit their vile acts as openly as in other parts of the Indies. And although some justice does prevail there, all the same, an infernal amount of killing is done. I have great hope that our Emperor Charles V will harken to and comprehend the evils and betrayals that afflict that land and its peoples, against the will of God and against the will of His Majesty, deeds still being perpetrated, because until now the truth has industriously been concealed, and it is my hope that His Majesty will abolish the evils and remedy conditions in the New World that God has entrusted to him, as the lover and motivator of justice that he is, and may God protect his glorious and felicitous life and the Imperial State that all-powerful God has given him, to heal the universal Church. And may his royal soul be saved at last, and may he prosper for many years to come on this earth. Amen.

After writing the above, there were promulgated certain laws and ordinances which His Majesty issued from the city of Barcelona, in the year one thousand five hundred and forty-two, the month of November, and from the palace in Madrid, the following year, by which it was ordained that henceforth such evil deeds and sins against God and our fellow men would cease in the New World. And finally, after having made these laws, His Majesty held many councils and conferences with persons of great authority, learning, and conscience and there were debates in the palace of Valladolid and the votes cast were set down in writing, the Counselors keeping close to the law of Jesus Christ, being good Christians. It was ordained that the Spanish conquerors should cease the corruption and the soiling of their hands and souls in robbing the Indians of their treasures.

The laws being published, the makers of the tyrants who were at the court had many transcriptions made of them, and these were sent to diverse parts of the Indies. (They did this unwillingly, for the laws seemed to shut them out of participating in the robberies and tyrannies.)

And those who, in the Indies, had charge of the ruin and the robberies have continued, as if no orders had been issued, being inspired by Lucifer, when they saw the transcriptions, to engage in still more disorders before the new judges should arrive to execute the laws. And the tyrants rioted and rebelled when the new judges did come to supplant those who had aided and abetted the tyrants (since they had lost all love and all fear of God, and lost all shame and all obedience to the King). And thus they agreed to adopt the fame of traitors, their extreme cruelties and tyrannies were now unleashed, especially in the kingdom of Peru, where today in the year one thousand five hundred and forty-six they are committing such horrible, frightful, nefarious acts as were never before committed in the Indies or anywhere else in the world.

And these acts were committed not only against the Indians, most of the Indians having been killed and their lands destroyed, but against each other, and since the laws of the King no longer operated, punishment came from Heaven, allowing each tyrant to be the executioner of the other.

In imitation of this rebellion against the King in this part of the Indies, the tyrants in other parts of the New World have disregarded the new laws and are behaving in the same way. For they cannot bring themselves to relinquish the estates and properties they have usurped, or let go their hold on the Indians, whom they maintain in perpetual subjection. And wherever killing with the sword has come to an end, they are killing the Indians little by little through subjecting them to servitude. And until now the King has been powerless to check them, for all the Spaniards, young and old, in the Indies, are occupied in pillage, some openly, others secretly and stealthily. And with the pretense of serving the King they are dishonoring God and robbing and destroying the King.

Questions:
1. *How favorably does Las Casas describe the Caribbean natives? What traits of theirs seem to particularly impress him?*
2. *To what overriding cause did Las Casas ascribe the Europeans' motivation to slaughter?*
3. *What role did the first Bishop play?*
4. *What, according to Las Casas' attestations, was the situation at the time of his writing his accounts? What were the results of his petition to King Charles V?*

14.8   The British Encounter Maoris: A Sailor's Impressions

Captain James Cook of Yorkshire was without doubt the greatest seafarer of the 18th century, circumnavigating the globe and opening the Pacific regions to the knowledge of the outside world. All too often, this eventually worked to the detriment of the native cultures of the islands. One of the most resilient nations of Oceania, however, were the Maori of New Zealand, first encountered during Cook's 1772–73 voyage. James Burney (1750–1821), a seaman with Cook who later became an admiral, left these impressions in his journals.

> **Source:** Beverly Hooper, ed., *James Burney: With Captain James Cook in the Pacific.* (Canberra, Australia: National Library of Australia), pp. 67–68, 72–74.

These Islands have been described in so satisfactory a manner, that there is no room left for me to hold forth without making frequent repetitions of what has before been said never the less I will venture a word or two & attempt to draw their characters according to my own opinions—

I must confess I was a little disappointed on my first coming here as I expected to find People nearly as white as Europeans. Some of the better sort are tolerably white, more so than a Spaniard or Portugueze, but the generality are of a dark olive Colour. the men are something larger than the common run in England—

The Similitude of Customs & Language scarce admits any doubt of these Islanders being sprung from the same stock as the Zealanders though from the difference of climate & country they are as opposite in their characters as the enervated, luxurious Italians & the rude unpolished Northern Nations of Europe—the Heavoh & Tattow are common to both though practised in different manners—the Islanders have I think, the Advantage of the Zealanders, in their persons, they are likewise very cleanly, washing both before & after every meal, & take a great deal of Pride in their Dress—any thing showy or Ornamental is much more esteemed here than at Zealand—especially by the girls who have almost as much Vanity as the Women of Europe—Hospitality & a love of Society reigns through all these Islands; I never in any of my Rambles met with an unwelcome reception—In short they are a friendly humane people, superior to the Zealanders in many aspects—I mean the men as to the women, they must not be mentiond together unless by way of contrast—they are reckon'd smaller here than the English Women & not in proportion to the men, but take away our high heads & high heels, the difference of Size would not be perceptible—there are much handsomer women in England & many, more ordinary. I mean as to the face—but for fine turned Limbs & well made persons I think they cannot be excelled—I only speak from my own notions, which are not infallible, for I have not the least pretence to set up for a Judge in this case—the Children are in general exceeding beautifull—as they grow up they lose it for want of that care which in Europe is taken to preserve Beauty, they are not in the least afraid "The Winds of the Heavens Should visit their faces too roughly"—were they brought up in the delicate manner European Women are, there would be a great many very fine women amongst these Islands— Colour, in my opinion, has very little to do with beauty provided it be a healthy one it is a handsome one whether fair, brown or black—I question if they have any Idea of Chastity being a virtue—you may see young Girls not more than 12 years old with bellies they can scarce carry—after Marriage they confine themselves to the Husband—if they are caught slipping the Husband commonly sends them home to their Relations, but the Gallant does not escape so well, his life often paying the forfeit of his incontinence. the Independent men, or Aree's are allowed to have 2 wives—If a women after 6 or 7 months cohabitation with her Husband does not prove with Child, their Union, if they please, may be dissolved & each party at liberty to choose another mate. the women always mess by themselves & are seldom allowed to eat flesh— if a girl becomes pregnant the man cannot be forced to marry her. When a man courts any girl for a wife, after having got her relations consent, he sleeps 3 nights at their house—if the bride is a Virgin he is allowed to take no liberties till the 3^d Night, though he lyes with her each Night—the 3^d Day he makes the Relations a present & the 4th takes the Bride home— they give no portions with the girls unless the Bride's father has no Male children or other Male Relations to bestow his property on. a case which must be very rare in these Islands—…

***

Opune—has but one child (a Girl) living; he has 2 Wives & 3 Concubines—Tereroa's Sister was formerly one of his wives—She has been dead some time his Daughter if She survives him will inherit his Dominions—for he is not likely to have any more Children, being now a very old man but is Still greatly loved by his own Subjects & feared by the other Islands—Opune, in spite of old age & Blindness, (his Eyes being very bad) nevertheless retains all the Chearfullness & Merriment of a Young Man, nor are his people ever happier than when in his Company—he is a great encourager of their Games & Revels (their Heavah of which I shall Speak presently) & has invented many new ones himself—I have given this Character of him from what Omy says, who stiles him a fighting man & a man of Laughter.—I never saw him—

Of these people's Character, I have as yet shewn you only the fair Side—My partiality towards them shall not induce me to Stop here—As I set down nought in Malice, so will I nothing extenuate.

In their dealings with us they are great thieves, our Goods being of such Value to them, that very few can withstand the temptation of a fair opportunity—nevertheless I have slept all Night in their houses 8 miles up the Country, without any attempt being made on me—theft amongst themselves is punished with Death—

They have some very barbarous customs, the worst of which is, when a man has as many children as he is able to maintain, all that come after are smothered: women will sometimes bargain with her husband on her first marrying him, for the Number of Children that shall be kept. They never keep any Children that are any ways deformed—every fifth Child if suffered to live is Seldom allowed to rank higher than a Towtow—yet notwithstanding all this, these Islands are exceeding populous—even the Smallest being full of inhabitants & perhaps were it not for the Custom just mentioned, these would be more than the Islands could well maintain—

Every Island has a high priest, some two, with inferior priests—of this latter Class was Omy—the Being whom they worship they call Mo-wee & sometime offer human sacrifices to him—this is not done at any particular sett times but when Mo-wee requires it—he appears to none but the high priests, who frequently pretend to see him flying—this gives the high priest great power & if he is a man of a vindictive temper, whoever offends him must feel it—Mo-wee always names the person & as soon as his desires are known to the high priest he sends his attendants to dispatch the destined victim who knows nothing of his fate till the minute of his death—having killed him, he is carried to the high Priest, who takes out his Eyes, which Mo-wee eats, & the body is buried—

Before they venture on any extraordinary Expedition, Mo-wee is consulted: if the priest brings bad News it is either laid aside or deferred till better success is promised. Temperance or Chastity is not in the least essential to the high priest's Character, he being at liberty to take any woman he chooses to honour so far, married or unmarried, for as long as he pleases. The great power of the high priest would be very inconvenient for the Chief Aree were it not that they most commonly exercise this office themselves.—The Kingsfisher is one of their inferior deities—& the high priest understands what they say—…

Questions:
1. In what ways does Bumey betray disappointment or bias in his descriptions of the natives? In what ways does he demonstrate a deeper appreciation or tolerance?
2. For what causes might a Maori marriage be terminated?
3. What seems to be the Maori attitude towards old age? Towards infanticide?
4. What are the attributes of the deity, Mo-wee?

14.9   The Prospects of Christian Conversion: Saint Francis Xavier

The following selection is an excerpt from the journals of Gaspar Correa, who sailed with Vasco da Gama in 1502. This incident occurred after a group of Portuguese had been killed in the trading station of Calcutta. Vasco da Gama sought to control the situation by exacting a bloody vengeance.

Source: "The Prospects of Christian Conversion" is from Henry James Coleridge, ed., *The Life and Letters of St. Francis Xavier,* 2nd edition (London: Burns and Oates, 1890), p. 86.

SAINT FRANCIS XAVIER

My own and only Father in the Heart of Christ, I think that the many letters from this place which have lately been sent to Rome will inform you how prosperously the affairs of religion go on in these parts, through your prayers and the good bounty of God. But there seem to be certain things which I ought myself to speak about to you; so I will just touch on a few points relating to these parts of the world which are so distant from Rome. In the first place, the whole race of the Indians, as far as I have been able to see, is very barbarous; and it does not like to listen to anything that is not agreeable to its own manners and customs, which, as I say, are barbarous. It troubles itself very little to learn anything about divine things and things which concern salvation. Most of the Indians are of vicious disposition, and are adverse to virtue. Their instability, levity, and inconstancy of mind are incredible; they have hardly any honesty, so inveterate are their habits of sin and cheating. We have hard work here, both in keeping the Christians up the mark and in this account you should take great care of us and help us continually by your prayers to God. You know very well what a hard business it is to teach people who neither have any knowledge of God nor follow reason, but think it a strange and intolerable thing to be told to give up their habits of sin, which have now gained all the force of nature by long possession. . . .

   The experience which I have of these countries makes me think that I can affirm with truth, that there is no prospect of perpetuating our Society out here by means of the natives themselves, and that the Christian religion will hardly survive us who are now in the country; so that it is quite necessary that continual supplies of ours should be sent out from Europe. . . .

   The Portuguese in these countries are masters only of the sea and of the coast. On the mainland they have only the towns in which they live. The natives themselves are so enormously addicted to vice as to be little adapted to receive the Christian religion. They so dislike it that it is most difficult to get them to hear us if we begin to preach about it, and they think it like death to be asked to become Christians. So for the present, we devote ourselves to keeping the Christians whom we have. Certainly, if the Portuguese were more remarkable for their kindness to the new converts, a great number would become Christians; as it is, the heathen see that the converts, are despised and looked down upon by the Portuguese, and so, as is natural, they are unwilling to become converts themselves. For all these reasons there is no need for me to labor in these countries, and as I have learned from good authorities that there is a country near China called Japan, the inhabitants of which are all heathen, quite untouched by Muslims or Jews, and very eager to learn what they do not know both in things divine and things natural, I have determined to go thither as soon as I can. . . .

Questions:
1. How does Xavier describe the Indians? By what criteria does he judge them?
2. According to Xavier, how are the Portuguese hindering the missionaries?

PART 15
Trade and Exploitation Across the Atlantic

15.1 The "Black Legend" of Spain: Bartolomé de las Casas

More than any other single individual, the Dominican friar Bartolomé de Las Casas was responsible for the birth of the "Black Legend," the vicious Spanish reputation that developed during the sixteenth and seventeenth centuries. Although the Black Legend became primarily an instrument of Anglo-Dutch propaganda against the Spanish, which Las Casas probably would never have accepted, his influence in its creation is undeniable. After witnessing the ravages and atrocities of Spanish colonists, Las Casas dedicated himself to the protection and defense of the Indians. He wrote the Short Account of the Destruction of the Indies in 1542 and dedicated it to the Spanish king Philip II in an effort to inform the crown of atrocities in the New World that, if not curtailed, would result in God's destruction of Spain. This book, a fierce and deeply atmospheric anatomy of genocide, established the image of the Spanish conquest of America for the next three centuries. It is testimony to the persuasive and enduring influence of the Black Legend that the Spanish government hoped to amend this pejorative image by hosting the 1992 Olympics in Barcelona.

Source: *A Short Account of the Destruction of the Indies* by Bartholome dé Las Casas, translated by Nigel Griffin (Penguin Classics, 1992) copyright © Nigel Griffin, 1992, pp. 14–15. Reproduced with permission of Penguin Books Ltd.

As we have said, the island of Hispaniola was the first to witness the arrival of Europeans and the first to suffer the wholesale slaughter of its people and the devastation and depopulation of the land. It all began with the Europeans taking native women and children both as servants and to satisfy their own base appetites; then not content with what the local people offered them of their own free will (and all offered as much as they could spare), they started taking for themselves the food that natives contrived to produce by the sweat of their brows, (which was in all honesty little enough). . . . Some of them started to conceal what food they had, others decided to send their women and children into hiding, and yet others took to the hills to get away from the brutal and ruthless cruelty that was being inflicted on them. The Christians punched them, boxed their ears and flogged them in order to track down the local leaders, and the whole shameful process came to a head when one of the European commanders raped the wife of the paramount chief of the entire island. It was then that the locals began to think up ways of driving the Europeans out of their lands and to take up arms against them. Their weapons, however, were flimsy and ineffective both in attack and in defense (and, indeed, war in the Americas is no more deadly than our jousting, or than many European children's games) and, with their horses and swords and lances, the Spaniards easily fended them off, killing them and committing all kind of atrocities against them.

They forced their way into native settlements, slaughtering everyone they found there, including small children, old men, pregnant women, and even women who had just given birth. They hacked them to pieces, slicing open their bellies with their swords as though they were so many sheep herded into a pen. They even laid wagers on whether they could manage to slice a man in two at a stroke, or cut an individual's head from his body, or disembowel him with a single blow of their axes. They grabbed suckling infants by the feet and, ripping them from their mothers' breasts, dashed them headlong against the rocks. . . . They slaughtered anyone and everyone in their path, on occasion running through a mother and her baby with a single thrust of their swords. They spared no one, erecting especially wide gibbets on which they could string their victims up with their feet just off the ground and then burn them alive thirteen at a time, in honor of our Savior and the twelve Apostles, or tie dry straw to their bodies and set fire to it. Some they chose to keep alive and simply cut their wrists, leaving their hands dangling, saying to them: "Take this letter"—meaning that their sorry condition would act as a warning to those hiding in the hills. The way they normally dealt with the native leaders and nobles was to tie them to a kind of griddle consisting of sticks resting on pitchforks driven into the ground and then grill them over a slow fire, with the result that they howled in agony and despair as they died a lingering death.

Questions:
1. What was the "Black Legend" of Spain?
2. What type of atrocities were committed by the Spanish conquistadors?

15.2 "Our Kingdom Is Being Lost": Nzinga Mbemba (Afonso I)

The next selection is a letter from the African King of Kongo, Nzinga Mbemba, who had converted to Christianity and adopted the name Afonso I (reigned ca. 1506–1543). Afonso had hoped to develop a prosperous state by cooperating with the Europeans. But by the time of his death, his kingdom had almost disintegrated. His concerns are expressed in a letter to the Portuguese king, Joao III, in 1526. It was evident that Portuguese exploitation and aggressive pursuit of slaves resulted in dissension and instability throughout the region.

Source: Copyright © 1964 by Basil Davidson, Reprinted by permission of Curtis Brown, Ltd.

Sir, Your Highness should know how our Kingdom is being lost in so many ways that it is convenient to provide for the necessary remedy, since this is caused by the excessive freedom given by your agents and officials to the men and merchants who are allowed to come to this Kingdom to set up shops with goods and many things which have been prohibited by us, and which they spread throughout our Kingdoms and Domains in such an abundance that many of our vassals, whom we had in obedience, do not comply because they have the things in greater abundance than we ourselves; and it was with these things that we had them content and subjected under our vassalage and jurisdiction, so it is doing a great harm not only to the service of God, but the security and peace of our Kingdoms and State as well.

And we cannot reckon how great the damage is, since the mentioned merchants are taking every day our natives, sons of the land and the sons of our noblemen and vassals and our relatives, because the thieves and men of bad conscience grab them wishing to have the things and wares of this Kingdom which they are ambitious of; they grab them and get them to be sold; and so great, Sir, is the corruption and licentiousness that our country is being completely depopulated, and Your Highness should not agree with this nor accept it as in your service. And to avoid it we need from your Kingdoms no more than some priests and a few people to teach in schools, and no other goods except wine and flour for the holy sacrament. That is why we beg of Your Highness to help and assist us in this matter, commanding your factors [agents] that they should not send here either merchants or wares, because it *our will that in these Kingdoms there should not be any trade of slaves nor outlet for them.* Concerning what is referred [to] above, again we beg of Your Highness to agree with it, since otherwise we cannot remedy such an obvious damage. Pray Our Lord in his mercy to have Your Highness under His guard and let you do forever the things of His service. . . .

Moreover, Sir, in our Kingdoms there is another great inconvenience which is of little service to God, and this is that many of our people, keenly desirous as they are of the wares and things of your Kingdoms, which are brought here by your people, and in order to satisfy their voracious appetite, seize many of our people, freed and exempt men, and very often it happens that they kidnap even noblemen and the sons of noblemen, and our relatives, and take them to be sold to the white men who are in our Kingdoms; and for this purpose they have concealed them; and others are brought during the night so that they might not be recognized.

And as soon as they are taken by the white men they are immediately ironed and branded with fire, and when they are carried to be embarked, if they are caught by our guards' men the whites allege that they have bought them but they cannot say from whom, so that it is our duty to do justice and to restore to the freemen their freedom, but it cannot be done if your subjects feel offended, as they claim to be.

And to avoid such a great evil we passed a law so that any white man living in our Kingdoms and wanting to purchase goods in any way should first inform three of our noblemen and officials of our court whom we rely upon in this matter, and these are Dom Pedro Manipanza and Dom Manuel Manissaba, our chief usher, and Gocalo Pires our chief freighter, who should investigate if the mentioned goods are captives or free men, and if cleared by them there will be no further doubt nor embargo for them to be taken and embarked. But if the white men do not comply with it they will lose the aforementioned goods. And if we do them this favor and concession it is for the part Your Highness has in it, since we know that it is in your service too that these goods are taken from our Kingdom, otherwise we should not consent to this. . . .

Question:
1. Why was his kingdom "out of balance" and what reforms did he suggest?

15.3 Olaudah Equiano, The Life of Olaudah Equiano, or Gustavus Vassa, The African

One African who survived the journey was Olaudah Equiano (ca. 1745–1797), an Ibo born in eastern Nigeria near Benin. When Equiano was ten years old, he and his sister were captured from their home by local robbers who quickly sold the children to slavers. Equiano served a series of masters, first in Barbados and later in Virginia; he was finally bought by a British naval officer who took him to Canada, England, and then back to the West Indies. This owner gave Equiano the new name of Gustavus Vassa. In 1766, by luck and frugal trading, Equiano had saved the hefty sum of forty pounds sterling, which was enough money to buy his freedom. As a free man, he returned to England, where he worked as a barber, a domestic servant, and a sailor.

In 1789, he published a two-volume set of memoirs in English, describing his life in Africa and his experiences as a slave. His account, excerpted in the following reading, became a best-seller in England and soon enabled Equiano; to become active in the English antislavery movement.

Source: From Olaudah Equiano, *The Life of Olaudah Equiano, or Gustavus Vassa, The African,* Written by Himself (Boston: I. Knapp, 1837), 31–32, 43–44, 47–48, 50–52.

One day, when all our people were gone out to their works as usual and only I and my dear sister were left to mind the house, two men and a woman got over our walls, and in a moment seized us both, and without giving us time to cry out or make resistance they stopped our mouths and ran off with us into the nearest wood. Here they tied our hands and continued to carry us as far as they could till night came on, when we reached a small house where the robbers halted for refreshment and spent the night. . . .

The first object which saluted my eyes when I arrived on the coast was the sea, and a slave ship which was then riding at anchor and waiting for its cargo. These filled me with astonishment, which was soon converted into terror when I was carried on board. I was immediately handled and tossed up to see if I were sound by some of the crew, and I was now persuaded that I had gotten into a world of bad spirits and that they were going to kill me. Their complexions too differing so much from ours, their long hair and the language they spoke (which was very different from any I had ever heard) united to confirm me in this belief. Indeed such were the horrors of my views and fears at the moment that, if ten thousand worlds had been my own, I would have freely parted with them all to have exchanged my condition with that of the meanest slave in my own country. When I looked round the ship too and saw a large furnace or copper boiling and a multitude of black people of every description chained together, every one of their countenances expressing dejection and sorrow, I no longer doubted of my fate; and quite overpowered with horror and anguish, I fell motionless on the deck and fainted. When I recovered a little I found some black people about me, who I believed were some of those who had brought me on board and had been receiving their pay; they talked to me in order to cheer me, but all in vain. I asked them if we were not to be eaten by those white men with horrible looks, red faces, and loose hair. They told me I was not, and one of the crew brought me a small portion of spirituous liquor in a wine glass, but being afraid of him I would not take it out of his hand. One of the blacks there took it from him and gave it to me, and I took a little down my palate, which instead of reviving me, as they thought it would, threw me into the greatest consternation at the strange feeling it produced, having never tasted any such liquor before. Soon after this the blacks who brought me on board went off, and left me abandoned to despair. . . .

The stench of the hold while we were on the coast was so intolerably loathsome that it was dangerous to remain there for any time, and some of us had been permitted to stay on the deck for the fresh air; but now that the whole ship's cargo were confined together it became absolutely pestilential. The closeness of the place and the heat of the climate, added to the number in the ship, which was so crowded that each had scarcely room to run himself, almost suffocated us. This produced copious perspirations, so that the air soon became unfit for respiration from a variety of loathsome smells, and brought on a sickness among the slaves, of which many died, thus falling victims to the improvident avarice, as I may call it, of their purchasers. This wretched situation was again aggravated by the galling of the chains, now become insupportable, and the filth of the necessary tubs, into which the children often fell and were almost suffocated. The shrieks of the women and the groans of the dying rendered the whole a scene of horror almost inconceivable. Happily perhaps for myself I was soon reduced so low here that it was thought necessary to keep me almost always on deck, and from my extreme youth I was not put in fetters. . . .

At last we came in sight of the island of Barbados, at which the whites on board gave a great shout and made many signs of joy to us. We did not know what to think of this, but as the vessel drew nearer we plainly saw the harbour and other ships of different kinds and sizes, and we soon anchored amongst them off Bridgetown. Many merchants and planters now came on board, though it was in the evening. They put us in separate parcels and examined us attentively. They also made us jump, and pointed to the land, signifying we were to go there. We thought by this we should be eaten by these ugly men, as they appeared to us; and when soon after we were all put down under the deck again, there was much dread and trembling among us, and nothing but bitter cries to be heard all the night from these apprehensions, insomuch that at last the white people got some old slaves from the land to pacify us. They told us we were not to be eaten but to work, and were soon to go on land where we should see many of our country people. This report eased us much; and sure enough soon after we were landed there came to us Africans of all languages. We were conducted immediately to the merchant's yard, where we were all pent up together like so many sheep in a fold without regard to sex or age. As every object was new to me everything I saw filled me with surprise. What struck me first was that the houses were built with storeys, and in every other respect different from those in Africa: but I was still more astonished on seeing people on horseback. I did not know what this could mean, and indeed I thought these people were full of nothing but magical arts. While I was in this astonishment one of my fellow prisoners spoke to a countryman of his about the horses, who said they were the same kind they had in their country. I understood them though they were from a distant part of Africa, and I thought it odd I had not seen any horses there; but afterwards when I came to converse with different Africans I found they had many horses amongst them, and much larger than those I then saw. We were not many days in the merchant's custody before we were sold after their usual manner, which is this: On a signal given, (as the beat of a drum) the buyers rush at once into the yard where the slaves are confined, and make choice of that parcel they like best. The noise and clamour with which this is attended and the eagerness visible in the countenances of the buyers serve not a little to increase the apprehensions of the terrified Africans, who may well be supposed to consider them as the ministers of that destruction to which they think themselves devoted. In this matter, without scruple, are relations and friends separated, most of them never to see each other again. I remember in the vessel in which I was brought over, in the men's apartment there were several brothers who, in the sale, were sold in different lots; and it was very moving on this occasion to see and hear their cries at parting. O, ye nominal Christians! might not an African ask you, Do unto all men as you would men should do unto you? Is it not enough that we are torn from our country and friends to toil for your luxury and lust of gain? Must every tender feeling be likewise sacrificed to your avarice? Are the dearest friends and relations, now rendered more dear by their separation from their kindred, still to be parted from each other and thus prevented from cheering the gloom of slavery with the small comfort of being together and mingling their sufferings and sorrows? Why are parents to lose their children, brothers their sisters, or husbands their wives? Surely this is a new refinement in cruelty which, while it has no advantage to atone for it, thus aggravates distress and adds fresh horrors even to the wretchedness of slavery.

Questions:
1. What does this memoir tell us about the organization and extent of slavery in the eighteenth-century Atlantic world?
2. What does this selection indicate about Equiano's African home and African culture?
3. What does the memoir, particularly its title, The Life of Olaudah Equiano, or Gustavus Vassa, The African, tell us about the cultural effects of slavery upon Africans in the eighteenth century?

15.4 Commerce, Slavery, and Religion in North Africa

The purchase of slaves by North African merchants through the agency of rulers on the southern Saharan fringes began as early as the ninth century a.d. and was brought to an end only at the beginning of the twentieth century. West African Muslim rulers played an important controlling role in all external trade, and North African merchants could operate only with their consent. From the nineteenth-century evidence we have from the northern regions of what is now Nigeria, it is clear that rulers had first choice of merchandise from the large caravans and paid for it in slaves—a commodity that could be obtained at will by raiding the large non-Muslim populations surrounding these Muslim states. The enslavement of non-Muslims was permitted by Islamic law as a by-product of jihād—"war for the expansion of the domain of Islam," but the random rounding up of non-Muslim populations to pay off a debt, such as is illustrated in the following piece, hardly comes under this rubric. Nevertheless, the narrator seeks some religious justification for carrying off black Africans into slavery inasmuch as their routinized mass "conversion" to Islam en route ensures their salvation. As he acknowledges, piety and commerce may be mutually reinforcing.

The following account was given to General E. Daumas, a French officer serving in Algeria in the 1830s, by a member of a caravan headed by a Tuareg guide (khabīr) called Cheggueun, which set out from Metlily in the Algerian Sahara to do business in Katsina in the far north of present-day Nigeria. Katsina was one of the emirates that formed part of a large Islamic empire founded in the early years of the nineteenth century with its capital at Sokoto.

Source: Abridged and trans. John O. Hunwick from Gen. E. Daumas, Le Grand Désert. *Itinéraire d'une* *caravane du Sahara au pays des nègres, royaume de Haoussa,* 4th ed., (Paris, 1860), pp. 199–247.

THE SLAVE TRADE

We had been at Katsina for ten days and when the story had got around in the surrounding villages that a rich caravan had arrived, all the petty merchants hastened to the town. Moreover, since those of Katsina were pressing us it was decided to put our merchandise on sale and Cheggueun went to tell Omar[1] what we intended to do. The response of the serki (ruler) was that we could do as we liked, but that he would reserve the sale of all our broadcloths, in the name of the sultan. His oukil (agent) made a list the same day and took us to the palace to discuss the price with the serki himself.

"Khabir (caravan leader)," said Omar to our chief, "according to what my agent has told me, the broadcloths of your merchants are of inferior quality and are worth no more than a single slave, negro or negress, per cubit." "Sir, it shall be done according to your justice. We are your servants," replied Cheggueun, and we all put our fist on our chest as a sign of consent, for in fact we were getting a good deal. "Go in peace, then," replied the serki, "I do not have enough slaves to pay you today. But, by the grace of God, Mohammed Omar shall not fail in his word."

As we went out of the palace a regular low pitched sound caught our attention. It came from the center of the town and we made for it. It led us to the Makhzen (army) square where, from every street, a crowd came running like us. At the center of the square was placed a huge drum which a strapping Negro beat with a knobbed stick with all his might. This is the sultan's drum. It is never beaten for anything but assembling the army.

We had discovered the secret of the strange noise that had moved us and this proclamation of the chief of the Mekhazenia informed us for what purpose they were gathered: "This is the will of the serki. In the name of sultan Bello the Victorious,[2] may God bless him, all of you, are summoned to present yourselves here at daybreak, armed and mounted, with sufficient provisions to go, some to Zenfra [Zamfara] and others to Zendeur [Zinder] to hunt the idolatrous Koholanes[3]—enemies of the glorious sultan our master—may God curse them." "All that the sultan orders is good," responded the soldiers. "Let it be done according to the will of our lord and master."

The following day, in fact, the Mekhazenia (soldiery), prompt to the appointed meeting, divided themselves into two goums (companies), one taking the east and the other the south-west with orders to attack places without defences and to carry off the inhabitants as well as seizing all peasants busy cultivating their fields. At the same time orders were given to track down the idolatrous Koholanes in the interior.

Whilst waiting for the return of the goums that Omar had despatched to hunt Negroes, we went every day to the slave market where we bought at the following prices:

A Negro with beard	10 or 15,000 cowries

They are not considered as merchandise since one has little chance of preventing them from escaping.

An adult Negress, same price for	10 or 15,000 cowries the same reasons
An adolescent Negro	30,000 cowries
A young Negress	50–60,000 cowries
(The price varies according to whether she is more or less beautiful.)	
A male Negro child	45,000 cowries
A female Negro child	35–40,000 cowries

The seller gives the buyer the greatest possible chance to examine the slaves and one has three days to give notice of concealed faults.

THE RETURN OF OMAR'S GOUM

The goum of serki Omar had been on campaign for about a month when we learnt from a messenger that the double raid launched against Zinder and Zamfara had been completely successful and that the makhzen, bringing back two thousand slaves would return to Katsina the next day. In a few hours this good news had spread throughout the town and at daybreak the next day the entire population crowded the gardens on the east side where the two armies that had the previous day joined up ought to arrive.

A cloud of dust soon announced it and as they crossed the outer wall where the route was better marked and the terrain more solid, their confused mass began to make itself out from the veil of sand that they had raised on the plain. The prisoners walked at the head, men, women, children, the elderly, almost all naked or half covered in rags of blue cloth. The women and the elderly were unbound but tightly packed together; the children were piled onto camels with some sitting on their mothers' backs in a piece of cloth doing duty as a bag. The men had been chained, five or six to the same chain, their necks fixed in a strong iron ring closed by a padlock and their hands bound with palm ropes. The strongest and most resistant were tied down to the tails of horses. Women moaned and children cried. Men, in general, seemed more resigned, but the bloody cuts that the whip had made on their shoulders bore witness to their tough struggle with the horsemen of the serki.

The convoy steered itself towards the palace and its arrival was announced to Mohammed Omar by musicians. At the first sound of the music the serki came out of his palace followed by his agent and some dignitaries. On seeing him all the slaves threw themselves on their knees and the musicians attacked their instruments with a passion that bordered on fury. The serki, approaching the goum, complimented its leaders, examined the slaves and gave the order for them to be taken to the market. There they were placed in two rows in sheds, women on one side and men on the other, and on the next day we were invited to go and choose those which suited us. Cheggueun and the palace agent went with us and after very careful examination each of us obtained as many Negroes and Negresses as he had handed over cubits of broadcloth to the serki. Nevertheless, we only accepted those whose sound constitutions were a surety against the hazards of the long journey we had to make. The elderly, small children and pregnant women were sold to the people of Katsina or given by Omar as gifts to the leaders of his mekhazenias.

DEPARTURE OF THE CARAVAN

We were now in the month of April and the season was favorable for leaving. We hastened to gather provisions of maize, millet, dried meat, butter and honey sufficient for each person for three months and we bought baggage camels in sufficient number to insure against accidents en route and some oxhide tents. Finally, our caravan which had set out from Metlily (in Algeria) with sixty-four camels and only sixteen persons, was now augmented by four hundred slaves, of whom three hundred were women, and had a total of almost six hundred camels.

The people of Touat [Tuwāt][4] who joined with us, had increased in number similarly. They had purchased fifteen hundred slaves and their camels had risen in number to two thousand. Altogether we formed a company of about two thousand one hundred men and two thousand six hundred camels. Katsina had no square big enough to contain us and so, under the name of the Touat caravan, we went to establish ourselves in one of the great empty spaces set up in the middle of the gardens.

Finally we saw successively arriving the three caravans of Ghadames, Ghat and the Fezzan.[5] The first had penetrated as far as Nupe on the banks of the Bahar-el-Nil [river Niger] to the south of Sokoto. It brought back three thousand slaves and three thousand five hundred camels. The second had pushed down to Kano to the south-east of Katsina. It only numbered seven or eight hundred camels and four or five hundred slaves. The third came back from Sokoto and was no larger than the preceding one.

At daybreak our camels were loaded, the Negro children perched atop the baggage, the male Negroes secured by their chains in the center of the convoy and the Negro females grouped in eights or tens under the watch of men carrying whips. The departure signal was given and the first caravan moved. It was at this point that suddenly a confused noise of cries and sobs passed from one group of slaves to another and reached our own. All, together, wept and moaned, called out and uttered farewells. They were terrified of being eaten during the journey. Some rolled on the ground, clung to bushes and absolutely refused to walk. Nothing had any effect on them, neither kind words nor threats. They could only be got up with mighty lashes of the whip and by rendering them completely bloody. Despite their obstinacy, no one of them resisted this extreme measure. Moreover, joined together as they were, the less fearful or more courageous, struggling with the weaker ones, forced them to walk.

The first day we halted at only three leagues[6] from Katsina on a huge plain where we found pools and plenty of grass and wood. Each caravan established its camp separately. As soon as our camels had crouched down and after having, first and foremost, chained up our Negresses by the foot in groups of eight or ten, we forced our Negroes to help us, using their left hand which we had left free, in unloading our animals, marking out a circle with our loads and putting up the oxhide tents we had brought from Katsina within this perimeter. Two or three of the older Negresses whom we had not chained together, but who nevertheless had their feet shackled, were set to preparing something for us to dine on.

The next day we loaded up early and this time the Ghat caravan took the lead. Although calmer than they were the evening before, our slaves were still very irritable. To tire them out and weaken them we made the slaves carry their irons, their dishes and the mortars for pounding maize and millet. And so that our entire attention could be concentrated on them, each of us tied his camels together in a single file. Watching over them thus became easier and if one of them fell down or a load fell off, we could in this way halt them all at once and we avoided the whole group bolting as we got one on its feet or reloaded another.

ESCAPE, RECAPTURE, PUNISHMENT

[The narrator's personal slave, Mebrouk, could not reconcile himself to his condition, despite his owner's blandishments, and led a party of six slaves—all chained together for the night—in an escape. Two were recaptured; two others chained together were attacked by a lion and one was mauled to death while the other eventually died of fright. Mebrouk and one other slave were never found.]

When news of this event was noised abroad our khebirs, each followed by fifteen horsemen, set off at a gallop and explored the countryside far and wide. But it is full of scrub and so dotted with hillocks that they could only find two of the fugitives. As a lesson for the future, it remained for us to learn from the two recaptured fugitives by what clever means they and their companions had slipped their chains. But neither kindness nor patience on the part of Cheggueun who was interrogating them, could make their tongues wag and, seized by anger, he ordered that they should be flogged in front of the other slaves. In no time all these pagans were lined up on the side of a hillock. Two powerful men seized one of the two Negroes, threw him to the ground and sat astride his heels and neck. At the same time two chaouchs (assistants) had taken up their stations, canes in hand, one on the right and the other on the left of the guilty one.

"Go to it," said Cheggueun. At the first blow the canes were white. At the fiftieth they were red and blood ran on the thighs and sides of the victim. But the obstinate fellow had still said nothing. Only his fitful breathing and some movement of his loins bore witness to the fact that they were not beating a corpse. Finally he cried out, "Abi (father)! Serki (chief)! I will tell all. Stop the beating." A gesture from Cheggueun brought the chaouchs to a halt.

"Speak," he said to the Negro. "What did you do to break your chains and what happened to them?"

"O Serki! I touched them with my kerikeri (amulet) and made them melt."

"Chaouchs!" responded Cheggueun, "Beat him harder. He lies."

The canes descended on the liar so hard that they removed a strip of his skin.

"Abi! Serki! I will talk. I will talk," he cried.

"Dog of a pagan," said Cheggueun, "I will have you killed if you lie to me again."

"By my father's neck," replied the slave, "here is the truth. During the night, by slithering on the sand, Mebrouk came over to us. He had some hot water in a calabash and he poured some of this in the lock of our chains. Thus wetted, when we tapped it on its side we made the bolt slide and we opened it. Out of the five, however, two had to escape attached to one another, carrying the chain with them."

"O my children," Cheggueun said to us, "you hear him. Above all, those of you whose Negroes are chained up with old chains, never go to sleep without seeing with your eye and touching with your hand the padlocks which protect your fortune. Let this be a good lesson to you all!"

The slave was seated and the chaouchs helped him to stand up. Limping and groaning he dragged himself to the feet of his master, prostrated with his face on the ground and poured sand over himself as a sign of his repentance and submission. It had taken no less than one hundred and twenty strokes of the cane to drag out his secret from him and good justice would have required that his accomplice receive the same. But his owner objected that two such wounded men would be an embarrassment for everyone, that they might die of exhaustion and that his loss was already great. Cheggueun, who had a heart of gold, was easily convinced by these good reasons and he gave orders that on departure the next morning the sick man should be put on a camel.

WITH THE MARABOUTS

[The caravan halted at a place called Aghezeur, probably near Agades in present-day Niger, to take on provisions and to reclaim some items they had deposited there on the southbound journey in the keeping of a community of "marabouts" (Muslim holymen).]

With our preparations for departure complete we were of a mind to set out on the third day after our arrival, but the marabouts of the zaouïa (lodge) of Sidi Ahmed who had come to our camp and called us together for prayer held us back with these words: "O Muslims! These negroes you are bringing are idolators. We must make them know the One God; we must teach them to pray and how to perform ablutions; we must circumcise them today. God will reward you for it. Make your slaves assemble. By God's grace we know their language; we will put ourselves in the middle of them and teach them what it is good for them to know."

We understood well, for the Lord loves him who causes the number of His servants to be increased; moreover, there is, from the point of view of sales, a great advantage in turning an idolator into a Muslim. Almost all of our slaves already knew the *shahāda* (declaration of faith) and the name of the Prophet and God. Frequently, during leisure time at camp we would teach them the basic tenets of the religion, speaking broken gnāwiyya[7] to them while they spoke broken Arabic to us. To the best behaved we offered some concessions; to the obdurate some harsh discipline; thus self-interest, if not conviction, had readied them for the solemn ceremony which would today make them into Muslims.

In front of the *zāwiya* of Sidi Ahmed is a huge open space. Each one of us led his Negroes there and made them sit on the ground and soon their number sketched out a gigantic thick semi-circle facing the zaouïa. Like a muezzin calling to prayer, the imam climbed up on the mosque and uttered these words:

"God is One; He has no associates. He is unique of His kind and none is comparable to Him. He is the Sovereign and Incomparable Lord. He is from all time and shall endure for all time. Eternity shall not destroy Him and time and the centuries do not change Him. He is the First, the Last, the Manifest and the Hidden. He knows what is in the inside of bodies. Nothing is similar to Him; He is superior to all things. His superiority and His exhaltation, instead of distancing Him from His worshippers, brings Him closer to His creatures. He is All-Seeing, All-Knowing, He is Omnipresent. He is Holy and no place can encompass Him. Only the saints can look upon Him in the places where His dwelling is sempiternal, as has been established by the verses of the Qur'ān and the accounts of the ancients. He is Living, He is Powerful, He is Almighty, He is Superb, He is Severe; idleness and weakness are remote from Him."

"He forgets not, He sleeps not. His is the command and to Him belongs the vastness of the universe. To Him belong honor and omnipotence. He created creatures and their acts. When He wishes a thing, it is. When He does not wish it, it is not. He is the Beginning and the End, the Doer of His will. Everything that is in the world—movement, rest, good, evil, profit, loss, faith, infidelity, obedience and disobedience—all come from God. There is no bird that flies with its wings, no beast that walks on its feet, no serpent that glides on its stomach, no leaf that grows or falls and no light or darkness without the almighty will of God. Everything that exists is created; God exists from eternity and all that has been created demonstrates His unity. Man's petition to God is prayer and prayer itself only exists by the will of God. If you put your confidence in God, He will care for you as He cares for the birds of the heavens who set out hungry and return full. He does not bring food to their nests, but he puts in them the instinct to search for it."

I would not dare to say that this speech made a lively impression on the Negroes, but the solemnity of the new spectacle for them, the receptivity with which we, their masters and the holy marabout, listened certainly made them ready for the carrying out of the religious act that would make them Muslims. When time for the operation came, though all or almost all showed themselves surprised, not one refused to undergo it, for they take pride in having no fear of pain. As soon as they had been marked with the symbol of the Muslims, they had their wounds staunched by us with an astringent powder made of dried ground leaves of arrar [juniper] and el-aazir, blended with butter.[8]

The marabouts then prayed over them in gnāwiyya, saying: "O you Negroes, give thanks to God! Yesterday you were idolators and today you are Muslims. Depart with your masters who will clothe you, feed you and love you like their brothers and children. Serve them well and they will give you your liberty in a while. If you are comfortable with them you shall stay there. If not you shall return to your land."

That day and the next we took particular care of our slaves. We fed them good meat and let them sleep in tents to keep them from the cold and dew of the nights. Thanks to such attentions our caravan did not lose a single one. In the other caravans, however, some of the older ones died.

Questions:
1. How did the Muslim Holy men (Marabouts) influence the commerce in African slavery?
2. How does the organization of the slave trade in North Africa in the nineteenth century compare with the organization of the slave trade in West Africa in the eighteenth century (see Reading 7)?

15.5   Thomas Nelson, Slavery and the Slave Trade of Brazil

Under pressure from Britain, Brazil agreed to abolish its slave trade in 1826, but contraband traffic in slaves continued unabated in subsequent decades. Meanwhile, Britain claimed the right to search and arrest suspected slave ships. During the 1840s, Thomas Nelson served as a surgeon aboard a British frigate, the H.M.S. Crescent, and his duties included the inspection and treatment of contraband slaves intercepted en route to Brazil. The following reading is an excerpt from his book describing the conditions of the Africans he encountered.

> **Source:** From Thomas Nelson, *Remarks on the Slavery and Slave Trade of the Brazils* (London: J. Halchard and Son, 1846), pp. 43–56 passim.

A few minutes after the vessel dropped her anchor, I went on board of her, and although somewhat prepared by the previous inspection of two full slavers to encounter a scene of disease and wretchedness, still my experience, aided by my imagination, fell short of the loathsome spectacle which met my eyes on stepping over the side. Huddled closely together on deck, and blocking up the gangways on either side, cowered, or rather squatted, three hundred and sixty-two negroes, with disease, want, and misery stamped upon them with such painful intensity as utterly beggars all powers of description. In one corner, apart from the rest, a group of wretched beings lay stretched, many in the last stage of exhaustion, and all covered with the pustules of smallpox. Several of these I noticed had crawled to the spot where the water had been served out, in the hope of procuring a mouthful more of the precious liquid; but unable to return to their proper places, lay prostrate around the empty tub. Here and there, amid the throng, were isolated cases of the same loathsome disease in its confluent or worst form, and cases of extreme emaciation and exhaustion, some in a state of perfect stupor, others looking piteously around, and pointing with their fingers to their parched mouths whenever they caught an eye who they thought would relieve them. On every side, squalid and sunken visages were rendered still more hideous by the swollen eyelids and the puriform discharge of a virulent ophthalmia, with which the majority appeared to be afflicted; added to this were figures shriveled to absolute skin and bone, and doubled up in a posture which originally want of space had compelled them to adopt, and which debility and stiffness of the joints compelled them to retain.

On looking more leisurely around, after the first paroxysm of horror and disgust had subsided, I remarked on the poop another wretched group, composed entirely of females. Some were mothers with infants who were vainly endeavoring to suck a few drops of moisture from the lank, withered, and skinny breasts of their wretched mothers; others were of every intermediate age. The most of them destitute even of the decency of a rag, and all presenting as woeful a spectacle of misery as it is possible to conceive.

While employed in examining the negroes individually, and separating and classifying the sick, who constituted by far the majority, I obtained a closer insight into their actual condition. Many I found afflicted with a confluent smallpox, still more with purulent ophthalmia, and the majority of what remained, with dysentery, ulcers, emaciation, and exhaustion. In several, two or three of these were met. Not the least distressing sight on that pest-laden deck was the negroes whom the ophthalmia had struck blind, and who cowered in seeming apathy to all that was going on around. This was indeed the ultimatum of wretchedness, the last drops of the cup of bitterness. Deprived of liberty, and torn from their native country, there was nothing more of human misery but to make them the victims of a physical darkness as deep as they had already been made of a moral one.

The stench on board was nearly overwhelming. The odor of the negroes themselves, rendered still stronger by their filthy and crowded condition, the sickening smell of the suppurative stage of smallpox, and the far more disgusting effluvium of dysenteric discharge, combined with bilge water, putrid jerked beef, and numerous other matters to form a stench, it required no little exertion of fortitude to withstand. To all this, hunger and thirst lent their aid to finish the scene; and so poignant were they, that the struggles to obtain the means of satisfying them were occasionally so great as to require the interference of the prize crew. The moment it could be done, water in abundance and a meal was provided them; and none but an eyewitness could form an idea of the eagerness with which the former luxury was coveted and enjoyed. For many days, it seems, the water had not only been reduced in quantity, but so filled with impurities, and so putrid, that nothing but the most stringent necessity could have induced the use of it. . . .

Early yesterday morning (11th of September, 1843) the decks of the *Crescent* were again thronged by a miserable crowd of liberated Africans. The vessel in which they had been conveyed from the "coast" was captured a few days ago by one of the boats belonging to H.M.S. *Frolic*, a little to the northward of Rio.

Previously to the removal of the negroes, Dr. Gunn (the surgeon of the *Crescent*) and myself went on board the slaver, and stepping over the side, were astonished at the smallness of the vessel, and the number of wretched negroes who had been thrust on board of her. Below, the hold was crowded to excess; and above, the deck was so closely packed with the poor creatures, that we had to walk along the top of the low bulwarks in order to get aft. Of the appearance of the negroes, no pen can give an adequate idea. In numbers, the different protuberances and anatomical peculiarities of the bones can be distinctly traced by the eye, and appear, on every motion, ready to break through the skin, which is, in fact, all that covers them. Nor has this been confined to appearance; in many, at the bend of the elbows and knee-joints, over the hip-joints and lower part of the spine, the integuments have given way, and caused the most distressing and ill-conditioned sores. A great number of the Africans, especially the younger, cannot stand upright even when assisted, and the moment they are left to themselves, they double up their knees under their chins, and draw their legs so closely to their bodies, that they scarcely retain the form of humanity. So weak and so cramped are the most of them that they had to be carried in the arms of the seamen, one by one, up the *Crescent's* ladder. All those not affected with contagious diseases are now on board the *Crescent,* and the most of them look like animated skeletons. From one of the Portuguese crew, who is at present under treatment for smallpox, I learn that the name of the vessel is the Vencedora, and that she left Benguela on the coast of Africa with four hundred and sixty slaves on board. But of this *number* only three hundred and thirty-eight have been counted over the side, a circumstance which will appear the less surprising when the space in which they were stowed comes to be considered. . . .

Just as the negroes who remained of the *Vencedora* had entirely recovered their wonted health and vigor, and were fit to be sent to one of our colonies, H.M.S. *Dolphin,* on the 15th of November, 1843, brought into harbor a full slaver, which she had captured a day or two before, a little to the northward of Rio. The crew of the slaver had actually run her ashore, and had begun to throw the negroes overboard into the sea, in order that they might be induced to swim for the land, when the boats of the *Dolphin* came up and obliged them to stop and effect their own escape.

This vessel is the largest I have yet seen employed in this traffic, and is better fitted and found than the common run of slavers; she is American built, and several of her fittings bear the name of American tradesmen. But, as usual, the Africans benefit nothing from the greater size of the vessel. The additional room has not been devoted to give increased accommodation, but to carry a greater number from the coast. The hold, instead of being fitted with one slave deck, has two; so that, in fact, the negroes have been as badly off, if not worse, than they would have been in a smaller vessel.

On attempting to go down into the hold, and satisfy myself with an examination before the Africans were removed, I was forced, after one or two unsuccessful attempts, to give it up;—the effluvium was perfectly overwhelming, and the heat so great, that the moment I left the square of the hatchway, the sensation approached suffocation. The decks furnished a melancholy spectacle of disease and wretchedness; but the most prominent and widely spread scourge is purulent ophthalmia. Numbers of the poor creatures are squatting down in corners or groping about the deck deprived of all sight. Their immensely swollen eyelids, contrasting with their haggard and wasted features, and the discharge which keeps constantly trickling down their cheeks, and which they have not even a rag to wipe away, gives them an appearance of ghastly, murky misery which it is impossible for me to describe.

Many eyes, I am afraid, are irretrievably lost, and several poor wretches must remain forever totally blind. Dysentery, too, that fellest of all diseases in the negro race, is at work amongst them, and will undoubtedly commit fearful ravages. Five hundred and seventy-two Africans were found on board. What the number was at starting there is no means of ascertaining. One of the crew, a slave, who acted on board in the capacity of a cook, and who preferred being captured by Englishmen to escaping with his master, told me that many had died and were thrown overboard during the passage. The exact number taken on board, however, he could not tell. In all probability, it was not under seven hundred; but of course this is only mere conjecture.

Questions:
1. *What diseases did Nelson describe as being most prevalent among the Africans who survived the Atlantic crossing? Roughly what proportion of slaves arrived in Brazil compared to those who left American ports?*
2. *Compare Nelson's account of conditions aboard slave ships with Equiano's personal memoir.*

PART 16
Late Traditional Asia

16.1 Matteo Ricci, Journals

Matteo Ricci reached Macao in 1582. He had to overcome seemingly insuperable difficulties before gaining a foothold in China, which was rigidly Confucian and xenophobic. Ricci was quick to realize that the Jesuits could not hope to succeed in China if they adopted the same proselytizing approach that other missionaries had used. Immediately he set out to work from the top down: He began to penetrate the Chinese ruling class, not so much as a Christian missionary but rather as a learned friend and scientist. To dispel suspicion on the part of Chinese scholars and officials, he at first wore the robes of the Buddhist monk and then changed to those of the Confucian scholar-official class. Besides his mastery of the Chinese language and the classics, he made an intense study of Chinese history, customs, geography, philosophy, and government. He also knew how to arouse the curiosity and fancy of Chinese officials and scholars by presenting them with gifts previously unknown to them, such as clocks, sundials, clavichords, and astrolabes. As a result, Ricci won the respect, admiration, and friendship of the Chinese scholar-officials. At last, in 1601, after eighteen strenuous years, Ricci was allowed by the Chinese emperor to establish his residence at the imperial capital, where he stayed until his death in 1610. Ricci was buried in a plot donated by the emperor.

For a period of twenty-eight years, with patience, keen intellect, tact, and dedication, Ricci laid a permanent foundation for Christianity in China. Hundreds of fellow Jesuits followed in his footsteps to China and won thousands of Chinese converts. At the same time, Ricci and many of the Jesuits who later came to China developed a respect and fascination for Chinese civilization. Because of this scholarly interest, many of these Jesuits, starting with Ricci, emerged as pioneers in sinology in the West. They built a bridge between the two worlds. They introduced Confucius to Europe, and the Bible, Copernicus, and Euclid to China. Their letters and writings on Chinese history, government, society, philosophy, geography, and customs became the chief reference sources on China for the Europeans.

In particular, Ricci's diary, De Propagatione Christiana apud Sinas (On the Propagation of Christianity Among the Chinese), contributed greatly to Europe's understanding of China. The diary was posthumously published in 1615 by Ricci's co-worker, the Belgian Jesuit Nicholas Trigault, who edited and translated the original Italian into Latin. This diary was widely read in seventeenth-century Europe and appeared in several European languages. Ricci described various aspects of Chinese life and institutions such as Confucian philosophy, the imperial examination system, the bureaucracy, the arts and sciences, customs, and religions. Thus, Ricci's journal reopened China to Europe three centuries after Marco Polo had first bridged the gap through his famous travelogue. The following selection is Ricci's description, as presented by Father Trigault, of China's pacifistic tradition and the triennial rotation system of the imperial government.

Source: From China in the Sixteenth Century: *The Journals of Matthew Ricci,* 1583–1610, by Matthew Ricci, translated by Louis J. Gallagher, S. J. (New York: Random House, 1953), pp. 54–56, 58–59. Copyright 1942 and renewed 1970 by Louis J. Gallagher, S. J. Reprinted by permission of Random House, Inc.

Before closing this chapter on Chinese public administration, it would seem to be quite worthwhile recording a few more things in which this people differ from Europeans. To begin with, it seems to be quite remarkable when we stop to consider it, that in a kingdom of almost limitless expanse and innumerable population, and abounding in copious supplies of every description, though they have a well-equipped army and navy that could easily conquer the neighboring nations, neither the King nor his people ever think of waging a war of aggression. They are quite content with what they have and are not ambitious of conquest. In this respect they are much different from the people of Europe, who are frequently discontent with their own governments and covetous of what others enjoy. While the nations of the West seem to be entirely consumed with the idea of supreme domination, they cannot even preserve what their ancestors have bequeathed them, as the Chinese have done through a period of some thousands of years. This assertion seems to have some bearing upon what many of our writers maintain relative to the initial founding of the empire, when they assert that the Chinese not only subjugated the neighboring nations but extended their sway even as far as India. After diligent study of the history of China, covering a period of more than four thousand years, I must admit that I have never seen any mention of such conquest, nor have I ever heard of them extending the boundaries of their empire. On the contrary, in frequent inquiry among learned Chinese historians, relative to this assertion, their answer has always been the same; that it was not so and could not possibly be so. Not to question the reputation of the writers who have recorded the error, the mistake may have arisen from the fact that certain evidences of the presence of the Chinese have been discovered beyond the confines of the kingdom. For example, one might cite the Philippine Islands, to which they found their way in private enterprise rather than on any official commission by their government.

Another remarkable fact and quite worthy of note as marking a difference from the West, is that the entire kingdom is administered by the Order of the Learned, commonly known as the Philosophers. The responsibility for orderly management of the entire realm is wholly and completely committed to their charge and care. The army, both officers and soldiers, hold them in high respect and show them the promptest obedience and deference, and not infrequently the military are disciplined by them as a schoolboy might be punished by his master. Policies of war are formulated and military questions are decided by the Philosophers only, and their advice and counsel has more weight with the King than that of the military leaders. In fact very few of these, and only on rare occasions, are admitted to war consultations. Hence it follows that those who aspire to be cultured frown upon war and would prefer the lowest rank in the philosophical order to the highest in the military, realizing that the Philosophers far excel military leaders in the good will and the respect of the people and in opportunities of acquiring wealth. What is still more surprising to strangers is that these same Philosophers, as they are called, with respect to nobility of sentiment and in contempt of danger and death, where fidelity to King and country is concerned, surpass even those whose particular profession is the defense of the fatherland. Perhaps this sentiment has its origin in the fact that the mind of man is ennobled by the study of letters. Or again, it may have developed from the fact that from the beginning and foundation of this empire the study of letters was always more acceptable to the people than the profession of arms, as being more suitable to a people who had little or no interest in the extension of the empire.

The order and harmony that prevails among magistrates, both high and low, in the provinces and in the regal Curia is also worthy of admiration. Their attitude toward the King, in exact obedience and in external ceremony, is a cause of wonderment to a foreigner. The literati would never think of omitting certain customary formal visits to one another or the regular practice of freely offering gifts. In the courts and elsewhere, inferiors always bend the knee when speaking to a superior, and address him in the most dignified language. The same is true of the people toward their prefects and toward the mayor of the city, even though these officers may have arisen from the lowest state in life before attaining their literary degrees and admittance to the magistracy. The term of office of all the dignitaries we have been discussing is three years, unless one be confirmed in his position or promoted by order of the crown. Usually they are promoted but not for the same locality, lest they should develop friendships and become lenient in the administration of justice, or develop a following in the province in which they are so influential. The experience of past ages has taught them that a magistrate burdened with favors is likely to incline toward the introduction of novelties and away from the rigor of the law.

No one is permitted to carry arms within city limits, not even soldiers or officers, military prefects or magistrates, unless one be en route to war or on the way to drill or to a military school. Certain of the higher magistrates, however, may be accompanied by an armed guard. Such is their dislike for arms that no one is allowed to have them in his home, except perhaps a metal dagger which might be needed on a journey as protection against robbers. Fighting and violence among the people are practically unheard of, save what might be concluded by hair pulling and scratching, and there is no requiting of injuries by wounds and death. On the contrary, one who will not fight and restrains himself from returning a blow is praised for his prudence and bravery.

Questions:

1. How do you compare the people and society of China described by Ricci with those of Europe in the sixteenth century?

2. How did Ricci describe China's pacifistic tradition? Do you agree or disagree with Ricci's assessment? Why?

16.2   Dynastic change in China Tears a Family Apart

By the 1640s the Ming dynasty, which had ruled China since 1368, was in decline and under heavy pressure from invading Manchus. By 1644, the Ming was crumbling and Manchu rulers had established their capital at Beijing, styling themselves as the Qing dynasty. However, resistance to the new order continued for years, and the conflict sometimes even divided families. Zheng Zhilong, a former pirate who had become a Ming functionary, transferred his allegiance to the Qing. However, his son Zheng Chenggong remained loyal to the Ming and waged a guerrilla war along the Southeastern coast. In the end, the distrustful Qing would execute Zheng Zhilong in 1661, and the son would die during an epidemic one year later. The exchange of letters shows the father's failed attempts to arrange an accomodation between his son and the Qing court.

Source: Lynn A. Stuve, ed./trans., *Voices from the Mina-Qing Cataclysm: China in Tiger's Jaws* (New Haven, CT: Yale University Press), pp. 184–189.

[1st month (February) of 1653]. Zhou Jiwu—having been deputed by Grand Preceptor and Duke of Pingguo [Zheng Zhi-long]—arrived at Xiamen from Beijing and transmitted a message from Zhilong informing the prince [Zheng Chenggong] that the Qing court wished to talk peace and ordering him to engage in such talks. The prince deputed Li De with a return letter to the grand preceptor, which said in part: "It has been several years since your son went southward, and he has already become a person beyond the pale. Zhang Xuesheng [the former Qing governor of Fujian] had no reason to start trouble arbitrarily [in the raids of 1651]. Your son could not but respond in kind. Now that he is riding a tiger, it's hard to get off; troops that have been gathered are hard to disperse."

***

[5th month (September–October)]. Li De, Zhou Jiwu, and others, having been deputed by the grand preceptor, the Duke of Pingguo, to present a letter in the duke's own hand to the prince, arrived and stated: "The Qing court wishes to confer land in exchange for peace. They wish to depute two high officials to present the seal of, and the documents bestowing the title of, Duke of Haicheng, authorizing the settlement of your followers in the lands of [Haicheng] Prefecture. The mission would be guaranteed by [the current viceroy for Zhejiang and Fujian] Liu Qingtai. They have sent us in advance to ascertain your willingness. After we report back, they will order the court envoys to come and make the presentation." The prince said, "The Qing court wants to trick me, eh? One way or another we'll use the situation to extract plenty of supplies to feed the troops."

Then he wrote a return missive to the Duke of Pingguo and ordered Li De to gallop [day and] night to the [Qing] capital to report. The missive said: "For eight years now I have failed to serve at my father's knee. But then, since my father no longer regarded his son as such, I did not presume to consider myself a son. Consequently our inquiries after one another utterly ceased; not one word has gone between us. Circumstances have been so extraordinary as to alienate even flesh and blood.

"Since ancient times, the principle that the greater righteousness [in serving one's ruler and state] extinguishes one's duty to family has been the instruction of men in sensible, not unstable, states of mind. When your son first learned to read, he straightaway respected this meaning of the *Spring and Autumn Annals*. I had been contemplating that principle for some time when, in the winter of 1646, Father's carriage entered the Qing capital and committed me to acting on it.

"Out of the blue I have received your stern directive that your son's capacity for loyalty be brought to reinforce filiality. As before, you transmit the oral edict of the Qing court, including talk about my having been an earl and a marquis [under the Ming, which would warrant] an expeditious elevation in rank. But if the Qing have lost credence with the father, how can the father's words bear credence with the son? When the Manchu prince [Boio] entered the pass [to Fujian], my father had long since retreated home to avoid the situation. They then used ingratiating phrases and clever language delivered by envoys who came to woo you in entourages of horses and carriages that went back and forth no fewer than ten times. They went as far as to bait my father with a princely title and control over three provinces. At first they said that once you had come to the provincial capital, you could go home again; later they said that after you entered the national capital, you could assume command of the three provinces. Now it's been several years. Let's not speak of the princely title or the assumption of command—now, even if you wanted to pass through your old neighborhood, you couldn't. How can their words be believed?

"When my father was in the Ming court, was he not the exalted Duke of Pingguo? Now that he's serving the Qing court, how is it that he's behind others? But it is that way even for those who went over to the Qing first. How much more so for the last to submit? Also laughable was that early on, your son sent Wang Yu to enter Beijing only because he had heard rumors about your circumstances and thought to have someone look into them. But Wang was abruptly put into prison and subjected to extremely cruel floggings. What could one Wang Yu have perpetrated? But seeing how they barked at shadows like that, the rest could be known.

"Nevertheless, in 1649 [I thought it safe] to sail into Guangdong Province to operate some colonies for a few years. I never expected that they would take advantage of your son's being far away to recklessly initiate hostilities. They attacked and destroyed our base, Zhongzuo [fig. 20], devastated our lands, took spoils from our soldiers and people, captured and raped our womenfolk, and robbed us of over 900,000 gold taels, several hundred pounds of pearls and jewels, and many hundreds of thousands of bushels of grain. The valuables stolen from our soldiers and common people are incalculable. When they heard that your son was about to return, they begged for mercy from Fourth Junior Uncle [Zheng Hongkui]. Fortunately for them, he gave them some room to get away, so they were able to make it back alive. But having returned, they again treated us with suspicion and involved us in disputation.

"All our generals and soldiers had such painful thoughts about the country's shame and our family's loss that their anger made their hair stand on end under their caps. That is why the military actions in Zhangzhou and Quanzhou prefectures ensued. The taking of [the former viceroy] Chen Jin's head and the repeated defeats of [Commander in Chief] Yang Minggao were assuredly in the natural course of getting back what one puts out. Not only that: troops from various neighboring foreign countries, such as Japan and Kampuchea, should arrive any day now. They, too, wish to practice the greater righteousness of the *Spring and Autumn Annals*.

"If I am to believe both my father's command and the Qing edict, then there is a contradiction: The edict that my father has transmitted says one thing, whereas the copy that I've obtained of the decree to be presented by Minister Liu Qingtai says another. There are thorny discrepancies between the former and the latter. We are already in full control of the seaboard. The resources of the eastern and western seas that we have propagated afford more than enough supplies for our offensive actions. Why should we be willing to revert from sitting and enjoying this surfeit to being constrained by others?

"Speaking in terms of Fujian, Guangdong, and Guangxi, the pros and cons [of the Qing effort to control these three provinces directly] are clear. Does no one at the Qing court understand this? The maritime provinces are several thousand li from the capital. The route is dauntingly long, exhausting for both men and horses. And their unfamiliarity with the environment once they arrive results in most of them dying off. Troop shortages are sure to make these regions hard for the Qing to hold. Increasing troop strength would necessitate recruitment from other regions. If that were done, it would surely prove difficult to sustain so many troops with provincial supplies. And if food for troops were not provided, then the regions certainly could not be held.

"To waste money and supplies trying to hold unholdable soil would bring harm but no advantage. Before, when my father had command over Fujian, Guangdong, and Guangxi, the lands and seas were as peaceful as could be, and the court did not have to expend so much as one arrow. Besides troop supplies, there was enough to send surpluses to the capital. The court enjoyed this service, and the people benefited. That brought advantage and no harm. If the Qing court is unable to learn from the astute calculation of my [Ming] dynasty, and instead sends its troops to labor in faraway ventures, year after year wasting unrenewable resources, how will they ever manage recovery later on?

"Perhaps they now intend to use an empty title to authority over three provinces—a title with which they previously baited the father—to turn around and bait the son. Your son truly does not categorically doubt his father's words, but under these particular circumstances, it is hard to believe them. If Liu Qingtai could actually take responsibility and truly confer control over the territory of three provinces on me, then the lands and seas could be free of the scourge of outlawry, and the Qing court would have no need to worry in looking southward—indeed, it would be their great good fortune....

"Besides, at present we have several hundred thousand troops, and conditions would make them hard to disperse. If dispersed, they would form disruptive groups among themselves and cause unrest in the area. Keeping them together entails numerous expenditures—a big ten thousand taels each day. Without the territory and revenues of a province, it would be like the old scheme that they used to bait my father. The father having been deceived before, how can the son allow himself to be deceived again later?

"The Ming dynasty has conferred the imperial surname and a princely title on your son. His official status already being the highest possible, how could the Qing add to it? Anyway, your son's concern for official titles has always been thin; much less is he interested in going through the hierarchy of conferrals again. I say this to someone who should know. Otherwise, if I were to display an empty, meaningless title while acquiescing in what actually was a disaster, then people's minds would tend to revolt against such falsity, and Jiangnan, too, would be hard to keep secure for long."

Questions:
1. *Under what pressures might the father have been from the Qing court to bring his son into compliance?*
2. *How did the son respond to his father's overtures? How does he explain the rift between the two of them?*
3. *Of what crimes does the son accuse the Qing? How does the son justify his continued defiance?*
4. *What advantages does the son assert that he possesses in his confrontations with Qing forces?*

16.3   Ceremonial for Visitors: Court Tribute

The following excerpt shows the rules and protocols governing the tributary missions developed by the Ch'ing [Qing] government in 1764.

> **Source:** From the *1764 Ch'ien-lung edition of the Statutes* (Ch'ien-lung hui-tien 56.1–8b), in John K. Fairbank and Ssù-yu Teng, *Ch'ing Administration: Three Studies* (Cambridge: Harvard University Press, 1960), pp. 170–73. Copyright © 1960 by the Harvard-Yenching Institute. These rules and regulations set the standard for the last century and a half of the Qing dynasty (1644–1911).

1. *"As to the countries of the barbarians on all sides that send tribute to Court,* on the east is Korea; on the southeast, Liu-ch'iu and Sulu; on the south, Annam and Siam; on the southwest, Western Ocean, Burma, and Laos. (For the barbarian tribes of the northwest, see under Court of Colonial Affairs.) All send officers as envoys to come to Court and present tributary memorials and pay tribute.

2.   *"As to the imperial appointment of kings of (tributary) countries,* whenever the countries which send tribute to Court have a succession to the throne, they first send an envoy to request an imperial mandate at the Court. In the cases of Korea, Annam, and Liu-ch'iu, by imperial command the principal envoy and secondary envoy(s) receive the imperial patent (of appointment) and go (to their country) to confer it. As for the other countries, the patent (of appointment) is bestowed upon the envoy who has come (from his country) to take it back, whereupon an envoy is sent (from that country) to pay tribute and offer thanks for the imperial favor.

3.   *"As to the king of Korea,* (the patent) is bestowed upon his wife the same as upon the king. When the son grows up, then he requests that it be bestowed upon him as the heir apparent. In all cases officials of the third rank or higher act as principal and secondary envoys. Their clothing and appearance, and ceremonial and retinue in each case are according to rank. In the cases of Annam and Liu-ch'iu, officials of the Hanlin Academy, the Censorate, or the Board of Ceremonies, of the fifth rank or below, act as principal and secondary envoys; (the Emperor) specially confers upon them 'unicorn' clothing of the first rank, in order to lend weight to their journey. In ceremonial and retinue they are all regarded as being of the first rank. When the envoys return, they hand back their clothing to the office in charge of it. . . .

6.   *"As to tribute objects,* in each case they should send the products of the soil of the country. Things that are not locally produced are not to be presented. Korea, Annam, Liu-ch'iu, Burma, Sulu, and Laos all have as tribute their customary objects. Western Ocean and Siam do not have a customary tribute. . . .

7.   *"As to the retainers* (who accompany an envoy), in the case of the Korean tribute envoy there are one attendant secretary, three chief interpreters, 24 tribute guards, 30 minor retainers who receive rewards, and a variable number of minor retainers who do not receive rewards. For Liu-ch'iu, Western Ocean, Siam, and Sulu, the tribute vessels are not to exceed three, with no more than 100 men per vessel; those going to the capital are not to exceed 20. When Annam, Burma, and Laos send tribute, the men are not to exceed 100, and those going to the capital are not to exceed 20. Those that do not go to the capital are to be retained at the frontier. The frontier officials give them a stipend from the government granary, until the envoy returns to the frontier, when he takes them back to their country.

[8.   Presentation of tributary memorials, after arrival at Peking.]

9.   *"As to the Court ceremony,* when a tribute envoy arrives at the capital at the time of a Great Audience or of an Ordinary Audience, His Majesty the Emperor goes to the T'ai Ho [Taihe] palace and, after the princes, dukes, and officials have audience and present their congratulations, the ushers lead in the tributary envoys and their attendant officers, each of them wearing his country's court dress. They stand in the palace courtyard on the west in the last place. When they hear (the command of) the ceremonial ushers they perform the ceremony of three kneelings and nine knockings of the head [the full kowtow]. They are graciously allowed to sit. Tea is imperially bestowed upon them. All this is according to etiquette (for details see under the Department of Ceremonies). If (a tribute envoy) does not come at the time of an Audience, he presents a memorial through the Board (of Ceremonies) asking for an imperial summons to Court. His Majesty the Emperor goes to a side hall of the palace . . . etc.

[10–13. There follow details concerning further ceremonies, with performances of the kowtow; banquets; and imperial escorts, including those provided for westerners because of their services as imperial astronomers.]

14.   *"As to trade,*—when the tribute envoys of the various countries enter the frontier, the goods brought along in their boats or carts may be exchanged in trade with merchants of the interior (China); either they may be sold at the merchants' hongs in the frontier province or they may be brought to the capital and marketed at the lodging house (i.e., the Residence for Tributary Envoys). At the customs stations (lit. passes and fords) which they pass en route, they are all exempted from duty. As to barbarian merchants who themselves bring their goods into the country for trade,—for Korea on the border of Shêng-ching [Shengjing] [Fengtien province], and at Chung-chiang [Zhongjiang] [northeast of Chengtu, Szechwan], there are spring and autumn markets, two a year; at Hui-ning [southeast of Lanchow, Kansu], one market a year; at Ch'ing-yüan [Qingyuan] [in Chihli, now Chao-hsien], one market every other year,—(each) with two Interpreters of the Board of Ceremonies, one Ninguta (Kirin) clerk, and one Lieutenant to superintend it. After twenty days the market is closed. For the countries beyond the seas, (the market) is at the provincial capital of Kwangtung [Guangdong]. Every summer they take advantage of the tide and come to the provincial capital (Canton). When winter comes they wait for a wind and return to their countries. All pay duties to the (local) officers in charge, the same as the merchants of the interior (China).

15.   *"As to the prohibitions,*—when a foreign country has something to state or to request, it should specially depute an officer to bring a document to the Board (of Ceremonies), or in the provinces it may be memorialized on behalf (of the country) by the Governor-General and Governor concerned. Direct communication to the Court is forbidden. For a tribute envoy's entrance of the frontier and the tribute route which he follows, in each case there are fixed places. Not to follow the regular route, or to go over into other provinces, is forbidden. It is forbidden secretly (i.e., without permission) to buy official costumes which violate the regulations, or books of history, weapons, copper, iron, oil, hemp, or combustible saltpetre; or to take people of the interior or rice and grain out

of the frontiers. There are boundaries separating the rivers and seas; to catch fish beyond the boundaries is forbidden. The land frontiers are places of defensive entrenchments where Chinese and foreign soldiers or civilians have established military colonies or signal-fire mounds, or cultivated rice-fields and set up huts; to abscond and take shelter (on either side) is forbidden. It is forbidden for civil or military officials on the frontier to communicate in writing with foreign countries not on public business. When commissioned to go abroad, to receive too many gifts, or when welcomed in coming and going, privately to demand the products of the locality (i.e., as "squeeze") is forbidden. Offenses against the prohibitions will be considered according to law.

[16.   Charity and sympathy to be shown regarding foreign rulers' deaths, calamities, etc.]

17.   "*As to the rescue* (of distressed mariners),—when ships of foreign merchants are tossed by the wind into the inner waters (of China), the local authorities should rescue them, report in a memorial the names and number of distressed barbarians, move the public treasury to give them clothing and food, take charge of the boat and oars, and wait for a wind to send them back. If a Chinese merchant vessel is blown by the wind into the outer ocean, the country there can rescue it and give it aid, put a boat in order and send them (the merchants) back, or it may bring them along on a tribute vessel so as to return them. In all such cases an imperial patent is to be issued, praising the king of the country concerned; imperial rewards are to be given to the officers (of the tributary country) in different degrees."

Questions:

1. *How analogous is China's tribute system to the Communist and Western alliance systems of post–World War II? What are the similarities and differences?*
2. *How do you relate this reading with Emperor Chien-lung's [Qianlong] letter to King George III of England?*

16.4   Taisuke Mitamura, The Palace Eunuchs of Imperial China

One of the most bizarre practices in history was the emasculation of young males who served as attendants to kings, queens, sultans, and maharajas or as members of the Vatican choirs. Often this act of mutilation of the genitals was voluntary and was performed for various reasons, both spiritual and mundane. Although the exact origins for the existence of eunuchs cannot be determined, they are known to have existed for many centuries before the common era, in both the East and the West, and persisted, in some cases, down to the early twentieth century. Some suggest that the Assyrian queen Semiramis, who founded New Babylonia, was the first to institute the system. Herodotus wrote accounts of the selling and buying of eunuchs by the Greeks at Ephesus and Sardis. The Bible also makes many references to the activities of eunuchs. Some early Christians are said to have emasculated themselves as an act of devotion to God.

Perhaps no other country had as enduring a eunuch system as Imperial China. As an integral part of the imperial court, the system persisted for at least three thousand years, until the end of the Qing (Ch'ing) dynasty in 1912. Thousands of eunuchs performed a wide variety of duties, from the menial, such as gardening, water carrying, and sedan-chair bearing, to stage acting, taking charge of the imperial bed chambers, and acting as informal counselors and tutors to the emperor and princes. The following excerpts include a brief account of the duties of the eunuchs in charge of the imperial bed chambers.

> **Source:** From Taisuke Mitamura, Chinese Eunuchs, *The Structure of Intimate Politics* (Rutland, VT: Charles E. Tuttle Co., 1970), pp. 111–15. Copyright © 1996, Chuo Koronsha, Tokyo, Japan.

Eunuchs participated in the nocturnal activities of the ruler. In the Ming dynasty, the office charged with the duty of looking after the Imperial bedchamber was called Ching Shih Fang, and the eunuch in charge was called the Ching Shih Fang T'ai Chien, or Chief of the Imperial Bedchamber. This office dealt exclusively with the nocturnal relations between the monarch and his consort and concubines.

When the Emperor had relations with the Empress, the date was recorded so that it would serve as proof in the case of conception. The procedure differed somewhat in the case of concubines. *Lu t'ou p'ai,* or nameplates painted green at the top, were prepared for the Emperor's favorite concubines. At dinner the eunuch in charge of the Imperial bedchamber would place as many as a score of these nameplates on a silver tray and take them to the Emperor with his meal. As soon as the Emperor finished eating, the eunuch would kneel before him, holding the silver tray high above his head, and await instructions. If the Emperor was not in the mood for love, he would dismiss the eunuch with a curt "Go." If he was interested he would pick up one of the nameplates and turn it over, face down. The eunuch would then hand the nameplate to the T'ai Chien in charge of carrying the concubines to his Majesty's bedchamber. When the time came, the T'ai Chien would strip the chosen concubine, wrap her in a feather garment, and carry her on his back to the Imperial bedchamber.

The eunuch in charge of the Imperial bedchamber and the T'ai Chien would then wait in front of the bedchamber a given length of time, at the end of which the T'ai Chien would shout, "Time is up" *(Shih shih Hou Le)*. If the Emperor didn't reply, the call was repeated, and if he still did not reply after the words were repeated a third time, the eunuch would enter the bedchamber and carry off the concubine. He would only ask the Emperor if he wanted the concubine to bear his child. If the Emperor answered in the negative, the T'ai Chien would take proper contraceptive measures; if the Emperor answered in the affirmative, he would record the date so that it would later serve as proof. This was no small matter since a concubine's future position depended on whether or not she bore a child for the Emperor.

Exactly when this system was made official in the Ming dynasty is not known, but it was adopted in the Ching dynasty because, it is said, Emperor Shih Tsu believed its enforcement would keep his descendants from indulging excessively in sex. Also, the system was undoubtedly enforced in order to ensure succession in the autocratic system. Imperial life was more flexible at the Yuan Ming Yuan Detached Palace, where Emperor Ch'ien Lung was said to have stepped out frequently for a change of air.

It should be noted that, in the seraglio, the words of the Empress carried much weight. The Emperor, for instance, could not visit the chambers of his concubines whenever he felt the urge to do so. In such cases, the concubine of the Emperor's choice would first receive from the Empress a written notice to the effect that his Majesty would pay her a visit. Without the Empress' seal, the notice would not be valid, and without the notice the Emperor would be turned back.

The eunuchs were also in charge of the Emperor's sex education. In the Ming dynasty, several Buddhist statues were enshrined in the Inner Court. Of esoteric Lamaist origin, these strange images were in the form of men and women and beasts locked in carnal ecstasy. Buddhist, Taoist, and Lamaist halls, where eunuch Taoists and priests served, were also set up in the Imperial court. In preparation for the nuptials of the Emperor or Imperial princes, the eunuchs would have them worship these images and then, by intimately caressing the images, educate them in sexual love.

Such intimate relations between the eunuchs and the rulers were established early in childhood. As soon as he was old enough to leave his nurse's side, an Imperial prince would be instructed in speech, table manners, deportment, etiquette, and knowledge by the eunuchs. In other words, he literally grew up with them. Emperor Wu Tsung of the Ming dynasty, who was profligate in his ways, always listened to his T'ai Chien, Wang Wei, although he never lent an ear to what his retainers had to say, because he had grown up with the eunuch, sharing the same desk and studying the same books. The Emperor called him *Pan Pan,* or friend.

Questions:
1. Compare and contrast the eunuch system of Imperial China with that of another civilization.
2. What were the reasons for a person to become a eunuch?

16.5   Letter to King George: China and Great Britain

In 1795. The British government decided to use the birthday celebration of the Manchu emperor of China, Ch'ien Lung (1711-1799), as an occasion to further their trading interests. So they dispatched their first ambassador, the Earl of Macartney, to the imperial court at Peking. The earl bore with him lavish birthday gifts but also a list of concessions for the advantage of England and of British merchants that he hoped to wrest from the aging emperor. The selection that follows contains the emperor's response to these English overtures.

Source: From Backhouse, E. and J. O. P. Bland, *Annals & Memoirs of the Court of Peking*

MANDATE TO KING GEORGE III

You, O King, live beyond the confines of many seas, nevertheless, impelled by your humble desire to partake of the benefits of our civilisation, you have dispatched a mission respectfully bearing your memorial. Your Envoy has crossed the seas and paid his respects at my Court on the anniversary of my birthday. To show your devotion, you have also sent offerings of your country's produce.

I have perused your memorial: the earnest terms in which it is couched reveal a respectful humility on your part, which is highly praiseworthy. In consideration of the fact that your Ambassador and his deputy have come a long way with your memorial and tribute, I have shown them high favour and have allowed them to be introduced into my presence. To manifest my indulgence, I have entertained them at a banquet and made them numerous gifts. I have also caused presents to be forwarded to the Naval Commander and six hundred of his officers and men, although they did not come to Peking, so that they too may share in my all-embracing kindness.

As to your entreaty to send one of your nationals to be accredited to my Celestial Court and to be in control of your country's trade with China, this request is contrary to all usage of my dynasty and cannot possibly be entertained. It is true that Europeans, in the service of the dynasty, have been permitted to live at Peking, but they are compelled to adopt Chinese dress, they are strictly confined to their own precincts and are never permitted to return home. You are presumably familiar with our dynastic regulations. Your proposed Envoy to my Court could not be placed in a position similar to that of European officials in Peking who are forbidden to leave China, nor could he, on the other hand, be allowed liberty of movement and the privilege of corresponding with his own country; so that you would gain nothing by his residence in our midst.

Moreover, our Celestial dynasty possesses vast territories, and tribute missions from the dependencies are provided for by the Department for Tributary States, which ministers to their wants and exercises strict control over their movements. It would be quite impossible to leave them to their own devices. Supposing that your Envoy should come to our Court, his language and national dress differ from that of our people, and there would be no place in which to bestow him. It may be suggested that he might imitate the Europeans permanently resident in Peking and adopt the dress and customs of China, but, it has never been our dynasty's wish to force people to do things unseemly and inconvenient. Besides, supposing I sent an Ambassador to reside in your country, how could you possibly make for him the requisite arrangements? Europe consists of many other nations besides your own: if each and all demanded to be represented at our Court, how could we possibly consent? The thing is utterly impracticable. How can our dynasty alter its whole procedure and system of etiquette, established for more than a century, in order to meet your individual views? If it be said that your object is to exercise control over your country's trade, your nationals have had full liberty to trade at Canton for many a year, and have received the greatest consideration at our hands. Missions have been sent by Portugal and Italy, preferring similar requests. The Throne appreciated their sincerity and loaded them with favours, besides authorising measures to facilitate their trade with China. You are no doubt aware that, when my Canton merchant, Wu Chao-ping, was in debt to the foreign ships, I made the Viceroy advance the monies due, out of the provincial treasury, and ordered him to punish the culprit severely. Why then should foreign nations advance this utterly unreasonable request to be represented at my Court? Peking is nearly two thousand miles from Canton, and at such a distance what possible control could any British representative exercise?

If you assert that your reverence for Our Celestial dynasty fills you with a desire to acquire our civilisation, our ceremonies and code of laws differ so completely from your own that, even if your Envoy were able to acquire the rudiments of our civilisation, you could not possibly transplant our manners and customs to your alien soil. Therefore, however adept the Envoy might become, nothing would be gained thereby.

Surveying the wide world, I have but one aim in view, namely, to maintain a perfect governance and to fulfil the duties of the State: strange and costly objects do not interest me. If I have commanded that the tribute offerings sent by you, O King, are to be accepted, this was solely in consideration for the spirit which prompted you to dispatch them from afar. Our dynasty's majestic virtue has penetrated unto every country under Heaven, and Kings of all nations have offered their costly tribute by land and sea. As your Ambassador can see for himself, we possess all things. I set no value on objects strange or ingenious, and have no use for your country's manufactures. This then is my answer to your request to appoint a representative at my Court, a request contrary to our dynastic usage, which would only result in inconvenience to yourself. I have expounded my wishes in detail and have commanded your tribute Envoys to leave in peace on their homeward journey. It behoves you, O King, to respect my sentiments and to display even greater devotion and loyalty in future, so that, by perpetual submission to our Throne, you may secure peace and prosperity for your country hereafter. Besides making gifts (of which I enclose an inventory) to each member of your Mission, I confer upon you, O King, valuable presents in excess of the number usually bestowed on such occasions, including silks and curios-a list of which is likewise enclosed. Do you reverently receive them and take note of my tender goodwill towards you! A special mandate.

[A further mandate to King George III dealt in detail with the British Ambassador's proposals and the Emperor's reasons for declining them.]

You, O King, from afar have yearned after the blessings of our civilisation, and in your eagerness to come into touch with our converting influence have sent an Embassy across the sea bearing a memorial. I have already taken note of your respectful spirit of submission, have treated your mission with extreme favour and loaded it with gifts, besides issuing a mandate to you, O King, and honouring you with the bestowal of valuable presents. Thus has my indulgence been manifested.

Yesterday your Ambassador petitioned my Ministers to memorialise me regarding your trade with China, but his proposal is not consistent with our dynastic usage and cannot be entertained. Hitherto, all European nations, including your own country's barbarian merchants, have carried on their trade with our Celestial Empire at Canton. Such has been the procedure for many years, although our Celestial Empire possesses all things in prolific abundance and lacks no product within its own borders. There was therefore no need to import the manufactures of outside barbarians in exchange for our own produce. But as the tea, silk and porcelain which the Celestial Empire produces, are absolute necessities to European nations and to yourselves, we have permitted, as a signal mark of favour, that foreign *hongs* should be established at Canton, so that your wants might be supplied and your country thus participate in our beneficence. But your Ambassador has now put forward new requests which completely fail to recognise the Throne's principle to 'treat strangers from afar with indulgence,' and to exercise a pacifying control over barbarian tribes, the world over. Moreover, our dynasty, swaying the myriad races of the globe, extends the same benevolence towards all. Your England is not the only nation trading at Canton. If other nations, following your bad example, wrongfully importune my ear with further impossible requests, how will it be possible for me to treat them with easy indulgence? Nevertheless, I do not forget the lonely remoteness of your island, cut off from the world by intervening wastes of sea, nor do I overlook your excusable ignorance of the usages of our Celestial Empire. I have consequently commanded my Ministers to enlighten your Ambassador on the subject, and have ordered the departure of the mission. But I have doubts that, after your Envoy's return he may fail to acquaint you with my view in detail or that he may be lacking in lucidity, so that I shall now proceed to take your requests *seriatim* and to issue my mandate on each question separately. In this way you will, I trust, comprehend my meaning.

(1) Your Ambassador requests facilities for ships of your nation to call at Ningpo, Chusan, Tientsin and other places for purposes of trade. Until now trade with European nations has always been conducted at Aomen, where the foreign *hongs* are established to store and sell foreign merchandise. Your nation has obediently complied with this regulation for years past without raising any objection. In none of the other ports named have *hongs* been established, so that even if your vessels were to proceed thither, they would have no means of disposing of their cargoes. Furthermore, no interpreters are available, so you would have no means of explaining your wants, and nothing but general inconvenience would result. For the future, as in the past, I decree that your request is refused and that the trade shall be limited to Aomen.

(2) The request that your merchants may establish a repository in the capital of my Empire for the storing and sale of your produce, in accordance with the precedent granted to Russia, is even more impracticable than the last. My capital is the hub and centre about which all quarters of the globe revolve. Its ordinances are most august and its laws are strict in the extreme. The subjects of our dependencies have never been allowed to open places of business in Peking. Foreign trade has hitherto been conducted at Aomen, because it is conveniently near to the sea, and therefore an important gathering place for the ships of all nations sailing to and fro. If warehouses were established in Peking, the remoteness of your country, lying far to the north-west of my capital, would render transport extremely difficult Before Kiakhta was opened, the Russians were permitted to trade at Peking, but the accommodation furnished to them was only temporary. As soon as Kiakhta was available, they were compelled to withdraw from Peking, which has been closed to their trade these many years. Their frontier trade at Kiakhta is on all fours with your trade at Aomen. Possessing facilities at the latter place, you now ask for further privileges at Peking, although our dynasty observes the severest restrictions respecting the admission of foreigners within its boundaries, and has never permitted the subjects of dependencies to cross the Empire's barriers and settle at will amongst the Chinese people. This request is also refused.

(3) Your request for a small island near Chusan, where your merchants may reside and goods be warehoused, arises from your desire to develop trade. As there are neither foreign *hongs* nor interpreters in or near Chusan, where none of your ships have ever called, such an island would be utterly useless for your purposes. Every inch of the territory of our Empire is marked on the map and the strictest vigilance is exercised over it all: even tiny islets and far-lying sand-banks are clearly defined as part of the provinces to which they belong. Consider, moreover, that England is not the only barbarian land which wishes to establish relations with our civilisation and trade with our Empire: supposing that other nations were all to imitate your evil example and beseech me to present them each and all with a site for trading purposes, how could I possibly comply? This also is a flagrant infringement of the usage of my Empire and cannot possibly be entertained.

(4) The next request, for a small site in the vicinity of Canton city, where your barbarian merchants may lodge or, alternatively, that there be no longer any restrictions over their movements at Aomen, has arisen from the following causes. Hitherto, the barbarian merchants of Europe have had a definite locality assigned to them at Aomen for residence and trade, and have been forbidden to encroach an inch beyond the limits assigned to that locality. Barbarian merchants having business with the *hongs* have never been allowed to enter the city of Canton; by these measures, disputes between Chinese and barbarians are prevented, and a firm barrier is raised between my subjects and those of other nations. The present request is quite contrary to precedent; furthermore, European nations have been trading with Canton for a number of years and, as they make large profits, the number of traders is constantly increasing. How would it be possible to grant such a site to each country? The merchants of the foreign *hongs* are responsible to the local officials for the proceedings of barbarian merchants and they carry out periodical inspections. If these restrictions were withdrawn, friction would inevitably occur between the Chinese and your barbarian subjects, and the results would militate against the benevolent regard that I feel towards you. From every point of view, therefore, it is best that the regulations now in force should continue unchanged.

(5) Regarding your request for remission or reduction of duties on merchandise discharged by your British barbarian merchants at Aomen and distributed throughout the interior, there is a regular tariff in force for barbarian mer-

chants' goods, which applies equally to all European nations. It would be as wrong to increase the duty imposed on your nation's merchandise on the ground that the bulk of foreign trade is in your hands, as to make an exception in your case in the shape of specially reduced duties. In future, duties shall be levied equitably without discrimination between your nation and any other, and, in order to manifest my regard, your barbarian merchants shall continue to be shown every consideration at Aomen.

(6) As to your request that your ships shall pay the duties leviable by tariff, there are regular rules in force at the Canton Custom house respecting the amounts payable, and since I have refused your request to be allowed to trade at other ports, this duty will naturally continue to be paid at Canton as heretofore.

(7) Regarding your nation's worship of the Lord of Heaven, it is the same religion as that of other European nations. Ever since the beginning of history, sage Emperors and wise rulers have bestowed on China a moral system and inculcated a code, which from time immemorial has been religiously observed by the myriads of my subjects. There has been no hankering after heterodox doctrines. Even the European (missionary) officials in my capital are forbidden to hold intercourse with Chinese subjects; they are restricted within the limits of their appointed residences, and may not go about propagating their religion. The distinction between Chinese and barbarian is most strict, and your Ambassador's request that barbarians shall be given full liberty to disseminate their religion is utterly unreasonable.

It may be, O King, that the above proposals have been wantonly made by your Ambassador on his own responsibility, or peradventure you yourself are ignorant of our dynastic regulations and had no intention of transgressing them when you expressed these wild ideas and hopes. I have ever shown the greatest condescension to the tribute missions of all States which sincerely yearn after the blessings of civilisation, so as to manifest my kindly indulgence. I have even gone out of my way to grant any requests which were in any way consistent with Chinese usage. Above all, upon you, who live in a remote and inaccessible region, far across the spaces of ocean, but who have shown your submissive loyalty by sending this tribute mission, I have heaped benefits far in excess of those accorded to other nations. But the demands presented by your Embassy are not only a contravention of dynastic tradition, but would be utterly unproductive of good result to yourself, besides being quite impracticable. I have accordingly stated the facts to you in detail, and it is your bounden duty reverently to appreciate my feelings and to obey these instructions henceforward for all time, so that you may enjoy the blessings of perpetual peace. If, after the receipt of this explicit decree, you lightly give ear to the representations of your subordinates and allow your barbarian merchants to proceed to Chêkiang and Tientsin, with the object of landing and trading there, the ordinances of my Celestial Empire are strict in the extreme, and the local officials, both civil and military, are bound reverently to obey the law of the land. Should your vessels touch the shore, your merchants will assuredly never be permitted to land or to reside there, but will be subject to instant expulsion. In that event your barbarian merchants will have had a long journey for nothing. Do not say that you were not warned in due time! Tremblingly obey and show no negligence! A special mandate!

Questions:
1. How does the Emperor Chi'en Lung depict the relationship between China and the European countries?
2. What type of restrictions were placed on foreigners trading with the Chinese? Why were these restrictions necessary?

16.6   Japan Encounters the West

The Portuguese reached Japan in 1543. The Japanese were curious and eager to interact with the Westerners at first. Japanese ships already dominated an active Asian trade network centered on the East China Sea and began vigorous interaction with Portuguese, Spanish, and Dutch merchants. Along with the merchants came Christian missionaries. Japan has a long history of intellectual and religious openness. In addition to native Shinto beliefs, various forms of Buddhism were well established in Japan and Confucian philosophy was influential among the educated. Christianity became very popular in the western regions of Japan in the century after contact with the West.

By 1638, however, missionaries had been expelled, foreign merchants were virtually banned, and Japanese were prohibited from leaving. There are several reasons for this abrupt turn of events. First, European explorers arrived in Japan during a time of civil war among powerful landlords called daimyo. Over time, Europeans were seen as supporting certain factions in return for the opportunity to spread Christianity in territories of those daimyo. Once Japan was unified by Toyotomi Hideyoshi and his successors, the Tokugawas, Europeans influence became even more suspect. Japanese Christians were suspected of having loyalties to religious leaders outside Japan. After the Spanish conquered the Philippines, the Tokugawas worried that European merchants and missionaries were merely the vanguard of a conquering force. Finally, the new regime desired a monopoly on international trade. First missionaries were expelled, then Christianity was suppressed, and eventually all contact with the West was broken off, with the exception of one Dutch merchant vessel a year.

The first two documents. From, 1587, show the growing suspicion of Christian missionaries by Hideyoshi. At this point, Europeans are still allowed to trade, but not spread their religion. The second set of documents date from 1638 to 1640 and represent the final stages of the Closing of Japan, including the killing of Portuguese envoys from Macao, a trading colony on the south China coast.

Source: John David Lu, *Sources of Japanese History*, vol. II, (McGraw-Hill) rights reverted to author.

LIMITATION ON THE PROPAGATION OF CHRISTIANITY, 1587

1. Whether one desires to become a follower of the padre is up to that person's own conscience.
2. If one receives a province, a district, or a village as his fief, and forces farmers in his domain who are properly registered under certain temples to become followers of the padre against their wishes, then he has committed a most unreasonable illegal act.
3. When a vassal (*kyūnin*) receives a grant of a province or a district, he must consider it as a property entrusted to him on a temporary basis. A vassal may be moved from one place to another, but farmers remain in the same place. Thus if an unreasonable illegal act is committed [as described above], the vassal will be called upon to account for his culpable offense. The intent of this provision must be observed.
4. Anyone whose fief is over 200 *chō* and who can expect two to three thousand *kan* of rice harvest each year must receive permission from the authorities before becoming a follower of the padre.
5. Anyone whose fief is smaller than the one described above may, as his conscience dictates, select for himself from between eight and nine religions.
8. If a *daimyō* who has a fief over a province, a district or a village, forces his retainers to become followers of the padre, he is committing a crime worse than the followers of Honganji who assembled in their temple [to engage in the Ikko riōt]. This will have an adverse effect on [the welfare of] the nation. Anyone who cannot use good judgment in this matter will be punished.

EXPULSION OF MISSIONARIES, 1587

1. Japan is the country of gods, but has been receiving false teachings from Christian countries. This cannot be tolerated any further.
2. The [missionaries] approach people in provinces and districts to make them their followers, and let them destroy shrines and temples. This is an unheard of outrage. When a vassal receives a province, a district, a village or another form of a fief, he must consider it as a property entrusted to him on a temporary basis. He must follow the laws of this country, and abide by their intent. However, some vassals illegally [commend part of their fiefs to the church]. This is a culpable offense.
3. The padres, by their special knowledge [in the sciences and medicine], feel that they can at will entice people to become their believers. In so doing they commit the illegal act of destroying the teachings of Buddha prevailing in Japan. These padres cannot be permitted to remain in Japan. They must prepare to leave the country within twenty days of the issuance of this notice. However, the vassals must not make unreasonable demands on the padres, which shall be treated as a culpable offense.
4. The black [Portuguese and Spanish] ships come to Japan to engage in trade. Thus the matter is a separate one. They can continue to engage in trade.
5. Hereafter, anyone who does not hinder the teachings of Buddha, whether he be a merchant or not, may come and go freely from Christian countries to Japan.

This is our wish, and so ordered.
Fifteenth year of Tenshō [1587], sixth month, 19th day.

THE EDICT OF 1635 ORDERING THE CLOSING OF JAPAN: ADDRESSED TO THE JOINT BUGYŌ OF NAGASAKI

1. Japanese ships are strictly forbidden to leave for foreign countries.
2. No Japanese is permitted to go abroad. If there is anyone who attempts to do so secretly, he must be executed. The ship so involved must be impounded and its owner arrested, and the matter must be reported to the higher authority.
3. If any Japanese returns from overseas after residing there, he must be put to death.
4. If there is any place where the teachings of padres (Christianity) is practiced, the two of you must order a thorough investigation.
5. Any informer revealing the whereabouts of the followers of padres (Christians) must be rewarded accordingly. If anyone reveals the whereabouts of a high ranking padre, he must be given one hundred pieces of silver. For those of lower ranks, depending on the deed, the reward must be set accordingly.
6. If a foreign ship has an objection [to the measures adopted] and it becomes necessary to report the matter to Edo, you may ask the Ōmura domain to provide ships to guard the foreign ship, as was done previously.
7. If there are any Southern Barbarians (Westerners) who propagate the teachings of padres, or otherwise commit crimes, they may be incarcerated in the prison maintained by the Ōmura domain, as was done previously.
8. All incoming ships must be carefully searched for the followers of padres.
9. No single trading city [see 12 below] shall be permitted to purchase all the merchandise brought by foreign ships.
10. Samurai are not permitted to purchase any goods originating from foreign ships directly from Chinese merchants in Nagasaki.
11. After a list of merchandise brought by foreign ships is sent to Edo, as before you may order that commercial dealings may take place without waiting for a reply from Edo.
12. After settling the price, all white yarns (raw silk) brought by foreign ships shall be allocated to the five trading cities and other quarters as stipulated.
13. After settling the price of white yarns (raw silk), other merchandise [brought by foreign ships] may be traded freely between the [licensed] dealers. However, in view of the fact that Chinese ships are small and cannot bring large consignments, you may issue orders of sale at your discretion. Additionally, payment for the goods purchased must be made within twenty days after the price is set.
14. The date of departure homeward of foreign ships shall not be later than the twentieth day of the ninth month. Any ships arriving in Japan later than usual shall depart within fifty days of their arrival. As to the departure of Chinese ships, you may use your discretion to order their departure after the departure of the Portuguese *galeota* (galleon).
15. The goods brought by foreign ships which remained unsold may not be deposited or accepted fro deposit.
16. The arrival in Nagaski of representatives of the five trading cities shall not be later that the fifth day of the seventh month. Anyone arriving later than that date shall lose the quota assigned to his city.
17. Ships arriving in Hirado must sell their raw silk at the price set in Nagasaki, and are not permitted to engage in business transactions until after the price is established in Nagaski.

You are hereby required to act in accordance with the provisions set above. It is so ordered.

Kaga no-kami Masamori et al., seals.

To: Sakakibara Hida no-kami, Sengoku Yamoto no-kami

COMPLETION OF THE EXCLUSION, 1639

1. The matter relating to the proscription of Christianity is known [to the Portuguese]. However, heretofore they have secretly transported those who are going to propagate that religion.
2. If those who believe in that religion band together in an attempt to do evil things, they must be subjected to punishment.
3. While those who believe in the preaching of padres are in hiding, there are incidents in which that country (Portugal) has sent gifts to them for their sustenance.

In view of the above, hereafter entry by the Portuguese *galeota* is forbidden. If they insist on coming [to Japan], the ships must be destroyed and anyone aboard those ships must be beheaded. We have received the above order and are thus transmitting it to you accordingly.

The above concerns our disposition with regard to the *galeota*.

Memorandum

With regard to those who believe in Christianity, you are aware that there is a proscription, and thus knowing, you are not permitted to let padres and those who believe in their preaching to come aboard your ships. If there is any violation, all of you who are aboard will be considered culpable. If there is anyone who hides the fact that he is a Christian and boards your ship, you may report it to us. A substantial reward will be given to you for this information.

This memorandum is to be given to those who come on Chinese ships. (A similar note to the Dutch ships.)

The Fate of the Embassy from Macao, 1640 by *Antonio Cardim, S.J.*

Because many serious crimes have been committed over a number of years by the propagation of the Christian religion in defiance of his decree, the shogun last year forbade under grave penalties all voyages from Macao to Japan, laying down that if any ship were to come to Japan despite this prohibition, the vessel would be burnt and the sailors and merchants executed. This edict was promulgated both summarily and in detail. Nevertheless, these men have blatantly violated the aforesaid decree by their voyage and are seriously at fault. Furthermore, in spite of their assertion that on no account will they send hereafter ministers of the Christian religion to Japan, the ambassadorial letters from Macao are silent on this point. Since, therefore, the *shogun* has prohibited such voyages on account of the Christian religion and since no mention of this matter is made in these letters, it is quite evident that the entire legation is but a pretence. For this reason, all who have come hither in this ship are to pay the extreme penalty.

It has accordingly been decided that the ship shall be consumed by flames and that the principal ambassadors shall be put to death along with their companions so that nothing may remain of this harbinger of evil. Thus the example which the *shogun* has made of them will be noticed abroad in Macao and the home country; as a consequence, all will learn to respect the rights of Princes and Kings. We nevertheless desire that the rabble among the crew be spared and sent back to Macao. But should any other ship come hither by force of adverse circumstances or for any other reason whatsoever, let it be known that, in whatsoever port it may call, one and all will be put to death.

Given on the 3rd day of the 6th moon of the 17th year of the Kanei era, that is, the 25th day of July in the year 1640.

At the same time they also asked what they would say about this punishment to foreign peoples in the Orient and even in Europe, if by chance they should go tither. They replied that they would tell the truth; to wit, that the shogun of Japan had put the Portuguese ambassadors to death and had set fire to their ship because they professed the Christian religion and had disobeyed his edict, and that they, to the number of thirteen, had been spared this punishment and sent back so that they could recount what had happened; but they added that the kings and all the peoples of the world would most certainly condemn what had been done as a crime against international law.

They were then taken thence to the mount of execution in order to identify the heads of the executed men, which they found affixed to boards in three groups. The heads of the ambassadors were set apart from the rest; they did not appear pale or washed out, but rather the freshness and beauty of their features well indicated their fate. Now they were set up near a large pole, from the top of which hung the Tyrant's proclamation. Not faraway they espied a house wherein the corpses had been buried and cairns of immense stones had been set up over them; thus if at any time the Japanese should be silent about these men, the very stones would speak.

Inscribed on a pole which emerged from the midst of these stones was the name of the legation and the reason for the executions; it was indeed their monument for posterity and an everlasting trophy of their glory. With unfeeling barbarity the Tyrant had added this inscription: *A similar penalty will be suffered by all those who henceforward come to these shores from Portugal, whether they be sailors, whether they come by error or whether they be driven hither by storm. Even more, if the King of Portugal, or Shaka, or even the GOD of the Christians were to come, they would all pay the very same penalty.*

. . .

Questions:
1. Why do Hideyoshi and the Tokugawas want to suppress Christianity?
2. How do the documents generally depict Europeans?

16.7   The Laws for the Military House (Buke Shohatto), 1615 (Tokugawa "Hostage" System)

For almost seven centuries, since General Minamoto Yoritomo assumed the title of shogun in 1192, a dualistic political tradition evolved in Japan. At the apex of the political hierarchy, two authorities shared leadership and maintained a symbiotic relationship. Theoretically, the shogun was recognized as the emperor's delegated military authority, but in practice, the shogun ruled the country as a virtual military dictator whereas the emperor merely reigned as a semi-divine monarch.

Source: Asiatic Society of Japan, *Transactions*, 38:4 (1911): 290, 293-97.

As to the rule that the Daimyos shall come (to the Shogun's Court at Edo) to do service.

In the *Shoku Nihon ki* (i.e., the Continuation of the Chronicles of Japan) it is recorded amongst the enactments:-

"Except when entrusted with some official duty no one (dignitary) is allowed at his own pleasure to assemble his whole tribe within the limits of the capital, no one is to go about attended by more than twenty horsemen, etc." Hence it is not permissible to lead about a large force of soldiers. For Daimyos whose revenues range from 1,000,000 koku[1] down to 200,000 koku, the number of twenty horsemen is not to be exceeded. For those whose revenues are 100,000 koku and under the number is to be in the same proportion.

On occasions of official service, however (i.e., in time of warfare), the number of followers is to be in proportion to the social standing of each Daimyo.

Laws for the Barons (The Buke Shohatto) of Kwan-ei 22 (5th August, 1635).

[Promulgated by Iyemitsu.]

1. The taste for the Way of literature, arms, archery and horsemanship is to be the chief object of cultivation.

2. It is now settled that the Daimyos and Shomyos (i.e., the greater and lesser Barons) are to do service by turns at Yedo. They shall proceed hither on service every year in summer during the course of the fourth month. Latterly the numbers of their followers have become excessive. This is at once a cause of wastefulness to the provinces and districts and of hardship to the people. Henceforward suitable reductions in this respect must be made. On the occasions of going up to Kyoto, however, the directions given may be followed. On occasions of government service (i.e., military service) the full complement of each Baron must be in attendance.

3. The erection or repairing of new castles is strictly forbidden. When the moats or ramparts of the present residential castles are to be repaired, whether as regards the stonework, plaster, or earth-work, a report must be made to the *Bugyosho* (i.e., the Mag-istracy at Yedo) and its direction taken. As regards the *(Yagura, hei and mon)* armories, fences and gates, repairs may be made to restore them to their previous conditions.

4. Whether at Yedo or in any of the provinces whatsoever, if an occurrence of any sort whatsoever should take place, those (Barons and their retainers) who are there at the time are to stay where they are and to await the Shogun's orders (from Yedo).

5. Whenever capital punishment is to be inflicted, no matter where, nobody except the functionaries in charge is to be present. But the coroner's directions are to be followed.

6. The scheming of innovations, the forming of parties and the taking of oaths is strictly forbidden.

7. There must be no private quarrels whether amongst the *(Kokushu)* greater Barons or *(Ryoshu)* the other Feudatories. Ordinary circumspection and carefulness must be exercised. If matters involving a lengthy arrangement should arise they must be reported to the Magistracy and its pleasure ascertained.

8. Daimyos of over 10,000 koku income, whether they be lords of provinces (domains) or lords of castles, and the heads of departments *(monogashira)* in personal attendance on them are not to form matrimonial alliances (between members of their families) at their private convenience (i.e., they must apply for the Shogun's permission before doing so).

9. In social observances of the present day, such as visits of ceremony, sending and return of presents, the formalities of giving and receiving in marriage, the giving of banquets and the construction of residences, the striving after elegance is carried to very great lengths.

Henceforth there must be much greater simplicity in these respects. And in all other matters there must be a greater regard for economy.

10. There must be no indiscriminate intermingling (of ranks) as regards the materials of dress. Undyed silk with woven patterns *(Shiro-aya)* is only to be worn by Court Nobles *(Kuge)* and others of the highest ranks. Wadded coats of undyed silk may be worn by Daimyos and others of higher rank. Lined coats of purple silk; silk coats with the lining of

purple; white gloss silk, coloured silk coats without the badge are not to be worn at random.

Coming down to retainers, henchmen, and men-at-arms, the wearing by such persons of ornamental dresses such as silks, damask, brocade or embroideries was quite unknown to the ancient laws, and a stop must be put to it.

11. Those who may ride in palaquins[2] are all persons of distinction who are connections of the Tokugawa clan; lords of domains *(Kuni)* and lords of castles having 10,000 koku and upwards; the sons of provincial Daimyo (beneficiaries), lords of castles; chamber lains and higher functionaries, and the legitimate sons of such (i.e., sons by their wives; but not sons by their concubines); persons (of any rank) above fifty years of age; of the two professions of doctors of medicine and soothsayers (astrologers, *onyoshi*) and invalids and sick persons. Apart from the above named, irregularities must be prohibited; but those who have applied for and received official permission to ride are not included in the prohibition.

As regard the feudal retainers in the provinces, those who may ride are to be
definitely specified in each fief. Court Nobles, Abbots of royal or noble birth, and ecclesiastics of distinction are not to be included in this regulation.

12. Retainers who have had a disagreement with their original lord are not to be taken into employment by other Daimyos. If any such are reported as having been guilty of rebellion or homicide they are to be sent back (to their former lord). Any who manifest a refractory disposition must either be sent back or expelled.

13. When the hostages given by subvassals to their mesne lords have committed an offence requiring punishment by banishment or death, a report in writing of the circumstances must be made to the Magistrates' office and their decision awaited. In case the circumstances were such as to necessitate or justify the instant cutting down of the offender, a personal account of the matter must be given to the Magistrate.

14. The lesser beneficiaries must honestly discharge the duties of their position and refrain from giving unlawful or arbitrary orders (to the people of their benefices): they must take care not to impair the resources or well-being of the province or district in which they are.

15. The roads, relays of post horses, boats, ferries and bridges must be carefully attended to, so as to ensure that there shall be no delays or impediments to quick communication.

16. No private toll-bars may be erected, nor may any existing ferry be discontinued.

17. No vessels of over 500 koku burden are to be built.

18. The glebelands of shrines and temples scattered throughout the provinces (domains) having been attached to them from ancient times to the present day, are not to be taken from them.

19. The Christian sect is to be strictly prohibited in all the provinces and in all places.

20. In case of any unfilial conduct the offender will be dealt with under the penal law.

21. In all matters the example set by the laws of Yedo is to be followed in all the provinces and places.

All the foregoing provisions, being in conformity with the previous enactments
of this (Tokugawa) House, are hereby reimposed and definitely established and must be carefully observed.

The "Buke Shohatto" were again promulgated by the 4th Shogun Iyetsuna in 1663 (June 28th): only alterations made on this occasion are noted below, the body of the code remaining as before.

In Art. 2—As regards the taking of turns of duty, the Daimyos and Shomyos shall come to Yedo on service every year at the time when the Shogun fixes the posts which they are to guard....

Questions:
1. *How would you compare the alternate attendance system of Tokugawa Japan with a similar system of political control in European history?*
2. *Can Tokugawa Japan be called "a premodern police state"? Why? Why not?*

---

[1] One koku is equivalent to 4/96 bushels (of rice).

PART 17
New Science and Enlightenment

17.1   The Heliocentric Statement (ca. 1520): Nicolaus Copernicus

One of the most important and fundamental areas of investigation during the Scientific Revolution was astronomy. For centuries, humans had subscribed to a geocentric theory that placed earth at the center of the universe with all the planets orbiting around it. This theory, ascribed to the Egyptian astronomer Ptolemy (fl. 150 c.e.) and supported by Aristotelian physics, maintained that the earth had to be the center of the universe because of its heaviness and that the stars and other planets existed in surrounding crystalline spheres. Beyond these crystalline spheres lay the realm of God and the angels. This view was supported by the Catholic Church, which saw humanity as the central focus of God's creation and therefore at the epicenter of all existence. Biblical support for the geocentric theory included Psalm 104: "Thou didst set the earth on its foundation, so that it should never be shaken." Still, there were mathematical problems associated with this theory. For one, it was difficult to explain the motion of the planets, which seemed to be moving in noncircular patterns around the earth. At times the planets actually appeared to be going backward. This was explained by epicycles. Ptolemy maintained that planets make a second revolution in an orbit tangent to the first. It was therefore difficult to predict the location of a planet at any given time. A Polish astronomer named Nicolaus Copernicus (1473–1543) attempted to eliminate many of the mathematical inconsistencies by proposing that the sun, not the earth, was the center of the universe. In most other ways, including the acceptance of epicycles and the circular orbit of planets, Copernicus' system was still Ptolemaic. Yet Copernicus freed scientists from a rigid conception of cosmic structure and in essence proposed the empirical evidence of mathematics as the cornerstone of scientific thought.

The first selection is the simple statement by Copernicus proposing the heliocentric theory; it is excerpted from a letter entitled Commentariolus, written sometime after 1520. In 1543, Copernicus published On the Revolutions of the Heavenly Spheres.

Source: From *Three Copernican Treatises* by Edward Rosen, translator, copyright © 1939 Columbia University Press, p. 58. Reprinted with the permission of the publisher.

THE HELIOCENTRIC STATEMENT (CA. 1520)
NICOLAUS COPERNICUS

What appears to us as motions of the sun arise not from its motion but from the motion of the earth and our sphere, with which we revolve about the sun like any other planet. The earth has, then, more than one motion.

ON THE MOVEMENT OF THE EARTH (1543)
NICOLAUS COPERNICUS

Source: "On the Movement of the Earth" is from Copernicus, *De Revolutionibus Orbium Caelestium* (1543), trans. John F. Dobson and Selig Brodetsky, published in Occasional Notes of the Royal Astronomical Society, vol. 2, no. 1 (London: Royal Astronomical Society, 1947), excerpts from the preface and Book I.

I may well presume, most Holy Father, that certain people, as soon as they hear that in this book about the Revolutions of the Spheres of the Universe I ascribe movement to the earthly globe, will cry out that, holding such views, I should at once be hissed off the stage. . . .

So I should like your Holiness to know that I was induced to think of a method of computing the motions of the spheres by nothing else than the knowledge that the mathematicians [who had previously considered the problem] are inconsistent in these investigations.

For, first, the mathematicians are so unsure of the movements of the sun and Moon that they cannot even explain or observe the constant length of the seasonal year. Secondly, in determining the motions of these and of the other five planets, they use neither the same principles and hypotheses nor the same demonstrations of the apparent motions and revolutions. . . . Nor have they been able thereby to discern or deduce the principal thing—namely the shape of the Universe and the unchangeable symmetry of its parts. . . .

I pondered long upon this uncertainty of mathematical tradition in establishing the motions of the system of the spheres. At last I began to chafe that philosophers could by no means agree on any one certain theory of the mechanism of the Universe, wrought for us by a supremely good and orderly Creator. . . . I therefore took pains to read again the works of all the philosophers on whom I could lay hand to seek out whether any of them had even supposed that the motions of the spheres were other than those demanded by the [Ptolemaic] mathematical schools. I found first in Cicero that Hicetas [of Syracuse, fifth century b.c.e.] had realized that the Earth moved. Afterwards I found in Plutarch that certain others had held the like opinion. . . .

Thus assuming motions, which in my work I ascribe to the Earth, by long and frequent observations I have at last discovered that, if the motions of the rest of the planets be brought into relation with the circulation of the Earth and be reckoned in proportion to the circles of each planet, . . . the orders and magnitudes of all stars and spheres, nay the heavens themselves, become so bound together that nothing in any part thereof could be moved from its place without producing confusion of all the other parts of the Universe as a whole.

Questions:
1. What reasons does Copernicus give for supporting the heliocentric theory? Is he convincing?
2. Why is it significant that Copernicus refers to ancient authors like Cicero and Plutarch?

17.2 "I Think, Therefore I Am": Discourse on Method (1637)

René Descartes was born in 1596 in western France but lived primarily in Holland for the last twenty years of his life. He attended Jesuit schools and graduated in law from the university in Poitiers. He was not attracted to a legal career, however, and became a soldier in the German wars of the time. It was while he was billeted in a German town that he had an intellectual revelation akin, as he later maintained, to a religious conversion. He had a vision of the great potential for progress, if mathematical method were to be applied to all fields of knowledge. He thus pursued a career devoted to the propagation of a strict method, best exemplified by his invention of analytical geometry. Descartes believed that human beings were endowed by God with the ability to reason and that God served as the guarantor of the correctness of clear ideas. The material world could thus be understood through adherence to mathematical laws and methods of inquiry. Descartes championed the process of deductive reasoning whereby specific information could be logically deduced from general information. His method was influential well into the eighteenth century, when it was supplanted by the method of scientific induction, whereby generalizations could be drawn from the observation of specific data.

The following selection is drawn from Descartes' most famous work, Discourse on the Method of Rightly Conducting the Reason (1636).

Source: *"'I Think, Therefore I Am'" is from René Descartes, The Discourse on Method and Metaphysical Meditations, trans. G. B. Rawlings (London: Walter Scott, 1901), pp. 32–35, 60–61, 75–76.*

RENÉ DESCARTES

As a multitude of laws often furnishes excuses for vice, so that a state is much better governed when it has but few, and those few strictly observed, so in place of the great number of precepts of which logic is composed, I believed that I should find the following four sufficient, provided that I made a firm and constant resolve not once to omit to observe them.

The first was, never to accept anything as true when I did not recognize it clearly to be so, that is to say, to carefully avoid precipitation and prejudice, and to include in my opinions nothing beyond that which should present itself so clearly and so distinctly to my mind that I might have no occasion to doubt it.

The second was, to divide each of the difficulties which I should examine into as many parts as were possible, and as should be required for its better solution.

The third was, to conduct my thoughts in order, by beginning with the simplest objects, and those most easy to know, so as to mount little by little, as if by steps, to the most complex knowledge, and even assuming an order among those which do not naturally precede one another.

And the last was, to make everywhere enumerations so complete, and reviews so wide, that I should be sure of omitting nothing. . . .

I had long remarked that, in conduct, it is sometimes necessary to follow opinions known to be very uncertain, just as if they were indisputable, as has been said above; but then, because I desired to devote myself only to the research of truth, I thought it necessary to do exactly the contrary, and reject as absolutely false all in which I could conceive the least doubt, in order to see if afterwards there did not remain in my belief something which was entirely indisputable. Thus, because our senses sometimes deceive us, I wanted to suppose that nothing is such as they make us imagine it; and because some men err in reasoning . . . and judging that I was as liable to fail as any other, I rejected as false all the reasons which I had formerly accepted as [true]; . . . I resolved that everything which had ever entered into my mind was no more true than the illusions of my dreams. But immediately afterwards I observed that while I thus desired everything to be false, I, who thought, must of necessity [exist]; and remarking that this truth, I think, therefore I am, was so firm and so assured that all the most extravagant suppositions of the skeptics were unable to shake it, I judged that I could unhesitatingly accept it as the first principle of the philosophy I was seeking. . . .

After this, and reflecting upon the fact that I doubted, and that in consequence my being was not quite perfect (for I saw clearly that to know was a greater perfection than to doubt), I [wondered where] I had learned to think of something more perfect than I; and I knew for certain that it must be from some nature which was in reality more perfect. [And I clearly recognized that] this idea . . . had been put in me by a nature truly more perfect than I, which had in itself all perfections of which I could have any idea; that is, to explain myself in one word, God. . . .

Finally, whether awake or asleep, we ought never to allow ourselves to be persuaded of the truth of anything unless on the evidence of our Reason. And it must be noted that I say of our Reason, and not of our imagination or of our senses: thus, for example, although we very clearly see the sun, we ought not therefore to determine that it is only of the size which our sense of sight presents; and we may very distinctly imagine the head of a lion joined to the body of a goat, without being therefore shut up to the conclusion that a chimaera exists; for it is not a dictate of Reason that what we thus see or imagine is in reality existent; but it plainly tells us that all our ideas or notions contain in them some truth; for otherwise it could not be that God, who is wholly perfect and veracious, should have placed them in us.

Questions:
1. *What did Descartes mean by the phrase "I think, therefore I am"? Why was this so fundamental to his method?*
2. *Reconstruct his logic for the existence of God. Do you find it compelling?*

17.3 "I Learn and Teach from the Fabric of Nature": On the Circulation of the Blood (1628)

William Harvey has been termed the father of modern physiology. He was heir to a legacy of interest in the internal workings of the human body that had been most recently in evidence among artists during the Renaissance. But whereas Michelangelo studied the body to better represent the human form, Harvey sought to discover the internal workings on their own scientific merit. In this, he was more closely akin to the earlier scientific studies of Leonardo da Vinci. Harvey built upon the work of the Greek physician Galen (fl. 150 c.e.), who demonstrated that the arteries carried blood instead of air. Harvey's exacting methods set the pattern of scientific research for generations. In the following selection, which was an address to the Royal College of Physicians in 1628, he gave the results of his methodical dissections and experiments.

> **Source:** *"'I Learn and Teach from the Fabric of Nature'" is from R. Willis, trans., The Works of William Harvey (London: Sydenham Society, 1847), pp. 5–7, 31–32, 45–47.*

WILLIAM HARVEY

As this book alone declares the blood to course and revolve by a new route, very different from the ancient and beaten pathway trodden for so many ages, and illustrated by such a host of learned and distinguished men, I was greatly afraid lest I might be charged with presumption did I lay my work before the public at home, or send it beyond seas for impression, unless I had first proposed its subject to you, had confirmed its conclusions by ocular demonstrations in your presence, had replied to your doubts and objections, and secured the assent and support of our distinguished President. For I was most intimately persuaded, that if I could make good my proposition before you and our College, . . . I had less to fear from others. . . . For true philosophers, who are only eager for truth and knowledge, never regard themselves as already so thoroughly informed, but that they welcome further information from whomsoever and from whencesoever it may come; nor are they so narrow- minded as to imagine any of the arts or sciences transmitted to us by the ancients, in such a state of forwardness or completeness, that nothing is left for the ingenuity and industry of others. . . . Neither do they swear such fealty to their mistress Antiquity, that they openly, and in sight of all, deny and desert their friend Truth. . . .

My dear colleagues . . . I profess both to learn and to teach anatomy, not from books, but from dissections; not from the positions of philosophers, but from the fabric of nature. . . .

From these and other observations of the like kind, I am persuaded it will be found that the motion of the heart is as follows:

First of all, the auricle contracts, and in the course of its contraction throws the blood, (which it contains in ample quantity as the head of the veins, the store-house and cistern of the blood,) into the ventricle, which being filled, the heart raises itself straightway, makes all its fibers tense, contracts the ventricles, and performs a beat, by which beat it immediately sends the blood supplied to it by the auricle into the arteries; the right ventricle sending its charge into the lungs by the vessel which is called vena arteriosi, but which, in structure and function, and all things else, is an artery; the left ventricle sending its charge into the aorta, and through this by the arteries to the body at large. . . .

Thus far I have spoken of the passage of the blood from the veins into the arteries, and of the manner in which it is transmitted and distributed by the action of the heart. . . . But what remains to be said upon the quantity and source of the blood which thus passes, is of so novel and unheard-of character, that I not only fear injury to myself from the envy of a few, but I tremble lest I have mankind at large for my enemies. . . . Still, the die is cast, and my trust is in my love of truth, and the candor that inheres in cultivated minds. And when I surveyed my mass of evidence, ... I revolved in my mind, what might be the quantity of blood which was transmitted, in how short a time its passage might be effected, and the like; . . . I began to think whether there might not be A MOTION, AS IT WERE, IN A CIRCLE. Now this I afterwards found to be true; and I finally saw that the blood, forced by the action of the left ventricle into the arteries, was distributed to the body at large . . . impelled by the right ventricle . . . through the veins, and so round to the left ventricle in the manner already indicated. . . .

The heart, consequently, is the beginning of life; the sun of the microcosm, even as the sun in his turn might well be designated the heart of the world; for it is the heart by whose virtue and pulse the blood is moved, perfected, made apt to nourish, and is preserved from corruption and coagulation; it is the household divinity which, discharging its function, nourishes, cherishes, quickens the whole body, and is indeed the foundation of life, the source of all action.

Questions:

1. Why did William Harvey want to present his findings in an address before the Royal College of Physicians? What was he afraid of?
2. Why were his discoveries about the heart and circulation of blood so important and perhaps so threatening?

17.4   Isaac Newton

Isaac Newton (1642-1727) had formulated his theory of universal gravitation by the time he was twenty-four. But it was not until several years later, in 1687, that he published it, at the insistence of friends, under the title The Mathematical Principles of Natural Philosophy—the culmination of a scientific development that had been in progress for well over a hundred years and had included such names as Copernicus, Kepler, and Galileo. But Newton was the heir of other thinkers in an even broader sense. The selection from his Optics (1704) begins with a reaffirmation of the atomistic theory of matter, which was first developed by Democritus, an ancient Greek.

Source: Issac Newton, *Optics,* or a *Treatise of the Reflections, Refractions, Inflections and colours of Light,* 4th ed. (London, 1730). [Capitalization and spelling have been modernized—*Ed.*]

OPTICS

. . .

All these things being considered, it seems probable to me, that God in the beginning formed matter in solid, massy, hard, impenetrable, moveable particles, of such sizes and figures, and with such other properties, and in such proportion to space, as most conduced to the end for which he formed them; and that these primitive particles, being solids, are incomparably harder than any porous bodies compounded of them; even so very hard, as never to wear or break in pieces; no ordinary power being able to divide what God himself made one in the first creation. While the particles continue entire, they may compose bodies of one and the same nature and texture in all ages: But should they wear away, or break in pieces, the nature of things depending on them would be changed. Water and earth, composed of old worn particles and fragments of particles, would not be of the same nature and texture now, with water and earth composed of entire particles in the beginning. And therefore, that nature may be lasting, the changes of corporeal things are to be placed only in the various separations and new associations and motions of these permanent particles; compound bodies being apt to break, not in the midst of solid particles, but where those particles are laid together, and only touch in a few points.

It seems to me farther, that those particles have not only a force of inertia accompanied with such passive laws of motion as naturally result from that force, but also that they are moved by certain active principles, such as is that of gravity, and that which causes fermentation, and the cohesion of bodies. These principles I consider, not as *occult qualities*, supposed to result from the specific forms of things, but as general laws of nature, by which the things themselves are formed; their truth appearing to us by phenomena, though their causes be not yet discovered. For these are manifest qualities, and their causes only are occult. And the Aristotelians gave the name of occult qualities, not to manifest qualities, but to such qualities only as they supposed to lie hid in bodies, and to be the unknown causes of manifest effects: Such as would be the causes of gravity, and of magnetic and electric attractions, and of fermentations, if we should suppose that these forces or actions arose from qualities unknown to us, and incapable of being discovered and made manifest. Such occult qualities put a stop to the improvement of natural philosophy, and therefore of late years have been rejected. To tell us that every species of things is endowed with an occult specific quality by which it acts and produces manifest effects, is to tell us nothing: But to derive two or three general principles of motion from phenomena, and afterwards to tell us how the properties and actions of all corporeal things follow from those manifest principles, would be a very great step in philosophy, though the causes of those principles were not yet discovered: And therefore I scruple not to propose the principles of motion above-mentioned, they being of very general extent, and leave their causes to be found out.

Now by the help of these principles, all material things seem to have been composed of the hard and solid particles above-mentioned, variously associated in the first creation by the counsel of an intelligent agent. For it became him who created them to set them in order. And if he did so, it's unphilosophical to seek for any other origin of the world, or to pretend that it might arise out of a chaos by the mere laws of nature; though being once formed, it may continue by those laws for many ages. For while comets move in very eccentric orbs in all manner of positions, blind fate could never make all the planets move one and the same way in orbs concentric, some inconsiderable irregularities excepted, which may have risen from the mutual actions of comets and planets upon one another, and which will be apt to increase, till this system wants a reformation. Such a wonderful uniformity in the planetary system must be allowed the effect of choice. And so much the uniformity in the bodies of animals, they having generally a right and a left side shaped alike, and on either side of their bodies two legs behind, and either two arms, or two legs, or two wings before their shoulders, a neck running down into a backbone, and a head upon it; and in the head two ears, two eyes, a nose, a mouth, and a tongue, alike situated. Also the first contrivance of those very artificial parts of animals, the eyes, ears, brain, muscles, heart, lungs, midriff, glands, larynx, hands, wings, swimming bladders, natural spectacles, and other organs of sense and motion; and the instinct of brutes and insects, can be the effect of nothing else than the wisdom and skill of a powerful ever-living agent, who being in all places, is more able by his will to move the bodies within his boundless uniform sensorium, and thereby to form and reform the parts of the universe, than we are by our will to move the parts of our bodies. And yet we are not to consider the world as the body of God, or the several parts thereof, as the parts of God. He is a uniform being, void of organs, members, or parts, and they are his creatures subordinate to him, and subservient to his will; and he is no more the soul of them, than the soul of man is the soul of the species of things carried through the organs of sense into the place of its sensation, where it perceives them by means of its immediate presence, without the intervention of any third thing. The organs of sense are not for enabling the soul to perceive the species of things in its sensorium, but only for conveying them thither; and God had no need of such organs, he being everywhere present to the things themselves. And since space is divisible in *infinitum*, and matter is not necessarily in all places, it may be also allowed that God is able to create particles of matter of several sizes and figures, and in several proportions to space, and perhaps of different densities and forces, and thereby to vary the laws of nature, and make worlds of several sorts in several parts of the universe. At least, I see nothing of contradiction in all this.

As in mathematics, so in natural philosophy, the investigation of difficult things by the method of analysis, ought ever to precede the method of composition. This analysis consists in making experiments and observations, and in drawing general conclusions from them by induction and admitting of no objections against the conclusions, but such as are taken from experiments, or other certain truths. For hypotheses are not to be regarded in experimental philosophy. And although the arguing from experiments and observations by induction be no demonstration of general conclusions; yet it is the best way of arguing which the nature of things admits of, and may be looked upon as so much the stronger, by how much the induction is more general. And if no exception occur from phenomena, the conclusion may be pronounced generally. But if at any time afterwards any exception shall occur from experiments, it may then begin to be pronounced with such exceptions as occur. By this way of analysis we may proceed from compounds to ingredients, and from motions to the forces producing them; and in general, from effects to their causes, and from particular causes to more general ones, till the argument ends in the most general. This is the method of analysis: And the synthesis consists in assuming the causes discovered, and established as principles, and by them explaining the phenomena proceeding from them, and proving the explanations.

THE MATHEMATICAL PRINCIPLES OF NATURAL PHILOSOPHY

The Rules of Reasoning in Philosophy

Rule I. We are to admit no more causes of natural things, than such as are both true and sufficient to explain their appearances.

To this purpose the philosophers say, that Nature does nothing in vain, and more is in vain, when less will serve; for Nature is pleased with simplicity, and affects not the pomp of superfluous causes.

Rule II. Therefore to the same natural effects we must, as far as possible, assign the same causes.

As to respiration in a man, and in a beast; the descent of stones in Europe and in America; the light of our culinary fire and of the sun; the reflection of light in the earth, and in the planets.

Rule III. The qualities of bodies, which admit neither intension nor remission of degrees, and which are found to belong to all bodies within reach of our experiments, are to be esteemed the universal qualities of all bodies whatsoever.

For since the qualities of bodies are only known to us by experiments, we are to hold for universal, all such as universally agree with experiments; and such as are not liable to diminution, can never be quite taken away. We are certainly not to relinquish the evidence of experiments for the sake of dreams and vain fictions of our own devising; nor are we to recede from the analogy of Nature, which is wont to be simple, and always consonant to itself. We no other way know the extension of bodies, than by our senses, nor do these reach it in all bodies; but because we perceive extension in all that are sensible, therefore we ascribe it universally to all others, also. That abundance of bodies are hard we learn by experience. And because the hardness of the whole arises from the hardness of the parts, we therefore justly infer the hardness of the undivided particles not only of the bodies we feel but of all others. That all bodies are impenetrable, we gather not from reason, but from sensation. The bodies which we handle we find impenetrable, and thence conclude impenetrability to be a universal property of all bodies whatsoever. That all bodies are moveable, and endowed with certain powers (which we call the forces of inertia) or persevering in their motion or in their rest, we only infer from the like properties observed in the bodies which we have seen. The extension, hardness, impenetrability, mobility, and force of inertia of the whole, result from the extension, hardness, impenetrability, mobility, and forces of inertia of the parts: and thence we conclude that the least particles of all bodies to be also all extended, and hard, and impenetrable, and moveable, and endowed with their proper forces of inertia. And this is the foundation of all philosophy. Moreover, that the divided but contiguous particles of bodies may be separated from one another, is a matter of observation; and, in the particles that remain undivided, our minds are able to distinguish yet lesser parts, as is mathematically demonstrated. But whether the parts so distinguished, and not yet divided, may, by the powers of nature, be actually divided and separated from one another, we cannot certainly determine. Yet had we the proof of but one experiment, that any undivided particle, in breaking a hard and solid body, suffered a division, we might by virtue of this rule, conclude, that the undivided as well as the divided particles, may be divided and actually separated into infinity.

Lastly, if it universally appears, by experiments and astronomical observations, that all bodies about the earth, gravitate toward the earth; and that in proportion to the quantity of matter which they severally contain; that the moon likewise, according to the quantity of its matter, gravitates toward the earth; that on the other hand our sea gravitates toward the moon; and all the planets mutually one toward another; and the comets in like manner towards the sun; we must, in consequence of this rule, universally allow, that all bodies whatsoever are endowed with a principle of mutual gravitation. For the argument from the appearances concludes with more force for the universal gravitation of all bodies, than for their impenetrability, of which among those in the celestial regions, we have no experiments, nor any manner of observation. Not that I affirm gravity to be essential to all bodies. By their inherent force I mean nothing but their force of inertia. This is immutable. Their gravity is diminished as they recede from the earth.

Rule IV. In experimental philosophy we are to look upon propositions collected by general induction from phenomena as accurately or very nearly true, notwithstanding any contrary hypotheses that may be imagined, till such time as other phenomena occur, by which they may either be made more accurate, or liable to exceptions.

This rule we must follow that the argument of induction may not be evaded by hypotheses.

Questions:
1. Describe Newton's method. How does he arrive at his conclusions?
2. According to rule four, what can we imply about scientific conclusions? Are they definite? Why or why not?

17.5 Francis Bacon

Francis Bacon (1561 - 1626) was a prophet of the scientific revolution of the seventeenth century-a revolution that transformed the foundations of thought and ushered in the Age of Science. Like the prophets of the Old Testament, Bacon concentrated first on the evils around him. Although for him these evils were intellectual rather than moral or religious, he couched his criticism of the science of his day in biblical terms. Like the medieval schoolmen, the leading thinkers of his age, he argued, had wandered from the path of truth into the worship of idols. In the selection that follows he lists four such idols, to which he gives the picturesque titles of idols of the Tribe, the Cave, the Market-place, and the Theatre. To avoid falling prey to these idols, people must turn their backs on scholastic philosophy and develop a new science based on a true knowledge of the workings of nature. Such knowledge, Bacon held, was to be derived from careful and continued observation of specific natural occurrences. This observational method, which he called induction, is explained and illustrated in his major work, the Instauratio Magna (Great Renewal). In his opinion, this treatise represented a "total reconstruction of the sciences, arts, and all human knowledge."

Although he was a prophet of the new science, Bacon himself did not fully grasp the nature of the method that men like Galileo and Newton were to employ in their work. His concept of induction fails to take adequate account of two other basic elements of the modern scientific method-the formulation of hypotheses and the deduction and verification of their consequences.

Living at the height of the English Renaissance (which followed by a hundred years the Italian Renaissance), Bacon exemplified many of the attitudes found in previous Renaissance writers: the rejection of the medieval worldview as pernicious error, the somewhat naïve optimism about his ability to take the whole of human knowledge as his sphere of activity, and the faith that he stood on the threshold of a new intellectual era. Finally, in his assertion that "knowledge is power" Bacon repeated a central concept of Machiavelli-but with a significant difference. Machiavelli was concerned with the power that a prince could wield over his subjects, but Bacon was concerned with the power, derived from scientific understanding, that all humans could wield over nature.

The following selection is from Novum Organum (the New Organon written in 1620), which forms a part of Instauratio Magna.

Source: Trans. J. Spedding

NOVUM ORGANUM

Aphorisms Concerning the Interpretation of Nature and the Kingdom of Man

I. Man, being the servant and interpreter of Nature, can do and understand so much and so much only as he has observed in fact or in thought in the course of nature: beyond this he neither knows anything nor can do anything.

II. Neither the naked hand nor the understanding left to itself can effect much. It is by instruments and helps that the work is done, which are as much wanted for the understanding as for the hand. And as the instruments of the hand either give motion or guide it, so the instruments of the mind supply either suggestions for the understanding or cautions.

III. Human knowledge and human power meet in one; for where the cause is not known the effect cannot be produced. Nature to be commanded must be obeyed; and that which in contemplation is as the cause is in operation as the rule.

IV. Towards the effecting of works, all that man can do is to put together or put asunder natural bodies. The rest is done by nature working within.

. . .

VI. It would be an unsound fancy and self-contradictory to expect that things which have never yet been done can be done except by means which have never yet been tried.

. . .

XI. As the sciences which we now have do not help us in finding out new works, so neither does the logic which we now have help us in finding out new sciences.

XII. The logic now in use serves rather to fix and give stability to the errors which have their foundations in commonly received notions than to help the search after truth. So it does more harm than good.

• • •

XVIII. The discoveries which have hitherto been made in the sciences are such as lie close to vulgar notions, scarcely beneath the surface. In order to penetrate into the inner and further recesses of nature, it is necessary that both notions and axioms be derived from things by a more sure and guarded way; and that a method of intellectual operation be introduced altogether better and more certain.

XIX. There are and can be only two ways of searching into and discovering truth. The one flies from the senses and particulars to the most general axioms, and from these principles, the truth of which it takes for settled and immovable, proceeds to judgment and to the discovery of middle axioms. And this way is now in fashion. The other derives axioms from the senses and particulars, rising by a gradual and unbroken ascent, so that it arrives at the most general axioms last of all. This is the true way, but as yet untried.

• • •

XXII. Both ways set out from the senses and particulars, and rest in the highest generalities; but the difference between them is infinite. For the one just glances at experiment and particulars in passing, the other dwells duly and orderly among them. The one, again, begins at once by establishing certain abstract and useless generalities, the other rises by gradual steps to that which is prior and better known in the order of nature.

• • •

XXXI. It is idle to expect any great advancement in science from the superinducing and engrafting of new things upon old. We must begin anew from the very foundations, unless we would revolve forever in a circle with mean and contemptible progress.

• • •

XXXV. It was said by Borgia of the expedition of the French into Italy, that they came with chalk in their hands to mark out their lodgings, not with arms to force their way in. I in like manner would have my doctrine enter quietly into the minds that are fit and capable of receiving it; for confutations cannot be employed, when the difference is upon first principles and very notions and even upon forms of demonstration.

XXXVI. One method of delivery alone remains to us; which is simply this: we must lead men to the particulars themselves, and their series and order; while men on their side must force themselves for awhile to lay their notions by and begin to familiarize themselves with facts.

XXXVII. The doctrine of those who have denied that certainty could be attained at all, has some agreement with my way of proceeding at the first setting out; but they end in being infinitely separated and opposed. For the holders of that doctrine assert simply that nothing can be known; I also assert that not much can be known in nature by the way which is now in use. But then they go on to destroy the authority of the senses and understanding; whereas I proceed to devise and supply helps for the same.

XXXVIII. The idols and false notions which are now in possession of the human understanding, and have taken deep root therein, not only so beset men's minds that truth can hardly find entrance, but even after entrance is obtained, they will again in the very instauration of the science meet and trouble us, unless men being forewarned of the danger fortify themselves as far as may be against their assaults.

XXXIX. There are four classes of Idols which beset men's minds. To these for distinction's sake I have assigned names, calling the first class *Idols of the Tribe;* the second, *Idols of the Cave;* the third, *Idols of the Marketplace;* the fourth, *Idols of the Theatre.*

XL. The formation of ideas and axioms by true induction is no doubt the proper remedy to be applied for the keeping off and clearing away of idols. To point them out, however, is of great use; for the doctrine of Idols is to the Interpretation of Nature what the doctrine of the refutation of Sophisms is to common Logic.

XLI. The Idols of the Tribe have their foundation in human nature itself, and in the tribe or race of men. For it is a false assertion that the sense of man is the measure of things. On the contrary, all perceptions as well of the sense as of the mind are according to the measure of the universe. And the human understanding is like a false mirror, which, receiving rays irregularly, distorts and discolours the nature of things by mingling its own nature with it.

XLII. The Idols of the Cave are the idols of the individual man. For every one (besides the errors common to human nature in general) has a cave or den of his own, which refracts and discolors the light of nature; owing either to his own proper and peculiar nature; or to his education and conversation with others; or to the reading of books, and the authority of those whom he esteems and admires; or to the differences of impressions, accordingly as they take place in a mind preoccupied and predisposed or in a mind indifferent and settled; or the like. So that the spirit of man (according as it is meted out to different individuals) is in fact a thing variable and full of perturbation, and governed as it were by chance. Whence it was observed by Heraclitus[1] that men look for sciences in their own lesser worlds, and not in the greater or common world.

XLIII. There are also Idols formed by the intercourse and association of men with each other, which I call Idols of the Marketplace, on account of the commerce and consort of men there. For it is by discourse that men associate; and words are imposed according to the apprehension of the vulgar. And therefore the ill and unfit choice of words wonderfully obstructs the understanding. Nor do the definitions or explanations wherewith in some things learned men are wont to guard and defend themselves, by any means set the matter right. But words plainly force and overrule the understanding, and throw all into confusion, and lead men away into numberless empty controversies and idle fancies.

XLIV. Lastly, there are Idols which have immigrated into men's minds from the various dogmas of philosophies, and also from wrong laws of demonstration. These I call Idols of the Theatre; because in my judgment all the received systems are but so many stage-plays, representing worlds of their own creation after an unreal and scenic fashion. Nor is it only of the systems now in vogue, or only of the ancient sects and philosophies, that I speak; for many more plays of the same kind may yet be composed and in like artificial manner set forth; seeing that errors the most widely different have nevertheless causes for the most part alike. Neither again do I mean this only of entire systems, but also of many principles and axioms in science, which by tradition, credulity, and negligence have come to be received.

Questions:
1. How does Bacon propose to find truth?
2. What are the strengths and weaknesses of his inductive method?

17.6   On Universal Toleration: Voltaire

The Enlightenment is often characterized as an era of empirical reasoning and critical thought, of doubt and skepticism, of individual assertion at the expense of formal control by the state or church. For the most part, this is a fair assessment. God, if he existed, was prone to be antiseptic, the "great clock-winder," who created the universe and then sat back, uninvolved in the lives of his creations. This philosophy, called deism, generally prevailed among the philosophes. It did not deny the existence of God, but it gave virtually no support to organized religion. The deists particularly denounced the mysteries of the Christian religion such as the Trinity and miracles like the Virgin Birth and the Eucharist. Since God was disinterested in the affairs of the world, formal prayers were useless. Deism enabled many of the philosophes to effect a reconciliation between a perfect God and an imperfect world.

Voltaire was the quintessential personality of the Enlightenment. An author of dramas, histories, and scathing satires, his wit and intellectual power dominated the age. Voltaire was an adamant opponent of organized religion, but one of the most enthusiastic advocates of religious toleration and the deist viewpoint. The first selection is from his famous Treatise on Toleration. In the letter that follows, Voltaire argues for the logic and necessity of a supreme deity. His ideas are generally representative of the enlightened thinkers of the age.

Source: "On Universal Toleration," is from Tobias Smollett, ed., *The Works of Voltaire* (London: E. R. DuMont, 1901), vol. 4, pp. 272–273, 275–276, 278. Text modernized by the editor.

VOLTAIRE

It does not require any great art or studied elocution to prove that Christians ought to tolerate one another. Nay, I shall go still farther and say that we ought to look upon all men as our brethren. How! Call a Turk, a Jew, and a Siamese, my brother? Yes, doubtless; for are we not all children of the same parent, and the creatures of the same Creator?

But these people hold us in contempt, and call us idolaters! Well, then, I should tell them that they were to blame. And I fancy that I could stagger the headstrong pride of an imam, or a talapoin [religious leaders], were I to address them in the following manner:

"This little globe, which is no more than a point, rolls, together with many other globes, in that immensity of space in which we are all alike confounded. Man, who is an animal, about five feet high, is certainly a very inconsiderable part of the creation; but one of those hardly visible beings says to others of the same kind inhabiting another spot of the globe: Hearken to me, for the God of all these worlds has enlightened me. There are about nine hundred millions of us little insects who inhabit the earth, but my ant-hill is alone cherished by God, who holds all the rest in horror and detestation; those who live with me upon my spot will alone be happy, and all the rest eternally wretched."

They would here stop me short and ask, "What madman could have made so ridiculous a speech?" I should then be obliged to answer them, "It is yourselves.". . .

O you different worshippers of a God of mercy! If you have cruel hearts, if, while you adore that Deity who has placed the whole of His law in these few words, "Love God and your neighbor," you have loaded that pure and holy law with sophistical and unintelligible disputes, if you have lighted the flames of discord sometimes for a new word, and at others for a single letter only; if you have annexed eternal punishment to the omission of some few words, or of certain ceremonies which other people cannot comprehend, I must say to you with tears of compassion for mankind: "Transport yourselves with me to that great instant in which all men are to receive judgment from the hand of God, who will then do unto every one according to their works, and with me behold all the dead of past ages appearing in His presence. Are you very sure that our heavenly Father and Creator will say to the wise and virtuous Confucius, to the great legislator Solon, to Pythagoras, Socrates, Plato, the divine Antoninus, the good Trajan, to Titus, the delight of humankind, and to many others who have been the models of humankind: 'Depart from me, wretches! into torments that know neither alleviation nor end; but are, like Himself, everlasting.'"

I think I see you start with horror at these words. . . .

May all men remember that they are brethren! May they alike abhor that tyranny which seeks to subject the freedom of the will, as they do the rapine which tears from the arms of industry the fruits of its peaceful labors! And if the scourge of war is not to be avoided, let us not mutually hate and destroy each other in the midst of peace; but rather make use of the few moments of our existence to join in praising, in a thousand different languages, from one extremity of the world to the other, Thy goodness, O all-merciful Creator, to whom we are indebted for that existence!

"IF GOD DID NOT EXIST, HE WOULD HAVE TO BE INVENTED"
VOLTAIRE

Source: "'If God Did Not Exist, He Would Have to Be Invented,'" is from S. G. Tallentyre, trans., *Voltaire in His Letters* (New York: G. P. Putnam's Sons, 1919).

To Frederick William, Prince of Prussia:

Monseigneur, the royal family of Prussia has excellent reasons for not wishing the annihilation of the soul. It has more right than anyone to immortality.

It is very true that we do not know any too well what the soul is: no one has ever seen it. All that we do know is that the eternal Lord of nature has given us the power of thinking, and of distinguishing virtue. It is not proved that this faculty survives our death: but the contrary is not proved either. It is possible, doubtless, that God has given thought to a particle to which, after we are no more, He will still give the power of thought: there is no inconsistency in this idea.

In the midst of all the doubts which we have discussed for four thousand years in four thousand ways, the safest course is to do nothing against one's conscience. With this secret, we can enjoy life and have nothing to fear from death.

There are some charlatans who admit no doubts. We know nothing of first principles. It is surely very presumptuous to define God, the angels, spirits, and to pretend to know precisely why God made the world, when we do not know why we can move our arms at our pleasure. Doubt is not a pleasant condition, but certainty is an absurd one.

What is most repellent in the System of Nature [by the Baron d'Holbach] . . . is the audacity with which it decides that there is no God, without even having tried to prove the impossibility. There is some eloquence in the book: but much more rant, and no sort of proof. It is a pernicious work, alike for princes and people: "Si Dieu n'existait pas, il faudrait l'inventer." [If God did not exist, he would have to be invented].

But all nature cries aloud that He does exist: that there is a supreme intelligence, an immense power, an admirable order, and everything teaches us our own dependence on it.

From the depth of our profound ignorance, let us do our best: this is what I think, and what I have always thought, amid all the misery and follies inseparable from seventy-seven years of life. . . . I am, with deep respect, Voltaire

Questions:
1. Why was toleration so important to Voltaire?
2. Do you regard him as a religious individual? Why is deism a comfortable philosophy?

17.7 "The Greatest Happiness of the Greatest Number": On Crimes and Punishments (1764)

Cesare Beccaria was the son of a Milanese aristocrat of modest means. He was educated initially at a Jesuit school, an experience that he later described as "fanatical" and stifling to "the development of human feelings." At the age of 26, he became an international celebrity with the publication of his work on criminal law in 1764. Translated into several languages, it enjoyed a remarkable success in France, where it went through seven editions in six months. In it, Beccaria lashed out against the barbarities of the day, including the torture of prisoners in order to induce confession, the corruption of judges, and degrading and brutal punishments. Penalties, he concluded, should be scaled to the offense. Beccaria was the first modern writer to advocate the complete abolition of capital punishment, and his treatise remains the most important and influential volume written on criminal justice.

Source: "'The Greatest Happiness of the Greatest Number'" is from Cesare Beccaria, *An Essay on Crimes and Punishments,* trans. E. D. Ingraham (Philadelphia: H. Nicklin, 1819), pp. xii, 18–19, 47, 59–60, 93–94, 104–105, 148–149.

CESARE BECCARIA

If we look into history, we shall find that laws, which are, or ought to be, conventions between men in a state of freedom, have been, for the most part the work of the passions of a few, or the consequences of a fortuitous or temporary necessity; not dictated by a cool examiner of human nature, who knew how to collect in one point the actions of a multitude, and had only this end in view, the greatest happiness of the greatest number. . . .

Observe that by justice I understand nothing more than that bond which is necessary to keep the interest of individuals united, without which men would return to their original state of barbarity. All punishments which exceed the necessity of preserving this bond are in their nature unjust. . . .

The end of punishment, therefore, is no other than to prevent the criminal from doing further injury to society, and to prevent others from committing the like offence. Such punishments, therefore, and such a mode of inflicting them ought to be chosen, as will make the strongest and most lasting impressions on the minds of others, with the least torment to the body of the criminal.

The torture of a criminal during the course of his trial is a cruelty consecrated by custom in most nations. It is used with an intent either to make him confess his crime, or to explain some contradiction into which he had been led during his examination, or discover his accomplices, or for some kind of metaphysical and incomprehensible purgation of infamy, or, finally, in order to discover other crimes of which he is not accused, but of which he may be guilty.

No man can be judged a criminal until he be found guilty; nor can society take from him the public protection until it has been proved that he has violated the conditions on which it was granted. What right, then, but that of power, can authorise the punishment of a citizen so long as there remains any doubt of his guilt? This dilemma is frequent. Either he is guilty, or not guilty. If guilty, he should only suffer the punishment ordained by the laws, and torture becomes useless, as his confession is unnecessary. If he be not guilty, you torture the innocent; for in the eye of the law, every man is innocent whose crime has not been proved. . . .

Crimes are more effectually prevented by the certainty than by the severity of punishment. . . . In proportion as punishments become more cruel, the minds of men, as a fluid rises to the same height with that which surrounds it, grow hardened and insensible; and the force of the passions still continuing, in the space of an hundred years the wheel [torture device] terrifies no more than formerly the prison. That a punishment may produce the effect required, it is sufficient that the evil it occasions should exceed the good expected from the crime, including in the calculation the certainty of the punishment, and the privation of the expected advantage. All severity beyond this is superfluous, and therefore tyrannical.

The punishment of death is pernicious to society, from the example of barbarity it affords. If the passions, or the necessity of war, have taught men to shed the blood of their fellow creatures, the laws, which are intended to moderate the ferocity of mankind, should not increase it by examples of barbarity, them more horrible as this punishment is usually attended with formal pageantry. Is it not absurd, that the laws, which detest and punish homicide, should, in order to prevent murder, publicly commit murder themselves? . . .

It is better to prevent crimes than to punish them. This is the fundamental principle of good legislation, which is the art of conducting men to the maximum of happiness, and to the minimum of misery, if we may apply this mathematical expression to the good and evil of life. . . .

Would you prevent crimes? Let the laws be clear and simple, let the entire force of the nation be united in their defence, let them be intended rather to favour every individual than any particular classes of men; let the laws be feared, and the laws only. The fear of the laws is salutary, but the fear of men is a fruitful and fatal source of crimes.

Questions:
1. How do you think Cesare Beccaria might have reacted to our modern concern over capital punishment?
2. Ultimately, how does a society prevent crime?

17.8 An Inquiry Into the Nature and Causes of the Wealth of Nations: Adam Smith

European economic practices before Adam Smith were guided by the theory of mercantilism. Often described as the doctrine that a nation's wealth consists in the amount of money, in the form of precious metals, it possesses, it follows from mercantile theory that the nation should adopt the policy of maximizing its exports (particularly in the form of valuable manufactured goods) and minimizing its imports, thus increasing its intake of bullion. But this is only a superficial account of a much more complex theory. To understand mercantilism one must view it in its historical context-that of the emerging nation-states of Europe. So understood, mercantilism, like warfare, can be seen as one of the methods employed by these burgeoning nations to increase their power, particularly in relation to that of their neighbors. Although one of the means to this end was to achieve a favorable balance of trade, others included the encouragement of manufacturing industries, the increase of an urban over a rural population, the acquisition of colonies (particularly in the Western Hemisphere), and others. But most important was the idea that economics was an organ of national power and that, therefore, the state should exercise tight control over every facet of its economy.

Although the mercantilist system was by no means a failure in serving the needs of the times, it began to come under attack during the eighteenth century. Perhaps the sharpest, and certainly the most influential, of its critics was the Scot, Adam Smith (1723-1790). By profession Smith was not an economist but a philosopher, being for several years a professor of moral philosophy at the University of Glasgow. His great work, whose full title is An Inquiry into the Nature and Causes of the Wealth of Nations, was published in 1776.

Smith focused his attack on mercantilism on its central tenet-that the economic life of a nation should be under the strict control of the government. Rather than encouraging economic activity, he argued, such a policy increasingly stifles it. In his mind the best way to maximize the wealth of a nation is to allow each individual to pursue his own interests with a minimum of restraints. Thus he advocated the economics that has come to be known as the free enterprise system and his book The Wealth of Nations laid the theoretical foundations on which modern capitalism was to develop.

Smith believed that, if each individual pursued his own economic interests, the interests of all would be enhanced. But, as the later history of capitalism has made us realize, the pursuit of unbridled self-interest- particularly by large corporations-has often had a quite different effect. To critics of his economic theory Smith would undoubtedly have replied that, when he spoke of self-interest, he always meant enlightened self-interest, or the individual's recognition that his own best interests could be realized only with the realization of those of society as a whole. To what extent such a reply would constitute a repudiation of the capitalism his economic theory engendered is a question worthy of debate.

Source: Adam Smith, *An Inquiry into the Nature and Causes of the Wealth of Nations*, 8th ed.

BOOK IV, CHAPTER II

Of Restraints upon the Importation from Foreign Countries of Such Goods as Can Be Produced at Home

By restraining, either by high duties, or by absolute prohibitions, the importation of such goods from foreign countries as can be produced at home, the monopoly of the home-market is more or less secured to the domestic industry employed in producing them. Thus the prohibition of importing either live cattle or salt provisions from foreign countries secures to the graziers of Great Britain the monopoly of the home market for butchers' -meat. The high duties upon the importation of corn, which in times of moderate plenty amount to a prohibition, give a like advantage to the growers of that commodity. The prohibition of the importation of foreign woollens is equally favourable to the woollen manufactures. The silk manufacture, though altogether employed upon foreign materials, has lately obtained the same advantage. The linen manufacture has not yet obtained it, but is making great strides towards it. Many other sorts of manufactures have, in the same manner, obtained in Great Britain, either altogether, or very nearly a monopoly against their countrymen. The variety of goods of which the importation into Great Britain is prohibited, either absolutely, or under certain circumstances, greatly exceeds what can easily be suspected by those who are not well acquainted with the laws of the customs.

That this monopoly of the home-market frequently gives great encouragement to that particular species of industry which enjoys it, and frequently turns toward that employment a greater share of both the labour and stock of the society than would otherwise have gone to it, cannot be doubted. But whether it tends either to increase the general industry of the society, or to give it the most advantageous direction, is not, perhaps, altogether so evident.

The general industry of the society never can exceed what the capital of the society can employ. As the number of workmen that can be kept in employment by any particular person must bear a certain proportion to his capital, so the number of those that can be continually employed by all the members of a great society, must bear a certain proportion to the whole capital of that society, and never can exceed that proportion. No regulation of commerce can increase the quantity of industry in any society beyond what its capital can maintain. It can only divert a part of it into a direction into which it might not otherwise have gone; and it is by no means certain that this artificial direction is likely to be more advantageous to the society than that into which it would have gone of its own accord.

Every individual is continually exerting himself to find out the most advantageous employment for whatever capital he can command. It is his own advantage, indeed, and not that of the society, which he has in view. But the study of his own advantage naturally, or rather necessarily leads him to prefer that employment which is most advantageous to the society.

First, every individual endeavours to employ his capital as near home as he can, and consequently as much as he can in the support of domestic industry; provided always that he can thereby obtain the ordinary, or not a great deal less than the ordinary profits of stock.

Thus, upon equal or nearly equal profits, every wholesale merchant naturally prefers the home-trade to the foreign trade of consumption, and the foreign trade of consumption to the carrying trade. In the home-trade his capital is never so long out of his sight as it frequently is in the foreign trade of consumption. He can know better the character and situation of the persons whom he trusts, and if he should happen to be deceived, he knows better the laws of the country from which he must seek redress. . . . Upon equal, or only nearly equal profits, therefore, every individual naturally inclines to employ his capital in the manner in which it is likely to afford the greater support to domestic industry, and to give revenue and employment to the greatest number of people of his own country.

Secondly, every individual who employs his capital in the support of domestic industry, necessarily endeavours so to direct that industry, that its produce may be of the greatest possible value.

The produce of industry is what it adds to the subject or materials upon which it is employed. In proportion as the value of this produce is great or small, so will likewise be the profits of the employer. But it is only for the sake of profit that any man employs a capital in the support of industry; and he will always, therefore, endeavour to employ it in the support of that industry of which the produce is likely to be of the greatest value, or to exchange for the greatest quantity either of money or of other goods.

But the annual revenue of every society is always precisely equal to the exchangeable value of the whole annual produce of its industry, or rather is precisely the same thing with that exchangeable value. As every individual, therefore, endeavours as much as he can both to employ his capital in the support of domestic industry, and so to direct that industry that its produce may be of the greatest value; every individual necessarily labours to render the annual revenue of the society as great as he can. He generally, indeed, neither intends to promote the public interest, nor knows how much he is promoting it. By preferring the support of domestic to that of foreign industry, he intends only his own security; and by directing that industry in such a manner as its produce may be of the greatest value, he intends only his own gain, and he is in this, as in many other cases, led by an invisible hand to promote an end which was no part of his intention. Nor is it always the worse for the society that it was no part of it. By pursuing his own interest he frequently promotes that of the society more effectually than when he really intends to promote it. I have never known much good done by those who affected to trade for the public good. It is an affectation, indeed, not very common among merchants, and very few words need be employed in dissuading them from it.

What is the species of domestic industry which his capital can employ, and of which the produce is likely to be of the greatest value, every individual, it is evident, can, in his local situation, judge much better than any statesman or lawgiver can do for him. The statesman, who should attempt to direct private people in what manner they ought to employ their capitals, would not only load himself with a most unnecessary attention, but assume an authority which could safely be trusted, not only to no single person, but to no council or senate whatever, and which would nowhere be so dangerous as in the hands of a man who had folly and presumption enough to fancy himself fit to exercise it.

To give the monopoly of the home-market to the produce of domestic industry, in any particular art or manufacture, is in some measure to direct private people in what manner they ought to employ their capitals, and must, in almost all cases, be either a useless or a hurtful regulation. If the produce of domestic can be brought there as cheap as that of foreign industry, the regulation is evidently useless. If it cannot, it must generally be hurtful. It is the maxim of every prudent master of a family, never to attempt to make at home what it will cost him more to make than to buy. The taylor does not attempt to make his own shoes, but buys them of the shoemaker. The shoemaker does not attempt to make his own clothes, but employs a taylor. The farmer attempts to make neither the one nor the other, but employs those different artificers. All of them find it for their interest to employ their whole industry in a way in which they have some advantage over their neighbours, and to purchase with a part of its produce, or what is the same thing, with the price of a part of it, whatever else they have occasion for.

What is prudence in the conduct of every family, can scarce be folly in that of a great kingdom. If a foreign country can supply us with a commodity cheaper than we ourselves can make it, better buy it of them with some part of the produce of our own industry, employed in a way in which we have some advantage. The general industry of the country, being always in proportion to the capital which employs it, will not thereby be diminished, no more than that of the above-mentioned artificers; but only left to find out the way in which it can be employed with the greatest advantage. It is certainly not employed to the greatest advantage, when it is thus directed towards an object which it can buy cheaper than it can make. The value of its annual produce is certainly more or less diminished, when it is thus turned away from producing commodities evidently of more value than the commodity which it is directed to produce. According to the supposition, that commodity could be purchased from foreign countries cheaper than it can be made at home. It could, therefore, have been purchased with a part only of the commodities, or, what is the same thing, with a part only of the price of the commodities, which the industry employed by an equal capital would have produced at home, had it been left to follow its natural course. The industry of the country, therefore, is thus turned away from a more to a less advantageous employment, and the exchangeable value of its annual produce, instead of being increased, according to the intention of the lawgiver, must necessarily be diminished by every such regulation.

By means of such regulations, indeed, a particular manufacture may sometimes be acquired sooner than it could have been otherwise, and after a certain time may be made at home as cheap or cheaper than in the foreign country. But though the industry of the society may be thus carried with advantage into a particular channel sooner than it could have been otherwise, it will by no means follow that the sum total, either of its industry, or of its revenue, can ever be augmented by any such regulation. The industry of the society can augment only in proportion as its capital augments, and its capital can augment only in proportion to what can be gradually saved out of its revenue. But the immediate effect of every such regulation is to diminish its revenue, and what diminishes its revenue is certainly not very likely to augment its capital faster than it would have augmented of its own accord, had both capital and industry been left to find out their natural employments.

Though for want of such regulations the society should never acquire the proposed manufacture, it would not, upon that account, necessarily be the poorer in any one period of its duration. In every period of its duration its whole capital and industry might still have been employed, though upon different objects, in the manner that was most advantageous at the time. In every period its revenue might have been the greatest which its capital could afford, and both capital and revenue might have been augmented with the greatest possible rapidity.

The natural advantages which one country has over another in producing particular commodities are sometimes so great, that it is acknowledged by all the world to be in vain to struggle with them. By means of glasses, hotbeds, and hotwalls, very good grapes can be raised in Scotland, and very good wine too can be made of them at about thirty times the expense for which at least equally good can be brought from foreign countries. Would it be a reasonable law to prohibit the importation of all foreign wines, merely to encourage the making of claret and burgundy in Scotland? But if there would be a manifest absurdity in turning towards any employment thirty times more of the capital and industry of the country, than would be necessary to purchase from foreign countries an equal quantity of the commodities wanted, there must be an absurdity, though not altogether so glaring, yet exactly of the same kind, in turning towards any such employment a thirtieth, or even a three hundredth part more of either. Whether the advantages which one country has over another be natural or acquired, is in this respect of no consequence. As long as the one country has those advantages, and the other wants them, it will always be more advantageous for the latter, rather to buy of the former than to make. It is an acquired advantage only, which one artificer has over his neighbour, who exercises another trade; and yet they both find it more advantageous to buy of one another, than to make what does not belong to their particular trades.

Merchants and manufacturers are the people who derive the greatest advantage from this monopoly of the home-market. The prohibition of the importation of foreign cattle, and of salt provisions, together with the high duties upon foreign corn, which in times of moderate plenty amount to a prohibition, are not near so advantageous to the graziers and farmers of Great Britain, as other regulations of the same kind are to its merchants and manufacturers. Manufactures, those of the finer kind especially, are more easily transported from one country to another than corn or cattle. It is in the fetching and carrying manufactures, accordingly, that foreign trade is chiefly employed. In manufactures, a very small advantage will enable foreigners to undersell our own workmen, even in the home-market. It will require a very great one to enable them to do so in the rude produce of the soil. If the free importation of foreign manufactures were permitted, several of the home manufactures would probably suffer, and some of them, perhaps, go to ruin altogether, and a considerable part of the stock and industry at present employed in them would be forced to find out some other employment. But the freest importation of the rude produce of the soil could have no such effect upon the agriculture of the country.

. . .

Even the free importation of foreign corn could very little affect the interest of the farmers of Great Britain. Corn is a much more bulky commodity than butchers'-meat. A pound of wheat at a penny is as dear as a pound of butchers'-meat at fourpence. The small quantity of foreign corn imported even in times of the greatest scarcity, may satisfy our farmers that they can have nothing to fear from the freest importation. The average quantity imported one year with another, amounts only, according to the very well-informed author of the tracts upon the corn trade, to twenty-three thousand seven hundred and twenty-eight quarters of all sorts of grain, and does not exceed the five hundredth and seventy-one part of the annual consumption. But as the bounty upon corn occasions a greater exportation in years of plenty, so it must of consequence occasion a greater importation in years of scarcity, than in the actual state of tillage would otherwise take place. By means of it, the plenty of one year does not compensate the scarcity of another, and as the average quantity exported is necessarily augmented by it, so much likewise, in the actual state of tillage, the average quantity imported. If there were no bounty, as less corn would be exported, so it is probable that, one year with another, less would be imported than at present. The corn merchant, the fetchers and carriers of corn between Great Britain and foreign countries, would have much less employment, and might suffer considerably; but the country gentlemen and farmers could suffer very little. It is in the corn merchants accordingly, rather than in the country gentlemen and farmers, that I have observed the greatest anxiety for the renewal and continuation of the bounty.

Country gentlemen and farmers are, to their great honour, of all people, the least subject to the wretched spirit of monopoly. The undertaker of a great manufactory is sometimes alarmed if another work of the same kind is established within twenty miles of him. The Dutch undertaker of all the woollen manufacture at Abbeville stipulated, that no work of the same kind should be established within thirty leagues of that city. Farmers and country gentlemen, on the contrary, are generally disposed rather to promote than to obstruct the cultivation and improvement of their neighbours' farms and estates. They have no secrets, such as those of the greater part of manufacturers, but are generally rather fond of communicating to their neighbours, and of extending as far as possible any new practice which they have found to be advantageous. . . . Country gentlemen and farmers, dispersed in different parts of the country, cannot so easily combine as merchants and manufacturers, who being collected into towns, and accustomed to that exclusive corporation spirit which prevails in them, naturally endeavour to obtain against all their countrymen, the same exclusive privilege which they generally possess against the inhabitants of their respective towns. They accordingly seem to have been the original inventors of those restraints upon the importation of foreign goods, which secure to them the monopoly of the home-market. It was probably in imitation of them, and to put themselves upon a level with those who, they found, were disposed to oppress them, that the country gentlemen and farmers of Great Britain so far forgot the generosity which is natural to their station, as to demand the exclusive privilege of supplying their countrymen with corn and butchers'-meat. They did not perhaps take time to consider, how much less their interest could be affected by the freedom of trade than that of the people whose example they followed.

To prohibit by a perpetual law the importation of foreign corn and cattle, is in reality to enact, that the population and industry of the country shall at no time exceed what the rude produce of its own soil can maintain.

There seem, however, to be two cases in which it will generally be advantageous to lay some burden upon foreign, for the encouragement of domestic industry.

The first is, when some particular sort of industry is necessary for the defense of the country. The defense of Great Britain, for example, depends very much upon the number of its sailors and shipping. The act of navigation, therefore, very properly endeavours to give the sailors and shipping of Great Britain the monopoly of the trade of their own country, in some cases, by absolute prohibitions, and in others by heavy burdens upon the shipping of foreign countries. The following are the principal dispositions of this act.

First, all ships, of which the owners, masters, and three-fourths of the mariners are not British subjects, are prohibited, upon pain of forfeiting ship and cargo, from trading to the British settlements and plantations, or from being employed in the coasting trade of Great Britain.

Secondly, a great variety of the most bulky articles of importation can be brought into Great Britain only, either in such ships as are above described, or in ships of the country where those goods are produced, and of which the owners, masters, and three-fourths of the mariners, are of that particular country; and when imported even in ships of this latter kind, they are subject to double aliens duty. If imported in ships of any other country, the penalty is forfeiture of ship and goods. When this act was made, the Dutch were, what they still are, the great carriers of Europe, and by this regulation they were entirely excluded from being carriers to Great Britain, or from importing to us the goods of any other European country.

Thirdly, a great variety of the most bulky articles of importation are prohibited from being imported, even in British ships, from any country but that in which they are produced; under pain of forfeiting ship and cargo. This regulation too was probably intended against the Dutch. Holland was then, as now, the great emporium for all European goods, and by this regulation, British ships were hindered from loading in Holland the goods of any other European country.

Fourthly, salt fish of all kinds, whale fins, whale-bone, oil, and blubber, not caught by and cured on board British vessels, when imported into Great Britain, are subjected to double aliens duty. The Dutch, as they are still the principal, were then the only fishers in Europe that attempted to supply foreign nations with fish. By this regulation, a very heavy burden was laid upon their supplying Great Britain.

When the act of navigation was made, though England and Holland were not actually at war, the most violent animosity subsisted between the two nations. It had begun during the government of the long parliament, which first framed this act, and it broke out soon after in the Dutch wars during that of the Protector and of Charles the second. It is not impossible, therefore, that some of the regulations of this famous act may have proceeded from national animosity. They are as wise, however, as if they had all been dictated by the most deliberate wisdom. National animosity at that particular time aimed at the very same object which the most deliberate wisdom would have recommended, the diminution of the naval power of Holland, the only naval power which could endanger the security of England.

The act of navigation is not favourable to foreign commerce or to the growth of that opulence which can arise from it. The interest of a nation in its commercial relations to foreign nations is, like that of a merchant with regard to the different people with whom he deals, to buy as cheap and to sell as dear as possible. But it will be most likely to buy cheap, when by the most perfect freedom of trade it encourages all nations to bring to it the goods which it has occasion to purchase; and, for the same reason, it will be most likely to sell dear, when its markets are thus filled with the greatest number of buyers. The act of navigation, it is true, lays no burden upon foreign ships that come to export the produce of British industry. Even the ancient aliens duty, which used to be paid upon all goods exported as well as imported, has, by several subsequent acts, been taken off from the greater part of the articles of exportation. But if foreigners, either by prohibitions or high duties, are hindered from coming to sell, they cannot always afford to come to buy; because coming without a cargo, they must lose the freight from their own country to Great Britain. By diminishing the number of sellers, therefore, we necessarily diminish that of buyers, and are thus likely not only to buy foreign goods dearer, but to sell our own cheaper, than if there was a more perfect freedom of trade. As defense, however, is of much more importance than opulence, the act of navigation is, perhaps, the wisest of all the commercial regulations of England.

The second case, in which it will generally be advantageous to lay some burden upon foreign for the encouragement of domestic industry, is when some tax is imposed at home upon the produce of the latter. In this case, it seems reasonable that an equal tax should be imposed upon the like produce of the former. This would not give the monopoly of the home-market to domestic industry, not turn towards a particular employment a greater share of the stock and labour of the country, than what would naturally go to it. It would only hinder any part of what would naturally go to it from being turned away by the tax, into a less natural direction, and would leave the competition between foreign and domestic industry, after the tax, as nearly as possible upon the same footing as before it. In Great Britain, when any such tax is laid upon the produce of domestic industry, it is usual at the same time, in order to stop the clamorous complaints of our merchants and manufacturers, that they will be undersold at home, to lay a much heavier duty upon the importation of all foreign goods of the same kind.

This second limitation of the freedom of trade according to some people should, upon some occasions, be extended much farther than to the precise foreign commodities which could come into competition with those which had been taxed at home. When the necessaries of life have been taxed in any country, it becomes proper, they pretend, to tax not only the like necessaries of life imported from other countries, but all sorts of foreign goods which can come into competition with any thing that is the produce of domestic industry. Subsistence, they say, becomes necessarily dearer in consequence of such taxes; and the price of labour must always rise with the price of the labourers' subsistence. Every commodity, therefore, which is the produce of domestic industry, though not immediately taxed itself, becomes dearer in consequence of such taxes, because the labour which produces it becomes so. Such taxes, therefore, are really equivalent, they say, to a tax upon every particular commodity produced at home. In order to put domestic upon the same footing with foreign industry, therefore, it becomes necessary, they think, to lay some duty upon every foreign commodity, equal to this enhancement of the price of the home commodities with which it can come into competition.

Whether taxes upon the necessaries of life, such as those in Great Britain upon soap, salt, leather, candles, etc. necessarily raise the price of labour, and consequently that of all other commodities, I shall consider hereafter, when I come to treat of taxes. Supposing, however, in the mean time, that they have this effect, and they have it undoubtedly, this general enhancement of the price of all commodities, in consequence of that of labour, is a case which differs in the two following respects from that of a particular commodity, of which the price was enhanced by a particular tax immediately imposed upon it.

First, it might always be known with great exactness how far the price of such a commodity could be enhanced by such a tax: but how far the general enhancement of the price of labour might affect that of every different commodity about which labour was employed, could never be known with any tolerable exactness. It would be impossible, therefore, to proportion with any tolerable exactness the tax upon every foreign, to this enhancement of the price of every home commodity.

Secondly, taxes upon the necessaries of life have nearly the same effect upon the circumstances of the people as a poor soil and a bad climate. Provisions are thereby rendered dearer in the same manner as if it required extraordinary labour and expense to raise them. As in the natural scarcity arising from soil and climate, it would be absurd to direct the people in what manner they ought to employ their capitals and industry, so is it likewise in the artificial scarcity arising from such taxes. To be left to accommodate, as well as they could, their industry to their situation, and to find out those employments in which, notwithstanding their unfavourable circumstances, they might have some advantage either in the home or in the foreign market, is what in both cases would evidently be most for their advantage. To lay a new tax upon them, because they are already overburdened with taxes, and because they already pay too dear for the necessaries of life, to make them likewise pay too dear for the greater part of other commodities, is certainly a most absurd way of making amends.

Such taxes, when they have grown up to a certain height, are a curse equal to the barrenness of the earth and the inclemency of the heavens; and yet it is in the richest and most industrious countries that they have been most generally imposed. No other countries could support so great a disorder. As the strongest bodies only can live and enjoy health, under an unwholesome regimen; so the nations only, that in every sort of industry have the greatest natural and acquired advantages, can subsist and prosper under such taxes. Holland is the country in Europe in which they abound most, and which from peculiar circumstances continues to prosper, not by means of them, as has been most absurdly supposed, but in spite of them.

. . .

To expect, indeed, that the freedom of trade should ever be entirely restored in Great Britain, is as absurd as to expect that an Oceana or Utopia should ever be established in it. Not only the prejudices of the public, but what is much more unconquerable, the private interests of many individuals, irresistibly oppose it. Were the officers of the army to oppose with the same zeal and unanimity any reduction in the number of forces, with which master manufacturers set themselves against every law that is likely to increase the number of their rivals in the home-market; were the former to animate their soldiers, in the same manner as the latter inflame their workmen, to attack with violence and outrage the proposers of any such regulation; to attempt to reduce the army would be as dangerous as it has now become to attempt to diminish in any respect the monopoly which our manufacturers have obtained against us. This monopoly has so much increased the number of some particular tribes of them, that, like an overgrown standing army, they have become formidable to the government, and upon many occasions intimidate the legislature. The member of parliament who supports every proposal for strengthening this monopoly is sure to acquire not only the reputation of understanding trade, but great popularity and influence with the order of men whose numbers and wealth render them of great importance. If he opposes them, on the contrary, and still more if he has authority enough to be able to thwart them, neither the most acknowledged probity, nor the highest rank, nor the greatest public services, can protect him from the most infamous abuse and detraction, from personal insults, nor sometimes from real danger, arising from the insolent outrage of furious and disappointed monopolists.

Questions:
1. *Briefly restate, in your own words, Adam Smith's argument.*
2. *Which classes of people in nineteenth century Europe would be most likely to favor free enterprise? Which would be most likely to oppose it? Why?*

17.9   What Is Enlightenment? (1784): Immanuel Kant

Immanuel Kant was a German philosopher whose comprehensive and systematic work in the theory of knowledge, ethics, and aesthetics greatly influenced subsequent philosophy. Kant's entire life was spent in Königsberg, where he was educated and served as a popular teacher and lecturer at the local university. In his writings, he hoped to avoid the confusion of earlier thinkers by examining the possibilities and limitations of applied reason. He sought to accept the rationalism of the Enlightenment while still preserving a belief in human freedom, immortality, and the existence of God. In fact, Kant found the world open to pure reason to be quite limited and postulated a sphere of moral reality known only by "practical reason and conscience." Although he hoped to raise philosophy to the level of a science, he believed that all things could not be proved by discursive reasoning—God and eternal life among them.

In the following selection, Kant seeks to define the Enlightenment by empowering the individual to break away from a somnolent dependence toward an active intellectual existence. Only through such personal initiative could one attain true enlightenment.

Source: *Foundations of the Metaphysics of Morals*, 2/E, by Kant, (trans. L. W. Beck), © 1990, pp. 83–85, 88. Reprinted by permission of Pearson Education, Inc., Upper Saddle River, NJ.

Enlightenment is man's release from his selfincurred tutelage. Tutelage is man's inability to make use of his understanding without direction from another. Self-incurred is this tutelage when its cause lies not in lack of reason but in lack of resolution and courage to use it without direction from another. Dare to Know! Have courage to use your own reason!—that is the motto of enlightenment.

Laziness and cowardice are the reasons why so great a portion of mankind, after nature has long since discharged them from external direction, nevertheless remains under lifelong tutelage, and why it is so easy for others to set themselves up as their guardians. It is so easy not to be of age. If I have a book which understands for me, a pastor who has a conscience for me, a physician who decides my diet, and so forth, I need not trouble myself. I need not think, if I can only pay—others will readily undertake the irksome work for me.

That the step to competence is held to be very dangerous by the far greater portion of mankind (and by the entire fair sex)—quite apart from its being arduous—is seen to by those guardians who have so kindly assumed superintendence over them. After the guardians have first made their domestic cattle dumb and have made sure that these placid creatures will not dare take a single step without the harness of the cart to which they are confined, the guardians then show them the danger which threatens if they try to go alone. Actually, however, this danger is not so great, for by falling a few times they would finally learn to walk alone. But an example of this failure makes them timid and ordinarily frightens them away from all further trials.

For any single individual to work himself out of the life under tutelage which has become almost his nature is very difficult. He has come to be fond of this state, and he is for the present really incapable of making use of his reason, for no one has ever let him try it out. Statutes and formulas, those mechanical tools of the rational employment or rather misemployment of his natural gifts, are the fetters of an everlasting tutelage. Whoever throws them off makes only an uncertain leap over the narrowest ditch because he is not accustomed to that kind of free motion. Therefore, there are only few who have succeeded by their own exercise of mind both in freeing themselves from incompetence and in achieving a steady pace.

But that the public should enlighten itself is more possible; indeed, if only freedom is granted, enlightenment is almost sure to follow. For there will always be some independent thinkers, even among the established guardians of the great masses, who, after throwing off the yoke of tutelage from their own shoulders, will disseminate the spirit of the rational appreciation of both their own worth and every man's vocation for thinking for himself. . . .

For this enlightenment, however, nothing is required but freedom, and indeed the most harmless among all the things to which this term can properly be applied. It is the freedom to make public use of one's reason at every point. But I hear on all sides, "Do not argue!" The officer says: "Do not argue but drill!" The tax collector: "Do not argue but pay!" The cleric: "Do not argue but believe!" Only one prince in the world [Frederick the Great of Prussia] says, "Argue as much as you will, and about what you will, but obey!" Everywhere there is restriction on freedom. . .

Question:
1. How does Immanuel Kant answer the question "What is Enlightenment?"

PART 18
From Old Regime to Revolution

18.1 "The Mortal God": Leviathan (1651)

Thomas Hobbes was one of the great political philosophers of the seventeenth century. His major work, entitled Leviathan, was published in 1651 and reflects the insecurity and fear of the English Revolution that had resulted in civil war (1642–1646) and had just seen the decapitation of a sovereign monarch in 1649. Hobbes himself, because of his aristocratic associations, had been forced to flee England. Not surprisingly, Leviathan is a treatise that advocates political absolutism. Its theme is power, and it justifies absolute rule as necessary in order to subdue man's violent nature and promote a reasonable existence. For Hobbes, the authority of the absolute monarch did not lie in hereditary right or in divine sanction, but only in his ability to achieve power and maintain it. In this sense, Hobbes borrowed much from the Renaissance political philosopher Niccolò Machiavelli. But Hobbes went much further by providing an integrated social and political philosophy of government.

> **Source:** "The Mortal God: Leviathan" is from W. Molesworth, ed., *The English Works of Thomas Hobbes*, vol. 3 (London: John Bohn, 1839), from chapters 13 and 17, pp. 110–113, 153, 157–158. Text modernized by the editor.

THOMAS HOBBES

Nature has made men so equal, in the faculties of the body and mind; as that though there be found one man sometimes manifestly stronger in body, or of quicker mind than another; yet when all is reckoned together, the differences between man and man, is not so considerable. . . . For as to the strength of body, the weakest has strength enough to kill the strongest, either by secret machination, or by confederacy with others, that are in the same danger with himself. And as to the faculties of the mind. . . . I find yet a greater equality among men, than that of strength. . . . Such is the nature of men, that howsoever they may acknowledge many others to be more witty, or more eloquent, or more learned; yet they will hardly believe there are many so wise as themselves; for they see their own wit at hand, and other men's at a distance. . . .

From this equality of ability, arises equality of hope in the attaining of our ends. And therefore if any two men desire the same thing, which nevertheless they cannot both enjoy, they become enemies; and in the way to their end, which is principally their own conservation . . . endeavour to destroy, or subdue one another. And from hence it comes to pass, that . . . an invader has no more to fear than another man's single power; if one plants, sows, builds, and possesses a convenient seat, others may probably be expected to come prepared with forces united, to dispossess, and deprive him, not only of the fruit of his labour, but also of his life, or liberty. And the invader again is in the like danger of another. . . . [Thus], men have no pleasure, but on the contrary a great deal of grief, in keeping company, where there is no power able to over-awe them all. . . .

So that in the nature of man, we find three principal causes of quarrel. First, competition; secondly, insecurity; thirdly, glory.

The first, makes men invade for gain; the second, for safety; and the third, for reputation. The first use violence, to make themselves master of other men's persons, wives, children, and cattle; the second, to defend them; the third, for trifles, as a word, a smile, a different opinion, and any other sign of undervalue, either direct in their persons, or by reflection in their kindred, their friends, their nation, their profession, or their name.

[Therefore, it is clear] that during the time men live without a common power to keep them all in awe, they are in that condition which is called war; and such a war is of every man, against every man. . . . In such condition, there is no place for industry; because the fruit thereof is uncertain: and consequently no culture of the earth; no navigation, nor use of the commodities that may be imported by sea; no commodious building; no instruments of moving, and removing, such things as require much force; no knowledge of the face of the earth; no account of time; no arts; no letters; no society; and which is worst of all, continual fear, and danger of violent death; and the life of man, solitary, poor, nasty, brutish, and short. . . .

The final cause, end, or design of men, who naturally love liberty, and dominion over others, [is] the introduction of that restraint upon themselves, [by] which we see them live in commonwealths. . . . The only way to erect such a common power, as may be able to defend them from the invasion of foreigners, and the injuries of one another, and thereby to secure them in such sort, as that by their own industry, and by the fruits of the earth, they may nourish themselves and live contentedly; is, to confer all their power and strength upon one man, or upon one assembly of men, that may reduce all their wills, by plurality of voices, unto one will. . . . [All men shall] submit their wills . . . to his will, and their judgments, to his judgment. This is more than consent, or concord; it is a real unity of them all, in one and the same person, made by covenant of every man with every man, in such manner, as if every man should say to every man, I authorize and give up my right of governing myself, to this man, or to this assembly of men, on this condition, that you give up your right to him, and authorize all his actions in like manner. This done, the multitude so united in one person, is called a COMMONWEALTH. . . . This is the generation of that great LEVIATHAN, or rather, to speak more reverently, of that mortal god, to which we own under the immortal God, our peace and defence. For by this authority, given him by every particular man in the commonwealth, he hath the use of so much power and strength conferred on him, that by terror thereof, he is enabled to perform the wills of them all, to peace at home, and mutual aid against their enemies abroad. And in him consists the essence of the commonwealth; which, to define it, is one person of whose acts a great multitude, by mutual covenants one with another, have made themselves every one the author, to the end he may use the strength and means of them all, as he shall think expedient, for their peace and common defence.

And . . . this person, is called SOVEREIGN, and said to have sovereign power; and every one besides, his SUBJECT.

Questions:
1. *Discuss the ideas of Thomas Hobbes contained in Leviathan. What is his view of human nature, and how does he justify absolute monarchy? Be specific in your assessment.*
2. *How does Hobbes's Leviathan reflect the uncertainty of the time?*

18.2   The Ideal Absolute State (1697): Jean Domat

The stable monarchy that Louis XIV inherited was largely the product of two master political craftsmen, cardinals Richelieu and Mazarin. These statesmen actually ran the day-to-day affairs of the French state under Louis XIII and during Louis XIV's minority, respectively. Under their strict control, the French nobility was subdued and made to realize that the king was absolute in his authority and would tolerate no defiance. It was under their direction, from 1610 to 1661, that absolutism was advanced out of the realm of theory and made a part of the political life of France. The practical rule of any government must be justified through some doctrine, whether it be a devotion to the principles of democracy or to the more blatant dictum "might makes right." Louis XIV justified his absolutism through the belief that God so willed it. Such a "divine-right" monarch ruled with the authority of God and was beholden to no power except that of God. For his part, the king was accountable to God and was expected to rule with the best interests of his people at heart.

The following selection explains the theoretical basis of Louis's absolutism. Jean Domat (1624–1696), one of the most renowned jurists and legal scholars of his age, was responsible for a codification of French law that was sponsored by the king himself. This document is from his treatment of French public law and may be regarded as the official statement of divine-right absolutism.

> **Source:** Church, William F., ed. & trans., *The Impact of Absolutism in France: National Experience Under Richelieu, Mazarin and Louis XIV*, pp. 377–381. Copyright © 1969. This material is used by permission of John Wiley & Sons, Inc.

All men being equal by nature because of the humanity that is their essence, nature does not cause some to be inferior to others. But in this natural equality, they are separated by other principles that render their conditions unequal and give rise to relationships and dependencies that determine their varying duties toward others and render government necessary. . . .

The first distinction that subjects some persons to others is that which birth introduces between parents and children. . . . The second distinction among persons is that which requires different employments in society and unites all in the body of which each is a member. . . . And it is these varying occupations and dependencies that create the ties that form society among men, as those of its members form a body. This renders it necessary that a head coerce and rule the body of society and maintain order among those who should give the public the benefit of the different contributions that their stations require of them. . . .

Since government is necessary for the common good and God himself established it, it follows that those who are its subjects must be submissive and obedient. For otherwise they would resist God, and the government which should be the source of the peace and unity that make possible the public good would suffer from dissension and trouble that would destroy it. . . .

As obedience is necessary to preserve the order and peace that unite the head and members of the body of the state, it is the universal obligation of all subjects in all cases to obey the ruler's orders without assuming the liberty of judging them. For otherwise each man would be master because of his right to examine what might be just or unjust, and this liberty would favor sedition. Thus every man owes obedience even to unjust laws and orders, provided that he may execute and obey them without injustice. And the only exception that may exempt him from this obligation is limited to cases in which he may not obey without violating divine law. . . .

According to these principles, which are the natural foundations of the authority of those who govern, their power should have two essential attributes: first, to cause justice to rule without exception and, second, to be as absolute as the rule of justice, that is, as absolute as the rule of God Himself who is justice, rules according to its principles, and desires rulers to do likewise. . . .

Since the power of princes comes to them from God and is placed in their hands as an instrument of his providence and his guidance of the states that He commits to their rule, it is clear that princes should use their power in proportion to the objectives that providence and divine guidance seek . . . and that power is confided to them to this end. This is without doubt the foundation and first principle of all the duties of sovereigns that consist of causing God Himself to rule, that is, regulating all things according to His will, which is nothing more than justice. The rule of justice should be the glory of the rule of princes. . . .

The power of sovereigns includes the authority to exercise the functions of government and to use the force that is necessary to their ministry. For authority without force would be despised and almost useless, while force without legitimate authority would be mere tyranny. . . .

There are two uses of sovereign power that are necessary to the public tranquillity. One consists of constraining the subjects to obey and repressing violence and injustice, the other of defending the state against the aggressions of its enemies. Power should be accompanied by the force that is required for these two functions.

The use of force for the maintenance of public tranquillity within the state includes all that is required to protect the sovereign himself from rebellions that would be frequent if authority and force were not united, and all that is required to keep order among the subjects, repress violence against individuals and the general public, execute the orders of the sovereign, and effect all that is required for the administration of justice. Since the use of force and the occasions that require it are never-ending, the government of the sovereign must maintain the force that is needed for the rule of justice. This requires officials and ministers in various functions and the use of arms whenever necessary. . . .

One should include among the rights that the law gives the sovereign that of acquiring all the evidences of grandeur and majesty that are needed to bring renown to the authority and dignity of such great power and to instill awe in the minds of the subjects. For although the latter should view royal power as from God and submit to it regardless of tangible indications of grandeur, God accompanies his own power with a visible majesty that extends over land and sea. . . . When He wishes to exercise his August power as lawgiver, He proclaims his laws with prodigies that inspire reverence and unspeakable terror. He is therefore willing that sovereigns enhance the dignity of their power . . . in such manner as to win the respect of the people. . . .

The general duties . . . of those who have sovereign authority include all that concern the administration of justice, the general polity of the state, public order, tranquillity of the subjects, security of families, attention to all that may contribute to the general good, the choice of skillful ministers who love justice and truth . . . discrimination between justice and clemency whenever justice might suffer from relaxation of its rigor, wise distribution of benefits, rewards, exemptions, privileges and other concessions, wise administration of the public funds, prudence regarding foreigners, and all that may render government agreeable to the good, terrible to the wicked, and entirely worthy of the divine function of ruling men by wielding power that comes only from God and is a participation in his own.

As the final duty of the sovereign, one may add the following which stems from the administration of justice and includes all others. Although his power seems to place him above the law, since no man has the right to call him to account for his conduct, he should observe the laws that concern himself not only because he should be an example to his subjects and render their duty pleasant but because he is not dispensed from his own duty by his sovereign power. On the contrary, his rank obliges him to subordinate his personal interests to the general good of the state, which it is his glory to regard as his own.

Questions:
1. Louis XIV was a divine-right monarch. What does this mean, and how did Louis use religion to strengthen his political position in the state?
2. What are the responsibilities of the king and the political advantages of absolute rule?

18.3   The Sighs of Enslaved France (1690): Pierre Jurieu

On October 22, 1685, Louis XIV annulled the Edict of Nantes, which had provided political and religious freedom for the French Protestants, or Huguenots, since 1598. Louis was determined to control a nation that was unified politically under his rule and religiously under his faith; Catholicism was to be the only accepted religion for the French people. As a result of the revocation of the Edict of Nantes, the persecution of Huguenots began in earnest. The author of the following memoirs cannot be positively identified, but they are probably from the pen of Pierre Jurieu, a Calvinist pastor who had fled to Holland. Louis endured much criticism from such dissidents in exile. Jurieu's memoirs are among the most provocative because they characterize Louis's absolutism as oppressive and responsible for many of the ills of France.

Source: Church, William F., ed. & trans., *The Impact of Absolutism in France: National Experience Under Richelieu, Mazarin and Louis XIV,* pp. 102–105. Copyright © 1969. This material is used by permission of John Wiley & Sons, Inc.

The oppression of the people is caused primarily by the prodigious number of taxes and excessive levies of money that are everywhere taken in France. Taxes and finance are a science today, and one must be skilled to speak knowledgeably of them, but it suffices for us to relate what we all feel and what the people know of the matter. There are the personal and [land taxes]. There are taxes on salt, wine, merchandise, principal, and revenue. This miserable century has produced a flood of names [of taxes], most of which were unknown to our ancestors or, if some were known, they were not odious because of the moderation with which they were imposed and levied. . . . It does not serve my purpose to acquaint you with the details of these taxes so that you may feel their weight and injustice. It will suffice to enable you to understand the horrible oppression of these taxes by showing (1) the immense sums that are collected, (2) the violence and abuses that are committed in levying them, (3) the bad use that is made of them, and (4) the misery to which the people are reduced.

First, dear unfortunate compatriots, you should realize that the taxes that are taken from you comprise a sum perhaps greater than that which all the other princes of Europe together draw from their states. One thing is certain, that France pays two hundred million in taxes of which about three-fourths go into the coffers of the king and the rest to expenses of collection, tax-farmers, officials, keepers, receivers, the profits of financiers, and new fortunes that are created in almost a single day. For the collection of the salt tax alone, there is a great army of officers and constables. . . .

If tyranny is clear and evident in the immense sums that are levied in France, it is not less so in the manner of collecting them. Kings were established by the people to preserve their persons, lives, liberty, and properties. But the government of France has risen to such excessive tyranny that the prince today regards everything as belonging to him alone. He imposes taxes at will without consulting the people, the nobles, the Estates, or the Parlements. I shall tell you something that is true and that thousands know but most Frenchmen do not. During Colbert's ministry [supervisor of the royal finances] it was discussed whether the king should take immediate possession of all real and personal property in France and reduce it to royal domain, to be used and assigned to whomever the court judged appropriate without regard for former possession, heredity, or other rights. . . .

How much abuse and violence is committed in the collection of taxes? The meanest agent is a sacred person who has absolute power over gentlemen, the judiciary, and all the people. A single blow is capable of ruining the most powerful subject. They confiscate houses, furnishings, cattle, money, grain, wine, and everything in sight. The prisons are full of wretches who are responsible for sums that they impose upon other wretches who cannot pay what is demanded of them. Is there anything more harsh and cruel than the salt tax? They make you buy for ten or twelve sous per pound something that nature, the sun, and the sea provide for nothing and may be had for two farthings. Under pretext of exercising this royal right, the realm is flooded with a great army of scoundrels called constables of the gabelle [salt tax] who enter houses, penetrate the most secret places with impunity, and do not fail to find unauthorized salt wherever they think there is money. They condemn wretches to pay huge fines, cause them to rot in prison, and ruin families. They force salt upon people everywhere and give each family more than three times as much as they can consume. In the provinces by the sea, they will not permit a poor peasant to bring home salt water; they break jugs, beat people, and imprison them. In a word, every abuse is committed in levying this and other taxes which is done with horrible expense, seizures, imprisonments, and legal cases before the collectors and courts with costs far above the sums involved. . . .

This is how all of France is reduced to the greatest poverty. In earlier reigns, that is, during the ministries of Cardinal Richelieu and Cardinal Mazarin, France was already burdened with heavy taxes. But the manner of collecting them, although not entirely just, nevertheless exhausted the realm much less than the way in which they are collected today. . . . The government of today has changed all of this. M. de Colbert made a plan to reform the finances and applied it to the letter. But what was this reformation? It was not the diminution of taxes in order to relieve the people. . . . He increased the king's revenue by one half. . . .

After this, if we examine the use that is made of these immense sums that are collected with such abuses and extortion, we shall find all the characteristics of oppression and tyranny. It sometimes happens that princes and sovereigns exact levies that appear excessive and greatly inconvenience individuals, but are required by what are called the needs and necessities of the state. In France there is no such thing. There are neither needs nor state. As for the state, earlier it entered into everything; one spoke only of the interests of the state, the needs of the state, the preservation of the state, and the service of the state. To speak this way today would literally be a crime of lese majesty [treason]. The king has taken the place of the state. It is the service of the king, the interest of the king, the preservation of the provinces and wealth of the king. Therefore the king is all and the state nothing. And these are no mere figures of speech but realities. At the French court, no interest is considered but the personal interest of the king, that is, his grandeur and glory. He is the idol to which are sacrificed princes, great men and small, families, provinces, cities, finances and generally everything. Therefore, it is not for the good of the state that these horrible exactions are made, since there is no more state. . . .

This money is used solely to nourish and serve the greatest self-pride and arrogance that ever existed. It is so deep an abyss that it would have swallowed not only the wealth of the whole realm but that of all other states if the king had been able to take possession of it as he attempted to do. The king has caused himself to receive more false flattery than all the pagan demi-gods did with true flattery. Never before was flattery pushed to this point. Never has man loved praise and vainglory to the extent that this prince has sought them. In his court and around himself he supports a multitude of flatterers who constantly seek to outdo each other. He not only permits the erection of statues to himself, on which are inscribed blasphemies in his honor and below which all the nations of the earth are shown in chains; he causes himself to be represented in gold, silver, bronze, copper, marble, silk, in paintings, arches of triumph, and inscriptions. He fills all Paris, all his palaces, and the whole realm with his name and his exploits, as though he far surpasses the Alexanders, the Caesars, and all the heroes of antiquity.

Question:
1. Do the criticisms of Pierre Jurieu seem valid to you? Why should a historian be somewhat careful in the judgments drawn from this evidence?

18.4 Declaration of Independence: Revolutionary Declarations

The Declaration of Independence on the Declaration of the Rights of Man and Citizen share a number of similarities particularly in their general statements about the nature and justification of government The first was written in 1776; the second was promulgated fifteen years later, in 1791. The French revolutionaries were well aware of events in America and sympathetic to the colonists' cause so it is hardly an undue speculation to reason that their thoughts and actions were stimulated by the American example.

THE DECLARATION OF INDEPENDENCE

IN CONGRESS, JULY 4, 1776 THE UNANIMOUS DECLARATION OF THE THIRTEEN UNITED STATES OF AMERICA

When in the course of human events, it becomes necessary for one people to dissolve the political bands which have connected them with another, and to assume among the powers of the earth, the separate and equal station to which the Laws of Nature and of Nature's God entitle them, a decent respect to the opinions of mankind requires that they should declare the causes which impel them to the separation.

We hold these truths to be self-evident, that all men are created equal, that they are endowed by their Creator with certain unalienable rights, that among these are life, liberty and the pursuit of happiness. That to secure these rights, governments are instituted among men, deriving their just powers from the consent of the governed. That whenever any form of government becomes destructive of these ends, it is the right of the people to alter or to abolish it, and to institute new government, laying its foundation on such principles and organizing its powers in such form, as to them shall seem most likely to effect their safety and happiness. Prudence, indeed, will dictate that governments long established should not be changed for light and transient causes; and accordingly all experience hath shown, that mankind are more disposed to suffer, while evils are sufferable, than to right themselves by abolishing the forms to which they are accustomed. But when a long train of abuses and usurpations, pursuing invariably the same object evinces a design to reduce them under absolute despotism, it is their right, it is their duty, to throw off such government, and to provide new guards for their future security. Such has been the patient sufferance of these Colonies; and such is now the necessity which constrains them to alter their former systems of government. The history of the present King of Great Britain is a history of repeated injuries and usurpations, all having in direct object the establishment of an absolute tyranny over these States. To prove this, let facts be submitted to a candid world.

He has refused his assent to laws, the most wholesome and necessary for the public good.

He has forbidden his Governors to pass laws of immediate and pressing importance, unless suspended in their operation till his assent should be obtained; and when so suspended, he has utterly neglected to attend to them.

He has refused to pass other laws for the accommodation of large districts of people, unless those people would relinquish the right of representation in the Legislature, a right inestimable to them and formidable to tyrants only.

He has called together legislative bodies at places unusual, uncomfortable, and distant from the depository of their public records, for the sole purpose of fatiguing them into compliance with his measures.

He has dissolved representative houses repeatedly, for opposing with manly firmness his invasions on the rights of the people.

He has refused for a long time, after such dissolutions, to cause others to be elected; whereby the legislative powers, incapable of annihilation, have returned to the people at large for their exercise; the State remaining in the meantime exposed to all the dangers of invasion from without and convulsions within.

He has endeavoured to prevent the population of these states; for that purpose obstructing the laws of naturalization of foreigners; refusing to pass others to encourage their migration hither, and raising the conditions of new appropriations of lands.

He has obstructed the administration of justice, by refusing his assent to laws for establishing judiciary powers.

He has made judges dependent on his will alone, for the tenure of their offices, and the amount and payment of their salaries.

He has erected a multitude of new offices, and sent hither swarms of officers to harass our people, and eat out their substance.

He has kept among us, in times of peace, standing armies without the consent of our legislatures.

He has affected to render the military independent of and superior to the civil power.

He has combined with others to subject us to a jurisdiction foreign to our constitution, and unacknowledged by our laws; giving his assent to their acts of pretended legislation:

For quartering large bodies of armed troops among us:

For protecting them, by a mock trial, from punishment for any murders which they should commit on the inhabitants of these States:

For cutting off our trade with all parts of the world:

For imposing taxes on us without our consent:

For depriving us in many cases, of the benefits of trial by jury:

For transporting us beyond seas to be tried for pretended offences:

For abolishing the free system of English laws in a neighbouring Province, establishing therein an arbitrary government, and enlarging its boundaries so as to render it at once an example and fit instrument for introducing the same absolute rule into these Colonies:

For taking away our Charters, abolishing our most valuable laws, and altering fundamentally the forms of our governments:

For suspending our own Legislatures, and declaring themselves invested with power to legislate for us in all cases whatsoever.

He has abdicated government here, by declaring us out of his protection and waging war against us.

He has plundered our seas, ravaged our coasts, burnt our towns, and destroyed the lives of our people.

He is at this time transporting large armies of foreign mercenaries to complete the works of death, desolation and tyranny, already begun with circumstances of cruelty and perfidy scarcely par0alleled in the most barbarous ages, and totally unworthy the head of a civilized nation.

He has constrained our fellow citizens taken captive on the high seas to bear arms against their country, to become the executioners of their friends and brethren, or to fall themselves by their hands.

He has excited domestic insurrections amongst us, and has endeavoured to bring on the inhabitants of our frontiers, the merciless Indian savages, whose known rule of warfare, is an undistinguished destruction of all ages, sexes, and conditions.

In every stage of these oppressions we have petitioned for redress in the most humble terms: our repeated petitions have been answered only by repeated injury. A prince whose character is thus marked by every act which may define a tyrant is unfit to be the ruler of a free people.

Nor have we been wanting in attention to our British brethren. We have warned them from time to time of attempts by their legislature to extend an unwarrantable jurisdiction over us. We have reminded them of the circumstances of our emigration and settlement here. We have appealed to their native justice and magnanimity, and we have conjured them by the ties of our common kindred to disavow these usurpations, which would inevitably interrupt our connections and correspondence.

They too have been deaf to the voice of justice and of consanguinity. We must, therefore, acquiesce in the necessity, which denounces our separation, and hold them, as we hold the rest of mankind, enemies in war, in peace friends.

We, therefore, the Representatives of the United States of America, in General Congress assembled, appealing to the Supreme Judge of the world for the rectitude of our intentions, do, in the name, and by authority of the good people of these Colonies, solemnly publish and declare, That these United Colonies are, and of right ought to be Free and Independent States; that they are absolved from all allegiance to the British Crown, and that all political connection between them and the State of Great Britain, is and ought to be totally dissolved; and that as Free and Independent States, they have full power to levy war, conclude peace, contract alliances, establish commerce, and to do all other acts and things which Independent States may of right do. And for the support of this declaration, with a firm reliance on the protection of Divine Providence, we mutually pledge to each other our lives, our fortunes, and our sacred honor.

Question:

1. *In what ways does the Declaration of the Rights of Man show the influence of the Declaration of Independence? In what ways is it unlike the Declaration of Independence?*

18.5 "What Is the Third Estate?" (January 1789): The Abbé Sieyès

The wars and extravagance of King Louis XIV had sent France to the brink of bankruptcy by 1715—and Louis was a competent and diligent administrator. His heirs, on the other hand, were not particularly dedicated to the governance of France. Louis XV (1715–1774) was poorly educated and preferred to allow his mistresses (one of whom had been a Parisian prostitute) to control the politics of state. Louis XVI (1774–1792) was well educated but more interested in hunting than in administration. From 1715 to 1789, the French economy spiraled into chaos. With the nobility and church exempt from taxation, the burden fell upon the Third Estate.

The French Revolution drew much of its support from the Third Estate, a conglomeration of middle-class professionals, artisans, and peasants. As a group, the middle class or bourgeoisie was ambitious, educated, and competent. Could they be expected to sit idly by while the nobility held offices that should have been theirs? Inspired by philosophical ideals as well as by potential economic and social advantages, they provided the leadership for the revolution. Lower members of the Third Estate, the artisans and peasants, generally could not read and were not concerned with philosophical justifications. It was the peasantry that labored under intolerable taxes, rents, and corvées (feudal services), which they were forced to undertake by the nobility without payment. What were their demands? Did their needs justify revolution?

By August 1788, Louis XVI had decided to summon the Estates-General, a convocation of the three estates, which had not met since 1614, in order to solve the government's financial problems. Louis was in debt, and he wanted the Estates-General to raise new taxes. This pamphlet by the Abbé Sieyès (1748–1836) was issued in January 1789, before the Estates-General met. It was intended to unite the various interests within the Third Estate toward a common cause: reform of the unequal voting procedure that gave advantage to the first two estates.

Source: *Documentary Survey of the French Revolution* by Stewart, John Hall, © 1951, pp. 46, 51–52. Reprinted by permission of Pearson Education, Inc., Upper Saddle River, NJ.

What Does the Third Estate Demand?
To Become Something

The true petitions of this order may be appreciated only through the authentic claims directed to the government by the large municipalities of the kingdom. What is indicated therein? That the people wishes to be something, and, in truth, the very least that is possible. It wishes to have real representatives in the Estates General, that is to say, deputies drawn from its order, who are competent to be interpreters of its will and defenders of its interests. But what will it avail it to be present at the Estates General if the predominating interest there is contrary to its own! Its presence would only consecrate the oppression of which it would be the external victim. Thus, it is indeed certain that it cannot come to vote at the Estates General unless it is to have in that body an influence at least equal to that of the privileged classes; and it demands a number of representatives equal to that of the first two orders together. Finally, this equality of representation would become completely illusory if every chamber voted separately. The third estate demands, then, that votes be taken by head and not by order. This is the essence of those claims so alarming to the privileged classes, because they believed that thereby the reform of abuses would become inevitable. The real intention of the third estate is to have an influence in the Estates General equal to that of the privileged classes. I repeat, can it ask less?

What Remains to Be Done: Development of Some Principles

The time is past when the three orders, thinking only of defending them-selves from ministerial despotism, were ready to unite against the common enemy. . . .

•••

The third estate awaits, to no purpose, the meeting of all classes, the restitution of its political rights, and the plenitude of its civil rights; the fear of seeing abuses reformed alarms the first two orders far more than the desire for liberty inspires them. Between liberty and some odious privileges, they have chosen the latter. Their soul is identified with the favors of servitude. Today they dread this Estates General which but lately they invoked so ardently. All is well with them; they no longer complain, except of the spirit of innovation. They no longer lack anything; fear has given them a constitution.

The third estate must perceive in the trend of opinions and circumstances that it can hope for nothing except from its own enlightenment and courage. Reason and justice are in its favor; . . . there is no longer time to work for the conciliation of parties. What accord can be anticipated between the energy of the oppressed and the rage of the oppressors?

They have dared pronounce the word secession. They have menaced the King and the people. Well! Good God! How fortunate for the nation if this desirable secession might be made permanently! How easy it would be to dispense with the privileged classes! How difficult to induce them to be citizens!

•••

In vain would they close their eyes to the revolution which time and force of circumstances have effected; it is none the less real. Formerly the third estate was serf, the noble order everything. Today the third estate is everything, the nobility but a word. . . .

In such a state of affairs, what must the third estate do if it wishes to gain possession of its political rights in a manner beneficial to the nation? There are two ways of attaining this objective. In following the first, the third estate must assemble apart: it will not meet with the nobility and the clergy at all; it will not remain with them, either by order or by head. I pray that they will keep in mind the enormous difference between the assembly of the third estate and that of the other two orders. The first represents 25,000,000 men, and deliberates concerning the interests of the nation. The two others, were they to unite, have the powers of only about 200,000 individuals, and think only of their privileges. The third estate alone, they say, cannot constitute the Estates General. Well! So much the better! It will form a National Assembly.

Question:
1. What were the specific demands made by the Third Estate? Do they seem reasonable to you?

18.6   The Tennis Court Oath (June 20, 1789)

From the outset, the Estates-General was hampered by organizational disputes. After several weeks of frustration, the Third Estate invited the clergy and nobility to join them in organizing a new legislative body. Only a few of the lower clergy accepted, but the National Assembly was thus formed on June 17, 1789. Three days later they were accidentally locked out of their usual meeting place, and they marched to a nearby tennis court, where they took an oath to draft a new constitution for France. This is one of the most important documents of the revolution. The oath was taken orally and individually with but one vote in dissension. The president of the National Assembly was barely able to save the dissenter from bodily harm.

Source: "The Tennis Court Oath" is reprinted with permission of Macmillan Publishing Company from *A Documentary Survey of the French Revolution*, edited by John Hall Stewart, p. 88. Copyright 1951 by Macmillan Publishing Company, renewed 1979 by John Hall Stewart.

The National Assembly, considering that it has been summoned to establish the constitution of the kingdom, to effect the regeneration of public order, and to maintain the true principles of monarchy; that nothing can prevent it from continuing its deliberations in whatever place it may be forced to establish itself; and, finally, that wheresoever its members are assembled, there is the National Assembly;

Decrees that all members of this Assembly shall immediately take a solemn oath not to separate, and to reassemble wherever circumstances require, until the constitution of the kingdom is established and consolidated upon firm foundations; and that, the said oath taken, all members and each one of them individually shall ratify this steadfast resolution by signature.

Question:
1. Does The Tennis Court Oath call for radical action? Why is it considered to be one of the most important documents of the French Revolution?

18.7 Declaration of the Rights of Man and Citizen

If one conceives the genesis of modernity in political terms, the following document may well be considered one of the pivotal documents in the modern era. It sets out, in dramatic language, both the philosophical assumptions that underlie the modern democratic state and the prerogatives that must be secured for its citizens if such a state is to be realized in practice. Thus, along with and influenced by the Declaration of Independence, the Declaration of the Rights of Man and the Citizen initiated modern democracy, a form of society that has been adopted in large part first throughout the West and later in various other areas of the world. The Declaration was written in 1791 during the French Revolution.

Source: Reprinted with permission of the Macmillan Company from *A Documentary Survey of the French Revolution* by John Hall Stewart. Copyright © 1979, John Hall Stewart.

The representatives of the French people, organized in National Assembly, considering that ignorance, forgetfulness, or contempt of the rights of man are the sole causes of public misfortunes and of the corruption of governments, have resolved to set forth in a solemn declaration the natural, inalienable, and sacred rights of man, in order that such declaration, continually before all members of the social body, may be a perpetual reminder of their rights and duties; in order that the acts of the legislative power and those of the executive power may constantly be compared with the aim of every political institution and may accordingly be more respected; in order that the demands of the citizens, founded henceforth upon simple and incontestable principles, may always be directed towards the maintenance of the Constitution and the welfare of all.

Accordingly, the National Assembly recognizes and proclaims, in the presence and under the auspices of the Supreme Being, the following rights of man and citizen.

1. Men are born and remain free and equal in rights; social distinctions may be based only upon general usefulness.

2. The aim of every political association is the preservation of the natural and inalienable rights of man; these rights are liberty, property, security, and resistance to oppression.

3. The source of all sovereignty resides essentially in the nation; no group, no individual may exercise authority not emanating expressly therefrom.

4. Liberty consists of the power to do whatever is not injurious to others; thus the enjoyment of the natural rights of every man has for its limits only those that assure other members of society the enjoyment of those same rights; such limits may be determined only by law.

5. The law has the right to forbid only actions which are injurious to society. Whatever is not forbidden by law may not be prevented, and no one may be constrained to do what it does not prescribe.

6. Law is the expression of the general will; all citizens have the right to concur personally, or through their representatives, in its formation; it must be the same for all, whether it protects or punishes. All citizens, being equal before it, are equally admissible to all public offices, positions, and employments, according to their capacity, and without other distinction than that of virtues and talents.

7. No man may be accused, arrested, or detained except in the cases determined by law, and according to the forms prescribed thereby. Whoever solicit, expedite, or execute arbitrary orders, or have them executed, must be punished; but every citizen summoned or apprehended in pursuance of the law must obey immediately; he renders himself culpable by resistance.

8. The law is to establish only penalties that are absolutely and obviously necessary; and no one may be punished except by virtue of a law established and promulgated prior to the offence and legally applied.

9. Since every man is presumed innocent until declared guilty, if arrest be deemed indispensable, all unnecessary severity for securing the person of the accused must be severely repressed by law.

10. No one is to be disquieted because of his opinions, even religious, provided their manifestation does not disturb the public order established by law.

11. Free communication of ideas and opinions is one of the most precious of the rights of man. Consequently, every citizen may speak, write, and print freely, subject to responsibility for the abuse of such liberty in the cases determined by law.

12. The guarantee of the rights of man and citizen necessitates a public force; such a force, therefore, is instituted for the advantage of all and not for the particular benefit of those to whom it is entrusted.

13. For the maintenance of the public force and for the expenses of administration a common tax is indispensable; it must be assessed equally on all citizens in proportion to their means.

14. Citizens have the right to ascertain, by themselves or through their representatives, the necessity of the public tax, to consent to it freely, to supervise its use, and to determine its quota, assessment, payment, and duration.

15. Society has the right to require of every public agent an accounting of his administration.

16. Every society in which the guarantee of rights is not assured or the separation of powers not determined has no constitution at all.

17. Since property is a sacred and inviolate right, no one may be deprived thereof unless a legally established public necessity obviously requires it, and upon condition of a just and previous indemnity.

Questions:
1. What basic rights are enumerated in the document?
2. What is the role of the government envisioned in this document?

18.8   Edmund Burke, Reflections on the Revolution in France

Edmund Burke (1729–1797) was a leading voice of conservatism who denounced the French Revolution even before it had moved into its most radical phase. In 1790, he published Reflections on the Revolution in France, in which he condemned the destructiveness of the revolutionary movement and questioned whether the newly elected assembly could produce a better government and society.

Source: From Edmund Burke, *The Works of Edmund Burke,* Vol. 3 (Boston: Chas. C. Little and James Brown, 1839), pp. 57–62, 71–73, 81–83, 97–101, passim.

France, by the perfidy of her leaders, has utterly disgraced the tone of lenient council in the cabinets of princes, and disarmed it of its most potent topics. She has sanctified the dark suspicious maxims of tyrannous distrust; and taught kings to tremble at (what will hereafter be called) the delusive plausibilities, of moral politicians. Sovereigns will consider those who advise them to place an unlimited confidence in their people, as subverters of their thrones; as traitors who aim at their destruction, by leading their easy good nature, under specious pretences, to admit combinations of bold and faithless men into a participation of their power. This alone (if there were nothing else) is an irreparable calamity to you and to mankind. . . .

Laws overturned; tribunals subverted; industry without vigor; commerce expiring; the revenue unpaid, yet the people impoverished; a church pillaged, and a state not relieved; civil and military anarchy made the constitution of the kingdom; every thing human and divine sacrificed to the idol of public credit, and national bankruptcy the consequence; and to crown all, the paper securities of new, precarious, tottering power, the discredited paper securities of impoverished fraud, and beggared rapine, held out as a currency for the support of an empire, in lieu of the two great recognised species that represent the lasting conventional credit of mankind, which disappeared and hid themselves in the earth from whence they came, when the principle of property, whose creatures and representatives they are, was systematically subverted.

Were all these dreadful things necessary? Were they the inevitable results of the desperate struggle of determined patriots, compelled to wade through blood and tumult, to the quiet shore of a tranquil and prosperous liberty? No! nothing like it. The fresh ruins of France, which shock our feelings wherever we can turn our eyes, are not the devastation of civil war; they are the sad but instructive monuments of rash and ignorant counsel in time of profound peace. They are the display of inconsiderate and presumptuous, because unresisted and irresistible authority.

This unforced choice, this fond election of evil, would appear perfectly unaccountable, if we did not consider the composition of the national assembly; I do not mean its formal constitution, which, as it now stands, is exceptionable enough, but the materials of which, in a great measure, it is composed, which is of ten thousand times greater consequence than all the formalities in the world. If we were to know nothing of this assembly but by its title and function, no colors could paint to the imagination any thing more venerable. . . .

After I had read over the list of the persons and descriptions elected into the Tiers Etat, nothing which they afterwards did could appear astonishing. Among them, indeed, I saw some of known rank; some of shining talents; but of any practical experience in the state, not one man was to be found. The best were only men of theory. But whatever the distinguished few may have been, it is the substance and mass of the body which constitutes its character, and must finally determine its direction. . . .

Judge, sir, of my surprise, when I found that a very great proportion of the assembly (a majority, I believe, of the members who attended,) was composed of practitioners in the law. It was composed, not of distinguished magistrates, who had given pledges to their country of their science, prudence, and integrity; not of leading advocates, the glory of the bar; not of renowned professors in universities; but for the far greater part, as it must in such a number, of the inferior, unlearned, mechanical, merely instrumental members of the profession. There were distinguished exceptions; but the general composition was of obscure provincial advocates, of stewards of petty local jurisdictions, country attorneys, notaries, and the whole train of the ministers of municipal litigation, the fomenters and conductors of the petty war of village vexation. From the moment I read the list, I saw distinctly, and very nearly as it has happened, all that was to follow. . . .

Whenever the supreme authority is vested in a body so composed, it must evidently produce the consequences of supreme authority placed in the hands of men not taught habitually to respect themselves; who had no previous fortune in character at stake; who could not be expected to bear with moderation, or to conduct with discretion, a power, which they themselves, more than any others, must be surprised to find in their hands. . . .

Nothing is a due and adequate representation of a state, that does not represent its ability, as well as its property. But as ability is a vigorous and active principle, and as property is sluggish, inert and timid, it never can be safe from the invasions of ability, unless it be, out of all proportion, predominant in the representation. It must be represented too in great masses of accumulation, or it is not rightly protected. The characteristic essence of property, formed out of the combined principles of its acquisition and conservation, is to be *unequal.* . . .

The power of perpetuating our property in our families is one of the most valuable and interesting circumstances belonging to it, and that which tends the most to the perpetuation of society itself. It makes our weakness subservient to our virtue; it grafts benevolence even upon avarice. The possessors of family wealth, and of the distinction which attends hereditary possession (as most concerned in it) are the natural securities for this transmission. With us, the house of peers is formed upon this principle. It is wholly composed of hereditary property and hereditary distinction; and made therefore the third of the legislature; and in the last event, the sole judge of all property in all its subdivisions. The house of commons too, though not necessarily, yet in fact, is always so composed in the far greater part. Let those large proprietors be what they will, and they have their chance of being among the best, they are at the very worst, the ballast in the vessel of the commonwealth. For though hereditary wealth, and the rank which goes with it, are too much idolized by creeping sycophants, and the blind abject admirers of power, they are too rashly slighted in shallow speculations of the petulant, assuming, short-sighted coxcombs of philosophy. Some decent regulated preëminence, some preference (not exclusive appropriation) given to birth, is neither unnatural, nor unjust, nor impolitic.

It is said, that twenty-four millions ought to prevail over two hundred thousand. True; if the constitution of a kingdom be a problem of arithmetic. This sort of discourse does well enough with the lamp-post for its second: to men who may reason calmly, it is ridiculous. The will of the many, and their interest, must very often differ; and great will be the difference when they make an evil choice. A government of five hundred country attorneys and obscure curates is not good for twenty-four millions of men, though it were chosen by eight and forty millions; nor is it the better for being guided by a dozen persons of quality, who have betrayed their trust in order to obtain that power. At present, you seem in every thing to have strayed out of the high-road of nature. The property of France does not govern it. Of course property is destroyed, and rational liberty has no existence. All you have got for the present is a paper circulation, and a stockjobbing constitution: and as to the future, do you seriously think that the territory of France, upon the republican system of eighty-three independent municipalities (to say nothing of the parts that compose them) can ever be governed as one body, or can ever be set in motion by the impulse of one mind? When the national assembly has completed its work, it will have accomplished its ruin. . . .

Government is not made in virtue of natural rights, which may and do exist in total independence of it; and exist in much greater clearness, and in a much greater degree of abstract perfection: but their abstract perfection is their practical defeat. By having a right to every thing, they want every thing. Government is a contrivance of human wisdom to provide for human *wants.* Men have a right that these wants should be provided for by this wisdom. Among these wants is to be reckoned the want, out of civil society, of a sufficient restraint upon their passions. Society requires not only that the passions of individuals should be subjected, but that even in the mass and body as well as in the individuals, the inclinations of men should frequently be thwarted, their will controlled, and their passions brought into subjection. This can only be done *by a power out of themselves;* and not, in the exercise of its function, subject to that will and to those passions which it is its office to bridle and subdue. In this sense the restraints on men, as well as their liberties, are to be reckoned among their rights. But as the liberties and the restrictions vary with times and circumstances, and admit of infinite modifications, they cannot be settled upon any abstract rule; and nothing is so foolish as to discuss them upon that principle.

The moment you abate any thing from the full rights of men, each to govern himself, and suffer any artificial positive limitation upon those rights, from that moment the whole organization of government becomes a consideration of convenience. This it is which makes the constitution of a state, and the due distribution of its powers, a matter of the most delicate and complicated skill. It requires a deep knowledge of human nature and human necessities, and of the things which facilitate or obstruct the various ends which are to be pursued by the mechanism of civil institutions. The state is to have recruits to its strength, and remedies to its distempers. What is the use of discussing a man's abstract right to food or medicine? The question is upon the method of procuring and administering them. In that deliberation I shall always advise to call in the aid of the farmer and the physician, rather than the professor of metaphysics.

The science of constructing a commonwealth, or renovating it, or reforming it, is, like every other experimental science, not to be taught a priori. Nor is it a short experience that can instruct us in that practical science; because the real effects of moral causes are not always immediate; but that which in the first instance is prejudicial may be excellent in its remoter operation; and its excellence may arise even from the ill effects it produces in the beginning. . . .

The nature of man is intricate; the objects of society are of the greatest possible complexity: and therefore no simple disposition or direction of power can be suitable either to man's nature, or to the quality of his affairs. When I hear the simplicity of contrivance aimed at and boasted of in any new political constitutions, I am at no loss to decide that the artificers are grossly ignorant of their trade, or totally negligent of their duty. The simple governments are fundamentally defective, to say no worse of them. If you were to contemplate society in but one point of view, all these simple modes of polity are infinitely captivating. In effect each would answer its single end much more perfectly than the more complex is able to attain all its complex purposes. But it is better that the whole should be imperfectly and anomalously answered, than that, while some parts are provided for with great exactness, others might be totally neglected, or perhaps materially injured, by the overcare of a favorite member.

Questions:

1. What did Edmund Burke find so offensive about the leadership of the French Revolution? What elements of Burke's essay may be cited as the basis for modern political conservatism?
2. In light of Burke's attack on the French Revolution, how could he champion the rights of the American colonists to rebel against King George III?

PART 19
The Industrial Revolution

19.1   Sybil (1845) Benjamin Disraeli

One of the most ardent reformers who criticized working conditions was Benjamin Disraeli. A novelist and politician, he served as prime minister of Britain from 1867 to 1868 and from 1874 to 1880. His most famous novel, Sybil, or the Two Nations, vividly describes working and living conditions in factory towns. Disraeli hoped to gain working-class support for a group of reforming aristocrats in his Tory party. The following selection from this novel demonstrates the power of his prose.

> **Source:** "Sybil" is from Benjamin Disraeli, *Sybil, or the Two Nations* (New York: M. Walter Dunne, 1904), pp. 199–200.

They come forth: the mine delivers its gang and the pit its bondsmen, the forge is silent and the engine is still. The plain is covered with the swarming multitude: bands of stalwart men, broad-chested and muscular, wet with the toil, and black as the children of the tropics; troops of youth, alas! of both sexes, though neither their raiment nor their language indicates the difference; all are clad in male attire; and oaths that men might shudder at issue from lips born to breathe words of sweetness. Yet these are to be, some are, the mothers of England! But can we wonder at the hideous coarseness of their language, when we remember the savage rudeness of their lives? Naked to the waist, an iron chain fastened to a belt of leather runs between their legs clad in canvas trousers, while on hands and feet an English girl, for twelve, sometimes for sixteen hours a day, hauls and hurries tubs of coals up subterranean roads, dark, precipitous, and plashy; circumstances that seem to have escaped the notice of the Society for the Abolition of Negro Slavery. Those worthy gentlemen, too, appear to have been singularly unconscious of the sufferings of the little trappers, which was remarkable, as many of them were in their own employ.

See, too, these emerge from the bowels of the earth! Infants of four and five years of age, many of them girls, pretty and still soft and timid; entrusted with the fulfillment of responsible duties, the very nature of which entails on them the necessity of being the earliest to enter the mine and the latest to leave it. Their labour indeed is not severe, for that would be impossible, but it is passed in darkness and in solitude. They endure that punishment which philosophical philanthropy has invented for the direst criminals, and which those criminals deem more terrible than the death for which it is substituted. Hour after hour elapses, and all that reminds the infant trappers of the world they have quitted, and that which they have joined, is the passage of the coal-wagons for which they open the air-doors of the galleries, and on keeping which doors constantly closed, except at this moment of passage, the safety of the mine and the lives of the persons employed in it entirely depend.

Question:
1. What was the "factory system"? How and why did it originate? What was it intended to do?

19.2   Women Miners in the English Coal Pits

Political revolution was not the only catalyst changing the global experience. Great Britain was the first country to undergo an industrial revolution, fueled in large part by the abundant coal deposits of Wales, Yorkshire, and Lancashire. Mining, like textile manufacture, was an occupation that exploited women and children. Not only did women and children work for less, their small bodies and nimble limbs permitted them to crawl the narrow tunnels to mine and haul the coal much more easily than men. Despite the clear economic advantages of using women and children in the English mines, by the 1840s there was a growing concern that the social and moral consequences of this exploitation were ruining the miners' family life. Agitation for reform in the mines compelled Parliament to investigate working conditions there and enact reform legislation to correct abuses. The following parliamentary reports printed in 1842 describe the working conditions for English women miners.

> **Source:** From Great Britain, *Parliamentary Papers,* 1842, Vol. XVI, pp. 24, 196.

In England, exclusive of Wales, it is only in some of the colliery districts of Yorkshire and Lancashire that female Children of tender age and young and adult women are allowed to descend into the coal mines and regularly to perform the same kinds of underground work, and to work for the same number of hours, as boys and men; but in the East of Scotland their employment in the pits is general; and in South Wales it is not uncommon.

West Riding of Yorkshire: Southern Part.—In many of the collieries in this district, as far as relates to the underground employment, there is no distinction of sex, but the labour is distributed indifferently among both sexes, except that it is comparatively rare for the women to hew or get the coals, although there are numerous instances in which they regularly perform even this work. In great numbers of the coalpits in this district the men work in a state of perfect nakedness, and are in this state assisted in their labour by females of all ages, from girls of six years old to women of twenty-one, these females being themselves quite naked down to the waist.

"Girls," says the Sub-Commissioner [J. C. Symons], "regularly perform all the various offices of trapping, hurrying [Yorkshire terms for drawing the loaded coal corves],[1] filling, riddling,[2] tipping, and occasionally getting, just as they are performed by boys. One of the most disgusting sights I have ever seen was that of young females, dressed like boys in trousers, crawling on all fours, with belts round their waists and chains passing between their legs, at day pits at Hunshelf Bank, and in many small pits near Holmfirth and New Mills: it exists also in several other places. I visited the Hunshelf Colliery on the 18th of January: it is a day pit; that is, there is no shaft or descent; the gate or entrance is at the side of a bank, and nearly horizontal. The gate was not more than a yard high, and in some places not above 2 feet.

"When I arrived at the board or workings of the pit I found at one of the sideboards down a narrow passage a girl of fourteen years of age in boy's clothes, picking down the coal with the regular pick used by the men. She was half sitting half lying at her work, and said she found it tired her very much, and 'of course she didn't like it.' The place where she was at work was not 2 feet high. Further on were men lying on their sides and getting. No less than six girls out of eighteen men and children are employed in this pit.

"Whilst I was in the pit the Rev Mr Bruce, of Wadsley, and the Rev Mr Nelson, of Rotherham, who accompanied me, and remained outside, saw another girl of ten years of age, also dressed in boy's clothes, who was employed in hurrying, and these gentlemen saw her at work. She was a nice-looking little child, but of course as black as a tinker, and with a little necklace round her throat.

"In two other pits in the Huddersfield Union I have seen the same sight. In one near New Mills, the chain, passing high up between the legs of two of these girls, had worn large holes in their trousers; and any sight more disgustingly indecent or revolting can scarcely be imagined than these girls at work—no brothel can beat it.

"On descending Messrs Hopwood's pit at Barnsley, I found assembled round a fire a group of men, boys, and girls, some of whom were of the age of puberty; the girls as well as the boys *stark naked* down to the waist, their hair bound up with a tight cap, and trousers supported by their hips. (At Silkstone and at Flockton they work in their shifts and trousers.) Their sex was recognizable only by their breasts, and some little difficulty occasionally arose in pointing out to me which were girls and which were boys, and which caused a good deal of laughing and joking. In the Flockton and Thornhill pits the system is even more indecent; for though the girls are clothed, at least three-fourths of the men for whom they "hurry" work stark naked, or with a flannel waistcoat only, and in this state they assist one another to fill the corves 18 or 20 times a day: I have seen this done myself frequently.

"When it is remembered that these girls hurry chiefly for men who are *not* their parents; that they go from 15 to 20 times a day into a dark chamber (the bank face), which is often 50 yards apart from any one, to a man working naked, or next to naked, it is not to be supposed but that where opportunity thus prevails sexual vices are of common occurrence. Add to this the free intercourse, and the rendezvous at the shaft or bullstake, where the corves are brought, and consider the language to which the young ear is habituated, the absence of religious instruction, and the early age at which contamination begins, and you will have before you, in the coal-pits where females are employed, the picture of a nursery for juvenile vice which you will go far and wide above ground to equal."

TWO WOMEN MINERS[3]

Betty Harris, age 37: I was married at 23, and went into a colliery when I was married. I used to weave when about 12 years old; can neither read nor write. I work for Andrew Knowles, of Little Bolton (Lancs), and make sometimes 7s a week, sometimes not so much. I am a drawer, and work from 6 in the morning to 6 at night. Stop about an hour at noon to eat my dinner; have bread and butter for dinner; I get no drink. I have two children, but they are too young to work. I worked at drawing when I was in the family way. I know a woman who has gone home and washed herself, taken to her bed, been delivered of a child, and gone to work again under the week.

I have a belt round my waist, and a chain passing between my legs, and I go on my hands and feet. The road is very steep, and we have to hold by a rope; and when there is no rope, by anything we can catch hold of. There are six women and about six boys and girls in the pit I work in; it is very hard work for a woman. The pit is very wet where I work, and the water comes over our clog-tops always, and I have seen it up to my thighs; it rains in at the roof terribly. My clothes are wet through almost all day long. I never was ill in my life, but when I was lying in.

My cousin looks after my children in the day time. I am very tired when I get home at night; I fall asleep some-times before I get washed. I am not so strong as I was, and cannot stand my work so well as I used to. I have drawn till I have had the skin off me; the belt and chain is worse when we are in the family way. My feller (husband) has beaten me many a time for not being ready. I were not used to it at first, and he had little patience.

I have known many a man beat his drawer. I have known men take liberties with the drawers, and some of the women have bastards.

Patience Kershaw, age 17, Halifax: I go to pit at 5 o'clock in the morning and come out at 5 in the evening; I get my break-fast, porridge and milk, first; I take my dinner with me, a cake, and eat it as I go; I do not stop or rest at any time for the purpose, I get nothing else until I get home, and then have potatoes and meat, not every day meat.

I hurry in the clothes I have now got on—trousers and a ragged jacket; the bald place upon my head is made by thrusting the corves; I hurry the corves a mile and more under ground and back; they weigh 3 cwt. I hurry eleven a day. I wear a belt and chain at the workings to get the corves out. The getters that I work for are naked except their caps; they pull off all their clothes; I see them at work when I go up.

Sometimes they beat me if I am not quick enough, with their hands; they strike me upon my back. The boys take liberties with me sometimes; they pull me about. I am the only girl in the pit; there are about 20 boys and 15 men; all the men are naked. I would rather work in mill than in coal-pit.

Note by Sub-Commissioner Scriven: This girl is an ignorant, filthy, ragged, and deplorable looking object, and such a one as the uncivilized natives of the prairies would be shocked to look upon.

Questions:
1. *Why would so many women miners prefer to work in the mines without clothing? Why did the women need the heavy belts around their waists and chains between their legs?*
2. *What was the average workday of these female miners? What was their daily diet? What would be the social and familial cost for these female miners?*
3. *Karl Marx and Friedrich Engels argue that capitalism and industrialism are inherently exploitive of women so that "The bourgeois sees in his wife only an instrument of production." Based upon an analysis of this document, how would you respond to Marx and Engels's argument?*

19.3 Sadler Report: Child Labor

By the early nineteenth century, the Industrial Revolution had spread from England and was beginning to transform Europe from a rural to an urban society. In England, this transformation often depressed the living standards of workers beneath even those of the cottage manufacturing system of an earlier era. In doing so, however, it paved the way for its own reform, for it bared to the public eye in an aggravated form conditions that had long existed but had passed relatively unnoticed. Poverty and misery could be overlooked as long as the workers remained scattered about the countryside, but once they were con-gregated in the hideous slums of the Midlands industrial centers, their plight became too obvious to remain unheeded. Consequently, social reform became the order of the day.

Among the most prominent of the English reformers was the seventh Earl of Shaftesbury (1801-1885), who concentrated on working conditions in the factories. At Shaftesbury's instigation, another reformer, Michael Sadler, introduced a bill in Parliament in 1831 designed to regulate the working conditions of children in textile mills. The bill was referred to a committee, with Sadler as chairman. The selection that follows is an excerpt from the evidence presented before that committee. The committee's recommen-dations resulted in the Factory Act of 1833, which limited the working hours of children and set up a system of inspection to insure that its regulations would be carried out.

The Sadler Report requires no comment; it speaks for itself. The selection included here was picked almost at random from a bulky volume of testimony provided by hundreds of witnesses. Although these witnesses were presumably selected with some care, their accounts provide a generally accurate picture of the conditions of many factory workers, children in particular, in early-nineteenth-century England.

Source: *The Sadler Rep ort: Report from the Committee on the Bill to Regulate the Labour of Children in the Mills and Factories of the United Kingdom* (London: House of Commons, 1832).

THE SADLER REPORT
VENERIS, 18° DIE MAII, 1832

Michael Thomas Sadler, Esquire, in the Chair

MR. MATTHEW CRABTREE, *called in; and Examined.*

What age are you? —Twenty—two.

What is your occupation? —A blanket manufacturer.

Have you ever been employed in a factory?-Yes.

At what age did you first go to work in one?-Eight.

How long did you continue in that occupation?-Four years.

Will you state the hours of labour at the period when you first went to the factory, in ordinary times? —From 6 in the morning to 8 at night.

Fourteen hours? — Yes.

With what intervals for refreshment and rest? — An hour at noon.

Then you had no resting time allowed in which to take your breakfast, or what is in Yorkshire called your "drinking"? — No.

When trade was brisk what were your hours? —From 5 in the morning to 9 in the evening.

Sixteen hours? —Yes.

With what intervals at dinner?-An hour.

How far did you live from the mill?-About two miles.

Was there any time allowed for you to get your breakfast in the mill?-No.

Did you take it before you left your home?-Generally.

During those long hours of labour could you be punctual; how did you awake? — I seldom did awake spontaneously; I was most generally awoke or lifted out of bed, sometimes asleep, by my parents.

Were you always in time?-No.

What was the consequence if you had been too late?-I was most commonly beaten.

Severely?-Very severely, I thought.

In whose factory was this?-Messrs. Hague & Cook's, of Dewsbury.

Will you state the effect that those long hours had upon the state of your health and feelings?-I was, when working those long hours, commonly very much fatigued at night, when I left my work; so much so that I sometimes should have slept as I walked if I had not stumbled and started awake again; and so sick often that I could not eat, and what I did eat I vomited.

Did this labour destroy your appetite?-It did.

In what situation were you in that mill?-I was a piecener.

Will you state to this Committee whether piecening is a very laborious employment for children, or not?-It is a very laborious employment. Pieceners are continually running to and fro, and on their feet the whole day.

The duty of the piecener is to take the cardings from one part of the machinery, and to place them on another?-Yes.

So that the labour is not only continual, but it is unabated to the last?-It is unabated to the last.

Do you not think, from your own experience, that the speed of the machinery is so calculated as to demand the utmost exertions of a child supposing the hours were moderate?-It is as much as they could do at the best; they are always upon the stretch, and it is commonly very difficult to keep up with their work.

State the condition of the children toward the latter part of the day, who have thus to keep up with the machinery.-It is as much as they do when they are not very much fatigued to keep up with their work, and toward the close of the day, when they come to be more fatigued, they cannot keep up with it very well, and the consequence is that they are beaten to spur them on.

Were you beaten under those circumstances? — Yes.

Frequently?-Very frequently.

And principally at the latter end of the day?-Yes.

And is it your belief that if you had not been so beaten, you should not have got through the work?-I should not if I had not been kept up to it by some means.

Does beating then principally occur at the latter end of the day, when the children are exceedingly fatigued?-It does at the latter end of the day, and in the morning sometimes, when they are very drowsy, and have not got rid of the fatigue of the day before.

What were you beaten with principally?-A strap.

Anything else?-Yes, a stick sometimes; and there is a kind of roller which runs on the top of the machine called

362

a billy, perhaps two or three yards in length, and perhaps an inch and a half or more in diameter; the circumference would be four or five inches; I cannot speak exactly.

Were you beaten with that instrument?-Yes.

Have you yourself been beaten, and have you seen other children struck severely with that roller?-I have been struck very severely with it myself, so much so as to knock me down, and I have seen other children have their heads broken with it.

You think that it is a general practice to beat the children with the roller?-It is.

You do not think then that you were worse treated than other children in the mill?-No, I was not, perhaps not so bad as some were.

In those mills is chastisement towards the latter part of the day going on perpetually?-Perpetually.

So that you can hardly be in a mill without hearing constant crying?-Never an hour, I believe.

Do you think that if the over—looker were naturally a humane person it would be still found necessary for him to beat the children, in order to keep up their attention and vigilance at the termination of those extraordinary days of labour?-Yes, the machine turns off a regular quantity of cardings, and of course they must keep as regularly to their work the whole of the day; they must keep with the machine, and therefore however humane the slubber may be, as he must keep up with the machine or be found fault with, he spurs the children to keep up also by various means but that which he commonly resorts to is to strap them when they become drowsy.

At the time when you were beaten for not keeping up with your work, were you anxious to have done it if you possibly could?-Yes; the dread of being beaten if we could not keep up with our work was a sufficient impulse to keep us to it if we could.

When you got home at night after this labour, did you feel much fatigued?-Very much so.

Had you any time to be with your parents, and to receive instruction from them?-No.

What did you do?-All that we did when we got home was to get the little bit of supper that was provided for us and go to bed immediately. If the supper had not been ready directly, we should have gone to sleep while it was preparing.

Did you not, as a child, feel it a very grievous hardship to be roused so soon in the morning?-I did.

Were the rest of the children similarly circumstanced? —Yes, all of them; but they were not all of them so far from their work as I was.

And if you had been too late you were under the apprehension of being cruelly beaten?-I generally was beaten when I happened to be too late; and when I got up in the morning the apprehension of that was so great, that I used to run, and cry all the way as I went to the mill.

That was the way by which your punctual attendance was secured?-Yes.

And you do not think it could have been secured by any other means?-No.

Then it is your impression from what you have seen, and from your own experience, that those long hours of labour have the effect of rendering young persons who are subject to them exceedingly unhappy?-Yes.

You have already said it had a considerable effect upon your health?-Yes.

Do you conceive that it diminished your growth?-I did not pay much attention to that; but I have been examined by some persons who said they thought I was rather stunted, and that I should have been taller if I had not worked at the mill.

What were your wages at that time?-Three shillings *[per week—Ed]*.

And how much a day had you for over—work when you were worked so exceedingly long?-A half—penny a day.

Did you frequently forfeit that if you were not always there to a moment?-Yes; I most frequently forfeited what was allowed for those long hours.

You took your food to the mill; was it in your mill, as is the case in cotton mills, much spoiled by being laid aside?-It was very frequently covered by flues from the wool; and in that case they had to be blown off with the mouth, and picked off with the fingers before it could be eaten.

So that not giving you a little leisure for eating your food, but obliging you to take it at the mill, spoiled your food when you did get it?-Yes, very commonly.

And that at the same time that this over—labour injured your appetite?-Yes.

Could you eat when you got home?-Not always.

What is the effect of this piecening upon the hands? —It makes them bleed; the skin is completely rubbed off, and in that case they bleed in perhaps a dozen parts.

The prominent parts of the hand?-Yes, all the prominent parts of the hand are rubbed down till they bleed; every day they are rubbed in that way.

All the time you continue at work? —All the time we are working. The hands never can be hardened in that work, for the grease keeps them soft in the first instance, and long and continual rubbing is always wearing them down, so that if they were hard they would be sure to bleed.

Is it attended with much pain? —Very much.

Do they allow you to make use of the back of the hand? —No; the work cannot be so well done with the back of the hand, or I should have made use of that.

Is the work done as well when you are so many hours engaged in it, as it would be if you were at it a less time? —I believe it is not done so well in those long hours; toward the latter end of the day the children become completely bewildered, and know not what they are doing, so that they spoil their work without knowing.

Then you do not think that the masters gain much by the continuance of the work to so great a length of time? — I believe not.

Were there girls as well as boys employed in this manner? —Yes.

Were they more tenderly treated by the overlookers, or were they worked and beaten in the same manner? —There was no difference in their treatment.

Were they beaten by the overlookers, or by the slubber? —By the slubber.

But the overlooker must have been perfectly aware of the treatment that the children endured at the mill? —Yes; and sometimes the overlooker beat them himself; but the man that they wrought under had generally the management of them.

Did he pay them their wages? —No; their wages were paid by the master.

But the overlooker of the mill was perfectly well aware that they could not have performed the duty exacted from them in the mill without being thus beaten? — I believe he was.

You seem to say that this beating is absolutely necessary, in order to keep the children up to their work; is it universal throughout all factories? —I have been in several other factories, and I have witnessed the same cruelty in them all.

Did you say that you were beaten for being too late? —Yes.

Is it not the custom in many of the factories to impose fines upon children for being too late, instead of beating them?-It was not in that factory.

What then were the fines by which you lost the money you gained by your long hours? — The spinner could not get on so fast with his work when we happened to be too late; he could not begin his work so soon, and therefore it was taken by him.

Did the slubber pay you your wages? —No, the master paid our wages.

And the slubber took your fines from you? —Yes.

Then you were fined as well as beaten? —There was nothing deducted from the ordinary scale of wages, but only from that received for over—hours, and I had only that taken when I was too late, so that the fine was not regular.

When you were not working over—hours, were you so often late as when you were working over—hours? —Yes.

You were not very often late whilst you were not working over—hours? —Yes, I was often late when I was not working over—hours; I had to go at six o'clock in the morning, and consequently had to get up at five to eat my breakfast and go to the mill, and if I failed to get up by five I was too late; and it was nine o'clock before we could get home, and then we went to bed; in the best times I could not be much above eight hours at home, reckoning dressing and eating my meals, and everything.

Was it a blanket—mill in which you worked? —Yes.

Did you ever know that the beatings to which you allude inflicted a serious injury upon the children? —I do not recollect any very serious injury, more than that they had their heads broken, if that may be called a serious injury; that has often happened; I, myself, had no more serious injury than that.

You say that the girls as well as the boys were employed as you have described, and you observed no difference in their treatment? —No difference.

The girls were beat in this unmerciful manner? —They were.

They were subject, of course, to the same bad effects from this over working? —Yes.

Could you attend an evening—school during the time you were employed in the mill? —No, that was completely impossible.

Did you attend the Sunday—school? —Not very frequently when I work at the mill.

How then were you engaged during the Sunday?- I very often slept till it was too late for school time or for divine worship, and the rest of the day I spent in walking out and taking a little fresh air.

Did your parents think that it was necessary for you to enjoy a little fresh air? —I believe they did; they never said anything against it; before I went to the mill I used to go to the Sunday—school.

Did you frequently sleep nearly the whole of the day on Sunday? —Very often.

At what age did you leave that employment? — I was about 12 years old.

Why did you leave that place? — I went very late one morning, about seven o'clock, and I got severely beaten by the spinner, and he turned me out of the mill, and I went home, and never went any more.

Was your attendance as good as the other children? —Being at rather a greater distance than some of them, I was generally one of the latest.

Where was your next work? —I worked as bobbin—winder in another part of the works of the same firm.

How long were you a bobbin—winder? —About two years, I believe.

What did you become after that? —A weaver.

How long were you a weaver? —I was a weaver till March in last year.

A weaver of what? —A blanket—weaver.

With the same firm? —With the same firm.

Did you leave them? — No; I was dismissed from my work for a reason which I am willing and anxious to explain.

Have you had opportunities of observing the way in which the children are treated in factories up to a late period? —Yes.

You conceive that their treatment still remains as you first found it, and that the system is in great want of regulation? —It does.

Children you still observe to be very much fatigued and injured by the hours of labour? —Yes.

From your own experience, what is your opinion as to the utmost labour that a child in piecening could safely undergo? —If I were appealed to from my own feelings to fix a limit, I should fix it at ten hours, or less.

And you attribute to longer hours all the cruelties that you describe? —A good deal of them.

Are the children sleepy in mills? —Very.

Are they more liable to accidents in the latter part of the day than in the other part? —I believe they are; I believe a greater number of accidents happen in the latter part of the day than in any other. I have known them so sleepy that in the short interval while the others have been going out, some of them have fallen asleep, and have been left there.

Is it an uncommon case for children to fall asleep in the mill, and remain there all night? —Not to remain there all night; but I have known a case the other day, of a child whom the overlooker found when he went to lock the door, that had been left there.

So that you think there has been no change for the better in the treatment of those children; is it your opinion that there will be none, except Parliament interfere in their behalf? —It is my decided conviction.

Have you recently seen any cruelties in mills? — Yes; not long since I was in a mill and I saw a girl severely beaten; at a mill called Hicklane Mill, in Batley; I happened to be in at the other end of the room, talking; and I heard the blows, and I looked that way, and saw the spinner beating one of the girls severely with a large stick. Hearing the sound, led me to look round, and to ask what was the matter, and they said it was "Nothing but paying *[beating—Ed.]* 'his ligger—on.' "

What age was the girl? — About 12 years.

Was she very violently beaten? —She was.

Was this when she was over—fatigued? —It was in the afternoon.

Can you speak as to the effect of this labour in the mills and factories on the morals of the children, as far as you have observed? — As far as I have observed with regard to morals in the mills, there is everything about them that is disgusting to every one conscious of correct morality.

Do you find that the children, the females especially, are very early demoralized in them? —They are.

Is their language indecent? —Very indecent; and both sexes take great familiarities with each other in the mills, without at all being ashamed of their conduct.

Do you connect their immorality of language and conduct with their excessive labour? —It may be somewhat connected with it, for it is to be observed that most of that goes on toward night, when they begin to be drowsy; it is a kind of stimulus which they use to keep them awake; they say some pert thing or other to keep themselves from drowsiness, and it generally happens to be some obscene language.

Have not a considerable number of the females employed in mills illegitimate children very early in life? —I believe there are; I have known some of them have illegitimate children when they were between 16 and 17 years of age.

How many grown—up females had you in the mill? — I cannot speak to the exact number that were grown up; perhaps there might be thirty—four or so that worked in the mill at that time.

How many of those had illegitimate children? A great many of them; eighteen or nineteen of them, I think.

Did they generally marry the men by whom they had the children? —No; it sometimes happens that young women have children by married men, and I have known an instance, a few weeks since, where one of the young women had a child by a married man.

Is it your opinion that those who have the charge of mills very often avail themselves of the opportunity they have to debauch the young women? —No, not generally; most of the improper conduct takes place among the younger part of those that work in the mill.

Do you find that the children and young persons in those mills are moral in other respects, or does their want of education tend to encourage them in a breach of the law? —I believe it does, for there are very few of them that can know anything about it; few of them can either read or write.

Are criminal offences then very frequent? —Yes, theft is very common; it is practised a great deal in the mills, stealing their bits of dinner, or something of that sort. Some of them have not so much to eat as they ought to have, and if they can fall in with the dinner of some of their partners they steal it. The first day my brother and I went to the mill we had our dinner stolen, because we were not up to the tricks; we were more careful in future, but still we did not always escape.

Was there any correction going on at the mills for indecent language or improper conduct? —No, I never knew of any.

From what you have seen and known of those mills, would you prefer that the hours of labour should be so long with larger wages, or that they should be shortened with a diminution of wages? — If I were working at the mill now, I would rather have less labour and receive a trifle less, than so much labour and receive a trifle more.

Is that the general impression of individuals engaged in mills with whom you are acquainted? —I believe it is.

What is the impression in the country from which you come with respect to the effect of this Bill upon wages? —They do not anticipate that it will affect wages at all.

They think it will not lower wages? —They do.

Do you mean that it will not lower wages by the hour, or that you will receive the same wages per day? —They anticipate that it may perhaps lower their wages at a certain time of the year when they are working hard, but not at other times, so that they will have their wages more regular.

Does not their wish for this Bill mainly rest upon their anxiety to protect their children from the consequences of this excessive labour, and to have some opportunity of affording them a decent education? —Yes; such are the wishes of every humane father that I have heard speak about the thing.

Have they not some feeling of having the labour equalized? — That is the feeling of some that I have heard speak of it.

Did your parents work in the same factories? —No.

Were any of the slubbers' children working there? —Yes.

Under what slubber did you work in that mill? —Under a person of the name of Thomas Bennett, in the first place; and I was changed from him to another of the name of James Webster.

Did the treatment depend very much upon the slubber under whom you were? —No, it did not depend directly upon him, for he was obliged to do a certain quantity of work, and therefore to make us keep up with that.

Were the children of the slubbers strapped in the same way? —Yes, except that it is very natural for a father to spare his own child.

Did it depend upon the feelings of a slubber toward his children? —Very little.

Did the slubbers fine their own spinners? — I believe not.

You said that the piecening was very hard labour; what labour is there besides moving about; have you anything heavy to carry or to lift? —We have nothing heavy to carry, but we are kept upon our feet in brisk times from 5 o'clock in the morning to 9 at night.

How soon does the hand get sore in piecening? —How soon mine became sore I cannot speak to exactly; but they get a little hard on the Sunday, when we are not working, and they will get sore again very soon on the Monday.

Is it always the case in piecening that the hand bleeds, whether you work short or long hours? —They bleed more when we work more.

Do they always bleed when you are working? —Yes.

Do you think that the children would not be more competent to this task, and their hands far less hurt, if the hours were fewer every day, especially when their hands had become seasoned to the labour? —I believe it would have an effect for the longer they are worked the more their hands are worn, and the longer it takes to heal them, and they do not get hard enough after a day's rest to be long without bleeding again; if they were not so much worn down, they might heal sooner, and not bleed so often or so soon.

After a short day's work, have you found your hands hard the next morning? — They do not bleed much after we have ceased work; they then get hard; they will bleed soon in the morning when in regular work.

Do you think if the work of the children were confined to about ten hours a day, that they would not be able to perform this piecening without making their hands bleed? —I believe they would.

So that it is your opinion, from your experience, that if the hours were mitigated, their hands would not be so much worn, and would not bleed by the business of piecening? —Yes.

Do you mean to say that their hands would not bleed at all? — I cannot say exactly, for I always wrought long hours, and therefore my hands always did bleed.

Have you any experience of mills where they only work ten hours? —I have never wrought at such mills, and in most of the mills I have seen their hands bleed.

At a slack time, when you were working only a few hours, did your hands bleed? —No, they did not for three or four days, after we had been standing still for a week; the mill stood still sometimes for a week together, but when we did work we worked the common number of hours.

Were all the mills in the neighbourhood working the same number of hours in brisk times? —Yes.

So that if any parent found it necessary to send his children to the mill for the sake of being able to maintain them, and wished to take them from any mill where they were excessively worked, he could not have found any other place where they would have been less worked? —No, he could not; for myself, I had no desire to change, because I thought I was as well off as I could be at any other mill.

And if the parent, to save his child, had taken him from the mill, and had applied to the parish for relief, would the parish, knowing that he had withdrawn his child from its work, have relieved him?-No.

So that the long labour which you have described, or actual starvation, was, practically, the only alternative that was presented to the parent under such circumstances? — It was; they must either work at the mill they were at or some other, and there was no choice in the mills in that respect.

What, in your opinion, would be the effect of limiting the hours of labour upon the happiness, and the health, and the intelligence of the rising generation? —If the hours are shortened, the children may, perhaps, have a chance of attending some evening—school, and learning to read and write; and those that I know who have been to school and learned to read and write; have much more comfort than those who have not. For myself, I went to a school when I was six years old, and I learned to read and write a little then.

At a free—school? —Yes, at a free—school in Dewsbury; but I left school when I was six years old. The fact is, that my father was a small manufacturer, and in comfortable circumstances, and he got into debt with Mr. Cook for a wool bill, and as he had no other means of paying him, he came and agreed with my father, that my brother and I should go to work at his mill till that debt was paid; so that the whole of the time that we wrought at the mill we had no wages.

THOMAS BENNETT, *called in; and Examined.*

Where do you reside? — At Dewsbury.

What is your business? — A slubber.

What age are you? —About 48.

Have you had much experience regarding the working of children in factories? —Yes, about twenty—seven years.

Have you a family? —Yes, eight children.

Have any of them gone to factories? —All.

At what age? —The first went at six years of age.

To whose mill? —To Mr. Halliley's, to piece for myself.

What hours did you work at that mill? —We have wrought from 4 to 9, from 4 to 10, and from 5 to 9, and from 5 to 10.

What sort of a mill was it? —It was a blanket—mill; we sometimes altered the time, according as the days increased and decreased.

What were your regular hours? —Our regular hours when we were not so throng, was from 6 to 7. And when you were the throngest, what were your hours then? —From 5 to 9, and from 5 to 10, and from 4 to 9.

Seventeen hours? —Yes.

What intervals for meals had the children at that period? —Two hours; an hour for breakfast, and an hour for dinner.

Did they always allow two hours for meals at Mr. Halliley's? —Yes, it was allowed, but the children did not get it, for they had business to do at that time, such as fettling and cleaning the machinery.

But they did not stop in at that time, did they? —They all had their share of the cleaning and other work to do.

That is, they were cleaning the machinery? —Cleaning the machinery at the time of dinner.

How long a time together have you known those excessive hours to continue? —I have wrought so myself very nearly two years together.

Were your children working under you then? —Yes, two of them.

State the effect upon your children. —Of a morning when they have been so fast asleep that I have had to go up stairs and lift them out of bed, and have heard them crying with the feelings of a parent; I have been much affected by it.

Were not they much fatigued at the termination of such a day's labour as that? —Yes; many a time I have seen their hands moving while they have been nodding, almost asleep; they have been doing their business almost mechanically.

While they have been almost asleep, they have attempted to work? —Yes; and they have missed the carding and spoiled the thread, when we have had to beat them for it.

Could they have done their work towards the termination of such a long day's labour, if they had not been chastised to it? —No.

You do not think that they could have kept awake or up to their work till the seventeenth hour, without being chastised? —No.

Will you state what effect it had upon your children at the end of their day's work? —At the end of their day's work, when they have come home, instead of taking their victuals, they have dropped asleep with the victuals in their hands; and sometimes when we have sent them to bed with a little bread or something to eat in their hand, I have found it in their bed the next morning.

Had it affected their health? —I cannot say much of that; they were very hearty children.

Do you live at a distance from the mill? —Half a mile.

Did your children feel a difficulty in getting home? —Yes, I have had to carry the lesser child on my back, and it has been asleep when I got home.

Did these hours of labour fatigue you? —Yes, they fatigued me to that excess, that in divine worship I have not been able to stand according to order; I have sat to worship.

So that even during the Sunday you have felt fatigue from your labour in the week? —Yes, we felt it, and always took as much rest as we could.

Were you compelled to beat your own children, in order to make them keep up with the machine? —Yes, that was forced upon us, or we could not have done the work; I have struck them often, though I felt as a parent.

If the children had not been your own, you would have chastised them still more severely? —Yes.

What did you beat them with? — A strap sometimes; and when I have seen my work spoiled, with the roller.

Was the work always worse done at the end of the day? —That was the greatest danger.

Do you conceive it possible that the children could do their work well at the end of such a day's labour as that? —No.

Matthew Crabtree, the last Witness examined by this Committee, I think mentioned you as one of the slubbers under whom he worked? —Yes.

He states that he was chastised and beaten at the mill? —Yes, I have had to chastise him.

You can confirm then what he has stated as to the length of time he had to work as a child, and the cruel treatment that he received? Yes, I have had to chastise him in the evening, and often in the morning for being too late; when I had one out of the three wanting I could not keep up with the machine, and I was getting behindhand compared with what another man was doing; and therefore I should have been called to account on Saturday night if the work was not done.

Was he worse than others? — No.

Was it the constant practice to chastise the children? —Yes.

It was necessary in order to keep up your work? —Yes.

And you would have lost your place if you had not done so? —Yes; when I was working at Mr. Wood's mill, at Dewsbury, which at present is burnt down, but where I slubbed for him until it was, while we were taking our meals he used to come up and put the machine agoing; and I used to say, 'You do not give us time to eat"; he used to reply, "Chew it at your work"; and I often replied to him, "I have not yet become debased like a brute, I do not chew my cud." Often has that man done that, and then gone below to see if a strap were off, which would have shown if the machinery was not working, and then he would come up again.

Was this at the drinking time? —Yes, at breakfast and at drinking.

Was this where the children were working? —Yes, my own children and others.

Were your own children obliged to employ most of their time at breakfast and at the drinking in cleansing the machine, and in fettling the spindles? I have seen at that mill, and I have experienced and mentioned it with grief, that the English children were enslaved worse than the Africans. Once when Mr. Wood was saying to the carrier who brought his work in and out, "How long has that horse of mine been at work?" and the carrier told him the time, and he said "Loose him directly, he has been in too long," I made this reply to him, 'You have more mercy and pity for your horse than you have for your men."

Did not this beating go on principally at the latter part of the day? —Yes.

Was it not also dangerous for the children to move about those mills when they became so drowsy and fatigued? —Yes, especially by lamplight.

Do the accidents principally occur at the latter end of those long days of labour? — Yes, I believe mostly so.

Do you know of any that have happened? I know of one; it was at Mr. Wood's mill; part of the machinery caught a lass who had been drowsy and asleep, and the strap which ran close by her caught her at about her middle, and bore her to the ceiling, and down she came, and her neck appeared to be broken, and the slubber ran up to her and pulled her neck, and I carried her to the doctor myself.

Did she get well? —Yes, she came about again.

What time was that? — In the evening.

You say that you have eight children who have gone to the factories? —Yes.

There has been no opportunity for you to send them to a day—school? —No; one boy had about twelve months' schooling.

Have they gone to Sunday—schools? —Yes.

Can any of them write? —Not one.

They do not teach writing at Sunday—schools? —No; it is objected to, I believe.

So that none of your children can write? —No.

What would be the effect of a proper limitation of the hours of labour upon the conduct of the rising generation? —I believe it would have a very happy effect in regard to correcting their morals; for I believe there is a deal of evil that takes place in one or other in consequence of those long hours.

Is it your opinion that they would then have an opportunity of attending night—schools? —Yes; I have often regretted, while working those long hours, that I could not get my children there.

Is it your belief that if they were better instructed, they would be happier and better members of society? —Yes, I believe so.

Questions:
1. *Summarize conditions in the factories.*
2. *What effect did factory work have on other aspects of the worker's lives?*

19.4   A Defense of the Factory System (1835): Andrew Ure

The factory system was not without its advocates. One of the most influential was Andrew Ure, a professor of applied science at the University of Glasgow. He was supportive of the efficiency and productive capabilities of mechanized manufacturing. Note how the major criticisms of the reformers (child labor, degrading and unhealthy work conditions, etc.) are methodically countered. Ure argued that the owners of the mills and mines were not devils, but were actually abused themselves by the demands of the workers.

> **Source:** "A Defense of the Factory System" is from Andrew Ure, *The Philosophy of Manufactures* (London: Charles Knight, 1835), pp. 282–284, 290, 300–301, 309–311, 398–399.

Proud of the power of malefaction, many of the cotton-spinners, though better paid, as we have shown, than any similar set of artisans in the world, organized the machinery of strikes through all the gradations of their people, terrifying or cajoling the timid or the passive among them to join their vindictive union. They boasted of possessing a dark tribunal, by the mandates of which they could paralyze every mill whose master did not comply with their wishes, and so bring ruin on the man who had given them profitable employment for many a year. By flattery or intimidation, they levied contributions from their associates in the privileged mills, which they suffered to proceed, in order to furnish spare funds for the maintenance of the idle during the decreed suspension of labour. In this extraordinary state of things, when the inventive head and the sustaining heart of trade were held in bondage by the unruly lower members, a destructive spirit began to display itself among some partisans of the union. Acts of singular atrocity were committed, sometimes with weapons fit only for demons to wield, such as the corrosive oil of vitriol, dashed in the faces of most meritorious individuals, with the effect of disfiguring their persons, and burning their eyes out of the sockets with dreadful agony.

The true spirit of turn-outs [strikes] among the spinners is well described in the following statement made on oath to the Factory Commission, by Mr. George Royle Chappel, a manufacturer of Manchester, who employs 274 hands, and two steam-engines of sixty-four horse power.

"I have had several turn-outs, and have heard of many more, but never heard of a turn-out for short time. I will relate the circumstances of the last turn-out, which took place on the 16th October, 1830, and continued till the 17th January, 1831. The whole of our spinners, whose average (weekly) wages were 2£. 13s. 5d., turned out at the instigation, as they told us at the time, of the delegates of the union. They said they had no fault to find with their wages, their work, or their masters, but the union obliged them to turn out. The same week three delegates from the spinners' union waited upon us at our mill, and dictated certain advances in wages, and other regulations, to which, if we would not adhere, they said neither our own spinners nor any other should work for us again! Of course we declined, believing our wages to be ample, and our regulations such as were necessary for the proper conducting of the establishment. The consequences were, they set watches on every avenue to the mill, night and day, to prevent any fresh hands coming into the mill, an object which they effectually attained, by intimidating some, and promising support to others (whom I got into the mill in a caravan), if they would leave their work. Under these circumstances, I could not work the mill, and advertised it for sale, without any applications, and I also tried in vain to let it. At the end of twenty-three weeks the hands requested to be taken to the mill again on the terms that they had left it, declaring, as they had done at first, that the union alone had forced them to turn out. . . ."

Nothing shows in a clearer point of view the credulity of mankind in general, and of the people of these islands in particular, than the ready faith which was given to the tales of cruelty exercised by proprietors of cotton-mills towards young children. The systems of calumny somewhat resembles that brought by the Pagans against the primitive Christians, of enticing children into their meetings in order to murder and devour them. . . . .

No master would wish to have any wayward children to work within the walls of his factory, who do not mind their business without beating, and he therefore usually fines or turns away any spinners who are known to maltreat their assistants. Hence, ill-usage of any kind is a very rare occurrence. I have visited many factories, both in Manchester and in the surrounding districts, during a period of several months, entering the spinning rooms, unexpectedly, and often alone, at different times of the day, and I never saw a single instance of corporal chastisement inflicted on a child, nor indeed did I ever see children in ill-humour. They seemed to be always cheerful and alert, taking pleasure in the light play of their muscles, enjoying the mobility natural to their age. The scene of industry, so far from exciting sad emotions in my mind, was always exhilarating. It was delightful to observe the nimbleness with which they pieced the broken ends, as the mule-carriage began to recede from the fixed roller-beam, and to see them at leisure, after a few seconds' exercise of their tiny fingers, to amuse themselves in any attitude they chose, till the stretch and winding-on were once more completed. The work of these lively elves seemed to resemble a sport, in which habit gave them a pleasing dexterity. Conscious of their skill, they were delighted to show it off to any stranger. As to exhaustion by the day's work, they evinced no trace of it on emerging from the mill in the evening; for they immediately began to skip about any neighbouring playground, and to commence their little amusements with the same alacrity as boys issuing from a school. It is moreover my firm conviction, that if children are not ill-used by bad parents or guardians, but receive in food and raiment the full benefit of what they earn, they would thrive better when employed in our modern factories, than if left at home in apartments too often ill-aired, damp, and cold. . . . .

Of all the common prejudices that exist with regard to factory labour, there is none more unfounded than that which ascribes to it excessive tedium and irksomeness above other occupations, owing to its being carried on in conjunction with the "unceasing motion of the steam- engine." In an establishment for spinning or weaving cotton, all the hard work is performed by the steam-engine, which leaves for the attendant no hard labour at all, and literally nothing to do in general; but at intervals to perform some delicate operation, such as joining the threads that break, taking the cops off the spindle, &c. And it is so far from being true that the work in a factory is incessant, because the motion of the steam-engine is incessant, that the fact is, that the labour is not incessant on that very count, because it is performed in conjunction with the steam-engine. Of all manufacturing employments, those are by far the most irksome and incessant in which steam-engines are not employed, as in lace-running and stocking-weaving; and the way to prevent an employment from being incessant, is to introduce a steam-engine into it. These remarks certainly apply more especially to the labour of children in factories. Three-fourths of the children so employed are engaged in piecing at the mules. "When the carriages of these have receded a foot and a half or two feet from the rollers," says Mr. Tufnell, "nothing is to be done, not even attention is required from either spinner or piecer." Both of them stand idle for a time, and in fine spinning particularly, for three-quarters of a minute, or more. Consequently, if a child remains at this business twelve hours daily, he has nine hours of inaction. And though he attends two mules, he has still six hours of non-exertion. Spinners sometimes dedicate these intervals to the perusal of books. The scavengers, who, in Mr. Sadler's report, have been described as being "constantly in a state of grief, always in terror, and every moment they have to spare stretched all their length upon the floor in a state of perspiration," may be observed in cotton factories idle for four minutes at a time, or moving about in a sportive mood, utterly unconscious of the tragical scenes in which they were dramatized. . . . .

Mr. Hutton, who has been in practice as a surgeon at Stayley Bridge upwards of thirty-one years, and, of course, remembers the commencement, and has had occasion to trace the progress and effect, of the factory system, says that the health of the population has much improved since its introduction, and that they are much superior in point of comfort to what they were formerly. He also says that fever has become less common since the erection of factories, and that the persons employed in them were less attacked by the influenza in 1833, than other classes of work-people. Mr. Bott, a surgeon, who is employed by the operatives in Messrs. Lichfield's mills to attend them in all cases of sickness or accident, at the rate of one halfpenny a week (a sum which indicates pretty distinctly their small chances of ailment), says that the factory workmen are not so liable to epidemics as other persons; and that though he has had many cases of typhus fever in the surrounding district, nearly all the mill-hands have escaped, and not one was attacked by the cholera during its prevalence in the neighbourhood.

Question:
1. How does Andrew Ure defend the factory system? What specific points does he address? Are his arguments persuasive? Why or why not?

19.5 The Chartist Demands (1838)

Although the Factory Act of 1833 resulted in an improvement in factory working conditions and in restrictions on child labor, many critics favored more radical reform. The Chartist movement in Great Britain, which was popular in the 1840s, sought political participation and especially universal manhood suffrage as means of improving the living conditions of the working poor. The following is an excerpt from the People's Petition of 1838, which articulated Chartist demands to the British House of Commons.

Source: "The Chartist Demands" is from *The Life and Struggles of William Lovett* (New York: Knopf, 1920), pp. 478–481.

We, your petitioners, dwell in a land whose merchants are noted for enterprise, whose manufacturers are very skillful, and whose workmen are proverbial for their industry.

The land itself is goodly, the soil rich, and the temperature wholesome; it is abundantly furnished with the materials of commerce and trade; it has numerous and convenient harbours; in facility of internal communication it exceeds all others. For three-and-twenty years we have enjoyed a profound peace.

Yet, with all these elements of national prosperity, and with every disposition and capacity to take advantage of them, we find ourselves overwhelmed with public and private suffering.

We are bowed down under a load of taxes; which, notwithstanding, fall greatly short of the wants of our rulers; our traders are trembling on the verge of bankruptcy; our workmen are starving; capital brings no profit, and labour no remuneration; the home of the artificer is desolate, and the warehouse of the pawnbroker is full; the workhouse is crowded, and the manufactory is deserted. . . .

It was the found expectation of the people that a remedy for the greater part, if not for the whole, of their grievances, would be found in the Reform Act of 1832.

They were taught to regard that Act as a wise means to a worthy end; as the machinery of an improved legislation, when the will of the masses would be at length potential.

They have been bitterly and basely deceived.

The fruit which looked so fair to the eye has turned to dust and ashes when gathered.

The Reform Act has effected a transfer of power from one domineering faction to another, and left the people as helpless as before. . . .

Required as we are, universally, to support and obey the laws, nature and reason entitle us to demand, that in the making of the laws, the universal voice shall be implicitly listened to.

We perform the duties of freemen; we must have the privileges of freemen.

WE DEMAND UNIVERSAL SUFFRAGE

The suffrage to be exempt from the corruption of the wealthy, and the violence of the powerful, must be secret. . . .

WE DEMAND THE BALLOT

The connection between the representatives and the people, to be beneficial must be intimate. . . . To public safety as well as public confidence, frequent elections are essential.

WE DEMAND ANNUAL PARLIAMENTS

With power to choose, and freedom in choosing, the range of our choice must be unrestricted.

We are compelled, by the existing laws, to take for our representatives, men who are incapable of appreciating our difficulties, or who have little sympathy with them; merchants who have retired from trade, and no longer feel its harassings; proprietors of land who are alike ignorant of its evils and their cure; lawyers, by whom the honours of the senate are sought after only as means of obtaining notice in the courts. . . .

We demand that in the future election of members of your Honourable House, the approbation of the constituency shall be the sole qualification; and that to every representative so chosen shall be assigned, out of the public taxes, a fair and adequate remuneration for the time which he is called upon to devote to the public service.

Finally, we would most earnestly impress on your Honourable House, that this petition has not been dictated by an idle love of change; that it springs out of no inconsiderate attachment to fanciful theories; but that it is the result of much and long deliberation, and of convictions, which the events of each succeeding year tend more and more to strengthen.

Question:
1. *Who were the Chartists and what were their demands for reform? Was this a political or social reform program?*

19.6 Luddism: An Assault on Technology

Anti-technologists of the late-twentieth century were foreshadowed over 150 years earlier by the Luddites: traditional English framework knitters who felt threatened by labor-saving machines and the trend towards the domination of the factory, mass-producing economy. Some framework knitters and sympathizers resorted to surreptitiously sabotaging machines and factories. Many Luddites were never apprehended; even the origin of the term is uncertain, though theories, such as the one advanced in this pamphlet, have been presented. The most frequent instances of Luddite activity occurred between 1810–1840; thereafter they petered out.

Source: Kenneth Carpenter, ed, *The Luddites: 3 pamphlets,* 1812–1839, (N.Y.: Arno Press, 1972), pp. 98–112.

LUDDISM

IT will no doubt, be gratifying to some Readers, to be made acquainted with the origin of *Luddism.* From the enquiries I made in Nottinghamshire, where Luddism originated, I learnt the following particulars, namely, that a good many years ago, there lived a poor man at Loughborough, in Leicestershire, about fifteen miles from Nottingham, vhose name was *Edward Ludd:* This man was not one of the brightest cast; in regard to his intellects; and, as is commonly the case with such characters, was of an irritable temper. This *Edward Ludd,* called by his neighbours *Ned Ludd,* was by trade a *Frame Work Knitter:* or in plainer language, and which is all the same, a *Stocking Weaver.* This man, being irritated, either by his Employer, or his work, or both took the desperate resolution of avenging himself, by breaking his *Stocking Frame.* As the value of a common Stocking Frame is considerable, being not much less than Forty Pounds, Ned's exploit was much more admired for its temerity than its utility.

However, the consequence of this affair was, a *Bon Mot:* for, whenever any Stocking Weaver was out of patience with his Employer or his Employment, he would say, speaking of his Frame, I have good mind to *Ned Ludd* it:" meaning, *I have a good mind to break it, &c.*

About the latter end of the year 1811, the Stocking and Lace Weavers of Nottingham, having been for a long time harrassed by abridged wages, and want of employment, in whole or in part, and consequently with want of bread, entered into a combination, (as report says, upon oath) to break certain proscribed Frames. But it should here be observed, that the interdicted Frames were not all of a new-invented kind, there being many destined to destruction for the sake of their *owner;* the owner having rendered himself notorious by abridging the workmen's wages, and underselling other manufacturers: therefore many Frames of an ordinary construction were broken.

These Frame-Breakers assumed the name of their proto-type *Ned Ludd.* Hence when they entered a house in order to break Frames, they would say *Ned Ludd* or *General Ludd,* commands us to break these Frames, &c. These men, collectively, were therefore called *Luddites,* and their system was, and is, called *Luddism.*

This system has been communicated to thousands; and as rumour says, to hundreds of thousands, and is still in existence. But it does not always exist where report places it; for every thief and highwayman now takes the name of *Ned Ludd* in his mouth when he is about to commit his depredations; and News Printers seem very willing to have it so; most of them caring very little about the difference betwixt truth and falsehood; their drift too commonly is, to enhance the value of their Papers, by saying something that will surprise and astonish their readers. The old and stale names of *thief, highwayman, and robber,* will not now adorn the *great news* columns of those Papers which are ever seeking to treat their Readers with a mess of Wonderment! Therefore *Ned Ludd* being a new character, is made to bear the heat and burden of the day; for whatever enormities are committed in the counties where *Ned* lives, they are, for the most part, very carefully ascribed to him.

Of the fourteen unfortunate men who were executed at York, on the 15th Jan. 1813, not one-half of them, as I am informed, were in reality Luddites. Either five or six of them were Luddites, who were convicted of entering houses and demanding fire-arms, or breaking, or attempting to break machinery; part of them upon one charge, and part of them upon the other. As to the rest of the fourteen, they were, as I am informed, utter strangers to the system of Luddism: but knowing something of Luddism by popular rumour, they had designated themselves Luddites. Wherefore on entering a house they would preface their demand of money, by telling the people General Ludd was come: or that Ned Ludd had sent them to make such and such demand. Information of the transaction soon reached the ears of a News Printer: who, glad enough of something fresh to tell his Readers, soon laid it before the public: his fellow News-men would copy his statement, and thus this wonderful news which was half true and half false, ran, in the compass of a week, all over the three kingdoms.

With regard to the conduct of the Luddites in breaking machinery, I wholly disapprove of it: it is altogether condemnable: for in my opinion, Machinery Ought to be encouraged to any extent whatever. It is also my opinion, that every man that invents any thing that will lessen human labour, is a benefactor to mankind, and ought to be rewarded, not by a patent, as is commonly the case, but out of the national purse, in order that he and others may be encouraged to new exertions, and the public benefitted by the free use of such inventions!

I pity the poor, and should hardly think myself innocent if any man felt more for them than I do; but the remedy for their grievances, lies not in the destruction of Machinery. They are oppressed exceedingly, but not by Machinery. Those who accuse Machinery of causing any part of the distresses of the poor, have very contracted views and narrow minds, and see but a little way. They do not seem to consider that almost every thing was new Machinery once. There was a time when corn was ground by the hand; and when Cora Mills and Wind Mills were first invented they were *New Machinery;* and therefore why not break and burn these as soon as any other kind of Machinery; for if they were all stopped, and corn again ground by the Hand, there would be plenty of employment; for many hands! Much the same observations might be made respecting every other kind of Machinery, and I have asked this question in order to shew the silliness of the practice.

The grievous distresses of the poor are occasioned by the Monopolization of Landed Property Rack Rents—Large Farms—War, and its Concomitants, Bad Trade and Excessive Taxation. The remedy for all which is, PEACE and REFORM; without these, bad will become worse and worse will be utter *ruin!*

Nor can l foregister the present opportunity of noticing the practice that has long obtained among Journeymen of various callings, respecting Apprentices. Ever since I can remember, feuds and quarrels have subsisted betwixt the Employers and the Employed respecting workmen called *illegal men;* and also an *allowed* number of *Apprentices:* and the proper, or *lawful time* of servitude in Apprenticeships, &c. &c. To me these altercations have always appeared highly reprehensible because at the best they originate in ignorance, and not unfrequently in something less excuseable. But be their origin what it may, they commonly generate litigations and enmity; and sometimes they separate chief friends, and greatly exasperate and injure individuals.

Now, is it not folly, or something worse for one man to, vex and harrass another, either respecting his servants as a Master, or his servitude as an Apprentice? What right, either in law or reason has one man to teaze and distress another on these considerations? There is nothing, there can be nothing but what is both unjust and unreasonable in such conduct. With regard to Apprentices, there ought in reason to be no constraints or restrictions laid upon them or their Masters, respecting the length or shortness of their servitude: let the parties concerned arbitrate the conditions according to their own discretion.

And is it not notorious also, that there are some branches of trade, some arts and callings, that are not half so mysterious and difficult of attainment as others? and some young men there are who by dint of superior gifts and mental endowments from nature will learn a trade in three, or even two years, as perfectly as others will learn the same trade in seven years. Is it not unjust these, is it not highly unreasonable that the narrow minded policy of selfish ignorance, should institute schemes of restriction to superscede the bounties of nature. Would it be equitable to compel a man of two yards high, to take as many strides in walking a mile, as a man of five feet? And is it any more equitable to compel young men of all geniuses and capacities, to run over the same precise round of seven years in the acquisition of a trade. It is in vain to declaim against aristocracies and priviledged orders, until this selfish and vexatious conduct be abandoned: for what are all these petty monopolies and sinister exclusious, but the exhibitions of aristocracy in low life!...

Questions:
1. *What does the author postulate as having been the origins of Luddism?*
2. *What is the author's position, and what arguments does he bring out, pro-and-con, concerning the Luddites?*
3. *Does the author view Luddites as criminals or victims? Explain.*

19.7 Utopian Socialism (1816): Robert Owen

One of the great personal success stories of the nineteenth century was Robert Owen. Born the son of a saddle maker, Owen left school at the age of 9 and went to work in a draper's shop. At the age of 18, he borrowed money and set up a small cotton mill in Manchester. Within ten years, he was very wealthy and was joint owner of the New Lanark mills, the largest textile operation in Scotland. But Robert Owen was possessed with a desire to improve the lot of humanity. He provided higher wages and better working conditions for his employees and established free schools for their children. The New Lanark mills also returned a handsome profit. Owen sought government intervention and regulation to change conditions in industry. He could not understand why all factories could not be run on his utopian model. He is generally accepted in England as the founder of British socialism. The following address was delivered in 1816 on the opening of an "Institution for the Formation of Character" at New Lanark. Note the emphasis on morality as an essential ingredient of change.

Source: "Utopian Socialism" is from Robert Owen, *Address to the Workers of New Lanark* (1816).

Every society which exists at present, as well as every society which history records, has been formed and governed on a belief in the following notions, assumed as *first principles:*

First,—That it is in the power of every individual to form his own character.

Hence the various systems called by the name of religion, codes of law, and punishments. Hence also the angry passions entertained by individuals and nations towards each other.

Second,—That the affections are at the command of the individual. Hence insincerity and degradation of character. Hence the miseries of domestic life, and more than one-half of all the crimes of mankind.

Third,—That it is necessary that a large portion of mankind should exist in ignorance and poverty, in order to secure to the remaining part such a degree of happiness as they now enjoy.

Hence a system of counteraction in the pursuits of men, a general opposition among individuals to the interests of each other, and the necessary effects of such a system,—ignorance, poverty, and vice.

Facts prove, however—

First,—That character is universally formed *for,* and not *by,* the individual.

Second,—That any habits and sentiments may be given to mankind.

Third,—That the affections are not under the control of the individual.

Fourth,—That every individual may be trained to produce far more than he can consume, while there is a sufficiency of soil left for him to cultivate.

Fifth,—That nature has provided means by which population may be at all times maintained in the proper state to give the greatest happiness to every individual, without one check of vice or misery.

Sixth,—That any community may be arranged, on a due combination of the foregoing principles, in such a manner, as not only to withdraw vice, poverty, and, in a great degree, misery, from the world, but also to place *every* individual under circumstances in which he shall enjoy more permanent happiness than can be given to *any* individual under the principles which have hitherto regulated society.

Seventh,—That all the assumed fundamental principles on which society has hitherto been founded are erroneous, and may be demonstrated to be contrary to fact. And—

Eighth,—That the change which would follow the abandonment of those erroneous maxims which bring misery into the world, and the adoption of principles of truth, unfolding a system which shall remove and for ever exclude that misery, may be effected without the slightest injury to any human being.

Here is the groundwork,—these are the data, on which society shall ere long be re-arranged; and for this simple reason, that it will be rendered evident that it will be for the immediate and future interest of every one to lend his most active assistance gradually to reform society on this basis. I say gradually, for in that word the most important considerations are involved. Any sudden and coercive attempt which may be made to remove even misery from men will prove injurious rather than beneficial. Their minds must be gradually prepared by an essential alteration of the circumstances which surround them, for any great and important change and amelioration in their condition. They must be first convinced of their blindness: this cannot be effected, even among the least unreasonable, or those termed the best part of mankind, in their present state, without creating some degree of irritation. This irritation, must then be tranquillized before another step ought to be attempted; and a general conviction must be established of the truth of the principles on which the projected change is to be founded. Their introduction into practice will then become easy,—difficulties will vanish as we approach them,—and, afterwards, the desire to see the whole system carried immediately into effect will exceed the means of putting it into execution.

The principles on which this practical system is founded are not new; separately, or partially united, they have been often recommended by the sages of antiquity, and by modern writers. But it is not known to me that they have ever been thus combined. Yet it can be demonstrated that it is only by their being *all brought into practice* together that they are to be rendered beneficial to mankind; and sure I am that this is the earliest period in the history of man when they could be successfully introduced into practice.

Questions:
1. *How would you define Utopian Socialism? How important is character to success?*
2. *Why was Robert Owens's factory at New Lanark successful? Do the most successful capitalists place an emphasis on people over profit?*

19.8   Karl Marx and Friedrich Engels

According to Lenin, Marxism was derived from three sources: German philosophy, English political economy, and French socialism. The German philosophy was the absolute idealism of G. W. F. Hegel, which Karl Marx had imbibed while a student at the University of Berlin. Central to this philosophy was the notion of dialectic, the theory that history is a series of struggles between opposing forces, with each successive struggle occurring on a higher level than the one that preceded it. Hegel viewed the struggles as taking place between opposing ideas embodied in distinct national cultures. But Marx shifted the struggles from the ideational plane to the economic or material plane, and transformed the antagonists from nations to classes. In other words, he replaced Hegel's dialectical idealism with his own dialectical materialism; or, as he put it, he turned the dialectic, which Hegel had stood on its head, back on its feet again.

The English political economy that Lenin referred to consisted of the writings of the classical economists, Adam Smith and David Ricardo, whose labor theory of value provided Marx with the basic assumption underlying his greatest work, Capital. But Marx reversed the argument of the classical economists: Where they found in the labor theory of value a defense of capitalism, he found a weapon to attack it.

Finally, in his reference to French socialism Lenin had in mind the works of a group of writers, including Claude Saint-Simon, François Fourier, Pierre Proudhon, and Louis Blanc, whose views on the elimination of capitalism and the establishment of the ideal society greatly influenced Marx-even though later he scornfully brushed their theories aside as "utopian" socialism, while claiming that his own were "scientific."

Although Lenin and most other orthodox Marxists would undoubtedly deny it, Marxism owes a debt to a fourth source. This is a moral tradition, stretching back all the way to Socrates and the Old Testament prophets. Marx, the philosopher, historian, and economist, was above all else a moral reformer. Although he clothed his critique of capitalism in an elaborate intellectual framework, at heart it was a moral protest against the human misery and degradation resulting from early-nineteenth-century industrialism. And though he assiduously repeated that his socialism was scientific, the new era of human happiness that he envisioned in the classless society following the revolution was an ideal as utopian as that of Plato's Republic.

The Communist Manifesto, one of the greatest revolutionary documents in history, was the joint production of Marx (1818-1883) and his lifelong friend and collaborator Friedrich Engels (1820-1895). Composed in 1848 as a platform for the Communist League, a small organization of radical workmen, it contains in capsule form most of the major Marxist doctrines. The Manifesto is reproduced here complete except for Part III, in which the authors criticize other forms of socialism.

Source: Trans S. Moore

MANIFESTO OF THE COMMUNIST PARTY

A specter is haunting Europe-the specter of Communism. All the powers of Old Europe have entered into a holy alliance to exorcise this specter; Pope and Czar, Metternich and Guizot, French Radicals and German police-spies.

Where is the party in opposition that has not been decried as communistic by its opponents in power? Where is the opposition that has not hurled back the branding reproach of Communism, against the more advanced opposition parties, as well as against its reactionary adversaries?

Two things result from this fact.

I. Communism is already acknowledged by all European powers to be in itself a power.

II. It is high time that Communists should openly, in the face of the whole world, publish their views, their aims, their tendencies, and meet this nursery tale of the specter of Communism with a Manifesto of the party itself.

To this end Communists of various nationalities have assembled in London, and sketched the following Manifesto to be published in the English, French, German, Italian, Flemish, and Danish languages.

BOURGEOIS AND PROLETARIANS[1]

The history of all hitherto existing society is the history of class struggles.

Freeman and slave, patrician and plebeian, lord and serf, guild-master and journey-man, in a word, oppressor and oppressed, stood in constant opposition to one another, carried on an uninterrupted, now hidden, now open fight, that each time ended, either in a revolutionary reconstitution of society at large, or in the common ruin of the contending classes.

In the earlier epochs of history we find almost everywhere a complicated arrangement of society into various orders, a manifold gradation of social rank. In ancient Rome we have patricians, knights, plebeians, slaves; in the Middle

Ages, feudal lords, vassals, guild-masters, journeymen, apprentices, serfs; in almost all of these classes, again, subordinate gradations.

The modern bourgeois society that has sprouted from the ruins of feudal society, has not done away with class antagonisms. It has but established new forms of struggle in place of the old ones.

Our epoch, the epoch of the bourgeoisie, possesses, however, this distinctive feature; it has simplified the class antagonisms. Society as a whole is more and more splitting up into two great hostile camps, into two great classes directly facing each other: Bourgeoisie and Proletariat.

From the serfs of the Middle Ages sprang the chartered burghers of the earliest towns. From these burgesses the first elements of the bourgeoisie were developed.

The discovery of America, the rounding of the Cape, opened up fresh ground for the rising bourgeoisie. The East-Indian and Chinese markets, the colonization of America, trade with the colonies, the increase in the means of exchange and in commodities generally, gave to commerce, to navigation, to industry, an impulse never before known, and thereby, to the revolutionary element in the tottering feudal society, a rapid development.

The feudal system of industry, under which industrial production was monopolized by closed guilds, now no longer sufficed for the growing wants of the new market. The manufacturing system took its place. The guild-masters were pushed on one side by the manufacturing middle class; division of labor between the different corporate guilds vanished in the face of division of labor in each single workshop.

Meantime the markets kept ever growing, the demand ever rising. Even manufacture no longer sufficed. Thereupon steam and machinery revolutionized industrial production. The place of manufacture was taken by the giant, Modern Industry, the place of the industrial middle class, by industrial millionaires, the leaders of whole industrial armies, the modern bourgeois.

Modern Industry has established the world's market, for which the discovery of America paved the way. This market has given an immense development to commerce, to navigation, to communication by land. This development has, in its turn, reacted on the extension of industry; and in proportion, as industry, commerce, navigation, railways extended, in the same proportion, the bourgeoisie developed, increased its capital, and pushed into the background every class handed down from the Middle Ages.

We see, therefore, how the modern bourgeoisie is itself the product of a long course of development, of a series of revolutions in the modes of production and of exchange.

Each step in the development of the bourgeoisie was accompanied by a corresponding political advance of that class. An oppressed class under the sway of the feudal nobility, an armed and self-governing association in the mediaeval commune, here independent urban republic (as in Italy and Germany), here taxable "third estate" of the monarchy (as in France), afterwards, in the period of manufacture proper, serving either the semi-feudal or the absolute monarchy as a counterpoise against the nobility, and, in fact, cornerstone of the great monarchies in general, the bourgeoisie has at last, since the establishment of Modern Industry and of the world's market, conquered for itself, in the modern representative State, exclusive political sway. The executive of the modern State is but a committee for managing the common affairs of the whole bourgeoisie.

The bourgeoisie, historically, has played a most revolutionary part.

The bourgeoisie, wherever it has got the upper hand, has put an end to all feudal, patriarchal, idyllic relations. It has pitilessly torn asunder the motley feudal ties that bound man to his "natural superiors," and has left remaining no other nexus between man and man than naked self-interest, than callous "cash payment." It has drowned the most heavenly ecstasies of religious fervor, of chivalrous enthusiasm, of Philistine sentimentalism, in the icy water of egotistical calculation. It has resolved personal worth into exchange value, and in place of the numberless indefeasible chartered freedoms, has set up that single, unconscionable freedom-Free Trade. In one word, for exploitation, veiled by religious and political illusions, it has substituted naked, shameless; direct, brutal exploitation.

The bourgeoisie has stripped of its halo every occupation hitherto honored and looked up to with reverent awe. It has converted the physician, the lawyer, the priest, the poet, the man of science, into its paid wage-laborers.

The bourgeoisie has torn away from the family its sentimental veil, and has reduced the family relation to a mere money relation.

The bourgeoisie has disclosed how it came to pass that the brutal display of vigor in the Middle Ages, which reactionists so much admire, found its fitting complement in the most slothful indolence. It has been the first to show what man's activity can bring about. It has accomplished wonders far surpassing Egyptian pyramids, Roman aqueducts, and Gothic cathedrals; it has conducted expeditions that put in the shade all former Exoduses of nations and crusades.

The bourgeoisie cannot exist without constantly revolutionizing the instruments of production, and thereby the relations of production, and with them the whole relations of society. Conservation of the old modes of production in unaltered form, was, on the contrary, the first condition of existence for all earlier industrial classes. Constant revolutionizing of production, uninterrupted disturbance of all social conditions, everlasting uncertainty and agitation, distinguish the bourgeois epoch from all earlier ones. All fixed, fast-frozen relations, with their train of ancient and venerable prejudices and opinions, are swept away; all new-formed ones become antiquated before they can ossify. All that is solid melts into air, all that is holy is profaned, and man is at last compelled to face with sober senses his real conditions of life, and his relations with his kind.

The need of a constantly expanding market for its products chases the bourgeoisie over the whole surface of the globe. It must nestle everywhere, settle everywhere, establish connections everywhere.

The bourgeoisie has through its exploitation of the world's market given a cosmopolitan character to production and consumption in every country. To the great chagrin of reactionists, it has drawn from under the feet of industry the national ground on which it stood. All old established national industries have been destroyed or are daily being destroyed. They are dislodged by new industries, whose introduction becomes a life and death question for all civilized nations, by industries that no longer work up indigenous raw material, but raw material drawn from the remotest zones, industries whose products are consumed, not only at home, but in every quarter of the globe. In place of the old wants, satisfied by the productions of the country, we find new wants, requiring for their satisfaction the products of distant lands and climes. In place of the old local and national seclusion and self-sufficiency we have had intercourse in every direction, universal interdependence of nations. And as in material, so also in intellectual production. The intellectual creations of individual nations become common property. National onesidedness and narrow-mindedness become more and more impossible, and from the numerous national and local literatures, there arises a world-literature.

The bourgeoisie, by the rapid improvement of all instruments of production, by the immensely facilitated means of communication, draws all, even the most barbarian, nations into civilization. The cheap prices of its commodities are the heavy artillery with which it batters down all Chinese walls, with which it forces the barbarians' intensely obstinate hatred of foreigners to capitulate. It compels all nations, on pain of extinction, to adopt the bourgeois mode of production; it compels them to introduce what it calls civilization into their midst, i.e., to become bourgeois themselves. In one word, it creates a world after its own image.

The bourgeoisie has subjected the country to the rule of the towns. It has created enormous cities, has greatly increased the urban population as compared with the rural, and has thus rescued a considerable part of the population from the idiocy of rural life. Just as it has made the country dependent on the towns, so it has made barbarian and semi-barbarian countries dependent on the civilized ones, nations of peasants on nations of bourgeois, the East on the West.

The bourgeoisie keeps more and more doing away with the scattered state of the population, of the means of production, and of property. It has agglomerated population, centralized means of production, and has concentrated property in a few hands. The necessary consequence of this was political centralization. Independent, or but loosely connected provinces, with separate interests, laws, governments, and systems of taxation, became lumped together into one nation, with one government, one code of laws, one national class interest, one frontier, and one customs tariff.

The bourgeoisie, during its rule of scarce one hundred years, has created more massive and more colossal productive forces than have all preceding generations together. Subjection of Nature's forces to man, machinery, application of chemistry to industry and agriculture, steam-navigation, railways, electric telegraphs, clearing of whole continents for cultivation, canalization of rivers, whole populations conjured out of the ground-what earlier century had even a presentiment that such productive forces slumbered in the lap of social labor?

We see then: the means of production and of exchange on whose foundation the bourgeoisie built itself up, were generated in feudal society. At a certain stage in the development of these means of production and of exchange, the conditions under which feudal society produced and exchanged, the feudal organization of agriculture and manufacturing industry, in one word, the feudal relations of property, became no longer compatible with the already developed productive forces; they became so many fetters. They had to be burst asunder; they were burst asunder.

Into their places stepped free competition, accompanied by a social and political constitution adapted to it, and by the economical and political sway of the bourgeois class.

A similar movement is going on before our own eyes. Modern bourgeois society with its relations of production, of exchange, and of property, a society that has conjured up such gigantic means of production and of exchange, is like the sorcerer, who is no longer able to control the powers of the nether world whom he has called up by his spells. For many a decade past the history of industry and commerce is but the history of the revolt of modern productive forces against modern conditions of production, against the property relations that are the conditions for the existence of the bourgeoisie and of its rule. It is enough to mention the commercial crises that by their periodical return put on its trial, each time more threateningly, the existence of the bourgeois society. In these crises a great part not only of the existing products, but also of the previously created productive forces, is periodically destroyed. In these crises there breaks out an epidemic that, in all earlier epochs, would have seemed an absurdity-the epidemic of over-production. Society suddenly finds itself put back into a state of momentary barbarism; it appears as if a famine, a universal war of devastation, had cut off the supply of every means of subsistence; industry and commerce seem to be destroyed; and why? because there is too much civilization, too much means of subsistence, too much industry, too much commerce. The productive forces at the disposal of society no longer tend to further the development of the conditions of bourgeois property; on the contrary, they have become too powerful for these conditions, by which they are fettered, and as soon as they overcome these fetters, they bring disorder into the whole of bourgeois society, endanger the existence of bourgeois property. The conditions of bourgeois society are too narrow to comprise the wealth created by them. And how does the bourgeoisie get over these crises? On the one hand by enforced destruction of a mass of productive forces; on the other, by the conquest of new markets, and by the more thorough exploitation of the old ones. That is to say, by paving the way for more extensive and more destructive crises, and by diminishing the means whereby crises are prevented.

The weapons with which the bourgeoisie felled feudalism to the ground are now turned against the bourgeoisie itself.

But not only has the bourgeoisie forged the weapons that bring death to itself; it has also called into existence the men who are to wield those weapons-the modern working class-the proletarians.

In proportion as the bourgeoisie, i.e., capital, is developed, in the same proportion is the proletariat, the modern working class, developed; a class of laborers, who live only so long as they find work, and who find work only so long as their labor increases capital. These laborers, who must sell themselves piece-meal, are a commodity, like every other article of commerce, and are consequently exposed to all the vicissitudes of competition, to all the fluctuations of the market.

Owing to the extensive use of machinery and to division of labor, the work of the proletarians has lost all individual character, and consequently, all charm for the workman. He becomes an appendage of the machine, and it is only the most simple, most monotonous, and most easily acquired knack, that is required of him. Hence, the cost of production of a workman is restricted almost entirely to the means of subsistence that he requires for his maintenance, and for the propagation of his race. But the price of a commodity, and therefore also of labor, is equal to its cost of production. In proportion, therefore, as the repulsiveness of the work increases, the wage decreases. Nay, more, in proportion as the use of machinery and division of labor increases, in the same proportion the burden of toil also increases, whether by prolongation of the working hours, by increase of the work enacted in a given time, or by increased speed of the machinery, etc.

Modern industry has converted the little workshop of patriarchal master into the great factory of the industrial capitalist. Masses of laborers, crowded into factories, are organized like soldiers. As privates of the industrialized army they are placed under the command of a perfect hierarchy of officers and sergeants. Not only are they the slaves of the bourgeois class, and of the bourgeois State, they are daily and hourly enslaved by the machine, by the over-looker, and, above all, by the individual bourgeois manufacturer himself. The more openly this despotism proclaims gain to be its end and aim, the more petty, the more hateful and the more embittering it is.

The less skill and exertion of strength implied in manual labor, in other words, the more modern industry becomes developed, the more is the labor of men superseded by that of women. Differences of age and sex have no longer any distinctive social validity for the working class. All are instruments of labor, more or less expensive to use, according to age and sex.

No sooner is the exploitation of the laborer by the manufacturer, so far at an end, that he receives his wages in cash, than he is set upon by the other portions of the bourgeoisie, the landlord, the shopkeeper, and pawnbroker, etc.

The lower strata of the middle class-the small tradespeople, shopkeepers, and retired tradesmen generally, the handicraftsmen and peasant-all these sink gradually into the proletariat, partly because their diminutive capital does not suffice for the scale on which modern industry is carried on, and is swamped in the competition with the large capitalists, partly because their specialized skill is rendered worthless by new methods of production. Thus the proletariat is recruited from all classes of the population.

The proletariat goes through various stages of development. With its birth begins its struggle with the bourgeoisie. At first the contest is carried on by individual laborers, then by the workpeople of a factory, then by the operatives of one trade, in one locality, against the individual bourgeois who directly exploits them. They direct their attacks not against the bourgeois conditions of production, but against the instruments of production themselves; they destroy imported wares that compete with their labor, they smash to pieces machinery, they set factories ablaze, they seek to restore by force the vanished status of the workman of the Middle Ages.

At this stage the laborers still form an incoherent mass scattered over the whole country, and broken up by their mutual competition. If anywhere they unite to form more compact bodies, this is not yet the consequence of their own active union, but of the union of the bourgeoisie, which class, in order to attain its own political ends, is compelled to set the whole proletariat in motion, and is moreover yet, for a time, able to do so. At this stage therefore, the proletarians do not fight their enemies, but the enemies of their enemies, the remnants of absolute monarchy, the landowners, the non-industrial bourgeois, the petty bourgeoisie. Thus the whole historical movement is concentrated in the hands of the bourgeoisie; every victory so obtained is a victory for the bourgeoisie.

But with the development of industry the proletariat not only increases in number; it becomes concentrated in greater masses, its strength grows and it feels that strength more. The various interests and conditions of life within the ranks of the proletariat are more and more equalized, in proportion as machinery obliterates all distinctions of labor, and nearly everywhere reduces wages to the same low level. The growing competition among the bourgeois, and the resulting commercial crises, make the wages of the workers even more fluctuating. The unceasing improvement of machinery, ever more rapidly developing, makes their livelihood more and more precarious; the collisions between individual workmen and individual bourgeois take more and more the character of collisions between two classes. Thereupon the workers begin to form combinations (Trades' Unions) against the bourgeois; they club together in order to keep up the rate of wages; they found permanent associations in order to make provision beforehand for these occasional revolts. Here and there the contest breaks out into riots.

Now and then the workers are victorious, but only for a time. The real fruit of their battles lies not in the immediate results but in the ever-improved means of communication that are created by modern industry, and that place the workers of different localities in contact with one another. It was just this contact that was needed to centralize the numerous local struggles, all of the same character, into one national struggle between classes. But every class struggle is a political struggle. And that union, to attain which the burghers of the Middle Ages, with their miserable highways, required centuries, the modern proletarians, thanks to railways, achieve in a few years.

This organization of the proletarians into a class, and consequently into a political party, is continually being upset again by the competition between the workers themselves. But it ever rises up again; stronger, firmer, mightier. It compels legislative recognition of particular interests of the workers, by taking advantage of the divisions among the bourgeoisie itself. Thus the ten-hours' bill in England was carried.

Altogether, collisions between the classes of the old society further, in many ways, the course of development of the proletariat. The bourgeoisie finds itself involved in a constant battle. At first with the aristocracy; later on, with those portions of the bourgeoisie itself, whose interests have become antagonistic to the progress of industry; at all times with the bourgeoisie of foreign countries. In all these countries it sees itself compelled to appeal to the proletariat, to ask for its help, and thus to drag it into the political arena. The bourgeoisie itself, therefore, supplies the proletariat with its own elements of political and general education, in other words, it furnishes the proletariat with weapons for fighting the bourgeoisie.

Further, as we have already seen, entire sections of the ruling classes are, by the advance of industry, precipitated into the proletariat, or are at least threatened in their conditions of existence. These also supply the proletariat with fresh elements of enlightenment and progress.

Finally, in times when the class struggle nears the decisive hour, the process of dissolution going on within the ruling class, in fact, within the whole range of an old society, assumes such a violent glaring character, that a small section of the ruling class cuts itself adrift, and joins the revolutionary class, the class that holds the future in its hands. Just as, therefore, at an earlier period, a section of the nobility went over to the bourgeoisie, so now a portion of the bourgeoisie goes over to the proletariat, and in particular, a portion of the bourgeoisie ideologists, who have raised themselves to the level of comprehending theoretically the historical movement as a whole.

Of all the classes that stand face to face with the bourgeoisie today the proletariat alone is a really revolutionary class. The other classes decay and finally disappear in the face of modern industry; the proletariat is its special and essential product.

The lower middle class, the small manufacturer, the shopkeeper, the artisan, the peasant, all these fight against the bourgeoisie to save from extinction their existence as fractions of the middle class. They are therefore not revolutionary, but conservative. Nay, more, they are reactionary, for they try to roll back the wheel of history. If by chance they are revolutionary, they are so only in view of their impending transfer into the proletariat; they thus defend not their present, but their future interests, they desert their own standpoint to place themselves at that of the proletariat.

The "dangerous class," the social scum, that passively rotting class thrown off by the lowest layers of old society, may, here and there, be swept into the movement by a proletarian revolution; its conditions of life, however, prepare it far more for the part of a bribed tool of reactionary intrigue.

In the conditions of the proletariat, those of the old society at large are already virtually swamped. The proletarian is without property; his relation to his wife and children has no longer anything in common with the bourgeois family relations; modern industrial labor, modern subjection to capital, the same in England as in France, in America as in Germany, has stripped him of every trace of national character. Law, morality, religion, are to him so many bourgeois prejudices, behind which lurk in ambush just as many bourgeois interests.

All the preceding classes that got the upper hand sought to fortify their already acquired status by subjecting society at large to their conditions of appropriation. The proletarians cannot become masters of the productive forces of society, except by abolishing their own previous mode of appropriation, and thereby also every other previous mode of appropriation. They have nothing of their own to secure and to fortify; their mission is to destroy all previous securities for, and insurances of, individual property.

All previous historical movements were movements of minorities, or in the interest of minorities. The proletarian movement is the self-conscious, independent movement of the immense majority, in the interest of the immense majority. The proletariat, the lowest stratum of our present society, cannot stir, cannot raise itself up, without the whole superincumbent strata of official society being sprung into the air.

Though not in substance, yet in form, the struggle of the proletariat with the bourgeoisie is at first a national struggle. The proletariat of each country must, of course, first of all settle matters with its own bourgeoisie.

In depicting the most general phases of the development of the proletariat, we traced the more or less veiled civil war, raging within existing society, up to the point where the war breaks out into open revolution, and where the violent overthrow of the bourgeoisie lays the foundation for the sway of the proletariat.

Hitherto every form of society has been based, as we have already seen, on the antagonism of oppressing and oppressed classes. But in order to oppress a class certain conditions must be assured to it under which it can, at least, continue its slavish existence. The serf, in the period of serfdom, raised himself to membership in the commune, just as the petty bourgeois, under the yoke of feudal absolutism, managed to develop into a bourgeois. The modern laborer, on the contrary, instead of rising with the progress of industry, sinks deeper and deeper below the conditions of existence of his own class. He becomes a pauper and pauperism develops more rapidly than population and wealth. And here it becomes evident that the bourgeoisie is unfit any longer to be the ruling class in society and to impose its conditions of existence upon society as an overriding law. It is unfit to rule because it is incompetent to assure an existence to its slave within his slavery, because it cannot help letting him sink into such a state that it has to feed him instead of being fed by him. Society can no longer live under this bourgeoisie, in other words its existence is no longer compatible with society.

The essential condition for the existence and for the sway of the bourgeois class, is the formation and augmentation of capital; the condition for capital is wage-labor. Wage-labor rests exclusively on competition between the laborers. The advance of industry, whose involuntary promoter is the bourgeoisie, replaces the isolation of the laborers, due to competition, by their revolutionary combination, due to association. The development of modern industry, therefore, cuts from under its feet the very foundation on which the bourgeoisie produces and appropriates products. What the bourgeoisie therefore produces above all, are its own gravediggers. Its fall and the victory of the proletariat are equally inevitable.

II

PROLETARIANS AND COMMUNISTS

In what relation do the Communists stand to the proletarians as a whole?

The Communists do not form a separate party opposed to other working class parties.

They have no interests separate and apart from those of the proletariat as a whole.

They do not set up any sectarian principles of their own by which to shape and mould the proletarian movement.

The Communists are distinguished from the other working class parties by this only: 1. In the national struggles of the proletarians of the different countries, they point out and bring to the front the common interests of the entire proletariat, independently of all nationality. 2. In the various stages of development which the struggle of the working class against the bourgeoisie has to pass through, they always and everywhere represent the interests of the movement as a whole.

The Communists, therefore, are on the one hand, practically, the most advanced and resolute section of the working class parties of every country, that section which pushes forward all others; on the other hand, theoretically, they have over the great mass of the proletariat the advantage of clearly understanding the line of march, the conditions, and the ultimate general results of the proletarian movement.

The immediate aim of the Communists is the same as that of all the other proletarian parties: formation of the proletariat into a class, overthrow of the bourgeois supremacy, conquest of political power by the proletariat.

The theoretical conclusions of the Communists are in no way based on ideas or principles that have been invented, or discovered, by this or that would-be universal reformer.

They merely express, in general terms, actual relations springing from an existing class struggle, from a historical movement going on under our very eyes. The abolition of existing property relations is not at all a distinctive feature of Communism.

All property relations in the past have continually been subject to historical change, consequent upon the change in historical conditions.

The French Revolution, for example, abolished feudal property in favor of bourgeois property.

The distinguishing feature of Communism is not the abolition of property generally, but the abolition of bourgeois property. But modern bourgeois private property is the final and most complete expression of the system of producing and appropriating products, that is based on class antagonisms, on the exploitation of the many by the few.

In this sense the theory of the Communists may be summed up in the single sentence: Abolition of private property.

We Communists have been reproached with the desire of abolishing the right of personally acquiring property as the fruit of a man's own labor, which property is alleged to be the groundwork of all personal freedom, activity, and independence.

Hard-won, self-acquired, self-earned property! Do you mean the property of the petty artisan and of the small peasant, a form of property that preceded the bourgeois form? There is no need to abolish that; the development of industry has to a great extent already destroyed it, and is still destroying it daily.

Or do you mean modern bourgeois private property?

But does wage-labor create any property for the laborer? Not a bit. It creates capital, i.e., that kind of property which exploits wage-labor, and which cannot increase except upon condition of begetting a new supply of wage-labor for fresh exploitation. Property, in its present form, is based on the antagonism of capital and wage-labor. Let us examine both sides of this antagonism.

To be a capitalist, is to have not only a purely personal, but a social *status* in production. Capital is a collective product, and only by the united action of many members, nay, in the last resort, only by the united action of all members of society, can it be set in motion.

Capital is therefore not a personal, it is a social power.

When, therefore, capital is converted into common property, into the property of all members of society, personal property is not thereby transformed into social property. It is only the social character of the property that is changed. It loses its class character.

Let us now take wage-labor.

The average price of wage-labor is the minimum wage, i.e., that quantum of the means of subsistence, which is absolutely requisite to keep the laborer in bare existence as a laborer. What, therefore, the wage-laborer appropriates by means of his labor, merely suffices to prolong and reproduce a bare existence. We by no means intend to abolish this personal appropriation of the products of labor, an appropriation that is made for the maintenance and reproduction of human life, and that leaves no surplus wherewith to command the labor of others. All that we want to do away with, is the miserable character of this appropriation, under which the laborer lives merely to increase capital, and is allowed to live only in so far as the interest of the ruling class requires it.

In bourgeois society living labor is but a means to increase accumulated labor. In Communist society accumulated labor is but a means to widen, to enrich, to promote the existence of the laborer.

In bourgeois society, therefore, the past dominates the present; in Communist society, the present dominates the past. In bourgeois society capital is independent and has individuality, while the living person is dependent and has no individuality.

And the abolition of this state of things is called by the bourgeois: abolition of individuality and freedom! And rightly so. The abolition of bourgeois individuality, bourgeois independence, and bourgeois freedom is undoubtedly aimed at.

By freedom is meant, under the present bourgeois conditions of production, free trade, free selling, and buying.

But if selling and buying disappears, free selling and buying disappears also. This talk about free selling and buying, and all the other "brave words" of our bourgeoisie about freedom in general, have a meaning, if any, only in contrast with restricted selling and buying, with the fettered traders of the Middle Ages, but have no meaning when opposed to the Communistic abolition of buying and selling, of the bourgeois conditions of production, and of the bourgeoisie itself.

You are horrified at our intending to do away with private property. But in your existing society private property is already done away with for nine-tenths of the population; its existence for the few is solely due to its non-existence in the hands of those nine-tenths. You reproach us, therefore, with intending to do away with a form of property, the necessary condition for whose existence is, the nonexistence of any property for the immense majority of society.

In one word, you reproach us with intending to do away with your property. Precisely so: that is just what we intend.

From the moment when labor can no longer be converted into capital, money, or rent, into a social power capable of being monopolized, i.e., from the moment when individual property can no longer be transformed into bourgeois property, into capital, from that moment, you say, individuality vanishes!

You must, therefore, confess that by "individual" you mean no other person than the bourgeois, than the middle-class owner of property. This person must, indeed, be swept out of the way, and made impossible.

Communism deprives no man of the power to appropriate the products of society: all that it does is to deprive him of the power to subjugate the labor of others by means of such appropriation.

It has been objected, that upon the abolition of private property all work will cease, and universal laziness will overtake us.

According to this, bourgeois society ought long ago to have gone to the dogs through sheer idleness; for those of its members who work, acquire nothing, and those who acquire anything, do not work. The whole of this objection is but another expression of the tautology: that there can no longer be any wage-labor when there is no longer any capital.

All objections against the communistic mode of producing and appropriating material products, have, in the same way, been urged against the communistic modes of producing and appropriating intellectual products. Just as, to the bourgeois, the disappearance of class property is the disappearance of production itself, so the disappearance of class structure is to him identical with the disappearance of all culture.

That culture, the loss of which he laments, is, for the enormous majority, a mere training to act as a machine.

But don't wrangle with us so long as you apply to our intended abolition of bourgeois property, the standard of your bourgeois notions of freedom, culture, law, etc. Your very ideas are but the outgrowth of the conditions of your bourgeois production and bourgeois property, just as your jurisprudence is but the will of your class made into a law for all, a will, whose essential character and direction are determined by the economical conditions of existence of your class.

The selfish misconception that induces you to transform into eternal laws of nature and of reason, the social forms springing from your present mode of production and form of property-historical relations that rise and disappear in the progress of production-this misconception you share with every ruling class that has preceded you. What you see clearly in the case of ancient property, what you admit in the case of feudal property, you are of course forbidden to admit in the case of your own bourgeois form of property.

Abolition of the family! Even the most radical flare up at this infamous proposal of the Communists.

On what foundation is the present family, the bourgeois family, based? On capital, on private gain. In its completely developed form this family exists only among the bourgeoisie. But this state of things finds its complement in the practical absence of the family among the proletarians and in public prostitution.

The bourgeois family will vanish as a matter of course when its complement vanishes, and both will vanish with the vanishing of capital.

Do you charge us with wanting to stop the exploitation of children by their parents? To this crime we plead guilty.

But, you will say, we destroy the most hallowed of relations, when we replace home education by social.

And your education! Is not that also social and determined by the social conditions under which you educate, by the intervention, direct or indirect, of society by means of schools, etc? The Communists have not invented the intervention of society in education; they do but seek to alter the character of that intervention, and to rescue education from the influence of the ruling class.

The bourgeois clap-trap about the family and education, about the hallowed co-relation of parent and child becomes all the more disgusting, as, by the action of modern industry, all family ties among the proletarians are torn asunder and their children transformed into simple articles of commerce and instruments of labor.

But you Communists would introduce community of women; screams the whole bourgeoisie in chorus.

The bourgeois sees in his wife a mere instrument of production. He heard that the instruments of production are to be exploited in common, and, naturally, can come to no other conclusion than that the lot of being common to all will likewise fall to the women.

He has not even a suspicion that the real point aimed at is to do away with the status of women as mere instruments of production.

For the rest nothing is more ridiculous than the virtuous indignation of our bourgeois at the community of women which, they pretend, is to be openly and officially established by the Communists. The Communists have no need to introduce community of women; it has existed almost from time immemorial.

Our bourgeois, not content with having the wives and daughters of their proletarians at their disposal, not to speak of common prostitutes, take the greatest pleasure in seducing each other's wives.

Bourgeois marriage is in reality a system of wives in common and thus, at the most, what the Communists might possibly be reproached with, is that they desire to introduce, in substitution for a hypocritically concealed, an openly legalized community of women. For the rest it is self-evident that the abolition of the present system of production must bring with it the abolition of the community of women springing from that system, i.e., of prostitution both public and private.

The Communists are further reproached with desiring to abolish countries and nationality.

The workingmen have no country. We cannot take from them what they have not got. Since the proletariat must first of all acquire political supremacy, must rise to be the leading class of the nation, must constitute itself the nation, it is, so far, itself national though not in the bourgeois sense of the word.

National differences and antagonisms between peoples are daily more and more vanishing, owing to the development of the bourgeoisie, to freedom of commerce, to the world's market, to uniformity in the mode of production and in the conditions of life corresponding thereto.

The supremacy of the proletariat will cause them to vanish still faster. United action, of the leading civilized countries at least, is one of the first conditions for the emancipation of the proletariat.

In proportion as the exploitation of one individual by another is put an end to, the exploitation of one nation by another will also be put an end to. In proportion as the antagonism between classes within the nation vanishes, the hostility of one nation to another will come to an end.

The charges against Communism made from a religious, a philosophical, and, generally, from an ideological standpoint, are not deserving of serious examination.

Does it require deep intuition to comprehend that man's ideas, views, and conceptions, in one word, man's consciousness changes with every change in the conditions of his material existence, in his social relations and in his social life?

What else does the history of ideas prove than that intellectual production changes its character in proportion as material production is changed? The ruling ideas of each age have ever been the ideas of its ruling class.

When people speak of ideas that revolutionize society they do but express the fact that within the old society the elements of a new one have been created, and that the dissolution of the old ideas keeps even pace with the dissolution of the old conditions of existence.

When the ancient world was in its last throes, the ancient religions were overcome by Christianity. When Christian ideas succumbed in the eighteenth century to rationalist ideas, feudal society fought its death-battle with the then revolutionary bourgeoisie. The ideas of religious liberty and freedom of conscience merely gave expression to the sway of free competition within the domain of knowledge.

"Undoubtedly," it will be said, "religious, moral, philosophical," and juridical ideas have been modified in the course of historic development. But religion, morality, philosophy, political science, and law, constantly survived this change.

"There are besides, eternal truths, such as Freedom, Justice, etc., that are common to all states of society. But Communism abolishes eternal truths, it abolishes all religion and all morality, instead of constituting them on a new basis; it therefore acts as a contradiction to all past historical experience."

What does this accusation reduce itself to? The history of all past society has consisted in the development of class antagonisms, antagonisms that assumed different forms at different epochs.

But whatever form they may have taken, one fact is common to all past ages, viz., the exploitation of one part of society by the other. No wonder, then, that the social consciousness of past ages, despite all the multiplicity and variety it displays, moves within certain common forms, or general ideas, which cannot completely vanish except with the total disappearance of class antagonisms.

The Communist revolution is the most radical rupture with traditional property relations; no wonder that its development involves the most radical rupture with traditional ideas.

But let us have done with the bourgeois objections to Communism.

We have seen above that the first step in the revolution by the working class is to raise the proletariat to the position of the ruling class, to win the battle of democracy.

The proletariat will use its political supremacy to wrest, by degrees, all capital from the bourgeoisie; to centralize all instruments of production in the hands of the State, i.e., of the proletariat organized as the ruling class; and to increase the total of productive forces as rapidly as possible.

Of course, in the beginning this cannot be effected except by means of despotic inroads on the rights of property and on the conditions of bourgeois production; by means of measures, therefore, which appear economically insufficient and untenable, but which, in the course of the movement, outstrip themselves, necessitate further inroads upon the old social order and are unavoidable as a means of entirely revolutionizing the mode of production.

These measures will of course be different in different countries.

Nevertheless in the most advanced countries the following will be pretty generally applicable:

1. *Abolition of property in land and application of all rents of land to public purposes.*
2. *A heavy progressive or graduated income tax.*
3. *Abolition of all rights of inheritance.*
4. *Confiscation of the property of all emigrants and rebels.*
5. *Centralization of credit in the hands of the State, by means of a national bank with State capital and an exclusive monopoly.*
6. *Centralization of the means of communication and transport in the hands of the State.*
7. *Extension of factories and instruments of production owned by the State; the bringing into cultivation of waste lands, and the improvement of the soil generally in accordance with a common plan.*
8. *Equal liability of all to labor Establishment of industrial armies, especially for agriculture.*
9. *Combination of agriculture with manufacturing industries: gradual abolition of the distinction between town and country, by a more equable distribution of the population over the country.*
10. *Free education for all children in public schools. Abolition of children's factory labor in its present form. Combination of education with industrial production, etc.*

When, in the course of development, class distinctions have disappeared and all production has been concentrated in the hands of a vast association of the whole nation, the public power will lose its political character. Political power, properly so called, is merely the organized power of one class for oppressing another. If the proletariat during its contest with the bourgeoisie is compelled, by the force of circumstances, to organize itself as a class, if, by means of a revolution, it makes itself the ruling class, and, as such, sweeps away by force the old conditions of production, then it will, along with these conditions, have swept away the conditions for the existence of class antagonism, and of classes generally, and will thereby have abolished its own supremacy as a class.

In place of the old bourgeois society with its classes and class antagonisms we shall have an association in which the free development of each is the condition for the free development of all.

• • •

IV

POSITION OF THE COMMUNISTS IN RELATION TO THE VARIOUS EXISTING OPPOSITION PARTIES

Section II has made clear the relations of the Communist to the existing working class parties, such as the Chartists in England and the Agrarian Reformers in America.

The Communists fight for the attainment of the immediate aims, for the enforcement of the momentary interests of the working class; but in the movement of the present they also represent and take care of the future of that movement. In France the Communists ally themselves with Social-Democrats, against the conservative and radical bourgeoisie, reserving, however, the right to take up a critical position in regard to phrases and illusions traditionally handed down from the great Revolution.

In Switzerland they support the Radicals, without losing sight of the fact that this party consists of antagonistic elements, partly of Democratic Socialists, in the French sense, partly of radical bourgeois.

In Poland they support the party that insists on an agrarian revolution, as the prime condition for national emancipation, that party which fomented the insurrection of Cracow in 1846.

In Germany they fight with the bourgeoisie whenever it acts in a revolutionary way against the absolute monarchy, the feudal squirearchy, and the petty bourgeoisie.

But they never cease, for a single instant, to instill into the working class the clearest possible recognition of the hostile antagonism between bourgeoisie and proletariat, in order that the German workers may straightway use, as so many weapons against the bourgeoisie the social and political conditions that the bourgeoisie must necessarily introduce along with its supremacy, and in order that, after the fall of the reactionary classes in Germany, the fight against the bourgeoisie itself may immediately begin.

The Communists turn their attention chiefly to Germany, because that country is on the eve of a bourgeois revolution that is bound to be carried out under more advanced conditions of European civilization, and with a much more developed proletariat, than that of England was in the seventeenth, and of France in the eighteenth century, and because the bourgeois revolution in Germany will be but the prelude to an immediately following proletarian revolution.

In short, the Communists everywhere support every revolutionary movement against the existing social and political order of things.

In all these movements they bring to the front, as the leading question in each, the property question, no matter what its degree of development at the time.

Finally, they labor everywhere for the union and agreement of the democratic parties of all countries.

The Communists disdain to conceal their views and aims. They openly declare that their ends can be attained only by the forcible overthrow of all existing social conditions. Let the ruling classes tremble at a communistic revolution. The proletarians have nothing to lose but their chains. They have a world to win.

Working men of all countries, unite!

Questions:
1. *What do Marx and Engels mean by the terms "bourgeois" and "proletariat"?*
2. *How do you think a nineteen century factory worker, as described in the last section, would have responded to the Communist Manifesto? Why?*

PART 20
Nationalism and Imperialism

20.1 Program of the Serb Society of National Defense [Narodna Odbrana]

Certainly one of the most violent national movements throughout the nineteenth and twentieth centuries, one that combined both the irredentist and militant strains of nationalism, was Balkan nationalism. "Balkan" is the Turkish word for mountain, and the rugged topography of the Balkan peninsula of southeastern Europe contributed mightily to the development of Balkan nationalism. Serbia, the largest of all the Balkan states, long considered itself the natural leader of all Balkan peoples and bitterly resented the interference of Austria-Hungary and Ottoman Turkey in Balkan affairs. After nearly five centuries of subjugation, Serbia gained its independence from Turkey in 1878 and aggressively sought to assert its hegemony over the entire Balkan peninsula. Early in the twentieth century, the executive committee of a Serbian patriotic society, the Society of National Defense, published its program for Serbian nationalism. Unlike many abstract, theoretical statements of nationalism, this document is a practical step-by-step blueprint for igniting Serbian nationalism to resist continued foreign interference and to prepare for a greater Serbian role in Balkan politics.

Source: *Narodna Odbrana Izdanje Stredisnog Odbora Odbrane* (Belgrade, 1911), translated into German and printed in *Die Kriegsschuldfrage* (Berlin, 1927), V, 192–225 *in Europe in the Nineteenth Century: A Documentary Analysis of Change and Conflict,* ed., Eugene N. Anderson. Stanley J. Pinceti, Jr., and Donald J. Ziegler 2:329–31; 316–22. Reprinted by permission of Prentice-Hall, Inc., Upper Saddle River, NJ.

It is quite wrong to think Kossowo[1] once existed, is past, and that today it must simply be avenged. Kossowo is still among us, or, to put it differently, we are today in the middle of Kossowo, and we are not avenging it but fighting on its battlefield.

The Serbian people are always fighting the battle of Kossowo, only the battlefield changes form. Our present Kossowo is the darkness and ignorance in which the Serbs live. Barbarism of every kind, unhygienic conditions, lack of national consciousness, party and other feuds—these are the Turks of today against whom we must set out to a new Kossowo. These internal causes of a new Kossowo are considerable; there are external causes too, however, beyond our boundaries in the north and west—the Germans, the Austrians, and the Swabians with their drive toward our Serb and Slavic south. Darkness and ignorance among our people within and the German invasion from outside are the new Turks whom we must meet today on the Serb battlefield of Kossowo and with whom we have to resume the struggle for the Serbian name and Serbian freedom.

The freedom of a people is just as incomplete when it is in bondage to ignorance as when it is in physical bondage. Man can be enserfed also to errors, prejudices, ignorance, love of drink, barbarism. War must be waged against all these evils. Just as we once rebelled against the Turks, we must now rebel against these evil national conditions and fight for freedom from them.

The view that there is war only when the guns thunder and the rifles crack is a false one. Among nations there is never peace, but always a condition of war; life goes forward under the sign of struggle. Even today in the middle of peace the Serbs are waging a desperate war. Woe to him who does not know it. This war is our present fight for our soil, our health, civilization, knowledge, schools, physical culture—as we have described it already in the section "The New Contemporary *Narodna Odbrana.*"

The *Narodna Odbrana,* convinced of this conception of our present position, expects that it will find among the unknown teachers and priests, among the students, merchants, and other modest workers displaying private initiative in all directions, new heroes such as are demanded by today's Kossowo, today's war for our freedom. Milosch Obilitsch fought his way through Turkish swords and lances to the tent of Mured to murder him. Our new contemporary hero, whether teacher or priest or some other national worker, must make his way through insults, humiliations, and injustice in order to drive darkness and ignorance from the soul of the people. Singjelitsch in the defense of the newly created Serbia blew himself and his companions up along with the breastwork. The national worker today must often sacrifice his personal happiness and his family in order to agitate day by day for the freeing of our society from the sins of disease, poverty, lack of national consciousness, and so on.

---

[1] The Turks crushed the Serbian-Albanian-Croatian army at Kossowo (also spelled as Kosovo or Kossovo) in 1389 and conquered the country, but Milosch Obilitsch, a Serb hero of the battle, succeeded in penetrating the Turkish line and slaying the Turkish sultan. The anniversary of the battle and of the assassination has been commemorated on June 28, a Serbian national holiday.

Questions:
1. *Scholars have both praised and criticized the Serbs for celebrating June 28, the battle of Kossowo, one of their greatest defeats, as their national holiday. What does this choice of national holiday, commemorating a defeat in the fourteenth century, tell us about Serbian nationalism?*
2. *Why would the Society of National Defense choose the present tense to describe the significance of the battle of Kossowo, a battle that took place in 1389? What does this insistence upon using the present tense and avenging the battle of Kossowo suggest about the character and spirit of Serbian nationalism?*
3. *As a part of its plan to develop Serbian nationalism, the Society of National Defense lists the following five elements: national consciousness, physical development, new methods of work, rifle clubs, and gymnastic societies. Which of these elements do you think is most important for the development of Serbian nationalism? Why?*
4. *How would you compare the Society of National Defense's definition of nationalism with that of Fustel de Coulanges?*
5. *Even though this document was written nearly a century ago, do you see any contemporary implications in the Program of the Serb Society of National Defense? What are they?*

20.2   Irish National Identity and Destiny: Three Views

Although once independent, from the early twelfth to the early twentieth centuries Ireland was governed by Great Britain. For more than four hundred years, the bitter tensions between the oppressed Irish Catholic majority and the dominant English-Protestant ruling minority frequently erupted in grim scenes of bloody, sectarian violence. In 1912, while the British Parliament was seriously considering greater internal autonomy for Ireland (Home Rule), the powerful Ulster Unionist Party, representing the Protestant majority of the six northern counties of Ireland, declared its unalterable opposition to Home Rule. Fearing that the British government's proposed Home Rule of 1912 would threaten their political and religious rights, the Ulster Unionist leaders declared September 12, 1912, "Ulster Day." In imitation of their seventeenth-century Presbyterian ancestors who pledged to establish the Presbyterian creed in England and Ireland, about 450,000 men and women signed this document (some with their own blood) denouncing Home Rule for Ireland's Catholic majority.

The outbreak of World War I in 1914 temporarily shelved the issue of Home Rule for Ireland until 1916 when the Sinn Fein ("we ourselves") movement vigorously resisted British military recruitment in Ireland for the fighting in France and urged an immediate reopening of the stalled debate on Home Rule. During Easter week 1916, Sinn Fein led a bloody, week-long rebellion in Dublin protesting British rule, culminating in the Declaration of a Provisional Government for an Irish Republic. The Easter Rising was brutally suppressed, but the political agitation, violence, and fighting among Irish Republicans, Ulster Unionists, and the British troops continued until a truce was signed on December 6, 1921, recognizing the twenty-six counties of southern Ireland as the Irish Free State within the British Commonwealth of Nations. During that Easter-week rising, four hundred people were killed and one thousand wounded. This event, perhaps more than any other, sealed the connections between militant Irish nationalism and the future Irish Republic.

The six counties of Northern Ireland (Ulster) withdrew from this Irish Free State and chose to remain part of the United Kingdom. In 1937, the Irish Free State changed its name to Érie and in 1947, Érie ceased to be a member of the British Commonwealth. Unfortunately, these political arrangements did not end the bloodshed or the violence. The outlawed Irish Republican Army (IRA) has advanced its goal of unity for the two Irelands by attacking British military units in Northern Ireland and by terror-bombing its political enemies throughout the United Kingdom. So, too, the political authorities of Northern Ireland, supported by the British military government, have a well-established record of denying the Catholic minority of Northern Ireland civic, political, and economic rights and have used brutality and torture in interrogating IRA suspects and their supporters.

The last statement in the following reading was made by Eamon De Valera (1882–1975), who served as the Republic of Ireland's (Érie) prime minister for twenty-one years. In a radio broadcast beamed to the United States on February 12, 1933, Lincoln's birthday, he explained his views on Irish nationalism and his dream of a united Ireland.

Source: First part from *The Times*, May 1, 1916; second part from *The Times*, September 20, 1912; third part from Maurice Moynihan, ed., *Speeches and Statements by Eamon De Valera*, 1917–1973, p. 234. Copyright © Maurice Moynihan. Reprinted by permission of St. Martin's Press, Incorporated.

IRISH DECLARATION OF INDEPENDENCE

The Provisional Government of the Irish republic to the people of Ireland

Irishmen and Irishwomen: In the name of God and of the dead generations from which she receives her old tradition of nationhood, Ireland, through us, summons her children to her flag and strikes for her freedom.

Having organized and trained her manhood through her secret revolutionary organization, the Irish Republican Brotherhood, and through her open military organizations, the Irish Volunteers, and the Irish Citizen Army, having patiently perfected her discipline, having resolutely waited for the right moment to reveal itself, she now seizes that moment, and, supported by her exiled children in America and by gallant allies in Europe, but relying in the first on her own strength, she strikes in full confidence of victory.

We declare the right of the people of Ireland to the ownership of Ireland, and to the unfettered control of Irish destinies, to be sovereign and indefeasible. The long usurpation of that right by a foreign people and government has not extinguished the right, nor can it ever be extinguished except by the destruction of the Irish people. In every generation the Irish people have asserted their right to national freedom and sovereignty; six times during the past three hundred years they have asserted it in arms. Standing on that fundamental right and again asserting it in arms in the face of the world, we hereby proclaim the Irish republic as a sovereign independent state, and we pledge our lives and the lives of our comrades-in-arms to the cause of its freedom, of its welfare, and of its exaltation among the nations.

The Irish republic is entitled to, and hereby claims, the allegiance of every Irishman and Irishwoman. The republic guarantees religious and civil liberty, equal rights and equal opportunities to all its citizens, and declares its resolve to pursue the happiness and prosperity of the whole nation and of all its parts, cherishing all the children of the nation equally, and oblivious of the differences carefully fostered by an alien government, which have divided a minority from the majority in the past.

Until our arms have brought the opportune moment for the establishment of a permanent national government, representative of the whole people of Ireland, and elected by the suffrages of all her men and women, the Provisional Government, hereby constituted, will administer the civil and military affairs of the republic in trust for the people. We place the cause of the Irish republic under the protection of the Most High God, whose blessing we invoke upon our arms, and we pray that no one who serves that cause will dishonour it by cowardice, inhumanity, or rapine. In this supreme hour the Irish nation must, by its valour and discipline, and by the readiness of its children to sacrifice themselves for the common good, prove itself worthy of the august destiny to which it is called.

Signed on behalf of the provisional government,

THOMAS J. CLARKE, SEAN MACDIARMADA, THOMAS MACDONAGH, P.H. PEARSE, EAMONN CEANNT, JAMES CONNOLLY, JOSEPH PLUNKETT.

ULSTER'S SOLEMN LEAGUE AND COVENANT

Being convinced in our consciences that Home Rule would be disastrous to the material well-being of Ulster, as well as of the whole of Ireland, subversive of our civil and religious freedom, destructive of our citizenship, and perilous to the unity of the Empire, we, whose names are underwritten, men of Ulster, loyal subjects of His Gracious Majesty King George V, humbly relying on the God Whom our fathers in the days of stress and trial confidently trusted, do hereby pledge ourselves in solemn Covenant throughout this our time of threatened calamity to stand by one another in defending for ourselves and our children our cherished position of equal citizenship in the United Kingdom and in using all means which may be found necessary to defeat the present conspiracy to set up a home rule parliament in Ireland. And in the event of such a Parliament being forced upon us we further and mutually pledge ourselves to refuse to recognize its authority. In sure confidence that God will defend the right, we hereto subscribe our names. And further we individually declare that we have not already signed this Covenant. God Save the King.

EAMON DE VALERA ON IRISH NATIONALISM

Ireland is more than a political union of states. It has been a nation from the dawn of history, united in traditions, in political institutions, in territory. The island is too small to be divided; it does not need and cannot afford two governments, with all the duplication of services and expenses which that involves. The pretext that partition was necessary to save a minority of Irishmen from religious persecution at the hands of the majority was an invention without any basis in the facts of our time or in the history of the past. No nation respects the rights of conscience more than Ireland, whose people too long bore persecution themselves to desire to inflict it on others. But British policy was not even consistent with the pretext invented to justify it; on the plea of saving one religious minority, it created two; on the plea of protecting the rights of a powerful and well-organised Protestant minority of twenty-five per cent, it split that minority, leaving part of it as a helpless remnant scattered through twenty-six counties.

Partition has no political or economic justification. The six counties cut off from the rest of Ireland had never been a political or administrative unit, and they could never hope to be in any measure an economic entity. They did not even comprise the whole of Ulster; that province itself, which British politicians affect to regard as holy ground, was not spared from mutilation. The erection of this six-county area into a petty state, under the ultimate control of the British Parliament and subsidised by the British Treasury, was a purely arbitrary act, inspired solely by considerations of British imperial policy and contrary to every interest of the Irish people. Imposed by force and maintained by subsidies, partition is the worst of all the many crimes committed by British statesmen against the Irish people during the last 750 years.

The area that Ireland has lost contains many of her holiest and most famous places. There is Armagh, the See of St Patrick; Downpatrick, his burial place, where lies also the body of Brian, who drove out the Danish invaders; Bangor, the site of one of the greatest of Ireland's ancient schools; Derry of St Columcille; Tyrone of the O'Neills; MacArt's Fort, where Wolfe Tone swore to work for Irish freedom; Belfast, the birthplace of the Irish Republican movement.1 Ireland never can abandon the hope of regaining a territory hallowed by so many memories, the scene of so many of the most heroic incidents of her history. The efforts of her people will inevitably be bent upon the undoing of partition until all the land within her four seas is once more united.

"Ireland not free merely but Gaelic as well," wrote Pádraig Pearse, who died before partition was effected. "Ireland not free and Gaelic merely but united also"—that is the objective of the Irish people today, and it will remain their unshakable resolve until it has been finally attained.

Questions:

1. How does the first document suggest the historic fault lines of religion and politics in the shaping of Irish nationalism?
2. Why would the Ulster Unionists choose to title their pledge a "Solemn League and Covenant"?
3. Why would the Provisional Government cite the "exiled children in America" but omit mentioning "Great Britain" or "King George V"?
4. How would you compare this definition of Irish nationalism with the documents on Serbian and French nationalism?
5. In light of centuries of sectarian violence between Catholics and Protestants, how persuasive is De Valera's argument that Ireland is simply too small a country for two separate governments?
6. De Valera argues that the erection of the six counties of Ulster "was a purely arbitrary act, inspired solely by considerations of British imperial policy and contrary to every interest of the Irish people." In light of the 1912 "Ulster's Solemn League and Covenant," is this true?

20.3 Fustel de Coulanges, "What Is a Nation?" A Reply to Mr. Mommsen, Professor in Berlin

An expression of French nationalism, incorporating both elements of nineteenth-century nationalism, was written by Fustel de Coulanges in the early autumn of 1870. In the midst of the Franco-Prussian War, de Coulanges, a French historian teaching in Alsace at the University of Strasbourg, wrote an open letter to the German historian Theodor Mommsen explaining why the French-controlled province of Alsace should remain French and not become part of any new German state. Prussia defeated France, and despite de Coulanges's arguments, the two French provinces of Alsace and Lorraine were taken from France in 1871 and appended to a new, united Germany. In 1919, as part of the Treaty of Versailles, Alsace and Lorraine were returned to France. In many ways, the arguments of de Coulanges, though focused on two small provinces, exemplified the contentious spirit and emotional fervor of late-nineteenth-century European nationalism.

Source: From *Fustel de Coulanges, Questions historiques revues et completées d'après les notes de l'auteur par Camille Jullian* (Paris: Librarie Hachette, 1893), pp. 505–11. Trans. G. de Bertier de Sauvigny and Philip F. Riley.

PARIS, OCTOBER 27, 1870

Sir:

You have lately addressed three letters to the Italian people. These letters, which were first published in Milan newspapers and were afterwards brought together in a pamphlet, are a real manifesto against our nation. You have relinquished your historical studies to drive an attack upon France; I therefore leave mine in order to reply. . . .

This past August, you indicated with perfect clarity that the true bone of contention between France and Prussia is Alsace and Lorraine. Bismarck [the Prussian premier] has not made this pronouncement as yet. He has not admitted that you are making war to take Alsace and Lorraine, but you are a discerning prophet and you have revealed the intentions and the goal of Prussia. You have clearly announced that it will be the object of this new war against our nation. Today no one can ignore that the issue that has engaged the young men of Germany and of France is clearly the question: Does Alsace belong to France or to Germany?

Prussia is determined to resolve this question by force, but force alone will not suffice for there is also the question of what is right. While your armies invade Alsace and bombard Strasbourg, you strive to prove that it is legitimate and lawful to control Alsace and Strasbourg. Alsace, according to you, is a German country: therefore she should belong to Germany. She was part of Germany in times past; from there you conclude that she should be handed back. She uses the German language, and you draw inferences now that Prussia may seize her. You call that the principle of nationality.

It is on this score that I want to reply because it is true that in this horrible duel, we know that right is not on the same side as force. It is also true that we know that Alsace has been wronged and that she is defending herself because Prussia has bombarded Strasbourg. You invoke the principle of nationality, but you understand it much differently than the rest of Europe. According to you, this principle would allow a powerful state to take hold of a province by force on the sole condition that this province is inhabited by the same race as that state. But according to Europe and to common sense, nationalism would also allow for a population or a province to refuse to submit to a foreign master against her will. I shall explain this by an example: the principle of nationality did not allow Piedmont to conquer by force Milan and Venice; but it authorized Milan and Venice to free themselves from Austria and join voluntarily to Piedmont. You see the difference. This principle may well give Alsace the right, but it does not give you any upon her.

I beg you to examine this question maturely, loyally! By what do you distinguish nationality? By what do you recognize the fatherland?

You believe you have proved that Alsace is of German nationality because its population is of Germanic race and because its language is German. But I am surprised that a historian like you feigns to ignore that it is neither race nor language that makes nationality.

It is not race. Have a look at Europe, and you will see that the people are almost never constituted after their primitive origins. Geographical conveniences, political or commercial interests are those which have brought populations together and founded states. Each nation has thus slowly been formed, each fatherland has taken shape without taking in account these ethnographical factors that you would like to bring into fashion. Your theory of race is contrary to the present state of Europe. If nations only corresponded to race, Belgium would belong to France, Portugal would belong to Spain, and Holland would belong to Prussia. By the same token, Scotland should detach itself from England to whom she has been closely tied for a century and one-half. And Russia and Austria should each divide into three or four pieces; Switzerland should be split into two parts, and most assuredly Poznan (a Polish-speaking city) should not be controlled by Berlin. If your idea would prevail the entire world would have to be reformed.

Language is no more a characteristic sign of nationality. Five languages are spoken in France, and nevertheless no one would dare challenge our national unity. Three languages are spoken in Switzerland. Is Switzerland less of a nation, and would you say she is lacking in patriotism? Americans speak English: do you think that the United States should reestablish ties with England? You take pride in noting that in the city of Strasbourg German is spoken, but it is also true that it was in Strasbourg that one heard for the first time our *Marseillaise*.

What distinguishes nations is neither race nor language. Men feel in their hearts that they belong to a same people when they have a community of ideas, of interests, of affections, of memories and hopes. This is what makes a fatherland. This is why men want to march together, work together, live and die for one another. The fatherland is what one loves. It may be that Alsace is German by race and language. But by nationality and the sentiment of fatherland she is French. And do you know what has made Alsace French? It was not the conquests of Louis XIV, but it was our Revolution of 1789. Since that moment, Alsace has followed our destinies and lived our life. Everything that we have thought, she has thought. All that we have felt, she has felt. She has been part of our victories and part of our defeats, part of our success and part of our mistakes, part of all of our joys and all of our sorrows. She has nothing in common with you. For Alsace the fatherland is France, and Germany is the foreigner.

All the reasoning in the world will change nothing. It might be impressive to invoke ethnology and philology, but we are not in a university classroom. We are at the very center of the human heart. Your reasoning and your arguments insist that Alsace should have a German heart, but my eyes and my ears assure me that her heart is French. You insist that for a long time Alsace has harbored a spirit of provincial opposition to France, but based upon my close examination here of men from all classes, religions and political parties, I have never encountered this spirit of opposition to France. You insinuate that Alsatians have a great antipathy to Parisians, but I find that they are warmly welcomed here. In its heart and in its spirit, Alsace is one of the most Francophile of all our provinces. The Strasbourgers have, as we all do, two fatherlands: their native city, and then above all France. No thought is given to Germany because she is not considered a fatherland.

You are certainly an eminent historian, but when we speak of the present let us not fix our eyes only on the past. Race is part of history, but it is of the past. Language is certainly part of history, but it remains a sign of the distant past. That which is present and living are the aspirations, the ideas, the interests and the affections. History tells you perhaps that Alsace is a German country; but the present proves that she is a French country. It would be childish to assert she must return to Germany because she was part of it some centuries ago. Are we going to reinstate all that was in past times? If so, I ask, what Europe shall we go back to? That of the eighteenth century or that of the fifteenth century, or to that time when old Gaul possessed the whole of the Rhine, and when Strasbourg, Saverne, and Colmar were Roman cities?

Let us live in our times. We have today something better than history to guide us. We have in the nineteenth century a principle of public law which is infinitely clearer and more indisputable than your pretended principle of nationality. Our principle is that a population can be governed only by the institutions it accepts freely and that it must be part of a state only by its will and free consent. This is the modern principle. It is today the only foundation of order, and it is to this that must rally whoever is at the same time friend of peace and supporter of progress of mankind. Whether Prussia wishes it or not this principle will triumph. If Alsace remains French it is because she wishes to be. You can only make her German if she herself wishes to be German.

Questions:

1. Why does Fustel de Coulanges argue that language is not the proper basis of nationality? According to de Coulanges, what is the proper basis of nationality?
2. Why does de Coulanges reject the legitimacy of Louis XIV's seventeenth-century conquest of Alsace and, instead, invoke the French Revolution as the basis of Alsace's affiliation with France?
3. According to de Coulanges, what is the definition of a nation?

20.4 Lord William Bentinck, Comments on Ritual Murder and the Limits of Religious Toleration

The pros and cons of intervening in these cases are weighed in the following selection by Lord William Bentinck (1774–1839), who was appointed governor-general of the East India Company in 1828.

> **Source:** From "Lord William Bentinck on the Suppression of *Sati*, 8 November 1829," in *Speeches and Documents on Indian Policy*, 1750–1921, ed. Arthur B. Keith (Oxford: Oxford University Press, 1922), Vol. 1, pp. 208–26.

Whether the question be to continue or to discontinue the practice of *sati*, the decision is equally surrounded by an awful responsibility. To consent to the consignment year after year of hundreds of innocent victims to a cruel and untimely end, when the power exists of preventing it, is a predicament which no conscience can contemplate without horror. But, on the other hand, if heretofore received opinions are to be considered of any value, to put to hazard by a contrary course the very safety of the British Empire in India, and to extinguish at once all hopes of those great improvements—affecting the condition not of hundreds and thousands but of millions—which can only be expected from the continuance of our supremacy, is an alternative which even in the light of humanity itself may be considered as a still greater evil. It is upon this first and highest consideration alone, the good of mankind, that the tolerance of this inhuman and impious rite can in my opinion be justified on the part of the government of a civilized nation. While the solution of this question is appalling from the unparalleled magnitude of its possible results, the considerations belonging to it are such as to make even the stoutest mind distrust its decision. On the one side, Religion, Humanity, under the most appalling form, as well as vanity and ambition—in short, all the most powerful influences over the human heart—are arrayed to bias and mislead the judgment. On the other side, the sanction of countless ages, the example of all the Mussulman conquerors, the unanimous concurrence in the same policy of our own most able rulers, together with the universal veneration of the people, seem authoritatively to forbid, both to feeling and to reason, any interference in the exercise of their natural prerogative. In venturing to be the first to deviate from this practice it becomes me to show that nothing has been yielded to feeling, but that reason, and reason alone, has governed the decision.

It must be first observed that of the 463 *satis* occurring in the whole of the Presidency of Fort William, 420 took place in Bengal, Behar, and Orissa, or what is termed the Lower Provinces, and of these latter 287 in the Calcutta Division alone.

It might be very difficult to make a stranger to India understand, much less believe, that in a population of so many millions of people as the Calcutta Division includes, and the same may be said of all the Lower Provinces, so great is the want of courage and of vigour of character, and such the habitual submission of centuries, that insurrection or hostile opposition to the will of the ruling power may be affirmed to be an impossible danger. . . .

If, however, security was wanting against extensive popular tumult or revolution, I should say that the Permanent Settlement, which, though a failure in many other respects and in its most important essentials, has this great advantage at least, of having created a vast body of rich landed proprietors deeply interested in the continuance of the British Dominion and having complete command over the mass of the people. . . .

Were the scene of this sad destruction of human life laid in the Upper instead of the Lower Provinces, in the midst of a bold and manly people, I might speak with less confidence upon the question of safety. In these Provinces the *satis* amount to forty-three only upon a population of nearly twenty millions. It cannot be expected that any general feeling, where combination of any kind is so unusual, could be excited in defense of a rite in which so few participate, a rite also notoriously made too often subservient to views of personal interest on the part of the other members of the family. . . .

But I have taken up too much time in giving my own opinion when those of the greatest experience and highest official authority are upon our records. In the report of the Nizamat Adalat for 1828, four out of five of the Judges recommended to the Governor-General in Council the immediate abolition of the practice, and attest its safety. The fifth Judge, though not opposed to the opinions of the rest of the Bench, did not feel then prepared to give his entire assent. In the report of this year the measure has come up with the unanimous recommendation of the Court. . . . No documents exist to show the opinions of the public functionaries in the interior, but I am informed that nine-tenths are in favour of the abolition. . . .

Having made inquiries, also, how far *satis* are permitted in the European foreign settlements, I find from Dr. Carey that at Chinsurah no such sacrifices had ever been permitted by the Dutch Government. That within the limits of Chandarnagar itself they were also prevented, but allowed to be performed in the British territories. The Danish Government of Serampur has not forbidden the rite, in conformity to the example of the British Government.

It is a very important fact that, though representations have been made by the disappointed party to superior authority, it does not appear that a single instance of direct opposition to the execution of the prohibitory orders of our civil functionaries has ever occurred. How, then, can it be reasonably feared that to the Government itself, from whom all authority is derived, and whose power is now universally considered to be irresistible, anything bearing the semblance of resistance can be manifested? Mr. Wilson also is of opinion that no immediate overt act of insubordination would follow the publication of the edict. The Regulation of Government may be evaded, the police may be corrupted, but even here the price paid as hush money will operate as a penalty, indirectly forwarding the object of Government.

I venture, then, to think it completely proved that from the native population nothing of extensive combination, or even of partial opposition, may be expected from the abolition. . . .

I have now to submit for the consideration of Council the draft of a regulation enacting the abolition of *satis*. . . . It is only in the previous process, or during the actual performance of the rite, when the feelings of all may be more or less roused to a high degree of excitement, that I apprehend the possibility of affray or of acts of violence through an indiscreet and injudicious exercise of authority. It seemed to me prudent, therefore, that the police, in the first instance, should warn and advise, but not forcibly prohibit, and if the sati, in defiance of this notice, were performed, that a report should be made to the magistrate, who would summon the parties and proceed as in any other case of crime. . . .

The first and primary object of my heart is the benefit of the Hindus. I know nothing so important to the improvement of their future condition as the establishment of a purer morality, whatever their belief, and a more just conception of the will of God. The first step to this better understanding will be dissociation of religious belief and practice from blood and murder. They will then, when no longer under this brutalizing excitement, view with more calmness acknowledged truths. They will see that there can be no inconsistency in the ways of Providence, that to the command received as divine by all races of men, "No innocent blood shall be spilt," there can be no exception; and when they shall have been convinced of the error of this first and most criminal of their customs, may it not be hoped that others, which stand in the way of their improvement, may likewise pass away, and that, thus emancipated from those chains and shackles upon their minds and actions, they may no longer continue, as they have done, the slaves of every foreign conqueror, but that they may assume their first places among the great families of mankind? I disown in these remarks, or in this measure, any view whatever to conversion to our own faith. I write and feel as a legislator for the Hindus, and as I believe many enlightened Hindus think and feel.

Descending from these higher considerations, it cannot be a dishonest ambition that the Government of which I form a part should have the credit of an act which is to wash out a foul stain upon British rule, and to stay the sacrifice of humanity and justice to a doubtful expediency; and finally, as a branch of the general administration of the Empire, I may be permitted to feel deeply anxious that our course shall be in accordance with the noble example set to us by the British Government at home, and that the adaptation, when practicable to the circumstances of this vast Indian population, of the same enlightened principles, may promote here as well as there the general prosperity, and may exalt the character of our nation.

Questions:
1. Why does Bentinck think it advisable and necessary for the Company to abolish the custom of sati?
2. What does sati have to do with the British policy of religious toleration?
3. What reaction does Bentinck expect from the Hindus if sati is abolished?
4. If sati is abolished, what advice does he give for handling possible violations?
5. Would you have approached this situation in the same way as Bentinck, or would you have used different reasoning?

20.5   The Scramble for Africa

After the political unification of Germany and Italy by 1871, a stabilized Europe embarked upon the "Great Hunt," the "scramble for empire" in Africa that provided the economic resources for industry and the image of authority so important in the vigorous competition for national prestige. Colonial enthusiasm had waned during the 1840s and 1850s when many politicians had denounced colonies as unprofitable and burdensome. But Europe's population was growing rapidly at a rate second only to the United States, while the populations of Asia and Africa were essentially static. New colonies acted as a safety valve for a domestic population often burdened and unemployed by the great push toward industrialization. The latter movement actually created the need for new markets and resources to keep the factories producing at full capacity. Added to this were the exhortations of explorers and missionaries, who fed the imperial impulse with romantic visions of adventure and the will of God.

The following selection is from a general history of the period written by Charles Seignobos, a prominent French scholar at the time. Note his disdain for the importance of African history. The quest for power and its symbols among great nations were all that mattered. European imperialism became a state of mind that subverted the relevance of indigenous peoples and denied them a past.

Source: "'The Great African Hunt'" is from James Harvey Robinson and Charles A. Beard, *Readings in Modern European History*, Vol. II (Boston: Gin & Company, 1909), p. 448.

"THE GREAT AFRICAN HUNT"
CHARLES SEIGNOBOS

By about 1880, the political geography of Europe was fixed; the attempt of any country to acquire territory at the expense of a neighbor would have precipitated an instantaneous armed conflict. Moreover, Europe had recovered from the fatigues which had accompanied the wars for the unification of the great nations, and regained its spirit of action; but its desire for expansion could now be satisfied only outside of Europe. All the continents, however, were occupied, except Africa, until then despised. The powers threw themselves upon that continent, so long scorned, and fairly dashed into the work of partition. The rivalry and the haste of the competitors was so great that one might well speak of "the great African hunt." Within twenty years almost everything was appropriated in Africa, and when the rivals wished to extend their borders further, they could only do so at the expense of the weaker among themselves.

The annals of Africa for twenty years (1880–1900) are practically limited to the story of the partition of the continent to its very heart. Its improvement and civilization have hardly begun; it has not yet passed out of the most rudimentary industrial state; and its development, of which there can be no question, will serve as a subject for the investigation of future historians. In itself the history of native Africa offers, with some few exceptions, no events of general interest. One may say, however, that the numberless African races have been happy because they have had no history. Some of them have had a little, but it is so confused that it cannot be told. Torrents of blood, which still flow in Africa, have been caused by the exploits of slave hunters, and by internecine pillage resulting from the general anarchy prevailing on a large scale; but the details of these horrors are so microscopic that they must be passed by with this general mention. The real object of our study should be the partition of Africa among the civilized nations.

The Lure of Diamonds and the Colossus of Rhodes:
"To Take As Much of the World As Possible"

In 1841, the British doctor David Livingstone (1813–1873) left for southern Africa to begin a fascinating career as a missionary and explorer. His journals enthralled the world with images of exotic animals, magnificent waterfalls, tangled jungles, and strange native customs. A great humanitarian, Dr. Livingstone decried the internecine strife between rival African tribes and described the horrors of the Arab slave trade in the region. His accounts inspired a generation of adventurers such as the journalist, Henry Stanley, who explored the Congo river in the 1880s and began to penetrate the "darkness" of central Africa. These explorations attracted investors and other businessmen who sought to tap the potential wealth of Africa.

This potential had already been demonstrated when in the mid-1860s diamonds were discovered on the De Beer family farm in Kimberley, South Africa. Like the American Gold Rush of 1849, South Africa soon became a battleground between Dutch settlers called Boers, who decades earlier had established themselves as farmers in the region, and British imperial interests. Looming over the events of this period was the image of Cecil Rhodes (1853–1902), a British entrepreneur who controlled 90 percent of the world's output of diamonds by the time he was 38 years old through his ownership and management of De Beers Consolidated Mines, Ltd. He also acquired a large stake in the Transvaal gold mines and formed the Gold Fields of South Africa Company in 1887.

An ardent British nationalist, Rhodes had great dreams of controlling all of Africa for Britain by building a railway from the Cape to Cairo, reconciling the Boers under the British flag, and even recovering the American colonies for Britain. Rhodes never regarded moneymaking as an end in itself, but certainly used its influence in his political maneuvers as prime minister of Cape Colony in the 1890s.

The following selection by Cecil Rhodes's anonymous biographer (who called himself "The Imperialist") demonstrates the attractions of Africa to Europeans seeking wealth and competitive advantage.

Source: "The Lure of Diamonds" is from "The Imperialist" (Pseudonym), *Cecil Rhodes* (London: Chapman & Hall, Ltd., 1897), pp. 326–328.

"THE IMPERIALIST"

Cecil Rhodes was the appointed instrument to preserve for and present to England the most permanently valuable, the most habitable portion of the last great continent that waited to be annexed; and his love of the excitement of money-making and his remarkable genius for finance were to supply the first of the two necessary instruments by which the realization of the dream of empire to the north might be made practicable—the instrument of money and the command of moneyed men. . . .

Little did his fellow-miners think as they passed the dreamy youth with impassive face gazing into vacancy, that the building of an empire, the occupation of the last unoccupied continent, was gradually assuming form under the shaping power of that youthful diamond digger's imagination. The paramount ideas in his mind—the expansion of our empire and its supremacy in South Africa—was of course developed, and gained shape and consistency under the influence of the study of history and the experience of life. An enlightened patriotism has gradually become the one paramount sentiment of the great South African's life; and putting one's self in his place and looking with his eyes upon the world, one can understand his far-reaching saying that territory is everything—that is to say, territory fit to support and breed a fine race of men. He sees with his mind's eye the vicious weaklings of our overcrowded English cities, and compares with them the magnificent race of Englishmen that might be reared on the fertile soil and in the fine air of the upland of Rhodesia, and, as he reflects, the great need for England seems to be territory. England can supply the men in ever-increasing numbers to colonize it, but suitable land for them to colonize is strictly limited, and therefore to England such territory for her expansion is all-important. "Having read the histories of other countries," to quote Rhodes upon himself, "I saw that expansion was everything, and that the world's surface being limited, the great object of present humanity should be to take as much of the world as it possibly could."

To the judgment of the future Cecil Rhodes may appeal with the certainty that it will applaud the unrivaled achievements of his energy and estimate justly the whole patriotic purpose of his life. The expansion of which he will be the acknowledged author will then be seen to have been not only an expansion of the empire but an expansion of the race, and expansion of English ideas and English principles. Men of that time who stand on the verge of the twentieth, will wonder at the shortsighted judgment and narrow spirit that failed to recognize the greatness and the patriotism of the statesman [Cecil Rhodes]. . . .

Zulu Dawn: The Battle At Isandhlwana (1879)

Although native resistance to the European presence in Africa was always a concern among imperial governments, it was sporadic and rarely organized on a grand scale. Perhaps the most important expression of African resistance occurred in January 1879 at the Battle of Isandhlwana in eastern South Africa.

The king of the Zulus was Cetshwayo (1826–1884), whose strong military leadership and political acumen had restored the prestige of the Zulu nation to the level established by his illustrious uncle, Shaka. Cetshwayo had assembled a disciplined force of 40,000 men armed with spears (assegai), bows, and arrows. Perceiving a threat and seeking to incorporate Zululand into the British colony of Natal, the High

Commissioner, Sir Henry Bartle Frere, sent an ultimatum to Cetshwayo in December 1878 demanding the dissolution of the Zulu military system. When the demand was not met, the British invaded Zululand.

The rains in January, 1879 impeded the British expeditionary force, which failed to take normal precautions in scouting the region and posting sentries. The Zulu army attacked the central British column at Isandhlwana on January 22, 1879, killing about 1,700 men. Although the Zulus lost 3,000 to 4,000 men, they captured over 1,000 rifles with ammunition. The Zulu rear guard then advanced to the British base at Rorke's Drift, which was well-fortified but guarded by only about 120 men. In fierce fighting, the soldiers at Rorke's Drift were able to fend off the Zulu attack and this led to an eventual British victory in March. By July 1879, Cetshwayo was decisively defeated at Ulundi and Zululand came under informal British control. It was annexed to Natal in 1887. Cetshwayo was driven from power and died in 1884. His grave, deep in the Nkandla forest, is still considered sacred land.

The following selections highlight the action at Isandhlwana and Rorke's Drift. The first excerpt comes from the diary of British Private Owen Ellis, who reveals the confidence of the British before the massacre in which he perished. It is followed by the accounts of Uguku, a Zulu warrior, and British Lieutenant, Horace Smith-Dorrien, who were both involved in the action. They testify to the price paid for freedom—and empire.

Source: "Zulu Dawn" is from *The North Wales Express* [February 21, 28 and March 7, 1879: Pvt. Owen Ellis]; Francis E. Colenso and E. Durnford, *History of the Zulu War and Its Origin* (London,1880), pp. 410–413 [Uguku]; and The Brecon County Times [March 15, 1879: Lt. Horace Smith-Dorrian].

Private Owen Ellis

January 11, 1879

Since the time I sent you my last letter I have removed about ten miles inland to the border of Zululand. We are about to march from this place at an early date in order to proceed through and occupy the country of the Zulus, in as much as King Cetshwayo did not submit to the terms demanded by the British government. It is now too late for him as we have crossed the Buffalo River by means of pontoons. Rorke's Drift is the name by which the place where we crossed is known. Sooner the better we march through Cetshwayo's country, as we have about one hundred miles to travel from this locality to the place where the King resides, called the "Grand Kraals." After arriving there, the Queen's flag will be hoisted and King Cetshwayo will be made into atoms or captured by us. . . . This war will be over in two months' time and then we shall all be hurrying towards England. We are about to capture all the cattle belonging to the Zulus and also to burn their kraals; and if they dare to face us with the intention of fighting, well, woe be to them! They shall be killed as they come across us.

January 19, 1879

It is now Sunday afternoon—just after dinner—and I am sitting on a small box to write to you these few lines, hoping very much that they will meet you healthy and hearty, as I am at present; and thanks be to the Almighty God for keeping us as we are. . . . I send you this letter in order that you may understand that we are shifting from Rorke's Drift at six a.m. tomorrow morning, 20 January, for the "Grand Kraals" of King Cetshwayo and perhaps it will take us a week or nine days to reach that place. All the regiments . . . will meet each other at the "Grand Kraals" and occupy the country and appoint English magistrates to administer the law unless Cetshwayo will submit to the terms now laid before him. Not a single word has yet been received from him, but it is said that he is willing to conform to every demand except one and that is giving up his arms. The English government will therefore do with him as was done with [other defeated tribal chiefs]. . . .

Well, I now conclude; pardon me for being so short, as I have not much time to comment, and as we are about to pack everything ready after tea. Therefore, I have only to hope that everybody at home are in good health, as all the boys are here. Dear father, perhaps I shall be for a long time after this without writing, therefore don't be uneasy about a letter. I will send one as early as possible. Good afternoon.

Uguku–Zulu Warrior

January 22, 1879

It was our intention to have rested for a day in the valley where we arrived the night before the battle, but having heard firing of the English advance guard, . . . we went up from the valley to the top of Nqutu which was between us and the camp. . . . We saw a body of horse coming up the hill towards us from the Isandhlwana side. We opened fire on them, and then the whole of our army rose and came up the hill. The enemy returned our fire. . . . We were not checked by them, but continued our march on the camp until the artillery opened upon us. . . .

As we got nearer, we saw the soldiers were beginning to fall from the effects of our fire. . . . As we rushed on, the soldiers retired on the camp, fighting all the way, and as they got into the camp [at Rorke's Drift], we were intermingled with them. . . . One party of soldiers came out from among the tents and formed up a little above the ammunition wagons. They held their ground there until their ammunition failed them, when they were nearly all speared. Those who were not killed at this place formed again in a solid square in the neck of Isandhlwana. They were completely surrounded on all sides, and stood back to back, surrounding some men who were in the center. Their ammunition was now done, except that they had some revolvers which they fired at us at close quarters. We were quite unable to break their square until we had killed a great many of them, by throwing our spears at short distances. We eventually overcame them in this way.

Lieutenant Horace Smith-Dorrien

Since I wrote the first part of my letter, a dreadful disaster has happened to us. It seems to me a pure miracle that I am alive to tell you about it. On the 21st of January an order came to me, then stationed at Rorke's Drift, to go out to advanced camp to escort a convoy of twenty-five wagons from there to Rorke's Drift and bring them back loaded with supplies. . . .

When I arrived back in camp, I found the greater part of the column gone out with the General to meet the Zulu force, so that there was really only a caretaking force left in the camp. . . . The first Zulu force appeared about six o'clock in the morning. Two companies of the 24th were sent out after them. The Zulus seemed to retire and there was firing kept up at long ranges. At about ten thirty, the Zulus were seen coming over the hills in thousands. They were in most perfect order, and seemed to be in about twenty rows of skirmishers one behind the other. They were in a semi-circle round our two flanks and in front of us and must have covered several miles of ground. Nobody knows how many there were of them, but the general idea is at least 20,000.

Well, to cut the account short, in half an hour they were right up to the camp. I was out with the front companies of the 24th, handing them spare ammunition. Bullets were flying all over the place, but I never seemed to notice them. The Zulus nearly all had firearms of some kind and lots of ammunition. Before we knew where we were they came right into the camp, spearing everybody right and left. Everybody then who had a horse turned to fly. The enemy were going at a kind of very fast half-walk and half-run. On looking round, we saw that we were completely surrounded and the road to Rorke's Drift was cut off. The place where they seemed thinnest was where we all made for. Everybody went scattered over ground covered with huge boulders and rocks until we got to a deep gully. Lots of our men were killed there. I had lots of marvelous escapes, and was firing away at them with my revolver as I galloped along. The ground there down to the river was so broken that the Zulus went as fast as the horses, and kept killing all the way. . . .

Well, to cut it short, I struggled into Helpmakaar, about twenty miles off, at nightfall, to find a few men who had escaped, about ten or twenty. . . . We sat up all night, momentarily expecting attack. . . . We have not a single thing left. The men have no coats or anything, all being taken by the Zulus. We shall have another dreadful night of it tonight, I expect, lying on the wet ground. I have just had to drop this for a minute for one of our numerous alarms. I have no time for more now. What excitement this will cause in England, and what indignation! The troops of course were badly placed, and the arrangements for defending the camp indifferent, but there should have been enough troops; and the risk of leaving a small force to be attacked by ten or fifteen times its number should not have been allowed. As you have heard, there were no wounded, all the wounded were killed, and in a most horrible way. Every white man that was killed or wounded was ripped up and the bowels torn out, so there was no chance of anyone being left alive on the field. I saw several wounded men during the retreat all crying out for help, as they knew the terrible fate in store for them. I thank God I am alive and well, having only a few bruises. God bless you.

"A Natural Inclination to Submit to a Higher Authority" (1893)

In spite of the organized resistence of the Zulus in 1879, British tenacity and power prevailed. In his analysis of the "Scramble for Africa," Sir Frederick Lugard, British soldier and administrator of some of Britain's colonial possessions in the late nineteenth century, focused on the necessity of British action and the benefits that would naturally ensue. In 1893, fourteen years after the Zulu destruction of British forces at Isandhlwana, Lugard confidently proclaimed that Africans possessed "a natural inclination to submit to a higher authority."

Source: "'A Natural Inclination to Submit to a Higher Authority'" is from Sir Frederick Dealtry Lugard, *The Rise of Our East African Empire*, vol. 1 (London: William Blackwood and Sons, 1893), pp. 379–382.

SIR FREDERICK DEALTRY LUGARD

The Chambers of Commerce of the United Kingdom have unanimously urged the retention of East Africa on the grounds of commercial advantage. The Presidents of the London and Liverpool chambers attended a deputation to her Majesty's Minister for Foreign Affairs to urge "the absolute necessity, for the prosperity of this country, that new avenues for commerce such as that in East Equatorial Africa should be opened up, in view of the hostile tariffs with which British manufacturers are being everywhere confronted." Manchester followed with a similar declaration; Glasgow, Birmingham, Edinburgh, and other commercial centers gave it as their opinion that "there is practically no middle course for this country, between a reversal of the free trade policy to which it is pledged, on the one hand, and a prudent but continuous territorial extension for the creation of new markets, on the other hand. . . .

The "Scramble for Africa" by the nations of Europe—an incident without parallel in the history of the world—was due to the growing commercial rivalry, which brought home to civilised nations the vital necessity of securing the only remaining fields for industrial enterprise and expansion. It is well, then, to realise that it is for our advantage—and not alone at the dictates of duty—that we have undertaken responsibilities in East Africa. It is in order to foster the growth of the trade of this country, and to find an outlet for our manufactures and our surplus energy, that our far-seeing statesmen and our commercial men advocate colonial expansion. . . .

There are some who say we have no right in Africa at all, that "it belongs to the natives." I hold that our right is the necessity that is upon us to provide for our ever-growing population—either by opening new fields for emigration, or by providing work and employment which the development of over-sea extension entails—and to stimulate trade by finding new markets, since we know what misery trade depression brings at home.

While thus serving our own interests as a nation, we may, by selecting men of the right stamp for the control of new territories, bring at the same time many advantages to Africa. Nor do we deprive the natives of their birthright of freedom, to place them under a foreign yoke. It has ever been the key-note of British colonial method to rule through and by the natives, and it is this method, in contrast to the arbitrary and uncompromising rule of Germany, France, Portugal, and Spain, which has been the secret of our success as a colonising nation, and has made us welcomed by tribes and peoples in Africa, who ever rose in revolt against the other nations named. In Africa, moreover, there is among the people a natural inclination to submit to a higher authority. That intense detestation of control which animates our Teutonic races does not exist among the tribes of Africa, and if there is any authority that we replace, it is the authority of the Slavers and Arabs, or the intolerable tyranny of the "dominant tribe."

Questions:
1. Why was Africa so attractive to competing European powers in the late nineteenth century?
2. Who was Cecil Rhodes and what was his perspective about "the expansion of English ideas and English principles"? Was he a great patriot or a vicious exploiter?
3. How did Sir Frederick Lugard connect nationalism with the economic argument for imperialism? How did he respond to the arguments presented by critics of imperialism? How did he justify his support of imperial expansion?
4. After reading the letters and eyewitness accounts of the Battle of Isandhlwana in 1879, what are your impressions? What price did the British pay for their imperialism? Was it worth it? And what does this say about the nature of native resistance? Were Zulu warriors inferior to British forces? What did the Zulus have to lose?

20.6 Rudyard Kipling

This selection, by Rudyard Kipling, concerns both African and Indian colonization. Of special interest is the assumption that the colonizing powers did the natives a favor by bringing civilization to them. No mention is made of the fact that these same powers exploited their colonies economically and kept them in bondage.

Source: Rudyard Kipling, *Rudyard Kipling's Verse* (1885–1918) (Garden City, NY: Doubleday, Page & Co. 1919).

THE WHITE MAN'S BURDEN (1899)

Take up the White Man's burden—
    Send forth the best ye breed—
Go bind your sons to exile
    To serve your captives' need;
To wait in heavy harness,
    On fluttered folk and wild—
Your new-caught, sullen peoples,
    Half-devil and half—child.

Take up the White Man's Burden—
    In patience to abide,
To veil the threat of terror
    And check the show of pride;
By open speech and simple,
    An hundred times made plain,
To seek another's profit,
    And work another's gain.

Take up the White Man's burden—
    The savage wars of peace—
Fill full the mouth of Famine
    And bid the sickness cease;
And when your goal is nearest
    The end for others sought,
Watch Sloth and heathen Folly
    Bring all your hope to nought.

Take up the White Man's burden—
    No tawdry rule of kings,
But toil of serf and sweeper—
    The tale of common things.
The ports ye shall not enter,
    The roads ye shall not tread,
Go make them with your living,
    And mark them with your dead.

Take up the White Man's burden—
    And reap his old reward:
The blame of those ye better,
    The hate of those ye guard—
The cry of hosts ye humour
    (Ah, slowly!) toward the light:—
"Why brought ye us from bondage,"
    "Our loved Egyptian night?"

Take up the White Man's burden—
    Ye dare not stoop to less—
Nor call too loud on Freedom
    To cloak your weariness;
By all ye cry or whisper,
    By all ye leave or do,
The silent, sullen peoples
    Shall weight your Gods and you.

Take up the White Man's burden—
    Have done with childish days—
The lightly proffered laurel,
    The easy, ungrudged praise.
Comes now, to search your manhood
    Through all the thankless years,
Cold, edged with dear-bought wisdom,
    The judgment of your peers!

Question:
1. In your own words, what is the "White Man's Burden"?

20.7   Francisco García Calderón, "The North American Peril"

In this selection, Francisco García Calderón, a Peruvian diplomat and writer, sharply criticizes U.S. policy and private commercial interests for exploiting Latin Americans. He also warns of the dangers of cultural imperialism.

Source: From Francisco García Calderón, *Latin America: Its Rise and Progress* (London: T.F. Unwin, 1913), pp. 300–12, passim.

Against the policy of respect for Latin liberties are ranged the instincts of a triumphant plutocracy. The center of North American life is passing from Boston to Chicago; the citadel of the ideal gives way to the material progress of the great porcine metropolis. There is a conflict of dissimilar currents of morality. The Puritan tradition of New England seems useless in the struggle of the Far West; the conquest of the desert demands another morality; the morality of conflict, aggression and success. The trusts raise their heads above the impotent clamor of the weak. The conflict between the new-comers is tumultuous and brutal; as in the time of imperial Rome, the latter-day republicans are becoming aware of their defeat by a new caste, animated by an impetuous love of conflict. It is the struggle between idealism and plutocracy, between the tradition of the Pilgrim Fathers and the morality of Wall Street; the patricians of the Senate and the bosses of Tammany Hall.

The great historical parties are divided; while the democrats do not forget the ideal of Washington and Lincoln, the republicans think only of imperialism.

Will a generous elite succeed in withstanding this racial tendency? Perhaps, but nothing can check the onward march of the United States. Their imperialism is an unavoidable phenomenon.

The nation which was peopled by nine millions of men in 1820 now numbers eighty millions—an immense demographic power; in the space of ten years, from 1890 to 1900, this population increased by one-fifth. By virtue of its iron, wheat, oil, and cotton, and its victorious industrialism, the democracy aspires to a world-wide significance of destiny; the consciousness of its powers is creating fresh international duties. Yankee pride increases with the endless multiplication of wealth and population, and the patriotic sentiment has reached such an intensity that it has become transformed into imperialism.

The United States buy the products they themselves lack from tropical nations. To rule in these fertile zones would to them appear the geographical ideal of a northern people. Do not their industries demand new outlets in America and Asia? So to the old mystic ambition are added the necessities of utilitarian progress. An industrial nation, the States preach a practical Christianity to the older continents, to Europe, and to lands yet barbarous; as to South America, they profess a doctrine of aggressive idealism, a strange fusion of economic tendencies and Puritan fervor. The Christian Republic imposes its tutelage upon inferior races, and so prepares them for self-government. . . .

Interventions have become more frequent with the expansion of frontiers. The United States have recently intervened in the territory of Acre,[1] there to found a republic of rubber gatherers; at Panama, there to develop a province and construct a canal; in Cuba, under the cover of the Platt Amendment,[2] to maintain order in the interior; in San Domingo, to support the civilizing revolution and overthrow the tyrants; in Venezuela, and in Central America, to enforce upon these nations, torn by internecine disorders, the political and financial tutelage of the imperial democracy. In Guatemala and Honduras the loans concluded with the monarchs of North American finance have reduced the people to a new slavery. Supervision of the customs and the dispatch of pacificatory squadrons to defend the interests of the Anglo-Saxon have enforced peace and tranquility: such are the means employed. *The New York American* announces that Mr. Pierpont Morgan proposes to encompass the finances of Latin America by a vast network of Yankee banks. Chicago merchants and Wall Street financiers created the Meat Trust in the Argentine. The United States offer millions for the purpose of converting into Yankee loans the moneys raised in London in the last century by the Latin American States; they wish to obtain a monopoly of credit. It has even been announced, although the news hardly appears probable, that a North American syndicate wished to buy enormous belts of land in Guatemala, where the English tongue is the obligatory language. The fortification of the Panama Canal, and the possible acquisition of the Galapagos Islands in the Pacific, are fresh manifestations of imperialistic progress.

The Monroe Doctrine takes an aggressive form with Mr. Roosevelt, the politician of the "big stick," and intervention *a outrance*. Roosevelt is conscious of his sacred mission: he wants a powerful army and a navy majestically sailing the two oceans. . . .

He recognizes the fact that the progress accomplished by the United States is not of a nature to tranquillize the South American; "that the Yankee believes that his Southern neighbors are trivial and childish peoples, and above all incapable of maintaining a proper self-government." He thinks the example of Cuba, liberated "from the rule of Spain, but not from internal troubles, will render the American of the States skeptical as to the aptitude of the Latin-American populations of mixed blood to govern themselves without disorder," and recognizes that the "pacific penetration" of Mexico by American capital constitutes a possible menace to the independence of that Republic, were the death of Diaz to lead to its original state of anarchy and disturb the peace which the millionaires of the North desire to see untroubled.

Warnings, advice, distrust, invasion of capital, plans of financial hegemony—all these justify the anxiety of the southern peoples. . . .

For geographical reasons, and on account of its very inferiority, South America cannot dispense with the influence of the Anglo-Saxon North, with its exuberant wealth and its industries. South America has need of capital, of enterprising men, of bold explorers, and these the United States supply in abundance. The defense of the South should consist in avoiding the establishment of privileges or monopolies, whether in favor of North Americans or Europeans.

It is essential to understand not only the foundations of North American greatness, but also the weaknesses of the Anglo-Saxon democracy, in order to escape from the dangers of excessive imitation.

The Anglo-Saxons of America have created an admirable democracy upon a prodigious expanse of territory. A caravan of races has pitched its tents from the Atlantic to the Pacific, and has watered the desert with its impetuous blood. Dutch, French, Anglo-Saxons, and Germans, people of all sects, Quakers, Presbyterians, Catholics, Puritans, all have mingled their creed in a single multiform nation. At the contact of new soil men have felt the pride of creation and of living. Initiative, self-assertion, self-reliance, audacity, love of adventure, all the forms of the victorious will are united in this Republic of energy. A triumphant optimism quickens the rhythm of life; an immense impulse of creation builds cities in the wilderness, and founds new plutocracies amidst the whirlpool of the markets. Workshops, factories, banks; the obscure unrest of Wall Street; the architectural insolence of the skyscraper; the many-colored, material West; all mingle perpetually in the wild, uncouth hymn which testifies the desperate battle of will and destiny, of generation against death. . . .

But this civilization, in which men of strong vitality win wealth, invent machines, create new cities, and profess a Christianity full of energy and accomplishment, has not the majesty of a harmonious structure. It is the violent work of a people of various origin, which has not yet been ennobled by the *patina* of tradition and time. In the cities which restless workers hastily raise on barren soil, one can as yet perceive no definitive unity. Race antagonism disturbs North America; the Negroes swarm in the South; Japanese and Orientals aspire to the conquest of the West. Neo-Saxon civilization is still seeking its final form, and in the meantime it is piling up wealth amid the prevailing indiscipline. "We find in the United States," says M. André Chevrillon, "a political system, but not a social organization." The admirable traditions of Hamilton and Jefferson have been subjected to the onslaught of new influences, the progress of plutocracy, the corruption of the administrative functions, the dissolution of parties, the abuse of the power of monopolies. The axis of the great nation is becoming displaced towards the West, and each step in advance marks the triumph of vulgarity.

An octopus of a city, New York, might be taken as the symbol of this extraordinary nation; it displays the vertigo, the audacity, and all the lack of proportion that characterize American life. Near the poverty of the Ghetto and the disturbing spectacle of Chinatown you may admire the wealth of Fifth Avenue and the marble palaces which plagiarize the architecture of the Tuscan cities. Opposite the obscure crowds of emigrants herded in the docks you will see the refined luxury of the plutocratic hotels, and facing the majestic buildings of Broadway, the houses of the parallel avenues, which are like the temporary booths of a provincial fair. Confusion, uproar, instability—these are the striking characteristics of the North American democracy. Neither irony nor grace nor skepticism, gifts of the old civilizations, can make way against the plebeian brutality, the excessive optimism, the violent individualism of the people.

All these things contribute to the triumph of mediocrity; the multitude of primary schools, the vices of utilitarianism, the cult of the average citizen, the transatlantic M. Homais, and the tyranny of opinion noted by Tocqueville; and in this vulgarity, which is devoid of traditions and has no leading aristocracy, a return to the primitive type of the redskin, which has already been noted by close observers, is threatening the proud democracy. From the excessive tension of wills, from the elementary state of culture, from the perpetual unrest of life, from the harshness of the industrial struggle, anarchy and violence will be born in the future. In a hundred years men will seek in vain for the "American soul," the "genius of America," elsewhere than in the undisciplined force or the violence which ignores moral laws.

Among the Anglo-Saxon nations individualism finds its limits in the existence of a stable home; it may also struggle against the State, according to the formula consecrated by Spencer, "the man versus the State." It defends its jealous autonomy from excessive legislation, from the intervention of the Government in economic conflicts or the life of the family. And it is precisely the family spirit which is becoming enfeebled in North America, under the pressure of new social conditions. The birth-rate is diminishing, and the homes of foreign immigrants are contributing busily to the formation of the new generations; the native stock inheriting good racial traditions would seem to be submerged more and more by the new human tide. A North American official writes that "the decrease in the birth-rate will lead to a complete change in the social system of the Republic." From this will result the abandonment of the traditional austerity of the race, and the old notions of sacrifice and duty. The descendants of alien races will constitute the nation of the future. The national heritage is threatened by the invasion of Slavs and Orientals, and the fecundity of the negroes; a painful anxiety weighs upon the destinies of the race.

The family is unstable, and divorces are increasing at an extraordinary rate. Between 1870 and 1905 the population doubled; during the same period the divorces increased sixfold and the marriages decreased. There is no fixity in the elements of variety, and the causes of this state of transition will not disappear, as they are intimately allied with the development of the industrial civilization which has brought with it a new ideal of happiness. By emancipating men and women from the old moral principles it has modified sexual morality; by accelerating social progress it has brought an additional bitterness into the social melee, a greater egoism into human conflict.

Excessive and heterogenous immigration prevents any final crystallization; in the last ten years 8,515,000 strangers have entered into the great hospitable Union. They came from Germany, Ireland, Russia, or Southern Italy. It is calculated that the United States are able to assimilate 150,000 to 200,000 immigrants each year, but they certainly cannot welcome such an overwhelming host without anxiety.

Criminality increases; the elaboration of a common type among these men of different origin is proceeding more slowly. Doubtless beneath the shelter of the political federation of the various States a confused agglomeration of races is forming itself, and this justifies the query of Professor Ripley: "The Americans of the North," he says, "have witnessed the disappearance of the Indians and the buffalo, but can they be certain today that the Anglo-Saxons will survive them?"

In seeking to imitate the United States we should not forget that the civilization of the peoples of the North presents these symptoms of decadence.

Europe offers the Latin-American democracies what the latter demand of Anglo-Saxon America, which was formed in the school of Europe. We find the practical spirit, industrialism, and political liberty in England; organization and education in Germany; and in France inventive genius, culture, wealth, great universities, and democracy. From these ruling peoples the new Latin world must indirectly receive the legacy of Western civilization.

Essential points of difference separate the two Americas. Differences of language and therefore of spirit; the difference between Spanish Catholicism and the multiform Protestantism of the Anglo-Saxons; between the Yankee individualism and the omnipotence of the State natural to the nations of the South. In their origin, as in their race, we find fundamental antagonisms; the evolution of the North is slow and obedient to the lessons of time, to the influences of custom; the history of the southern peoples is full of revolutions, rich with dreams of an unattainable perfection.

The people of the United States hate the half-breed, and the impure marriages of whites and blacks which take place in southern homes; no manifestation of Pan-Americanism could suffice to destroy the racial prejudice as it exists north of Mexico. The half-breeds and their descendants govern the Ibero-American democracies, and the Republic of English and German origin entertains for the men of the tropics the same contempt which they feel for the slaves of Virginia whom Lincoln liberated.

In its friendship for them there will always be disdain; in their progress, a conquest; in their policy, a desire of hegemony. It is the fatality of blood, stronger than political affinities or geographical alliances.

Instead of dreaming of an impossible fusion the Neo-Latin peoples should conserve the traditions which are proper to them. The development of the European influences which enrich and improve them, the purging of the nation from the strain of miscegenation, and immigration of a kind calculated to form centers of resistance against any possibilities of conquest, are the various aspects of this Latin Americanism.

Questions:

1. *Would you agree with García Calderón's statement that "interventions [in Latin America] have become more frequent with the expansion of frontiers"? Why does he warn about the dangers of the U.S. shift from the "tradition of the Pilgrim fathers" to that of the "morality of Wall Street"?*
2. *According to the author, what were some of the differences that divided the two Americas? Were his judgments valid, or were they based on false assumptions? How have these differences exacerbated U.S. relations with Latin America?*
3. *Why did García Calderón regard the United States as a threat to Latin America's cultural identity? Were his concerns justified?*
4. *Compare Calderón's views of the American character with those expressed by Alexis de Tocqueville. Are there similarities? If so, what are they, and why do they exist? Also, compare his beliefs with Simón Bolívar's.*

PART 21
East Asia Responds to the West

21.1 Lin Tse-hsü [Lin Zexu], Letter of Moral Admonition to Queen Victoria

Although the English East India Company's trade with China was profitable, the overall balance of trade had remained in China's favor until the early decades of the nineteenth century. European traders bought tea, silk, rhubarb, and other goods from China, but the Chinese found little need for Western goods. A reversal in the trade balance came in the 1830s, and opium importation was one of the most important factors. Opium, forbidden in China, was smuggled into the country from India in ever-increasing quantities, primarily by English East India Company ships through the port of Canton [Guanzhou]. During the years of 1838–1839 alone, more than five million pounds of opium were imported illegally by East India Company ships.

The effects of the illicit trade on Chinese morality and health, as well as on the economy, were so deleterious that Emperor Tao-kuang [Daoguang] (r. 1821–1850) was gravely concerned. He searched for an official who would be able to deal with the opium menace effectively and resolutely. In Lin Tse-hsü [Lin Zexu] he found such a person. A high official in the Imperial government, Lin had enjoyed a wide reputation for his competence and integrity and for his hard-line approach toward the proliferation of opium. In December 1838, he was appointed imperial commissioner at Canton, with full power to stop the Canton opium traffic.

Lin Tse-hsü arrived in Canton in March 1839 and immediately began to stamp out the opium traffic; however, it became clear to him that the solution was to stop the supply at its source. The following selection is his letter to Queen Victoria, appealing to the British conscience and demanding an end to the opium trade. The letter was written in the summer of 1839, only a few months before the outbreak of the Opium War in November 1839. The fact that Lin Tse-hsü refers to Queen Victoria as "king" might suggest how knowledgeable the Chinese government was of English politics.

Source: Reprinted by permission of the publisher from *China's Response to the West: A Documentary Survey, 1839–1923* by Ssu-yu Teng and John K. Fairbank, Cambridge, Mass.: Harvard University Press, pp. 24–27. Copyright © 1954 by the President and Fellows of Harvard College; Copyright © renewed 1982 by Ssu-yu Teng and John K. Fairbank, Copyright © for new preface 1979 by the President and Fellows of Harvard College.

A communication: magnificently our great Emperor soothes and pacifies China and the foreign countries, regarding all with the same kindness. If there is profit, then he shares it with the peoples of the world; if there is harm, then he removes it on behalf of the world. This is because he takes the mind of heaven and earth as his mind.

The kings of your honorable country by a tradition handed down from generation to generation have always been noted for their politeness and submissiveness. We have read your successive tributary memorials saying, "In general our countrymen who go to trade in China have always received His Majesty the Emperor's gracious treatment and equal justice," and so on. Privately we are delighted with the way in which the honorable rulers of your country deeply understand the grand principles and are grateful for the Celestial grace. For this reason the Celestial Court in soothing those from afar has redoubled its polite and kind treatment. The profit from trade has been enjoyed by them continuously for two hundred years. This is the source from which your country has become known for its wealth.

But after a long period of commercial intercourse, there appear among the crowd of barbarians both good persons and bad, unevenly. Consequently there are those who smuggle opium to seduce the Chinese people and so cause the spread of the poison to all provinces. Such persons who only care to profit themselves, and disregard their harm to others, are not tolerated by the laws of heaven and are unanimously hated by human beings. His Majesty the Emperor, upon hearing of this, is in a towering rage. He has especially sent me, his commissioner, to come to Kwangtung, and together with the governor-general and governor jointly to investigate and settle this matter.

All those people in China who sell opium or smoke opium should receive the death penalty. If we trace the crime of those barbarians who through the years have been selling opium, then the deep harm they have wrought and the great profit they have usurped should fundamentally justify their execution according to law. We take into consideration, however, the fact that the various barbarians have still known how to repent their crimes and return to their allegiance to us by taking the 20,183 chests of opium from their storeships and petitioning us, through their consular officer [superintendent of trade], Elliot, to receive it. It has been entirely destroyed and this has been faithfully reported to the Throne in several memorials by this commissioner and his colleagues.

Fortunately we have received a specially extended favor from His Majesty the Emperor, who considers that for those who voluntarily surrender there are still some circumstances to palliate their crime, and so for the time being he has magnanimously excused them from punishment. But as for those who again violate the opium prohibition, it is difficult for the law to pardon them repeatedly. Having established new regulations, we presume that the ruler of your honorable country, who takes delight in our culture and whose disposition is inclined towards us, must be able to instruct the various barbarians to observe the law with care. It is only necessary to explain to them the advantages and disadvantages and then they will know that the legal code of the Celestial Court must be absolutely obeyed with awe.

We find that your country is sixty or seventy thousand *li* [three *li* make one mile] from China. Yet there are barbarian ships that strive to come here for trade for the purpose of making a great profit. The wealth of China is used to profit the barbarians. That is to say, the great profit made by barbarians is all taken from the rightful share of China. By what right do they then in return use the poisonous drug to injure the Chinese people? Even though the barbarians may not necessarily intend to do us harm, yet in coveting profit to an extreme, they have no regard for injuring others. Let us ask, where is your conscience? I have heard that the smoking of opium is very strictly forbidden by your country; that is because the harm caused by opium is clearly understood. Since it is not permitted to do harm to your own country, then even less should you let it be passed on to the harm of other countries—how much less to China! Of all that China exports to foreign countries, there is not a single thing which is not beneficial to people: they are of benefit when eaten, or of benefit when used, or of benefit when resold; all are beneficial. Is there a single article from China which has done any harm to foreign countries? Take tea and rhubarb, for example; the foreign countries cannot get along for a single day without them. If China cuts off these benefits with no sympathy for those who are to suffer, then what can the barbarians rely upon to keep themselves alive? Moreover the woolens, camlets, and longells [i.e., textiles] of foreign countries cannot be woven unless they obtain Chinese silk. If China, again, cuts off this beneficial export, what profit can the barbarians expect to make? As for other food-stuffs, beginning with candy, ginger, cinnamon, and so forth, and articles for use, beginning with silk, satin, chinaware, and so on, all the things that must be had by foreign countries are innumerable. On the other hand, articles coming from the outside to China can only be used as toys. We can take them or get along without them. Since they are not needed by China, what difficulty would there be if we closed the frontier and stopped the trade? Nevertheless our Celestial Court lets tea, silk, and other goods be shipped without limit and circulated everywhere without begrudging it in the slightest. This is for no other reason but to share the benefit with the people of the whole world.

The goods from China carried away by your country not only supply your own consumption and use, but also can be divided up and sold to other countries, producing a triple profit. Even if you do not sell opium, you still have this threefold profit. How can you bear to go further, selling products injurious to others in order to fulfill your insatiable desire?

Suppose there were people from another country who carried opium for sale to England and seduced your people into buying and smoking it; certainly your honorable ruler would deeply hate it and be bitterly aroused. We have heard heretofore that your honorable ruler is kind and benevolent. Naturally you would not wish to give unto others what you yourself do not want. We have also heard that the ships coming to Canton have all had regulations promulgated and given to them in which it is stated that it is not permitted to carry contraband goods. This indicates that the administrative orders of your honorable rule have been originally strict and clear. Only because the trading ships are numerous, heretofore perhaps they have not been examined with care. Now after this communication has been dispatched and you have clearly understood the strictness of the prohibitory laws of the Celestial Court, certainly you will not let your subjects dare again to violate the law.

We have further learned that in London, the capital of your honorable rule, and in Scotland (Su-ko-lan), Ireland (Ai-lun), and other places, originally no opium has been produced. Only in several places of India under your control such as Bengal, Madras, Bombay, Patna, Benares, and Malwa has opium been planted from hill to hill, and ponds have been opened for its manufacture. For months and years work is continued in order to accumulate the poison. The obnoxious odor ascends, irritating heaven and frightening the spirits. Indeed you, O King, can eradicate the opium plant in these places, hoe over the fields entirely, and sow in its stead the five grains [i.e., millet, barley, wheat, etc.]. Anyone who dares again attempt to plant and manufacture opium should be severely punished. This will really be a great, benevolent government policy that will increase the common weal and get rid of evil. For this, Heaven must support you and the spirits must bring you good fortune, prolonging your old age and extending your descendants. All will depend on this act.

As for the barbarian merchants who come to China, their food and drink and habitation are all received by the gracious favor of our Celestial Court. Their accumulated wealth is all benefit given with pleasure by our Celestial Court. They spend rather few days in their own country but more time in Canton. To digest clearly the legal penalties as an aid to instruction has been a valid principle in all ages. Suppose a man of another country comes to England to trade, he still has to obey the English laws; how much more should he obey in China the laws of the Celestial Dynasty?

Now we have set up regulations governing the Chinese people. He who sells opium shall receive the death penalty and he who smokes it also the death penalty. Now consider this: if the barbarians do not bring opium, then how can the Chinese people resell it, and how can they smoke it? The fact is that the wicked barbarians beguile the Chinese people into a death trap. How then can we grant life only to these barbarians? He who takes the life of even one person still has to atone for it with his own life; yet is the harm done by opium limited to the taking of one life only? Therefore in the new regulations, in regard to those barbarians who bring opium to China, the penalty is fixed at decapitation or strangulation. This is what is called getting rid of a harmful thing on behalf of mankind.

Moreover we have found that in the middle of the second month of this year [April 9] Consul [Superintendent] Elliot of your nation, because the opium prohibition law was very stern and severe, petitioned for an extension of the time limit. He requested a limit of five months for India and its adjacent harbors and related territories, and ten months for England proper, after which they would act in conformity with the new regulations. Now we, the commissioner and others, have memorialized and have received the extraordinary Celestial grace of His Majesty the Emperor, who has redoubled his consideration and compassion. All those who within the period of the coming one year (from England) or six months (from India) bring opium to China by mistake, but who voluntarily confess and completely surrender their opium, shall be exempt from their punishment. After this limit of time, if there are still those who bring opium to China then they will plainly have committed a willful violation and shall at once be executed according to law, with absolutely no clemency or pardon. This may be called the height of kindness and the perfection of justice.

Our Celestial Dynasty rules over and supervises the myriad states, and surely possesses unfathomable spiritual dignity. Yet the Emperor cannot bear to execute people without having first tried to reform them by instruction. Therefore he especially promulgates these fixed regulations. The barbarian merchants of your country, if they wish to do business for a prolonged period, are required to obey our statutes respectfully and to cut off permanently the source of opium. They must by no means try to test the effectiveness of the law with their lives. May you, O King, check your wicked and sift your vicious people before they come to China, in order to guarantee the peace of your nation, to show further the sincerity of your politeness and submissiveness, and to let the two countries enjoy together the blessings of peace. How fortunate, how fortunate indeed! After receiving this dispatch will you immediately give us a prompt reply regarding the details and circumstances of your cutting off the opium traffic. Be sure not to put this off. The above is what has to be communicated. [Vermilion endorsement:] This is appropriately worded and quite comprehensive.

Questions:
1. *What moral arguments did Commissioner Lin present against the British importation of opium into China?*
2. *On the basis of Lin's letter to Queen Victoria and Emperor Ch'ien-lung's letter to King George III, describe China's view of the West, especially of Great Britain. Contrast these views with those expressed by Rudyard Kipling in "The White Man's Burden."*

21.2 "Use the Barbarians to Fight the Barbarians" (1842): Wei Yuan

As the British continued to pressure the Chinese government for free trade and protection for the legal rights of their citizens in treaty ports, Chinese officials saw beyond the "fairness" argument and accused the British of pushing opium. In 1830, Chinese officials destroyed 20,000 chests of British opium, and war broke out. From 1839 to 1842, the British demonstrated their superiority in arms by sieging forts and seizing cities, soundly defeating Chinese troops equipped with their antiquated weapons. The Opium War ended in August 1842 with the Treaty of Nanjing, the first of a series of "unequal treaties" that expanded foreign access to Chinese markets. Britain got control of Hong Kong, a huge indemnity, and access to five new ports. France and the United States also made similar treaties and the Russians were active on the northern border with China.

This selection is by Wei Yuan (1794–1856), a scholar and author of the Illustrated Gazetteer of the Maritime Countries. This was the first systematic attempt to provide educated individuals with a view of the outside world. Wei Yuan's argument can be put succinctly: Western barbarians in their vicious pursuit of power and profit have exercised their technologies to threaten the virtuous Chinese society; China must awaken to the threat by applying its superior moral strength to finding practical solutions. That China had difficulty in "catching up" to the West technologically and defending itself against foreign domination is demonstrated in the succeeding source by You Zan, an economic scholar, who was still complaining about the opium poison in 1894.

Source: From *Sources of Chinese Tradition* by de Bary, William Theodore, et al., eds., © 1958 Columbia University Press, pp. 675–677. Reprinted with the permission of the publsiher.

Keep in Mind . . .

•   What did Wei Yuan mean when he said "use the barbarians to fight the barbarians?"

•   What were the economic drawbacks of the opium trade for China?

What is the purpose of the present work? Its purpose is to show how to use barbarians to fight barbarians, how to make the barbarians pacify one another [to our advantage], and how to employ the techniques of the barbarians in order to bring the barbarians under control. . . .

    Yet, the steady poisoning of our people by the barbarians with their opium represents a crime ten thousand times worse than [any in the past]. However, our present emperor, His Majesty, is so benevolent and diligent. His virtue matches that of His ancestors. The operations of Heaven in time and of man through his own efforts are conjoined for our advantage. Why should we fear that the time is not ripe for extermination of the barbarians; why should we fear that there may be no chance to show our might? Thus all of our courageous people must show their eagerness for the achievement of such a task, and anyone who has not lost his senses must devise some means for its accomplishment. Away with hypocrisy! Away with all window dressing! Away with the nurturing of internal evils and the tolerating of private gain at the expense of the public interest! Then the minds of men will be aroused from their ignorant lethargy.

    First of all, through practical projects we must advance practical effort; and through practical effort advance practical projects. . . . Our nets must be made ready before we can go fishing in the lake. . . .

    Secondly, once rid of our ignorant lethargy, the sun will shine more brightly in the sky; once the dearth of men with practical abilities is remedied, government orders will be carried out with the speed of wind and lightning. . . .

Questions:
1. *What did Wei Yuan mean when he said "use the barbarians to fight the barbarians?"*
2. *Wei Yuan's argument against the "barbarians" seems to be a call for Chinese unity. What did he mean when he said "away with hypocrisy" and "away with window dressing"?*

21.3   "Why Are Western Nations Small and Yet Strong?": Feng Guifen

This selection is by Feng Guifen (1809–1874), a teacher and official who hoped to awaken China from its complacency. In this struggle, some Chinese even admired the Japanese ability to respond quickly to the Western threat.

Source: From *Sources of Japanese Tradition* by de Bary, William Theodore, et al., eds., copyright © 1958 Columbia University Press, pp. 708–709. Reprinted with the permission of the publisher.

FENG GUIFEN

Keep in Mind . . .

•   What elements does Feng Guifen think were important in the self-strengthening movement? What must the Chinese learn from the Western barbarians?

Why are the Western nations small and yet strong? Why are we large and yet weak? We must search for the means to become their equal, and that depends solely upon human effort. . . . We have only one thing to learn from the barbarians, and that is strong ships and effective guns.... Funds should be allotted to establish a shipyard and arsenal in each trading port. A few barbarians should be employed, and Chinese who are good in using their minds should be selected to receive instruction so that in turn they may teach many craftsmen. . . .

    Our nation's emphasis on civil service examinations has sunk deep into people's minds for a long time. Intelligent and brilliant scholars have exhausted their time and energy in such useless things as the stereo-typed examination essays, examination papers, and formal calligraphy. . . . We should now order one-half of them to apply themselves to the manufacturing of instruments and weapons and to the promotion of physical studies. . . . The intelligence and ingenuity of the Chinese are certainly superior to those of the various barbarians; it is only that hitherto we have not made use of them. . . . There ought to be some people of extraordinary intelligence who can have new ideas and improve on Western methods. At first they may take the foreigners as their teachers and models; then they may come to the same level and be their equals; finally they may move ahead and surpass them. Herein lies the way to self-strengthening. . . .

When we speak of repelling the barbarians, we must have the actual means to repel them, and not just empty bravado. If we live in the present day and speak of repelling the barbarians, we should ask with what instruments we are to repel them? . . . [The answer is that] we should use the instruments of the barbarians, but not adopt the ways of the barbarians. We should use them so that we can repel them.

Question:

1. What elements does Feng Guifen think were important in the self-strengthening movement? What must the Chinese learn from the Western barbarians?

21.4 The Treaty of Nanking: Treaty of Peace, Friendship, Commerce, Indemnity, etc., Between Great Britain and China, August 29, 1842

From ancient times trade existed between China and the West, particularly over the long "silk road." Besides silk other Chinese products like tea, spices, and porcelain ("china") were greatly prized in Europe and later in America. But the overland route was long and difficult, so increasingly efforts were made to develop trade by sea. Two ports were opened on the south coast of China, Macao by the Portuguese in 1557 and nearby Canton by the British and others in the early eighteenth century. Because these allowed only a limited and restricted trade, European merchants and their governments began to apply pressure to have China opened more widely to them commercially. In their turn, the Chinese, suspicious and disdainful of the West, offered stiff and continuing resistance to any change. The British, rebuffed in their efforts to gain a privileged trading relationship with China, soon turned to illicit endeavors. They began the mass production of opium in India, which was then smuggled into China. This underground trade led eventually to the Opium War in 1839, in which the British were quickly victorious. The following document, the Treaty of Nanking, stipulates the concessions that China made to the British following the Opium War.

> **Source:** *Changing China: Readings in the History of China from the Opium War to the Present,* edited by J. Mason Gentzler. Copyright © 1977 by Praeger Publishers, A Division of Holt, Rinehart and Winston. Reproduced by permission of Holt, Rinehart and Winston.

Her Majesty the Queen of the United Kingdom of Great Britain and Ireland, and His Majesty the Emperor of China, being desirous of putting an end to the misunderstandings and consequent hostilities which have arisen between the two countries, have resolved to conclude a treaty for that purpose, and have therefore named as their Plenipotentiaries, that is to say:—

Her Majesty the Queen of Great Britain and Ireland, Sir Henry Pottinger, Bart, a Major-General in the service of the East India Company, &c.;

And His Imperial Majesty the Emperor of China, the High Commissioners Keying, a Member of the Imperial House, a guardian of the Crown Prince, and General of the garrison of Canton; and Elepoo, of the Imperial Kindred, graciously permitted to wear the insignia of the first rank, and the distinction of a peacock's feather, lately Minister and Governor-General, &c., and now Lieutenant-General Commanding at Chapoo.

Who, after having communicated to each other their respective full powers, and found them to be in good and due form, have agreed upon and concluded the following Articles:—

ARTICLE I

Peace and Friendship. Protection of Persons and Property.

There shall henceforward be peace and friendship between Her Majesty the Queen of the United Kingdom of Great Britain and Ireland and His Majesty the Emperor of China, and between their respective subjects, who shall enjoy full security and protection for their persons and property within the dominions of the other.

ARTICLE II

Canton, Amoy, Foochow, Ningpo, and Shanghai opened to British Subjects and their Trade.

His majesty the Emperor of China agrees, that British subjects, with their families and establishments, shall be allowed to reside, for the purpose of carrying on their mercantile pursuits, without molestation or restraint, at the cities and towns of Canton, Amoy, Foochowfoo, Ningpoo, and Shanghai.

Appointment of British Superintendents or Consuls at those places; their Duties.

And Her Majesty the Queen of Great Britain, &c., will appoint Superintendents, or Consular Officers, to reside at each of the above named cities or towns, to be the medium of communication between the Chinese authorities and the said merchants, and to see that the just duties and other dues of the Chinese Government, as hereafter provided for, are duly discharged by Her Britannic Majesty's subjects.

ARTICLE III

Cession of Hong Kong to Great Britain.

It being obviously necessary and desirable that British subjects should have some port at which they may careen and refit their ships, when required, and keep stores for that purpose, His Majesty the Emperor of China cedes to Her Majesty the Queen of Great Britain, &c., the Island of Hong Kong. To be possessed in perpetuity by Her Britannic Majesty, her heirs and successors, and to be governed by such laws and regulations as Her Majesty the Queen of Great Britain, &c., shall see fit to direct.

ARTICLE 1V

Indemnity, Payment by China of 6,000,000 dollars for value of Opium delivered up as a Ransom for British Subjects.

The Emperor of China agrees to pay the Sum of 6,000,000 dollars, as the value of the Opium which was delivered up at Canton in the month of March, 1839, as a ransom for the lives of Her Britannic Majesty's Superintendent and subjects, who had been imprisoned and threatened with death by the Chinese High Officers.

ARTICLE V

Abolition of Privileges of Hong Merchants at Ports of residence of British Merchants. Payment by China of 3,000,000 dollars, for Debts due to British Subjects by certain Hong Merchants.

The Government of Chin having compelled the British merchants trading at Canton to deal exclusively with certain Chinese merchants, called Hong merchants (or Co-Hong), who had been licensed by the Chinese Government for that purpose, the Emperor of China agrees to abolish that practice in future at all ports where British merchants may reside, and to permit them to carry their mercantile transactions with whatever persons they please; and His Imperial Majesty further agrees to pay to the British Governments the sum of 3,000,000 dollars, on account of debts due to British subjects by some of the Hong merchants on Co-Hong, who have become insolvent, and who owe very large sums of money to subjects of Her Britannic Majesty.

ARTICLE VI

Indemnity, Payment by China of 12,000,000 dollars for Expenses of British Expedition to demand Redress. Deduction of ransom received by British Forces for Chinese towns.

The Government of Her Britannic Majesty having obliged to send out an expedition to demand and obtain redress for the violent and unjust proceedings of the Chinese High Authorities towards Her Britannic Majesty's Officers and subjects, the Emperor of China agrees to pay the sum of 12,000,000 dollars, on account of the expenses incurred; and Her Britannic /Majesty's Plenipotentiary voluntarily agrees, on behalf of Her Majesty, to deduct from said amount of 12,000,000 dollars, any sum which may have been received by Her Majesty's combined forces, as ransom for cities and towns in China, subsequent to the 1st day of August, 1841.

ARTICLE VII

Periods for payment to be made by China of Indemnities of 21,000,000 dollars.

It is agreed, that the total amount of 21,000,000 dollars, described in the 3 preceding Articles, shall be paid as follows:
6,000,000 immediately.
6,000,000 in 1843; that is, 3,000,000 on or before the 30th of the month of June, and 3,000,000 on or before the 31st of December.
5,000,000 in 1844; that is, 2,500,000 on or before the 30th day of June, and 2,500,000 on or before the 31st of December.
4,000,000 in 1845; that is, 2,000,000 on or before the 30th of June, and 2,000,000 on or before the 31st of December.

Interest on Arrears

And it is further stipulated, that interest, at the rate of 5 per cent per annum, shall be paid by the Government of China on any portion of the above sums that are not punctually discharged at the periods fixed.

ARTICLE VIII

All British Subjects (European and Indian) confined in China to be released.

ARTICLE IX.

Amnesty. Release and Indemnity to Chinese formerly in British employ.

ARTICLE X

Tariff to be issued of Import, Export, and Transit Duties.

His Majesty the Emperor of China agrees to establish at all the ports which are, by Article II of this Treaty, to be thrown open for the resort of British merchants, a fair and regular tariff of export and import customs and other dues, which tariff shall be publicly notified and promulgated for general information.

Transit Duties on British Goods conveyed by Chinese into the Interior.

And the Emperor further engages, that when British merchandise shall have once paid at any of the said ports the regulated customs and dues, agreeable to the tariff to be hereafter fixed, such merchandise may be conveyed by Chinese merchants to any province or city in the interior of the Empire of China, on paying a further amount as transit duties, which shall not exceed ??? percent on the tariff value of such goods.

ARTICLE XI

Correspondence between British and Chinese Authorities

It is agreed that Her Britannic Majesty's Chief High Officer in China shall correspond with Chinese High Officers, both at the capital and in the provinces, under the term "communication"; the subordinate British Officers and Chinese High Officers in the provinces, under the terms "statement" on the part of the former, and on the part of the latter, "declaration"; and the subordinates of both countries on a footing of perfect equality: merchants and others not holding official situations, and therefore not included in the above, on both sides, to use the term "representation" in all papers addressed to, or intended for the notice of, the respective Governments.

ARTICLE XII

Evacuation of Nanking and Grand Canal by British Forces.-Kulangsu and Chusan to be held by British Forces until Settlement of Money Payments.

On the assent of the Emperor of China to this Treaty being received, and the discharge of the first installment of money, Her Britannic Majesty's forces will retire from Nanking and the Grand Canal, and will no longer molest or stop the trade of China. The military post at Chinhai will also be withdrawn; but the Islands of Kulangsu, and that of Chusan, will continue to be held by Her Majesty's forces until the money payments, and the arrangements for opening the ports to British merchants, be completed.

ARTICLE XIII

Ratifications. Provisions of Treaty to take effect in the meantime.

The ratification of this Treaty by Her Majesty the Queen of Great Britain, &c., and His Majesty the Emperor of China, shall be exchanged as soon as the great distance which separates England from China will admit; but, in the meantime, counterpart copies of it, signed and sealed by the Plenipotentiaries, on behalf of their respective Sovereigns, shall be mutually delivered, and all its provisions and arrangements shall take effect.

Done at Nanking, and signed and sealed by the Plenipotentiaries on board Her Britannic Majesty's ship "Cornwallis," this 29th day of August, 1842; corresponding with the Chinese date, 24th day of the seventh month, in the 22nd year of Taoukwang.

(L.S.) HENRY POTTINGER.
Her Majesty's Plenipotentiary

Seal of the Chinese High Commissioner
Signature of the 3rd Chinese Plenipotentiary.
Signature of the 2nd Chinese Plenipotentiary.
Signature of the 1st Chinese Plenipotentiary.

Questions:

1. *The Treaty of Nanking was the first of many treaties that European powers signed with China after the Opium War. These treaties are often referred to as "Unequal Treaties." Why is this?*
2. *How is the Opium War depicted in this document?*

21.5   The Abdication Decree (1912): Long Yu

In the first decade of the twentieth century, Sun's greatest opposition came from those who were committed to reform, but thought that this could be attained without a change of government. By 1911, however, even these reformers knew that the Manchus had to go. An uprising in October paved the way for the establishment of a republic. The formal abdication notice, signed by the empress dowager, Long Yu, on behalf of the 6-year-old emperor, Pu Yi (1906–1967), came on February 12, 1912. Sun's new Nationalist Party (Guomintang) won the elections in 1913, but the republic faced decades of turmoil as rival warlord armies continued to tear China apart. When Sun died in 1925, his successor as head of the Guomindang, Jiang Jieshi (Chiang Kai-shek), would have to face a new rival: Mao Zedong and his Communist faction.

> **Source:** "The Abdication Decree" is from Harley Farnsworth MacNair, *Modern Chinese History: Selected Readings* (Shanghai: The Commercial Press, 1927), p. 722.

It is clear that the minds of the majority of the people are favorable to the establishment of a republican form of government. . . . The universal desire clearly expresses the will of Heaven, and it is not for us to oppose the desire and incur the disapproval of the millions of the People merely for the sake of the privileges and powers of a single House. It is right that this general situation should be considered and due deference given to the opinion of the People. I, the Empress Dowager, therefore, together with the Emperor, hereby hand over the sovereignty to be the possession of the whole people, and declare that the constitution shall henceforth be Republican, in order to satisfy the demands of those within the confines of the nation, hating disorder and desiring peace, and anxious to follow the teaching of the sages, according to which the country is the possession of the People.

Consider This:

• Why did the last emperor, Pu Yi, abdicate? Why was it essential that the Qing dynasty come to an end?

Question:

1. *Why did the last emperor, Pu Yi, abdicate?*

21.6 Geisha: Glimpse of Unfamiliar Japan

The term "geisha" was first used in the middle of the eighteenth century during the Tokugawa period (1600–1868), and the first geisha were male entertainers. But in time, women came to dominate the profession. Aspiring geisha had to have good looks and, more important, good training in various traditional arts such as classical dancing, playing a stringed instrument called the samisen, singing, games, and flirtatious conversation. Some of the ambitious geisha were even trained in the tea ceremony, flower arranging, calligraphy, and painting. Training began early for girls—often as young as eight or nine—from poor families who were adopted into geisha houses and worked as maid servants for a few years as part of their early apprenticeship. When they reached the age of about thirteen, they were admitted to full apprenticeship, which lasted about five years. Upon successful completion of the apprenticeship, these girls had to pass an examination of their artistic skills at their local geisha registry before the senior members of the geisha union. Successful geisha candidates then registered at the local registry and were ready to receive assignments. They were hired to entertain customers at dinner parties or at certain restaurants. In recent decades, the profession of geisha has suffered a decline as a result of the inroad of the Western-style bar hostesses. But the geisha house today still enjoys the special favor of the Japanese politicians who prefer to conduct political negotiations at a geisha house rather than at Western-style restaurants.

The following excerpt is an account of the Japanese geisha and a geisha party described by Lafcadio Hearn (1850–1904), an Anglo-Irish-Greek who went to Japan in 1890 and became a Japanese citizen, taking the Japanese name Koizumi Yagumo. He became one of the most popular Western writers on Japan at the turn of the century.

Source: From Lafcadio Hearn, *Glimpse of Unfamiliar Japan,* Vol. II (Boston: Houghton Mifflin and Co., 1894), pp. 525–33.

The robed guests take their places, quite noiselessly and without speech, upon the kneeling-cushions. The lacquered services are laid upon the matting before them by maidens whose bare feet make no sound. For a while there is only smiling and flitting, as in dreams. You are not likely to hear any voices from without, as a banqueting-house is usually secluded from the street by spacious gardens. At last the master of ceremonies, host or provider, breaks the hush with the consecrated formula: *"O-somatsu degozarimasu ga!—dōzo o-hashi!"* whereat all present bow silently, take up their hashi (chopsticks), and fall to. But hashi, deftly used, cannot be heard at all. The maidens pour warm saké into the cup of each guest without making the least sound; and it is not until several dishes have been emptied, and several cups of saké absorbed, that tongues are loosened.

Then, all at once, with a little burst of laughter, a number of young girls enter, make the customary prostration of greeting, glide into the open space between the ranks of the guests, and begin to serve the wine with a grace and dexterity of which no common maid is capable. They are pretty; they are clad in very costly robes of silk; they are girdled like queens; and the beautifully dressed hair of each is decked with mock flowers, with wonderful combs and pins, and with curious ornaments of gold. They greet the stranger as if they had always known him; they jest, laugh, and utter funny little cries. These are the geisha,[1] or dancing-girls, hired for the banquet.

Samisen[2] tinkle. The dancers withdraw to a clear space at the farther end of the banqueting-hall, always vast enough to admit of many more guests than ever assemble upon common occasions. Some form the orchestra, under the direction of a woman of uncertain age; there are several samisen, and a tiny drum played by a child. Others, singly or in pairs, perform the dance. It may be swift and merry, consisting wholly of graceful posturing,—two girls dancing together with such coincidence of step and gesture as only years of training could render possible. But more frequently it is rather like acting than like what we Occidentals call dancing,—acting accompanied with extraordinary waving of sleeves and fans, and with a play of eyes and features, sweet, subtle, subdued, wholly Oriental. There are more voluptuous dances known to geisha, but upon ordinary occasions and before refined audiences they portray beautiful old Japanese traditions, like the legend of the fisher Urashima, beloved by the Sea God's daughter; and at intervals they sing ancient Chinese poems, expressing a natural emotion with delicious vividness by a few exquisite words. And always they pour the wine,—that warm, pale yellow, drowsy wine which fills the veins with soft contentment, making a faint sense of ecstasy, through which, as through some poppied sleep, the commonplace becomes wondrous and blissful, and the geisha Maids of Paradise, and the world much sweeter than, in the natural order of things, it could ever possibly be.

The banquet, at first so silent, slowly changes to a merry tumult. . . .

Notwithstanding all this apparent comradeship, a certain rigid decorum between guest and geisha is invariably preserved at a Japanese banquet. However flushed with wine a guest may have become, you will never see him attempt to caress a girl; he never forgets that she appears at the festivities only as a human flower, to be looked at, not to be touched. The familiarity which foreign tourists in Japan frequently permit themselves with geisha or with waiter-girls, though endured with smiling patience, is really much disliked, and considered by native observers an evidence of extreme vulgarity.

For a time the merriment grows; but as midnight draws near, the guests begin to slip away, one by one, unnoticed. Then the din gradually dies down, the music stops; and at last the geisha, having escorted the latest of the feasters to the door, with laughing cries of *Sayōnara,* can sit down alone to break their long fast in the deserted hall.

Such is the geisha's rôle. But what is the mystery of her? What are her thoughts, her emotions, her secret self? What is her veritable existence beyond the night circle of the banquet lights, far from the illusion formed around her by the mist of wine? . . .

The girl begins her career as a slave, a pretty child bought from miserably poor parents under a contract, according to which her services may be claimed by the purchasers for eighteen, twenty, or even twenty-five years. She is fed, clothed, and trained in a house occupied only by geisha; and she passes the rest of her childhood under severe discipline. She is taught etiquette, grace, polite speech; she has daily lessons in dancing; and she is obliged to learn by heart a multitude of songs with their airs. Also she must learn games, the service of banquets and weddings, the art of dressing and looking beautiful. Whatever physical gifts she may have are carefully cultivated. Afterwards she is taught to handle musical instruments: first, the little drum (tsudzumi), which cannot be sounded at all without considerable practice; then she learns to play the samisen a little, with a plectrum of tortoise-shell or ivory. At eight or nine years of age she attends banquets, chiefly as a drum-player. She is then the most charming little creature imaginable, and already knows how to fill your wine-cup exactly full, with a single toss of the bottle and without spilling a drop, between two taps of her drum.

Thereafter her discipline becomes more cruel. Her voice may be flexible enough, but lacks the requisite strength. In the iciest hours of winter nights, she must ascend to the roof of her dwelling-house, and there sing and play till the blood oozes from her fingers and the voice dies in her throat. The desired result is an atrocious cold. After a period of hoarse whispering, her voice changes its tone and strengthens. She is ready to become a public singer and dancer.

In this capacity she usually makes her first appearance at the age of twelve or thirteen. If pretty and skillful, her services will be much in demand, and her time paid for at the rate of twenty to twenty-five sen (Japanese cent) per hour. Then only do her purchasers begin to reimburse themselves for the time, expense, and trouble of her training; and they are not apt to be generous. For many years more all that she earns must pass into their hands. She can own nothing, not even her clothes.

At seventeen or eighteen she has made her artistic reputation. She has been at many hundreds of entertainments, and knows by sight all the important personages of her city, the character of each, the history of all. Her life has been chiefly a night life; rarely has she seen the sun rise since she became a dancer. She has learned to drink wine without ever losing her head, and to fast for seven or eight hours without ever feeling the worse. She has had many lovers. To a certain extent she is free to smile upon whom she pleases; but she has been well taught, above all else, to use her power of charm for her own advantage. She hopes to find Somebody able and willing to buy her freedom,—which Somebody would almost certainly thereafter discover many new and excellent meanings in those Buddhist texts that tell about the foolishness of love and the impermanency of all human relationships.

Questions:
1. *How do you compare geisha with women in a comparable entertainment profession in the West?*
2. *Why do you think Japanese politicians generally prefer geisha houses to Western-style restaurants for conducting political negotiations?*
3. *Why would a woman become a geisha?*

21.7 President Fillmore, "Letter to the Emperor of Japan"

Millard Fillmore, the thirteenth president of the United States (1850–1853), sent a letter to the emperor of Japan seeking friendly commercial relations between the two countries. For this historic mission, Commodore Matthew C. Perry of the U.S. Navy was chosen. He led three steam frigates and five other ships—a quarter of the American navy—to Japan. The following is President Fillmore's letter dated November 13, 1852.

Source: Roger Pineau, ed., *The Japan Expedition, 1852–1854. The Personal Journal of Commodore Matthew C. Perry* (Washington, DC: Smithsonian Institution Press, 1968), pp. 220–21.

LETTER OF THE PRESIDENT OF THE UNITED STATES TO THE EMPEROR OF JAPAN

Great and Good Friend!

I send you this public letter by Commodore Matthew C. Perry, an officer of highest rank in the Navy of the United States, and commander of the squadron now visiting Your Imperial Majesty's dominions.

I have directed Commodore Perry to assure Your Imperial Majesty that I entertain the kindest feelings toward Your Majesty's person and government, and that I have no other object in sending him to Japan but to propose to Your Imperial Majesty that the United States and Japan should live in friendship and have commercial intercourse with each other.

The constitution and laws of the United States forbid all interference with the religious or political concerns of other nations. I have particularly charged Commodore Perry to abstain from every act which could possibly disturb the tranquility of Your Imperial Majesty's dominions.

The United States of America reach from ocean to ocean, and our territory of Oregon and state of California lie directly opposite to the dominions of Your Impe-rial Majesty. Our steamships can go from California to Japan in eighteen days.

Our great state of California produces about sixty millions of dollars in gold every year, besides silver, quicksilver, precious stones, and many other valuable articles. Japan is also a rich and fertile country and produces many very valuable articles. Your Imperial Majesty's subjects are skilled in many of the arts. I am desirous that our two countries should trade with each other for the benefit both of Japan and the United States.

We know that the ancient laws of Your Imperial Majesty's government do not allow of foreign trade except with the Dutch. But as the state of the world changes, and new governments are formed, it seems to be wise from time to time to make new laws. There was a time when the ancient laws of Your Imperial Majesty's government were first made.

About the same time America, which is sometimes called the New World, was first discovered and settled by the Europeans. For a long time there were but a few people, and they were poor. They have now become quite numerous; their commerce is very extensive; and they think that if your Imperial Majesty were so far to change the ancient laws as to allow a free trade between the two countries, it would be extremely beneficial to both.

If Your Imperial Majesty is not satisfied that it would be safe, altogether, to abrogate the ancient laws which forbid foreign trade, they might be suspended for five or ten years, so as to try the experiment. If it does not prove as beneficial as was hoped, the ancient laws can be restored. The United States often limits its treaties with foreign states to a few years, and then renew them or not, as they please.

I have directed Commodore Perry to mention another thing to Your Imperial Majesty. Many of our ships pass every year from California to China, and great numbers of our people pursue the whale fishery near the shores of Japan. It sometimes happens in stormy weather that one of our ships is wrecked on Your Imperial Majesty's shores. In all such cases we ask and expect that our unfortunate people should be treated with kindness, and that their property should be protected till we can send a vessel and bring them away. We are very much in earnest in this.

Commodore Perry is also directed by me to represent to Your Imperial Majesty that we understand that there is a great abundance of coal and provisions in the empire of Japan. Our steam ships, in crossing the great ocean, burn a great deal of coal, and it is not convenient to bring it all the way from America. We wish that our steam ships and other vessels should be allowed to stop in Japan and supply themselves with coal, provisions, and water. They will pay for them in money, or anything else Your Imperial Majesty's subjects may prefer, and we request Your Imperial Majesty to appoint a convenient port in the southern part of the empire where our vessels may stop for this purpose. We are very desirous of this.

These are the only objects for which I have sent Commodore Perry with a powerful squadron to pay a visit to Your Imperial Majesty's renowned city of Edo: friendship, commerce, a supply of coal, and provisions and protection for our shipwrecked people.

We have directed Commodore Perry to beg Your Imperial Majesty's acceptance of a few presents. They are of no great value in themselves, but some of them may serve as specimens of the articles manufactured in the United States, and they are intended as tokens of our sincere and respectful friendship.

May the Almighty have Your Imperial Majesty in his great and holy keeping!

In witness whereof I have caused the great seal of the United States to be hereunto affixed, and have subscribed the same with my name, at the city of Washington in America, the seal of my government, on the thirteenth day of the month of November, in the year one thousand eight hundred and fifty-two.

Your good friend,
Millard Fillmore

By the President
Edward Everett
Secretary of State

Questions:
1. *Why was it necessary for the United States among other Western nations to spearhead and open Japan, which had been following a policy of self-imposed isolationism for over two centuries?*
2. *Why did the Tokugawa government in Edo succumb to the American pressure without any resistance and abandon its two-centuries'-old seclusion policy? What were the significant consequences of Tokugawa's signing of the Treaty of Kanagawa with the United States?*

21.8   Russo-Japanese War, 1904–1905, Imperial Rescript

During the Meiji period (1868–1912), Japan enjoyed phenomenal success as it transformed from a small, obscure, feudal, agrarian island-state into a modern industrial and imperial power. After having successfully modernized its government, economy, society, and military, Japan began to turn its attention abroad and show its expansionistic impulses. The first major victims of Japan's imperialistic thrust into the Asian continent were the Chinese Empire, which had been in steady decline since the Opium War (1839–1842), and its small neighbor, the Kingdom of Korea. China was humiliated and shocked by its defeat at the hands of such a small insular nation in the Sino-Japanese War (1894–1895). Invigorated by easy victory, Japan stepped up its expansionism against Manchuria, a northeastern province of China, and against Korea. Here, Japan's expansionism collided with tsarist Russia's territorial ambitions. Impatient with the impasse of bilateral negotiations, Japan declared war on Russia on February 10, 1904, two days after it had launched devastating naval attacks on Russian warships at Inchon, Korea, and Port Arthur in Manchuria. After an eighteen-month-long bitter fight, the Russo-Japanese War came to an end when the two powers signed the Portsmouth Treaty in 1905. American President Theodore Roosevelt acted as mediator at the negotiation for peace at Portsmouth, New Hampshire. Through this victory, Japan was catapulted into the ranks of the world powers. The following excerpts are from Japan's declaration of war against Russia, and Russia's communiqué in response.

Source: From K. Asakawa, *The Russo-Japanese Conflict: Its Causes and Issues* (Port Washington, NY: Kennikat Press, 1904), pp. 346–49.

DECLARATION OF WAR ON RUSSIA: *IMPERIAL RESCRIPT*

The Japanese Imperial Rescript, countersigned by all the members of the Cabinet, and declaring war against Russia, read as follows:—

"We, by the Grace of Heaven, the Emperor of Japan, seated on the Throne occupied by the same dynasty from time immemorial, do hereby make proclamation to all our loyal and brave subjects:—

"We hereby declare war against Russia. We command our army and navy to carry on hostilities against her with all their strength, and we also command all our officials to make effort, in pursuance of their duties and in accordance with their powers, to attain the national aim, with all the means within the limits of the law of nations.

"We deem it essential to international relations, and make it our constant aim, to promote the pacific progress of our Empire in civilization, to strengthen our friendly ties with other States, and thereby to establish a state of things which would maintain enduring peace in the East, and assure the future security of our Empire without injury to the rights and interests of other Powers. Our officials also perform their duties in obedience to our will, so that our relations with all Powers grow steadily in cordiality.

"It is thus entirely against our wishes that we have unhappily come to open hostilities against Russia.

"The integrity of Korea has long been a matter of the gravest concern to our Empire, not only because of the traditional relations between the two countries, but because the separate existence of Korea is essential to the safety of our Empire. Nevertheless, Russia, despite her explicit treaty pledges to China and her repeated assurances to other Powers, is still in occupation of Manchuria, and has consolidated and strengthened her hold upon it, and is bent upon its final absorption,. Since the possession of Manchuria by Russia would render it impossible to maintain the integrity of Korea, and would, in addition, compel the abandonment of all hope for peace in the Far East, we expected, in these circumstances, to settle the question by negotiations and secure thereby a permanent peace. With this object in view, our officials by our order made proposals to Russia, and frequent conferences were held during the last half year. Russia, however, never met such proposals in a spirit of conciliation, but by her prolonged delays put off the settlement of the pending question, and, by ostensibly advocating peace on the one hand, and on the other secretly extending her naval and military preparations, sought to bring about our acquiescence. It is not possible in the least to admit that Russia had from the first a sincere desire for peace. She has rejected the proposals of our Empire; the safety of Korea is in danger; the interests of our Empire are menaced. At this crisis, the guarantees for the future which the Empire has sought to secure by peaceful negotiations can now only be sought by an appeal to arms.

"It is our earnest wishes that, by the loyalty and valor of our faithful subjects, peace may soon be permanently restored and the glory of our Empire preserved."[1]

OFFICIAL RESPONSE FROM RUSSIA

On February 18, the Russian Government issued the following official communiqué:—

"Eight days have now elapsed since all Russia was shaken with profound indignation against an enemy who suddenly broke off negotiations, and, by a treacherous attack, endeavored to obtain an easy success in a war long desired. The Russian nation, with natural impatience, desires prompt vengeance, and feverishly awaits news from the Far East. The unity and strength of the Russian people leave no room for doubt that Japan will receive the chastisement she deserves for her treachery and her provocation of war at a time when our beloved Sovereign desired to maintain peace among all nations.

"The conditions under which hostilities are being carried on compel us to wait with patience for news of the success of our troops, which cannot occur before decisive actions have been fought by the Russian army. The distance of the territory now attacked and the desire of the Czar to maintain peace were causes of the impossibility of preparations for war being made a long time in advance. Much time is now necessary in order to strike at Japan blows worthy of the dignity and might of Russia, and, while sparing as much as possible the shedding of blood of her children, to inflict just chastisement on the nation which has provoked the struggle.

"Russia must await the event in patience, being sure that our army will avenge that provocation a hundred-fold. Operations on land must not be expected for some time yet, and we cannot obtain early news from the theatre of war. The useless shedding of blood is unworthy of the greatness and power of Russia. Our country displays such unity and desire for self-sacrifice on behalf of the national cause that all true news from the scene of hostilities will be immediately due to the entire nation."[2]

Questions:
1. What were the underlying and immediate causes of the war? Was the war avoidable? How? Evaluate the Russian response to Japan's war declaration. What were the important consequences of the war?
2. Define the word "imperialism" in your own words and illustrate it by citing one or two specific historical examples.
3. Why did Russia, the largest country in the world, lose the war to one of the smallest countries in the world, the newly emerging, modern state of Japan? What role did American President Theodore Roosevelt play at the peace talks between Japan and Russia in Portsmouth, New Hampshire?
4. How would you compare the Japanese attack on the Russian naval base at Port Arthur on February 8, 1904, with the Japanese attack on the American naval base at Pearl Harbor on December 7, 1941? In what ways were they similar? How did they differ?

PART 22
World War I

22.1 The Horror of Battle

The German strategy in August 1914 had been planned long in advance by Count Alfred von Schlieffen, German chief of staff until 1905. The essence of the strategy was to sweep through Belgium and over-whelm French defenses in one swift onslaught; about 90 percent of the German army would be used for that purpose, while the remaining fraction, together with the Austrians, would hold off Russia. Once France was defeated, Germany and Austria-Hungary could concentrate their forces against the Russian army. Quite unexpectedly, however, the Belgians put up a gallant resistance, and the German attack was stalled long enough to upset the timetable. The British were able to land troops in Europe, and the war degenerated into a struggle for position that was characterized by trench warfare. New weapons such as the machine gun, the tank, and barbed wire eliminated thousands of men as attacks failed and comrades were left to die in the region between the trenches called "no man's land."

The following accounts of soldiers testify to the horrors of ceaseless shelling and destruction. The Battle of Verdun in 1916 raged for ten months, resulting in a combined total of about one million casualties. The Battle of the Somme lasted five months, with well over one million killed or wounded. Very little ground or tactical advantage was gained. Battle cries such as the French "They Shall Not Pass" were indicative of the stalemated defensive war.

THE BATTLE OF THE SOMME (JULY–NOVEMBER 1916)

Source: "The Battle of the Somme" is from Charles F. Horne, ed., *Source Records of the Great War,* vol. 4 (Indianapolis, IN: The American Legion, 1931), pp. 248–251. Reprinted by permission of The American Legion.

The German Command was not thinking much about the human suffering of its troops. It was thinking, necessarily, of the next defensive line upon which they would have to fall back if the pressure of the British offensive could be maintained. . . . It was getting nervous. Owing to the enormous efforts made in the Verdun offensive the supplies of ammunition were not adequate to the enormous demand.

The German gunners were trying to compete with the British in continuity of bombardments and the shells were running short. Guns were wearing out under this incessant strain, and it was difficult to replace them. General von Gallwitz received reports of "an alarmingly large number of bursts in the bore, particularly in the field guns."

In all the letters written during those weeks of fighting and captured by us from dead or living men there is one great cry of agony and horror.

"I stood on the brink of the most terrible days of my life," wrote one of them. "They were those of the battle of the Somme. It began with a night attack on August 13th–14th. The attack lasted till the evening of the 18th, when the English wrote on our bodies in letters of blood: 'It is all over with you.' A handful of the half-mad, wretched creatures, worn out in body and mind, were all that was left of a whole battalion. We were that handful."

In many letters this phrase was used. The Somme was called the "Bath of Blood" by the German troops who waded across its shell-craters, and in the ditches which were heaped with their dead. But what I have described is only the beginning of the battle, and the bath was to be filled deeper in the months that followed.

It was in no cheerful mood that men went away to the Somme battlefields. Those battalions of gray-clad men entrained without any of the old enthusiasm with which they had gone to earlier battles. Their gloom was noticed by the officers.

"Sing, you sheep's heads, sing!" they shouted.

They were compelled to sing, by order.

"In the afternoon," wrote a man of the 18th Reserve Division, "we had to go out again: we were to learn to sing. The greater part did not join in, and the song went feebly. Then we had to march round in a circle, and sing, and that went no better."

"After that we had an hour off, and on the way back to billets we were to sing 'Deutschland über Alles,' but this broke down completely. One never hears songs of the Fatherland any more."

They were silent, grave-eyed men who marched through the streets of French and Belgian towns to be entrained for the Somme front, for they had forebodings of the fate before them. Yet none of their forebodings were equal in intensity of fear to the frightful reality into which they were flung.

A GERMAN WAR LETTER: "ONE BLOOD-SOAKED, CORPSE-STREWN FIELD"

Source: "A German War Letter" is from *German Students' War Letters,* translated and arranged from the original edition of Dr. Philipp Witkop by A. F. Wedd (New York: E. P. Dutton, 1929), pp. 208–209. Reprinted by permission of Methuen and Company.

RICHARD SCHMIEDER, Student of Philosophy, Leipzig
Born January 24th, 1888.
Killed July 14th, 1916, near Bethenville.
In the Trenches near Vaudesincourt, March 13th, 1915

Anybody who, like myself, has been through the awful days near Penthy since the 6th of February, will agree with me that a more appalling struggle could not be imagined. It has been a case of soldier against soldier, equally matched and both mad with hate and anger, fighting for days on end over a single square of ground, till the whole tract of country is one blood-soaked, corpse-strewn field. . . .

On February 27th, tired out and utterly exhausted in body and mind, we were suddenly called up to reinforce the VIIIth Reserve Corps, had to reoccupy our old position at Ripont, and were immediately attacked by the French with extraordinary strength and violence. It was a gigantic murder, by means of bullets, shells, axes, and bombs, and there was such a thundering, crashing, bellowing and screaming as might have heralded the Day of Judgment.

In three days, on a front of about 200 yards, we lost 909 men, and the enemy casualties must have amounted to thousands. The blue French cloth mingled with the German grey upon the ground, and in some places the bodies were piled so high that one could take cover from shell-fire behind them. The noise was so terrific that orders had to be shouted by each man into the ear of the next. And whenever there was a momentary lull in the tumult of battle and the groans of the wounded, one heard, high up in the blue sky, the joyful song of birds! Birds singing just as they do at home in spring-time! It was enough to tear the heart out of one's body!

Don't ask about the fate of the wounded! Anybody who was incapable of walking to the doctor had to die a miserable death; some lingered in agony for hours, some for days, and even for a week. And the combatants stormed regardlessly to and fro over them: "I can't give you a hand,—You're for the Promised Land,—My Comrade good and true." A dog, dying in the poorest hovel at home, is enviable in comparison.

There are moments when even the bravest soldier is so utterly sick of the whole thing that he could cry like a child. When I heard the birds singing at Ripont, I could have crushed the whole world to death in my wrath and fury. If only those gentlemen—Grey, Asquith, and Poincaré—could be transported to this spot, instead of the war lasting ten years, there would be peace tomorrow!

Questions:
1. What are your most vivid impressions from the personal accounts of combat?
2. Granted that all wars are horrible, what made this war unique?

22.2   Slaughter on the Somme

The following are excerpts from the diaries of three British soldiers who participated in the Battle of the Somme.

Source: From Michael Kernan, "Day of Slaughter on the Somme," *The Washington Post,* June 27, 1976, pp. C1, C5, passim. © 1976, The Washington Post. Reprinted by permission.

DIARY OF PRIVATE TOM EASTON

A beautiful summer morning, though we'd had a bit of rain earlier. The skylarks were just singing away. Then the grand mine went up, it shook the earth for nearly a minute, and we had to wait for the fallout. The whistles blew and we stepped off one yard apart going straight forward. We were under orders not to stop or look or help the wounded. Carry on if you're fit, it was. . . .

Men began to fall one by one. . . . One officer said we were OK, all the machine-guns were firing over our heads. This was so until we passed our own front line and started to cross No Man's Land. Then trench machine-guns began the slaughter from the La Boiselle salient [German positions]. Men fell on every side screaming. Those who were unwounded dare not attend to them, we must press on regardless. Hundreds lay on the German barbed wire which was not all destroyed and their bodies formed a bridge for others to pass over and into the German front line.

There were few Germans, mainly in machine-gun posts. These were bombed out, and there were fewer still of us, but we consolidated the lines we had taken by preparing firing positions on the rear of the trenches gained, and fighting went on all morning and gradually died down as men and munitions on both sides became exhausted.

When we got to the German trenches we'd lost all our officers. They were all dead, there was no question of wounded. About 25 of us made it there. . . .

Yes, as we made our way over the latter stages of the charge, men dropped all around like ninepins. Apart from machine-guns, the German artillery was also very active, great sheets of earth rose up before one. Every man had to fend for himself as we still had to face the Germans in their trenches when we got there.

I kept shouting for my mother to guide me, strange as it may seem. Mother help me. Not the Virgin Mother but my own maternal Mother, for I was then only 20 years of age.

DIARY OF CAPTAIN REGINALD LEETHAM

I got to my position and looked over the top. The first thing I saw in the space of a tennis court in front of me was the bodies of 100 dead or severely wounded men lying there in our own wire. . . . I sent my runner 200 yards on my right to get into touch with our right company, who should have been close beside me. He came back and reported he could find nothing of them. It subsequently transpired that they never reached the front line as their communication trenches had caught it so much worse than mine, and the communication trench was so full of dead and dying, that they could not get over them. . . . Those three battalions [2500 men] who went over were practically annihilated. Every man went to his death or got wounded without flinching. Yet in this war, nothing will be heard about it, the papers have glowing accounts of great British success. . . . 60 officers went out, lots of whom I knew. I believe 2 got back without being wounded. . . .

The dead were stretched out on one side [of the trench], one on top of the other, six high. . . . To do one's duty was continually climbing over corpses in every position. . . . Of the hundreds of corpses I saw I only saw one pretty one—a handsome boy called Schnyder of the Berkshires who lay on our firestep shot through the heart. There he lay with a sand-bag over his face: I uncovered it as I knew he was an officer. I wish his Mother could have seen him—one of the few whose faces had not been mutilated.

The 2nd Middlesex came back with 22 men out of 600. . . .

DIARY OF SUBALTERN EDWARD G.D. LIVEING

There was the freshness and splendor of a summer morning over everything. . . .

Just in front the ground was pitted by innumerable shellholes. . . . More holes opened suddenly every now and then. Here and there a few bodies lay about. Farther away, before our front line and in No Man's Land, lay more. In the smoke one could distinguish the second line advancing. One man after another fell down in a seemingly natural manner, and the wave melted away. In the background, where ran the remains of the German lines and wire, there was a mask of smoke, the red of the shrapnel bursting amid it. As I advanced I felt as if I was in a dream, but I had all my wits about me. We had been told to walk. Our boys, however, rushed forward with splendid impetuosity. . . .

A hare jumped up and rushed towards me through the dry yellowish grass, its eyes bulging with fear. . . . At one time we seemed to be advancing in little groups. I was at the head of one for a moment or two only to realize shortly afterwards that I was alone. I came up to the German wire. Here one could hear men shouting to one another and the wounded groaning above the explosion of shells and bombs and the rattle of machine-guns. . . .

Suddenly I cursed. I had been scalded in the left hip. A shell, I thought, had blown up in a waterlogged crump hole and sprayed me with boiling water. Letting go of my rifle, I dropped forward full length on the ground. My hip began to smart unpleasantly, and I felt a curious warmth stealing down my left leg. I thought it was the boiling water that had scalded me. Certainly my breeches looked as if they were saturated with water. I did not know they were saturated with blood.

Questions:
1. What do the diary entries reveal about the soldiers' views of authority, the enemy, and the press?
2. What do the diary entries reveal about the soldiers' sense of duty?

22.3 "World War I: A Frenchman's Recollections"

Not all the casualties were on the battlefield. Certainly one of the most devastating aspects of World War I was its effect upon the civilian populations, particularly in the small towns and villages. This particular account is from the recollections of François Carlotti (1907–   ), who draws upon his boyhood memories to describe the effects of the Great War upon the French town of Auneau, located fifteen kilometers west of the cathedral city of Chartres.

Source: François Carlotti, "World War I: A Frenchman's Recollections," *The American Scholar* 57:2 (Spring 1988), pp. 286–88. Copyright © 1988 by the author. By permission of the publishers.

The first leaves fell at the end of October. After the defeat at the frontiers, the retreat, the miracle of the Marne, the stabilization of the line in the trenches was necessary to give France time to recover her balance.

And then the High Command and government, appalled by the losses that surpassed imagining, probably found themselves little disposed to reveal the truth.

Up to this point we had only bad news of those wounded who, evacuated to the interior, had succeeded in getting a letter or a message through, and they were not many. One had lost a leg and another had been hit in the stomach. We had showed them much sympathy, them and their families. We should soon envy them.

When the two gendarmes who had stayed at headquarters started to go on their rounds with the official notices, "Died on the field of Honor," a terrified silence fell on the town, the villages, and the hamlets.

Gustave was killed, the little clerk who had once worked for my father and who had looked so handsome in his cavalryman's uniform.

Arsène, Alcide, Jules, Léon, Kléber, Maurice, Rémi, Raoul—all killed. Georges, the son of the fat ironmonger in the marketplace, who had studied in Paris and come back with advanced ideas—talking English, putting up little hurdles in the field to jump over as he ran, teaching the boys to play with a queer sort of ball that wasn't even round—killed.

Alphonse, Clothaire, Emile, Etienne, Firmin, Marceau, Raymond, Victor—killed, killed. . . .

The grief was often the more terrible because in most cases it was an only son.

And then there were the three Cochon brothers.

The Cochons were one of those families of small market-gardeners who grew their crops by the banks of the river. Every morning, the wife threaded on her shoulder straps, took up the shafts of the enormous wheelbarrow, and set out through the town to sell her mountain of fresh vegetables while her husband stayed home working in the garden.

Tall, spare, bony, mother Cochon was always the first to set out and the last to return. She had four men in the house.

The eldest daughter, married to an employee of the railway from far away, had made her home with him there in the Capdenac region where he had a good job.

The father remained at home with his three sons, who had been born one after the other within the space of five years. The three boys had all done very well at school, while also giving a helping hand at home when required. They had passed their leaving certificates before rejoining their father to toil with him from dawn to dusk.

Yet, despite all their work, their plot of land did not suffice to provide a livelihood for the whole family, and, in turn, one or two of the boys went to work for wages. They were not living as lodgers, like Belgians or Bretons who, at St. Jean, poured from the trains in serried ranks with their round hats and their clogs, their working boots slung round their necks—no, they worked as neighbors who were well favored, eating at their master's table. These Cochons were good boys who would never have worked less than their father.

Happy lads, not bothered by jokes on their name, always the first to sound the trumpet and bang the drum of the town band, first over the parallel bars or the vaulting horse, or leaders at the dance in the *mairie* on holidays.[1]

The father died while the eldest boy was away doing his training. The other two boys slaved away in the garden, working all the harder because the first born did not return home when the youngest son left. And after his three years' service, this youngest son faced mobilization and war.

When the gendarmes arrived that morning, Mme. Cochon received them standing, with the one word: "Which?" "Auguste," replied one of them and laid the little notice on the table.

"Ah, Auguste, my first born, my strongest and my bravest." A slow shudder passed across her face, but she didn't flinch.

And then, as the gendarmes stood their ground, shifting from one foot to the other, she looked them full in the face, till one of them, gathering all his courage, managed to say, "And Désiré," putting the official notification on the table as he left. "Désiré, my most handsome, my most gentle, the golden-haired one." Now she trembled from head to foot, murmuring. "Auguste . . . Désiré . . . Auguste . . . Désiré . . . ," ever more softly, as though she was clasping them.

When the gendarmes returned, a month later, she turned towards them from her seat in the corner of the fireplace without looking at them and asked: "Is it Marcel?" They bowed their heads, unable to speak.

"Ah, Marcel, my baby, my last, my dearest, O Marcel." And then suddenly a terrible cry rent the air and carried down to the river. "Marcel, Marcel. Now there are no more Cochons."

Without hearing, the gendarme forced himself to read the paper. "Cochon, Marcel, sergeant, infantry . . . heroic conduct . . . citation . . . *croix de guerre.*"[2] She repeated her crazy, despairing threnody, "No more Cochons, no more Cochons."

From that day she hardly ever went out except to walk to her husband's grave. Those who met her would often hear her muttering. "No more Cochons . . . there are no more." But no one ever saw her cry.

She died at the onset of winter.

And there were still four years of war to come. The long hopeless agonies in the military hospitals, the boys of *classe 16,*[3] called up at eighteen, who would never see their twentieth year, men who were wounded three times, bandaged up, nursed and healed, who returned yet again to the line never to return, the atrocious deaths in the gas attacks. There was the terrible winter of 1916–17 when even wild animals were frozen to death; and the insane spring offensives of 1917 when for a moment one thought oneself back in the bloodiest days of the summer of 1914, when training regiments were rushed into the line to plug the yawning gaps that held fast, never bending under the shells and the hail of the machine guns. The Americans arrived, the diabolical long-range guns shelled Paris, the last great German offensive began, which again reached the Marne, and the final victorious counter-offensive was launched.

There was the great Roger who fell on November 8.

When it was all ended and there was no family left to ask for the return of their corpses, they remained on their battlefields—the three brothers, with the vast army of shadows in the great military cemeteries, neat and orderly where they rest, hidden forever, the bravery, the gaiety, the youth of this people of France, who were—like the men of Athens before them—the adornment of the world.

Questions:
1. *Does this set of recollections suggest anything about the quality of civilian morale in France during the Great War?*
2. *Do these recollections coupled with the diary entries help to explain the appeal of fascism to some of the men and women who survived the battles and devastation of World War I?*

22.4 The Perversion of Technology: War in "No Man's Land"

What distinguishes the two great wars of the twentieth century is not so much the degree of savagery by which they were waged—very little changed in that respect—but the fact that dramatic advances in the technology of killing made it possible to liquidate masses of human beings on a previously unheard-of scale. World War I (1914–1918) was, at least prior to 1939, called the "Great War"—machine guns; barbed wire; mustard gas; and thunderous artillery effectively halted troop movement and mired the major antagonists (French and British vs. Germans) in dehumanizing trench warfare for the better part of four years. Erich Maria Remarque (1898–1970) was drafted into the German army and wrote one of the most uncompromising antiwar books of all time, "All Quiet on the Western Front," around what he had observed, heard, and lived through.

Source: Erich Maria Remarque *All Quiet on the Western Front* (Greenwich, CT: Fawcett Publications, (Crest Reprint), 1965), pp. 43–47, 68–74, 80–85, 174–175.

…Müller has a pair of glasses. We see a dark group, bearers with stretchers, and larger black clumps moving about. Those are the wounded horses. But not all of them. Some gallop away in the distance, fall down, and then run on farther. The belly of one is ripped open, the guts trail out. He becomes tangled in them and falls, then he stands up again.

Detering raises his gun and aims. Kat hits it up in the air. "Are you mad—?"
Detering trembles and throws his rifle on the ground.
We sit down and hold our ears. But this appalling noise, these groans and screams penetrate, they penetrate everywhere.

We can bear almost anything. But now the sweat breaks out on us. We must get up and run, no matter where, but where these cries can no longer be heard. And it is not men, only horses.

From the dark group stretchers move off again. Then single shots crack out. The black heap is convulsed and becomes thinner. At last! But still it is not the end. The men cannot overtake the wounded beasts which fly in their pain, their wide open mouths full of anguish. One of the men goes down on his knee, a shot—one horse drops—another. The last one props himself on his forelegs and drags himself round in a circle like a merry-go-round; squatting, it drags round in circles on its stiffened fore-legs, apparently its back is broken. The soldier runs up and shoots it. Slowly, humbly, it sinks to the ground.

We take our hands from our ears. The cries are silenced. Only a long-drawn, dying sigh still hangs on the air.

Then again only the rockets, the singing of the shells, and the stars—and they shine out wonderfully.

Detering walks up and down cursing: "Like to know what harm they've done." He returns to it once again. His voice is agitated, it sounds almost dignified as he says: "I tell you it is the vilest baseness to use horses in the war."

We go back. It is time we returned to the lorries. The sky is become a bit brighter. Three o'clock in the morning. The breeze is fresh and cool, the pale hour makes our faces look grey.

We trudge onward in single file through the trenches and shell-holes and come again to the zone of mist. Katczinsky is restive, that's a bad sign.

"What's up, Kat?" says Kropp.

"I wish I were back home." Home—he means the huts.

"It won't last much longer, Kat."

He is nervous. "I don't know, I don't know—"

We come to the communication-trench and then to the open fields. The little wood reappears; we know every foot of ground here. There's the cemetery with the mounds and the black crosses.

That moment it breaks out behind us, swells, roars, and thunders. We duck down—a cloud of flame shoots up a hundred yards ahead of us.

The next minute under a second explosion part of the wood rises slowly in the air, three or four trees sail up and then crash to pieces. The shells begin to hiss like safety-valves—heavy fire—

"Take cover!" yells somebody—"Cover!"

The fields are flat, the wood is too distant and dangerous—the only cover is the graveyard and the mounds. We stumble across in the dark and as though spirited away every man lies glued behind a mound.

Not a moment too soon. The dark goes mad. It heaves and raves. Darknesses blacker than the night rush on us with giant strides, over us and away. The flames of the explosions light up the graveyard.

There is no escape anywhere. By the light of the shells I try to get a view of the fields. They are a surging sea, daggers of flame from the explosions leap up like fountains. It is impossible for anyone to break through it.

The wood vanishes, it is pounded, crushed, torn to pieces. We must stay here in the graveyard.

The earth bursts before us. It rains clods. I feel a smack. My sleeve is torn away by a splinter. I shut my fist. No pain. Still that does not reassure me: wounds don't hurt till afterwards. I feel the arm all over. It is grazed but sound. Now a crack on the skull, I begin to lose consciousness. Like lightning the thought comes to me: Don't faint, sink down in the black broth and immediately come up to the top again. A splinter slashes into my helmet, but has travelled so far that it does not go through. I wipe the mud out of my eyes. A hole is torn up in front of me. Shells hardly ever land in the same hole twice, I'll get into it. With one bound I fling myself down and lie on the earth as flat as a fish; there it whistles again, quickly I crouch together, claw for cover, feel something on the left, shove in beside it, it gives way, I groan, the earth leaps, the blast thunders in my ears, I creep under the yielding thing, cover myself with it, draw it over me, it is wood, cloth, cover, cover, miserable cover against the whizzing splinters.

I open my eyes—my fingers grasp a sleeve, an arm. A wounded man? I yell to him—no answer—a dead man. My hand gropes farther, splinters of wood—now I remember again that we are lying in the graveyard.

But the shelling is stronger than everything. It wipes out the sensibilities, I merely crawl still deeper into the coffin, it should protect me, and especially as Death himself lies in it too.

Before me gapes the shell-hole. I grasp it with my eyes as with fists. With one leap I must be in it. There, I get a smack in the face, a hand clamps on to my shoulder—has the dead man waked up?—The hand shakes me, I turn my head, in the second of light I stare into the face of Katczinsky, he has his mouth wide open and is yelling. I hear nothing, he rattles me, comes nearer, in a momentary lull his voice reaches me: "Gas—Gaas—Gaaas—Pass it on."

I grab for my gas-mask. Some distance from me there lies someone. I think of nothing but this: That fellow there must know: Gaaas—Gaaas—

I call, I lean toward him, I swipe at him with the satchel, he doesn't see—once again, again—he merely ducks—it's a recruit—I look at Kat desperately, he has his mask ready—I pull out mine too, my helmet falls to one side, it slips over my face, I reach the man, his satchel is on the side nearest me, I seize the mask, pull it over his head, he understands, I let go and with a jump drop back into the shell-hole.

The dull thud of the gas-shells mingles with the crashes of the high explosives. A bell sounds between the explosions, gongs, and metal clappers wanting everyone—Gas— Gas—Gaas.

Someone plumps down behind me, another. I wipe the goggles of my mask clear of the moist breath. It is Kat, Kropp, and someone else. All four of us lie there in heavy, watchful suspense and breathe as lightly as possible.

These first minutes with the mask decide between life and death: is it tightly woven? I remember the awful sights in the hospital: the gas patients who in day-long suffocation cough their burnt lungs up in clots.

Cautiously, the mouth applied to the valve, I breathe. The gas still creeps over the ground and sinks into all hollows. Like a big, soft jelly-fish it floats into our shell-hole and lolls there obscenely. I nudge Kat, it is better to crawl out and lie on top than to stay here where the gas collects most. But we don't get as far as that; a second bombardment begins. It is no longer as though the shells roared; it is the earth itself raging.

With a crash something black bears down on us. It lands close beside us; a coffin thrown up.

I see Kat move and I crawl across. The coffin has hit the fourth man in our hole on his out-stretched arm. He tries to tear off his gas-mask with the other hand. Kropp seizes him just in time, twists the hand sharply behind his back and holds it fast.

Kat and I proceed to free the wounded arm. The coffin lid is loose and bursts open, we are easily able to pull it off, we toss the corpse out, it slides down to the bottom of the shell-hole, then we try to loosen the under-part.

Fortunately the man swoons and Kropp is able to help us. We no longer have to be careful, but work away till the coffin gives with a sigh before the spade that we have dug in under it.

It has grown lighter. Kat takes a piece of the lid, places it under the shattered arm, and we wrap all our bandages round it. For the moment we can do no more.

Inside the gas-mask my head booms and roars—it is nigh bursting. My lungs are tight, they breathe always the same hot, used-up air, the veins on my temples are swollen, I feel I am suffocating.

A grey light filters through to us. I climb out over the edge of the shell-hole. In the dirty twilight lies a leg torn clean off; the boot is: quite whole, I take that all in at a glance. Now someone stand up a few yards distant. I polish the windrows, in my excitement they are immediately dimmed again, I peer through them, the man there no longer wears his mask.

I wait some seconds—he has not collapsed—he looks around and makes a few paces—rattling in my throat I tear my mask off too and fall down, the air streams into me like cold water, my eyes are bursting, the wave sweeps over me and extinguishes me.

The shelling has ceased. I drag myself to the crater and tell the others. They take off their masks. We lift up the wounded man, one taking his splintered arm. And so we stumble off hastily.

The graveyard is a mass of wreckage. Coffins and corpses lie strewn about. They have been killed once again; but each of them that was flung up saved one of us.

The hedge is destroyed the rails of the light railway are torn up and rise stiffly in the air in great arches. Someone lies in front of us. We stop; Kropp goes on alone with the wounded man.

The man on the ground is a recruit. His hip is covered with blood; he is so exhausted that I feel for my water-bottle where I have rum and tea. Kat restrains my hand and stoops over him.

"Where's it got you, comrade?"

His eyes move. He is too weak to answer.

We cut off his trousers carefully. He groans. "Gently, gently, it is much better—"

If he has been hit in the stomach, he oughtn't to drink anything. There's no vomiting, that's a good sign. We lay the hip bare. It is one mass of mincemeat and bone splinters. The joint has been hit. This lad won't walk any more.

I wet his temples with a moistened finger and give him swig. His eyes move again. We see now that the right arm is bleeding as well.

Kat spreads out two wads of dressing as wide as possible so that they will cover the wound. I look for something to bind loosely round it. We have nothing more, so I slit up the man's trouser leg still farther in order to use a piece of his underpants as a bandage. But he is wearing none. I now look at him closely. He is the fair-headed boy of a little while ago.

In the meantime, Kat has taken a bandage from a dead man's pocket and we carefully bind the wound. I say to the youngster who looks at us fixedly: "We're going for a stretcher now—"

Then he opens his mouth and whispers: "Stay here—"

"We'll be back again soon," says Kat. "We are only going to get a stretcher for you."

We don't know if he understands. He wimpers like a child and plucks at us: "Don't go away——"

Kat looks around and whispers: "Shouldn't we just take a revolver and put an end to it?"

The youngster will hardly survive the carrying, and at the most he will only last a few days. What he has gone through so far is nothing to what he's in for till he dies. Now he is numb and feels nothing. In an hour he will become one screaming bundle of intolerable pain. Every day that he can live will be a howling torture. And to whom does it matter whether he has them or not—

421

I nod. "Yes, Kat, we ought to put him out of his misery."

He stands still a moment. He has made up his mind. We look round—but we are no longer alone. A little group is gathering, from the trenches appear heads.

We get a stretcher.

Kat shakes his head. "Such a kid——" He repeats it: "Young innocents——"

Our losses are less than was to be expected—five killed and eight wounded. It was quite a short bombardment. Two of our dead lie in the upturned graves. We had merely to throw the earth in on them.

The night is unbearable. We cannot sleep, but stare ahead of us and doze. Tjaden regrets that we wasted the gnawed pieces of bread on the rats. We would gladly have them again to eat now. We are short of water, too, but not seriously yet.

Towards morning, while it is dark, there is some excitement. Through the entrance rushes in a swarm of fleeing rats that try to storm the walls. Torches light up the confusion. Everyone yells and curses and slaughters. The madness and despair of many hours unloads itself in this outburst. Faces are distorted, arms strike out, the beasts scream; we just stop in time to avoid attacking one another.

The onslaught has exhausted us. We lie down to wait again. It is a marvel that our post has had no casualties so far. It is one of the few deep dug-outs.

A corporal creeps in; he has a loaf of bread with him. Three people have had the luck to get through during the night and bring some provisions. They say the bombardment extends undiminished as far the artillery lines. It is a mystery where the enemy gets all his shells.

We wait and wait. By midday what I expected happens. One of the recruits has a fit. I have been watching him for a long time, grinding his teeth and opening and shutting his fists. These hunted, protruding eyes, we know them too well. During the last few hours he has had merely the appearance of calm. He had collapsed like a rotten tree.

Now he stands up, stealthily, creeps across the floor, hesitates a moment and then glides towards the door. I intercept him and say: "Where are you going?"

"I'll be back in a minute," says he, and tries to push past me.

"Wait a bit, the shelling will stop soon."

He listens and for a moment his eye becomes clear. Then again he has the glowering eyes of a mad dog, he is silent, he shoves me aside.

"One minute, lad," I say. Kat notices. Just as the recruit shakes me off Kat jumps in and we hold him.

Then he begins to rave. "Leave me alone, let me go out, I will go out!"

He won't listen to anything and hits out, his mouth is wet and pours out words, half choked, meaningless words. It is a case of claustrophobia, he feels as though he is suffocating here: and wants to get out at any price. If we let him go he would run about everywhere regardless of cover. He is not the first.

Though he raves and his eyes roll, it can't be helped, and we have to give him a hiding to bring him to his senses. We do it quickly and mercilessly, and at last he sits down quietly. The others have turned pale; let's hope it deters them. This bombardment is too much for the poor devils, they have been sent straight from a recruiting-depot into a barrage that is enough to turn and old soldier's hair grey.

After this affair the sticky, close atmosphere works more than ever on our nerves. We sit as if in our grave: waiting only to be closed in.

Suddenly it howls and flashes terrifically the dugout cracks in all its joints under a direct hit, fortunately only a light one that the concrete blocks are able to withstand. It rings metallically, the walls reel, rifles, helmets, earth, mud, and dust fly everywhere. Sulphur fumes pour in.

If we were in one of those light dug-outs that they have been building lately instead of this deep one, not one of us would now be alive.

But the effect is bad enough even so. The recruit starts to rave again and two others follow suit. One jumps up and rushes out, we have trouble with the other two. I start after the one who escapes and wonder whether to shoot him in the leg—then it shrieks again, I fling myself down and when I stand up the wall of the trench is plastered with smoking splinters, lumps of flesh, and bits of uniform. I scramble back.

The first recruit seems actually to have gone insane. He butts his head against the wall like a goat. We must try to take him to the rear. Meanwhile, we bind him, but so that in case of attack he can be released.

Kat suggests a game of skat: it is easier when a man has something to do. But it is no use, we listen for every explosion that comes close, miscount the tricks, and fail to follow suit. We have to give it up. We sit as though in a hissing boiler that is being belaboured from without on all sides.

Night again. We are deadened by the strain—a deadly tension that scrapes along one's spine like a gapped knife. Our legs refuse to move, our hands tremble, our bodies are a thin skin stretched painfully over repressed madness, over an almost irresistible, bursting roar. We have neither flesh nor muscles any longer, we dare not look at one another for fear of some incalculable thing. So we shut our teeth—it will end—it will end—perhaps we will come through.

Suddenly the nearer explosions cease. The shelling continues but it has lifted and falls behind us, our trench is free. We seize the hand-grenades pitch them out in front of the dug-out and jump after them. The bombardment has stopped and a heavy barrage now falls behind us. The attack has come.

No one would believe that in this howling waste there could still be men; but steel helmets now appear on all sides out of the trench, and fifty yards from us a machine-gun is already in position and barking.

The wire-entanglements are torn to pieces. Yet they offer some obstacle. We see the storm-troops coming. Our artillery opens fire. Machine-guns rattle, rifles crack. The charge works its way across. Haie and Kropp begin with the hand-grenades. They throw as fast as they can, others pass them, the handles with the strings already pulled. Haie throws seventy-five yards, Kropp sixty, it has been measured, the distance is important. The enemy as they run cannot do much before they are within forty yards.

We recognize the distorted faces, the smooth helmets: they are French. They have already suffered heavily when they reach the remnants of the barbed-wire entanglements. A whole line has gone down before our machine-guns; then we have a lot of stoppages and they come nearer.

I see one of them, his face upturned, fall into a wire cradle. His body collapses, his hands remain suspended as though he were praying. Then his body drops clean away and only his hands with the stumps of his arms shot off, now hang in the wire.

The moment we are about to retreat three faces rise up from the ground in front of us. Under one of the helmets a dark pointed beard and two eyes that are fastened on me. I raise my hand, but I cannot throw into those strange eyes; for one mad moment the whole slaughter whirls like a circus round me, and these two eyes that are alone motionless; then the head rises up, a hand, a movement, and my hand-grenade flies through the air and into him.

We make for the rear, pull wire cradles into the trench and leave bombs behind us with the string pulled, which ensure us a fiery retreat. The machine-guns are already firing from the next position.

We have become wild beasts. We do not fight, we defend ourselves against annihilation. It is not against men that we fling our bombs, what do we know of men, in this moment when Death with hands and helmets is hunting us down— now, for the first time in three days we can see his face, now, for the first time in three days we can oppose him; we feel a mad anger. No longer do we lie helpless, waiting on the scaffold, we can destroy, and kill, to save ourselves, to save ourselves and be revenged.

We crouch behind every corner, behind every barrier of barbed wire, and hurl heaps of explosives at the feet of the advancing enemy before we run. The blast of the hand-grenades impinges powerfully on our arms and legs; crouching like cats we run on, overwhelmed by this wave that bears us along, that fills us with ferocity, turning us into thugs, into murderers, into God only knows what devils; this wave that multiplies our strength with fear and madness and greed of life, seeking and fighting for nothing but our deliverance. If your father came over with them you would not hesitate to fling a bomb into him

The forward trenches have been abandoned. Are they still trenches? They are blown to pieces, annihilated—there are only broken bits of trenches, holes linked by tracks, nests of craters, that is all. But the enemy's casualties increase. They did not count on so much resistance.

It is nearly noon. The sun blazes hotly, the sweat stings in our eyes, we wipe it off on our sleeves, and often blood with it. At last we reach a trench that is in a somewhat better condition. It is manned and ready for the counter-attack, it receives us. Our guns open up in full blast and cut off the enemy attack.

The lines behind us stop. They can advance no farther. The attack is crushed by our artillery. We watch. The fire lifts a hundred yards and we break forward. Beside me a lance-corporal has his head torn off. He runs a few steps more while the blood spouts from his neck like a fountain.

It does not come quite to hand-to-hand fighting; they are driven back. We arrive once again at our shattered trench and pass on beyond it.

Oh, this turning back again! We reach the shelter of the reserves and yearn to creep in and disappear;—but instead we must turn round and plunge again into the horror. If we were not automata at that moment we would continue lying there, exhausted, and without will. But we are swept forward again, powerless, madly savage and raging; we will kill, for they are still our mortal enemies; their rifles and bombs are aimed against us, and if we don't destroy them, they will destroy us.

The brown earth, the torn, blasted earth, with a greasy shine under the sun's rays; the earth is the background of this restless, gloomy world of automatons, our gasping is the scratching of a quill, our lips are dry, our heads are debauched with stupor—thus we stagger forward, and into our pierced and shattered souls bores the torturing image of the brown earth with the greasy sun and the convulsed and dead soldiers, who lie there—it can't be helped—who cry and clutch at our legs as we spring away over them.

We have lost all feeling for one another. We can hardly control ourselves when our hunted glance lights on the form of some other man. We are insensible, dead men, who through some trick, some dreadful magic, are still able to run and to kill.

A young Frenchman lags behind, he is overtaken, he puts up his hands, in one he still holds his revolver—does he mean to shoot or to give himself up?—a blow from a spade cleaves through his face. A second sees it and tries to run farther; a bayonet jabs into his back. He leaps in the air, his arms thrown wide, his mouth wide open, yelling; he staggers, in his back the bayonet quivers. A third throws away his rifle, cowers down with his hands before his eyes. He is left behind with a few other prisoners to carry off the wounded.

Suddenly in the pursuit we reach the enemy line. We are so close on the heels of our retreating enemies that we reach it almost at the same time as they. In this way we suffer few casualties. A machine-gun barks: but is silenced with a bomb. Nevertheless, the couple of seconds has sufficed to give us five stomach wounds. With the butt of his rifle Kat smashes to pulp the face of one of the unwounded machine-gunners. We bayonet the others before they have time to get out their bombs. Then thirstily we drink the water they have for cooling the gun.

Everywhere wire-cutters are snapping, planks are thrown across the entanglements, we jump through the narrow entrances into the trenches. Haie strikes his spade into the neck of a gigantic Frenchman and throws the first hand-grenade; we duck behind a breastwork for a few seconds, then the whole section of trench before us is empty. The next throw whizzes obliquely over the corner and clears a passage; as we run past we toss handfuls down into the dug-outs, the earth shudders, it crashes; dully and stifled, we stumble over slippery lumps of flesh, over yielding bodies; I fall into an open belly on which lies a clean, new officer's cap.

The fight ceases. We lose touch with the enemy. We cannot stay here long but must retire under cover of our artillery to our own position. No sooner do we know this than we dive into the nearest dug-outs, and with the utmost haste seize on whatever provisions we can see, especially the tins of corned beef and butter, before we clear out.

We get back pretty well. There has been no further attack by the enemy. We lie for an hour panting and resting before anyone speaks. We are so completely played out that in spite of our great hunger we do not think of the provisions. Then gradually we become something like men again.

The corned beef over there is famous along the whole front. Occasionally it has been the chief reason for a flying raid on our part, for our nourishment is generally bad; we have a constant hunger.

We bagged five tins altogether. The fellows over there are well looked after; it seems a luxury to us with our hunger-pangs, our turnip jam, and meat so scarce that we simply grab at it. Haie has scored a thin loaf of white French bread, and stuck it in behind his belt like a spade. It is a bit bloody at one corner, but that can be cut off.

It is a good thing we have something decent to eat at last; we still have a use for all our strength. Enough to eat is just as valuable as a good dug-out; it can save our lives; that is the reason we are so greedy for it.

Tjaden has captured two water-bottles full of cognac. We pass them round.

The evening benediction begins. Night comes, out of the craters rise the mists. It looks as though the holes were full of ghostly secrets. The white vapour creeps painfully round before it ventures to steal away over the edge. Then long streaks stretch from crater to crater.

It is chilly. I am on sentry and stare into the darkness. My strength is exhausted as always after an attack, and so it is hard for me to be alone with my thoughts. They are not properly thoughts; they are memories which in my weakness turn homeward and strangely move me.

The parachute-lights shoot upwards—and I see a picture, a summer evening, I am in the cathedral cloister and look at the tall rose trees that bloom in the middle of the little cloister garden where the monks lie buried. Around the walls are the stone carvings of the Stations of the Cross. No one is there. A great quietness rules in this blossoming quadrangle, the sun lies warm on the heavy grey stones, I place my hand upon them and feel the warmth. At the right-hand corner the green cathedral spire ascends into the, pale blue sky of the evening. Between the glowing columns of the cloister is the cool darkness that only churches have, and I stand there and wonder whether, when I am twenty, I shall have experienced the bewildering emotions of love.

The image is alarmingly near; it touches me before it dissolves in the light of the next star-shell.

I lay hold of my rifle to see that it is in trim. The barrel is wet, I take it in my hand and rub off the moisture with my fingers.

Between the meadows behind our town there stands a line of old poplars by a stream. They were visible from a great distance, and although they grew on one bank only, we called them the poplar avenue. Even as children we had a great love for them, they drew us vaguely thither, we played truant the whole day by them and listened to their rustling. We sat beneath them on the bank of the stream and let our feet hang over in the bright, swift waters. The pure fragrance of the water and the melody of the wind in the poplars held our fancies. We loved them dearly, and the image of those days still makes my heart pause in its beating.

It is strange that all the memories that come have these two qualities. They are always completely calm, that is predominant in them; and even if they are not really calm, they become so. They are soundless apparitions that speak to me, with looks and gestures, silently, without a any word—and it is the alarm of their silence that forces me to lay hold of my sleeve and my rifle lest I should abandon myself to the liberation and allurement in which my body would dilate and gently pass away into the still forces that lie behind these things.

They are quiet in this way, because quietness is so unattainable for us now. At the front there is no quietness…

One morning two butterflies play in front of our trench. They are brimstone-butterflies, with red spots on their yellow wings. What can they be looking for here? There is not a plant nor a flower for miles. They settle on the teeth of a skull. The birds too are just as carefree, they have long since accustomed themselves to the war. Every morning larks ascend from No Man's Land. A year ago we watched them nesting; the young ones grew up too.

We have a spell from the rats in the trench. They are in No Man's Land—we know what for. They grow fat; when we see one we have a crack at it. At night we hear again, the rolling behind the enemy lines. All day we have only the normal shelling, so that we are able to repair the trenches. There is always plenty of amusement, the airmen see to that. There are countless fights for us to watch every day.

Battle planes don't trouble us, but the observation planes we hate like the plague; they put the artillery on to us. A couple of minutes after they appear, shrapnel and high-explosives begin to drop on us. We lose eleven men in one day that way, and five of them stretcher-bearers. Two are so smashed that Tjaden remarks you could scrape them off the wall of the trench with a spoon and bury them in a mess-tin. Another has the lower part of his body and his legs torn off. Dead, his chest leans against the side of the trench, his face is lemon-yellow, in his beard still burns a cigarette. It glows until it dies out on his lips.

We put the dead in a large shell-hole. So far there are three layers; one on top of the other.

Suddenly the shelling begins to pound again. Soon we are sitting up, once more with the rigid tenseness of blank anticipation.

Attack, counter-attack, charge, repulse—these are words but what things they signify! We have lost a good many men, mostly recruits. Reinforcements have again been sent up to our sector. It is one of the new regiments, composed of young fellows called up during last year. They have had hardly any training, and are sent into the field with only a theoretical knowledge. They do know what a hand-grenade is, it is true, but they have very little idea of cover, and what is most important of all, have no eye for it. A fold in the ground has to be quite eighteen inches high before they can see it.

Although we need reinforcements, the recruits give us almost more trouble than they are worth. They are helpless in this grim fighting area, they fall like flies. The present method of fighting from posts demands knowledge and experience; a man must have a feeling for the contours of the ground, an ear for the sound and character of the shells, must be able to decide beforehand where they drop, how they burst, and how to take shelter.

The young recruits of course know none of these things. They get killed simply because they can hardly tell shrapnel from high-explosive, they are mown down because they are listening anxiously to the roar of the big coal-boxes falling far in the rear, and miss the light, piping whistle of the low spreading little daisy-cutters. They flock together like sheep instead of scattering, and even the wounded are shot down like hares by the airmen.

Their pale turnip faces, their pitiful clenched hands, the miserable courage of these poor devils, the desperate charges and attacks made by these poor brave devils, who are so terrified that they dare not cry out loudly, but with battered chests and torn bellies and arms and legs only whimper softly for their mothers and cease as soon as one looks at them.

Their sharp, downy, dead faces have the awful expressionlessness of dead children.

It brings a lump into the throat to see how they go over, and run and fall. A man would like to spank them, they are so stupid, and to take them by the arm and lead them away from here where they have no business to be. They wear grey coats and trousers and boots, but for most of them the uniform is far too big, it hangs on their limbs, their shoulders are too narrow, their bodies too slight; no uniform was ever made to these childish measurements.

Between five and ten recruits fall to every old hand.

A surprise gas-attack carries off a lot of them. They have not yet learned what to do. We found one dug-out full of them, with blue heads and black lips. Some of them in a shell hole took their masks off too soon; they did not know that the gas lies longest in the hollows; when they saw others on top without masks they pulled theirs off too and swallowed enough to scorch their lungs. Their condition is hopeless, they choke to death with hæmorrhages and suffocation.

In one part of the trench I suddenly run into Himmelstoss. We dive into the same dug-out. Breathless we are all lying one beside the other waiting for the charge.

When we run out again, although I am very excited, I suddenly think: "Where's Himmelstoss?" Quickly I jump back into the dug-out and find him with a small scratch lying in a corner pretending to be wounded. His face looks sullen. He is in a panic; he is new to it too. But it makes me mad that the young recruits should be out there and he here.

"Get out!" I spit.

He does not stir, his lips quiver, his moustache twitches.

"Out!" I repeat.

He draws up his legs, crouches back against the wall, and shows his teeth like a cur.

I seize him by the arm and try to pull him up. He barks.

That is too much for me. I grab him by the neck and shake him like a sack, his head jerks from side to side.

"You lump, will you get out—you hound, you skunk, sneak out of it, would you?" His eye becomes glassy, I knock his head against the wall—"You cow"—I kick him in the ribs—"You swine"—I push him toward the door and shove him out head first.

Another wave of our attack has just come up. A lieutenant is with them. He sees us and yells: "Forward, forward join in, follow." And the word of command does what all my banging could not. Himmelstoss hears the order looks round him as if awakened, and follows on.

I come after and watch him go over. Once more he is the smart Himmelstoss of the parade-ground, he has even outstripped the lieutenant and is far ahead.

Bombardment, barrage, curtain-fire, mines, gas, tanks machine-guns, hand-grenades—words, words, but they hold the horror of the world.

Our faces are encrusted, our thoughts are devastated, we are weary to death; when the attack comes we shall have to strike many of the men with our fists to waken them and make them come with us—our eyes are burnt, our hands are torn, our knees bleed, our elbows are raw.

How long has it been? Weeks—months—years? Only days. We see time pass in the colourless faces of the dying, we cram food into us, we run, we throw, we shoot, we kill, we lie about, we are feeble and spent, and nothing supports us but the knowledge that there are still feebler, still more spent, still more helpless ones there who, with staring eyes, look upon us as gods that escape death many times.

In the few hours of rest we teach them. "There, see that waggle-top? That's a mortar coming. Keep down, it will go clean over. But if it comes this way, then run for it. You can run from a mortar."

We sharpen their ears to the malicious, hardly audible buzz of the smaller shells that are not so easily distinguished. They must pick them out from the general din by their insect-like hum—we explain to them that these are far more dangerous than the big ones that can be heard long beforehand.

We show them how to take cover from aircraft, how to simulate a dead man when one is overrun in an attack, how to time hand-grenades so that they explode half a second before hitting the ground; we teach them to fling themselves into holes as quick as lightning before the shells with instantaneous fuses; we show them how to clean up a trench with a handful of bombs; we explain the difference between the fuse-length of the enemy bomb: and our own; we put them wise to the sound of gas shells;—show them all the tricks that can save them from death.

They listen, they are docile—but when it begins again, in their excitement they do everything wrong.

Haie Westhus drags off with a great wound in his back, through which the lung pulses at every breath. I can only press his hand; "It'll all up, Paul," he groans and bites his arm because of the pain.

We see men living with their skulls blown open; we see soldiers run with their two feet cut off, they stagger on their splintered stumps into the next shell-hole; a lance-corporal crawls a mile and half on his hands dragging his smashed knee after him; another goes to the dressing-station and over his clasped hands bulge his intestines; we see men without mouths, without jaws, without faces; we find one man who has held the artery of his arm in his teeth for two hours in order not to bleed to death. The sun goes down, night comes, the shells whine, life is at an end.

Still the little piece of convulsed earth in which we lie is held. We have yielded no more than a few hundred yards of it as a prize to the enemy. But on every yard there lies a dead man.

We have been relieved. The wheels roll beneath us, we stand dully, and when the call "Mind—wire" comes, we bend our knees. It was summer when we came up, the trees were still green, now it is autumn and the night is grey and wet. The lorries stop, we climb out—a confused heap, a remnant of many names. On either side stand people, dark, calling out the numbers of the regiments, the companies. And at each call a little group separates itself off, a small, handful of dirty, pallid soldiers, a dreadfully small handful, and a dreadfully small remnant.

Now someone is calling the number of our company, it is, yes, the company-commander, he has got one too, his arm is in a sling. We go over to him and I recognize Kat and Albert; we stand together, lean against each other, and look at one another.

And we hear the number of our company called again and again. He will call a long time, they do not hear him in the hospitals and shell-holes.

Once again: "Second Company, this way!"

And then more softly: "Nobody else Second Company?"

He is silent, and then huskily he says: "Is that all?" and gives the order: "Number!"

The morning is grey, it was still summer when we came up, and we were one hundred and fifty strong. Now we freeze, it is autumn, the leaves rustle, the voices flutter out wearily: "One—two—three—four" and cease at thirty-two. And there is a long silence before the voice asks: "Anybody else?"—and waits and then says softly: "In squads—" and then breaks off and is only able to finish: "Second Company—" with difficulty: "Second Company-march easy!"

A line, a short line, trudges off into the morning. Thirty-two men.

***

It is autumn. There are not many of the old hands left. I am the last of the seven fellows from our class.

Everyone talks of peace and armistice. All wait. If it again proves an illusion, then they will break up; hope is high, it cannot be taken away again without an upheaval. If, there is not peace, then there will be revolution.

I have fourteen days' rest, because I have swallowed a bit of gas; in a little garden I sit the whole day long in the sun. The armistice is coming soon, I believe it now too. Then we will go home.

Here my thoughts stop and will not go any farther. All that meets me, all that floods over me are but feelings— greed of life, love of home, yearning of the blood, intoxication of deliverance. But no aims.

Had we returned home in 1916, out of the suffering and the strength of our experiences we might have unleashed a storm. Now if we go back we will be weary, broken, burnt out, rootless, and without hope. We will not be able to find our way any more.

And men will not understand us—for the generation that grew up before us, though it has passed these years with us here, already had a home and a calling; now it will return to its old occupations, and the war will be forgotten— and the generation that has grown up after will be strange to us and push us aside. We will be superfluous even to ourselves, we will grow older, a few will adapt themselves, some others will merely submit, and most will be bewildered;—the years will pass by and in the end we shall fall into ruin.

But perhaps all this that I think is mere melancholy and dismay, which will fly away as the dust, when I stand once again beneath the poplars and listen to the rustling of their leaves. It cannot be that it has gone, the yearning that made our blood unquiet, the unknown, the perplexing, the oncoming things, the thousand faces of the future, the melodies from dreams and from books, the whispers and divinations of women, it cannot be that fills has vanished in bombardment, in despair, in brothels.

Here the trees show gay and golden, the berries of the rowan stand red among the leaves, country roads run white out to the sky-line, and the canteens hum like beehives with rumours of peace.

I stand up.

I am very quiet. Let the months and years come, they bring me nothing more, they can bring me nothing more. I am so alone, and so without hope that I can confront them without fear. The life that has borne me through these years is still in my hands and my eyes. Whether I have subdued it, I know not. But so long as it is there it will seek its own way out, heedless of the will that is within me.

He fell in October, 1918, on a day that was so quiet and still on the whole front, that the army report confined itself to the single sentence: All quiet on the Western Front.

He had fallen forward and lay on the earth as though sleeping. Turning him over one saw that he could not have suffered long; his face had an expression of calm, as though almost glad the end had come.

Questions:
1. *Compare the passages to previous battle narratives in this volume; what similarities and/or differences are there?*
2. *What effects do a face-to-face encounter with the enemy have on soldiers?*
3. *What passage(s) and what points brought out in the passage(s), in your opinion, are used to greatest effect by Remarque in contradicting notions of "glory" in war? Why?*

22.5   Sir Henry McMahon, Letter to Ali Ibn Husain

Sir Henry McMahon, the British high commissioner in Egypt, and Ali Ibn Husain, the sherif of Mecca, exchanged ten letters from 1915 to 1916. The following excerpt from a letter written October 24, 1915, shows Britain's aim—to enlist Arab support against Britain's enemy Turkey in return for hints of British support of an independent Arab state.

Source: From Great Britain, *Parliamentary Papers*, 1939, Misc. No. 3, Cmd. 5957.

As for those regions lying within those frontiers wherein Great Britain is free to act without detriment to the interests of her ally, France, I am empowered in the name of the Government of Great Britain to give the following assurances and make the following reply to your letter:

1. Subject to the above modifications, Great Britain is prepared to recognise and support the independence of the Arabs in all the regions within the limits demanded by the Sherif of Mecca.

2. Great Britain will guarantee the Holy Places against all external aggression and will recognise their inviolability.

3. When the situation admits, Great Britain will give to the Arabs her advice and will assist them to establish what may appear to be the most suitable forms of government in those various territories.

4. On the other hand, it is understood that the Arabs have decided to seek the advice and guidance of Great Britain only, and that such European advisers and officials as may be required for the formation of a sound form of administration will be British.

5. With regard to the vilayets [provinces] of Bagdad and Basra, the Arabs will recognise that the established position and interests of Great Britain necessitate special administrative arrangements in order to secure these territories from foreign aggression, to promote the welfare of the local populations and to safeguard our mutual economic interests.

I am convinced that this declaration will assure you beyond all possible doubt of the sympathy of Great Britain towards the aspirations of her friends the Arabs and will result in a firm and lasting alliance, the immediate results of which will be the expulsion of the Turks from the Arab countries and the freeing of the Arab peoples from the Turkish yoke, which for so many years has pressed heavily upon them.

Questions:
1. *Do the suggestions made in the McMahon letter provide a perspective on the contemporary political problems in the Middle East?*
2. *Did the British government have the legal and moral authority to promise the birth of an Arab state?*

22.6   The Balfour Declaration

To enlist Jewish support for the war, British Foreign Secretary, Arthur James Balfour wrote the following letter to Lord Rothschild, a prominent Jewish leader, and had it printed in The Times. The letter contains the official statement that soon became known as the Balfour Declaration.

Source: From *The Times* (London), November 9, 1917.

Foreign Office
November 2nd, 1917

Dear Lord Rothschild:

I have much pleasure in conveying to you, on behalf of His Majesty's Government, the following declaration of sympathy with Jewish Zionist aspirations which has been submitted to, and approved by, the Cabinet:

His Majesty's Government view with favor the establishment in Palestine of a national home for the Jewish people, and will use their best endeavors to facilitate the achievement of this object, it being clearly understood that nothing shall be done which may prejudice the civil and religious rights of existing non-Jewish communities in Palestine, or the rights and political status enjoyed by Jews in any other country.

I should be grateful if you would bring this declaration to the knowledge of the Zionist Federation.

Yours,

Arthur James Balfour

Questions:
1. *Why did the British government wait until 1917 to publicly support the desire of the Jewish people for a state?*
2. *What are the contemporary implications of Lord Balfour's statement: ". . . it being clearly understood that nothing shall be done which may prejudice the civil and religious rights of existing non-Jewish communities in Palestine"?*

22.7 Woodrow Wilson, "Speech on the Fourteen Points"

On January 8, 1918, U.S. President Woodrow Wilson, speaking before a joint session of Congress, put forth his Fourteen Points proposal for ending the war. In this speech, he established the basis of a peace treaty and the foundation of a League of Nations.

Source: From Woodrow Wilson, "Speech on the Fourteen Points," *Congressional Record,* 65th Congress, 2nd Session, 1918, pp. 680–81.

We entered this war because violations of right had occurred which touched us to the quick and made the life of our own people impossible unless they were corrected and the world secured once and for all against their recurrence. What we demand in this war, therefore, is nothing peculiar to ourselves. It is that the world be made fit and safe to live in; and particularly that it be made safe for every peace-loving nation which, like our own, wishes to live its own life, determine its own institutions, be assured of justice and fair dealing by the other peoples of the world as against force and selfish aggression. All the peoples of the world are in effect partners in this interest, and for our own part we see very clearly that unless justice be done to others it will not be done to us. The programme of the world's peace, therefore, is our programme; and that programme, the only possible programme, as we see it, is this:

I.   Open covenants of peace, openly arrived at, after which there shall be no private international understanding of any kind but diplomacy shall proceed always frankly and in the public view.

II. Absolute freedom of navigation upon the seas, outside territorial waters, alike in peace and in war, except as the seas may be closed in whole or in part by international action for the enforcement of international covenants.

III. The removal, so far as possible, of all economic barriers and the establishment of an equality of trade conditions among all the nations consenting to the peace and associating themselves for its maintenance.

IV. Adequate guarantees given and taken that national armaments will be reduced to the lowest point consistent with domestic safety.

V.   A free, open-minded, and absolutely impartial adjustment of all colonial claims, based upon a strict observance of the principle that in determining all such questions of sovereignty the interests of the populations concerned must have equal weight with the equitable claims of the government whose title is to be determined.

VI. The evacuation of all Russian territory and such a settlement of all questions affecting Russia as will secure the best and freest cooperation of the other nations of the world in obtaining for her an unhampered and unembarrassed opportunity for the independent determination of her own political development and national policy and assure her a sincere welcome into the society of free nations under institutions of her own choosing; and, more than a welcome, assistance also of every kind that she may need and may herself desire. The treatment accorded Russia by her sister nations in the months to come will be the acid test of their good will, of their comprehension of her needs as distinguished from their own interests, and of their intelligent and unselfish sympathy.

VII. Belgium, the whole world will agree, must be evacuated and restored, without any attempt to limit the sovereignty which she enjoys in common with all other free nations. No other single act will serve as this will serve to restore confidence among the nations in the laws which they have themselves set and determined for the government of their relations with one another. Without this healing act the whole structure and validity of international law is forever impaired.

VIII. All French territory should be freed and the invaded portions restored, and the wrong done to France by Prussia in 1871 in the matter of Alsace-Lorraine, which has unsettled the peace of the world for nearly fifty years, should be righted, in order that peace may once more be made secure in the interest of all.

IX. A readjustment of the frontiers of Italy should be effected along clearly recognizable lines of nationality.

X. The peoples of Austria-Hungary, whose place among the nations we wish to see safeguarded and assured, should be accorded the freest opportunity of autonomous development.

XI. Rumania, Serbia, and Montenegro should be evacuated; occupied territories restored; Serbia accorded free and secure access to the sea; and the relations of the several Balkan states to one another determined by friendly counsel along historically established lines of allegiance and nationality; and international guarantees of the political and economic independence and territorial integrity of the several Balkan states should be entered into.

XII. The Turkish portions of the present Ottoman Empire should be assured a secure sovereignty, but the other nationalities which are now under Turkish rule should be assured an undoubted security of life and an absolutely unmolested opportunity of autonomous development, and the Dardanelles should be permanently opened as a free passage to the ships and commerce of all nations under international guarantees.

XIII. An independent Polish state should be erected which should include the territories inhabited by indisputably Polish populations, which should be assured a free and secure access to the sea, and whose political and economic independence and territorial integrity should be guaranteed by international covenant.

XIV. A general association of nations must be formed under specific covenants for the purpose of affording mutual guarantees of political independence and territorial integrity to great and small states alike.

Questions:
1. What was the political impact of the Fourteen Points on the peoples living under colonial rule? Was Wilson's idea of self-determination for colonial peoples to decide their own fate?
2. An underlying assumption of the Fourteen Points is that America should use its power to ensure that the world "be made fit and safe to live in." Is this the proper policy of the United States? Why? Why not?

22.8   The Covenant of the League of Nations

President Woodrow Wilson insisted that the Covenant of the League be included as an integral part of the peace treaties signed at the conclusion of the First World War. The League of Nations functioned sporadically throughout the interwar period, until it was eclipsed by the outbreak of the Second World War. Although weakened from the outset by the refusal of the United States to become a member - the U.S. Senate thus repudiating Wilson - it achieved some significant results. It sponsored and supported treaties on the reduction of armaments, settled border disputes between nations, and averted a possible war between Greece and Bulgaria.

The high contracting parties, in order to promote international cooperation and to achieve international peace and security by the acceptance of obligations not to resort to war, by the prescription of open, just and honourable relations between nations, by the first establishment of the understandings of international law as the actual law of conduct among Governments, and by the maintenance of justice and a scrupulous respect for all treaty obligations in the dealings of organized peoples with one another, agree to this Covenant of the League of Nations.

ARTICLE 1

1. The original Members of the League of Nations shall be those of the Signatories which are named in the Annex to this Covenant and also such of those other States named in the Annex as shall accede without reservation to this Covenant. Such accession shall be effected by a Declaration deposited with the Secretariat within two months of the coming into force of the Covenant. Notice thereof shall be sent to all other Members of the League.

2. Any fully self-governing State, Dominion or Colony not named in the Annex may become a Member of the League if its admission is agreed to by two-thirds of the Assembly, provided that it shall give effective guarantees of its sincere intention to observe its international obligations, and shall accept such regulations as may be prescribed by the League in regard to its military, naval and air forces and armaments.

3. Any Member of the League may, after two years' notice of its intention so to do, withdraw from the League, provided that all its international obligations and all its obligations under this Covenant shall have been fulfilled at the time of its withdrawal.

ARTICLE 2

The action of the League under this Covenant shall be effected through instrumentality of an Assembly and of a Council, with a permanent Secretariat.

ARTICLE 3

1. The Assembly shall consist of Representatives of the Members of the League.
2. The Assembly shall meet at stated intervals and from time to time as occasion may require, at the Seat of the League or at such other place as may be decided upon.
3. The Assembly may deal at its meetings with any matter within the sphere of action of the League or affecting the peace of the world.
4. At meetings of the Assembly, each Member of the League shall have one vote, and may have not more than three Representatives.

ARTICLE 4

1. The Council shall consist of Representatives of the Principal Allied and Associated Powers, together with Representatives of four other Members of the League. These four Members of the League shall be selected by the Assembly from time to time in its discretion. Until the appointment of the Representatives of the four Members of the league first selected by the Assembly, Representatives of Belgium, Brazil, Spain, and Greece shall be members of the Council.
2. With the approval of the majority of the Assembly, the Council may name additional Members of the League whose Representatives shall always be members of the Council; the Council with like approval may increase the number of Members of the League to be selected by the Assembly for representation on the Council. The Assembly shall fix by a two-thirds majority the rules dealing with the election of the non-permanent Members of the Council, and particularly such regulations as relate to their term of office and the conditions of re-eligibility.
3. The Council shall meet from time to time as occasion may require, and at least once a year, at the Seat of the League, or at such other place as may be decided upon.
4. The Council may deal at its meetings with any matter within the sphere of action of the League or affecting the peace of the world.
5. Any Member of the League not represented on the Council shall be invited to send a Representative to sit as a member at any meeting of the Council during the consideration of matters specially affecting the interest of that Member of the League.
6. At meetings of the Council each member of the League represented on the Council shall have one vote, and may have not more than one Representative.

ARTICLE 5

1. Except where otherwise expressly provided in this Covenant or by the terms of the present Treaty, decisions at any meeting of the Assembly or of the Council shall require the agreement of all the Members of the League represented at the meeting.
2. All matters of procedure at meetings of the Assembly or of the Council, including the appointment of Committees to investigate particular matters, shall be regulated by the Assembly or by the Council, and may be decided by a majority of the Members of the League represented at the meeting.
3. The first meeting of the Assembly and the first meeting of the Council shall be summoned by the President of the United States of America.

ARTICLE 6

1. The permanent Secretariat shall be established at the Seat of the League. The Secretariat shall comprise a Secretary-General and such secretaries and staff as may be required.

2. The first Secretary-General shall be the person named in the Annex; thereafter the Secretary-General shall be appointed by the Council with the approval of the majority of the Assembly.

3. The secretaries and staff of the Secretariat shall be appointed by the Secretary-General with the approval of the Council.

4. The Secretary-General shall act in that capacity at all meetings of the Assembly and of the Council.

5. The expenses of the League shall be borne by the Members of the League in the proportion decided by the Assembly.

ARTICLE 7

1. The Seat of the League is established at Geneva.

2. The Council may at any time decide that the Seat of the League shall be established elsewhere.

3. All positions under or in connection with the League, including the Secretariat, shall be open equally to men and women.

4. Representatives of the Members of the League and officials of the League when engaged on the business of the League shall enjoy diplomatic privileges and immunities.

5. The buildings and other property occupied by the League or its officials or by Representatives attending its meetings shall be inviolable.

ARTICLE 8

1. The Members of the League recognize that the maintenance of peace requires the reduction of national armaments to the lowest point consistent with national safety and the enforcement by common action of international obligations.

2. The Council, taking account of the geographical situation and circumstances of each state, shall formulate plans for such reduction for the consideration and action of the several Governments.

3. Such plans shall be subject to re-consideration and revision at least every ten years.

4. After these plans shall have been adopted by the several Governments, the limits of armaments therein fixed shall not be exceeded without the concurrence of the Council.

5. The Members of the League agree that the manufacture by private enterprise of munitions and implements of war is open to grave objections. The Council shall advise how the evil effects attendant upon such manufacture can be prevented, due regard being had to the necessities of those Members of the League which are not able to manufacture the munitions and implements of war necessary for their safety.

6. The Members of the League undertake to interchange full and frank information as to the scale of their armaments, their military, naval and air programmes and the condition of such of their industries as are adaptable to war-like purposes.

ARTICLE 9

A permanent Commission shall be constituted to advise the Council on the execution of the provisions of Articles 1 and 8 and on military, naval and air questions generally.

ARTICLE 10

The Members of the League undertake to respect and preserve as against external aggression the territorial integrity and existing political independence of all Members of the League. In case of any such aggression or in case of any threat or danger of such aggression the Council shall advise upon the means by which this obligation shall be fulfilled.

ARTICLE 11

1. Any war or threat of war, whether immediately affecting any of the members of the League or not, is hereby declared a matter of concern to the whole League, and the League shall take any action that may be deemed wise and effec-

tual to safeguard the peace of nations. In case any such emergency should arise the Secretary-General shall on the request of any Member of the League forthwith summon a meeting of the Council.

2. It is also declared to be the friendly right of each Member of the League to bring to the attention of the Assembly or of the Council any circumstances whatever affecting international relations which threatens to disturb international peace or the good understanding between nations upon which peace depends.

ARTICLE 12

1. The Members of the League agree that if there should arise between them any dispute likely to lead to a rupture, they will submit the matter either to arbitration or judicial settlement or to inquiry by the Council, and they agree in no case to resort to war until three months after the award by the arbitrators or the judicial decision or the report by the Council.

2. In any case under this Article the award of the arbitrators or the judicial decision shall be made within a reasonable time, and the report of the Council shall be made within six months after the submission of the dispute.

ARTICLE 13

1. The Members of the League agree that whenever any dispute shall arise between them which they recognize to be suitable for submission to arbitration or judicial settlement and which cannot be satisfactorily settled by diplomacy, they will submit the whole subject-matter to arbitration or judicial settlement.

2. Disputes as to the interpretation of a treaty, as to any question of international law, as to the existence of any fact which if established would constitute a breach of any international obligation, or as to the extent and nature of the reparation to be made for any such breach, are declared to be among those which are generally suitable for submission to arbitration or judicial settlement.

3. For the consideration of any such dispute, the court to which the case is referred shall be the Permanent Court of International Justice, established in accordance with Article 14, or any tribunal agreed on by the parties to the dispute or stipulated in any convention existing between them.

4. The Members of the League agree that they will carry out in full good faith any award or decision that may be rendered and that they will not resort to war against a Member of the League which complies therewith. In the event of any failure to carry out such an award or decision, the Council shall propose what steps should be taken to give effect thereto.

ARTICLE 14

The Council shall formulate and submit to the Members of the League for adoption plans for the establishment of a Permanent Court of International Justice. The Court shall be competent to hear and determine any dispute of an international character which the parties thereto submit to it. The Court may also give an advisory opinion upon any dispute or question referred to it by the Council or by the Assembly.

ARTICLE 15

1. If there should arise between Members of the League any dispute likely to lead to a rupture, which is not submitted to arbitration or judicial settlement in accordance with Article 13, the Members of the League agree that they will submit the matter to the Council. Any party to the dispute may effect such submission by giving notice of the existence of the dispute to the Secretary-General, who will make all necessary arrangements for a full investigation and consideration thereof.

2. For this purpose the parties to the dispute will communicate to the Secretary-General, as promptly as possible, statements of their case with all the relevant facts and papers, and the Council may forthwith direct the publication thereof.

3. The Council shall endeavour to effect a settlement of the dispute, and if such efforts are successful, a statement shall be made public giving such facts and explanations regarding the dispute and the terms of settlement thereof as the Council may deem appropriate.

4. If the dispute is not thus settled, the Council, either unanimously or by a majority vote, shall make and publish a report containing a statement of the facts of the dispute and the recommendations which are deemed just and proper in regard thereto.

5. Any Member of the League represented on the Council may make public a statement of the facts of the dispute and of its conclusions regarding the same.

6. If a report by the Council is unanimously agreed to by the members thereof other than the Representatives of one or more of the parties to the dispute, the Members of the League agree that they will not go to war with any party to the dispute which complies with the recommendations of the report.

7. If the Council fails to reach a report which is unanimously agreed to by the members thereof, other than the Representatives of one or more of the parties to the dispute, the Members of the League reserve to themselves the right to take such action as they shall consider necessary for the maintenance of right and justice.

8. If the dispute between the parties is claimed by one of them, and is found by the Council to arise out of a matter which by international law is solely within the domestic jurisdiction of that party, the Council shall so report, and shall make no recommendation as to its settlement.

9. The Council may in any case under this Article refer the dispute to the Assembly. The dispute shall be so referred at the request of either party to the dispute, provided that such a request be made within fourteen days after the submission of the dispute to the Council.

10. In any case referred to the Assembly, all the provisions of this Article and Article 12 relating to the action and powers of the Council shall apply to the action and powers of the Assembly, provided that a report made by the Assembly, if concurred in by the Representatives of those Members of the League represented on the Council and of a majority of the other Members of the League, exclusive in each case of the Representatives of the parties to the dispute, shall have the same force as a report by the Council concurred in by all the members thereof other than the Representatives of one or more of the parties to the dispute.

ARTICLE 16

1. Should any Member of the League resort to war in disregard of its covenants under Articles 12, 13 or 15, it shall *ipso facto* be deemed to have committed an act of war against all other Members of the League, which hereby undertake immediately to subject it to the severance of all trade or financial relations, the prohibition of all intercourse between their nationals and the nationals of the covenant-breaking State, and the prevention of all financial, commercial or personal intercourse between the nationals of the covenant-breaking State and the nationals of any other State, whether a Member of the League or not.

2. It shall be the duty of the Council in such case to recommend to the several Governments concerned what effective military, naval or air force the Members of the League shall severally contribute to the armed forces to be used to protect the covenants of the League.

3. The Members of the League agree further, that they will mutually support one another in the financial and economic measures which are taken under this article, in order to minimize the loss and inconvenience resulting from the above measures, and that they will mutually support one another in resisting any special measures aimed at one of their number by the covenant-breaking State, and that they will take the necessary steps to afford passage through their territory to the forces of any of the Members of the League which are co-operating to protect the covenants of the League.

4. Any Member of the League which has violated any covenant of the League may be declared to be no longer a Member of the League by a vote of the Council concurred in by the Representatives of all the other Members of the League represented thereon.

ARTICLE 17

1. In the event of a dispute between a Member of the League and a State which is not a Member of the League, or between States not Members of the League, the State or States not Members of the League shall be invited to accept the obligations of membership in the League for the purposes of such dispute, upon such conditions as the Council may deem just. If such invitation is accepted, the provisions of Articles 12 to 16 inclusive shall be applied with such modifications as may be deemed necessary by the Council.

2. Upon such invitation being given the council shall immediately institute an inquiry into the circumstances of the dispute and recommend such action as may seem best and most effectual in the circumstances.

3. If a State so invited shall refuse to accept the obligations of membership in the League for the purposes of such dispute, and shall resort to war against a Member of the League, the provisions of Article 16 shall be applicable as against the State taking such action.

4. If both parties to the dispute when so invited refuse to accept the obligations of membership in the League for the purpose of such dispute, the Council may take such measures and make such recommendations as will prevent hostilities and will result in the settlement of the dispute.

ARTICLE 18

Every treaty or international engagement entered into hereafter by any Member of the League shall be forthwith registered with the Secretariat and shall as soon as possible be published by it. No such treaty or international engagement shall be binding until so registered.

ARTICLE 19

The Assembly may from time to time advise the reconsideration by Members of the League of treaties which have become inapplicable and the consideration of international conditions whose continuance might endanger the peace of the world.

ARTICLE 20

1. The Members of the League severally agree that this Covenant is accepted as abrogating all obligations or understandings inter se which are inconsistent with the terms thereof, and solemnly undertake that they will not hereafter enter into any engagements inconsistent with the terms thereof.

2. In case any Member of the League shall, before becoming a Member of the League, have undertaken any obligations inconsistent with the terms of this covenant, it shall be the duty of such Member to take immediate steps to procure its release from such obligations.

ARTICLE 21

Nothing in this Covenant shall be deemed to affect the validity of international engagements, such as treaties of arbitration or regional understandings like the Monroe Doctrine, for securing the maintenance of peace.

ARTICLE 22

1. To those colonies and territories which as a consequence of the late war have ceased to be under the sovereignty of the States which formerly governed them and which are inhabited by the peoples not yet able to stand by themselves under the strenuous conditions of the modern world, there should be applied the principle that the well-being and development of such peoples form a sacred trust of civilization and that securities for the performance of this trust should be embodied in this Covenant.

2. The best method of giving practical effect to this principle is that the tutelage of such peoples should be entrusted to advanced nations who by reason of their resources, their experience or their geographical position can best undertake this responsibility, and who are willing to accept it, and that this tutelage should be exercised by them as Mandatories on behalf of the League.

3. The character of the mandate must differ according to the stage of the development of the people, the geographical situation of the territory, its economic conditions and other similar circumstances.

4. Certain communities formerly belonging to the Turkish Empire have reached a stage of development where their existence as independent nations can be provisionally recognized subject to the rendering of administrative advice and assistance by a Mandatory until such time as they are able to stand alone. The wishes of these communities must be a principal consideration in the selection of the Mandatory.

5. Other peoples, especially those of Central Africa, are at such a stage that the Mandatory must be responsible for the administration of the territory under conditions which will guarantee freedom of conscience and religion, subject only to the maintenance of public order and morals, the prohibition of abuses such as the slave trade, the arms traffic and the liquor traffic, and the prevention of the establishment of fortifications or military and naval bases and of military training of the natives for other than police purposes and the defence of territory, and will also secure equal opportunities for the trade and commerce of other Members of the League.

6. There are territories, such as Southwest Africa and certain of the South Pacific Islands, which, owing to the sparseness of their population, or their small size, or their remoteness from the centres of civilization, or their geographical contiguity to the territory of the Mandatory, and other circumstances, can be best administered under the laws of the Mandatory as integral portions of its territory, subject to the safeguards above mentioned in the interests of the indigenous population.

7. In every case of mandate, the Mandatory shall render to the Council an annual report in reference to the territory committed to its charge.

8. The degree of authority, control, or administration to be exercised by the Mandatory shall, if not previously agreed upon by the Members of the League, be explicitly defined in each case by the Council.

9. A permanent Commission shall be constituted to receive and examine the annual reports of the Mandatories and to advise the Council on all matters relating to the observance of the mandates.

ARTICLE 23

Subject to and in accordance with the provisions of international conventions existing or hereafter to be agreed upon, the Members of the League:

(a) will endeavour to secure and maintain fair and humane conditions and labour for men, women, and children, both in their own countries and in all countries to which their commercial and industrial relations extend, and for that purpose will establish and maintain the necessary international organizations;

(b) undertake to secure just treatment of the native inhabitants of territories under their control;

(c) will entrust the League with the general supervision over the execution of agreements with regard to the traffic in women and children, and the traffic in opium and other dangerous drugs;

(d) will entrust the League with the general supervision of the trade in arms and ammunition with the countries in which the control of this traffic is necessary in the common interest;

(e) will make provision to secure and maintain freedom of communications and of transit and equitable treatment for the commerce of all Members of the League. In this connexion, the special necessities of the regions devastated during the war of 1914-1918 shall be borne in mind;

(f) will endeavour to take steps in matters of international concern for the prevention and control of disease.

ARTICLE 24

1. There shall be placed under the direction of the League all international bureaux already established by general treaties if the parties to such treaties consent. All such international bureaux and all commissions for the regulation of matters of international interest hereafter constituted shall be placed under the direction of the League.

2. In all matters of international interest which are regulated by general conventions but which are not placed under the control of international bureaux or commissions, the Secretariat of the League shall, subject to the consent of the Council and if desired by the parties, collect and distribute all relevant information and shall render any other assistance which may be necessary or desirable.

3. The Council may include as part of the expenses of the Secretariat the expenses of any bureau or commission which is placed under the direction of the League.

ARTICLE 25

The Members of the League agree to encourage and promote the establishment and co-operation of duly authorized voluntary national Red Cross organizations having as purposes the improvement of health, the prevention of disease and the mitigation of suffering throughout the world.

ARTICLE 26

1. Amendments to this Covenant will take effect when ratified by the Members of the League whose Representatives compose the Council and by a majority of the Members of the League whose Representatives compose the Assembly.

2. No such amendments shall bind any Member of the League which signifies its dissent therefrom, but in that case it shall cease to be a Member of the League.

Questions:
1. What are the goals of the League of Nations?
2. What provisions are there for meeting those goals?

PART 23
Authoritarian and Totalitarian Experiments in Europe

23.1 The Bolshevik Seizure of Power (November–December 1917)

World War I proved especially disastrous for Russia. The army suffered tremendous losses against a German onslaught of superior force and preparation. Misery, famine, and disease descended on the Russian people, and thousands were dislocated and wandered aimlessly as refugees. Tsar Nicholas II feared a general uprising and finally decided to abdicate his throne in March 1917.

A temporary body called the Provisional Government was installed to maintain stability in the country until a representative Constituent Assembly could be elected by the Russian people. The Petrograd Soviet, an elected council of workers and soldiers, immediately threatened the authority of the Provisional Government. The Marxist revolutionary, Vladimir Ulyanov, better known as Lenin (1870–1924), arrived from Switzerland to reassert his leadership of the Bolshevik party and in November 1917, persuaded his faction that the time was ripe for a coup. The first selection is Lenin's speech after his successful storming of the tsar's Winter Palace in Petrograd. Note the critical editorial from the newspaper Izvestia on November 8. It was the last before the Bolsheviks censored the press. Lenin's seizure of power also included the establishment of a secret police (Cheka), an institution that had been used (in another form) by the autocratic tsar to eliminate opposition.

SPEECH AFTER THE OVERTHROW OF THE PROVISIONAL GOVERNMENT
V. I. LENIN

> **Source:** "Speech after the Overthrow of the Provisional Government" is from Frank A. Golder, ed., *Documents of Russian History* (1914–1917), trans. Emanuel Aronsberg (New York: The Century Company, 1927), pp. 618–619.

Comrades, the workmen's and peasant's revolution, the need of which the Bolsheviks have emphasized many times, has come to pass.

What is the significance of this revolution? Its significance is, in the first place, that we shall have a soviet government, without the participation of bourgeoisie of any kind. The oppressed masses will of themselves form a government. The old state machinery will be smashed into bits and in its place will be created a new machinery of government by the soviet organizations. From now on there is a new page in the history of Russia, and the present, third Russian revolution shall in its final result lead to the victory of Socialism.

One of our immediate tasks is to put an end to the war at once. But in order to end the war, which is closely bound up with the present capitalistic system, it is necessary to overthrow capitalism itself. In this work we shall have the aid of the world labor movement, which has already begun to develop in Italy, England, and Germany.

A just and immediate offer of peace by us to the international democracy will find everywhere a warm response among the international proletariat masses. In order to secure the confidence of the proletariat, it is necessary to publish at once all secret treaties.

In the interior of Russia a very large part of the peasantry has said: Enough playing with the capitalists; we will go with the workers. We shall secure the confidence of the peasants by one decree, which will wipe out the private property of the landowners. The peasants will understand that their only salvation is in union with the workers.

We will establish a real labor control on production.

We have now learned to work together in a friendly manner, as is evident from this revolution. We have the force of mass organization which has conquered all and which will lead the proletariat to world revolution.

We should now occupy ourselves in Russia in building up a proletarian socialist state.

Long live the world-wide socialistic revolution!

"LITTLE GOOD IS TO BE EXPECTED" (NOVEMBER 8, 1917)
IZVESTIA

Source: "'Little Good Is to Be Expected'" is from Frank A. Golder, ed., *Documents of Russian History* (1914–1917), trans. Emanuel Aronsberg (New York: The Century Company, 1927), p. 619.

Yesterday we said that the Bolshevik uprising is a made adventure and today, when their attempt is crowned with success, we are of the same mind. We repeat: that which is before us is not a transfer of power to the Soviets, but a seizure of power by one party—the Bolsheviks. Yesterday we said that a successful attempt meant the breaking up of the greatest of the revolution—the Constituent Assembly. Today we add that it means, also, the breaking up of the Congress of Soviets, and perhaps the whole soviet organization. They can call themselves what they please; the fact remains that the Bolsheviks alone took part in the uprising. All the other socialistic and democratic parties protest against it.

How the situation may develop we do not know, but little good is to be expected. We are quite confident that the Bolsheviks cannot organize a state government. As yesterday, so today, we repeat that what is happening will react worst of all on the question of peace.

CENSORSHIP OF THE PRESS (NOVEMBER 9, 1917)
V. I. LENIN

Source: "Censorship of the Press" is from Martin McCauley, ed., *The Russian Revolution and the Soviet State* (New York: Barnes & Noble, 1975), pp. 190–191. Permission granted by Barnes & Noble Books, Totowa, New Jersey.

In the trying critical period of the revolution and the days that immediately followed it the Provisional Revolutionary Committee was compelled to take a number of measures against the counter-revolutionary press of different shades.

Immediately outcries were heard from all sides that the new, socialist power had violated a fundamental principle of its programme by encroaching upon the freedom of the press.

The Workers' and Peasants' Government calls the attention of the population to the fact that what this liberal facade actually conceals is freedom for the propertied classes, having taken hold of the lion's share of the entire press, to poison, unhindered, the minds and obscure the consciousness of the masses.

Every one knows that the bourgeois press is one of the most powerful weapons of the bourgeoisie. Especially at the crucial moment when the new power, the power of workers and peasants, is only affirming itself, it was impossible to leave this weapon wholly in the hands of the enemy, for in such moments it is no less dangerous than bombs and machine-guns. That is why temporary extraordinary measures were taken to stem the torrent of filth and slander in which the yellow and green press would be only too glad to drown the recent victory of the people.

As soon as the new order becomes consolidated, all administrative pressure on the press will be terminated and it will be granted complete freedom within the bounds of legal responsibility, in keeping with a law that will be broadest and most progressive in this respect.

However, being aware that a restriction of the press, even at critical moments, is permissible only within the limits of what is absolutely necessary, the Council of People's Commissars resolves:

General Provisions on the Press

1. Only those publications can be suppressed which (1) call for open resistance or insubordination to the Workers' and Peasants' Government; (2) sow sedition through demonstrably slanderous distortion of facts; (3) instigate actions of an obviously criminal, i.e. criminally punishable, nature.

2. Publications can be proscribed, temporarily or permanently, only by decision of the Council of People's Commissars.

3. The present ordinance is of a temporary nature and will be repealed by a special decree as soon as normal conditions of social life set in.

Chairman of the Council of People's Commissars,
VLADIMIR ULYANOV (LENIN)

ESTABLISHMENT OF THE SECRET POLICE (DECEMBER 20, 1917)
V. I. LENIN

Source: "Establishment of the Secret Police" is from Martin McCauley, ed., *The Russian Revolution and the Soviet State* (New York: Barnes & Noble, 1975), pp. 181–182. Permission granted by Barnes & Noble Books, Totowa, New Jersey.

The Commission is to be called the All-Russian Extraordinary Commission for the Struggle with Counter-Revolution and Sabotage and is to be attached to the Council of People's Commissars.

The duties of the Commission are to be as follows:

1. To investigate and nullify all acts of counter-revolution and sabotage throughout Russia, irrespective of origin.

2. To bring before the Revolutionary Tribunal all counter-revolutionaries and saboteurs and to work out measures to combat them.

3. The Commission is to conduct the preliminary investigation only, sufficient to suppress (the counter-revolutionary act). The Commission is to be divided into sections: (1) the information (section) (2) the organization section (in charge of organizing the struggle with counter-revolution throughout Russia) with branches, and (3) the fighting section.

The Commission shall be set up finally tomorrow. Then the fighting section of the All-Russian Commission shall start its activities. The Commission shall keep an eye on the press, saboteurs, right Socialist Revolutionaries and strikers. Measures to be taken are confiscation, imprisonment, confiscation of cards, publication of the names of the enemies of the people, etc.

Chairman of the Council of People's Commissars
V. ULYANOV (LENIN)

Questions:
1. *What measures did Lenin take to protect the position of the Bolsheviks once they had achieved power? How does Lenin justify censorship of the press? Do fallacies or inconsistencies exist in his argument? Note especially the vocabulary. For example, how is the phrase "workmen's and peasants' revolution" used? How was the Izvestia newspaper editorial dangerous to the Bolshevik revolution?*
2. *What are the duties of the secret police? What elements of society was this organization directed against? The tsar also had an active secret police that protected against "enemies of the monarchy." What is the difference between "enemies of the monarchy" and "enemies of the people"? Is a secret police therefore a necessary instrument for maintaining power, regardless of political philosophy?*

23.2   Nadezhda K. Krupskaya, "What a Communist Ought to Be Like"

Nadezhda Konstantinova Krupskaya (1869–1939), a Russian social worker who married Lenin in 1898, aided Lenin in his revolutionary program as long as he lived and supported Bolshevik programs as his legacy after he died. From 1900 to 1917, she served as the secretary of the Bolshevik wing of the Social Democratic Party in Russia, which after the Revolution became the Communist Party of the USSR. (It was later as "General" Secretary of the Communist Party's Central Committee that Stalin ruled the Soviet Union; Krupskaya's long secretaryship was of a more conventional nature.) Stalin's rude treatment of Krupskaya not long before her husband's death provoked the stroke-weakened Lenin into a rebuke of the future dictator, but Krupskaya had no inclination to publicize their differences and subsequently treated Stalin as Lenin's more or less rightful successor. In the following selection, she elaborates on Lenin's discussion of Communist ethics and morality.

Source: From *Bolshevik Visions: First Phase of the Cultural Revolution in Soviet Russia,* ed. and trans. William G. Rosenberg (Ann Arbor: University of Michigan Press, 1992). Copyright © 1992 University of Michigan Press. Reprinted with permission. Krupskaya, Lenin's wife and closest friend, played an active role in educational and cultural matters at the time of the revolution, and for a brief period was Deputy Commissar of Education.

A communist is, first and foremost, *a person involved in society,* with strongly developed social instincts, who desires that all people should live well and be happy.

Communists can come from all classes of society, but most of all they are workers by birth. Why? Because the conditions of workers' lives are such as to nurture in them social instincts: collective labor, the success of which depends on the separate efforts of each; the same conditions of labor; common experiences; the common struggle for humane conditions of existence. All this brings workers closer together and unites them with the bonds of class solidarity. Let us take the capitalist class. The conditions of life for this class are completely different. Competition forces each capitalist to see another capitalist primarily as an opponent, who has to be tripped up. In the worker the capitalist sees only "worker's hands" which must labor for the creation of his, the capitalist's, profits. Of course, the common struggle against the working class unites capitalists, but that internal unity, that formation into a collective which we see among workers—they have nothing to divide among themselves—does not exist in the capitalist class, where solidarity is corroded by competition. That is why in the working class the person with well-developed social instincts is the rule, while among the capitalists such a person is the exception.

Social instinct means a great many things. Often it offers a clue for finding a way out of a situation, for choosing the correct path. That is why during the purge of the RKP [Russian Communist Party], attention was paid to whether this or that member of the party had been born in a working family or not. He who comes from a worker's background will more easily straighten himself out. The Russian intelligentsia, seeing how easily a worker, thanks to this class instinct, comprehends that which an intellectual, for example, perceives only with great difficulty, was inclined, in the end of the nineties and in the first half of the first decade of the twentieth century (1896–1903) to exaggerate the significance of class instinct. *Rabochaya Mysl' [Workers' Thought],* one of the underground Social Democratic newspapers, even came to the conclusion that no one other than people from workingman backgrounds could be accepted as socialists. Since Marx and Engels were not workers, *Rabochaya Mysl'* wrote "We don't need Marx and Engels!"

Class instinct, which among workers coincides with a social one, is a necessary condition for being a communist. Necessary, but not sufficient.

A communist must also know quite a lot. First, he must understand what is happening around him, and must gain an understanding of the existing system. When the workers' movement began to develop in Russia, Social Democrats were concerned from the very first with the widespread distribution of such pamphlets as Dikshtein's "Who Lives by What," "Worker's Day," etc. But it is not enough to understand the mechanics of the capitalist system. The communist must also study the laws of the development of human society. He must know the history of the development of economic forms, of the development of property, of division into classes, of the development of state forms. He must understand their interdependence and know how religious and moral notions will develop out of a particular social structure. Understanding the laws of the development of human society, the communist must clearly picture to himself where social development is heading. Communism must be seen by him as not only a desired system, where the happiness of some will not be based on the misfortune of others; he must further understand that communism is that very system toward which mankind is moving, and that communists must clear a path to this system, and promote its speedy coming.

In workers' circles at the dawn of the workers' movement in Russia, commonly studied courses were, on the one hand, political economy, which had the aim of explaining the structure of contemporary society, and the history of culture (the history of culture was usually opposed to the regular exposition of history, which often presented just a set of heterogeneous historical data). That is why in the circles of those days they read the first volume of Marx's *Capital* and F. Engels' *The Origins of the Family, Property and State.*

In 1919, in one of the villages of Nizhny Novgorod province, in the village of Rabotki, I happened to come across this phenomenon. Teachers told me that in the intermediate school they taught political economy and the history of culture; that the students unanimously demanded the introduction of these subjects into the curriculum of the intermediate school.

Where could such a desire, and such a definitely formulated one, have come from among peasant youth in a Volga village whose population was occupied exclusively with Volga river trades and agriculture? Obviously, interest in political economy and the history of culture was brought into Rabotki by some worker, who at one time had attended some circle and who explained to the children what they needed to know.

However, at the present moment the Russian communist must know not only that. The October Revolution opened for Russia an opportunity for widespread building in the direction of communism. But in order to utilize these possibilities it is necessary to know what one can do at the moment in order to make at least one first step toward communism, and what one cannot, and it is necessary to know how to build a new life. It is necessary first and foremost to know thoroughly that sphere of work which you have undertaken, and then to master the method of a communist *approach* to the matter. Let us take an example. In order to organize correctly medical affairs in the country, it is first necessary to know the situation itself, secondly, how it was organized earlier in Russia and is currently organized in other states, and thirdly, how to approach the problem in a communist manner, namely, to conduct agitation among wide strata of workers, to interest them, to attract them to work, to create with their efforts a powerful organization in regard to medical affairs. It is necessary not only to know how to do all this, but to be able to *do* it. Thus it follows that a communist must know not only what communism is and why it is inevitable, but also know his own affairs well, and be able to approach the masses, influence them, and convince them.

In his personal life, a communist must always conduct himself in the interests of communism. What does this mean? It means, for example, that however nice it might be to stay in a familiar, comfortable home environment, that if for the sake of the cause, for the success of the communist cause, it is necessary to abandon everything and expose oneself to danger, the communist will do this. It means that however difficult and responsible the task the communist is called upon to perform, he will take it upon himself and try to carry it out to the best of his strength and skill, whether it is at the front, during the confiscation of valuables, etc. It means that the communist puts his personal interests aside, subordinates them to the common interest. It means that the communist is not indifferent to what is happening around him and that he actively struggles with that which is harmful to the interests of the toiling masses, and that he on the other hand actively defends these interests and makes them his own. . . .

Who was discarded during the purging of the party? (a) the self-seekers and their adherents, that is, those who put their personal interests above the communist cause; (b) those who were indifferent to communism, who did nothing to help it make headway, who stood far from the masses and made no efforts to draw closer to them; (c) those who did not enjoy the respect and love of the masses; (d) those who were distinguished by a coarse manner, conceit, insincerity and other such characteristics.

Thus, in order to be a communist: (1) it is necessary to know what is bad about the capitalist system, where social development is heading and how to promote the speediest coming of the communist system; (2) it is necessary to know how to apply one's knowledge to the cause; and (3) it is necessary to be spiritually and physically devoted to the interests of the working masses and to communism.

Questions:
1. *Why does Krupskaya find well-developed social instincts to characterize most workers most of the time but to be rare among capitalists?*
2. *What are some of the areas in which Communists should acquire extensive knowledge?*
3. *What are some aspects of a Communist's personal life, according to Krupskaya?*

23.3   John Scott, Behind the Urals

In 1932, John Scott (1912–1976), a twenty-year-old American college student, left the United States to work as a welder in the Soviet Union. Disturbed by the conditions of the American depression, Scott hoped that the Russian Revolution of 1917 had destroyed social inequality and injustice and that a better society was being created. Soviet reality turned out to be quite different from his expectations, but Scott remained in the Soviet Union for five years and eventually returned to the United States with a Russian wife. In Behind the Urals, he offers a vivid description of life in Magnitogorsk, Russia's new city of steel, located on the eastern slopes of the Ural Mountains. These were the years of the first Five-Year Plan, whose two major goals were industrialization and collectivization of the countryside. Scott lived and worked in the harsh, freezing conditions along with Soviet workers—some of whom had been sent there as punishment for being rich peasants (kulaks). He vividly describes the chronic shortages of everything from bread to welding rods; the frequent, often fatal, accidents of inexperienced, underfed workers; and the ever-present bureaucratic red tape. Yet Scott also was a witness to the hope, optimism, and commitment of many of these people who believed that their personal sacrifices would benefit all humankind. This work offers a detached and penetrating documentation of the tensions, problems, and heroic tasks confronting the men and women engaged in attempting to erect the first Communist society.

Source: From John Scott, *Behind the Urals: An American Worker in Russia's City of Steel* (Bloomington: Indiana University Press, 1973), pp. 9–10, 15–21, passim.

The big whistle on the power house sounded a long, deep, hollow six o'clock. All over the scattered city-camp of Magnitogorsk, workers rolled out of their beds or bunks and dressed in preparation for their day's work.

I climbed out of bed and turned on the light. I could see my breath across the room as I woke my roommate, Kolya. Kolya never heard the whistle. Every morning I had to pound his shoulder for several seconds to arouse him.

We pushed our coarse brown army blankets over the beds and dressed as quickly as we could—I had good American long woolen underwear, fortunately; Kolya wore only cotton shorts and a jersey. We both donned army shirts, padded and quilted cotton pants, similar jackets, heavy scarves, and then ragged sheepskin coats. We thrust our feet into good Russian "valinkis"—felt boots coming up to the knee. We did not eat anything. We had nothing on hand except tea and a few potatoes, and there was no time to light a fire in our little home-made iron stove. We locked up and set out for the mill.

It was January, 1933. The temperature was in the neighborhood of thirty-five below. A light powdery snow covered the low spots on the ground. The high spots were bare and hard as iron. A few stars cracked in the sky and some electric lights twinkled on the blast furnaces. Otherwise the world was bleak and cold and almost pitch-dark.

It was two miles to the blast furnaces, over rough ground. There was no wind, so our noses did not freeze. I was always glad when there was no wind in the morning. It was my first winter in Russia and I was not used to the cold. . . .

By the time the seven o'clock whistle blew, the shanty was jammed full of riggers, welders, cutters, and their helpers. It was a varied gang, Russians, Ukrainians, Tartars, Mongols, Jews, mostly young and almost all peasants of yesterday, though a few, like Ivanov, had long industrial experience. There was Popov, for instance. He had been a welder for ten years and had worked in half a dozen cities. On the other hand, Khaibulin, the Tartar, had never seen a staircase, a locomotive, or an electric light until he had come to Magnitogorsk a year before. His ancestors for centuries had raised stock on the flat plains of Kazakhstan. They had been dimly conscious of the Czarist government; they had had to pay taxes. Reports of the Kirghiz insurrection in 1916 had reached them. They had heard stories of the October Revolution; they even saw the Red Army come and drive out a few rich landlords. They had attended meetings of the Soviet, without understanding very clearly what it was all about, but through all this their lives had gone on more or less as before. Now Shaimat Khaibulin was building a blast furnace bigger than any in Europe. He had learned to read and was attending an evening school, learning the trade of electrician. He had learned to speak Russian, he read newspapers. His life had changed more in a year than that of his antecedents since the time of Tamerlane. . . .

I took my mask and electrodes and started out for No. 3. On the way I met Shabkov, the ex-kulak; a great husky youth with a red face, a jovial voice, and two fingers missing from his left hand.

"Well, Jack, how goes it?" he said, slapping me on the back. My Russian was still pretty bad, but I could carry on a simple conversation and understood almost everything that was said.

"Badly," I said. "All our equipment freezes. The boys spend half their time warming their hands."

"Nichevo, that doesn't matter," said the disfranchised rigger's brigadier. "If you lived where I do, in a tent, you wouldn't think it so cold here."

"I know you guys have it tough," said Popov, who had joined us. "That's what you get for being kulaks."

Shabkov smiled broadly. "Listen, I don't want to go into a political discussion, but a lot of the people living down in the special section of town are no more kulaks than you."

Popov laughed. "I wouldn't be surprised. Tell me, though, how did they decide who was to be dekulakized?"

"Ah," said Shabkov, "that's a hell of a question to ask a guy that's trying to expiate his crimes in honest labor. Just between the three of us, though, the poor peasants of the village get together in a meeting and decide: 'So-and-so has six horses; we couldn't very well get along without those in the collective farm; besides he hired a man last year to help on the harvest.' They notify the GPU, and there you are. So-and-so gets five years. They confiscate his property and give it to the new collective farm. Sometimes they ship the whole family out. When they came to ship us out, my brother got a rifle and fired several shots at the GPU officers. They fired back. My brother was killed. All of which, naturally, didn't make it any better for us. We all got five years, and in different places. I heard my father died in December, but I'm not sure." . . .

Popov and I set about welding up a section of the bleeder pipe on the blast furnace. He gave me a break and took the outside for the first hour. Then we changed around. From the high scaffolding, nearly a hundred feet above the ground, I could see Kolya making the rounds of his thirty-odd welders, helping them when they were in trouble, swearing at them when they spent too much time warming their hands. People swore at Kolya a good deal too, because the scaffolds were unsafe or the wages bad.

It was just about nine-fifteen when I finished one side of the pipe and went around to start the other. The scaffold was coated with about an inch of ice, like everything else around the furnaces. The vapor rising from the large hot-water cooling basin condensed on everything and formed a layer of ice. But besides being slippery, it was very insecure, swung down on wires, without any guys to steady it. It swayed and shook as I walked on it. I always made a point of hanging on to something when I could. I was just going to start welding when I heard someone sing out, and something swished down past me. It was a rigger who had been working up on the very top.

He bounced off the bleeder pipe, which probably saved his life. Instead of falling all the way to the ground, he landed on the main platform about fifteen feet below me. By the time I got down to him, blood was coming out of his mouth in gushes. He tried to yell, but could not. There were no foremen around, and the half-dozen riggers that had run up did not know what to do. By virtue of being a foreigner I had a certain amount of authority, so I stepped in and said he might bleed to death if we waited for a stretcher, and three of us took him and carried him down to the first-aid station. About halfway there the bleeding let up and he began to yell every step we took.

I was badly shaken when we got there, but the two young riggers were trembling like leaves. We took him into the little wooden building, and a nurse with a heavy shawl over her white gown showed us where to put him. "I expect the doctor any minute," she said; "good thing, too, I wouldn't know what the hell to do with him."

The rigger was gurgling and groaning. His eyes were wide open and he seemed conscious, but he did not say anything. "We should undress him, but it is so cold in here that I am afraid to," said the nurse. Just then the doctor came in. I knew him. He had dressed my foot once when a piece of pig iron fell on it. He took his immense sheepskin off and washed his hands. "Fall?" he asked, nodding at the rigger.

"Yes," I said.

"How long ago?"

"About ten minutes."

"What's that?" asked the doctor, looking at the nurse and indicating the corner of the room with his foot. I looked and for the first time noticed a pair of ragged valinkis sticking out from under a very dirty blanket on the floor.

"Girder fell on his head," said the nurse.

"Well," said the doctor, rolling up his sleeves, "let's see what we can do for this fellow." He moved over toward the rigger, who was lying quietly now and looking at the old bearded doctor with watery blue eyes. I turned to go, but the doctor stopped me.

"On your way out, please telephone the factory board of health and tell them I simply must have more heat in this place," he said.

I did the best I could over the telephone in my bad Russian, but all I could get was, "Comrade, we are sorry, but there is no coal."

I was making my way unsteadily back to the bleeder pipe on No. 3 when Kolya hailed me. "Don't bother to go up for a while, the brushes burnt out on the machine you were working on. They won't be fixed for half an hour or so." I went toward the office with Kolya and told him about the rigger. I was incensed and talked about some thorough checkup on scaffoldings. Kolya could not get interested. He pointed out there was not enough planking for good scaffolds, that the riggers were mostly plowboys who had no idea of being careful, and that at thirty-five below without any breakfast in you, you did not pay as much attention as you should.

"Sure, people will fall. But we're building blast furnaces all the same, aren't we?" and he waved his hand toward No. 2 from which the red glow of flowing pig iron was emanating. He saw I was not satisfied. "This somewhat sissified foreigner will have to be eased along a little," he probably said to himself. He slapped me on the back. "Come on in the office. We are going to have a technical conference. You'll be interested."

Questions:
1. *According to John Scott's observations, what were some of the social problems encountered in trying to meet the goals for industrialization set by the first Five-Year Plan?*
2. *In the process of collectivization, how did the peasants and the Communist Party decide who were the rich peasants? What was their fate?*

23.4   Nadezhda Mandelstam, Hope Against Hope

In the 1930s, Nadezhda Mandelstam (1899–1980) experienced the Soviet terror. Her husband, Osip Mandelstam (1891–1938), recognized today as the greatest Russian poet of the twentieth century, was persecuted because he portrayed Stalin as a tyrant in one of his poems. He was sentenced in 1938 to five years of hard labor in a camp in Vladivostok, but he died within the first year. Nadezhda first learned that her husband had died when a package she had sent him was returned, and she was told that the addressee was dead.

Source: Excerpted from *Hope Against Hope: A Memoir* by Nadezhda Mandelstam, pp. 297–98, 304–05, 316–17, 369–71. Translated from the Russian by Max Hayward with introduction by Clarence Brown. Copyright © 1970 Atheneum Publishers. English translation copyright © 1970 Atheneum Publishers. Introduction copyright © 1970 Atheneum Publishers. Reprinted with the permission of Scribner, a Division of Simon & Schuster.

When I used to read about the French Revolution as a child, I often wondered whether it was possible to survive during a reign of terror. I now know beyond doubt that it is impossible. Anybody who breathes the air of terror is doomed, even if nominally he manages to save his life. Everybody is a victim—not only those who die, but also all the killers, ideologists, accomplices and sycophants who close their eyes or wash their hands—even if they are secretly consumed with remorse at night. Every section of the population has been through the terrible sickness caused by terror, and none has so far recovered, or become fit again for normal civic life. It is an illness that is passed on to the next generation, so that the sons pay for the sins of the fathers and perhaps only the grandchildren begin to get over it—or at least it takes on a different form with them.

Who was it who dared say that we have no "lost generation" here? The fact that he could utter such a monstrous untruth is also a consequence of terror. One generation after another was "lost" here, but it was a completely different process from what may have happened in the West. Here people just tried to go on working, struggling to maintain themselves, hoping for salvation, and thinking only about their immediate concerns. In such times your daily round is like a drug. The more you have to do, the better. If you can immerse yourself in your work, the years fly by more quickly, leaving only a gray blur in the memory. Among the people of my generation, only a very few have kept clear minds and memories. In M.'s generation, everybody was stricken by a kind of sclerosis at an early stage.

True as this is, however, I never cease to marvel at our hardiness. After Stalin's death my brother Evgeni said to me: "We still do not realize what we have been through." Not long ago, as I was traveling in an overcrowded bus, an old woman pushed up against me and I found my arm was bearing the whole weight of her body. "That must be killing you," she said suddenly. "No," I replied, "we're as tough as the devil." "As tough as the devil?" she said, and laughed. Somebody nearby also laughingly repeated the phrase, and soon the whole bus was saying it after us. But then the bus stopped and everybody started to push toward the exit, jostling each other in the usual way. The little moment of good humor was over. . . .

When life becomes absolutely intolerable, you begin to think the horror will never end. In Kiev during the bombardment I understood that even the unbearable can come to an end, but I was not yet fully aware that it often does so only at death. As regards the Stalinist terror, we always knew that it might wax or wane, but that it might end—this we could never imagine. What reason was there for it to end? Everybody seemed intent on his daily round and went smilingly about the business of carrying out his instructions. It was essential to smile—if you didn't, it meant you were afraid or discontented. This nobody could afford to admit—if you were afraid, then you must have a bad conscience. Everybody who worked for the State—and in this country even the humblest stall-keeper is a bureaucrat—had to strut around wearing a cheerful expression, as though to say: "What's going on is no concern of mine, I have very important work to do, and I'm terribly busy. I am trying to do my best for the State, so do not get in my way. My conscience is clear—if what's-his-name has been arrested, there must be good reason." The mask was taken off only at home, and then not always—even from your children you had to conceal how horror-struck you were; otherwise, God save you, they might let something slip in school. . . . Some people had adapted to the terror so well that they knew how to profit from it—there was nothing out of the ordinary about denouncing a neighbor to get his apartment or his job. But while wearing your smiling mask, it was important not to laugh—this could look suspicious to the neighbors and make them think you were indulging in sacrilegious mockery. We have lost the capacity to be spontaneously cheerful, and it will never come back to us. . . .

I think he exaggerated the extent to which our secret police went in for ordinary detective work. They were not in the least bit interested in *real* facts—all they wanted were lists of people to arrest, and these they got from their network of informers and the volunteers who brought them denunciations. To meet their quotas, all they needed were names of people, not details about their comings and goings. During interrogations they always, as a matter of routine, collected "evidence" against people whom they had no intention of arresting—just in case it was ever needed. I have heard of a woman who heroically went through torture rather than give "evidence" against Molotov! A man was asked for evidence against Liuba Ehrenburg, whom he had never even met. He managed to send word about this from the forced-labor camp, and Liuba was warned—apparently Akhmatova passed on the message to her. Liuba could not believe it: "What Spasski? I don't know him." She was still naïve in those days, but later she understood everything.

In the torture chambers of the Lubianka they were constantly adding to the dossiers of Ehrenburg, Sholokhov, Alexei Tolstoi, and others whom they had no intention of touching. Dozens, if not hundreds of people were sent to camps on a charge of being involved in a "conspiracy" headed by Tikhonov and Fadeyev! Among them was Spasski. Wild inventions and monstrous accusations had become an end in themselves, and officials of the secret police applied all their ingenuity to them, as though reveling in the total arbitrariness of their power. Their basic principle was just what Furmanov had told us at the end of the twenties: "Give us a man, and we'll make a case." On the day we had spent at Stenich's apartment, his name was almost certainly already on a list of persons due to be arrested—his telephone number would have been found in Diki's address book, and no further information about him was needed.

The principles and aims of mass terror have nothing in common with ordinary police work or with security. The only purpose of terror is intimidation. To plunge the whole country into a state of chronic fear, the number of victims must be raised to astronomical levels, and on every floor of every building there must always be several apartments from which the tenants have suddenly been taken away. The remaining inhabitants will be model citizens for the rest of their lives—this will be true for every street and every city through which the broom has swept. The only essential thing for those who rule by terror is not to overlook the new generations growing up without faith in their elders, and to keep on repeating the process in systematic fashion. Stalin ruled for a long time and saw to it that the waves of terror recurred from time to time, always on an even greater scale than before. But the champions of terror invariably leave one thing out of account—namely, that they can't kill everyone, and among their cowed, half-demented subjects there are always witnesses who survive to tell the tale. . . .

The only link with a person in prison was the window through which one handed parcels and money to be forwarded to him by the authorities. Once a month, after waiting three or four hours in line (the number of arrests was by now falling off, so this was not very long), I went up to the window and gave my name. The clerk behind the window thumbed through his list—I went on days when he dealt with the letter "M"—and asked me for my first name and initial. As soon as I replied, a hand stretched out of the window and I put my identity papers and some money into it. The hand then returned my papers with a receipt and I went away. Everybody envied me because I at least knew that my husband was alive and where he was. It happened only too often that the man behind the window barked: "No record. . . . Next!" All questions were useless—the official would simply shut his window in your face and one of the uniformed guards would come up to you. Order was immediately restored and the next in line moved up to the window. If anybody ever tried to linger, the guard found ready allies among the other people waiting.

There was generally no conversation in the line. This was the chief prison in the Soviet Union, and the people who came here were a select, respectable and well-disciplined crowd. There were never any untoward events, unless it was a minor case of someone asking a question—but persons guilty of such misconduct would speedily retreat in embarrassment. The only incident I saw was when two little girls in neatly starched dresses once came in. Their mother had been arrested the previous night. They were let through out of turn and nobody asked what letter their name began with. All the women waiting there were no doubt moved by pity at the thought that their own children might soon be coming here in the same way. Somebody lifted up the elder of the two, because she was too small to reach the window, and she shouted through it: "Where's my mummy?" and "We won't go to the orphanage. We won't go home." They just managed to say that their father was in the army before the window was slammed shut. This could have been the actual case, or it could have meant that he had been in the secret police. The children of Chekists were always taught to say that their father was "in the army"—this was to protect them from the curiosity of their schoolmates, who, the parents explained, might be less friendly otherwise. Before going abroad on duty, Chekists also made their children learn the new name under which they would be living there. . . . The little girls in the starched dresses probably lived in a government building—they told the people waiting in line that other children had been taken away to orphanages, but that they wanted to go to their grandmother in the Ukraine. Before they could say any more, a soldier came out of a side door and led them away. The window opened again and everything returned to normal. As they were being led away, one woman called them "silly little girls," and another said: "We must send ours away before it's too late."

These little girls were exceptional. Children who came and stood in line were usually as restrained and silent as grown-ups. It was generally their fathers who were arrested first—particularly if they were military people—and they would then be carefully instructed by their mothers on how to behave when they were left completely alone. Many of them managed to keep out of the orphanages, but that depended mainly on their parents' status—the higher it had been, the less chance the children had of being looked after by relatives. It was astonishing that life continued at all, and that people still brought children into the world and had families. How could they do this, knowing what went on in front of the window in the building on Sophia Embankment?

Questions:
1. *What was the justification given in Stalin's Russia for the arrest, imprisonment, and execution of "enemies of the state"?*
2. *How did those who had not been arrested behave during Stalin's terror?*
3. *What are the long-term consequences for the Soviet Union of Stalin's mass murders?*

23.5 The Rise of Benito Mussolini

Benito Mussolini (1883–1945) was perhaps fascism's most articulate spokesman. He was born the son of a blacksmith and worked as a school teacher and day laborer before becoming editor of a Socialist news-paper prior to World War I. He supported Italy's entry into the war and was wounded in the conflict. In 1919, he was one of many small-time candidates trying to make a mark in Italian politics. An amazing orator and opportunist, Mussolini presented a message of order and action that won him the support of working and middle-class Italians who had been hit hard by the inflation that plagued Europe after the war. Mussolini even organized terrorist squads to contribute to the very instability that drew him adherents.

By 1922, the fascists controlled local governments in many cities in northern Italy. Mussolini initiated a march on Rome that met with no resistance from King Victor Emmanuel III. Concerned with violence and his personal safety, the king asked Mussolini to become prime minister and form a government. Although Mussolini had achieved power legally, his Italian National Fascist party ("Blackshirts") did not enjoy even a near majority in the Chamber of Deputies. He immediately disrupted the parliamentary gov-ernment with threats and physical acts of violence against its elected members. Mussolini was then given temporary dictatorial powers by the king to stabilize the political situation; he soon turned these into a permanent and personal dominance.

Mussolini's vision of a "corporate state," in which each individual worked for the welfare of the entire nation, guaranteed employment and satisfactory wages for labor but did not permit strikes. He favored industrialists by allowing lucrative profits and gave respect to Italy by closely identifying his regime with the glorious heritage of the ancient Roman Empire. Mussolini succeeded in giving Italy direction and dignity, but he accomplished this through suppression of civil rights and individual liberties. He was, indeed, the quintessential fascist.

The following selection is perhaps the defining statement of fascism. Mussolini believed that the twen-tieth century was a new historical epoch that required a different political premise based on popular loyalty to the state and supported by violent force.

Source: Reprinted by permission of the publisher from "The Political and Social Doctrine of Fascism," Benito Mussolini, *International Conciliation*. Washington, DC: Carnegie Endowment for International Peace, January 1935, pp. 5–17.

THE DOCTRINE OF FASCISM: "THIS WILL BE THE CENTURY OF THE STATE"
BENITO MUSSOLINI

Fascism was not the nursling of a doctrine worked out beforehand with detailed elaboration; it was born of the need for action and it was itself from the beginning practical rather than theoretical; it was not merely another political party but, even in the first two years, in opposition to all political parties as such. . . . If one were to re-read . . . the report of the meeting in which the *Fasci Italiani di Combáttimento* [Italian Bands of Combat] were constituted, one would there find no ordered expression of doctrine, but a series of aphorisms, anticipations, and aspirations which, when refined by time from the original ore, were destined after some years to develop into an ordered series of doctrinal concepts, forming the Fascists' political doctrine—different from all others either of the past or the present day. . . .

We want to accustom the working-class to real and effectual leadership, and also to convince them that it is no easy thing to direct an industry or a commercial enterprise successfully. . . . We shall combat every retrograde idea, technical or spiritual. . . . When the succession to the seat of government is open, we must not be unwilling to fight for it. We must make haste; when the present regime breaks down, we must be ready at once to take its place. It is we who have the right to the succession, because it was we who forced the country into the War, and led her to victory. . . .

The years which preceded the March to Rome were years of great difficulty, during which the necessity for action did not permit research of any complete elaboration of doctrine. The battle had to be fought in the towns and villages. There was much discussion, but—what was more important and more sacred—men died. They knew how to die. Doctrine, beautifully defined and carefully elucidated, with headlines and paragraphs, might be lacking; but there was to take its place something more decisive—Faith. . . . But, since there was inevitably some lack of system, the adversaries of Fascism have disingenuously denied that it had any capacity to produce a doctrine of its own, though that doctrine was growing and taking shape under their very eyes . . . in the laws and institutions of the regime as enacted successively in the years 1926, 1927 and 1928. . . .

Above all, Fascism, the more it considers and observes the future and the development of humanity quite apart from political considerations of the moment, believes neither in the possibility nor the utility of perpetual peace. It thus repudiates the doctrine of Pacifism—born of a renunciation of the struggle and an act of cowardice in the face of sacrifice. War alone brings up to its highest tension all human energy and puts the stamp of nobility upon the peoples who have the courage to meet it. All other trials are substitutes, which never really put men into the position where they have to make the great decision—the alternative of life or death. Thus a doctrine which is founded upon this harmful postulate of peace is hostile to Fascism. . . . This anti-pacifist spirit is carried by Fascism even in the life of the individual. . . . The Fascist accepts life and loves it, knowing nothing of and despising suicide; he rather conceives of life as duty and struggle and conquest, life which would be high and full, lived for oneself, but above all for others—those who are at hand and those who are far distant contemporaries, and those who will come after. . . .

Such a conception of life makes Fascism the complete opposite of that doctrine, the base of the so-called scientific and Marxian Socialism, the materialist conception of history; according to which the history of human civilization can be explained simply through the conflict of interests among the various social groups and by the change and development in the means and instruments of production. That the changes in the economic field . . . have their importance no one can deny; but that these factors are sufficient to explain the history of humanity excluding all others is an absurd delusion. Fascism now and always, believes in holiness and in heroism; that is to say, in actions influenced by no economic motive, direct or indirect. . . . And above all Fascism denies that class war can be the preponderant force in the transformation of society. . . .

After Socialism, Fascism combats the whole complex system of democratic ideology; and repudiates it, whether in its theoretical premises or in its practical application. Fascism denies that the majority, by the simple fact that it is a majority, can direct human society; it denies that numbers alone can govern by means of a periodical consultation, and it affirms the immutable, beneficial, and fruitful inequality of mankind, which can never be permanently leveled through the mere operation of a mechanical process such as universal suffrage. The democratic regime may be defined as from time to time giving the people the illusion of sovereignty, while the real effective sovereignty lies in the hands of other concealed and irresponsible forces. Democracy is a regime nominally without a king, but it is ruled by many kings—more absolute, tyrannical, and ruinous than one sole king, even though a tyrant. . . .

Political doctrines pass, but humanity remains; and it may rather be expected that this will be a century of Fascism. For if the nineteenth century was the century of individualism (Liberalism always signifying individualism) it may be expected that this will be the century of collectivism, and hence the century of the State. . . .

The foundation of Fascism is the conception of the State. Fascism conceives of the State as an absolute, in comparison with which all individuals or groups are relative, only to be conceived of in their relation to the State. . . .

The Fascist State has drawn into itself even the economic activities of the nation, and through the corporative social and educational institutions created by it, its influence reaches every aspect of the national life and includes, framed in their respective organizations, all the political, economic and spiritual forces of the nation. A State which reposes upon the support of millions of individuals who recognize its authority, are continually conscious of its power and are ready at once to serve it, is not the old tyrannical State of the medieval lord nor has it anything in common with the absolute governments either before or after 1789. The individual in the Fascist State is not annulled but rather multiplied, just in the same way that a soldier in a regiment is not diminished but rather increased by the number of his comrades. The Fascist State organizes the nation, but leaves a sufficient margin of liberty to the individual; the latter is deprived of all useless and possibly harmful freedom, but retains what is essential. . . .

The Fascist State is an embodied will to power and government; the Roman tradition is here an ideal of force in action. According to Fascism, government is not so much a thing to be expressed in territorial or military terms as in terms of morality and the spirit. It must be thought of as an empire—that is to say, a nation which directly or indirectly rules other nations, without the need for conquering a single square yard of territory. For Fascism, the growth of empire, that is to say the expansion of the nation, is an essential manifestation of vitality, and its opposite a sign of decadence. Peoples which are rising, or rising again after a period of decadence, are always imperialist: any renunciation is a sign of decay and of death.

Fascism is the doctrine best adapted to represent the tendencies and the aspirations of a people, like the people of Italy, who are rising again after many centuries of abasement and foreign servitude. But empire demands discipline, the coordination of all forces and a deeply felt sense of duty and sacrifice; . . . for never before has the nation [Italy] stood more in need of authority, of direction, and of order. If every age has its own characteristic doctrine, there are a thousand signs which point to Fascism as the characteristic doctrine of our time. For if a doctrine must be a living thing, this is proved by the fact that Fascism has created a living faith; and that this faith is very powerful in the minds of men, is demonstrated by those who have suffered and died for it.

Questions:

1. *According to Benito Mussolini, what are the primary tenets of fascist doctrine? Why was he especially critical of socialism (Marxism) and democracy? Do you find his arguments compelling or flawed? Why is war such an important requirement for the fascist state?*
2. *What did Mussolini mean by "[the individual] is deprived of all useless and possibly harmful freedom, but retains what is essential"? What is "harmful freedom" as opposed to "essential freedom"?*

23.6 Adolf Hitler

Anyone who has doubts about the progress of civilization can find ample support for his pessimism in the career of Adolf Hitler (1889-1945), for this twentieth-century political leader was the greatest mass murderer in human history. Although the exact number will never be known, best estimates place the total of those killed on his orders in the region of six million people. These people, it should be emphasized, did not die in war or even incidentally in Hitler's prosecution of other projects but simply because he decided to exterminate them. Although most of his victims were Jews, others were murdered as well, including gypsies, Poles, Russians, and other "undesirables." Known to history as the Holocaust, these deaths were the result of the deliberate, systematic murder of innocent victims from all over Europe.

Hitler wrote the book Mein Kampf ("My Struggle") nearly twenty years before the Holocaust, while he was serving a term in a Bavarian prison following his unsuccessful Munich "Beer Hall Putsch" against the government in 1923. The book, in two volumes, covers a number of topics,

including an autobiography of the author up to the time of its writing, discussions of various political topics, Hitler's own theories of government, his plans for the development of his National Socialist (Nazi) party, and his eventual conquest of Europe following his release from jail. It has been remarked by an astute political observer that the nations of the world could have spared themselves much bloodshed, grief, and destruction had their leaders of the time read Mein Kampf carefully, taken its message seriously, and responded appropriately.

In the chapter "Nation and Race," from which the following selection is taken, Hitler cloaks his racism, including his slander of the Jewish people, in the garments of pseudoscience. Of special interest are his evaluation of the contributions of the Aryans (an undefined term) to culture and his understanding of the concept of idealism.

Hitler did not survive the Second World War. He committed suicide in his bunker far below the streets of Berlin as the Russian army was moving into the city, just after his partner in crime, the Italian dictator, Benito Mussolini, was captured by partisans and executed as he was trying to escape from Italy to Switzerland.

MEIN KAMPF

XI. Nation and Race

There are some truths which are so obvious that for this very reason they are not seen or at least not recognized by ordinary people. They sometimes pass by such truisms as though blind and are most astonished when someone suddenly discovers what everyone really ought to know. Columbus's eggs lie around by the hundreds of thousands, but Columbuses are met with less frequently.

Thus men without exception wander about in the garden of Nature; they imagine that they know practically everything and yet with few exceptions pass blindly by one of the more patent principles of Nature's rule: the inner segregation of the species of all living beings on this earth.

Even the most superficial observation shows that Nature's restricted form of propagation and increase is an almost rigid basic law of all the innumerable forms of expression of her vital urge. Every animal mates only with a member of the same species. The titmouse seeks the titmouse, the finch the finch, the stork the stork, the field mouse the field mouse, the dormouse the dormouse, the wolf the she-wolf, etc.

Only unusual circumstances can change this, primarily the compulsion of captivity or any other cause that makes it impossible to mate within the same species. But then Nature begins to resist this with all possible means, and her most visible protest consists either in refusing further capacity for propagation to bastards or in limiting the fertility of later offspring; in most cases, however, she takes away the power of resistance to disease or hostile attacks.

This is only too natural.

Any crossing of two beings not at exactly the same level produces a medium between the level of the two parents. This means: the offspring will probably stand higher than the racially lower parent, but not as high as the higher one. Consequently, it will later succumb in the struggle against the higher level. Such mating is contrary to the will of Nature for a higher breeding of all life. The precondition for this does not lie in associating superior and inferior, but in the total victory of the former. The stronger must dominate and not blend with the weaker, thus sacrificing his own greatness. Only the born weakling can view this as cruel, but he after all is only a weak and limited man; for if this law did not prevail, any conceivable higher development of organic living beings would be unthinkable.

The consequence of this racial purity, universally valid in Nature, is not only the sharp outward delimitation of the various races, but their uniform character in themselves. The fox is always a fox, the goose a goose, the tiger a tiger, etc., and the difference can lie at most in the varying measure of force, strength, intelligence, dexterity, endurance, etc., of the individual specimens. But you will never find a fox who in his inner attitude might, for example, show humanitarian tendencies toward geese, as similarly there is no cat with a friendly inclination toward mice.

Therefore, here, too, the struggle among themselves arises less from inner aversion than from hunger and love. In both cases, Nature looks on calmly, with satisfaction, in fact. In the struggle for daily bread all those who are weak and sickly or less determined succumb, while the struggle of the males for the female grants the right or opportunity to propagate only to the healthiest. And struggle is always a means for improving a species' health and power of resistance and, therefore, a cause of its higher development.

If the process were different, all further and higher development would cease and the opposite would occur. For, since the inferior always predominates numerically over the best, if both had the same possibility of preserving life and propagating, the inferior would multiply so much more rapidly that in the end the best would inevitably be driven into the background, unless a correction of this state of affairs were undertaken. Nature does just this by subjecting the weaker part to such severe living conditions that by them alone the number is limited, and by not permitting the remainder to increase promiscuously, but making a new and ruthless choice according to strength and health.

No more than Nature desires the mating of weaker with stronger individuals, even less does she desire the blending of a higher with a lower race, since, if she did, her whole work of higher breeding, over perhaps hundreds of thousands of years, might be ruined with one blow.

Historical experience offers countless proofs of this. It shows with terrifying clarity that in every mingling of Aryan blood with that of lower peoples the result was the end of the cultured people. North America, whose population consists in by far the largest part of Germanic elements who mixed but little with the lower colored peoples, shows a different humanity and culture from Central and South America, where the predominantly Latin immigrants often mixed with the aborigines on a large scale. By this one example, we can clearly and distinctly recognize the effect of racial mixture. The Germanic inhabitant of the American continent, who has remained racially pure and unmixed, rose to be master of the continent; he will remain the master as long as he does not fall a victim to defilement of the blood.

The result of all racial crossing is therefore in brief always the following:

(a)   Lowering of the level of the higher race;
(b)   Physical and intellectual regression and hence the beginning of a slowly but surely progressing sickness.

To bring about such a development is, then, nothing else but to sin against the will of the eternal creator....

Everything we admire on this earth today-science and art, technology and inventions-is only the creative product of a few peoples and originally perhaps of one race. On them depends the existence of this whole culture. If they perish, the beauty of this earth will sink into the grave with them.

However much the soil, for example, can influence men, the result of the influence will always be different depending on the races in question. The low fertility of a living space may spur the one race to the highest achievements; in others it will only be the cause of bitterest poverty and final undernourishment with all its consequences. The inner nature of peoples is always determining for the manner in which outward influences will be effective. What leads the one to starvation trains the other to hard work.

All great cultures of the past perished only because the originally creative race died out from blood poisoning.

The ultimate cause of such a decline was their forgetting that all culture depends on men and not conversely; hence that to preserve a certain culture the man who creates it must be preserved. This preservation is bound up with the rigid law of necessity and the right to victory of the best and stronger in this world.

Those who want to live, let them fight, and those who do not want to fight in this world of eternal struggle do not deserve to live.

Even if this were hard-that is how it is! Assuredly, however, by far the harder fate is that which strikes the man who thinks he can overcome Nature, but in the last analysis only mocks her. Distress, misfortune, and diseases are her answer.

The man who misjudges and disregards the racial laws actually forfeits the happiness that seems destined to be his. He thwarts the triumphal march of the best race and hence also the precondition for all human progress, and remains, in consequence, burdened with all the sensibility of man, in the animal realm of helpless misery.

It is idle to argue which race or races were the original representative of human culture and hence the real founders of all that we sum up under the word "humanity." It is simpler to raise this question with regard to the present, and here an easy, clear answer results. All the human culture, all the results of art, science, and technology that we see before us today, are almost exclusively the creative product of the Aryan. This very fact admits of the not unfounded inference that he alone was the founder of all higher humanity, therefore representing the prototype of all that we understand by the word "man." He is the Prometheus of mankind from whose bright forehead the divine spark of genius has sprung at all times, forever kindling anew that fire of knowledge which illumined the night of silent mysteries and thus caused man to climb the path to mastery over the other beings of this earth. Exclude him-and perhaps after a thousand years darkness will again descend on the earth, human culture will pass, and the world turn to a desert.

If we were to divide mankind into three groups, the founders of culture, the bearers of culture, the destroyers of culture, only the Aryan could be considered as the representative of the first group. From him originate the foundations and walls of all human creation, and only the outward form and color are determined by the changing traits of character of the various peoples. He provides the mightiest building stones and plans for all human progress and only the execution corresponds to the nature of the varying men and races....

The question of the inner causes of the Aryan's importance can be answered to the effect that they are to be sought less in a natural instinct of self-preservation than in the special type of its expression. The will to live, subjectively viewed, is everywhere equal and different only in the form of its actual expression. In the most primitive living creatures the instinct of self-preservation does not go beyond concern for their own ego. Egoism, as we designate this urge, goes so far that it even embraces time; the moment itself claims everything, granting nothing to the coming hours. In this condition the animal lives only for himself, seeks food only for his present hunger, and fights only for his own life. As long as the instinct of self-preservation expresses itself in this way, every basis is lacking for the formation of a group, even the most primitive form of family. Even a community between male and female, beyond pure mating, demands an extension of the instinct of self-preservation, since concern and struggle for the ego are now directed toward the second party; the male sometimes seeks food for the female, too, but for the most part both seek nourishment for the young. Nearly always one comes to the defense of the other, and thus the first, though infinitely simple, forms of a sense of sacrifice result. As soon as this sense extends beyond the narrow limits of the family, the basis for the formation of larger organisms and finally formal states is created.

In the lowest peoples of the earth this quality is present only to a very slight extent, so that often they do not go beyond the formation of the family. The greater the readiness to subordinate purely personal interests, the higher rises the ability to establish comprehensive communities.

This self-sacrificing will to give one's personal labor and if necessary one's own life for others is most strongly developed in the Aryan. The Aryan is not greatest in his mental qualities as such, but in the extent of his willingness to put all his abilities in the service of the community. In him the instinct of self-preservation has reached the noblest form, since he willingly subordinates his own ego to the life of the community and, if the hour demands, even sacrifices it.

Not in his intellectual gift lies the source of the Aryan's capacity for creating and building culture. If he had just this alone, he could only act destructively, in no case could he organize; for the innermost essence of all organization requires that the individual renounce putting forward his personal opinion and interests and sacrifice both in favor of a larger group. Only by way of this general community does he again recover his share. Now, for example, he no longer works directly for himself, but with his activity articulates himself with the community, not only for his own advantage, but for the advantage of all. The most wonderful elucidation of this attitude is provided by his word "work," by which he does not mean an activity for maintaining life in itself, but exclusively a creative effort that does not conflict with the interests of the community. Otherwise he designates human activity, in so far as it serves the instinct of self-preservation without consideration for his fellow men, as theft, usury, robbery, burglary, etc.

This state of mind, which subordinates the interests in the ego to the conservation of the community, is really the first premise for every truly human culture. From it alone can arise all the great works of mankind, which bring the founder little reward, but the richest blessings to posterity. Yes, from it alone can we understand how so many are able to bear up faithfully under a scanty life which imposes on them nothing but poverty and frugality, but gives the community the foundation of its existence. Every worker, every peasant, every inventor, official, etc., who works without ever being able to achieve any happiness or prosperity for himself, is a representative of his lofty idea, even if the deeper meaning of his activity remains hidden in him.

What applies to work as the foundation of human sustenance and all human progress is true to an even greater degree for the defense of man and his culture. In giving one's own life for the existence of the community lies the crown of all sense of sacrifice. It is this alone that prevents what human hands have built from being overthrown by human hands or destroyed by Nature.

Our own German language possesses a word which magnificently designates this kind of activity: *Pflichterfüllung* [fulfillment of duty]; it means not to be self-sufficient but to serve the community.

The basic attitude from which such activity arises, we call-to distinguish it from egoism and selfishness-idealism. By this we understand only the individual's capacity to make sacrifices for the community, for his fellow men.

How necessary it is to keep realizing that idealism does not represent a superfluous expression of emotion, but that in truth it has been, is, and will be, the premise for what we designate as human culture, yes, that it alone created the concept of "man." It is to this inner attitude that the Aryan owes his position in this world, and to it the world owes man; for it alone formed from pure spirit the creative force which, by a unique pairing of the brutal fist and the intellectual genius, created the monuments of human culture.

Without his idealistic attitude all, even the most dazzling faculties of the intellect, would remain mere intellect as such-outward appearance without inner value, and never creative force.

But, since true idealism is nothing but the subordination of the interests and life of the individual to the community, and this in turn is the precondition for the creation of organizational forms of all kinds, it corresponds in its innermost depths to the ultimate will of Nature. It alone leads men to voluntary recognition of the privilege of force and strength, and thus makes them into a dust particle of that order which shapes and forms the whole universe.

The purest idealism is unconsciously equivalent to the deepest knowledge.

How correct this is, and how little true idealism has to do with playful flights of the imagination, can be seen at once if we let the unspoiled child, a healthy boy, for example, judge. The same boy who feels like throwing up when he hears the tirades of a pacifist "idealist" is ready to give his young life for the ideal of his nationality.

Here the instinct of knowledge unconsciously obeys the deeper necessity of the preservation of the species, if necessary at the cost of the individual, and protests against the visions of the pacifist windbag who in reality is nothing but a cowardly, though camouflaged, egoist, transgressing the laws of development; for development requires willingness on the part of the individual to sacrifice himself for the community, and not the sickly imaginings of cowardly know-it-alls and critics of Nature.

Especially, therefore, at times when the ideal attitude threatens to disappear, we can at once recognize a diminution of that force which forms the community and thus creates the premises of culture. As soon as egoism becomes the ruler of a people, the bands of order are loosened and in the chase after their own happiness men fall from heaven into a real hell.

Yes, even posterity forgets the men who have only served their own advantage and praises the heroes who have renounced their own happiness.

The mightiest counterpart to the Aryan is represented by the Jew. In hardly any people in the world is the instinct of self-preservation developed more strongly than in the so-called "chosen." Of this, the mere fact of the survival of this race may be considered the best proof. Where is the people which in the last two thousand years has been exposed to so slight changes of inner disposition, character, etc., as the Jewish people? What people, finally, has gone through greater upheavals than this one-and nevertheless issued from the mightiest catastrophes of mankind unchanged? What an infinitely tough will to live and preserve the species speaks from these facts!

The mental qualities of the Jew have been schooled in the course of many centuries. Today he passes as "smart," and this in a certain sense he has been at all times. But his intelligence is not the result of his own development, but of visual instruction through foreigners. For the human mind cannot climb to the top without steps; for every step upward he needs the foundation of the past, and this in the comprehensive sense in which it can be revealed only in general culture. All thinking is based only in small part on man's own knowledge, and mostly on the experience of the time that has preceded. The general cultural level provides the individual man, without his noticing it as a rule, with such a profusion of preliminary knowledge that, thus armed, he can more easily take further steps of his own. The boy of today, for example, grows up among a truly vast number of technical acquisitions of the last centuries, so that he takes for granted and no longer pays attention to much that a hundred years ago was a riddle to even the greatest minds, although for following and understanding our progress in the field in question it is of decisive importance to him. If a very genius from the twenties of the past century should suddenly leave his grave today, it would be harder for him even intellectually to find his way in the present era than for an average boy of fifteen today. For he would lack all the infinite preliminary education which our present contemporary unconsciously, so to speak, assimilates while growing up amidst the manifestation of our present general civilization.

Since the Jew-for reasons which will at once become apparent-was never in possession of a culture of his own, the foundations of his intellectual work were always provided by others. His intellect at all times developed through the cultural world surrounding him.

The reverse process never took place.

For if the Jewish people's instinct of self-preservation is not smaller but larger than that of other peoples, if his intellectual faculties can easily arouse the impression that they are equal to the intellectual gifts of other races, he lacks completely the most essential requirement for a cultured people, the idealistic attitude.

In the Jewish people the will to self-sacrifice does not go beyond the individual's naked instinct of self-preservation. Their apparently great sense of solidarity is based on the very primitive herd instinct that is seen in many other living creatures in this world. It is a noteworthy fact that the herd instinct leads to mutual support only as long as a common danger makes this seem useful or inevitable. The same pack of wolves which has just fallen on its prey together disintegrates when hunger abates into its individual beasts. The same is true of horses which try to defend themselves against an assailant in a body, but scatter again as soon as the danger is past.

It is similar with the Jew. His sense of sacrifice is only apparent. It exists only as long as the existence of the individual makes it absolutely necessary. However, as soon as the common enemy is conquered, the danger threatening all averted and the booty hidden, the apparent harmony of the Jews among themselves ceases, again making way for their old causal tendencies. The Jew is only united when a common danger forces him to be or a common booty entices him; if these two grounds are lacking, the qualities of the crassest egoism come into their own, and in the twinkling of an eye the united people turns into a horde of rats, fighting bloodily among themselves.

If the Jews were alone in this world, they would stifle in filth and offal; they would try to get ahead of one another in hate-filled struggle and exterminate one another, in so far as the absolute absence of all sense of self-sacrifice, expressing itself in their cowardice, did not turn battle into comedy here too.

So it is absolutely wrong to infer any ideal sense of sacrifice in the Jews from the fact that they stand together in struggle, or, better expressed, in the plundering of their fellow men.

Here again the Jew is led by nothing but the naked egoism of the individual.

That is why the Jewish state- which should be the living organism for preserving and increasing a race-is completely unlimited as to territory. For a state formation to have a definite spatial setting always presupposes an idealistic attitude on the part of the state-race, and especially a correct interpretation of the concept of work. In the exact measure in which this attitude is lacking any attempt at forming, even of preserving, a spatially delimited state fails. And thus the basis on which alone culture can arise is lacking.

Hence the Jewish people, despite all apparent intellectual qualities, is without any true culture, and especially without any true culture of its own. For what sham culture the Jew today possesses is the property of other peoples, and for the most part it is ruined in his hands.

In judging the Jewish people's attitude on the question of human culture, the most essential characteristic we must always bear in mind is that there has never been a Jewish art and accordingly there is none today either; that above all the two queens of all the arts, architecture and music, owe nothing original to the Jews. What they do accomplish in the field of art is either patchwork or intellectual theft. Thus, the Jews lack those qualities which distinguish the races that are creative and hence culturally blessed.

To what an extent the Jew takes over foreign culture, imitating or rather ruining it, can be seen from the fact that he is mostly found in the art which seems to require the least original invention, the art of acting. But even here, in reality, he is only a "juggler," or rather an ape; for even here he lacks the last touch that is required for real greatness; even here he is not the creative genius, but a superficial imitator, and all the twists and tricks that he uses are powerless to conceal the inner lifelessness of his creative gift. Here the Jewish press most lovingly helps him along by raising such a roar of hosannahs about even the most mediocre bungler, just so long as he is a Jew, that the rest of the world actually ends up by thinking that they have an artist before them, while in truth it is only a pitiful comedian.

No, the Jew possesses no culture-creating force of any sort, since the idealism, without which there is no true higher development of man, is not present in him and never was present. Hence his intellect will never have a constructive effect, but will be destructive, and in very rare cases perhaps will at most be stimulating, but then as the prototype of the "force which always wants evil and nevertheless creates good."[1] Not through him does any progress of mankind occur, but in spite of him.

Questions:
1. How does Hitler justify his racist views?
2. What attributes do "Aryans" possess, according to Hitler?

---

[1] [Goethe's Faust, lines 1336–37: Mephistopheles to Faust.]

PART 24
Authoritarian and Totalitarian Experiments in Asia

24.1   Kita Ikki, Outline for the Reconstruction of Japan

Following World War I, Japan experimented with parliamentary democracy at home and pursued internationalism abroad. But Japanese radicals, both right- and left-wing, had little confidence in parliamentary solutions for social problems. Radical nationalists, particularly ultranationalistic young army officers, found inspiration for the future in the thought and writings of Kita Ikki (1885–1937). This advocate of national socialism was implicated in the abortive military coup d'état of February 26, 1936, and was executed in 1937.

> **Source:** From David John Lu, *Sources of Japanese History,* Vol. 2 (New York: McGraw-Hill, 1974), pp. 131–36. Reprinted by permission.

THE EMPEROR OF THE PEOPLE

Suspension of the Constitution: In order to establish a firm base for national reorganization, the Emperor, with the aid of the entire Japanese nation and by invoking his imperial prerogatives, shall suspend the Constitution for a period of three years, dissolve the two houses of the Diet, and place the entire country under martial law.

The true significance of the Emperor: We must make clear the fundamental principle that the Emperor is the sole representative of the people and the pillar of the state. . . .

Abolition of the peerage system: By abolishing the peerage system, we shall be able to remove the feudal aristocracy which constitutes a barrier between the Emperor and the people. In this way the spirit of the Meiji Restoration shall be proclaimed.

The House of Peers shall be replaced by the Deliberative Council which shall review decisions made by the House of Representatives. The Deliberative Council may reject for a single time only any decisions of the House of Representatives.

The members of the Deliberative Council shall consist of men distinguished in various fields of activities, elected by each other or appointed by the Emperor.

Popular election: All men twenty-five years of age and above shall have the right to elect and be elected to the House of Representatives, exercising their rights with full equality as citizens of Great Japan. Similar provisions shall apply to all local self-governing bodies. No women shall be permitted to participate in politics.

Restoration of people's freedom: Existing laws which restrict people's freedom and circumvent the spirit of the constitution shall be abolished. These laws include the civil ser-vice appointment ordinance, peace preservation law, press act, and publication law.

National reorganization Cabinet: A national reorganization Cabinet shall be formed during the time martial law is in effect. In addition to the existing ministries, the Cabinet shall establish such ministries of industries as described below and add a number of ministers without portfolio. Members of the reorganization Cabinet shall be selected from outstanding individuals throughout the country, avoiding those who are presently connected with military, bureaucratic, financial, or party cliques. . . .

Granting of imperial estate: The Emperor shall set a personal example by granting to the state, the lands, forests, shares and similar properties held by the Imperial Household. The expenses of the Imperial Household shall be limited to thirty million yen per annum appropriated from the national treasury. However, the Diet may authorize additional expenditure if the need arises.

LIMITATION ON PRIVATE PROPERTY

Limitation on private property: No Japanese family shall possess property in excess of one million yen. A similar limitation shall apply to Japanese citizens holding property overseas. No one shall be permitted to make a gift of property to those related by blood or to others, or to transfer his property by other means with the intent of circumventing this limitation.

Nationalization of excess amount over limitation on private property: Any amount which exceeds the limitation on private property shall revert to the state without compensation. No one shall be permitted to resort to the protection of present laws in order to avoid remitting such excess amount. Anyone who violates these provisions shall be deemed a person thinking lightly of the example set by the Emperor and endangering the basis of national reorganization. As such, during the time martial law is in effect, he shall be charged with the crimes of endangering the person of the Emperor and engaging in internal revolt and shall be punished by death.

THREE PRINCIPLES FOR DISPOSITION OF LANDS

Limitation on private landholding: No Japanese family shall hold land in excess of 100,000 yen in current market value. . . .
Lands held in excess of the limitation on private landholding shall revert to the state. . . .

Popular ownership of lands reverted to state: The state shall divide the lands granted by the Imperial Household and the lands reverted to it from those whose holdings exceed the limitation and distribute such lands to farmers who do not possess their own lands. These farmers shall gain title to their respective lands by making annual installment payments to the state. . . .

Lands to be owned by the state: Large forests, virgin lands which require large capital investment, and lands which can best be cultivated in large lots shall be owned and operated by the state.

CONTROL OF LARGE CAPITAL

Limitation on private property: No private industry shall exceed the limit of 10,000,000 yen in assets. A similar limitation shall apply to private industries owned by Japanese citizens overseas.

Nationalization of industries exceeding the limitation: Any industry whose assets exceed the limitation imposed on private industry shall be collectivized and operated under state control. . . .

INDUSTRIAL ORGANIZATION OF THE STATE

No. 1. Ministry of Banking: The assets of this ministry shall come from the money expropriated from large banks whose assets exceed the limitation on private industry and from individuals whose net worth exceeds the limitation on private property. . . .

No. 2. Ministry of Navigation: Ships and other assets expropriated from private lines in excess of the limitation on private property shall be utilized mainly for transoceanic voyages in order to attain supremacy of the seas. [The ministry shall also] engage in shipbuilding (naval and commercial) and other activities. . . .

No. 3. Ministry of Mines: Large mines whose assets or market values exceed the limitation on private industry shall be expropriated and operated by this ministry. . . .

No. 4. Ministry of Agriculture: Management of nationally owned lands; management of Taiwan sugar industry and forestry; development of Taiwan, Hokkaido, Karafuto (Southern Sakhalin), and Ch⁻osen (Korea); development of South and North Manchuria and colonies to be acquired in the future; and management of large farms when acquired by the state.

No. 5. Ministry of Industries: Various large industries expropriated by the state shall be reorganized, unified, and expanded to form a truly large industrial combine through which all types of industries may acquire competitive advantages now possessed by comparable foreign industries. The ministry shall also operate industries urgently needed by the nation but not undertaken by private parties. Naval Steel Works and Military Ordnance Factories shall be placed under this ministry's jurisdiction and be operated by it. . . .

Railways whose assets do not exceed the limitation on private industry shall be open to private operation.

Vast income of the national treasury: The vast income realized by the industrial ministries shall be sufficient for the expenditures of various service ministries and guarantee adequate living conditions for the people as described below. Therefore, with the exception of basic income taxes, all other inequitable taxes shall be abolished. Without exception, all industrial ministries shall be taxed in a manner similar to all private industries. . . .

RIGHTS OF WORKERS

Functions of the Ministry of Labor: A Ministry of Labor shall be established within the Cabinet to protect the rights of all workers employed by state-owned and privately owned industries. Industrial disputes shall be submitted to the Ministry of Labor for arbitration in accordance with a law to be enacted independently. . . .

Working hours: Working hours shall be uniformly set at eight hours a day. Wages shall be paid for Sundays and holidays when no work is performed. Farm workers shall receive additional wages for the overtime work performed during the busy farming seasons.

Distribution of profits to workers: One half of the net profits of private industries shall be distributed to workers employed in such industries. All workers, mental and physical, shall participate in the profit distribution proportionate to their salaries or wages. Workers shall elect their own representatives to participate in the industry's management planning and bookkeeping. Similar provisions shall apply to farm workers and landlords.

Workers employed in state-owned industries shall receive semi-annual bonuses in lieu of the profit distribution. . . .

Establishment of employee-shareholder system: Every private corporation shall set up a provision under which physical and mental workers in their employment shall have the right to become stockholders of the corporation.

Protection of tenant farmers: The state shall enact a separate law, based on the basic human rights, to protect tenant farmers tilling the lands owned by small landlords whose holdings do not exceed the limitation on private lands.

Women's labor: Women's labor shall be free and equal to that of men. However, after the reorganization, the state shall make it a matter of national policy that the burden of labor shall not rest on the shoulders of women. In order to prepare women to replace men in providing needed labor in a national emergency, women shall receive education equal to that of men.

PEOPLE'S RIGHT TO LIVE

Children's right to live: Children under fifteen years of age without both parents or father, having rights as children of the state, shall be uniformly supported and educated by the state. . . .

Support of the aged and disabled: The state shall assume the responsibility of supporting those men and women sixty years of age or over who are poor and not having their natural born or adopted sons. Similar support shall be given to those disabled and crippled persons who are poor, unable to work, and without fathers and sons.

Rights to education: National (compulsory) education shall last for a period of ten years from ages six to sixteen. Similar education shall be given to both male and female. There shall be instituted a fundamental reform in the educational system. . . .

English shall be abolished and Esperanto shall become the second language. . . .

RIGHTS OF THE STATE

Continuation of the conscript system: The state, having rights to existence and development among the nations of the world, shall maintain the present conscript system in perpetuity. . . .

Positive right to start war: In addition to the right to self-defense, the state shall have the right to start a war on behalf of other nations and races unjustly oppressed by a third power. (As a matter of real concern today, the state shall have the right to start a war to aid the independence of India and preservation of China's integrity.)

As a result of its own development, the state shall also have the right to start a war against those nations who occupy large colonies illegally and ignore the heavenly way of the co-existence of all humanity. (As a matter of real concern today, the state shall have the right to start a war against those nations which occupy Australia and Far Eastern Siberia for the purpose of acquiring them.)

Questions:
1. Why would Kita Ikki urge that the study of English be abolished?
2. Are there any parallels between Kita Ikki's and Mussolini's views of war and violence?
3. Compare and contrast national social socialism advocated by Adolf Hitler with Kita's ideas of restructuring Japan.

24.2 Japanese Imperialism

In the waning years of the nineteenth century, as European imperialism was beginning to ebb, a new imperial power was rising in the Far East-Japan. The Japanese embarked on their imperialistic expansion soon after beginning their own internal modernization following the Meiji Restoration in 1868. With the hope of becoming a world power, comparable to those in the West, they realized that they needed vast material resources, which their small islands could not provide, to attain their goal. So they turned their eyes to the mainland of Asia. After a preliminary move against the island of Formosa (Taiwan) in 1874, they put military and diplomatic pressure on Korea, gaining important economic concessions there. This effort was followed in 1894 by direct invasion, precipitating a war with China. The Japanese were easily victorious, taking over control of Korea (which was formally annexed in 1910) and forcing the Chinese to cede the island of Formosa and the strategically important Liaotung peninsula of Manchuria to them. Under pressure from the European powers, however, they were forced to return the Liaotung peninsula to China. After a successful war against Russia in 1904 Japan won important economic concessions (which the Russians had held) in Manchuria, as well as the southern half of Sakhalin Island, north of Hokkaido.

During the First World War, as the ally of England, Japan was able with little effort to take control of German colonies in Asia, both on the mainland and among the islands of the western Pacific. Also she saw the war as an opportunity for domination of China itself. In 1915 she presented the Chinese with a set of "Twenty-one Demands," which, had they been granted, would virtually have converted China into a colony of Japan. Although the new republican government of China was able to resist the most sweeping of these demands, Japan did gain some important economic concessions from it. Finally, in 1931, Japan launched her main drive for the conquest of East Asia, beginning with the invasion of Manchuria, which she quickly conquered and annexed. This led to further warfare in China, which was pursued relentlessly for a decade against stubborn Chinese resistance. By 1941 the Japanese had concluded that they needed to eliminate any possibility of American intervention in the war. This they (mistakenly) *believed they could do by the destruction of the United States Pacific fleet; hence the surprise attack on Pearl Harbor, which precipitated the American war against Japan.*

Outside of Japan little was known directly of the extent of her imperial ambitions. Only at the end of the war were documents uncovered revealing her long-range goals. One of the most important of these was a secret plan, prepared at the beginning of 1942 for the Japanese government by the Total War Research Institute. The product of this plan was to be called "The Greater East Asia Co-Prosperity Sphere."

Source: Theodore De Bary, ed., *Sources of the Japanese Tradition,* volume I, (Columbia University Press), 1958, pp. 801–805.

DRAFT OF BASIC PLAN FOR ESTABLISHMENT OF GREATER EAST ASIA CO-PROSPERITY SPHERE

PART I. OUTLINE OF CONSTRUCTION

....*The Plan.* The Japanese empire is a manifestation of morality and its special characteristic is the propagation of the Imperial Way. It strives but for the achievement of *Hakkō Ichiu*, the spirit of its founding. . . . .It is necessary to foster the increased power of the empire, to cause East Asia to return to its original form of independence and co-prosperity by shaking off the yoke of Europe and America, and to let its countries and peoples develop their respective abilities in peaceful cooperation and secure livelihood.

The Form of East Asiatic Independence and Co-Prosperity.

The states, their citizens, and resources, comprised in those areas pertaining to the Pacific, Central Asia, and the Indian Oceans formed into one general union are to be established as an autonomous zone of peaceful living and common prosperity on behalf of the peoples of the nations of East Asia. The area including Japan, Manchuria, North China, lower Yangtze River, and the Russian Maritime Province, forms the nucleus of the East Asiatic Union. The Japanese empire possesses a duty as the leader of the East Asiatic Union.

The above purpose presupposes the inevitable emancipation or independence of Eastern Siberia, China, Indo-China, the South Seas, Australia, and India.

Regional Division in the East Asiatic Union and the National Defense Sphere for the Japanese Empire.

In the Union of East Asia, the Japanese empire is at once the stabilizing power and the leading influence. To enable the empire actually to become the central influence in East Asia, the first necessity is the consolidation of the inner belt of East Asia; and the East Asiatic Sphere shall be divided as follows for this purpose:

The Inner Sphere-the vital sphere for the empire-includes Japan, Manchuria, North China, the lower Yangtze Area and the Russian Maritime area.

The Smaller Co-Prosperity Sphere-the smaller self-supplying sphere of East Asia-includes the inner sphere plus Eastern Siberia, China, Indo-China and the South Seas.

The Greater Co-Prosperity Sphere-the larger self-supplying sphere of East Asia-includes the smaller co-prosperity sphere, plus Australia, India, and island groups in the Pacific....

For the present, the smaller co-prosperity sphere shall be the zone in which the construction of East Asia and the stabilization of national defense are to be aimed at. After their completion there shall be a gradual expansion toward the construction of the Greater Co-Prosperity Sphere.

Outline of East Asiatic Administration.

It is intended that the unification of Japan, Manchoukuo, and China in neighborly friendship be realized by the settlement of the Sino-Japanese problems through the crushing of hostile influences in the Chinese interior, and through the construction of a new China in tune with the rapid construction of the Inner Sphere. Aggressive American and British influences in East Asia shall be driven out of the area of Indo-China and the South Seas, and this area shall be brought into our defense sphere. The war with Britain and America shall be prosecuted for that purpose.

The Russian aggressive influence in East Asia will be driven out. Eastern Siberia shall be cut off from the Soviet regime and included in our defense sphere. For this purpose, a war with the Soviets is expected. It is considered possible that this Northern problem may break out before the general settlement of the present Sino-Japanese and the Southern problems if the situation renders this unavoidable. Next the independence of Australia, India, etc. shall gradually be brought about. For this purpose, a recurrence of war with Britain and her allies is expected. The construction of a Greater Mongolian State is expected during the above phase. The construction of the Smaller Co-Prosperity Sphere is expected to require at least twenty years from the present time.

The Building of the National Strength.

Since the Japanese empire is the center and pioneer of Oriental moral and cultural reconstruction, the officials and people of this country must return to the spirit of the Orient and acquire a thorough understanding of the spirit of the national moral character.

In the economic construction of the country, Japanese and Manchurian national power shall first be consolidated, then the unification of Japan, Manchoukuo and China, shall be effected....Thus a central industry will be constructed in East Asia, and the necessary relations established with the Southern Seas.

The standard for the construction of the national power and its military force, so as to meet the various situations that might affect the stages of East Asiatic administration and the national defense sphere, shall be so set as to be capable of driving off any British, American, Soviet or Chinese counter influences in the future.

CHAPTER 3. POLITICAL CONSTRUCTION

Basic Plan.

The realization of the great ideal of constructing Greater East Asia Co-Prosperity requires not only the complete prosecution of the current Greater East Asia War but also presupposes another great war in the future. Therefore, the following two points must be made the primary starting points for the political construction of East Asia during the course of the next twenty years: 1) Preparation for war with the other spheres of the world; and 2) Unification and construction of the East Asia Smaller Co-Prosperity Sphere.

The following are the basic principles for the political construction of East Asia, when the above two points are taken into consideration:

a.   The politically dominant influence of European and American countries in the Smaller Co-Prosperity Sphere shall be gradually driven out and the area shall enjoy its liberation from the shackles hitherto forced upon it.

b.   The desires of the peoples in the sphere for their independence shall be respected and endeavors shall be made for their fulfillment, but proper and suitable forms of government shall be decided for them in consideration of military and economic requirements and of the historical, political and cultural elements peculiar to each area.

It must also be noted that the independence of various peoples of East Asia should be based upon the idea of constructing East Asia as "independent countries existing within the New Order of East Asia" and that this conception differs from an independence based on the idea of liberalism and national self-determination.

c.   During the course of construction, military unification is deemed particularly important, and the military zones and key points necessary for defense shall be directly or indirectly under the control of our country.

d.   The peoples of the sphere shall obtain their proper positions, the unity of the people's minds shall be effected and the unification of the sphere shall be realized with the empire as its center. . . .

CHAPTER 4. THOUGHT AND CULTURAL CONSTRUCTION

General Aim in Thought.

The ultimate aim in thought construction in East Asia is to make East Asiatic peoples revere the imperial influence by propagating the Imperial Way based on the spirit of construction, and to establish the belief that uniting solely under this influence is the one and only way to the eternal growth and development of East Asia.

And during the next twenty years (the period during which the above ideal is to be reached) it is necessary to make the nations and peoples of East Asia realize the historical significance of the establishment of the New Order in East Asia, and in the common consciousness of East Asiatic unity, to liberate East Asia from the shackles of Europe and America and to establish the common conviction of constructing a New Order based on East Asiatic morality.

Occidental individualism and materialism shall be rejected and a moral world view, the basic principle of whose morality shall be the Imperial Way, shall be established. The ultimate object to be achieved is not exploitation but co-prosperity and mutual help, not competitive conflict but mutual assistance and mild peace, not a formal view of equality but a view of order based on righteous classification, not an idea of rights but an idea of service, and not several world views but one unified world view.

General Aim in Culture.

The essence of the traditional culture of the Orient shall be developed and manifested. And, casting off the negative and conservative cultural characteristics of the continents (India and China) on the one hand, and taking in the good points of Western culture on the other, an Oriental culture and morality, on a grand scale and subtly refined, shall be created.

Questions:
1. What is Greater East Asia Co-Prosperity Sphere?
2. Were Japanese imperialist goals different from the goals of nineteenth century European imperialism? If so, how are they different?

24.3 Mao Tse-Tung: Report of an Investigation into the Peasant Movement in Hunan

If Karl Marx would have been surprised to see communism taking root in Russia he would have been astonished to see it conquer China; for China, even more than Russia, was a land of peasant farmers, with only a minuscule population of industrial proletarians. Clearly, it was no place for a Communist revolution, according to orthodox Marxist theory.

As in Russia, the success of communism in China was in large part the result of the activities of a single individual-in this case Mao Tse-tung, now called Mao Zedong (1893-1976). Mao was instrumental in accomplishing two goals. First, he revised Marxist theory and practice to fit the actual conditions in his country. Lacking a nucleus of industrial workers, but with hundreds of millions of agricultural laborers at hand, most living under conditions of dire poverty, he turned to these peasants for his revolutionary force. (He did suggest that China had undergone an earlier bourgeois revolution in 1911, when Dr. Sun Yat-sen had overthrown the Manchu dynasty and set up a republic.)

Mao's second task was a different, more formidable one that took him over twenty years to accomplish. This was to mount the revolution and to guarantee that it would lead to the establishment of a Communist regime in China. Two obstacles stood in his way; both were military. Scarcely had he begun organizing the peasants and getting the revolution under way than Japan invaded and occupied Manchuria (in 1931) and later much of the rest of China. The Japanese occupation frustrated Mao's revolutionary movement for over a decade until the end of the Second World War in 1945. The other military opposition was internal. During the long struggle against the Japanese a substantial portion of the Chinese army belonged to the Kuomintang, under the leadership of Chiang Kai-shek. Chiang, who had originally been a compatriot of Mao, had, over the years, become increasingly reactionary. So, after the expulsion of the Japanese, these two leaders became bitter antagonists, in a struggle for control of China. Mao won, forcing Chiang and his followers to flee to Formosa (Taiwan) in 1949. Finally, he was able to realize his goal of establishing a Communist state in China.

The selection that follows is Mao's account of the beginning phases of the peasant revolt that was to lead to a Communist victory over twenty years later. In 1926 peasants in the interior of China had begun to rise against their landlords, but many of Mao's co-workers belittled their efforts. Mao decided to go to the area himself to see what actually was happening. In the selection he reports on what he found.

> **Source:** Mao Tse-tung, *Selected Readings from the Works of Mao Tse-tung* (Peking: Foreign Languages Press, 1971). Courtesy of Foreign Languages Press.

THE IMPORTANCE OF THE PEASANT PROBLEM

During my recent visit to Hunan I conducted an investigation on the spot into the conditions in the five counties of Siangtan, Siangsiang, Hengshan, Liling and Changsha. In the thirty-two days from January 4 to February 5, in villages and in county towns, I called together for fact-finding conferences experienced peasants and comrades working for the peasant movement, listened attentively to their reports and collected a lot of material. Many of the hows and whys of the peasant movement were quite the reverse of what I had heard from the gentry in Hankow and Changsha. And many strange things there were that I had never seen or heard of before. I think these conditions exist in many other places.

All kinds of arguments against the peasant movement must be speedily set right. The erroneous measures taken by the revolutionary authorities concerning the peasant movement must be speedily changed. Only thus can any good be done for the future of the revolution. For the rise of the present peasant movement is a colossal event. In a very short time, in China's central, southern and northern provinces, several hundred million peasants will rise like a tornado or tempest, a force so extraordinarily swift and violent that no power, however great, will be able to suppress it. They will break all trammels that now bind them and rush forward along the road to liberation. They will send all imperialists, warlords, corrupt officials, local bullies and bad gentry to their graves. All revolutionary parties and all revolutionary comrades will stand before them to be tested, and to be accepted or rejected as they decide.

To march at their head and lead them? Or to follow at their rear, gesticulating at them and criticising them? Or to face them as opponents?

Every Chinese is free to choose among the three alternatives, but circumstances demand that a quick choice be made.

GET ORGANISED!

The peasant movement in Hunan, so far as it concerns the counties in the central and southern sections of the province, where the movement is already developed, can be roughly divided into two periods.

The first period was the period of organisation, extending from January to September of last year. In this period, there was the stage from January to June-a stage of underground activities, and the stage from July to September when the revolutionary army expelled Chao Hengti[1] —a stage of open activities. In this period, the membership of the peasant association totaled only 300,000–400,000, and the masses it could directly lead numbered but little more than a million; as there was hardly any struggle in the rural areas, very little criticism of the association was heard. Since its members served as guides, scouts and carriers, the officers in the Northern Expedition Army even had a good word or two for the peasant association.

The second period was the period of revolutionary action, extending from last October to this January. The membership of the peasant association jumped to two million and the masses over whom it could exercise direct leadership increased to ten million people. As the peasants mostly entered only one name for each family when joining the association, a membership of two million therefore means a mass following of about ten million. Of all the peasants in Hunan, almost half are organised. In counties like Siangtan, Siangsiang, Liuyang, Changsha, Liling, Ningsiang, Pingkiang, Siangyin, Hengshan, Hengyang, Leiyang, Chen and Anhwa, nearly all the peasants have rallied organisationally in the association and followed its leadership. The peasants, with their extensive organisation, went right into action and within four months brought about a great and unprecedented revolution in the countryside.

DOWN WITH THE LOCAL BULLIES AND BAD GENTRY! ALL POWER TO THE PEASANT ASSOCIATION!

The peasants attack as their main targets the local bullies and bad gentry and the lawless landlords, hitting in passing against patriarchal ideologies and institutions, corrupt officials in the cities and evil customs in the rural areas. In force and momentum, the attack is like a tempest or hurricane; those who submit to it survive and those who resist it perish. As a result, the privileges which the feudal landlords have enjoyed for thousands of years are being shattered to pieces. The dignity and prestige of the landlords are dashed to the ground. With the fall of the authority of the landlords, the peasant association becomes the sole organ of authority, and what people call "All power to the peasant association" has come to pass. Even such a trifle as a quarrel between man and wife has to be settled at the peasant association. Nothing can be settled in the absence of people from the association. The association is actually dictating in all matters in the countryside, and it is literally true that "what ever it says, goes." The public can only praise the association and must not condemn it. The local bullies and bad gentry and the lawless landlords have been totally deprived of the right to have their say, and no one dares mutter the word "No." To be safe from the power and pressure of the peasant association, the first-rank local bullies and bad gentry fled to Shanghai; the second-rank ones to Hankow; the third-rank ones to Changsha; and the fourth-rank ones to the county towns; the fifth-rank ones and even lesser fry can only remain in the countryside and surrender to the peasant association.

"I'll donate ten dollars, please admit me to the peasant association," one of the smaller gentry would say.

"Pshaw! Who wants your filthy money!" the peasants would reply.

Many middle and small landlords, rich peasants and middle peasants, formerly opposed to the peasant association, now seek admission in vain. Visiting various places, I often came across such people, who solicited my help. "I beg," they would say, "the committeeman from the provincial capital to be my guarantor."

The census book compiled by the local authorities under the Manchu régime consisted of a regular register and a special register; in the former honest people were entered, and in the latter burglars, bandits and other undesirables. The peasants in some places now use the same method to threaten people formerly opposed to the association: "Enter them in the special register!"

Such people, afraid of being entered in the special register, try various means to seek admission to the association and do not feel at ease until, as they eagerly desire, their names are entered in its register. But they are as a rule sternly turned down, and so spend their days in a constant state of suspense; barred from the doors of the association, they are like homeless people. In short, what was generally sneered at four months ago as the "peasants' gang" has now become something most honourable. Those who prostrated themselves before the power of the gentry now prostrate themselves before the power of the peasants. Everyone admits that the world has changed since last October.

"AN AWFUL MESS!" AND "VERY GOOD INDEED!"

The revolt of the peasants in the countryside disturbed the sweet dreams of the gentry. When news about the countryside reached the cities, the gentry there immediately burst into an uproar. When I first arrived in Changsha, I met people from various circles and picked up a good deal of street gossip. From the middle strata upwards to the rightwingers of the Kuomintang, there was not a single person who did not summarise the whole thing in one phrase: "An awful mess!" Even quite revolutionary people, carried away by the opinion of the "awful mess" school which prevailed like a storm over the whole city, became downhearted at the very thought of the conditions in the countryside, and could not deny the word "mess." Even very progressive people could only remark, "Indeed a mess, but inevitable in the course of the revolution." In a word, nobody could categorically deny the word "mess.

But the fact is, as stated above, that the broad peasant masses have risen to fulfill their historic mission, that the democratic forces in the rural areas have risen to overthrow the rural feudal power. The patriarchal-feudal class of local bullies, bad gentry and lawless landlords has formed the basis of autocratic government for thousands of years, the cornerstone of imperialism, warlordism and corrupt officialdom. To overthrow this feudal power is the real objective of the national revolution. What Dr. Sun Yat-sen wanted to do in the forty years he devoted to the national revolution but failed to accomplish, the peasants have accomplished in a few months. This is a marvellous feat which has never been achieved in the last forty or even thousands of years. It is very good indeed. It is not "a mess" at all. It is anything but "an awful mess."

"An awful mess"-that is obviously a theory which, in line with the interests of the landlords, aims at combating the rise of the peasants, a theory of the landlord class for preserving the old order of feudalism and obstructing the establishment of a new order of democracy, and a counterrevolutionary theory. No revolutionary comrade should blindly repeat it. If you have firmly established your revolutionary viewpoint and have furthermore gone the round of the villages for a look, you will feel overjoyed as never before. There, great throngs of tens of thousands of slaves, i.e., the peasants, are overthrowing their cannibal enemies. Their actions are absolutely correct; their actions are very good indeed! "Very good indeed!" is the theory of the peasants and of all other revolutionaries. Every revolutionary comrade should know that the national revolution requires a profound change in the countryside. The Revolution of 1911[2] did not bring about this change, hence its failure. Now the change is taking place, which is an important factor necessary for completing the revolution. Every revolutionary comrade must support this change, or he will be taking the counter-revolutionary stand.

THE QUESTION OF "GOING TOO FAR"

There is another section of people who say, "although the peasant association ought to be formed, it has gone rather too far in its present actions." This is the opinion of the middle-of-the-roaders. But how do matters stand in reality? True, the peasants do in some ways "act unreasonably" in the countryside. The peasant association, supreme in authority, does not allow the landlords to have their say and makes a clean sweep of all their prestige. This is tantamount to trampling the landlords underfoot after knocking them down. The peasants threaten: "Put you in the special register"; they impose fines on the local bullies and bad gentry and demand contributions; they smash their sedan-chairs. Crowds of people swarm into the homes of the local bullies and bad gentry who oppose the peasant association, slaughtering their pigs and consuming their grain. They may even loll for a minute or two on the ivory beds of the young mesdames and mademoiselles in the families of the bullies and gentry. At the slightest provocation they make arrests, crown the arrested with tall paperhats, and parade them through the villages: "You bad gentry, now you know who we are!" Doing whatever they like and turning everything upside down, they have even created a kind of terror in the countryside. This is what some people call "going too far," or "going beyond the proper limit to right a wrong," or "really too outrageous."

The opinion of this group, reasonable on the surface, is erroneous at bottom.

First, the things described above have all been the inevitable results of the doings of the local bullies and bad gentry and lawless landlords themselves. For ages these people, with power in their hands, tyrannised over the peasants and trampled them underfoot; that is why the peasants have now risen in such a great revolt. The most formidable revolts and the most serious troubles invariably occur at places where the local bullies and bad gentry and the lawless landlords were the most ruthless in their evil deeds. The peasants' eyes are perfectly discerning. As to who is bad and who is not, who is the most ruthless and who is less so, and who is to be severely punished and who is to be dealt with lightly, the peasants keep perfectly clear accounts and very seldom has there been any discrepancy between the punishment and the crime.

Secondly, a revolution is not the same as inviting people to dinner, or writing an essay, or painting a picture, or doing fancy needlework; it cannot be anything so refined, so calm and gentle, or so mild, kind, courteous, restrained and magnanimous. A revolution is an uprising, an act of violence whereby one class overthrows another. A rural revolution is a revolution by which the peasantry overthrows the authority of the feudal landlord class. If the peasants do not use the maximum of their strength, they can never overthrow the authority of the landlords which has been deeply rooted for thousands of years. In the rural areas, there must be a great, fervent revolutionary upsurge, which alone can arouse hundreds and thousands of the people of form a great force. All the action mentioned above, labelled as "going too far," are caused by the power of the peasants, generated by a great, fervent, revolutionary upsurge in the countryside. Such actions were quite necessary in the second period of the peasant movement (the period of revolutionary action). In this period, it was necessary to establish the absolute authority of the peasants. It was necessary to stop malicious criticisms against the peasant association. It was necessary to overthrow all the authority of the gentry, to knock them down and even trample them underfoot. All actions labelled as "going too far" had a revolutionary significance in the second period. To put it bluntly, it was necessary to bring about a brief reign of terror in every rural area; otherwise one could never suppress the activities of the counter-revolutionaries in the countryside or overthrow the authority of the gentry. To right a wrong it is necessary to exceed the proper limits, and the wrong cannot be righted without the proper limits being exceeded.

The opinion of this school that the peasants are "going too far" is on the surface different from the opinion of the other school mentioned earlier that the peasant movement is "an awful mess," but in essence it adheres to the same viewpoint, and is likewise a theory of the landlords which supports the interests of the privileged classes. Since this theory hinders the rise of the peasant movement and consequently disrupts the revolution, we must oppose it resolutely.

THE SO-CALLED "MOVEMENT OF THE RIFFRAFF"

The right wing of the Kuomintang says, "The peasant movement is a movement of the riffraff, a movement of the lazy peasants." This opinion has gained much currency in Changsha. I went to the countryside and heard the gentry say, "It is all right to set up the peasant association, but the people now running it are incompetent; better put others on the job." This opinion and the dictum of the right wing come to the same thing; both admit that the peasant movement may be carried on (as the peasant movement has already risen, no one dares say that it shouldn't); but both regard the people leading the movement as incompetent and hate particularly those in charge of the associations at the lower levels, labelling them "riffraff." In short, all those who were formerly despised or kicked into the gutter by the gentry, who had no social standing, and who were denied the right to have a say, have now, to everyone's surprise, raised their heads. They have not only raised their heads, but have also taken power into their hands. They are now running the township peasant associations (peasant associations at the lowest level), which have been turned into a formidable force in their hands. They raise their rough, blackened hands and lay them on the gentry. They bind the bad gentry with ropes, put tall paperhats on them and lead them in a parade through the villages. (This is called "parading through the township" in Siangtan and Siangsiang, and "parading through the fields" in Liling.) Every day the coarse, harsh sound of their denunciation assails the ears of the gentry. They are giving orders and directions in all matters. They rank above everybody else, they who used to rank below everybody else-that is what people mean by "upside down."

VANGUARD OF THE REVOLUTION

When there are two opposite approaches to a thing or a kind of people, there will be two opposite opinions. "An awful mess" and "very good indeed," "riffraff" and "vanguard of the revolution," are both suitable examples.

We have seen the peasants' accomplishment of a revolutionary task for many years left unaccomplished, and their important contributions to the national revolution. But have all the peasants taken part in accomplishing such a great revolutionary task and in making important contributions? No. The peasantry consist of three sections-the rich peasants, the middle peasants and the poor peasants. The circumstances of the three sections differ, and so do their reactions to the revolution. In the first period, what reached the ears of the rich peasants was that the Northern Expedition Army had met with a crushing defeat in Kiangsi, that Chiang Kai-shek had been wounded in the leg and had flown back to Kwangtung, and that Wu P'ei-fu had recaptured Yochow. So they thought that the peasant association certainly could not last long and that the Three People's Principles[3] could never succeed, because such things were never heard of before. The officials of a township peasant association (generally of the so-called "riffraff' type), bringing the membership register and entering the house of a rich peasant, would say to him, "Please join the peasant association." How would the rich peasant answer? "Peasant association? For years I have lived here and tilled the fields; I have not seen anything like the peasant association but I get along all the same. You had better give it up!"-this from a moderate rich peasant. "What peasant association? Association for having one's head chopped off-don't get people into trouble!"-this from a violent rich peasant.

Strangely enough, the peasant association has now been established for several months, and has even dared to oppose the gentry. The gentry in the neighbourhood have been arrested by the association and paraded through the villages because they refused to surrender their opium-smoking kits. In the county towns, moreover, prominent members of the gentry have been put to death, such as Yen Yung-ch'iu of Siangtan and Yang Chih-tse of Ningsiang. At the meeting celebrating the anniversary of the October Revolution, the anti-British rally and the grand celebration of the victory of the Northern Expedition, at least ten thousand peasants in every county, carrying big and small banners, with poles and hoes thrown in, marched in demonstrations in great columns like rolling waves. When all this happened, the rich peasants began to feel perplexed. In the grand celebration of the victory of the Northern Expedition, they learnt that Kiu-kiang had been taken, that Chiang Kai-shek had not been wounded in the leg and that Wu P'ei-fu had been finally defeated. Furthermore, "Long live the Three People's Principles!" "Long live the peasant association!" and "Long live the peasants!" were clearly written on the "decrees on red and green paper" [posters]. "Long live the peasants! Are these people to be regarded as emperors?" The rich peasants were greatly puzzled.

So the peasant association put on grand airs. People from the association said to the rich peasants, "We'll enter you in the special register," or, "In another month, the admission fee will be ten dollars!" It was only in these circumstances that the rich peasants tardily joined the peasant association, some paying fifty cents or a dollar (the regular fee being only one hundred cash), others securing admission only after people had put in a good word for them at their request. There are also quite a number of die-hards who, even up to the present, have not joined the association. When the rich peasants join the association they generally enter the name of some old man of sixty or seventy of their family, for they are always afraid of "the drafting of the adult males." After joining the association they never work for it enthusiastically. They remain inactive throughout.

How about the middle peasants? Their attitude is vacillating. They think that the revolution will not do them much good. They have rice in their pots and are not afraid of bailiffs knocking at their doors at midnight. They too, judging a thing by whether it ever existed before, knit their brows and think hard: "Can the peasant association really stand on its own feet?" "Can the Three People's Principles succeed?" Their conclusion is, "Afraid not." They think that all these things depend entirely on the will of Heaven; "To run a peasant association? Who knows if Heaven wills it or not?" In the first period, people from the peasant association, registers in hand, would enter the house of a middle peasant and say to him, "Please join the peasant association!" "No hurry!" replied the middle peasant. It was not until the second period, when the peasant association enjoyed great power, that the middle peasants joined up. In the association they behave better than the rich peasants, but are as yet not very active, and still want to wait and see. It is certainly necessary for the peasant association to explain a good deal more to the middle peasants in order to get them to join.

The main force in the countryside which has always put up the bitterest fight is the poor peasants. Throughout both the period of underground organisation and that of open organisation, the poor peasants have fought militantly all along. They accept most willingly the leadership of the Communist Party. They are the deadliest enemies of the local bullies and bad gentry and attack their strongholds without the slightest hesitation. They say to the rich peasants: "We joined the peasant association long ago, why do you still hesitate?" The rich peasants answer in a mocking tone, "You people have nei

ther a tile over your head nor a pinpoint of land beneath your feet, what should have kept you from joining!" Indeed, the poor peasants are not afraid of losing anything. Many of them really have "neither a tile over their head nor a pinpoint of land beneath their feet"-what should have kept them from joining the association?

According to a survey of Changsha county, the poor peasants comprise 70 per cent of the rural population; the middle peasants, 20 per cent; and the rich peasants and landlords, 10 per cent. The poor peasants who comprise 70 per cent can be subdivided into two groups, the utterly impoverished and the less impoverished. The completely dispossessed, i.e., those who have neither land nor money, and who, without any means of livelihood, are forced to leave home and become mercenary soldiers, or hired labourers, or tramp about as beggars-all belong to the "utterly impoverished" and comprise 20 per cent. The partly dispossessed, i.e., those who have a little land or a little money, but consume more than they receive and live in the midst of toil and worry all the year round, e.g. the handicraftsmen, tenant-peasants (except the rich tenant-peasants) and semi-tenant peasants-all belong to the "less impoverished" and comprise 50 per cent. The enormous mass of poor peasants, altogether comprising 70 per cent of the rural population, are the backbone of the peasant association, the vanguard in overthrowing the feudal forces, and the foremost heroes who have accomplished the great revolutionary undertaking left unaccomplished for many years. Without the poor peasants (the "riffraff" as the gentry call them) it would never have been possible to bring about in the countryside the present state of revolution, to overthrow the local bullies and bad gentry, or to complete the democratic revolution. Being the most revolutionary, the poor peasants have won the leadership in the peasant association. Almost all the posts of chairmen and committee members in the peasant associations at the lowest level were held by poor peasants in both the first and second periods (of the officials in the township associations in Hangshan the utterly impoverished comprise 50 per cent, the less impoverished comprise 40 per cent, and the impoverished intellectuals comprise 10 per cent). This leadership of the poor peasants is absolutely necessary. Without the poor peasants there can be no revolution. To reject them is to reject the revolution. To attack them is to attack the revolution. Their general direction of the revolution has never been wrong.

They have hurt the dignity of the local bullies and bad gentry. They have beaten the big and small local bullies and bad gentry to the ground and trampled them underfoot. Many of their deeds in the period of revolutionary action, described as "going too far," were in fact the very needs of the revolution. Some of the county governments, county headquarters of the party and county peasant associations in Hunan have committed a number of mistakes; there are even some which at the request of the landlords sent soldiers to arrest the lower officials of the peasant associations. Many chairmen and committeemen of the township associations are imprisoned in the jails in Hengshan and Siangsiang. This is a serious mistake, which greatly encourages the arrogance of the reactionaries. To judge whether or not it is a mistake, one need only see how, as soon as the chairmen and committeemen of the peasant associations are arrested, the local lawless landlords are elated and reactionary sentiments grow. We must oppose such counterrevolutionary calumnies as "riffraff movement" and "movement of the lazy peasants" and must be especially careful not to commit the mistake of helping the local bullies and bad gentry to attack the poor peasants.

As a matter of fact, although some of the poor peasant leaders certainly had shortcomings in the past, most of them have reformed themselves by now. They are themselves energetically prohibiting gambling and exterminating banditry. Where the peasant association is powerful, gambling and banditry have vanished. In some places it is literally true that people do not pocket articles dropped on the road and that doors are not bolted at night. According to a survey of Hengshan, 85 per cent of the poor peasant leaders have now turned out to be quite reformed, capable and energetic. Only 15 per cent of them retain some bad habits. They can only be regarded as "the few undesirables," and we must not echo the local bullies and bad gentry in condemning indiscriminately everybody as "riffraff." To tackle this problem of "the few undesirables," we can only, on the basis of the association's slogan of strengthening discipline, carry on propaganda among the masses and educate the undesirables themselves, so that the discipline of the association may be strengthened; but we must not wantonly send soldiers to make arrests, lest we should undermine the prestige of the poor peasantry and encourage the arrogance of the local bullies and the bad gentry. This is a point we must particularly attend to.

Questions:
1. *According to Mao, who were the revolutionary classes? Who were the counterrevolutionary classes?*
2. *In what ways has Mao changed the Communist ideas of Marx?*

24.4 "How to Be a Good Communist" (1939): Li Shaoqi

Just before his death in 1925, Sun Yat-sen had appointed the young military officer, Jiang Jieshi, to succeed him as leader of the Guomindang party and head of the National Revolutionary Army. It became Jiang's responsibility to organize a Northern Expedition to "crush the warlords and unify the country." The Guomindang party at that time was composed of a coalition of Nationalists and Communists, united in their opposition to the warlords and Western influence. But the Communist faction also viewed the campaign primarily as an anti-imperialist and anti-feudal struggle whereas the Nationalists were looking to end the interference of the West through negotiation. The Nationalists sought the support of Western powers while the Communists, true to their Marxist roots, wanted a domestic revolution and establishment of a workers' and peasants' state. By 1930, the Nationalist campaigns against warlord control had evolved into anti-Communist forays.

Mao's success in organizing peasants, promoting strikes against landlords, and eventually redistributing land to the needy peasants demonstrated his dangerous organizational genius. Jiang launched four military campaigns against Mao's new Chinese Soviet Republic from 1930 to 1932; all four proved unsuccessful. The Communist Red Army, though poorly trained and equipped, was incredibly motivated and able to resist these assaults. But by 1934, an effective economic blockade and a fifth Nationalist offensive proved too much for the Communists. Rather than risk total annihilation, Mao broke through Jiang's encirclement and began a retreat to the hills called the "Long March" on October 16, 1934. Attacked and harried by Nationalist forces during a 6,000 mile trek, the Red Army was decimated and but a skeleton force when the march ended a year later. As Mao recalled in 1971: "The Red Army had had 300,000 men prior to the Long March, but it was reduced to 25,000 men when it arrived in Shensi province." As Jiang's forces moved in for the kill, the Communists were rescued, most ironically, by a Japanese invasion of Manchuria in northern China. Encouraged by the Chinese civil war, the Japanese had seized the opportunity to attack, forcing Jiang to deflect his attention.

The Soviet Union's leader, Joseph Stalin, encouraged both Mao and Jiang to end their civil war, and China entered World War II against Japan in 1937. This reprieve of the Communists was a crucial turning point in the Chinese Revolution. For while Jiang directed the Chinese resistance against Japan, Mao reorganized his political movement. At the end of World War II in 1945, Mao stood ready to meet Jiang once again in a fight to the death.

The following selection is an indoctrination tract by Li Shaoqi (1898–1969), one of Mao's closest advisors and theoreticians. This was part of the Communist strengthening movement that focused Party discipline and revived Communist fortunes. Such instructive tracts gave inspiration to the peasants movement and Red Army in their duel with the Nationalists.

> **Source:** "How to Be a Good Communist" is from Li Shaoqi, *How to Be a Good Communist* (New York: New Century Press, 1952), pp. 15–16; 24; 29–32.

Comrades! What is the most fundamental and common duty of us Communist Party members? As everybody knows, it is to establish Communism, to transform the present world into a Communist world. Is a Communist world good or not? We all know that it is very good. In such a world there will be no exploiters, oppressors, landlords, capitalists, imperialists, or fascists. There will be no oppressed and exploited people, no darkness, ignorance, backwardness, etc. In such a society all human beings will become unselfish and intelligent Communists with a high level of culture and technique. The spirit of mutual assistance and mutual love will prevail among mankind. There will be no such irrational things as mutual deception, mutual antagonism, mutual slaughter and war, etc. Such a society will, of course, be the best, the most beautiful, and the most advanced society in the history of mankind. Who will say that such a society is not good? Here the question arises: Can Communist society be brought about? Our answer is "yes." About this the whole theory of Marxism-Leninism offers a scientific explanation that leaves no room for doubt. It further explains that as the ultimate result of the class struggle of mankind, such a society will inevitably be brought about. The victory of Socialism in the U.S.S.R. has also given us factual proof. Our duty is, therefore, to bring about at an early date this Communist society, the realization of which is inevitable in the history of mankind. . . .

Comrades! If you only possess great and lofty ideals but . . . do not carry on genuinely practical work, you are not a good Communist Party member. You can only be a dreamer, a prattler, or a pendant. If on the contrary, you only do practical work, but do not possess the great and lofty ideals of Communism, you are not a good Communist, but a common careerist. A good Communist Party member is one who combines the great and lofty ideals of Communism with practical work and the spirit of searching for the truth from concrete facts.

The Communist ideal is beautiful while the existing capitalist world is ugly. It is precisely because of its ugliness that the overwhelming majority of the people want to change it and cannot but change it. . . .

At all times and on all questions, a Communist Party member should take into account the interests of the Party as a whole, and place the Party's interests above his personal problems and interests. It is the highest principle of our Party members that the Party's interests are supreme. . . .

A Communist Party member should possess all the greatest and noblest virtues of man-kind. . . . Such ethics are not built upon the backward basis of safeguarding the interests of individuals or a small number of exploiters. They are built, on the contrary, upon the progressive basis of the interests of the proletariat, of the ultimate emancipation of mankind as a whole, of saving the world from destruction, and of building a happy and beautiful Communist world.

Questions:
1. *Li Shaoqi's 1939 political tract, "How to Be a Good Communist," sought to inspire unity and focus commitment to the Communist cause. Why was such an effort so important at the time? Note especially the link between idealism and practical necessity argued by Li Shaoqi. How does one become a "good Communist"?*
2. *Li notes that "Marxism-Leninism offers a scientific explanation that leaves no room for doubt" and that "such a society will inevitably be brought about." Over sixty years later, why has this "happy and beautiful Communist world" not materialized?*

24.5   The New Communist State (1940-1950)

Jiang Jieshi's decision, as leader of the Guomindang's Nationalist forces, to resist the Japanese invasion of Manchuria in summer 1937 was hailed by most Chinese as a valiant and proper decision in the face of foreign aggression. The Communist Chinese led by Mao Zedong were perhaps most elated, for they had been on the brink of annihilation by the Guomindang when the threat instantly disappeared. With the Japanese now viewed as the primary threat to China, the Communists entered a rather unnatural collaboration with the Guomindang from 1937 to 1941. They both pledged cooperation, but the distrust and even hatred of these rival factions immediately produced tension that exhausted their energies and made effective resistance to Japan an impossibility. Although the United States sent military advisors and diplomats, the gulf between the Nationalists and the Communists could not be breached.

After the surrender of Japan in 1945, the Nationalist forces of Jiang enjoyed tremendous prestige and even signed a treaty of friendship with the Soviet Union, which promised to recognize and support Jiang's government. As Mao emerged from the Yenan caves where he and his Communist supporters had directed their operations against the Nationalists, it was not clear whether he would concede authority to Jiang or renew the civil war. By 1947, despite the diplomatic efforts of American General George Marshall, it was evident that China was about to embark on a path of destruction even more brutal than had just been experienced in World War II. Millions of Chinese, Communist and Nationalist, were killed in the ensuing civil war. Finally, the Nationalist forces of the Guomindang were defeated and pushed to the coast where they fled to the island of Taiwan.

It is difficult to assess the reasons for the Guomindang's defeat; they are varied and complex. Ultimately, this was a struggle not only for China's sovereignty and national independence, as it had been since the beginning of the century, but for China's soul. The Communists won most importantly because they were committed and outstanding organizers of a new political force in Chinese history: the peasant masses. Mao knew quite early in the history of Chinese Communism that the social and economic welfare of the peasantry was the key to its mobilization as a revolutionary force. The vision of a peasant rarely extended past his village, but he understood exorbitant rents and landlord villains; he advocated land confiscations and redistribution, and he desired dignity as an individual. These had never been priorities in China's modern history and Mao directed his organizational genius to the hearts and minds of an underclass that had never known opportunity. The peasants rewarded the Communists with their loyalty as the backbone of the Red Army, and with their inspiration as the keystone of a new nation independent of foreign control. Under Mao's direction, the Chinese people envisioned a future of possibility.

As the year 1949 opened, the Nationalist forces were in disarray and the Red Army was marching toward Nanjing, the Nationalist capital. Mao demanded unconditional surrender and the punishment of war criminals; foremost among them was Jiang Jieshi, as noted in the first selection. It is followed by an assessment of the situation by U.S. Secretary of State, Dean Acheson.

> **Source:** "Jiang Jieshi Is China's Number One War Criminal" is from *Selected Works of Mao Zedong* (Beijing: Foreign Languages Press, 1967), Vol. 4, pp. 315–319.

"JIANG JIESHI IS CHINA'S NUMBER ONE WAR CRIMINAL" (JANUARY 1949)
MAO ZEDONG

Two and a half years have gone by since July, 1946, when the reactionary Nanjing Guomindang government, with the aid of the U.S. imperialists, violated the will of the people, tore up the truce agreement and the resolutions of the Political Consultative Conference, and launched the countrywide counter-revolutionary civil war. In these two and a half years of war, the reactionary Nanjing Guomindang government has, in violation of the will of the people, convened a bogus National Assembly, promulgated a bogus constitution, elected a bogus president, and issued a bogus decree on the so-called "mobilization for putting down the rebellion"; sold out the national interest wholesale to the U.S. government and received loans amounting to thousands of millions of U.S. dollars; invited the U.S. navy and air force to occupy China's territory and territorial sea and air; signed a large batch of treasonable treaties with the U.S. government and accepted the U.S. Military Advisory Group's participation in China's civil war; and obtained from the U.S. government huge quantities of aircraft, tanks, light and heavy artillery, machine-guns, rifles, shells, bullets and other war material for slaughtering the Chinese people.

And it was on the basis of these reactionary and traitorous basic policies, domestic and foreign, that the reactionary Nanjing Guomindang government ordered millions of troops to launch ruthless attacks on the Chinese People's Liberated Areas and the Chinese People's Liberation Army. . . . Wherever they went, they massacred and raped, burned and looted, and stopped at nothing.

In the areas under its rule, the reactionary Nanjing Guomindang government sucks the lifeblood of the broad masses of the people—the workers, peasants, soldiers, intellectuals, and businessmen—by exacting grain levies, taxes, and forced labor for "putting down the rebellion and suppressing the bandits." The reactionary Nanjing Guomindang government deprives the people of all their freedoms denying them their legal status; it suppresses the righteous movement of the students against civil war, hunger, and persecution and against U.S. interference in China's internal affairs. . . . In short, the reactionary Nanjing Guomindang government has plunged the whole nation into dire suffering by waging a civil war based on its reactionary and traitorous basic policies, domestic and foreign; it absolutely cannot escape full responsibility.

In contrast to the Guomindang, the Communist Party of China did all it could after Japan's surrender to press the Guomindang government to prevent and stop the civil war and realize domestic peace. Basing itself on this policy, the Communist Party of China struggled steadfastly and, with the support of the people of the whole country. . . . But it is regrettable that the reactionary Guomindang government showed no respect for any of the actions we took in defense of internal peace and the democratic rights of the people. On the contrary, they thought that the people could be bullied. . . . Therefore, the reactionary Guomindang government had the audacity to violate the will of the people of the whole country and to unleash the counter-revolutionary war.

Under the circumstances, the Communist Party of China had no choice but to rise resolutely against the Guomindang government's reactionary policies and to fight to safeguard the county's independence and the people's democratic rights. Since July, 1946, the Communist Party of China has led the heroic People's Liberation Army to repulse the attacks of . . . the reactionary Guomindang government and then to go over to the counter-offensive, recover all the lost territories of the Liberated Areas and liberate many large cities. . . . The People's Liberation Army has overcome unparalleled difficulties, grown in strength, and equipped itself with huge quantities of arms given to the Guomindang government by the U.S. government. In two and a half years, it has wiped out the main military forces of the reactionary Guomindang government and all its crack divisions. Today the People's Liberation Army is superior to the remnant military forces of the reactionary Guomindang government in numbers, morale, and equipment. It is only now that the Chinese people can begin to breathe freely. The Guomindang regime will crumble and perish if the People's Liberation Army launches a few more powerful attacks against its remnant forces.

Having pursued a policy of civil war, the reactionary Guomindang government is now reaping what it has sown: the masses are in rebellion, its close followers are deserting, and it can no longer maintain itself. . . . Jiang Jieshi, chieftain of the Guomindang bandit gang and bogus president of the Nanjing government, is China's number one war criminal.

Comrade Commanders and fighters of the People's Liberation Army, attention! You should not slacken your fighting efforts in the slightest until the reactionary Nanjing Guomindang government has accepted a genuine democratic peace and carried it out. Any reactionaries who dare to resist must be resolutely, thoroughly, wholly and completely annihilated.

Questions:
1. *Why did Mao Zedong regard Jiang Jieshi as "China's number one war criminal" in 1949?*
2. *According to Mao, why did the civil war take place, who was to blame, and what was the Communist role?*

24.6 "From the Countryside to the City"(May 1949): Mao Zedong

As the Communists rolled toward victory against Nationalist Chinese forces, Mao directed his rhetoric toward the establishment of a "people's democratic dictatorship" that would extend "from the countryside to the city" and integrate rural peasants and urban workers, as the following speech of May 1949 indicates. On October 1, 1949, Mao, flush with victory, proclaimed the establishment of the People's Republic of China.

Source: "From the Countryside to the City" is from *Selected Works of Mao Zedong* (Beijing: Foreign Languages Press, 1967), Vol. 4, pp. 363–365; 373–374.

From 1927 to the present, the center of gravity of our work has been in the villages—gathering strength in the villages, using the villages in order to surround the cities, and then taking the cities. The period for this method of work has now ended. The period of "from the city to the village" and of the city leading the village has now begun. The center of gravity of the party's work has shifted from the village to the city. In the south the People's Liberation Army will occupy first the cities and then the villages. Attention must be given to both city and village and it is necessary to link closely urban and rural work, workers and peasants, industry and agriculture. Under no circumstances should the village be ignored and only the city given attention; such thinking is entirely wrong. Nevertheless, the center of gravity of the work of the party and the army must be in the cities; we must do our utmost to learn how to administer and build the cities. In the cities we must learn how to wage political, economic, and cultural struggles against the imperialists, the Guomindang, and the bourgeoisie and also how to wage diplomatic struggles against the imperialists. . . .

On whom shall we rely in our struggles in the cities? Some muddle-headed comrades think we should rely not on the working class but on the masses of the poor. Some comrades who are even more muddle-headed think we should rely on the bourgeoisie. As for the direction of industrial development, some muddle-headed comrades maintain that we should chiefly help the development of private enterprise and not state enterprise, whereas others hold the opposite view, that it suffices to pay attention to state enterprise and that private enterprise is of little importance. We must criticize these muddled views. We must wholeheartedly rely on the working class, unite with the rest of the laboring masses, win over the intellectuals and win over to our side as many as possible of the national bourgeois elements and their representatives who can cooperate with us—or neutralize them—so that we can wage a determined struggle against the imperialists, the Guomindang and the bureaucrat-capitalist class and defeat these enemies step by step. Meanwhile we shall set about our task of construction and learn, step by step, how to administer cities and restore and develop their production. . . .

Very soon we shall be victorious throughout the country. This victory will breach the eastern front of imperialism and will have great international significance. To win this victory will not require much more time and effort, but to consolidate it will. The bourgeoisie doubts our ability to construct. The imperialists reckon that eventually we will beg alms from them in order to live. With victory, certain moods may grow within the party—arrogance, the airs of a self-styled hero, inertia and unwillingness to make progress, love of pleasure and distaste for continued hard living. With victory, the people will be grateful to us and the bourgeoisie will come forward to flatter us. . . .

We must guard against such a situation. To win country-wide victory is only the first step in a long march. . . . Even if this step is worthy of pride, it is comparatively tiny; what will be more worthy of pride is yet to come. . . . We are not only good at destroying the old world, we are also good at building the new. Not only can the Chinese people live without begging alms from the imperialists, they will live a better life than that in the imperialist countries.

Questions:
1. *Why did the Communists turn their attention to the cities in order to achieve the consolidation of Communism?*
2. *Who did he identify as "muddle-headed" and why?*

24.7 The Failure of the Nationalist Government: The American Assessment (1949)

Jiang Jieshi's decision, as leader of the Guomindang's Nationalist forces, to resist the Japanese invasion of Manchuria in summer 1937 was hailed by most Chinese as a valiant and proper decision in the face of foreign aggression. The Communist Chinese led by Mao Zedong were perhaps most elated, for they had been on the brink of annihilation by the Guomindang when the threat instantly disappeared. With the Japanese now viewed as the primary threat to China, the Communists entered a rather unnatural collaboration with the Guomindang from 1937 to 1941. They both pledged cooperation, but the distrust and even hatred of these rival factions immediately produced tension that exhausted their energies and made effective resistance to Japan an impossibility. Although the United States sent military advisors and diplomats, the gulf between the Nationalists and the Communists could not be breached.

After the surrender of Japan in 1945, the Nationalist forces of Jiang enjoyed tremendous prestige and even signed a treaty of friendship with the Soviet Union, which promised to recognize and support Jiang's government. As Mao emerged from the Yenan caves where he and his Communist supporters had directed their operations against the Nationalists, it was not clear whether he would concede authority to Jiang or renew the civil war. By 1947, despite the diplomatic efforts of American General George Marshall, it was evident that China was about to embark on a path of destruction even more brutal than had just been experienced in World War II. Millions of Chinese, Communist and Nationalist, were killed in the ensuing civil war. Finally, the Nationalist forces of the Guomindang were defeated and pushed to the coast where they fled to the island of Taiwan.

It is difficult to assess the reasons for the Guomindang's defeat; they are varied and complex. Ultimately, this was a struggle not only for China's sovereignty and national independence, as it had been since the beginning of the century, but for China's soul. The Communists won most importantly because they were committed and outstanding organizers of a new political force in Chinese history: the peasant masses. Mao knew quite early in the history of Chinese Communism that the social and economic welfare of the peasantry was the key to its mobilization as a revolutionary force. The vision of a peasant rarely extended past his village, but he understood exorbitant rents and landlord villains; he advocated land confiscations and redistribution, and he desired dignity as an individual. These had never been priorities in China's modern history and Mao directed his organizational genius to the hearts and minds of an underclass that had never known opportunity. The peasants rewarded the Communists with their loyalty as the backbone of the Red Army, and with their inspiration as the keystone of a new nation independent of foreign control. Under Mao's direction, the Chinese people envisioned a future of possibility.

As the year 1949 opened, the Nationalist forces were in disarray and the Red Army was marching toward Nanjing, the Nationalist capital. Mao demanded unconditional surrender and the punishment of war criminals; foremost among them was Jiang Jieshi, as noted in the first selection. It is followed by an assessment of the situation by U.S. Secretary of State, Dean Acheson.

Source: "The Failure of the Nationalist Government" is from U.S. Department of State, *United States Relations with China: With Special Reference to the Period 1944-1949* (China White Paper), pp. xiv–xvii.

DEAN ACHESON

The reasons for the failure of the Chinese National Government appear in some detail in the attached record. They do not stem from any inadequacy of American aid. Our military observers on the spot have reported that the Nationalist armies did not lose a single battle during the crucial year of 1948 through lack of arms or ammunition. The fact was that the decay which our observers had detected . . . early in the war had fatally sapped the powers of resistance of the Guomindang. Its leaders had proved incapable of meeting the crisis confronting them, its troops had lost the will to fight, and its Government had lost popular support. The Communists, on the other hand, through a ruthless discipline and fanatical zeal, attempted to sell themselves as guardians and liberators of the people. The Nationalist armies did not have to be defeated; they disintegrated. History has proved again and again that a regime without faith in itself and an army without morale cannot survive the test of battle. . . .

It must be admitted frankly that the American policy of assisting the Chinese people in resisting domination by any foreign power or powers is now confronted with the greatest difficulties. The heart of China is in Communist hands. The Communist leaders have foresworn their Chinese heritage and have publicly announced their subservience to a foreign power, Russia. . . . The foreign domination has been masked behind the facade of a vast crusading movement which apparently has seemed to many Chinese to be wholly indigenous and national. Under these circumstances, our aid has been unavailing. . . .

And now it is abundantly clear that we must face the situation as it exists in fact. We will not help the Chinese or ourselves by basing our policy on wishful thinking. We continue to believe that, however tragic may be the immediate future of China and however ruthlessly a major portion of this great people may be exploited by a party in the interest of a foreign imperialism, ultimately the profound civilization and the democratic individualism of China will reassert themselves and she will throw off the foreign yoke.

Question:

1. *Ultimately, why did the Communists win the civil war? On this point, compare the account of Mao Zedong on Jiang Jieshi.*

PART 25
World War II

25.1 Adolf Hitler, The Obersalzberg Speech

On August 22, 1939, Adolf Hitler invited his chief military commanders and commanding generals, including Air Marshall Hermann Göring, to his Bavarian retreat high in the Obersalzberg. Here in the rarified mountain air, he informed his military commanders of his plans for war. No complete text of this speech survives, so what we have here is a collation of notes of the generals who were in attendance. Although no one disputes the overall outline and argument of this speech, some historians caution that the graphic language attributed to Hitler in this speech, for example, his identification with Genghis Khan and such phrases as "Chamberlain or some other such pig of a fellow," might have been inserted afterward by his dissident generals, who wanted to portray Hitler as brutally as possible. This florid language, if inserted by a dissident, could have been used to alert his adversaries, such as British Prime Minister Neville Chamberlain, or the French Premier Édouard Daladier, that by August 1939, Hitler was determined to go to war immediately. Yet, one cannot dismiss entirely the authenticity of this speech. Hitler was quite unpredictable, and the sensational and vulgar rhetoric of this text can be found in many of his other speeches. Despite the emotional character and questions of attribution, the Obersalzberg speech remains important because it provides a good insight into Hitler's grasp of history and his strategic thinking just on the eve of his September 1, 1939, attack on Poland. Similar versions of this speech have been printed in the principal documents of the Nuremberg War Trials (1945–1946), as well as in the official U.S. and British government documents on Hitler and the coming of World War II.

> **Source:** From *Documents on British Foreign Policy*, 1919–1939, ed. E.L. Woodward and Rohan Butler, 3rd series (London: HMSO, 1954), 7:258–60.

Decision to attack Poland was arrived at in spring. Originally there was fear that because of the political constellation we would have to strike at the same time against England, France, Russia and Poland. This risk too we should have had to take. Göring had demonstrated to us that his Four-Year Plan is a failure and that we are at the end of our strength, if we do not achieve victory in a coming war.

Since the autumn of 1938 and since I have realised that Japan will not go with us unconditionally and that Mussolini is endangered by that nitwit of a King and the treacherous scoundrel of a Crown Prince, I decided to go with Stalin. After all there are only three great statesmen in the world, Stalin, I and Mussolini. Mussolini is the weakest, for he has been able to break the power neither of the crown nor of the Church. Stalin and I are the only ones who visualise the future. So in a few weeks hence I shall stretch out my hand to Stalin at the common German-Russian frontier and with him undertake to re-distribute the world.

Our strength lies in our quickness and in our brutality; Genghis Khan has sent millions of women and children into death knowingly and with a light heart. History sees in him only the great founder of States. As to what the weak Western European civilisation asserts about me, that is of no account. I have given the command and I shall shoot everyone who utters one word of criticism, for the goal to be obtained in the war is not that of reaching certain lines but of physically demolishing the opponent. And so for the present only in the East I have put my death-head formations[1] in place with the command relentlessly and without compassion to send into death many women and children of Polish origin and language. Only thus we can gain the living space that we need. Who after all is today speaking about the destruction of the Armenians?

Colonel-General von Brauchitsch has promised me to bring the war against Poland to a close within a few weeks. Had he reported to me that he needs two years or even only one year, I should not have given the command to march and should have allied myself temporarily with England instead of Russia for we cannot conduct a long war. To be sure a new situation has arisen. I experienced those poor worms Daladier and Chamberlain in Munich. They will be too cowardly to attack. They won't go beyond a blockade. Against that we have our autarchy and the Russian raw materials.

Poland will be depopulated and settled with Germans. My pact with the Poles was merely conceived of as a gaining of time. As for the rest, gentlemen, the fate of Russia will be exactly the same as I am now going through with in the case of Poland. After Stalin's death—he is a very sick man—we will break the Soviet Union. Then there will begin the dawn of the German rule of the earth.

---

[1] The S.S. Death's Head formations were principally employed in peacetime in guarding concentration camps. With the S.S. Verfügungstruppen, they formed the nucleus of the Waffen S.S.

The little States cannot scare me. After Kemal's death Turkey is governed by "cretins" and half idiots. Carol of Roumania is through and through the corrupt slave of his sexual instincts. The King of Belgium and the Nordic kings are soft jumping jacks who are dependent upon the good digestions of their over-eating and tired peoples.

We shall have to take into the bargain the defection of Japan. I gave Japan a full year's time. The Emperor is a counterpart to the last Czar—weak, cowardly, undecided. May he become a victim of the revolution. My going together with Japan never was popular. We shall continue to create disturbances in the Far East and in Arabia. Let us think as "gentlemen" and let us see in these peoples at best lacquered half maniacs who are anxious to experience the whip.

The opportunity is as favourable as never before. I have but one worry, namely that Chamberlain or some other such pig of a fellow ("Saukerl") will come at the last moment with proposals or with ratting ("Umfall"). He will fly down the stairs, even if I shall personally have to trample on his belly in the eyes of the photographers.

No, it is too late for this. The attack upon and the destruction of Poland begins Saturday early. I shall let a few companies in Polish uniform attack in Upper Silesia or in the Protectorate. Whether the world believes it is quite indifferent ("scheissegal"). The world believes only in success.

For you, gentlemen, fame and honour are beginning as they have not since centuries. Be hard, be without mercy, act more quickly and brutally than the others. The citizens of Western Europe must tremble with horror. That is the most human way of conducting a war. For it scares the others off.

The new method of conducting war corresponds to the new drawing of the frontiers. A war extending from Reval, Lublin, Kaschau to the mouth of the Danube. The rest will be given to the Russians. Ribbentrop has orders to make every offer and to accept every demand. In the West I reserve to myself the right to determine the strategically best line. Here one will be able to work with Protectorate regions, such as Holland, Belgium and French Lorraine.

And now, on to the enemy, in Warsaw we will celebrate our reunion.

The speech was received with enthusiasm. Göring jumped on a table, thanked blood-thirstily and made blood-thirsty promises. He danced like a wild man. The few that had misgivings remained quiet. (Here a line of the memorandum is missing in order no doubt to protect the source of information.)

Questions:

1. *What does Hitler think of Stalin, his Italian and Japanese allies, and the leaders of Britain, France, and Turkey?*
2. *Hitler asks, "Who after all is today speaking about the destruction of the Armenians?" What does this suggest about his views of the twentieth century's first large-scale genocide?*
3. *How does Hitler view the coming war? What does he plan for Poland and the Polish people? How closely did he follow these plans?*

25.2 The Atlantic Charter

President Franklin D. Roosevelt's concern over the war in Europe sharply increased in 1940 with the collapse of France and the potential expansion of Hitler's empire to the New World if Britain fell. In September, Roosevelt tried to strengthen Britain's ability to resist by exchanging American destroyers for the right to lease naval and air bases in British Commonwealth territories. The following spring, although the United States was technically neutral, Roosevelt urged the passage of the Lend-Lease Act to provide war materials to those nations fighting the Axis powers. While taking these important steps on the road to war, President Roosevelt outlined his objectives and the national interest in his 1941 State of the Union Address, which became known as his "Four Freedoms" speech.

Later that summer, Roosevelt and Churchill met for a shipboard conference off Argentia, Newfoundland, and forged a closer alignment with their joint statement of war aims known as the Atlantic Charter.

Source: From U.S. Department of State, Peace and War: United States Foreign Policy, 1931–1941, Publication 1983 (Washington, DC: Government Printing Office, 1943), pp. 718–19.

Joint declaration of the President of the United States of America and the Prime Minister, Mr. Churchill, representing His Majesty's Government in the United Kingdom, being met together, deem it right to make known certain common principles in the national policies of their respective countries on which they base their hopes for a better future for the world.

First, their countries seek no aggrandizement, territorial or other;

Second, they desire to see no territorial changes that do not accord with the freely expressed wishes of the peoples concerned;

Third, they respect the right of all peoples to choose the form of government under which they will live; and they wish to see sovereign rights and self-government restored to those who have been forcibly deprived of them;

Fourth, they will endeavor, with due respect for their existing obligations, to further the enjoyment by all states, great or small, victor or vanquished, of access, on equal terms, to the trade and to the raw materials of the world which are needed for their economic prosperity;

Fifth, they desire to bring about the fullest collaboration between all nations in the economic field with the object of securing, for all, improved labor standards, economic advancement, and social security;

Sixth, after the final destruction of the Nazi tyranny, they hope to see established a peace which will afford to all nations the means of dwelling in safety within their own boundaries, and which will afford assurance that all the men in all the lands may live out their lives in freedom from fear and want;

Seventh, such a peace should enable all men to traverse the high seas and oceans without hindrance;

Eighth, they believe that all the nations of the world, for realistic as well as spiritual reasons, must come to the abandonment of the use of force. Since no future peace can be maintained if land, sea, or air armaments continue to be employed by nations which threaten, or may threaten, aggression outside of their frontiers, they believe, pending the establishment of a wider and permanent system of general security, that the disarmament of such nations is essential. They will likewise aid and encourage all other practicable measures which will lighten for peace-loving peoples the crushing burden of armaments.

Franklin D. Roosevelt
Winston S. Churchill

Questions:
1. Why would the influential Japanese newspaper Asahi regard the Atlantic Charter, particularly its fourth article, as a de facto declaration of war by the United States and Great Britain?
2. Would Woodrow Wilson approve of this charter? Why? Why not?

25.3 The Rape of Nanjing

On December 13, 1937, Nanjing, the capital city of Nationalist China, fell to the onslaught of the invading Japanese army. For the Chinese forces of Jiang Jieshi, which had fought to defend the Yangtze Valley, this was a bitter defeat. The ancient walled city of Nanjing lay open to the fury of the Japanese who, for the next six weeks, pillaged and burned the town, executed tens of thousands of Chinese soldiers, slaughtered civilian men, and raped the women and children. This was no temporary lapse of military discipline in the Japanese ranks, but a methodical and horrific act of terror that resulted in the death of nearly 300,000 Chinese. The Rape of Nanjing, as it was immediately called, was not publicized after the war and has been termed by some historians, the "forgotten Holocaust." But its lingering memory has poisoned Chinese-Japanese relations for over sixty years. The following transcript of the 1947 sentencing of a convicted Japanese war criminal testifies to the savagery and tragedy of the Rape of Nanjing.

> **Source:** "The Rape of Nanjing" is from Military Tribunal for the Trial of War Criminals (March 10, 1947), contained in Dun J. Li, *The Road to Communism* (New York: Van Nostrand Reinhold Company,

Compare and Contrast:

•   Compare this account of the atrocities in Nanjing with those described in the Nazi death camps. What motivated the Japanese and German soldiers to commit such acts?

File Number: *Shen* 1, 1947

Defendant: Tani Hsiao, male, age 66, native of Japan; a former lieutenant general and division commander of the Japanese army. The above defendant was accused by the public prosecutor of this Tribunal as a war criminal. The trial has been duly conducted. The decision is as follows:

Decision: During the period of war, Tani Hsiao, the defendant, condoned and encouraged the soldiers under his command to commit mass murder against prisoners of war as well as civilians, in addition to rape, looting, and deliberate destruction of properties. The defendant is hereby sentenced to death.

Facts: The defendant is regarded as one of the most ferocious and ablest generals among the Japanese militarists. He joined the Japanese army as early as the Russo-Japanese War [1905] and distinguished himself repeatedly on the battlefield. He was the commander of the Japanese Sixth Division when the Sino-Japanese War began in 1937; in August of that year, he came to China with his command and participated in the war of aggression. . . . Since Nanjing was the capital of our country and the center of resistance against the Japanese aggression, the Japanese militarists mobilized their best and most ferocious military units, including the Sixth Division headed by the defendant . . . to launch an all-out attack under the overall supervision of General Matsu Iwane. Because of the fact that the defenders of the city had continued to resist and refused to surrender, the Japanese army, after capturing the city, conducted a systematic campaign of murder to show its revenge, hatred, and frustration.

On the afternoon of December 12, the invaders, led by the Sixth Division under the command of the defendant, captured the Zhonghua Gate. Massacre began the moment they roped over the city wall and descended upon the civilians. . . . The massacre was followed by looting, rape, and arson. The worst slaughter occurred between December 12 and 21, the time when the defendant's troops were stationed inside the city. . . . The total number of captured soldiers and civilians who were collectively machine-gunned and then burned into ashes amounted to more than 190,000. The total number of victims who were murdered on an individual basis and whose bodies were later buried by philanthropic organizations were more than 150,000. Thus, the grand total of civilians and prisoners of war who fell victim to this campaign of mass murder was well beyond 300,000. Dead bodies were piled from one street corner to another, and no words, however eloquent, were adequate enough to describe this atrocity of unprecedented scale. . . .

On December 12, Mrs. Wang of Xu, a peasant woman, was beheaded on the harbor outside of the Zhonghua Gate. . . . On December 14, Yao Qialong, a native of Nanjing, was ordered to watch the performance when Japanese soldiers took turns raping his wife. When his eight-year-old son and three-year-old daughter pleaded for mercy on behalf of their mother, the rapists picked them up with their bayonets and roasted them to death over a camp fire. . . . In another case, two Japanese officers entered a murder contest; later, the one who had killed 106 persons was declared the winner over the other who had killed 105. On December 19, Xie Shanzhen, a peasant woman more than sixty years old, was cut into pieces after a Japanese soldier had pierced her vagina with a bamboo stick. In each and every case, the atrocities committed by the Japanese army were brutal to the greatest extreme. From December 12 to 21, the total number of atrocity cases that can be documented amounts to 886.

Consider This:

*   Until recently, why did the Japanese brutality in Nanjing go relatively unnoticed? Why has Nanjing been called the "forgotten Holocaust"?

*   The poet W. H. Auden reflected on the holocausts of World War II: "And maps can really point to places/Where life is evil now: Nanjing; Dachau." What do you think? Can evil be defined by the atrocities conducted on these sites? Or is evil such a relative concept that it defies definition? Was Hitler evil?

Question:
1. What motivated the Japanese to commit such acts?

25.4   Hiroshima and Nagasaki

Although heavy fighting had been waged on the mainland of Asia since the Japanese invasion of Manchuria in 1931, the beginning of the Second World War is usually dated from September 1, 1939, when Nazi Germany launched its surprise attack on Poland. Unlike the First World War, in which hostilities were generally confined to relatively small areas of Europe, the Second World War was virtually global in extent. Land, sea, and aerial combat spread throughout most of Europe, large areas of Asia and Africa, along the coastlines of both North and South America, and on innumerable islands scattered across the Pacific Ocean. The United States entered the war following the Japanese surprise attack on the Pacific Fleet at Pearl Harbor, Hawaii, on December 7, 1941. The war finally came to an end, first with the German collapse in May 1945, and then the Japanese surrender three months later, following the American atomic bomb attacks on Hiroshima and Nagasaki. One of the unanswerable questions of history is that of how long the war would have continued and how many lives would have been lost had the United States not dropped the two atomic bombs.

The bomb had been developed over several years by American scientists and engineers working in great secrecy under the code name "Manhattan Project." It had been tested only once-in the desert of New Mexico-before being released over Hiroshima. The decision to drop the bomb in Japan, probably the most awesome decision ever to face a human being, was made by President Harry S. Truman.

It is difficult to describe in words the effects of the atomic explosions over the two Japanese cities. Nevertheless, the following selection, although written largely in factual, unemotional terms, succeeds in capturing something of the essence not only of the material destruction wreaked but also of the human suffering, both physical and psychological, of the victims of the attacks. It is taken from a report prepared shortly after the war by a team of American investigators who visited both cities, examined the effects of the bombing, and questioned many survivors of the attacks.

Source: *The Effects of Atomic Bombs on Hiroshima and Nagasaki* (Washington, D.C.: U.S. Government Printing Office, 1946).

THE EFFECTS OF ATOMIC BOMBS ON HIROSHIMA AND NAGASAKI

I. INTRODUCTION

The available facts about the power of the atomic bomb as a military weapon lie in the story of what it did at Hiroshima and Nagasaki. Many of these facts have been published, in official and unofficial form, but mingled with distortions or errors. The United States Strategic Bombing Survey, therefore, in partial fulfillment of the mission for which it was established, has put together in these pages a fairly full account of just what the atomic bombs did at Hiroshima and Nagasaki. Together with an explanation of how the bomb achieved these effects, this report states the extent and nature of the damage, the casualties, and the political repercussions from the two attacks. The basis is the observation, measurement, and analysis of the Survey's investigators. The conjecture that is necessary for understanding of the complex phenomena and for applying the findings to the problems of defense of the United States is clearly labelled.

When the atomic bombs fell, the United States Strategic Bombing Survey was completing a study of the effects of strategic bombing on Germany's ability and will to resist. A similar study of the effects of strategic bombing on Japan was being planned. The news of the dropping of the atomic bomb gave a new urgency to this project, for a study of the air war against Japan clearly involved new weapons and new possibilities of concentration of attack that might qualify or even change the conclusions and recommendations of the Survey as to the effectiveness of air power. The directors of the Survey, therefore, decided to examine exhaustively the effects of the atomic bombs, in order that the full impact on Japan and the implications of their results could be confidently analyzed. Teams of experts were selected to study the scenes of the bombings from the special points of emphasis of physical damage, civilian defense, morale, casualties, community life, utilities and transportation, various industries, and the general economic and political repercussions. In all, more than 110 men-engineers, architects, fire experts, economists, doctors, photographers, draftsmen-participated in the field study at each city, over a period of 10 weeks from October to December, 1945. Their detailed studies are now being published.

• • •

II. THE EFFECTS OF THE ATOMIC BOMBINGS

A. The Attacks and Damage

1. The attacks.

A single atomic bomb, the first weapon of its type ever used against a target, exploded over the city of Hiroshima at 0815 on the morning of 6 August 1945. Most of the industrial workers had already reported to work, but many workers were enroute and nearly all the school children and some industrial employees were at work in the open on the program of building removal to provide fire-breaks and disperse valuables to the country. The attack came 45 minutes after the "all clear" had been sounded from a previous alert. Because of the lack of warning and the populace's indifference to small groups of planes, the explosion came as an almost complete surprise, and the people had not taken shelter. Many were caught in the open, and most of the rest in flimsily constructed homes or commercial establishments.

The bomb exploded slightly northwest of the center of the city. Because of this accuracy and the flat terrain and circular shape of the city, Hiroshima was uniformly and extensively devastated. Practically the entire densely or moderately built-up portion of the city was leveled by blast and swept by fire. A "fire-storm," a phenomenon which has occurred infrequently in other conflagrations, developed in Hiroshima: fires springing up almost simultaneously over the wide flat area around the center of the city drew in air from all directions. The inrush of air easily overcame the natural ground wind, which had a velocity of only about 5 miles per hour. The "fire-wind" attained a maximum velocity of 30 to 40 miles per hour 2 to 3 hours after the explosion. The "fire-wind" and the symmetry of the built-up center of the city gave a roughly circular shape to the 4.4 square miles which were almost completely burned out.

The surprise, the collapse of many buildings, and the conflagration contributed to an unprecedented casualty rate. Seventy to eighty thousand people were killed, or missing and presumed dead, and an equal number were injured.

At Nagasaki, 3 days later, the city was scarcely more prepared, though vague references to the Hiroshima disaster had appeared in the newspaper of 8 August. From the Nagasaki Prefectural Report on the bombing, something of the shock of the explosion can be inferred:

The day was clear with not very much wind-an ordinary midsummer's day. The strain of continuous air attack on the city's population and the severity of the summer had vitiated enthusiastic air raid precautions. Previously, a general alert had been sounded at 0748, with a raid alert at 0750; this was canceled at 0830, and the alertness of the people was dissipated by a great feeling of relief.

The city remained on the warning alert, but when two B-29s were again sighted coming in the raid signal was not given immediately; the bomb was dropped at 1102 and the raid signal was given a few minutes later, at 1109. Thus only about 400 people were in the city's tunnel shelters, which were adequate for about 30 percent of the population.

When the atomic bomb exploded, an intense flash was observed first, as though a large amount of magnesium had been ignited, and the scene grew hazy with white smoke. At the same time at the center of the explosion, and a short while later in other areas, a tremendous roaring sound was heard and a crushing blast wave and intense heat were felt. The people of Nagasaki, even those who lived on the outer edge of the blast, all felt as though they had sustained a direct hit, and the whole city suffered damage such as would have resulted from direct hits everywhere by ordinary bombs.

The zero area, where the damage was most severe, was almost completely wiped out and for a short while after the explosion no reports came out of that area. People who were in comparatively damaged areas reported their condition under the impression that they had received a direct hit. If such a great amount of damage could be wreaked by a near miss, then the power of the atomic bomb is unbelievably great.

In Nagasaki, no fire-storm arose, and the uneven terrain of the city confined the maximum intensity of damage to the valley over which the bomb exploded. The area of nearly complete devastation was thus much smaller; only about 1.8 square miles. Casualties were lower also; between 35,000 and 40,000 were killed, and about the same number injured. People in the tunnel shelters escaped injury, unless exposed in the entrance shaft.

. . .

Hiroshima before the war was the seventh largest city in Japan, with a population of over 340,000, and was the principal administrative and commercial center of the southwestern part of the country. As the headquarters of the Second Army and of the Chugoku Regional Army, it was one of the most important military command stations in Japan, the site of one of the largest military supply depots, and the foremost military shipping point for both troops and supplies. Its shipping activities had virtually ceased by the time of the attack, however, because of sinkings and the mining of the Inland Sea. It had been relatively unimportant industrially before the war, ranking only twelfth, but during the war new plants were built that increased its significance. These factories were not concentrated, but spread over the outskirts of the city; this location, we shall see, accounts for the slight industrial damage.

The impact of the atomic bomb shattered the normal fabric of community life and disrupted the organizations for handling the disaster. In the 30 percent of the population killed and the additional 30 percent seriously injured were included corresponding proportions of the civic authorities and rescue groups. A mass flight from the city took place, as persons sought safety from the conflagration and a place for shelter and food. Within 24 hours, however, people were streaming back by the thousands in search of relatives and friends and to determine the extent of their property loss. Road blocks had to be set up along all routes leading into the city, to keep curious and unauthorized people out. The bulk of the dehoused population found refuge in the surrounding countryside; within the city the food supply was short and shelter virtually nonexistent.

On 7 August, the commander of the Second Army assumed general command of the counter-measures, and all military units and facilities in the area were mobilized for relief purposes. Army buildings on the periphery of the city provided shelter and emergency hospital space, and dispersed Army supplies supplemented the slight amounts of food and clothing that had escaped destruction. The need far exceeded what could be made available. Surviving civilians assisted; although casualties in both groups had been heavy, 190 policemen and over 2,000 members of the Civilian Defense Corps reported for duty on 7 August.

The status of medical facilities and personnel dramatically illustrates the difficulties facing authorities. Of more than 200 doctors in Hiroshima before the attack, over 90 percent were casualties and only about 30 physicians were able to perform their normal duties a month after the raid. Out of 1,780 nurses, 1,654 were killed or injured. Though some stocks of supplies had been dispersed, many were destroyed. Only three out of 45 civilian hospitals could be used, and two large Army hospitals were rendered unusable. Those within 3,000 feet of ground zero were totally destroyed, and the mortality rate of the occupants was practically 100 percent. Two large hospitals of reinforced concrete construction were located 4,900 feet from ground zero. The basic structures remained erect but there was such severe interior damage that neither was able to resume operation as a hospital for some time and the casualty rate was approximately 90 percent, due primarily to falling plaster, flying glass, and fire. Hospitals and clinics beyond 7,000 feet, though often remaining standing, were badly damaged and contained many casualties from flying glass or other missiles.

With such elimination of facilities and personnel, the lack of care and rescue activities at the time of the disaster is understandable; still, the eyewitness account of Father Siemes[1] shows how this lack of first-aid contributed to the seriousness of casualties. At the improvised first-aid stations, he reports:

. . . Iodine is applied to the wounds but they are left uncleansed. Neither ointment nor other therapeutic agents are available. Those that have been brought in are laid on the floor and no one can give them any further care. What could one do when all means are lacking? Among the passersby, there are many who are uninjured. In a purposeless, insensate manner, distraught by the magnitude of the disaster, most of them rush by and none conceives the thought of organizing help on his own initiative. They are concerned only with the welfare of their own families-in the official aid stations and hospitals, a good third or half of those that had been brought in died. They lay about there almost without care, and a very high percentage succumbed. Everything was lacking, doctors, assistants, dressings, drugs, etc. . . .

Effective medical help had to be sent in from the outside, and arrived only after a considerable delay.

Fire-fighting and rescue units were equally stripped of men and equipment. Father Siemes reports that 30 hours elapsed before any organized rescue parties were observed. In Hiroshima, only 16 pieces of fire-fighting equipment were available for fighting the conflagration, three of them borrowed. However, it is unlikely that any public fire department in the world, even without damage to equipment or casualties to personnel, could have prevented development of a conflagration in Hiroshima, or combatted it with success at more than a few locations along its perimeter. The total fire damage would not have been much different.

When the atomic bomb fell, Nagasaki was comparatively intact. Because the most intense destruction was confined to the Urukami Valley, the impact of the bomb on the city as a whole was less shattering than at Hiroshima. In addition, no fire-storm occurred; indeed, a shift in wind direction helped control the fires. Medical personnel and facilities were hard-hit, however. Over 80 percent of the city's hospital beds and the Medical College were located within 3,000 feet of the center of the explosion, and were completely gutted by fire; buildings of wooden construction were destroyed by fire and blast. The mortality rate in this group of buildings was between 75 and 80 percent. Exact casualty figures for medical personnel are unknown, but the city seems to have fared better than Hiroshima: 120 doctors were at work on 1 November, about one-half of the pre-raid roster. Casualties were undoubtedly high: 600 out of 850 medical students at the Nagasaki Medical College were killed and most of the others injured; and of the 20 faculty members, 12 were killed and 4 others injured.

. . .

The city's repair facilities were completely disorganized by the atomic bomb, so that with the single exception of shutting off water to the affected areas no repairs were made to roads, bridges, water mains, or transportation installations by city forces. The prefecture took full responsibility for such restoration as was accomplished, delegating to the scattered city help the task of assisting in relief of victims. There were only 3 survivors of 115 employees of the street car company, and as late as the middle of November 1945 no cars were running. A week after the explosion, the water works officials made an effort to supply water to persons attempting to live in the bombed-out areas, but the leakage was so great that the effort was abandoned. It fell to the prefecture, therefore, to institute recovery measures even in those streets normally the responsibility of the city. Of the entire public works construction group covering the Nagasaki city area, only three members appeared for work and a week was required to locate and notify other survivors. On the morning of 10 August, police rescue units and workers from the Kawaminami shipbuilding works began the imperative task of clearing the Omura-Nagasaki pike, which was impassable for 8,000 feet. A path 6-1/2 feet wide was cleared despite the intense heat from smouldering fires, and by 15 August had been widened to permit two-way traffic. No trucks, only rakes and shovels, were available for clearing the streets, which were filled with tile, bricks, stone, corrugated iron, machinery, plaster, and stucco. Street areas affected by blast and not by fire were littered with wood. Throughout the devastated area, all wounded had to be carried by stretcher, since no motor vehicles were able to proceed through the cluttered streets for several days. The plan for debris removal required clearance of a few streets leading to the main highway; but there were frequent delays caused by the heat of smouldering fires and by calls for relief work. The debris was simply raked and shoveled off the streets. By 20 August the job was considered complete. The streets were not materially damaged by the bomb nor were the surface or the abutments of the concrete bridges, but many of the wooden bridges were totally or partially destroyed by fire.

Under the circumstances-fire, flight of entire families, destruction of official records, mass cremation- identification of dead and the accurate count of casualties was impossible. As at Hiroshima, the season of the year made rapid disposal of bodies imperative, and mass cremation and mass burial were resorted to in the days immediately after the attack. Despite the absence of sanitary measures, no epidemics broke out here. The dysentery rate rose from 25 per 100,000 to 125 per 100,000. A census taken on 1 November 1945 found a population of 142,700 in the city.

At Nagasaki, the scale of destruction was greater than at Hiroshima, though the actual area destroyed was smaller because of the terrain and the point of fall of the bomb. The Nagasaki Prefectural Report described vividly the impress of the bomb on the city and its inhabitants:

Within a radius of 1 kilometer from ground zero, men and animals died almost instantaneously from the tremendous blast pressure and heat; houses and other structures were smashed, crushed and scattered; and fires broke out. The strong complex steel members of the structures of the Mitsubishi Steel Works were bent and twisted like jelly and the roofs of the reinforced concrete National Schools were crumpled and collapsed, indicating a force beyond imagination. Trees of all sizes lost their branches or were uprooted or broken off at the trunk.

Outside a radius of 1 kilometer and within a radius of 2 kilometers from ground zero, some men and animals died instantly from the great blast and heat, but the great majority were seriously or superficially injured. Houses and other structures were completely destroyed while fires broke out everywhere. Trees were uprooted and withered by the heat.

Outside a radius of 2 kilometers and within a radius of 4 kilometers from ground zero, men and animals suffered various degrees of injury from window glass and other fragments scattered about by the blast and many were burned by the intense heat. Dwelling and other structures were half damaged by blast.

Outside a radius of 4 kilometers and within a radius of 8 kilometers from ground zero, living creatures were injured by materials blown about by the blast; the majority were only superficially wounded. Houses were half or only partially damaged.

While the conflagration with its uniformly burnt-out area caught the attention at Hiroshima, the blast effects, with their resemblance to the aftermath of a hurricane, were most striking at Nagasaki. Concrete buildings had their sides facing the blast stove in like boxes. Long lines of steel-framed factory sheds, over a mile from ground zero, leaned their skeletons away from the explosion. Blast resistant objects such as telephone poles leaned away from the center of the explosion; on the surrounding hills trees were blown down within considerable areas. Although there was no general conflagration, fires contributed to the total damage in nearly all concrete structures. Evidence of primary fire is more frequent than at Hiroshima.

. . .

B. General Effects

1. Casualties.

The most striking result of the atomic bombs was the great number of casualties. The exact number of dead and injured will never be known because of the confusion after the explosions. Persons unaccounted for might have been burned beyond recognition in the falling buildings, disposed of in one of the mass cremations of the first week of recovery, or driven out of the city to die or recover without any record remaining. No sure count of even the pre-raid population existed. Because of the decline in activity in the two port cities, the constant threat of incendiary raids, and the formal evacuation programs of the Government, an unknown number of the inhabitants had either drifted away from the cities or been removed according to plan. In this uncertain situation, estimates of casualties have generally ranged between 100,000 and 180,000 for Hiroshima, and between 50,000 and 100,000 for Nagasaki. The Survey believes the dead at Hiroshima to have been between 70,000 and 80,000 with an equal number injured; at Nagasaki over 35,000 dead and somewhat more than that injured seems the most plausible estimate.

Most of the immediate casualties did not differ from those caused by incendiary or high-explosive raids. The outstanding difference was the presence of radiation effects, which became unmistakable about a week after the bombing. At the time of impact, however, the causes of death and injury were flash burns, secondary effects of blast and falling debris, and burns from blazing buildings. No records are available that give the relative importance of the various types of injury, especially for those who died immediately after the explosion. Indeed, many of these people undoubtedly died several times over, theoretically, since each was subjected to several injuries, any one of which would have been fatal.

Radiation disease. The radiation effects upon survivors resulted from the gamma rays liberated by the fission process rather than from induced radio-activity or the lingering radio-activity of deposits of primary fission products. Both at Nagasaki and at Hiroshima, pockets of radioactivity have been detected where fission products were directly deposited, but the degree of activity in these areas was insufficient to produce casualties. Similarly, induced radio-activity from the interaction of neutrons with matter caused no authenticated fatalities. But the effects of gamma rays-here used in a general sense to include all penetrating high-frequency radiations and neutrons that caused injury-are well established, even though the Allies had no observers in the affected areas for several weeks after the explosions.

Our understanding of radiation casualties is not complete. In part the deficiency is in our basic knowledge of how radiation effects animal tissue.

According to the Japanese, those individuals very near the center of the explosion but not affected by flash burns or secondary injuries became ill within 2 or 3 days. Bloody diarrhea followed, and the victims expired, some within 2 to 3 days after the onset and the majority within a week. Autopsies showed remarkable changes in the blood picture-almost complete absence of white blood cells, and deterioration of bone marrow. Mucous membranes of the throat, lungs, stomach, and the intestines showed acute inflammation.

The majority of the radiation cases, who were at greater distances, did not show severe symptoms until 1 to 4 weeks after the explosion, though many felt weak and listless on the following day. After a day or two of mild nausea and vomiting, the appetite improved and the person felt quite well until symptoms reappeared at a later date. In the opinion of some

Japanese physicians, those who rested or subjected themselves to less physical exertion showed a longer delay before the onset of subsequent symptoms. The first signs of recurrence were loss of appetite, lassitude, and general discomfort. Inflammation of the gums, mouth, and pharynx appeared next. Within 12 to 48 hours, fever became evident. In many instances it reached only 100° Fahrenheit and remained for only a few days. In other cases, the temperature went as high as 104° or 106° Fahrenheit. The degree of fever apparently had a direct relation to the degree of exposure to radiation. Once developed, the fever was usually well sustained, and in those cases terminating fatally it continued high until the end. If the fever subsided, the patient usually showed a rapid disappearance of other symptoms and soon regained his feeling of good health. The other symptoms commonly seen were shortage of white corpuscles, loss of hair, inflammation and gangrene of the gums, inflammation of the mouth and pharynx, ulceration of the lower gastro-intestinal tract, small livid spots (petechiae) resulting from escape of blood into the tissues of the skin or mucous membrane, and larger hemorrhages of gums, nose and skin.

Loss of hair usually began about 2 weeks after the bomb explosion, though in a few instances it is reported to have begun as early a 4 to 5 days afterward. The areas were involved in the following order of frequency with variations depending on the degree of exposure: scalp, armpits, beard, pubic region, and eyebrows. Complete baldness was rare. Microscopic study of the body areas involved has shown atrophy of the hair follicles. In those patients who survived after 2 months, however, the hair has commenced to re-grow. An interesting but unconfirmed report has it that loss of the hair was less marked in persons with grey hair than in those with dark hair. . .

The effects of the bomb on pregnant women are marked, however. Of women in various stages of pregnancy who were within 3,000 feet of ground zero, all known cases have had miscarriages. Even up to 6,500 feet they have had miscarriages or premature infants who died shortly after birth. In the group between 6,500 and 10,000 feet, about one-third have given birth to apparently normal children. Two months after the explosion, the city's total incidence of miscarriages, abortions, and premature births was 27 percent as compared with a normal rate of 6 percent. Since other factors than radiation contributed to this increased rate, a period of years will be required to learn the ultimate effects of mass radiation upon reproduction.

Treatment of victims by the Japanese was limited by the lack of medical supplies and facilities. Their therapy consisted of small amounts of vitamins, liver extract, and an occasional blood transfusion. Allied doctors used penicillin and plasma with beneficial effects. Liver extract seemed to benefit the few patients on whom it was used: It was given in small frequent doses when available. A large percentage of the cases died of secondary disease, such as septic bronchopneumonia or tuberculosis, as a result of lowered resistance. Deaths from radiation began about a week after exposure and reached a peak in 3 to 4 weeks. They had practically ceased to occur after 7 to 8 weeks.

Unfortunately, no exact definition of the killing power of radiation can yet be given, nor a satisfactory account of the sort and thickness of concrete or earth that will shield people. From the definitive report of the Joint Commission will come more nearly accurate statements on these matters. In the meanwhile the awesome lethal effects of the atomic bomb and the insidious additional peril of the gamma rays speak for themselves.

• • •

2. Morale.

As might be expected, the primary reaction to the bomb was fear- uncontrolled terror, strengthened by the sheer horror of the destruction and suffering witnessed and experienced by the survivors. Between one-half and two-thirds of those interviewed in the Hiroshima and Nagasaki areas confessed having such reactions, not just for the moment but for some time. As two survivors put it:

Whenever a plane was seen after that, people would rush into their shelters; they went in and out so much that they did not have time to eat. They were so nervous they could not work.

After the atomic bomb fell, I just couldn't stay home. I would cook, but while cooking I would always be watching out and worrying whether an atomic bomb would fall near me.

The behavior of the living immediately after the bombings, as described earlier, clearly shows the state of shock that hindered rescue efforts. A Nagasaki survivor illustrates succinctly the mood of survivors:

All I saw was the flash and I felt my body get warm and then I saw everything flying around. My grandmother was hit on the head by a flying piece of roof and she was bleeding. . . . I became hysterical seeing my grandmother bleeding and we just ran around without knowing what to do.

I was working at the office. I was talking to a friend at the window. I saw the whole city in a red flame, then I ducked. The pieces of the glass hit my back and face. My dress was torn off by the glass. Then I got up and ran to the mountain where the good shelter was.

The two typical impulses were these: Aimless, even hysterical activity or flight from the city to shelter and food.

Questions:
1. What is the purpose of this report?
2. What unexpected effects of the bombings did the investigators find?

25.5　"Tojo Makes Plea of Self Defense"

Soon after Japan's defeat in World War II, twenty-eight Japanese leaders[1] who had held high posts in the Japanese government and military between 1928 and 1945 were apprehended by the U.S. occupation authorities and charged with fifty-five counts of war crimes, which were grouped in three categories: (1) crimes against peace (first 36 counts), namely, the planning, preparation, initiation, or waging of a declared or undeclared war of aggression, or a war in violation of international law, treaties, agreements, or assurances, or participation in a common plan, or conspiring for the accomplishment of any of the foregoing; (2) murder (counts 37 through 52); and (3) conventional war crimes, namely, violations of the laws or customs of war, and crimes against humanity, namely, murder, extermination, enslavement, deportation, and other inhumane acts committed before or during the war (counts 53, 54, and 55).[2] They were tried by the International Military Tribunal for the Far East (I.M.T.F.E.), which was created on January 19, 1946, by the Supreme Commander of the Allied Powers in Japan in accordance with the directive of the U.S. Joint Chiefs of Staff. The Supreme Commander of the Allied Powers, General Douglas MacArthur, appointed eleven justices to the bench, one from each of the eleven victorious nations.[3] After nearly two and a half years of trial, despite a vigorous defense by the defense counsels, the defendants themselves and the jurists, including one of the justices, on the grounds that they had acted in self-defense of their nation, all twenty-five defendants were found guilty.[4] Seven of them—former Prime Minister General Hideki Tojo, former Foreign Minister Koki Hirota, and five generals—received death sentences by hanging, and the remaining eighteen received various prison terms, ranging from seven years to life. Eight of the eleven justices supported the judgment of the tribunal. Justice Radhabinod Pal of India, the leading dissenter, questioned, among other things, the justness of the victors' deciding whether or not the vanquished resorted to war in self-defense. Justice Pal was apprehensive that the notion that "might makes right" would become an accepted rule in the international system. On December 23, 1948, the seven defendants were hanged at Sugamo Prison in Tokyo.

During the trial, General Hideki Tojo, leader of the hawkish ultranationalistic faction of the Imperial Army of Japan, who became prime minister in October 1941, less than two months before the Pearl Harbor attack, and remained in that post until July 1944, justified what he and Japan did in the name of national survival and anticommunism. In a 60,000-word written testimony, he accused the United States and Britain of forcing Japan into war and accepted full responsibility for his and Japan's actions. He also strongly defended Emperor Hirohito's innocence in starting the war. The following excerpts are an edited version of a New York Times report of the trial.

Source: From "Tojo Makes Plea of Self Defense" by Lindsey Parrot, *The New York Times*, December 26, 1947. Copyright © 1947 by The New York Times Company. Reprinted by permission.

Defiantly the 63 year old career soldier who attempted suicide two years ago on the heels of the Japanese surrender, told the eleven-nation court that the Western Allies maneuvered so as to force Japan to fire the first shot "in self-defense" to preserve her "national existence."

Japan's leaders, including Emperor Hirohito, Tojo testified, went to war reluctantly and only after peaceful means of settlement had been exhausted. Economic pressure had brought the nation in 1941 "to the point of annihilation," he asserted. But Japan attempted to fight the war honorably, Tojo implied.

His government had no intention of making the Pearl Harbor attack a sneak affair, Tojo said. . . .

The treatment of prisoners, he indicated, could in part be explained by Japanese psychology.

As for the Doolittle fliers[5] who were caught after the attack on Tokyo in April 1942, their execution, he asserted, followed "the atrocities they committed in violation of international law and regulations" in the bombing of civilian population.

Tojo, the last but one of the remaining twenty-five top war leaders of Japan to open his defense, gave his testimony in a 60,000-word affidavit. A defense attorney began reading the document to the court while Tojo sat erect in the witness box, earphones clamped to his head. . . .

In effect a long bill of indictment against the Allied nations, restating in much detail Japan's pre-war charges of blockade, encirclement, bad faith and aid to a "hostile" China. Tojo's affidavit roundly attacked the prosecution's main contention that the Japanese leaders formed a conspiracy for war.

"I fail utterly to understand the reasoning of the prosecution in this fantastic accusation," Tojo wrote.

Under the Japanese imperial system with its "fundamental and unchangeable administrative processes," he asserted, such a conspiracy, continuing over a long period and involving many changes of administration was "unthinkable to persons of reason and intelligence."

For Japan's defeat in the war Tojo said he as Premier accepted full responsibility, but he challenged the "legal or criminal" responsibility that the Allied prosecutors attach to him.

"Never at any time did I ever conceive that the waging of this war would or could be challenged by the victors as an international crime," his affidavit concluded, "or that regularly constituted officials of the vanquished nation would be charged individually as criminals under any recognized international law or under alleged violations of treaties between nations."

In one long passage of the affidavit Tojo made vigorous effort to exculpate Emperor Hirohito from all blame for the war as a sovereign who constantly pressed his Ministers to seek other means of settlement but who eventually was powerless to alter the course of events.

"Even though some explanation of this point has previously been given by me, further exposition should be made so that, with regard to the Emperor's position, there be no possibility of misconstruction," Tojo wrote. "That to me is quite important."

"The Emperor had no free choice in the governmental structure setting up the Cabinet and Supreme Command. He was not in a position to reject the recommendations and advice of the Cabinet and the High Command."

Although Hirohito might have advanced personal "hopes and wishes" through Marquis Koichi Kido, Lord Keeper of the Privy Seal, Tojo said, even such imperial expressions were subject to Cabinet and military examination.

"The recommendations and suggestions after this careful examination had to be approved by the Emperor and never to be rejected," the statement said. "That was the position of the Emperor beforehand during this most perplexing period in the history of the Japanese Empire."

"These facts being what they are," this part of the argument concluded, "it was solely upon the Cabinet and the Supreme Command that responsibility lay for the political, diplomatic and military affairs of the nation. Accordingly, full responsibility for the decision of Dec. 1, 1941 for war is that of the Cabinet Ministers and members of the High Command and absolutely not the responsibility of the Emperor."

Tojo asserted two main factors forced Japan into war, first "pressure" by Britain and the United States and second national fear of communism.

While the United States and Britain, he wrote, would have been content with nothing less than Japan's evacuation of China and abandonment by the Japanese of all advantages they had gained there in almost ten years of warfare, Japan feared the "bolshevization of Asia" would be the result. To this thesis Tojo reverted several times.

In the Konoye Cabinet of 1939 in which he served as War Minister, Tojo said he expressed this viewpoint regarding the "unconditional withdrawal" from China as sought by the United States.

"Chinese contempt for Japan will expand if we retire from China unconditionally because of United States duress. Relations between Japan and China will grow worse coupled with the thorough-going resistance against Japan maintained by the Communists in China. Certainly China Incident No. 2 and China Incident No. 3 would result, and the repercussions at our loss of prestige would be keenly felt in Manchuria and Korea."

During his own Premiership (Oct. 18, 1941 to July 22, 1944) and up to the end of the war, Tojo asserted, Japan's policy was to preserve peace with Russia despite urgings from Germany, although the Soviet Union after Yalta[5] "actually had pledged itself to enter the war against Japan on the promise of territorial gains even while the (nonaggression) treaty was still valid and that nation actually attacked Japan while the agreement still was in force."

Japan has always been deeply concerned over communism in Asia, Tojo said.

"She realized that the activities of the Chinese Communist party were among the important causes preventing the establishment of peace between Japan and China in the China Incident," he went on. "Thus she made the joint prevention of communism one of the conditions for settlement of the Incident and also made prevention of communism an essential policy among the independent states of East Asia.

"This was all done with a view to saving East Asia from the danger of bolshevization and at the same time to making herself a barrier against world bolshevization. The present condition of the world two years after the end of World War II eloquently tells how important these barriers were for the peace of the world."

Tojo used a large part of his affidavit to set out what he argued was a "cold war" waged by Britain and the United States against Japan in the Nineteen Thirties and which, he argued, forced upon Japan nearly every step she took outside her borders, including her understanding with the Berlin-Rome Axis.

On more than one occasion, after Japan was cut off from food, rubber and petroleum by Allied economic measures after her credits had been frozen and after the United States began on a tremendously expanding arms program, Tojo said Japanese leaders feared armed attack in the Pacific.

"We did not anticipate at the time (1940–41) that America was so directing the war as to force Japan to make the first overt act," he wrote.

Such measures as the construction of air bases in French Indo-China, to which the Allies objected as presaging aggression, Tojo said were "protection against attacks from the south." From this direction, Japan's leaders thought, he said, might come an "onslaught by the 'have' nations against the Japanese Empire."[6]

Questions:
1. *Was the judgment at the Tokyo trial an exercise in victors' justice, as alleged by some jurists? Why? Why not?*
2. *How valid was the argument put up by Tojo and other defendants at the trial that Japan was forced by the United States and Britain into war?*
3. *Should a sovereign nation retain complete freedom of action concerning questions vital to its existence?*

25.6   The Charter of the United Nations[1]

As the Second World War was drawing to a close, representatives of most of the nations of the world came together in San Francisco in April of 1945 and drafted the Charter of the United Nations. Organized with a Security Council including the United States, Great Britain, France, the Soviet Union and China, each of which have veto power over any proposed action. Whether its authority and its ability to maintain peace and security in the future will prove effective remains to be seen.

We the Peoples of the United Nations Determined

to save succeeding generations from the scourge of war, which twice in our lifetime has brought untold sorrow to mankind, and

to reaffirm faith in fundamental human rights, in the dignity and worth of the human person, in the equal rights of men and women and of nations large and small, and

to establish conditions under which justice and respect for the obligations arising from treaties and other sources of international law can be maintained, and

to promote social progress and better standards of life in larger freedom,

And for These Ends

to practice tolerance and live together in peace with one another as good neighbours, and

to unite our strength to maintain international peace and security, and

to ensure by the acceptance of principles and the institution of methods, that armed force shall not be used, save in the common interest, and

to employ international machinery for the promotion of the economic and social advancement of all peoples,

Have Resolved to Combine Our Efforts to Accomplish These Aims

Accordingly, our respective Governments, through representatives assembled in the city of San Francisco, who have exhibited their full powers found to be in good and due form, have agreed to the present Charter of the United Nations and do hereby establish an international organization to be known as the United Nations.

CHAPTER I

Purposes and Principles

Article 1. The Purposes of the United Nations are:
1.   To maintain international peace and security, and to that end: to take effective collective measures for the prevention and removal of threats to the peace, and for the suppression of acts of aggression or other breaches of the peace, and

to bring about by peaceful means, and in conformity with the principles of justice and international law, adjustment or settlement of international disputes or situations which might lead to a breach of the peace;

2. To develop friendly relations among nations based on respect for the principle of equal rights and self-determination of peoples, and to take other appropriate measures to strengthen universal peace;
3. To achieve international cooperation in solving international problems of an economic, social, cultural or humanitarian character, and in promoting and encouraging respect for human rights and for fundamental freedoms for all without distinction as to race, sex, language, or religion; and
4. To be a centre for harmonizing the actions of nations in the attainment of these common ends.

Article 2. The Organization and its Members, in pursuit of the Purposes stated in Article 1, shall act in accordance with the following Principles.
1. The Organization is based on the principle of the sovereign equality of all its Members.
2. All Members, in order to ensure to all of them the rights and benefits resulting from membership, shall fulfill in good faith the obligations assumed by them in accordance with the present Charter.
3. All Members shall settle their international disputes by peaceful means in such a manner that international peace and security, and justice, are not endangered.
4. All Members shall refrain in their international relations from the threat or use of force against the territorial integrity or political independence of any state, or in any other manner inconsistent with the Purposes of the United Nations.
5. All Members shall give the United Nations every assistance in any action it takes in accordance with the present Charter, and shall refrain from giving assistance to any state against which the United Nations is taking preventive or enforcement action.
6. The Organization shall ensure that states which are not Members of the United Nations act in accordance with these Principles so far as may be necessary for the maintenance of international peace and security.
7. Nothing contained in the present Charter shall authorize the United Nations to intervene in matters which are essentially within the domestic jurisdiction of any state or shall require the Members to submit such matters to settlement under the present Charter; but this principle shall not prejudice the application of enforcement measures under Chapter VII.

CHAPTER II

Membership

Article 3. The original Members of the United Nations shall be the states which, having participated in the United Nations Conference on International Organization at San Francisco, or having previously signed the Declaration by United Nations of 1 January 1942, sign the present Charter and ratify it in accordance with Article 110.

Article 4.
1. Membership to the United Nations is open to all other peace-loving states which accept the obligations contained in the present Charter and, in the judgment of the Organization, are able and willing to carry out these obligations.
2. The admission of any such state to membership in the United Nations will be effected by a decision of the General Assembly upon the recommendation of the Security Council.

Article 5. A member of the United Nations against which preventive or enforcement action has been taken by the Security Council may be suspended from the exercise of the rights and privileges of membership by the General Assembly upon the recommendation of the Security Council. The exercise of these rights and privileges may be restored by the Security Council.

Article 6. A member of the United Nations which has persistently violated the Principles contained in the present Charter may be expelled from the Organization by the General Assembly upon the recommendation of the Security Council.

CHAPTER III

Organs

Article 7.
1. There are established as the principal organs of the United Nations: a General Assembly, a Security Council, an Economic and Social Council, a Trusteeship Council, an International Court of Justice, and a Secretariat.
2. Such subsidiary organs as may be found necessary may be established in accordance with the present Charter.

Article 8. The United Nations shall place no restrictions on the eligibility of men and women to participate in any capacity and under conditions of equality in its principal and subsidiary organs.

CHAPTER IV

The General Assembly

Composition

Article 9.
1. The General Assembly shall consist of all the members of the United Nations.
2. Each Member shall have not more than five representatives in the General Assembly.

Functions and Powers

Article 10. The General Assembly may discuss any questions or any matters within the scope of the present Charter or relating to the powers and functions of any organs provided for in the present Charter, and except as provided in Article 12, may make recommendations to the Members of the United Nations or to the Security Council or to both on any such questions or matters.

Article 11.
1. The General Assembly may consider the general principles of cooperation in the maintenance of international peace and security, including the principles governing disarmament and the regulation of armaments, and may make recommendations with regard to such principles to the Members or to the Security Council or to both.
2. The General Assembly may discuss any questions relating to the maintenance of international peace and security brought before it by any Member of the United Nations, or by the Security Council, or by a state which is not a Member of the United Nations in accordance with Article 35, paragraph 2, and, except as provided in Article 12, may make recommendations with regard to any such question to the state or states concerned or to the Security Council or to both. Any such question on which action is necessary shall be referred to the Security Council by the General Assembly either before or after discussion.
3. The General Assembly may call the attention of the Security Council to situations which are likely to endanger international peace and security.
4. The powers of the General Assembly set forth in this Article shall not limit the general scope of Article 10.

Article 12.
1. While the Security Council is exercising in respect of any dispute or situation the functions assigned to it in the present Charter, the General Assembly shall not make any recommendation with regard to that dispute or situation unless the Security Council so requests.
2. The Secretary-General, with the Security Council, shall notify the General Assembly at each session of any matters relative to the maintenance of international peace and security which are being dealt with by the Security Council and shall similarly notify the General Assembly or the Members of the United Nations if the General Assembly is not in session, immediately the Security Council ceases to deal with such matters.

Article 13.
1 The General Assembly shall initiate studies and make recommendations for the purpose of:
   a. promoting international cooperation in the political field and encouraging the progressive developments of international law and its codification;
   b. promoting international cooperation in the economic, social, cultural, educational, and health fields, and assisting in the realization of human rights and fundamental freedoms for all without distinction as to race, sex, language, or religion.
2 The further responsibilities, functions and powers of the General Assembly with respect to matters mentioned in paragraph 1b above are set forth in Chapters IX and X.

Article 14. Subject to the provisions of Article 12, the General Assembly may recommend measures for the peaceful adjustment of any situation, regardless of origin, which it deems likely to impair the general welfare or friendly relations among nations, including situations resulting from a violation of the provisions of the present Charter setting forth the Purposes and Principles of the United Nations.

Article 15.

1 The General Assembly shall receive and consider annual and special reports from the Security Council; these reports shall include an account of the measures that the Security Council has decided upon or taken to maintain international peace and security.

2 The General Assembly shall receive and consider reports from the other organs of the United Nations.

Article 16. The General Assembly shall perform such functions with respect to the international trusteeship system as are assigned to it under Chapters XII and XIII, including the approval of the trusteeship agreements for areas not designed as strategic.

Article 17.

1. The General Assembly shall consider and approve the budget of the Organization.
2. The expenses of the Organization shall be borne by the Members as apportioned by the General Assembly.
3. The General Assembly shall consider and approve any financial and budgetary arrangements with specialized agencies referred to in Article 57 and shall examine the administrative budgets of such specialized agencies with a view to making recommendations to the agencies concerned.

Voting

Article 18.

1. Each member of the General Assembly shall have one vote.
2. Decisions of the General Assembly on important questions shall be made by a two-thirds majority of the members present and voting. These questions shall include: recommendations with respect to the maintenance of international peace and security, the election of the nonpermanent members of the Security Council, the election of the members of the Economic and Social Council, the election of members of the Trusteeship Council in accordance with paragraph 1c of Article 86, the admission of new members to the United Nations, the suspension of the rights and privileges of membership, the expulsion of Members, questions relating to the operation of the trusteeship system, and budgetary questions.
3. Decisions on other questions including the determination of additional categories of questions to be decided by a two-thirds majority, shall be made by a majority of the members present and voting.

Article 19. A member of the United Nations which is in arrears in the payment of its financial contributions to the Organization shall have no vote in the General Assembly if the amount of its arrears equals or exceeds the amount of the contributions due from it for the preceding two full years. The General Assembly may, nevertheless, permit such a Member to vote if it is satisfied that the failure to pay is due to conditions beyond the control of the Member.

Procedure

Article 20. The General Assembly shall meet in regular annual sessions and in such special sessions as occasion may require. Special sessions shall be convoked by the Secretary-General at the request of the Security Council or of a majority of the Members of the United Nations.

Article 21. The General Assembly shall adopt its own rules of procedure. It shall elect its President for each session.

Article 22. The General Assembly may establish such subsidiary organs as it deems necessary for the performance of its functions.

CHAPTER V

The Security Council

Composition

Article 23.

1. The Security Council shall consist of fifteen members of the United Nations. The Republic of China, France, the Union of Soviet Socialist Republics, the United Kingdom of Great Britain and Northern Ireland, and the United States of America shall be permanent members of the Security Council. The General Assembly shall elect ten other Members of the United Nations to be nonpermanent members of the Security Council, due regard being specially paid, in the first instance to the contribution of Members of the United Nations to the maintenance of international peace and security and to the other purposes of the Organization, and also to equitable geographical distribution.

2. The nonpermanent members of the Security Council shall be elected for a term of two years. In the first election of the nonpermanent members after the increase of the membership of the Security Council from eleven to fifteen, two of the four additional members shall be chosen for a term of one year. A retiring member shall not be eligible for immediate re-election.

3. Each member of the Security Council shall have one representative.

Functions and Powers

Article 24.

1. In order to ensure prompt and effective action by the United Nations, its Members confer on the Security Council primary responsibility for the maintenance of international peace and security, and agree that in carrying out its duties under this responsibility the Security Council acts on their behalf.

2. In discharging these duties the Security Council shall act in accordance with the Purposes and Principles of the United Nations. The specific powers granted to the Security Council for the discharge of these duties are laid down in Chapters VI, VII, VIII, and XII.

3. The Security Council shall submit annual and, when necessary, special reports to the General Assembly for its consideration.

Article 25. The Members of the United Nations agree to accept and carry out the decisions of the Security Council in accordance with the present Charter.

Article 26. In order to promote the establishment and maintenance of international peace and security with the least diversion for armaments of the world's human economic resources, the Security Council shall be responsible for formulating, with the assistance of the Military Staff Committee referred to in Article 47, plans to be submitted to the Members of the United Nations for the establishment of a system for the regulation of armaments.

Voting

Article 27.

1. Each member of the Security Council shall have one vote.

2. Decisions of the Security Council on procedural matters shall be made by an affirmative vote of nine members.

3. Decisions of the Security Council on all other matters shall be made by an affirmative vote of nine members including the concurring votes of the permanent members; provided that, in decisions under Chapter VI, and under paragraph 3 of Article 52, a party to a dispute shall abstain from voting.

Procedure

Article 28.

1. The Security Council shall be so organized as to be able to function continuously. Each member of the Security Council shall for this purpose be represented at all times at the seat of the Organization.

2. The Security Council shall hold periodic meetings at which each of its members may, if it so desires, be represented by a member of the government or by some other specially designated representative.

3. The Security Council may hold meetings at such places other than the seat of the Organization as in its judgment will best facilitate its work.

Article 29. The Security Council may establish such subsidiary organs as it deems necessary for the performance of its functions.

Article 30. The Security Council shall adopt its own rules of procedure, including the method of selecting its President.

Article 31. Any Member of the United Nations which is not a member of the Security Council may participate, without vote, in the discussion of any question brought before the Security Council whenever the latter considers that the interests of that Member are specially affected.

Article 32. Any Member of the United Nations which is not a member of the Security Council or any state which is not a Member of the United Nations, if it is a party to a dispute under consideration by the Security Council, shall be invited to participate, without vote, in the discussion relating to the dispute. The Security Council shall lay down such conditions as it deems just for the participation of such a state which is not a Member of the United Nations.

CHAPTER VI

Pacific Settlement of Disputes

Article 33.
1. The parties to any dispute, the continuance of which is likely to endanger the maintenance of international peace and security, shall, first of all, seek a solution by negotiation, enquiry, mediation, conciliation, arbitration, judicial settlement, resort to regional agencies or arrangements, or other peaceful means of their own choice.
2. The Security Council shall, when it deems necessary, call upon the parties to settle their dispute by such means.

Article 34. The Security Council may investigate any dispute, or any situation which might lead to international friction or give rise to a dispute, in order to determine whether the continuance of the dispute or situation is likely to endanger the maintenance of international peace and security.

Article 35.
1. Any Member of the United Nations may bring any dispute, or any situation of the nature referred to in Article 34, to the attention of the Security Council or of the General Assembly.
2. A state which is not a Member of the United Nations may bring to the attention of the Security Council or of the General Assembly any dispute to which it is a party if it accepts in advance, for the purposes of the dispute, the obligations of pacific settlement provided in the present Charter.
3. The proceedings of the General Assembly in respect of matters brought to its attention under this Article will be subject to the provisions of Articles 11 and 12.

Article 36.
1. The Security Council may, at any stage of a dispute of the nature referred to in Article 33 or of a situation of like nature, recommend appropriate procedures or methods of adjustment.
2. The Security Council should take into consideration any procedures for the settlement of the dispute which have already been adopted by the parties.
3. In making recommendations under this Article the Security Council should also take into consideration that legal disputes should as a general rule be referred by the parties to the International Court of Justice in accordance with the provisions of the Statute of the Court.

Article 37.
1. Should the parties to a dispute of the nature referred to in Article 33 fail to settle it by the means indicated in that Article, they shall refer it to the Security Council.
2. If the Security Council deems that the continuance of the dispute is in fact likely to endanger the maintenance of international peace and security, it shall decide whether to take action under Article 36 or to recommend such terms of settlement as it may consider appropriate.

Article 38. Without prejudice to the provisions of Article 33 to 37, the Security Council may, if all the parties to any dispute so request, make recommendations to the parties with a view to a pacific settlement of the dispute.

CHAPTER VII

Action with Respect to Threats to the Peace, Breaches of the Peace, and Acts of Aggression

Article 39. The Security Council shall determine the existence of any threat to the peace, breach of the peace, or act of aggression and shall make recommendations, or decide what measures shall be taken in accordance with Articles 41 and 42, to maintain or restore international peace and security.

Article 40. In order to prevent an aggravation of the situation, the Security Council may, before making the recommendations or deciding upon the measures provided for in Article 39, call upon the parties concerned to comply with such provisional measures as it deems necessary or desirable. Such provisional measures shall be without prejudice to the rights, claims, or position of the parties concerned. The Security Council shall duly take account of failure to comply with such provisional measures.

Article 41. The Security Council may decide what measures not involving the use of armed forces are to be employed to give effect to its decisions, and it may call upon the Members of the United Nations to apply such measures.

These may include complete or partial interruption of economic relations and of rail, sea, air, postal, telegraphic, radio, and other means of communication, and the severance of diplomatic relations.

Article 42. Should the Security Council consider that measures provided for in Article 41 would be inadequate or have proved to be inadequate, it may take such action by air, sea, or land forces as may be necessary to maintain or restore international peace and security. Such action may include demonstrations, blockade, and other operations by air, sea, or land forces of Members of the United Nations.

Article 43.

1. All Members of the United Nations, in order to contribute to the maintenance of international peace and security, undertake to make available to the Security Council, on its call and in accordance with a special agreement or agreements, armed forces, assistance, and facilities, including rights of passage, necessary for the purpose of maintaining international peace and security.
2. Such agreement or agreements shall govern the numbers and types of forces, the degree of readiness and general location, and the nature of the facilities and assistance to be provided.
3. The agreement or agreements shall be negotiated as soon as possible on the initiative of the Security Council. They shall be concluded between the Security Council and Members or between the Security Council and groups of Members and shall be subject to ratification by the signatory states in accordance with their respective constitutional processes.

Article 44. When the Security Council has decided to use force it shall, before calling upon a Member not represented on it to provide armed forces in fulfillment of the obligations assumed under Article 43, invite that Member, if the Member so desires, to participate in the decisions of the Security Council concerning the employment of contingents of that Member's armed forces.

Article 45. In order to enable the United Nations to take urgent military measures, Members shall hold immediately available national air-force contingents for combined international enforcement action. The strength and degree of readiness of these contingents and plans for their combined action shall be determined, within the limits laid down in the special agreement or agreements referred to in Article 43, by the Security Council with the assistance of the Military Staff Committee.

Article 46. Plans for the application of armed force shall be made by the Security Council with the assistance of the Military Staff Committee.

Article 47.

1. There shall be established a Military Staff Committee to advise and assist the Security Council on all questions relating to the Security Council's military requirements for the maintenance of international peace and security, the employment and command of forces placed at its disposal, the regulation of armaments, and possible disarmament.
2. The Military Staff Committee shall consist of the Chiefs of Staff, of the permanent members of the Security Council or their representatives. Any Member of the United Nations not permanently represented on the Committee shall be invited by the Committee to be associated with it when the efficient discharge of the Committee's responsibilities requires the participation of that Member in its work.
3. The Military Staff Committee shall be responsible under the Security Council for the strategic direction of any armed forces placed at the disposal of the Security Council. Questions relating to the command of such forces shall be worked out subsequently.
4. The Military Staff Committee, with the authorization of the Security Council and after consultation with appropriate regional agencies, may establish regional subcommittees.

Article 48.

1. The action required to carry out the decisions of the Security Council for the maintenance of international peace and security shall be taken by all the Members of the United Nations or by some of them, as the Security Council may determine.
2. Such decisions shall be carried out by the Members of the United Nations directly and through their action in the appropriate international agencies of which they are members.

Article 49. The Members of the United Nations shall join in affording mutual assistance in carrying out the measures decided upon by the Security Council.

Article 50. If preventive or enforcement measures against any state are taken by the Security Council, any other state, whether a Member of the United Nations or not, which finds itself confronted with special economic problems arising from the carrying out of those measures shall have the right to consult the Security Council with regard to a solution of those problems.

Article 51. Nothing in the present Charter shall impair the inherent right of individual or collective self-defence if an armed attack occurs against a Member of the United Nations until the Security Council has taken measures necessary to maintain international peace and security. Measures taken by Members in the exercise of this right of self-defence shall be immediately reported to the Security Council and shall not in any way affect the authority and responsibility of the Security Council under the present Charter to take at any time such action as it deems necessary in order to maintain or restore international peace and security.

Questions:
1. *What are the requirements for joining the United Nations?*
2. *What is the purpose of the United Nations?*
3. *What is the function of the General Assembly? The Security Council?*

PART 26
The Cold War

26.1 The Soviet Victory: Capitalism versus Communism (February 1946): Joseph Stalin

The term "Cold War" describes the era of uneasy relations between the Western Allies and the Soviet Union after World War II. Each was competing for influence in Europe through propaganda and troop placement. In the first excerpt, the Soviet leader Joseph Stalin offered a glimpse of the ideological combat that was to be waged in the future. A month later, Winston Churchill, who had largely directed the British war effort, warned the West of the deceptive Soviet Union in his famous "Iron Curtain" speech.

Source: "The Soviet Victory" is from Embassy of the U.S.S.R., speech delivered by J. V. Stalin at a Meeting of Voters of the Stalin Electoral Area of Moscow (Washington, DC: Government Printing Office, 1946).

It would be wrong to believe that the Second World War broke out accidentally or as a result of the mistakes of some or other statesmen, though mistakes certainly were made. In reality, the war broke out as an inevitable result of the development of world economic and political forces on the basis of modern monopoly capitalism.

Marxists have stated more than once that the capitalist system of world economy conceals in itself the elements of general crisis and military clashes, that in view of this in our time the development of world capitalism takes place not as a smooth and even advance but through crises and war catastrophes.

The reason is that the unevenness of the development of capitalist countries usually results, as time passes, in an abrupt disruption of the equilibrium within the world system of capitalism, and that a group of capitalist countries which believes itself to be less supplied with raw materials and markets usually attempts to alter the situation and re-divide the "spheres of influence" in its own favour by means of armed force. . . .

This results in the splitting of the capitalist world into two hostile camps and in war between them. Perhaps the catastrophes of war could be avoided if there existed the possibility of re-distributing periodically raw materials and markets among the countries in accordance with their economic weight—by means of adopting coordinated and peaceful decisions. This, however, cannot be accomplished under present capitalist conditions of the development of world economy. . . .

As to our country, for her the war was the severest and hardest of all the wars our Motherland has ever experienced in her history. But the war was not only a curse. It was at the same time a great school in which all the forces of the people were tried and tested. The war laid bare all the facts and events in the rear and at the front, it mercilessly tore off all the veils and covers which had concealed the true faces of States, governments, and parties, and placed them on the stage without masks, without embellishments, with all their shortcomings and virtues.

. . .

And so, what are the results of the war? . . .

Our victory means, in the first place, that our Soviet social system has won, that the Soviet social system successfully withstood the trial in the flames of war and proved its perfect viability. It is well known that the foreign press more than once asserted that the Soviet social system is a "risky experiment" doomed to failure, that the Soviet system is a "house of cards," without any roots in life, imposed upon the people by the organs of the "Cheka" [secret police], that a slight push from outside would be enough to blow this "house of cards" to smithereens.

Now we can say that the war swept away all these assertions of the foreign press as groundless. The war has shown that the Soviet social system is a truly popular system, which has grown from the people and enjoys its powerful support, that the Soviet social system is a perfectly viable and stable form of organisation of society.

More than that, the point is now not whether the Soviet social system is viable or not, since after the objective lessons of the war no single skeptic now ventures to come out with doubts concerning the viability of the Soviet social system. The point now is that the Soviet social system has proved more viable and stable than a non-Soviet social system, that the Soviet social system is a better form of organisation of society than any non-Soviet social system.

Question:
1. What did Stalin mean in his speech of February 1946 by the phrase "Soviet victory"?

26.2 "An Iron Curtain Has Descended Across the Continent" (March 1946): Sir Winston Churchill

The term "Cold War" describes the era of uneasy relations between the Western Allies and the Soviet Union after World War II. Each was competing for influence in Europe through propaganda and troop placement. In the first excerpt, the Soviet leader Joseph Stalin offered a glimpse of the ideological combat that was to be waged in the future. A month later, Winston Churchill, who had largely directed the British war effort, warned the West of the deceptive Soviet Union in his famous "Iron Curtain" speech.

Source: "'An Iron Curtain Has Descended Across the Continent'" is from *Congressional Record*, 79th Congress, 2nd session, pp. A1145–A1147.

I now come to the . . . danger which threatens the cottage home and ordinary people, namely tyranny. We cannot be blind to the fact that the liberties enjoyed by individual citizens throughout the United States and British Empire are not valid in a considerable number of countries, some of which are very powerful. In these states control is forced upon the common people by various kinds of all-embracing police governments, to a degree which is overwhelming and contrary to every principle of democracy. The power of the state is exercised without restraint, either by dictators or by compact oligarchies operating through a privileged party and a political police. It is not our duty at this time, when difficulties are so numerous, to interfere forcibly in the internal affairs of countries whom we have not conquered in war, but we must never cease to proclaim in fearless tones the great principles of freedom and the rights of man, which are the joint inheritance of the English-speaking world and which, through Magna Carta, the Bill of Rights, the habeas corpus, trial by jury, and the English common law find their famous expression in the Declaration of Independence. . . .

A shadow has fallen upon the scenes so lately lighted by the Allied victory. Nobody knows what Soviet Russia and its Communist international organization intends to do in the immediate future, or what are the limits, if any, to their expansive and proselytizing tendencies. . . . From Stettin in the Baltic to Trieste in the Adriatic, an iron curtain has descended across the continent. Behind that line lie all the capitals of the ancient states of central and eastern Europe. Warsaw, Berlin, Prague, Vienna, Budapest, Belgrade, Bucharest, and Sofia, all these famous cities and the populations around them lie in the Soviet sphere and all are subject, in one form or another, not only to Soviet influence but to a very high and increasing measure of control from Moscow. Athens alone, with its immortal glories, is free to decide its future at an election under British, American, and French observation.

In a great number of countries, far from the Russian frontiers and throughout the world, Communist fifth columns are established and work in complete unity and absolute obedience to the directions they receive from the Communist center. Except in the British Commonwealth, and in the United States, where communism is in its infancy, the Communist parties and fifth columns constitute a growing challenge and peril to Christian civilization. These are somber facts for anyone to have to recite on the morrow of a victory gained by so much splendid comradeship in arms and in the cause of freedom and democracy, and we should be most unwise not to face them squarely while time remains. . . .

On the other hand, I repulse the idea that a new war is inevitable, still more that it is imminent. It is because I am so sure that our fortunes are in our own hands and that we hold the power to save the future, that I feel the duty to speak out now that I have occasion to do so. I do not believe that Soviet Russia desires war. What they desire is the fruits of war and the indefinite expansion of their power and doctrines. But what we have to consider here today while time remains, is the permanent prevention of war and the establishment of conditions of freedom and democracy as rapidly as possible in all countries.

Our difficulties and dangers will not be removed by closing our eyes to them; they will not be removed by mere waiting to see what happens; nor will they be relieved by a policy of appeasement. What is needed is a settlement, and the longer this is delayed, the more difficult it will be and the greater our dangers will become. From what I have seen of our Russian friends and allies during the war, I am convinced that there is nothing they admire so much as strength, and there is nothing for which they have less respect than for military weakness. For that reason the old doctrine of a balance of power is unsound. We cannot afford, if we can help it, to work on narrow margins, offering temptations to a trial of strength. If the western democracies stand together in strict adherence to the principles of the United Nations Charter, their influence for furthering these principles will be immense and no one is likely to molest them. If, however, they become divided or falter in their duty, and if these all-important years are allowed to slip away, then indeed catastrophe may overwhelm us all.

Questions:
1. *What policy was Churchill advocating in his "Iron Curtain" speech?*
2. *Was he pessimistic or optimistic about the possibility of war?*

26.3   The Truman Doctrine (March 1947): Harry S. Truman

In the first months of 1946, President Truman received urgent requests from the Greek government for economic assistance, which, it was hoped, would put an end to the chaos and strife hindering its recovery from the war. Hoping to forestall Communist dissidents who were threatening the stability of the government, Truman appealed to Congress to appropriate such financial assistance. He also asked for military as well as economic aid to Turkey. The controversial Truman Doctrine, as it came to be called, committed the United States to an active policy of promoting ideological divisions between it and the Soviet Union and further escalated Cold War tensions. The Marshall Plan of 1947, which advocated the rebuilding of West Germany after the war, is an example of this policy of Soviet containment.

> **Source:** "The Truman Doctrine" is from *Public Papers of the President,* Harry S. Truman, 1947 (Washington, DC: Government Printing Office, 1963), pp. 177–180.

One of the primary objectives of the foreign policy of the United States is the creation of conditions in which we and other nations will be able to work out a way of life free from coercion. This was a fundamental issue in the war with Germany and Japan. Our victory was won over countries which sought to impose their will, and their way of life, upon other nations.

To ensure the peaceful development of nations, free from coercion, the United States has taken a leading part in establishing the United Nations. The United Nations is designed to make possible lasting freedom and independence for all its members. We shall not realize our objectives, however, unless we are willing to help free peoples to maintain their free institutions and their national integrity against aggressive movements that seek to impose upon them totalitarian regimes. This is no more than a frank recognition that totalitarian regimes imposed upon free peoples, by direct or indirect aggression, undermine the foundations of international peace and hence the security of the United States.

The peoples of a number of countries of the world have recently had totalitarian regimes forced upon them against their will. The Government of the United States has made frequent protests against coercion and intimidation, in violation of the Yalta agreement, in Poland, Rumania, and Bulgaria. I must also state that in a number of other countries there have been similar developments.

At the present moment in world history nearly every nation must choose between alternative ways of life. The choice is too often not a free one.

One way of life is based upon the will of the majority, and is distinguished by free institutions, representative government, free elections, guarantees of individual liberty, freedom of speech and religion, and freedom from political oppression.

The second way of life is based upon the will of a minority forcibly imposed upon the majority. It relies upon terror and oppression, a controlled press and radio, fixed elections, and the suppression of personal freedoms.

I believe that it must be the policy of the United States to support free peoples who are resisting attempted subjugation by armed minorities or by outside pressures. I believe that we must assist free peoples to work out their own destinies in their own way. I believe that our help should be primarily through economic and financial aid which is essential to economic stability and orderly political processes.

The world is not static, and the status quo is not sacred. But we cannot allow changes in the status quo in violation of the Charter of United Nations by such methods as coercion, or by such subterfuges as political infiltration. In helping free and independent nations to maintain their freedom, the United States will be giving effect to the principles of the Charter of the United Nations. . . .

The seeds of totalitarian regimes are nurtured by misery and want. They spread and grow in the evil soil of poverty and strife. They reach their full growth when the hope of a people for a better life has died. We must keep that hope alive. The free peoples of the world look to us for support in maintaining their freedoms.

If we falter in our leadership, we may endanger the peace of the world—and we shall surely endanger the welfare of this Nation. Great responsibilities have been placed upon us by the swift movement of events. I am confident that the Congress will face these responsibilities squarely.

Questions:
1. *What prompted Truman to choose this course of action?*
2. *How much of the philosophy of the Truman Doctrine was vested in America's need to help free peoples and how much was vested in issues considered vital to national interests?*

26.4 The Marshall Plan (June 1947): George C. Marshall

In the first months of 1946, President Truman received urgent requests from the Greek government for economic assistance, which, it was hoped, would put an end to the chaos and strife hindering its recovery from the war. Hoping to forestall Communist dissidents who were threatening the stability of the government, Truman appealed to Congress to appropriate such financial assistance. He also asked for military as well as economic aid to Turkey. The controversial Truman Doctrine, as it came to be called, committed the United States to an active policy of promoting ideological divisions between it and the Soviet Union and further escalated Cold War tensions. The Marshall Plan of 1947, which advocated the rebuilding of West Germany after the war, is an example of this policy of Soviet containment.

Source: "The Marshall Plan" is from *Department of State Bulletin* (June 15, 1947), pp. 1159–1160.

The truth of the matter is that Europe's requirements for the next three or four years of foreign food and other essential products—principally from America—are so much greater than her present ability to pay that she must have substantial additional help or face economic, social, and political deterioration of a very grave character.

The remedy lies in breaking the vicious circle and restoring the confidence of the European people in the economic future of their own countries and of Europe as a whole. The manufacturer and the farmer throughout wide areas must be able and willing to exchange their products for currencies the continuing value of which is not open to question.

Aside from the demoralizing effect on the world at large and the possibilities of disturbances arising as a result of the desperation of the people concerned, the consequences to the economy of the United States should be apparent to all. It is logical that the United States should do whatever it is able to do to assist in the return of normal economic health in the world, without which there can be no political stability and no assured peace. Our policy is directed not against any country or doctrine but against hunger, poverty, desperation, and chaos. Its purpose should be the revival of a working economy in the world so as to permit the emergence of political and social conditions in which free institutions can exist. Such assistance, I am convinced, must not be on a piecemeal basis as various crises develop. Any assistance that this Government may render in the future should provide a cure rather than a mere palliative. Any government that is willing to assist in the task of recovery will find full cooperation, I am sure, on the part of the United States Government. Any government which maneuvers to block the recovery of other countries cannot expect help from us. Furthermore, governments, political parties, or groups which seek to perpetuate human misery in order to profit therefrom politically or otherwise will encounter the opposition of the United States.

It is already evident that, before the United States Government can proceed much further in its efforts to alleviate the situation and help start the European world on its way to recovery, there must be some agreement among the countries of Europe as to the requirements of the situation and the part those countries themselves will take in order to give proper effect to whatever action might be undertaken by this Government. It would be neither fitting nor efficacious for this Government to undertake to draw up unilaterally a program designed to place Europe on its feet economically. This is the business of the Europeans. The initiative, I think, must come from Europe. The role of this country should consist of friendly aid in the drafting of a European program and of later support of such a program so far as it may be practical for us to do so. The program should be a joint one, agreed to by a number, if not all, European nations.

An essential part of any successful action on the part of the United States is an understanding on the part of the people of America of the character of the problem and the remedies to be applied. Political passion and prejudice should have no part. With foresight, and a willingness on the part of our people to face up to the vast responsibility which history has clearly placed upon our country, the difficulties I have outlined can and will be overcome.

Questions:
1. How does this plan fit into the context of "containment"?
2. The plan states "our policy is not directed against any country or doctrine, but against hunger, poverty, desperation, and chaos." Was this true? Why was it necessary to articulate a disclaimer? What relation to hunger, poverty, desperation, and chaos have to political instability or political agendas?

26.5   Korea: The Thirty-eighth Parallel

On August 9, 1945, the Soviet Union declared war on Japan, and soon afterwards the Soviet Red Army crossed into Manchuria and Korea. The United States, whose armed forces were hundreds of miles away from Korea, had to draw up a military demarcation line across the Korean peninsula to prevent the Russians from overrunning the entire region. On August 11, the State-War-Navy Coordinating Committee ordered two former Rhodes scholars, Colonels Dean Rusk and Charles H. Bonesteel III, to determine a line within thirty minutes. They recommended the thirty-eighth parallel as a division between U.S. and Soviet occupation zones. By the time American troops entered Korea on September 8, the Russians were already entrenched along the thirty-eighth parallel. This line had been intended merely as a temporary military line to expedite the disarming of the Japanese troops in Korea. On August 14, Japan surrendered and Japanese rule in Korea ended; however, Korea found itself bisected and a focal point of intense rivalry between the United States and the Soviet Union. The following excerpt provides a detailed account of who actually drew the line and why.

Source: From James F. Schnabel, *United States Army in the Korean War. Policy and Direction: The First Year* (Washington, DC: Office of the Chief of Military History, Untied States Army, 1972), pp. 8–11.

At Potsdam, the chief of the Russian General Staff told General Marshall that Russia would attack Korea after declaring war on Japan. He asked whether the Americans could operate against Korean shores in co-ordination with this offensive. General Marshall told him that the United States planned no amphibious operation against Korea until Japan had been brought under control and Japanese strength in South Korea was destroyed. Although the Chiefs of Staff developed ideas concerning the partition of Korea, Manchuria, and the Sea of Japan into U.S. and USSR zones, these had no connection with the later decisions that partitioned Korea into northern and southern areas.

Russian entry into the war against Japan on 9 August, and signs of imminent Japanese collapse on 10 August 1945 changed U.S. Army planning from defeating Japan to accepting its surrender. Military planners in the War Department Operations Division began to outline surrender procedures in General Order No. 1, which General MacArthur would transmit to the Japanese Government after its surrender. The first paragraph of the order specified the nations and commands that were to accept the surrender of Japanese forces throughout the Far East.

The Policy Section of the Strategy and Policy Group in the Operations Division drafted the initial version of the order.

Under pressure to produce a paper as quickly as possible, members of the Policy Section began work late at night on 10 August. They discussed possible surrender zones, the allocation of American, British, Chinese, and Russian occupation troops to accept the surrender in the zones most convenient to them, the means of actually taking the surrender of the widely scattered Japanese military forces, and the position of Russia in the Far East. They quickly decided to include both provisions for splitting up the entire Far East for the surrender and definitions of the geographical limits of those zones.

The Chief of the Policy Section, Col. Charles H. Bonesteel, had thirty minutes in which to dictate Paragraph 1 to a secretary, for the Joint Staff Planners and the State-War-Navy Coordinating Committee were impatiently awaiting the result of his work. Colonel Bonesteel [along with Colonel Dean Rusk] thus somewhat hastily decided who would accept the Japanese surrender. His thoughts, with very slight revision, we incorporated into the final directive.

Bonesteel's prime consideration was to establish a surrender line as far north as he thought the Soviets would accept. He knew that Russian troops could reach the southern tip of Korea before American troops could arrive. He knew also that the Russians were on the verge of moving into Korea, or were already there. The nearest American troops to Korea were on Okinawa, 600 miles away. His problem therefore was to compose a surrender arrangement which, while acceptable to the Russians, would at the same time prevent them from seizing all of Korea. If they refused to confine their advance to North Korea, the United States would be unable to stop them.

At first Bonesteel had thought of surrender zones conforming to the provincial boundary lines. But the only map he had in his office, which was a small National Geographic map, a 1942 Gilbert Grosvenor Edition of "Asia and Adjacent Areas," was hardly adequate for this sort of distinction. The 38th Parallel, he noted, cut Korea approximately through the middle. If this line was agreeable to President Truman and to Generalissimo Stalin, it would place Seoul and a nearby prisoner of war camp in American hands. It would also leave enough land to be apportioned to the Chinese and British if some sort of quadripartite administration became necessary. Thus he decided to use the 38th Parallel as a hypothetical line dividing the zones within which Japanese forces in Korea would surrender to appointed American and Russian authorities. . . .

When Bonesteel's draft paper reached the Joint Planners in the predawn hours of 11 August, Admiral M.B. Gardner suggested moving the surrender line north to the 39th Parallel, a recommendation that the planners believed the Navy Secretary, James C. Forrestal, favored. Gardner pointed out that the 39th Parallel would place Dairen in the military zone to be occupied by the Americans. General Lincoln, however, felt that the Russians would hardly accept a surrender line that barred them from Dairen and other parts of the Liaotung Peninsula; besides, American units would have great difficulty reaching the Manchurian port ahead of the Russians. Calling Assistant Secretary of State James Dunn, Lincoln ascertained that his opinion was shared. Mr. Dunn believed that Korea was more important politically to the United States than Dairen, and he felt this to be the view of Secretary of State James F. Byrnes. As a result, the 38th Parallel remained in the draft when the Joint Planners handed the general order to the State-War-Navy Coordinating Committee.

While General Lincoln was shepherding the document through the State-War-Navy Coordinating Committee on 11 and 12 August, the Russians invaded Korea, landing on the northeast coast near Rashin. Russian troops then poured out of the maritime provinces of Siberia, down the Korean peninsula, and into the Kaesong-Ch'unch'on area above Seoul, where they looted much equipment, including locomotives and rolling stock. Reports of the Russian troop movements reaching Washington underscored the need for concurrence in the proposed general order. Otherwise, the Russian advance would render academic the American acceptance of the Japanese surrender in southern Korea. At the same time, swift Russian troop movements into key areas of southern Manchuria eliminated the possibility of including Dairen in the American surrender zone.

Between 11 and 14 August, the State-War-Navy Coordinating Committee and the Joint Chiefs of Staff discussed the wording of the surrender instrument. Meanwhile, General MacArthur informed the Joint Chiefs of Staff that he would adhere to three priorities for the use of the forces under his command. After the Japanese surrender, the occupation of Japan would come first, Korea second, China third.

In Washington, the War Department Operations Division rephrased General Order No. 1 to the satisfaction of the Joint Chiefs of Staff and the heads of the State, War, and Navy Departments. On 15 August 1945, clean copies of the draft order were sent to Fleet Admiral William D. Leahy's White House office. Within a few hours President Truman gave his approval, directing at the same time that General Order No. 1 be sent also to the capitals of Great Britain and the USSR with requests for concurrence by the heads of those states. . . .

Among the items it specified, General Order No. 1 stated that Japanese forces north of the 38th Parallel in Korea would surrender to the Russian commander, while those south of the parallel would surrender to the commanding general of the U.S. expeditionary forces. As Washington waited for the Moscow reaction to President Truman's message, there was a short period of suspense. Russian troops had entered Korea three days before the President accepted the draft of General Order No. 1. If the Russians failed to accept the proposal, and if Russian troops occupied Seoul, General Lincoln suggested that American occupation forces move into Pusan.

Stalin replied to President Truman on 16 August 1945. He said nothing specifically about the 38th Parallel but offered no objection to the substance of the President's message.

Questions:

1. *How do you assess the behind-the-scenes decision for the containing of the Soviet advance in the Korean peninsula? Was the decision to divide Korea at the thirty-eighth parallel a wise one? Would another approach have been feasible?*
2. *How did the decision to divide Korea shape the course of Korean history and influence the cold war?*

26.6 General Douglas MacArthur, Report to Congress, April 19, 1951: "Old Soldiers Never Die"

General of the Army Douglas MacArthur (1880–1964), who was much respected by the World War II generation of Americans as the successful Allied Supreme Commander of forces in the Pacific and then head of the military government of Japan, opposed "containment" as too passive at best and as "appeasement" at worst. Appointed as commander of UN forces at the outbreak of the Korean War, MacArthur's disagreements with President Truman over how aggressively the United States should pursue the Korean War led to his dismissal in April 1951. In possession of a substantial following among Americans, MacArthur was invited to address a joint session of Congress to report on the situation in the Far East, an occasion he used to advocate widening the scope of war measures against communism there. The ballad that he cites near the end gave the speech a familiar name. No less than five recording companies issued releases of the song, which became an immediate hit, at least one version including a new final verse, which began:

Washington and Grant and Lee were all tried and true,
Eisenhower, Bradley, [pause] and MacArthur too!

Source: From United States Congressional Record, "Address of General of the Army Douglas MacArthur," 82nd Congress, 1st Session, 19 April 1951, pp. 4123–25.

I address you with neither rancor nor bitterness in the fading twilight of life with but one purpose in mind—to serve my country.

The issues are global and so interlocked that to consider the problem of one sector, oblivious to those of another, is but to court disaster of the whole. . . .

The Communist threat is a global one. Its successful advance in one sector threatens the destruction of every other sector. You cannot appease or otherwise surrender to communism in Asia without simultaneously undermining our efforts to halt its advance in Europe.

Beyond pointing out these simple truisms, I shall confine my discussion to the general areas of Asia. Before one may objectively assess the situation now existing there, he must comprehend something of Asia's past and the revolutionary changes which have marked her course up to the present. Long exploited by the so-called colonial powers, with little opportunity to achieve any degree of social justice, individual dignity, or a higher standard of life such as guided our own noble administration of the Philippines, the peoples of Asia found their opportunity in the war just past to throw off the shackles of colonialism, and now see the dawn of new opportunity, a heretofore unfelt dignity and the self-respect of political freedom.

Mustering half of the earth's population and 60 percent of its natural resources, these peoples are rapidly consolidating a new force, both moral and material, with which to raise the living standard and erect adaptations of the design of modern progress to their own distinct cultural environments. . . .

Our strategic frontier [has] shifted to embrace the entire Pacific Ocean, which became a vast moat to protect us as long as we hold it. Indeed, it acts as a protective shield for all of the Americas and all free lands of the Pacific Ocean area. We control it to the shores of Asia by a chain of islands extending in an arc from the Aleutians to the Mariannas held by us and our free allies.

From this island chain we can dominate with sea and air power every Asiatic port from Vladivostok to Singapore and prevent any hostile movement into the Pacific. Any predatory attack from Asia must be an amphibious effort. No amphibious force can be successful without control of the sea lanes and the air over those lanes in its avenue of advance. With naval and air supremacy and modest ground elements to defend bases, any major attack from continental Asia toward us or our friends of the Pacific would be doomed to failure. . . .

The holding of this littoral defense line in the western Pacific is entirely dependent upon holding all segments thereof, for any major breach of that line by an unfriendly power would render vulnerable to determined attack every other major segment. This is a military estimate as to which I have yet to find a military leader who will take exception. For that reason I have strongly recommended in the past as a matter of military urgency that under no circumstances must Formosa fall under Communist control. Such an eventuality would at once threaten the freedom of the Philippines and the loss of Japan, and might well force our western frontier back to the coasts of California, Oregon, and Washington. . . .

At the turn of the century, . . . efforts toward greater homogeneity produced the start of a nationalist urge [in China]. This was further and more successfully developed under the leadership of Chiang Kai-shek, but has been brought to its greatest fruition under the present regime, to the point that it has now taken on the character of a united nationalism of increasingly dominant aggressive tendencies.

Through these past fifty years, the Chinese people have thus become militarized in their concepts and in their ideals. They now constitute excellent soldiers with competent staffs and commanders. This has produced a new and dominant power in Asia which for its own purposes is allied with Soviet Russia, but which in its own concepts and methods has become aggressively imperialistic with a lust for expansion and increased power normal to this type of imperialism. There is little of the ideological concept either one way or another in the Chinese make-up. The standard of living is so low and the capital accumulation has been so thoroughly dissipated by war that the masses are desperate and avid to follow any leadership which seems to promise the alleviation of local stringencies.

I have from the beginning believed that the Chinese Communists' support of the Koreans was the dominant one. Their interests are at present parallel to those of the Soviet, but I believe that the aggressiveness recently displayed not only in Korea, but also in Indochina and Tibet, and pointing potentially toward the south, reflects predominantly the same lust for the expansion of power which has animated every would-be conqueror since the beginning of time.

The Japanese people since the war have undergone the greatest reformation recorded in modern history. With a commendable will, eagerness to learn, and marked capacity to understand, they have, from the ashes left in war's wake, erected in Japan an edifice dedicated to the primacy of individual liberty and personal dignity, and in the ensuing process there has been created a truly representative government committed to the advance of political morality, freedom of economic enterprise, and social justice. Politically, economically and socially Japan is now abreast of many free nations of the earth and will not again fail the universal trust. . . .

I sent all four of our occupation divisions to the Korean battlefront without the slightest qualms as to the effect of the resulting power vacuum upon Japan. The results fully justified my faith. I know of no nation more serene, orderly and industrious—nor in which higher hopes can be entertained for future constructive service in the advance of the human race. . . .

On Formosa, the government of the Republic of China has had the opportunity to refute by action much of the malicious gossip which so undermined the strength of its leadership on the Chinese mainland. The Formosan people are receiving a just and enlightened administration with majority representation on the organs of government; and politically, economically, and socially they appear to be advancing along sound and constructive lines.

With this brief insight into the surrounding areas I now turn to the Korean conflict. While I was not consulted prior to the President's decision to intervene in support of the Republic of Korea, that decision, from a military standpoint, proved a sound one as we hurled back the invader and decimated his forces. Our victory was complete and our objectives within reach when Red China intervened with numerically superior ground forces. This created a new war and an entirely new situation—a situation not contemplated when our forces were committed against the North Korean invaders—a situation which called for new decisions in the diplomatic sphere to permit the realistic adjustment of military strategy. Such decisions have not been forthcoming.

While no man in his right mind would advocate sending our ground forces into continental China, and such was never given a thought, the new situation did urgently demand a drastic revision of strategic planning if our political aim was to defeat this new enemy as we had defeated the old.

Apart from the military need as I saw it to neutralize the sanctuary protection given the enemy north of the Yalu, I felt that military necessity in the conduct of the war made mandatory:

1. The intensification of our economic blockade against China;
2. The imposition of a naval blockade against the China coast;
3. Removal of restrictions on air reconnaissance of China's coastal areas and of Manchuria;
4. Removal of restrictions on the forces of the Republic of China on Formosa with logistical support to contribute to their effective operations against the common enemy.

For entertaining these views, all professionally designed to support our forces committed to Korea and bring hostilities to an end with the least possible delay and at a saving of countless American and Allied lives, I have been severely criticized in lay circles, principally abroad, despite my understanding that from a military standpoint the above views have been fully shared in the past by practically every military leader concerned with the Korean campaign, including our own Joint Chiefs of Staff.

I called for reinforcements, but was informed that reinforcements were not available. I made clear that if not permitted to destroy the [enemy] build-up bases north of the Yalu; if not permitted to utilize the friendly Chinese force of some 600,000 men on Formosa; if not permitted to blockade the China coast to prevent the Chinese Reds from getting succor from without; and if there were to be no hope of major reinforcements, the position of the command from the military standpoint forbade victory. We could hold in Korea by constant maneuver and at an approximate area where our supply line advantages were in balance with the supply line disadvantages of the enemy, but we could hope at best for only an indecisive campaign, with its terrible and constant attrition upon our forces if the enemy utilized his full military potential.

I have constantly called for the new political decisions essential to a solution. Efforts have been made to distort my position. It has been said, in effect, that I am a warmonger. Nothing could be further from the truth. I know war as few other men now living know it, and nothing to me is more revolting. I have long advocated its complete abolition as its very destructiveness on both friend and foe has rendered it useless as a means of settling international disputes. . . .

There are some who for varying reasons would appease Red China. They are blind to history's clear lesson; for history teaches with unmistakable emphasis that appeasement but begets new and bloodier war. It points to no single instance where the end has justified that means—where appeasement has led to more than a sham peace. Like blackmail, it lays the basis for new and successively greater demands, until, as in blackmail, violence becomes the only other alternative.

Why, my soldiers asked of me, surrender military advantages to an enemy in the field? I could not answer. Some may say to avoid spread of the conflict into an all-out war with China; others, to avoid Soviet intervention. Neither explanation seems valid. For China is already engaging with the maximum power it can commit and the Soviets will not necessarily mesh its actions with our moves. Like a cobra, any new enemy will more likely strike whenever it feels that the relativity in military or other potential is in its favor on a worldwide basis.

The tragedy of Korea is further heightened by the fact that as military action is confined to its territorial limits, it condemns that nation, which it is our purpose to save, to suffer the devastating impact of full naval and air bombardment, while the enemy's sanctuaries are fully protected from such attack and devastation. Of the nations of the world, Korea alone, up to now, is the sole one which has risked its all against communism. The magnificence of the courage and fortitude of the Korean people defies description. They have chosen to risk death rather than slavery. Their last words to me were "Don't scuttle the Pacific."

I have just left your fighting sons in Korea. They have met all tests there and I can report to you without reservation they are splendid in every way. It was my constant effort to preserve them and end this savage conflict honorably and with the least loss of time and a minimum sacrifice of life. Its growing bloodshed has caused me the deepest anguish and anxiety. Those gallant men will remain often in my thoughts and in my prayers always.

I am closing my fifty-two years of military service. When I joined the Army, even before the turn of the century, it was the fulfillment of all my boyish hopes and dreams. The world has turned over many times since I took the oath on the plain at West Point, and the hopes and dreams have long since vanished. But I still remember the refrain of one of the most popular barrack ballads of that day which proclaimed most proudly that "Old soldiers never die. They just fade away."

And like the old soldier of that ballad, I now close my military career and just fade away—an old soldier who tried to do his duty as God gave him the light to see that duty.

Goodbye.

Questions:

1. *In a speech to the Texas legislature some three months after his Report to Congress, MacArthur called the Truman administration's policy "appeasement on the battlefield, whereunder we soften our blows, withhold our power, and surrender military advantages, in apparent hope that some nebulous way by doing so a potential enemy be coerced to desist from attacking us."[1] Did Truman's policy or MacArthur's—outlined below—make more sense in the conflict in Korea? Was "containment" really "appeasement"? Did it tend to leave the initiative for international action with Communist adversaries during the cold war? Was it ultimately successful?*
2. *How does MacArthur allude to the relationship between China and Taiwan (Formosa)? How would you assess his proposed Taiwan policies and predictions half a century later?*
3. *Some forceful rhetoric in April 1951, including slogans on placards and bumper stickers, called for the impeachment of President Truman for his firing of MacArthur. How much chance do you think impeachment proceedings really had?*

26.7   Henry A. Myers, "East Berliners Rise Up Against Soviet Oppression," A Personal Account

After Stalin's death in March 1953, the less-threatening plural leadership in the USSR probably expected the people of Eastern Europe under Soviet control to look for some increase in political freedom and perhaps improvements in their standards of living. Those leaders seem not to have expected that a willingness on their part to listen to complaints would be taken as a sign of weakness and would lead to revolt.

In the early postwar period, East Germany appeared to have the native regime most obedient to the USSR and the most passive population in Soviet-occupied Eastern Europe. Yet even there demands for change rose in the spring of 1953. Student groups hoped for some freedom of the press. Workers sought improvements in pay and length of the workweek: A particular complaint was the regime's insistence on "voluntary," that is, unpaid, Saturday afternoon work of clearing away rubble at sites still not repaired or rebuilt since the end of the war—this following regular Saturday-morning work in the forty-five-hour workweek.

The Eisenhower-Nixon campaign for the American presidency in 1952 had stressed "rolling back the tide of communism in Eastern Europe" as a foreign policy objective along with an honorable end to the Korean War. Many East German students and workers took this to mean that if Eastern Europeans rose up against their Soviet occupiers, the new president would send American troops to help them. In June 1953, American-sponsored radio broadcasts did not promise American aid, but by reporting news of snowballing protests in major East German cities and Soviet inaction, these broadcasts did much to encourage dissidents to press their demands. By June 16, crowds in moods of rebellion appeared to be in control of main streets in many cities, most of all in East Berlin.

The author of the following piece, then a nineteen-year-old U.S. student in West Berlin, enjoyed a pleasantly exciting morning on June 17, the peak of revolutionary activity in East Berlin, when protesters spoke enthusiastically of the American support they thought was coming. In the afternoon, however, when Russian troops systematically put down the uprising with tanks followed by soldiers with sub-machine guns and others with bayonets, separating the massive crowds into manageable clusters, it became evident that the demonstrating, rock-throwing opponents of the regime were on their own.

Source: From *The Daily Mail,* Vol. CXXV, No. 148 (Hagerstown, Maryland: June 25, 1953), pp. 1–2. Reprinted by permission. Footnotes added.

Stretched across Berlin's broadest avenue, with massive bomb-scarred columns towering 40 feet above the street, stands a stone arch, the Brandenburger Tor. A red flag, large enough to be seen flapping miles away, flies day and night from the roof of the arch here on the border between East and West Berlin. The red flag is a symbol of Soviet control in East Germany, a control that for eight years has gone unquestioned and untested.

With the last subway to cross the East-West border before the anti-Soviet uprising shut down all means of transportation, I arrived at Alexanderplatz, Soviet Berlin's main business section, on the morning of June 17. Scattered crowds of protestors had been gathering since the evening before and now a full-scale riot was breaking out. The streets were jammed with Berliner workers by the thousands, who were jeering in chorus at the trucks of Russian troops being driven by to intimidate them. A week before, an open complaint against the puppet government (which clamors its single-minded purpose of running a "workers' government" while in reality exploiting the workers with extra long hours under the worst of working conditions coupled with high prices out of the workers' reach in the government-owned stores) could never have been heard on the street where giant posters of government bosses Pieck, Grotewohl, and Ulbricht,[1] stared from every flat wall surrounded by banners and slogans, and patrols of carbine-carrying "Vopos," German "People's Police," who do the dirty work of the Russian occupation, policed the streets. But that morning the defiant mob had ripped every poster within reach into pieces and trampled the fragments along with the red flags on the muddy cobblestones. As the troop-trucks of Russian soldiers continued to roll by, the demonstrators chanted in unison "Down with the clique of pointed beards," meaning Ulbricht and his hirelings, and "Bread! Free elections! A united Germany!" There was a mixture of surprise and anger on the faces of the Russian soldiers as if a workers' uprising against a "workers' government" just couldn't be. Some of them attempted to laugh it off and waved their hats with broad grins at the fist-shaking mob, who cleared up any doubts by showering the soldiers with stone fragments and yelling "Go home!" in German and Russian.

As the last troop truck rolled by, the crowd pressed into the street and surrounded several cars that were trying to make their way through. Car doors were ripped open and bureaucrats yanked out and thrown against the curb, while workers tore up and scattered their party-record books and wrecked their cars. One wrinkled little man clung fast to his steering wheel and pleaded with the crowd: "But I'm a worker!" "A worker!" shouted an exasperated young hausfrau, "If you were a worker, you wouldn't have a car to drive." Finally the little man produced papers to show that he was only a messenger for the film industry and was allowed to drive away on four wheels. Others weren't so lucky. A little farther down the street we came to a battered door, then a tire-rim followed by a battery and an inner-tube and finally a burning heap of unclassified rubbish. "What's that?" I asked. The answer was prompt but calm, "Oh, they found a real Bonzen [government boss] driving it."

Soon a parade of demonstrators, thousands strong, was headed for the headquarters of the hated Vopos. The crowd collected bricks from nearby ruins and began to heave them through the windows, when suddenly the Vopos swarmed out of the building and began beating the crowd back with riot clubs. Part of the crowd stampeded and we were forced through the narrow gateway of a courtyard opposite the headquarters. From the street we heard pistol volleys from the Vopos and a rain of brick fragments in answer, but it was not until we were able to push out of the courtyard again that we saw what had really happened. The Vopos had been driven back into their building by the enraged demonstrators who were helping some of their badly beaten wounded away. Four huge black squad cars lay on their side engulfed in flames.

The uprising was in full sway. Back at Alexanderplatz, children climbed to the top of the "Monument to German Soviet Friendship" and tore loose the wooden decorations and glass-framed pictures of Stalin, smashing them on the sidewalk below. By this time the panic-stricken government had sent out a general alarm. Help came in the form of Russian troops and Vopos, heavy tanks and gun wagons. At Alexanderplatz, a man was brutally smashed by a tank as the reenforcements rolled by. The groups of demonstrators were cut off from each other as the tanks zigzagged down the streets, churning up the cobblestones as they collided with the sidewalks. A Russian officer stood in the turret of the lead tank and directed the panzers with a pretentious sweep of his cane. Squads of soldiers sprang from the trucks and advanced on the demonstrators with fixed bayonets, firing machine gun bursts over their heads.

Yet the workers were far from finished. On the parade street "Unter den Linden," they reassembled and even erected a crude wooden cross where one of their members had been shot by a Vopo. An hour before, two East Berliners had scrambled atop the Brandenburger Tor and thrown down the symbolic red flag into a crowd on the West Berlin side, where it was burned under the arch. Now the East Berliners organized for a last march past the Soviet panzers and Vopo troops, down the parade street, and through the Brandenburger Tor into the West. We joined the ranks, which had been considerably thinned through the Soviet maneuvers, behind two young workers carrying the black, gold, and red German flag. Suddenly over the street-corner loudspeakers came a sharp announcement: "By order of the Soviet Commander, East Berlin has been placed under martial law. Curfew is declared from 9 p.m. until 5 a.m. Gatherings of more than three persons are strictly forbidden." Suddenly the demonstrators broke into a run. As the first ranks passed through under the arch into the free West, the marchers struck up a chorus of "Deutschland über alles,"[2] which was taken up by the waiting crowd on the other side.

A few minutes later, several young demonstrators appeared on the roof of the arch and fastened three flags to the huge mast. Others followed after them, bringing flags and emblems of all sorts. A tall blond girl stood in the middle of the assemblage on the roof and waved the black, gold, and red flag as the cheers from below reached a climax. Suddenly the little group stiffened and as the crowd looked on in silent horror, the girl walked to the West edge of the arch-roof and dropped the flag over the side. We soon learned why. From the East side of the arch, a Russian gun wagon had pulled up and focused its MGs on the arch-roof. Machine-gun bursts methodically strafed the small staircase leading down from the roof. Only with the aid of a long pole and a rope were the six able to reach the street on the western side where they were carried on the shoulders of the crowd and bestowed with presents of cigarettes—a tribute which in postwar Germany was no meager honor.

That evening as Russian troop trucks and tanks were still stationed behind the Brandenburger Tor and the East Berlin horizon was still discolored with smoke from burning government-owned booths and stands throughout the city, the Russians removed the rebellious German flags and hoisted a new red one over the arch. But the new flag was little more than half the size of the monstrous red banner Berliners were used to and looked conspicuously bare on the huge mast. Berliners on the way home could feel that, unconscious though it was, the change in the size of the red flag behind them also marked a whittling down of Soviet confidence as the Russians reviewed their control in East Germany and counted on its support in the Cold War.

Questions:
1. *Before 1953 the (West) German Federal Republic had no holidays commemorating national personages or events. Why was there a certain logic in celebrating June 17 as "Day of German Unity"?*
2. *Why do you suppose that although the June Uprising was generally applauded in Western Europe and the United States, there were some less than enthusiastic responses there also?*
3. *What lessons do you think other Eastern Europeans in the Soviet bloc drew (or failed to draw) from the June Uprising and the American response?*

26.8 "The Victory of Communism Is Inevitable!": Speech to the 22nd Communist Party Congress (1962): Nikita Khrushchev

After Stalin's death in 1953, the power vacuum was eventually filled by Sergeyevich (Nikita) Khrushchev. At the 20th Communist Party Congress, Khrushchev quite unexpectedly attacked Stalin and his legacy of fear. The Soviets were looking for a new beginning. Although there may have been hope that the fears of the Cold War would be reduced, the decade from 1955 to 1966 was especially intense in its rhetoric and ideological conflict. As Khrushchev menacingly said of capitalist states in 1956, "Whether you like it or not, history is on our side. We will bury you!" This was the era of Senator Joseph McCarthy, who played on the fears of Americans with his deceitful rantings that communists had infiltrated the highest echelons of government. It was during this time (1961) that the Berlin Wall was built, sealing off the city into communist and democratic sectors—a symbolic as well as practical measure. And finally, in 1962, the two superpowers nearly went to nuclear war as President Kennedy demanded the removal of Soviet missiles from Cuba. The following excerpt is from Khrushchev's speech to the 22nd Congress of the Communist party. Note the argument carefully.

Source: Translation copyright 1962 by *The Current Digest of the Soviet Press,* published weekly at Columbus, Ohio. Reprinted by permission of the *Digest.*

The most rabid imperialists, acting on the principle of "after us the deluge," openly voice their desire to undertake a new war venture. The ideologists of imperialism, intimidating the peoples, try to instill a kind of philosophy of hopelessness and desperation. Hysterically they cry: "Better death under capitalism than life under communism." They do not like free peoples to flourish, you see. They fear that the peoples in their countries too will take the path of socialism. Blinded by class hatred, our enemies are ready to doom all mankind to the catastrophe of war. The imperialists' opportunities to carry out their aggressive designs, however, are becoming smaller and smaller. They behave like a feeble and greedy old man whose powers have been exhausted, whose physical capacity has weakened, but whose avid desires remain. . . .

As long as the imperialist aggressors exist, we must be on guard, keep our powder dry, improve the defense of the socialist countries, their armed forces and the state security agencies. If, in the face of common sense, the imperialists dare attack the socialist countries and plunge mankind into the abyss of a world war of annihilation, this mad act of theirs would be their last, it would be the end of the whole system of capitalism. *(Applause.)*

Our party clearly understands its tasks, its responsibility, and will do everything in its power to see to it that the world socialist system continues to grow stronger, gathers fresh strength and develops. We believe that in the competition with capitalism socialism will win. *(Prolonged applause.)* We believe that this victory will be won in peaceful competition and not by way of unleashing a war. We have stood, we stand and we will stand by the positions of peaceful competition of states with different social systems; we will do everything to strengthen world peace. *(Prolonged applause.)*

The most important component of our party's foreign policy activities is *the struggle for general and complete disarmament.* The Soviet Union has been waging this struggle for many years now, and doing so firmly and perseveringly. We have always been resolutely opposed to the arms race, since rivalry in this sphere in the past not only saddled the peoples with a terrible burden but inevitably led to world wars. We are even more resolutely opposed to the arms race now that there has been a colossal technical revolution in the art of war and the use of today's weapons would inevitably entail the deaths of hundreds of millions of people.

The stockpiling of these weapons, proceeding as it is in a setting of cold war and war hysteria, is fraught with disastrous consequences. All that has to happen is for the nerves of some fellow in uniform to crack while he is on duty at a "push-button" somewhere in the West, and things may happen that will bring more than a little misfortune upon the peoples of the whole world.

Naturally, when we put forward a program of general and complete disarmament, we are talking not about the unilateral disarmament of socialism in the face of imperialism or vice versa, but about universal renunciation of arms as a means of solving problems at issue among states. . . .

The example of the Soviet Union inspires all progressive mankind. Never has the great vital force of Marxist-Leninist teaching been so clearly evident as in our days, now that socialism has triumphed fully and finally in the Soviet Union, the cause of socialism is winning new victories in the countries of the world socialist commonwealth, and the international Communist and workers' movement and the national liberation struggle of peoples are growing and expanding tempestuously.

The revolution awakened the great energy of peoples, which is transforming the world on the principles of socialism and communism. Colossal changes are taking place and will take place throughout the world under the influence of the successes of communism.

The victory of communism is inevitable! *(Stormy applause.)*

The great army of Communists and of Marxist- Leninists acts as the vanguard of the peoples in the struggle for peace, for social progress and for communism, the bright future of mankind. New and ever newer millions of people will assemble and rally under the great banner of communism. The cause of progress, the cause of communism will triumph! *(Stormy applause.)*

Long live the great and heroic Soviet people, the builders of communism! *(Stormy applause.)*

Long live the indestructible unity and fraternal friendship of the peoples of the world socialist camp! *(Stormy applause.)*

Long live the heroic party of the Communists of the Soviet Union, created and tempered in struggle by the great Lenin! *(Stormy applause.)*

Long live the indestructible unity of the international Communist and workers' movement and the fraternal solidarity of the proletarians of all countries! *(Stormy applause.)*

Long live peace the world over! *(Stormy applause.)*

Under the all-conquering banner of Marxism- Leninism, under the leadership of the Communist Party, forward to the victory of communism! *(Stormy, prolonged applause, turning into an ovation. All rise.)*

Question:
1. What are the main points about capitalism and communism that Khrushchev stressed in his speech to the 22nd Communist Party Congress?

PART 27
Decolonization

27.1 Mohandas K. Gandhi

Mohandas K. Gandhi (1869-1948), known and revered throughout the world as Mahatma ("the Great Souled"), was one of the most influential figures in the political history of the twentieth century. Largely because of his tireless activities over a period of more than thirty years, India finally won its independence from British rule in 1947.

Gandhi's method for gaining his goal of Swaraj, or Home Rule, for India was extraordinary. Unlike most nationalists, who relied on arms to expel their oppressors, Gandhi repudiated the use of force in any form. His weapon was, in his language, satyagraha. This is a difficult term to translate into English. It is usually translated as "passive resistance" and Gandhi himself does so in the selection that follows. But he nevertheless insisted that this rendering fails to capture its essence. Literally the term means "insistence on truth" and Gandhi generally equated it with such phrases as "truth-force" or "soul-force." In political action this meant the practice of disobeying laws imposed by the government that Gandhi considered to be unjust and then accepting the consequences of his disobedience. As a result of his use of satyagraha, Gandhi was arrested on innumerable occasions, spending nearly seven years of his life behind bars. But with every incarceration his reputation and the body of his followers grew.

Gandhi was a deeply religious man, drawing his faith from a variety of sources. Central was his native Hindu religion, with its emphasis on nonviolence and its indifference to the comforts of material existence. But this was overlaid with ideas he had imbibed as a youthful law student in London, including the Christianity of the Sermon on the Mount and the pacifistic anarchism of the Russian, Peter Kropotkin (1842-1921). Finally, he was imbued with a deep moral sense, which led him to follow the guidance of his conscience, whatever the personal consequences might be.

Gandhi's life ended tragically. Following India's independence, its Hindu and Muslim populations found themselves in bitter internal conflict. Gandhi did his best to resolve the differences between them, but this led to antagonism against him by extremists from both camps. Early in 1948 he was assassinated by a young Hindu zealot while kneeling at his morning prayers. But there may be an even greater tragedy to relate. Gandhi was strongly opposed to what he considered to be the materialism of modern Western civilization and tried throughout his career to prevent the Westernization of India. In this he had some success, leading a movement to return Indian civilization to an earlier, simpler mode of life. It is hard, therefore, to believe that Gandhi would have looked on the subsequent history of his native land with anything but despair.

Source: Gandhi, *Mohandas K., Hind Swaraj or Indian Home Rule* (Ahmedabad: Navajivan Publishing House, 1938). Courtesy of The Navajivan Trust.

HIND SWARAJ OR INDIAN HOME RULE

READER: ...Will you tell me something of what you have read and thought of [modern] civilization?

EDITOR: Let us first consider what state of things is described by the word "civilization." Its true test lies in the fact that people living in it make bodily welfare the object of life. We will take some examples. The people of Europe today live in better-built houses than they did a hundred years ago. This is considered an emblem of civilization, and this is also a matter to promote bodily happiness. Formerly, they wore skins, and used spears as their weapons. Now, they wear long trousers, and, for embellishing their bodies, they wear a variety of clothing, and, instead of spears, they carry with them revolvers containing five or more chambers. If people of a certain country, who have hitherto not been in the habit of wearing much clothing, boots, etc., adopt European clothing, they are supposed to have become civilized out of savagery. Formerly, in Europe, people ploughed their lands mainly by manual labour. Now, one man can plough a vast tract by means of steam engines and can thus amass great wealth. This is called a sign of civilization. Formerly, only a few men wrote valuable books. Now, anybody writes and prints anything he likes and poisons people's minds. Formerly, men traveled in wagons. Now, they fly through the air in trains at the rate of four hundred and more miles per day. This is considered the height of civilization. It has been stated that, as men progress, they shall be able to travel in airships and reach any part of the world in a few hours. Men will not need the use of their hands and feet. They will press a button, and they will have their clothing by their side. They will press another button, and they will have their newspaper. A third, and a motor-car will be in waiting for them. They will have a variety of delicately dished up food. Everything will be done by machinery. Formerly, when people wanted to fight with one another, they measured between them their bodily strength; now it is possible to take away thousands of lives by one man working behind a gun from a hill. This is civilization. Formerly, men worked in the open air only as much as they liked. Now thousands of workmen meet together and for the sake of maintenance work in factories or mines. Their condition is worse than that of beasts. They are obliged to work, at the risk of their lives, at most dangerous occupations, for the sake of millionaires. Formerly, men were made slaves under physical compulsion. Now they are enslaved by temptation of money and of the luxuries that money can buy. There are now diseases of which people never dreamt before, and an army of doctors is engaged in finding out their cures, and so hospitals have increased. This is a test of civilization. Formerly, special messengers were required and much expense was incurred in order to send letters; today, anyone can abuse his fellow by means of a letter for one penny. True, at the same cost, one can send one's thanks also. Formerly, people had two or three meals consisting of home-made bread and vegetables; now, they require something to eat every two hours so that they have hardly leisure for anything else. What more need I say? All this you can ascertain from several authoritative books. These are all true tests of civilization. And if anyone speaks to the contrary, know that he is ignorant. This civilization takes note neither of morality nor of religion. Its votaries calmly state that their business is not to teach religion. Some even consider it to be a superstitious growth. Others put on the cloak of religion, and prate about morality. But, after twenty years' experience, I have come to the conclusion that immorality is often taught in the name of morality.

Even a child can understand that in all I have described above there can be no inducement to morality. Civilization seeks to increase bodily comforts, and it fails miserably even in doing so.

. . .

READER: . . . What, then, is [true] civilization?

EDITOR: The answer to that question is not difficult. I believe that the civilization India has evolved is not to be beaten in the world. Nothing can equal the seeds sown by our ancestors. Rome went, Greece shared the same fate; the might of the Pharaohs was broken; Japan has become westernized; of China nothing can be said; but India is still, somehow or other, sound at the foundation. The people of Europe learn their lessons from the writings of the men of Greece or Rome, which exist no longer in their former glory. In trying to learn from them, the Europeans imagine that they will avoid the mistakes of Greece and Rome. Such is their pitiable condition. In the midst of all this India remains immoveable and that is her glory. It is a charge against India that her people are so uncivilized, ignorant and stolid, that it is not possible to induce them to adopt any changes. It is a charge really against our merit. What we have tested and found true on the anvil of experience, we dare not change. Many thrust their advice upon India, and she remains steady. This is her beauty; it is the sheet-anchor of our hope.

Civilization is that mode of conduct which points out to man the path of duty. Performance of duty and observance of morality are convertible terms. To observe morality is to attain mastery over our mind and our passions. So doing, we know ourselves. The Gujarati equivalent for civilization means "good conduct."

If this definition be correct, then India, as so many writers have shown, has nothing to learn from anybody else, and this is as it should be. We notice that the mind is a restless bird; the more it gets the more it wants, and still remains unsatisfied. The more we indulge our passions the more unbridled they become. Our ancestors, therefore, set a limit to our indulgences. They saw that happiness was largely a mental condition. A man is not necessarily happy because he is rich, or unhappy because he is poor. The rich are often seen to be unhappy, the poor to be happy. Millions will always remain poor. Observing all this, our ancestors dissuaded us from luxuries and pleasures. We have managed with the same kind of plough as existed thousands of years ago. We have retained the same kind of cottages that we had in former times and our indigenous education remains the same as before. We have had no system of life-corroding competition. Each followed his own occupation or trade and charged a regulation wage. It was not that we did not know how to invent machinery, but our forefathers knew that, if we set our hearts after such things, we would become slaves and lose our moral fibre. They, therefore, after due deliberation decided that we should only do what we could with our hands and feet. They saw that our real happiness and health consisted in a proper use of our hands and feet. They further reasoned that large cities were a snare and a useless encumbrance and that people would not be happy in them, that there would be gangs of thieves and robbers, prostitution and vice flourishing in them and that poor men would be robbed by rich men. They were, therefore, satisfied with small villages. They saw that kings and their swords were inferior to the sword of ethics, and they, therefore, held the sovereigns of the earth to be inferior to the Rishis and the Fakirs. A nation with a constitution like this is fitter to teach others than to learn from others. This nation had courts, lawyers and doctors, but they were all within bounds. Everybody knew that these professions were not particularly superior; moreover, these vakils and vaids did not rob people; they were considered people's dependants, not their masters. Justice was tolerably fair. The ordinary rule was to avoid courts. There were no touts to lure people into them. This evil, too, was noticeable only in and around capitals. The common people lived independently and followed their agricultural occupation. They enjoyed true Home Rule.

And where this cursed modern civilization has not reached, India remains as it was before. The inhabitants of that part of India will very properly laugh at your newfangled notions. The English do not rule over them, nor will you ever rule over them. Those in whose name we speak we do not know, nor do they know us. I would certainly advise you and those like you who love the motherland to go into the interior that has yet been not polluted by the railways and to live there for six months; you might then be patriotic and speak of Home Rule.

Now you see what I consider to be real civilization. Those who want to change conditions such as I have described are enemies of the country and are sinners.

READER: It would be all right if India were exactly as you have described it, but it is also India where there are hundreds of child widows, where two-year-old babies are married, where twelve-year-old girls are mothers and house wives, where women practice polyandry, where the practice of Niyoga obtains, where, in the name of religion, girls dedicate themselves to prostitution, and in the name of religion sheep and goats are killed. Do you consider these also symbols of the civilization that you have described?

EDITOR: You make a mistake. The defects that you have shown are defects. Nobody mistakes them for ancient civilization. They remain in spite of it. Attempts have always been made and will be made to remove them. We may utilize the new spirit that is born in us for purging ourselves of these evils. But what I have described to you as emblems of modern civilization are accepted as such by its votaries. The Indian civilization, as described by me, has been so described by its votaries. In no part of the world, and under no civilization, have all men attained perfection. The tendency of the Indian civilization is to elevate the moral being, that of the Western civilization is to propagate immorality. The latter is godless, the former is based on a belief in God. So understanding and so believing, it behooves every lover of India to cling to the old Indian civilization even as a child clings to the mother's breast.

READER: I appreciate your views about civilization. I will have to think over them. I cannot take them in all at once. What, then, holding the views you do, would you suggest for freeing India?

EDITOR: I do not expect my views to be accepted all of a sudden. My duty is to place them before readers like yourself. Time can be trusted to do the rest. We have already examined the conditions for freeing India, but we have done so indirectly; we will now do so directly. It is a world-known maxim that the removal of the cause of a disease results in the removal of the disease itself. Similarly if the cause of India's slavery be removed, India can become free.

READER: If Indian civilization is, as you say, the best of all, how do you account for India's slavery?

EDITOR: This civilization is unquestionably the best, but it is to be observed that all civilizations have been on their trial. That civilization which is permanent outlives it. Because the sons of India were found wanting, its civilization has been placed in jeopardy. But its strength is to be seen in its ability to survive the shock. Moreover, the whole of India is not touched. Those alone who have been affected by Western civilization have become enslaved. We measure the universe by our own miserable foot-rule. When we are slaves, we think that the whole universe is enslaved. Because we are in an abject condition, we think that the whole of India is in that condition. As a matter of fact, it is not so, yet it is as well to impute our slavery to the whole of India. But if we bear in mind the above fact, we can see that if we become free, India is free. And in this thought you have a definition of *Swaraj*. It is *Swaraj* when we learn to rule ourselves. It is, therefore, in the palm of our hands. Do not consider this *Swaraj* to be like a dream. There is no idea of sitting still. The *Swaraj* that I wish to picture is such that, after we have once realized it, we shall endeavour to the end of our life-time to persuade others to do likewise. But such *Swaraj* has to be experienced, by each one for himself. One drowning man will never save another. Slaves ourselves, it would be a mere pretension to think of freeing others. Now you will have seen that it is not necessary for us to have as our goal the expulsion of the English. If the English become Indianized, we can accommodate them. If they wish to remain in India along with their civilization, there is no room for them. It lies with us to bring about such a state of things.

. . .

READER: . . . You know that what the English obtained in their own country they obtained by using brute force. I know you have argued that what they have obtained is useless, but that does not affect my argument. They wanted useless things and they got them. My point is that their desire was fulfilled. What does it matter what means they adopted? Why should we not obtain our goal, which is good, by any means whatsoever, even by using violence?

EDITOR: . . .Two kinds of force can back petitions. "We shall hurt you if you do not give this," is one kind of force; it is the force of arms, whose evil results we have already examined. The second kind of force can thus be stated: "If you do not concede our demand, we shall be no longer your petitioners. You can govern us only so long as we remain the governed; we shall no longer have any dealings with you." The force implied in this may be described as love-force, soul-force, or more popularly, but less accurately, passive resistance. This force is indestructible. He who uses it perfectly understands his position. We have an ancient proverb which literally means: "One negative cures thirty-six diseases." The force of arms is powerless when matched against the force of love or the soul.

. . .

READER: Is there any historical evidence as to the success of what you have called soul-force or truth-force? No instance seems to have happened of any nation having risen through soul-force. I still think that the evildoers will not cease doing evil without physical punishment.

EDITOR: The poet Tulsidas has said:

"Of religion, pity, or love, is the root, as egotism of the body. Therefore, we should not abandon pity so long as we are alive." This appears to me to be a scientific truth. I believe in it as much as I believe in two and two being four. The force of love is the same as the force of the soul or truth. We have evidence of its working at every step. The universe would disappear without the existence of that force. But you ask for historical evidence. It is, therefore, necessary to know what history means. The Gujarati equivalent means: "It so happened." If that is the meaning of history, it is possible to give copious evidence. But, if it means the doings of kings and emperors, there can be no evidence of soul-force or passive resistance in such history. You cannot expect silver ore in a tin mine. History, as we know it, is a record of the wars of the world; and so there is a proverb among Englishmen that a nation which has no history, that is, no wars, is a happy nation. How kings played, how they became enemies of one another, how they murdered one another, is found accurately recorded in history, and if this were all that had happened in the world, it would have been ended long ago. If the story of the universe had commenced with wars, not a man would have been found alive today. Those people who have been warred against have disappeared as, for instance, the natives of Australia of whom hardly a man was left alive by the intruders. Mark, please, that these natives did not use soul-force in self-defense, and it does not require much foresight to know that the Australians will share the same fate as their victims. "Those that take the sword shall perish by the sword." With us the proverb is that professional swimmers will find a watery grave.

The fact that there are so many men still alive in the world shows that it is based not on the force of arms but on the force of truth or love. Therefore, the greatest and most unimpeachable evidence of the success of the force is to be found in the fact that, in spite of the wars of the world, it still lives on.

Thousands, indeed tens of thousands, depend for their existence on a very active working of this force. Little quarrels of millions of families in their daily lives disappear before the exercise of this force. Hundreds of nations live in peace. History does not and cannot take note of this fact. History is really a record of every interruption of the even working of the force of love or of the soul. Two brothers quarrel; one of them repents and re-awakens the love that was lying dormant in him; the two again begin to live in peace; nobody takes note of this. But if the two brothers, through the intervention of solicitors or some other reason take up arms or go to law-which is another form of the exhibition of brute force,-their doings would be immediately noticed in the press, they would be the talk of their neighbours and would probably go down to history. And what is true of families and communities is true of nations. There is no reason to believe that there is one law for families and another for nations. History, then, is a record of an interruption of the course of nature. Soul-force, being natural, is not noted in history.

READER: According to what you say, it is plain that instances of this kind of passive resistance are not to be found in history. It is necessary to understand this passive resistance more fully. It will be better, therefore, if you enlarge upon it.

EDITOR: Passive resistance is a method of securing rights by personal suffering; it is the reverse of resistance by arms. When I refuse to do a thing that is repugnant to my conscience, I use soul-force. For instance, the Government of the day has passed a law which is applicable to me. I do not like it. If by using violence I force the Government to repeal the law, I am employing what may be termed body-force. If I do not obey the law and accept the penalty for its breach, I use soul-force. It involves sacrifice of self.

Everybody admits that sacrifice of self is infinitely superior to sacrifice of others. Moreover, if this kind of force is used in a cause that is unjust, only the person using it suffers. He does not make others suffer for his mistakes. Men have before now done many things which were subsequently found to have been wrong. No man can claim that he is absolutely in the right or that a particular thing is wrong because he thinks so, but it is wrong for him so long as that is his deliberate judgment. It is therefore meet that he should not do that which he knows to be wrong, and suffer the consequence whatever it may be. This is the key to the use of soul-force.

READER: You would then disregard laws-this is rank disloyalty. We have always been considered a law-abiding nation. You seem to be going even beyond the extremists. They say that we must obey the laws that have been passed, but if the laws be bad, we must drive out the law-givers even by force.

EDITOR: Whether I go beyond them or whether I do not is a matter of no consequence to either of us. We simply want to find out what is right and to act accordingly. The real meaning of the statement that we are a law-abiding nation is that we are passive resisters. When we do not like certain laws, we do not break the heads of law-givers but we suffer and do not submit to the laws. That we should obey laws whether good or bad is a new-fangled notion. There was no such thing in former days. The people disregarded those laws they did not like and suffered the penalties for their breach. It is contrary to our manhood if we obey laws repugnant to our conscience. Such teaching is opposed to religion and means slavery. If the Government were to ask us to go about without any clothing, should we do so? If I were a passive resister, I would say to them that I would have nothing to do with their law. But we have so forgotten ourselves and become so compliant that we do not mind any degrading law.

A man who has realized his manhood, who fears only God, will fear no one else. Man-made laws are not necessarily binding on him. Even the Government does not expect any such thing from us. They do not say 'You must do such and such a thing," but they say; "If you do not do it, we will punish you." We are sunk so low that we fancy that it is our duty and our religion to do what the law lays down. If man will only realize that it is unmanly to obey laws that are unjust, no man's tyranny will enslave him. This is the key to self-rule or Home Rule.

It is a superstition and ungodly thing to believe that an act of a majority binds a minority. Many examples can be given in which acts of majorities will be found to have been wrong and those of minorities to have been right. All reforms owe their origin to the initiation of minorities in opposition to majorities. If among a band of robbers a knowledge of robbing is obligatory, is a pious man to accept the obligation? So long as the superstition that men should obey unjust laws exists, so long will their slavery exist. And a passive resister alone can remove such a superstition.

To use brute-force, to use gunpowder, is contrary to passive resistance, for it means that we want our opponent to do by force that which we desire but he does not. And if such a use of force is justifiable, surely he is entitled to do likewise by us. And so we should never come to an agreement. We may simply fancy, like the blind horse moving in a circle round a mill, that we are making progress. Those who believe that they are not bound to obey laws which are repugnant to their conscience have only the remedy of passive resistance open to them. Any other must lead to disaster.

READER: From what you say I deduce that passive resistance is a splendid weapon of the weak, but that when they are strong they may take up arms.

EDITOR: This is gross ignorance. Passive resistance, that is, soul-force, is matchless. It is superior to the force of arms. How, then, can it be considered only a weapon of the weak? Physical-force men are strangers to the courage that is requisite in a passive resister. Do you believe that a coward can ever disobey a law that he dislikes? Extremists are considered to be advocates of brute force. Why do they, then, talk about obeying laws? I do not blame them. They can say nothing else. When they succeed in driving out the English and they themselves have become governors, they will want you and me to obey their laws. And that is a fitting thing for their constitution. But a passive resister will say he will not obey a law that is against his conscience, even though he may be blown to pieces at the mouth of a cannon.

What do you think? Wherein is courage required-in blowing others to pieces from behind a cannon, or with a smiling face to approach a cannon and be blown to pieces? Who is the true warrior-he who keeps death always as a bosom-friend, or he who controls the death of others? Believe me that a man devoid of courage and manhood can never be a passive resister.

This, however, I will admit; that even a man weak in body is capable of offering this resistance. One man can offer it just as well as millions. Both men and women can indulge in it. It does not require the training of an army; it needs no jiu-jitsu. Control over the mind is alone necessary, and when that is attained, man is free like the king of the forest and his very glance withers the enemy.

Passive resistance is an all-sided sword, it can be used anyhow; it blesses him who uses it and him against whom it is used. Without drawing a drop of blood it produces far-reaching results. It never rusts and cannot be stolen. Competition between passive resisters does not exhaust. The sword of passive resistance does not require a scabbard. It is strange indeed that you should consider such a weapon to be a weapon merely of the weak.

READER: You have said that passive resistance is a specialty of India. Have cannons never been used in India?

EDITOR: Evidently, in your opinion, India means its few princes. To me it means its teeming millions on whom depends the existence of its princes and our own.

Kings will always use their kingly weapons. To use force is bred in them. They want to command, but those who have to obey commands do not want guns; and these are in a majority throughout the world. They have to learn either body-force or soul-force. Where they learn the former, both the rulers and the ruled become like so many madmen; but where they learn soul-force, the commands of the rulers do not go beyond the point of their swords, for true men disregard unjust commands. Peasants have never been subdued by the sword, and never will be. They do not know the use of the sword, and they are not frightened by the use of it by others. That nation is great which rests its head upon death as its pillow. Those who defy death are free from all fear. For those who are labouring under the delusive charms of brute-force, this picture is not overdrawn. The fact is that, in India, the nation at large has generally used passive resistance in all departments of life. We cease to co-operate with our rulers when they displease us. This is passive resistance.

• • •

In order to restore India to its pristine condition, we have to return to it. In our own civilization there will naturally be progress, retrogression, reforms, and reactions; but one effort is required, and that is to drive out Western civilization. All else will follow.

READER: When you speak of driving out Western civilization, I suppose you will also say that we want no machinery?

EDITOR: . . . Machinery has begun to desolate Europe. Ruination is now knocking at the English gates. Machinery is the chief symbol of modern civilization; it represents a great sin.

The workers in the mills of Bombay have become slaves. The condition of the women working in the mills is shocking. When there were no mills, these women were not starving. If the machinery craze grows in our country, it will become an unhappy land. It may be considered a heresy, but I am bound to say that it were better for us to send money to Manchester [England] and to use flimsy Manchester cloth than to multiply mills in India. By using Manchester cloth we only waste our money; but by reproducing Manchester in India, we shall keep our money at the price of our blood, because our very moral being will be sapped, and I call in support of my statement the very mill-hands as witnesses. And those who have amassed wealth out of factories are not likely to be better than other rich men. It would be folly to assume that an Indian Rockefeller would be better than the American Rockefeller. Impoverished India can become free, but it will be hard for any India made rich through immorality to regain its freedom. I fear we shall have to admit that moneyed men support British rule; their interest is bound up with its stability. Money renders a man helpless. The other thing which is equally harmful is sexual vice. Both are poison. A snake-bite is a lesser poison than these two, because the former merely destroys the body but the latter destroy body, mind, and soul. We need not, therefore, be pleased with the prospect of the growth of the mill-industry.

READER: Are the mills, then, to be closed down?

EDITOR: That is difficult. It is no easy task to do away with a thing that is established. We, therefore, say that the non-beginning of a thing is supreme wisdom. We cannot condemn the mill-owners; we can but pity them. It would be too much to expect them to give up their mills, but we may implore them not to increase them. If they would be good they would gradually contract their business. They can establish in thousands of households the ancient and sacred handlooms and they can buy out the cloth that may be thus woven. Whether the mill-owners do this or not, people can cease to use machine-made goods.

READER: You have so far spoken about machine-made cloth, but there are innumerable machine-made things. We have either to import them or to introduce machinery into our country.

EDITOR: Indeed, our goods even are made in Germany. What need, then, to speak of matches, pins, and glassware? My answer can be only one. What did India do before these articles were introduced? Precisely the same should be done today. As long as we cannot make pins without machinery so long will we do without them.

. . .

READER: What, then, would you say to the English?

EDITOR: To them I would respectfully say: "I admit you are my rulers. It is not necessary to debate the question whether you hold India by the sword or by my consent. I have no objection to your remaining in my country, but although you are the rulers, you will have to remain as servants of the people. It is not we who have to do as you wish, but it is you who have to do as we wish. You may keep the riches that you have drained away from this land, but you may not drain riches henceforth. Your function will be, if you so wish, to police India; you must abandon the idea of deriving any commercial benefit from us. We hold the civilization that you support to be the reverse of civilization. We consider our civilization to be far superior to yours. If you realize this truth, it will be to your advantage and, if you do not, according to your own proverb, you should only live in our country in the same manner as we do. You must not do anything that is contrary to our religions. It is your duty as rulers that for the sake of the Hindus you should eschew beef, and for the sake of Mahomedans you should avoid bacon and ham. We have hitherto said nothing because we have been cowed down, but you need not consider that you have not hurt our feelings by your conduct. We are not expressing our sentiments either through base selfishness or fear, but because it is our duty now to speak out boldly. We consider your schools and law courts to be useless. We want our own ancient schools and courts to be restored. The common language of India is not English but Hindi. You should, therefore, learn it. We can hold communication with you only in our national language.

"We cannot tolerate the idea of your spending money on railways and the military. We see no occasion for either. You may fear Russia; we do not. When she comes we shall look after her. If you are with us, we may then receive her jointly. We do not need any European cloth. We shall manage with articles produced and manufactured at home. You may not keep one eye on Manchester and the other on India. We can work together only if our interests are identical.

"This has not been said to you in arrogance. You have great military resources. Your naval power is matchless. If we wanted to fight with you on your own ground, we should be unable to do so, but if the above submissions be not acceptable to you, we cease to play the part of the ruled. You may, if you like, cut us to pieces. You may shatter us at the cannon's mouth. If you act contrary to our will, we shall not help you; and without our help, we know that you cannot move one step forward.

"It is likely that you will laugh at all this in the intoxication of your power. We may not be able to disillusion you at once; but if there be any manliness in us, you will see shortly that your intoxication is suicidal and that your laugh at our expense is an aberration of intellect. We believe that at heart you belong to a religious nation. We are living in a land which is the source of religions. How we came together need not be considered, but we can make mutual good use of our relations.

'You, English, who have come to India are not good specimens of the English nation, nor can we, almost half-Anglicized Indians, be considered good specimens of the real Indian nation. If the English nation were to know all you have done, it would oppose many of your actions. The mass of the Indians have had few dealings with you. If you will abandon your so-called civilization and search into your own scriptures, you will find that our demands are just. Only on condition of our demands being fully satisfied may you remain in India; and if you remain under those conditions, we shall learn several things from you and you will learn many from us. So doing we shall benefit each other and the world. But that will happen only when the root of our relationship is sunk in a religious soil."

READER: What will you say to the nation?

EDITOR: Who is the nation?

READER: For our purposes it is the nation that you and I have been thinking of, that is those of us who are affected by European civilization, and who are eager to have Home Rule.

EDITOR: To these I would say, "It is only those Indians who are imbued with real love who will be able to speak to the English in the above strain without being frightened, and only those can be said to be so imbued who conscientiously believe that Indian civilization is the best and that the European is a nine days' wonder. Such ephemeral civilizations have often come and gone and will continue to do so. Those only can be considered to be so imbued who, having experienced the force of the soul within themselves, will not cower before brute-force, and will not, on any account, desire to use brute-force. Those only can be considered to have been so imbued who are intensely dissatisfied with the present pitiable condition, having already drunk the cup of poison.

"If there be only one such Indian, he will speak as above to the English and the English will have to listen to him."

. . .

In my opinion, we have used the term "*Swaraj*" without understanding its real significance. I have endeavoured to explain it as I understand it, and my conscience testifies that my life henceforth is dedicated to its attainment.

Questions:

1. What does Gandhi mean by "love-force" or "soul-force"? Why does he think it will be effective?
2. How does Gandhi define civilization?

27.2   Gandhi and Nehru: "Two Utterly Different Standpoints": Jawaharlal Nehru

One of the most influential members of the Indian National Congress was the sophisticated and urbane Jawaharlal Nehru, a graduate of Cambridge University. He met Gandhi in 1916 and was impressed by his commitment to active civil disobedience. Nehru realized in 1919 "how brutal and immoral imperialism was and how it had eaten into the souls of the British upper classes." Although Nehru admired Gandhi's self-control and supported his emphasis on nonviolence, Nehru was no ascetic, but rather a practical politician with his own personal vision for India. In the following excerpt from his autobiography, Nehru discusses the differences between himself and Gandhi. Ultimately, their combined wisdom negotiated the path toward Indian independence.

Source: "Gandhi and Nehru" is from Jawaharlal Nehru, *The Autobiography of Jawaharlal Nehru* (New York: John Day Company, 1942), pp. 185–186.

Keep in Mind . . .

•   How did Nehru differ from Gandhi in his personal vision of life and in the future of India?

I imagine that Gandhiji is not so vague about the objective as he sometimes appears to be. He is passionately desirous of going in a certain direction, but this is wholly at variance with modern ideas and conditions, and he has so far been unable to fit the two, or to chalk out all the intermediate steps leading to his goal. Hence the appearance of vagueness and avoidance of clarity. . . .

"India's salvation consists," he wrote in 1909, "in unlearning what she has learned during the last fifty years. The railways, telegraphs, hospitals, lawyers, doctors, and suchlike have all to go; and the so-called upper classes have to learn consciously, religiously, and deliberately the simple peasant life, knowing it to be a life giving true happiness." And again: "Every time I get into a railway car or use a motor bus, I know that I am doing violence to my sense of what is right"; "to attempt to reform the world by means of highly artificial and speedy locomotion is to attempt the impossible."

All this seems to me utterly wrong and harmful doctrine, and impossible of achievement. Behind it lies Gandhiji's love and praise of poverty and suffering and the ascetic life. For him, progress and civilization consist not in the multiplication of wants, of higher standards of living, "but in the deliberate and voluntary restriction of wants, which promotes real happiness and contentment, and increases the capacity for service."

Personally, I dislike the praise of poverty and suffering. I do not think they are at all desirable, and they ought to be abolished. Nor do I appreciate the ascetic life as a social ideal, though it may suit individuals. I understand and appreciate simplicity, equality, self-control; but not the mortification of the flesh. . . . To be in good moral condition requires at least as much training as to be in good physical condition. But that certainly does not mean asceticism or self-mortification.

Nor do I appreciate in the least the idealization of the "simple peasant life." I have almost a horror of it, and instead of submitting to it myself, I want to drag out even the peasantry from it, not to urbanization, but to the spread of urban cultural facilities to rural areas. Far from this life's giving me true happiness, it would be almost as bad as imprisonment for me. . . .

Present-day civilization is full of evils, but also full of good; and it has the capacity in it to rid itself of those evils. To destroy it root and branch is to remove that capacity from it and revert to a dull, sunless, and miserable existence. But even if that were desirable, it is an impossible undertaking. We cannot stop the river of change or cut ourselves adrift from it, and psychologically we who have eaten of the apple of Eden cannot forget that taste and go back to primitiveness.

It is difficult to argue this, for the two standpoints are utterly different. Gandhiji is always thinking in terms of personal salvation and of sin, while most of us have society's welfare uppermost in our minds. I find it difficult to grasp the idea of sin, and perhaps it is because of this that I cannot appreciate Gandhiji's general outlook.

Consider This:

*   How was Nehru's approach to the future very practical in contrast to Gandhi's idealism? Did the eventual independence of India depend on both approaches?

Question:
1. How did Nehru differ from Gandhi in his personal vision of life and in the future of India?

27.3   Frantz Fanon, *The Wretched of the Earth*

One of the most articulate spokespersons for decolonization in the Third World was the French-educated Algerian psychiatrist Frantz Fanon (1925–1961). Fanon's writings, coupled with his struggle against French colonial rule in Algeria, ensured that he would become one of the most celebrated leaders of decolonization in the 1960s.

Source: From Frantz Fanon, *The Wretched of the Earth*, pp. 37–41, *passim*, trans. Constance Farrington. Copyright © 1963 by Presence Africaine. Used by permission of Grove/Atlantic, Inc. Reprinted by permission.

The colonial world is a world cut in two. The dividing line, the frontiers are shown by barracks and police stations. In the colonies it is the policeman and the soldier who are the official, instituted go-betweens, the spokesmen of the settler and his rule of oppression. . . . In the capitalist countries a multitude of moral teachers, counselors and "bewilderers" separate the exploited from those in power. In the colonial countries, on the contrary, the policeman and the soldier, by their immediate presence and their frequent and direct action maintain contact with the native and advise him by means of rifle butts and napalm not to budge. It is obvious here that the agents of government speak the language of pure force. The intermediary does not lighten the oppression, nor seek to hide the domination; he shows them up and puts them into practice with the clear conscience of an upholder of the peace; yet he is the bringer of violence into the home and into the mind of the native.

The zone where the natives live is not complementary to the zone inhabited by the settlers. The two zones are opposed, but not in the service of a higher unity. Obedient to the rules of pure Aristotelian logic, they both follow the principle of reciprocal exclusivity. No conciliation is possible, for of the two terms, one is superfluous. The settlers' town is a strongly built town, all made of stone and steel. It is a brightly lit town; the streets are covered with asphalt, and the garbage cans swallow all the leavings, unseen, unknown and hardly thought about. The settler's feet are never visible, except perhaps in the sea; but there you're never close enough to see them. His feet are protected by strong shoes although the streets of his town are clean and even, with no holes or stones. The settler's town is a well-fed town, an easygoing town; its belly is always full of good things. The settlers' town is a town of white people, of foreigners.

The town belonging to the colonized people, or at least the native town, the Negro village, the medina, the reservation, is a place of ill fame, peopled by men of evil repute. They are born there, it matters little where or how; they die there, it matters not where, nor how. It is a world without spaciousness; men live there on top of each other, and their huts are built—one on top of the other. The native town is a hungry town, starved of bread, of meat, of shoes, of coal, of light. The native town is a crouching village, a town on its knees, a town wallowing in the mire. It is a town of niggers and dirty Arabs. The look that the native turns on the settler's town is a look of lust, a look of envy; it expresses his dreams of possession—all manner of possession: to sit at the settler's table, to sleep in the settler's bed, with his wife if possible. The colonized man is an envious man. And this the settler knows very well; when their glances meet he ascertains bitterly, always on the defensive, "They want to take our place." It is true, for there is no native who does not dream at least once a day of setting himself up in the settler's place. . . .

The violence which has ruled over the ordering of the colonial world, which has ceaselessly drummed the rhythm for the destruction of native social forms and broken up without reserve the systems of reference of the economy, and the customs of dress and external life, that same violence will be claimed and taken over by the native at the moment when, deciding to embody history in his own person, he surges into the forbidden quarters. To wreck the colonial world is henceforward a mental picture of action which is very clear, very easy to understand and which may be assumed by each one of the individuals which constitute the colonized people. To break up the colonial world does not mean that after the frontiers have been abolished lines of communication will be set up between the two zones. The destruction of the colonial world is no more and no less than the abolition of one zone, its burial in the depths of the earth or its expulsion from the country.

The natives' challenge to the colonial world is not a rational confrontation of points of view. It is not a treatise on the universal, but the untidy affirmation of an original idea propounded as an absolute. The colonial world is a Manichean world. It is not enough for the settler to delimit physically, that is to say with the help of the army and the police force, the place of the native. As if to show the totalitarian character of colonial exploitation the settler paints the native as a sort of quintessence of evil. Native society is not simply described as a society lacking in values. It is not enough for the colonist to affirm that those values have disappeared from, or still better never existed in, the colonial world. The native is declared insensible to ethics; he represents not only the absence of values, but also the negation of values. He is, let us dare to admit, the enemy of values, and in this sense he is the absolute evil. He is the corrosive element, destroying all that comes near him; he is the deforming element, disfiguring all that has to do with beauty or morality; he is the depository of maleficent powers, the unconscious and irretrievable instrument of blind forces.

Questions:
1. *Are there any parallels between Frantz Fanon's diagnosis of colonialism and Francisco García Calderón's discussion of "The North American Peril"?*
2. *Fanon describes the colonial world as a "Manichean world." Would Rudyard Kipling agree? Why? Why not?*

27.4 Kwame Nkrumah, I Speak of Freedom: A Statement of African Ideology

Kwame Nkrumah (1909–1972) led the former British colony of the Gold Coast to become the independent country of Ghana in 1957. Until he was overthrown by a coup d'état in 1966, Kwame Nkrumah was one of Africa's most influential leaders.

> **Source:** From Kwame, Nkrumah, *I Speak of Freedom: A Statement of African Ideology* (New York: Frederick A. Praeger, 1961), pp. ix–xii, *passim*. Copyright and all rights reserved Panaf Books Ltd., 243 Regent Street, London WIR 8PN. Reprinted by permission.

For centuries, Europeans dominated the African continent. The white man arrogated to himself the right to rule and to be obeyed by the non-white; his mission, he claimed was to "civilise" Africa. Under this cloak, the Europeans robbed the continent of vast riches and inflicted unimaginable suffering on the African people.

All this makes a sad story, but now we must be prepared to bury the past with its unpleasant memories and look to the future. All we ask of the former colonial powers is their goodwill and co-operation to remedy past mistakes and injustices and to grant independence to the colonies in Africa. . . .

It is clear that we must find an African solution to our problems, and that this can only be found in African unity. Divided we are weak; united, Africa could become one of the greatest forces for good in the world.

Although most Africans are poor, our continent is potentially extremely rich. Our mineral resources, which are being exploited with foreign capital only to enrich foreign investors, range from gold and diamonds to uranium and petroleum. Our forests contain some of the finest woods to be grown anywhere. Our cash crops include cocoa, coffee, rubber, tobacco and cotton. As for power, which is an important factor in any economic development, Africa contains over 40% of the total potential water power of the world, as compared with about 10% in Europe and 13% in North America. Yet so far, less than 1% has been developed. This is one of the reasons why we have in Africa the paradox of poverty in the midst of plenty, and scarcity in the midst of abundance.

Never before have a people had within their grasp so great an opportunity for developing a continent endowed with so much wealth. Individually, the independent states of Africa, some of them potentially rich, others poor, can do little for their people. Together, by mutual help, they can achieve much. But the economic development of the continent must be planned and pursued as a whole. A loose confederation designed only for economic cooperation would not provide the necessary unity of purpose. Only a strong political union can bring about full and effective development of our natural resources for the benefit of our people.

The political situation in Africa today is heartening and at the same time disturbing. It is heartening to see so many new flags hoisted in place of the old; it is disturbing to see so many countries of varying sizes and at different levels of development, weak and, in some cases, almost helpless. If this terrible state of fragmentation is allowed to continue it may well be disastrous for us all.

There are at present some 28 states in Africa, excluding the Union of South Africa, and those countries not yet free. No less than nine of these states have a population of less than three million. Can we seriously believe that the colonial powers meant these countries to be independent, viable states? The example of South America, which has as much wealth, if not more than North America, and yet remains weak and dependent on outside interests, is one which every African would do well to study.

Critics of African unity often refer to the wide differences in culture, language and ideas in various parts of Africa. This is true, but the essential fact remains that we are all Africans, and have a common interest in the independence of Africa. The difficulties presented by questions of language, culture and different political systems are not insuperable. If the need for political union is agreed by us all, then the will to create it is born; and where there's a will there's a way.

The present leaders of Africa have already shown a remarkable willingness to consult and seek advice among themselves. Africans have, indeed, begun to think continentally. They realise that they have much in common, both in their past history, in their present problems and in their future hopes. To suggest that the time is not yet ripe for considering a political union of Africa is to evade the facts and ignore realities in Africa today.

The greatest contribution that Africa can make to the peace of the world is to avoid all the dangers inherent in disunity, by creating a political union which will also by its success, stand as an example to a divided world. A union of African states will project more effectively the African personality. It will command respect from a world that has regard only for size and influence. The scant attention paid to African opposition to the French atomic tests in the Sahara, and the ignominious spectacle of the U.N. in the Congo quibbing about constitutional niceties while the Republic was tottering into anarchy, are evidence of the callous disregard of African Independence by the Great Powers.

We have to prove that greatness is not to be measured in stock piles of atom bombs. I believe strongly and sincerely that with the deep-rooted wisdom and dignity, the innate respect for human lives, the intense humanity that is our heritage, the African race, united under one federal government, will emerge not as just another world bloc to flaunt its wealth and strength, but as a Great Power whose greatness is indestructible because it is built not on fear, envy and suspicion, nor won at the expense of others, but founded on hope, trust, friendship and directed to the good of all mankind.

The emergence of such a mighty stabilising force in this strife-worn world should be regarded not as the shadowy dream of a visionary, but as a practical proposition, which the peoples of Africa can, and should, translate into reality. There is a tide in the affairs of every people when the moment strikes for political action. Such was the moment in the history of the United States of America when the Founding Fathers saw beyond the petty wranglings of the separate states and created a Union. This is our chance. We must act now. Tomorrow may be too late and the opportunity will have passed, and with it the hope of free Africa's survival.

Questions:
1. *Why have Kwame Nkrumah's dreams of African unity had so little appeal for many modern African political leaders?*
2. *Is the dream of African unity too idealistic? Why? Why not?*

27.5 Israel's Proclamation of Independence

One day before the termination of the British mandate for Palestine, the Provisional State Council (a forerunner of the Israeli Parliament) declared the independence of Israel on May 14, 1948. The following selection is an excerpt from this official announcement.

Source: From "Proclamation of the New Jewish State," *The New York Times,* May 15, 1948, p. 2. Copyright © 1948 by The New York Times Company. Reprinted by permission.

The Land of Israel was the birthplace of the Jewish people. Here their spiritual, religious and national identity was formed. Here they achieved independence and created a culture of national and universal significance. Here they wrote and gave the Bible to the world.

Exiled from the Land of Israel the Jewish people remained faithful to it in all the countries of their dispersion, never ceasing to pray and hope for their return and the restoration of their national freedom.

Impelled by this historic association, Jews strove throughout the centuries to go back to the land of their fathers and regain their statehood. In recent decades they returned in their masses. They reclaimed the wilderness, revived their language, built cities and villages, and established a vigorous and ever-growing community, with its own economic and cultural life. They sought peace, yet were prepared to defend themselves. They brought the blessings of progress to all inhabitants of the country and looked forward to sovereign independence.

In the year 1897 the First Zionist Congress, inspired by Theodor Herzl's vision of the Jewish State, proclaimed the right of the Jewish people to national revival in their own country.

This right was acknowledged by the Balfour Declaration of November 2, 1917, and re-affirmed by the Mandate of the League of Nations, which gave explicit international recognition to the historic connection of the Jewish people with Palestine and their right to reconstitute their National Home.

The recent holocaust, which engulfed millions of Jews in Europe, proved anew the need to solve the problem of the homelessness and lack of independence of the Jewish people by means of the re-establishment of the Jewish State, which would open the gates to all Jews and endow the Jewish people with equality of status among the family of nations.

The survivors of the disastrous slaughter in Europe, and also Jews from other lands, have not desisted from their efforts to reach Eretz-Yisrael, in face of difficulties, obstacles and perils; and have not ceased to urge their right to a life of dignity, freedom and honest toil in their ancestral land.

In the second World War the Jewish people in Palestine made their full contribution to the struggle of the freedom-loving nations against the Nazi evil. The sacrifices of their soldiers and their war effort gained them the right to rank with the nations which founded the United Nations.

On November 29, 1947, the General Assembly of the United Nations adopted a Resolution requiring the establishment of a Jewish State in Palestine. The General Assembly called upon the inhabitants of the country to take all the necessary steps on their part to put the plan into effect. This recognition by the United Nations of the right of the Jewish people to establish their independent State is unassailable.

It is the natural right of the Jewish people to lead, as do all other nations, an independent existence in its sovereign State.

ACCORDINGLY WE, the members of the National Council, representing the Jewish people in Palestine and the World Zionist Movement, are met together in solemn assembly today, the day of termination of the British Mandate for Palestine; and by virtue of the natural and historic right of the Jewish people and of the Resolution of the General Assembly of the United Nations.

WE HEREBY PROCLAIM the establishment of the Jewish State in Palestine, to be called Medinath Yisrael (The State of Israel).

WE HEREBY DECLARE that, as from the termination of the Mandate at midnight, the 14th–15th May, 1948, and pending the setting up of the duly elected bodies of the State in accordance with a Constitution, to be drawn up by the Constituent Assembly not later than the 1st October, 1948, the National Council shall act as the Provisional State Council, and that the National Administration shall constitute the Provisional Government of the Jewish State, which shall be known as Israel.

THE STATE OF ISRAEL will be open to the immigration of Jews from all countries of their dispersion; will promote the development of the country for the benefit of all its inhabitants; will be based on the principles of liberty, justice and peace as conceived by the Prophets of Israel; will uphold the full social and political equality of all its citizens, without distinction of religion, race, or sex; will guarantee freedom of religion, conscience, education and culture; will safeguard the Holy Places of all religions; and will loyally uphold the principles of the United Nations Charter.

THE STATE OF ISRAEL will be ready to co-operate with the organs and representatives of the United Nations in the implementation of the Resolution of the Assembly of November 29, 1947, and will take steps to bring about the Economic Union over the whole of Palestine.

We appeal to the United Nations to assist the Jewish people in the building of its State and to admit Israel into the family of nations.

In the midst of wanton aggression, we yet call upon the Arab inhabitants of the State of Israel to preserve the ways of peace and play their part in the development of the State, on the basis of full and equal citizenship and due representation in all its bodies and institutions—provisional and permanent.

Questions:
1. *Can the historic and religious ties of the Jewish people to Israel accommodate the fact that for nearly two thousand years Israel was also the dwelling place of Arabs and other non-Jewish populations?*
2. *How does Israel's Proclamation of Independence suggest the influence of European and American history in this area?*

27.6   Palestinian Declaration of Independence

Forty years after the state of Israel declared its independence, the Palestine National Council, meeting in Algiers, further revised its 1964 charter and on November 15, 1988, proclaimed this Declaration of Independence for the Palestinian people.

Source: From Palestine National Council, "Palestinian Declaration of Independence," Algiers, November 15, 1988. *The Journal of Palestine Studies* 70 (Winter 1989), pp. 213–16. Copyright © Journal of Palestine Studies. Reprinted by permisison.

In the name of God, the Compassionate, the Merciful.

Palestine, the land of the three monotheistic faiths, is where the Palestinian Arab people was born, on which it grew, developed, and excelled. The Palestinian people was never separated from or diminished in its integral bonds with Palestine. Thus the Palestinian Arab people ensured for itself an everlasting union between itself, its land, and its history. . . .

Despite the historical injustice inflicted on the Palestinian Arab people resulting in their dispersion and depriving them of their right to self-determination, following upon UN General Assembly Resolution 181 (1947), which partitioned Palestine into two states, one Arab, one Jewish, yet it is this resolution that still provides those conditions of international legitimacy that ensure the right of the Palestinian Arab people to sovereignty and national independence. . . .

In Palestine and on its perimeters, in exile distant and near, the Palestinian Arab people never faltered and never abandoned its conviction in its rights of return and independence. Occupation, massacres, and dispersion achieved no gain in the unabated Palestinian consciousness of self and political identity, as Palestinians went forward with their destiny, undeterred and unbowed. And from out of the long years of trial in evermounting struggle, the Palestinian political identity emerged further consolidated and confirmed. And the collective Palestinian national will forge itself in a political embodiment, the Palestine Liberation Organization, its sole, legitimate representative, recognized by the world community as a whole, as well as by related regional and international institutions. . . .

The massive national uprising, the *intifadah,* now intensifying in cumulative scope and power on occupied Palestinian territories, as well as the unflinching resistance of the refugee camps outside the homeland, have elevated consciousness of the Palestinian truth and right into still higher realms of comprehension and actuality. Now at last the curtain has been dropped around a whole epoch of prevarication and negation. The Intifadah has set siege to the mind of official Israel, which has for too long relied exclusively upon myth and terror to deny Palestinian existence altogether. Because of the Intifadah and its revolutionary irreversible impulse, the history of Palestine has therefore arrived at a decisive juncture.

Whereas the Palestinian people reaffirms most definitely its inalienable rights in the land of its patrimony:

Now by virtue of natural, historical, and legal rights and the sacrifices of successive generations who gave of themselves in defense of the freedom and independence of their homeland;

In pursuance of resolutions adopted by Arab summit conferences and relying on the authority bestowed by international legitimacy as embodied in the resolutions of the United Nations Organization since 1947;

And in exercise by the Palestinian Arab people of its rights to self-determination, political independence, and sovereignty over its territory;

The Palestine National Council, in the name of God, and in the name of the Palestinian Arab people, hereby proclaims the establishment of the State of Palestine on our Palestinian territory with its capital Jerusalem (Al-Quds Ash-Sharif).

The State of Palestine is the state of Palestinians wherever they may be. The state is for them to enjoy in it their collective national and cultural identity, theirs to pursue in it a complete equality of rights. In it will be safeguarded their political and religious convictions and their human dignity by means of a parliamentary democratic system of governance, itself based on freedom of expression and the freedom to form parties. The rights of minorities will duly be respected by the majority, as minorities must abide by decisions of the majority. Governance will be based on principles of social justice, equality and nondiscrimination in public rights on grounds of race, religion, color, or sex under the aegis of a constitution which ensures the role of law and an independent judiciary. Thus shall these principles allow no departure from Palestine's age-old spiritual and civilizational heritage of tolerance and religious co-existence.

The State of Palestine is an Arab state, an integral and indivisible part of the Arab nation, at one with that nation in heritage and civilization, with it also in its aspiration for liberation, progress, democracy, and unity. The State of Palestine affirms its obligation to abide by the Charter of the League of Arab States, whereby the coordination of the Arab states with each other shall be strengthened. It calls upon Arab compatriots to consolidate and enhance the emergence in reality of our State, to mobilize potential, and to intensify efforts whose goal is to end Israeli occupation.

The State of Palestine proclaims its commitment to the principles and purposes of the United Nations, and to the Universal Declaration of Human Rights. It proclaims its commitment as well to the principles and policies of the Non-Aligned Movement.

It further announces itself to be a peace-loving state, in adherence to the principles of peaceful co-existence. It will join with all states and peoples in order to assure a permanent peace based upon justice and the respect of rights so that humanity's potential for well-being may be assured, an earnest competition for excellence be maintained, and in which confidence in the future will eliminate fear for those who are just and for whom justice is the only recourse.

In the context of its struggle for peace in the land of love and peace, the State of Palestine calls upon the United Nations to bear special responsibility for the Palestinian Arab people and its homeland. It calls upon all peace- and freedom-loving peoples and states to assist it in the attainment of its objectives, to provide it with security, to alleviate the tragedy of its people, and to help to terminate Israel's occupation of the Palestinian territories.

The State of Palestine herewith declares that it believes in the settlement of regional and international disputes by peaceful means, in accordance with the UN Charter and resolutions. Without prejudice to its natural right to defend its territorial integrity and independence, it therefore rejects the threat or use of force, violence, and terrorism against its territorial integrity, or political independence, as it also rejects their use against the territorial integrity of other states.

Therefore, on this day unlike all others, 15 November, 1988, as we stand at the threshold of a new dawn, in all honor and modesty we humbly bow to the sacred spirits of our fallen ones, Palestinian and Arab, by the purity of whose sacrifice for the homeland our sky has been illuminated and our land given life. . . .

Therefore, we call upon our great people to rally to the banner of Palestine, to cherish and defend it, so that it may forever be the symbol of our freedom and dignity in that homeland, which is a homeland for the free, now and always.

In the name of God, the Compassionate, the Merciful.

Questions:
1. *After a half century of bitter warfare between Palestinians and Israelis, can the Palestinian Declaration of Independence be reconciled with the state of Israel's concerns about national security? Can the two peoples ever find a way to live in peace?*
2. *In its Declaration of Independence, the Palestinian National Council "calls upon the United Nations to bear special responsibility for the Palestinian Arab people and its homeland." Do you believe that the UN should "bear a special responsibility" for ensuring the security of a Palestinian state? How should the UN exercise this responsibility?*

27.7 Views of a Viet Cong Official

Truong Nhu Tang was a founder of the National Liberation Front (NLF) and a minister of justice in the NLF's Provisional Revolutionary Government. In 1982, he gave the following account of the Viet Cong movement and the collapse of South Vietnam. The 1968 Tet offensive he refers to was a failed North Vietnamese and Viet Cong campaign against South Vietnamese cities. This occurred while General Thieu, Truong Nhu Tang's captor, was president of South Vietnam.

> **Source:** From Truong Nhu Tang, "Myth of a Liberation," *The New York Review of Books*, 39, no. 16 (October 21, 1982), pp. 31–36, *passim*. Reprinted with permission from *The New York Review of Books*. Copyright © 1982 Nyrev, Inc.

The North Vietnamese on their part never indicated that they wanted to impose communism on the South. On the contrary, they knew, they said, that the South must have a different program altogether, one that embodied our aspirations not just for independence but also for internal political freedom. I believe, in addition, that the Northern leadership would have the wisdom to draw from the experiences—both good and bad—of other communist countries, and especially of North Vietnam, and that they could avoid the errors made elsewhere. North Vietnam was, as Ho Chi Minh often declared, a special situation in which nationalists and communists had combined their efforts. Clearly South Vietnam was no less special, and the newly constituted NLF Permanent Committee felt a certain amount of confidence in working with our Northern compatriots. . . .

The great majority of our troops then were Southern resistance fighters many of whom were veterans of the French colonial wars. Others were peasants who joined us when the NLF was formed. Almost all of this latter group still lived at home. During the day they were loyal citizens of South Vietnam; at night they became Viet Cong.

For the most part these guerrillas cared nothing about Marxist-Leninism or any other ideology. But they despised the local officials who had been appointed over them by the Saigon dictatorship. Beyond this, joining the Viet Cong allowed them to stay clear of the ARVN draft and to remain near their families. They were treated as brothers by the NLF, and although Viet Cong pay was almost nonexistent, these peasant soldiers were loyal and determined fighters. Moreover, they had the support of much of the population: people in the countryside and even in the cities provided food and intelligence information and protected our cadres. Although South Vietnamese propaganda attacked us as communists and murderers, the peasants believed otherwise. To them we were not Marxist-Leninists but simply revolutionaries fighting against a hated dictatorship and foreign intervention.

Because it was a people's war, the Viet Cong cadres were trained carefully to exploit the peasants' sympathies. But our goals were in fact generally shared by the people. We were working for Southern self-determination and independence—from Hanoi as well as from Washington. While we in the Viet Cong were beholden to Hanoi for military supplies and diplomatic contacts, many of us still believed that the North Vietnamese leadership would respect and support the NLF political program, that it would be in their interest to do so.

As early as the 1968 Tet offensive, after I was released from Thieu's prisons, I protested to the communist leaders about the atrocities committed by North Vietnamese troops in Hue, where many innocent people were murdered and about a dozen American prisoners were shot. It was explained to me that these were political executions and also that a number of "errors" had been made. I managed to persuade myself then that no such "errors" would be necessary once the war was over.

Unfortunately the Tet offensive also proved catastrophic to our plans. It is a major irony of the Vietnamese war that our propaganda transformed this military debacle into a brilliant victory, giving us new leverage in our diplomatic efforts, inciting the American antiwar movement to even stronger and more optimistic resistance, and disheartening the Washington planners.

The truth was that Tet cost us half of our forces. Our losses were so immense that we were simply unable to replace them with new recruits. One consequence was that the Hanoi leadership began to move unprecedented numbers of troops into the South, giving them a new and much more dominant position in the NLF deliberations. The Tet failure also retarded the organization of the Alliance of National, Democratic, and Peace Forces, an opposition coalition that had formed around thirty prominent South Vietnamese intellectuals and opinion makers. . . .

The Hanoi leadership knew all this and orchestrated their position toward us accordingly. They accepted and supported the NLF platform at every point, and gave the firmest assurances of respect for the principle of South Vietnamese self-determination. Later, of course we discovered that the North Vietnamese communists had engaged in a deliberate deception to achieve what had been their true goal from the start, the destruction of South Vietnam as a political or social entity in any way separate from the North. They succeeded in their deception by portraying themselves as brothers who had fought the same battles we were fighting and by exploiting our patriotism in the most cynical fashion. Nevertheless, the eventual denouement would not have taken place except for several wholly unpredictable developments.

After the Paris peace agreement was signed in 1973, most of us were preparing to create a neutralist government, balanced between Northern leftists and Southern rightists. We hoped that America and other signers would play an active role in protecting the agreement. Certainly no one expected Watergate and Nixon's resignation. No one expected America's easy and startlingly rapid abandonment of the country. I myself, the soon-to-be minister of justice, was preparing a reconciliation policy that specifically excluded reprisals. But the sudden collapse of the South Vietnamese regime (caused partly by the hasty departure of many top Saigon leaders) together with the abandonment by the Americans left me and other "independent socialists" with no counterweight to the huge influx of Northern communists.

It is important to note that our views were not based solely on naivete. During the Sixties neither the NLF leaders nor the Politburo ever hoped for total military victory against the Americans and their clients. Our entire strategy was formulated with the expectation that eventually we would be involved in some kind of coalition government. Such a government would have been immune to outright North Vietnamese domination and could have expected substantial international support. . . .

Unfortunately when the war did end, North Vietnamese vindictiveness and fanaticism blossomed into a ferocious exercise of power. Hundreds of thousands of former officials and army officers of the Saigon regime were imprisoned in "re-education camps." Literally millions of ordinary citizens were forced to leave their homes and settle in so-called New Economic Zones.

Questions:
1. According to Truong Nhu Tang, was the Tet offensive a military victory for the insurgency? Why did the American public perceive Tet as an American defeat?
2. As a southerner in the NLF, what was Truong Nhu Tang's attitude toward the North Vietnamese? Did American policy take into account this division in the NLF ranks?

27.8   An American Prisoner of War

Congressional Medal of Honor winner and retired Vice Admiral James Bond Stockdale was a prisoner of war in Vietnam for eight years. In 1992, he was Ross Perot's running mate for the U.S. vice presidency. In the following essay, he recounts some of his experiences in Vietnam and offers his views on the lessons to be learned from the war.

Source: From James B. Stockdale, *A Vietnam Experience: Ten Years of Reflection* (Stanford, CA: Hoover Institution, 1984), pp. 109, 122–28. This material originally appeared in "The Most Important Lesson of Vietnam: Power of the Human Spirit," *San Jose Mercury News*, January 3, 1982, copyright 1982 by The San Diego Union; and "Dignity and Honor in Vietnam," *The Wall Street Journal*, April 16, 1982. Reprinted by the kind permission of James Bond Stockdale, *The San Diego Union*, and *The Wall Street Journal*.

My viewpoint of the Vietnam War was that Eisenhower's domino theory was probably valid: that if North Vietnam took over the south, a chain reaction could be expected to proceed to the southwest. I also knew that South Vietnam was not really like the western democracy our government tried to pretend it was. I knew there was a formidable framework of a Communist infrastructure in the south that would have to be burned out. I also knew how militant!y doctrinaire and disciplined the North Vietnamese were. Putting all this together, I thought, during the war, after it, and still today, that Barry Goldwater had the only sensible outlook: either move quickly against Hanoi with repeated high impact non-nuke hammer blows from the air or forget it. Vietnam was no place for the Army.

So how do I classify the tragedy of Vietnam, if not a crusade, a mistake, a crime or a conspiracy? I classify it as a misguided experiment of the Harvard Business School crowd—the "whiz kids"—in achieving foreign policy objectives by so-called rational game theory, while ignoring the reality and obstinacy of human nature.

These were some of the policy lessons of Vietnam: You can't finesse human nature, human will, or human obstinacy, with economic game theory. And you should never let those who think you can, call the shots in a war! . . .

The central strategy of the North Vietnamese prison system was extortion pressure—pressure to get us to contribute to what turned out to be their winning propaganda campaign beamed at the American man on the street, pressure to get us to inform on one another. These ideas were tied together as integral parts of the whole and were to be extracted by the imposition of loneliness, fear and guilt—fear of pain, guilt at having betrayed a fellow prisoner. . . .

Chivalry was dead in my prison. Its name was Hoa Lo, meaning "fiery furnace," located in downtown Hanoi, a prison the French built in 1895.

I arrived there, a prisoner of war in North Vietnam, in the late morning of a rainy Sunday in September 1965, a stretcher case. I had a broken leg (which my welcoming party, a street mob of civilians, had inflicted), a broken back (which I charge off to my carelessness in not having had the presence of mind to brace myself correctly before ejecting into low altitude, high-speed air from a tumbling airplane), and a gunshot wound in my good leg (which an irate farmer had pumped into my stretcher during my first night on the ground, an act I credit as morally neutral just to keep the score balanced). The North Vietnamese officer who presided over my arrival after three days in the back of a truck was about my age (42 at the time), also a career military man.

I asked him for medical attention for my broken bones and open wounds. "You have a medical problem and you have a political problem," he said. "In this country we handle political problems first, and if they are satisfactorily resolved, that is, if you demonstrate a proper understanding of the American war of imperialist aggression in Vietnam and take concrete actions to stop it, we will attend to your medical problems." That was the last time the subject of medical attention for me ever came up in my next eight years as a prisoner of war. . . .

These prisons are all the same; the name of the game is to unstring their victims with fear and polarize them with guilt. There are always more rules than can practically be obeyed, always a tripwire system to snare you in a violation that the jailers can brand as moral turpitude—and there is always an escape valve, a way to make amends if you repent.

The tripwire in Hanoi was based on the "no communication" rule. As with all tripwires, the prisoner had a choice to make and he stood to lose either way. If he obeyed and did not communicate with his comrades, he accrued the conscience problems of betraying his fellows and at the same time sentenced himself to a desperate loneliness which would likely get to him after a year or two. If he communicated, and this was the only way to go for loyalty, for a feeling of self-worth, for dignity, he would periodically be caught and tortured under the charge of ingratitude for the "humane and lenient treatment" he was being given.

(Incidentally, communication grew to be a very refined, high-volume, high-speed, highly accurate though dangerous art. We used the same code Koestler's fictional Commissar N.S. Rubashov used during his Moscow trial and execution period in the late 1930's.)

By torture, I don't mean leg irons or handcuffs or isolation. We were always careful to remind ourselves that those were just inconveniences, not to panic. By torture we meant the intentional imposition of pain and claustrophobia over as short a time as necessary to get the victim to "submit."

In my experience this is best done by heavily slapping the prisoner, seating him on the brick floor, reeving his upper arms with ropes, and while standing barefoot on his back cinching up the elaborate bindings by jerks, pulling his shoulders together while stuffing his head down between his feet with the heel of your foot. Numb arms under contorted tension produce an excruciating pain and a gnawing but sure knowledge that a clock is ticking while your blood is stopped and that the longer you wait before submitting the longer useless arms will dangle at your sides (45 minutes of blood stoppage usually cost about six months of dangle). The claustrophobia also concentrates the mind wonderfully.

How long to submission for a good man? About 30 minutes. Why not hold your silence and die? You can't just will yourself dead and have it happen—especially in that position. Why not just give them what they want and be done with it? Reasons that come to mind include dignity, self-esteem, contempt for B-grade pageants. They can make you tell them most anything they know you know. The trick is, year in and year out, never to level with your captors, never let them really know what you know. . . .

The political prison experience is an emotional experience in that you learn that your naked, most inner self is in the spotlight, and that any detected shame or deep fear, any chink in your moral armor is a perfect opening for the manipulative crowbar. And once the manipulator gets it into you, he can put you out front working for him because he has something on you of which you are genuinely ashamed; he has the means to destroy your reputation if you fail him. Fates like that are what prison nightmares are made of, not the fear of pain. . . .

Americans in Hanoi learned fast. They made no deals. They learned that "meeting them half way" was the road to degradation. My hypothetical young prison mate soon learned that impulses, working against the grain, are very important in political prisons, that one learns to enjoy fighting city hall, to enjoy giving the enemy upside-down logic problems, that one soon finds himself taking his lumps with pride and not merely liking but loving that tapping guy next door, the man he never sees, the man he bares his soul to after each torture session, until he realizes he is thereby expiating all residual guilt. Then he realizes he can't be hurt and he can't be had as long as he tells the truth and clings to that forgiving band of brothers who are becoming his country, his family.

This is the power of comradeship and high mindedness that ultimately springs up among people of good will under pressure in mutual danger. It is a source of power as old as man, one we forget in times of freedom, of affluence, of fearful pessimism—like now.

Eight years in a Hanoi prison, survival and dignity. What does it all come down to? It does not come down to coping or supplication or hatred or strength beyond the grasp of any normal person. It comes down to unselfish comradeship, and it comes down to pride, dignity, an enduring sense of self-worth and to that enigmatic mixture of conscience and egoism called personal honor.

Questions:
1. President Ronald Reagan described the Vietnam War as a "noble crusade." James B. Stockdale describes it "as a misguided experiment of the Harvard Business School crowd." Which description do you believe to be correct? Why?
2. What do the accounts of Truong Nhu Tang and James B. Stockdale suggest about the ambiguities and frustrations of the Second Indochina War?

PART 28
Race, Ethnicity, and Conflict in the Twentieth Century

28.1   Roupen of Sassoun, Eyewitness to Armenia's Genocide

All the belligerents in World War I had internal political problems, but the Turkish Empire had special problems with its large minority populations. Fearful that its huge Armenian population would be too sympathetic to its enemy, Russia, in the spring of 1915, the Turkish military authorities decided to remove Armenians from eastern Turkey and march them south to the city to Aleppo, where they would be sent into the Syrian desert or marched east into the Tigris-Euphrates valley. On April 24, 1915, the first roundup of Armenians began. Throughout the spring and summer of 1915, large elements of the Armenian population were removed from their homes, stripped of their property, and marched into the desert; in many cases, they were killed in their villages. Although the exact numbers are difficult to determine, it is likely that more than a million Armenians were slaughtered in 1915. Mr. Roupen, an Armenian resident of Sassoun District, provided this eyewitness account of the 1915 summer massacres in an interview with Mr. A.S. Safrastian. In his account, he refers to the Kurds, another minority under Turkish rule, who were frequently used by the Turks to attack the Armenians.

Source: From The Treatment of Armenians in the Ottoman Empire: Documents Presented to Viscount Grey of Fallodon, Secretary of State for Foreign Affairs, with a Preface by Viscount Bryce (London: HMSO, 1916), pp. 85–87.

Early in July, the authorities ordered the Armenians to surrender their arms, and pay a large money ransom. The leading Armenians of the town and the headmen of the villages were subjected to revolting tortures. Their finger nails and then their toe nails were forcibly extracted; their teeth were knocked out, and in some cases their noses were whittled down, the victims being thus done to death under shocking, lingering agonies. The female relatives of the victims who came to the rescue were outraged in public before the very eyes of their mutilated husbands and brothers. The shrieks and death-cries of the victims filled the air, yet they did not move the Turkish beast. The same process of disarmament was carried out in the large Armenian villages of Khaskegh, Franknorshen, etc., and on the slightest show of resistance men and women were done to death in the manner described above. On the 10th July, large contingents of troops, followed by bands of criminals released from the prisons, began to round up the able-bodied men from all the villages. In the 100 villages of the plain of Moush most of the villagers took up any arms they possessed and offered a desperate resistance in various favourable positions. In the natural order of things the ammunition soon gave out in most villages, and there followed what is perhaps one of the greatest crimes in all history. Those who had no arms and had done nothing against the authorities were herded into various camps and bayoneted in cold blood.

In the town of Moush itself the Armenians, under the leadership of Gotoyan and others, entrenched themselves in the churches and stone-built houses and fought for four days in self-defense. The Turkish artillery, manned by German officers, made short work of all the Armenian positions. Every one of the Armenians, leaders as well as men, was killed fighting; and when the silence of death reigned over the ruins of churches and the rest, the Moslem rabble made a descent upon the women and children and drove them out of the town into large camps which had already been prepared for the peasant women and children. The ghastly scenes which followed may indeed sound incredible, yet these reports have been confirmed from Russian sources beyond all doubt.

The shortest method for disposing of the women and children concentrated in the various camps was to burn them. Fire was set to large wooden sheds in Alidjan, Megrakom, Khaskegh, and other Armenian villages, and these absolutely helpless women and children were roasted to death. Many went mad and threw their children away; some knelt down and prayed amid the flames in which their bodies were burning; others shrieked and cried for help which came from nowhere. And the executioners, who seem to have been unmoved by this unparalleled savagery, grasped infants by one leg and hurled them into the fire, calling out to the burning mothers: "Here are your lions." Turkish prisoners who had apparently witnessed some of these scenes were horrified and maddened at remembering the sight. They told the Russians that the stench of the burning human flesh permeated the air for many days after.

Under present circumstances it is impossible to say how many Armenians, out of a population of 60,000 in the plain of Moush, are left alive; the one fact which can be recorded at present is that now and then some survivors escape through the mountains and reach the Russian lines to give further details of the unparalleled crime perpetrated in Moush during July.

The Massacres in Sassoun.—While the "Butcher" battalions of Djevdet Bey and the regulars of Kiazim Bey were engaged in Bitlis and Moush, some cavalry were sent to Sassoun early in July to encourage the Kurds who had been defeated by the Armenians at the beginning of June. The Turkish cavalry invaded the lower valley of Sassoun and captured a few villages after stout fighting. In the meantime the reorganized Kurdish tribes attempted to close on Sassoun from the south, west, and north. During the last fortnight of July almost incessant fighting went on, sometimes even during the night. On the whole, the Armenians held their own on all fronts and expelled the Kurds from their advanced positions. However, the people of Sassoun had other anxieties to worry about. The population had doubled since their brothers who had escaped from the plains had sought refuge in their mountains; the millet crop of the last season had been a failure; all honey, fruit, and other local produce had been consumed, and the people had been feeding on unsalted roast mutton (they had not even any salt to make the mutton more sustaining); finally, the ammunition was in no way sufficient for the requirements of heavy fighting. But the worst had yet to come. Kiazim Bey, after reducing the town and the plain of Moush, rushed his army to Sassoun for a new effort to overwhelm these brave mountaineers. Fighting was renewed on all fronts throughout the Sassoun district. Big guns made carnage among the Armenian ranks. Roupen tells me that Gorioun, Dikran, and twenty other of their best fighters were killed by a single shell, which burst in their midst. Encouraged by the presence of guns, the cavalry and Kurds pushed on with relentless energy.

The Armenians were compelled to abandon the outlying lines of their defence and were retreating day by day into the heights of Antok, the central block of the mountains, some 10,000 feet high. The non-combatant women and children and their large flocks of cattle greatly hampered the free movements of the defenders, whose number had already been reduced from 3,000 to about half that figure. Terrible confusion prevailed during the Turkish attacks as well as the Armenian counter-attacks. Many of the Armenians smashed their rifles after firing the last cartridge and grasped their revolvers and daggers. The Turkish regulars and Kurds, amounting now to something like 30,000 altogether, pushed higher and higher up the heights and surrounded the main Armenian position at close quarters. Then followed one of those desperate and heroic struggles for life which have always been the pride of mountaineers. Men, women and children fought with knives, scythes, stones, and anything else they could handle. They rolled blocks of stone down the steep slopes, killing many of the enemy. In a frightful hand-to-hand combat, women were seen thrusting their knives into the throats of Turks and thus accounting for many of them. On the 5th August, the last day of the fighting, the blood-stained rocks of Antok were captured by the Turks. The Armenian warriors of Sassoun, except those who had worked round to the rear of the Turks to attack them on their flanks, had died in battle. Several young women, who were in danger of falling into the Turks' hands, threw themselves from the rocks, some of them with their infants in their arms. The survivors have since been carrying on a guerilla warfare, living only on unsalted mutton and grass. The approaching winter may have disastrous consequences for the remnants of the Sassounli Armenians, because they have nothing to eat and no means of defending themselves.

Questions:
1. *How would you compare this eyewitness account of "ethnic cleansing" with other accounts in this section? Are there any common characteristics?*
2. *Why would the Turkish military use Kurdish troops against Armenians?*
3. *Are Armenian women targeted for any special treatment? Why would women be a special target in genocide?*
4. *Were the Turkish concerns about Armenians supporting Russians justified? Why? Why not?*

28.2 "The Struggle Is My Life" (1961): Nelson Mandela

The 1950s was a difficult decade for the African National Congress. The South African government was consolidating the system of apartheid with new laws and trigger reflexes, an aggressive policy against civil protest, a disposition for violence and quick imprisonment. In March 1960, as demonstrators marched toward a police station to protest pass laws, the police panicked at the size of the crowds and opened fire: sixty-nine were killed and 180 wounded. The "Sharpeville Massacre," as it was called, focused international criticism on the Nationalist government. Uncomfortable under the spotlight, South Africa withdrew from the British Commonwealth and declared itself a republic; this began a twenty-year retreat from the international community as South Africa staggered into a self-imposed isolation. Within the country, the Nationalist government began a forced relocation of Africans into their "homelands" where dispossessed Blacks could be removed from the sight of White citizens, restricted, and better controlled.

It was in this environment that the protests of Oliver Tambo (1917–1993), Walter Sisulu (1912–), and Nelson Mandela (1918–) exacerbated the situation and focused the sentiment of many Africans. All three men had been active in organizing the ANC during the 1950s. In response to the Sharpeville Massacre, the ANC went underground and decided that peaceful protest and nonviolent action had not been effective against the violent tactics of the government. The time had arrived, in their minds, for active confrontation.

In many ways, Nelson Mandela's life encapsulates the setbacks and successes of Black nationalist politics in South Africa. The son of a minor tribal chief, Mandela was raised by his Christian mother before being taken into the household of a Thembu chief for education. Expelled from school for organizing resistence, Mandela trained as a lawyer in 1941 and became part of Oliver Tambo's legal practice. Encouraged by older and experienced protesters like his friend, Walter Sisulu, Mandela became an important and articulate advocate for the pain and alienation of native sentiment. In 1961, Mandela moved through the country in disguise, a renegade from South African law.

The first selection is from one of Mandela's underground letters dictated on June 26, 1961, where he made clear his decision to oppose the government. On August 5, 1962, Mandela was arrested in Natal and brought to trial in Pretoria from October 15 to November 7. Mandela was accused on two counts of inciting people to strike illegally and of leaving the country without a valid passport. The second excerpt from the trial transcript reveals much about Mandela's character and purpose. He conducted his own defense.

Source: *"The Struggle Is My Life" is from Freedom, Justice and Dignity for All South Africa: Statements and Articles by Mr. Nelson Mandela* (New York: Centre Against Apartheid, United Nations Department of Political and security Council Affairs, 1978), pp. 6–8.

Keep in Mind . . .

- Why did Mandela want to launch a campaign of noncollaboration and militant action against the Nationalist government?

NONCOLLABORATION IS OUR WEAPON

A full-scale and country-wide campaign of noncooperation with the Government will be launched immediately. The precise form of the contemplated actions, its scope and dimensions and duration, will be announced to you at the appropriate time.

At the present moment, it is sufficient to say that we plan to make government impossible. Those who are voteless cannot be expected to continue paying taxes to a Government which is not responsible to them. People who live in poverty and starvation cannot be expected to pay exorbitant house rents to the government and industry. We produce the work of the gold mines, the diamonds, and the coal, of the farms and industry, in return for miserable wages.

Why should we continue enriching those who steal the products of our sweat and blood? Those who side with the Government when we stage peaceful demonstrations to assert our claims and aspirations? . . . Which African does not burn with indignation when thousands of our people are sent to jail every month under cruel pass laws? Why should we continue carrying badges of slavery?

Noncollaboration is a dynamic weapon. We must refuse. We must use this weapon to send this Government to the grave. It must be used vigorously and without delay. The entire resources of the black people must be mobilized to withdraw all cooperation with the Nationalist Government.

Various forms of industrial and economic action will be employed to undermine the already tottering economy of the country. We will call upon the international bodies to expel South Africa and upon nations of the world to sever economic and diplomatic relations with the country.

THE STRUGGLE IS MY LIFE

I am informed that a warrant for my arrest has been issued, and that the police are looking for me. The National Action Council has given full and serious consideration to this question, and has sought advice of many trusted friends and bodies, and they have advised me not to surrender myself. I have accepted this advice and will not give myself up to a Government I do not recognize. Any serious politician will realize that, under the present-day conditions in this country to seek for cheap martyrdom by handing myself to the police is naive and criminal. We have an important program before us and it is important to carry it out very seriously and without delay.

I have chosen this latter course which is more difficult and which entails more risk and hardship than sitting in jail. I have had to separate myself from my dear wife and children, from my mother and sisters, to live as an outlaw in my own land. I have had to close my business, to abandon my profession, and to live in poverty and misery, as many of my people are doing. I will continue to act as the spokesman of the National Action Council during the phase that is unfolding and in the tough struggles that lie ahead.

I shall fight the Government side by side with you, inch by inch, and mile by mile, until victory is won.

What are you going to do? Will you come along with us, or are you going to cooperate with the Government in its efforts to suppress the claims and aspirations of your own people? Or are you going to remain silent and neutral in a matter of life and death to my people, to our people?

For my part, I have made the choice, I will not leave South Africa, nor will I surrender. Only through hardship, sacrifice and militant action can freedom be won. The struggle is my life.

I will continue fighting for freedom until the end of my days.

Consider This:

*   In this underground letter from Mandela, is his call for noncollaboration a plea for nonviolent protest? How do you interpret the phrase, "Only through hardship, sacrifice, and militant action can freedom be won"?

*   Compare Mandela's methods of resistance with those of Mohandas Gandhi in the selection entitled the "Doctrine of the Sword." Did these men share the same spirit of protest?

BLACK MAN IN A WHITE COURT (1962)

Source: Copyright © 1978 by Pathfinder Press. Reprinted by permission.

Keep in Mind . . .

*   Why did Mandela want the Court to recuse itself from his case?

Mandela: Your Worship, before I plead to the charge, there are one or two points I would like to raise. . . . I want to apply for Your Worship's recusal from this case. I challenge the right of this Court to hear my case on two grounds:

Firstly, I challenge it because I fear that I will not be given a fair and proper trial. Secondly, I consider myself neither legally nor morally bound to obey laws made by a Parliament in which I have no representation.

In a political trial such as this one, which involves a clash of the aspirations of the African people and those of whites, the country's courts, as presently constituted, cannot be impartial and fair. . . .

The Universal Declaration of Human Rights provides that all men are equal before the law, and are entitled without any discrimination to equal protection of the law. . . . It is true that an African who is charged in a court of law enjoys, on the surface the same rights and privileges as an accused who is white in so far as the conduct of this trial is concerned. He is governed by the same rules of procedure and evidence as apply to a white accused. But it would be grossly inaccurate to conclude from this fact that an African consequently enjoys equality before the law.

In its proper meaning equality before the law means the right to participate in the making of the laws by which one is governed, a constitution which guarantees democratic rights to all sections of the population, the right to approach the court for protection or relief in the case of the violation of rights guaranteed in the constitution, and the right to take part in the administration of justice as judges, magistrates, attorneys-general, law advisers and similar positions.

In the absence of these safeguards the phrase "equality before the law," in so far as it is intended to apply to us, is meaningless and misleading. All the rights and privileges to which I have referred are monopolized by whites, and we enjoy none of them.

The white man makes all the laws, he drags us before his courts and accuses us, and he sits in judgment over us.

It is fit and proper to raise the question sharply, what is this rigid colour-bar in the administration of justice? Why is it that in this courtroom, I face a white magistrate, am confronted by a white prosecutor, and escorted into the dock by a white orderly? Can anyone honestly and seriously suggest that in this type of atmosphere, the scales of justice are evenly balanced?

Why is it that no African in the history of this country has ever had the honour of being tried by his own kith and kin, by his own flesh and blood?

I will tell Your Worship why: the real purpose of this rigid colour-bar is to ensure that the justice dispensed by the courts should conform to the policy of the country, however much that policy might be in conflict with the norms of justice accepted in judiciaries throughout the civilized world.

I feel oppressed by the atmosphere of white domination that lurks all around in this courtroom. Somehow this atmosphere calls to mind the inhuman injustices caused to my people outside this courtroom by this same white domination.

It reminds me that I am voteless because there is a Parliament in this country that is white-controlled. I am without land because the white minority has taken a lion's share of my country and forced me to occupy poverty-stricken Reserves, over-populated and over-stocked. We are ravaged by starvation and disease. . . .

Magistrate: What has that got to do with the case, Mr. Mandela?

Mandela: Your Worship, this to me is an extremely important ground which the Court must consider.

Magistrate: I fully realise your position, Mr. Mandela, but you must confine yourself to the application and not go beyond it. I don't want to know about starvation. That in my view has got nothing to do with the case or the present moment.

Mandela: Well, Your Worship has already raised the point that here in the country there is only a white Court. What is the point of all this? Now if I can demonstrate to Your Worship that outside this Courtroom race discrimination has been used in such a way as to deprive me of my rights, not to treat me fairly, certainly this is a relevant fact from which to infer that wherever race discrimination is practised, this will be the same result, and this is the only reason why I am using this point.

Magistrate: I am afraid that I will have to interrupt you, and you will have to confine yourself to the reasons, the real reasons for asking me to recuse myself. . . .

Consider This:

*   What was Mandela's primary argument before the Court? Why didn't an African "enjoy equality before the law"?

*   In the decree entitled "Protection of the White Race," the National Party characterized apartheid as a policy "based on Christian principles of justice and reasonableness." How did Mandela's argument in Court disprove this point?

*   Would you agree that in the eyes of the White government and Court, the concept of equal rights was not a principle of "justice and reasonableness"?

Question:
1. *In this underground letter from Mandela, is his call for noncollaboration a plea for nonviolent protest? How do you interpret the phrase, "Only through hardship, sacrifice, and militant action can freedom be won"?*

28.3   Martin Luther King, Jr.

The letter that follows was written by Dr. King while he was serving a jail sentence in Birmingham, Alabama, in 1963. The offense for which he was jailed consisted of his participation in civil rights demonstrations throughout Alabama. He joined a growing number of demonstrators in this activity and several others also were jailed by the authorities. The civil rights movement had its origins in the Second World War in which many black soldiers participated with distinction and valor. Their experiences taught them that there was a better life possible than what they had endured as second-class citizens in the south. Many of these men became active in attempts to improve conditions for black people in their home areas. Dr. King is a notable example of such a person. He bases his case on the idea of justice and the American commitment, expressed so well by Thomas Jefferson in the Declaration of Independence, to the idea that all people are equal. As Dr. King makes clear, segregation is the opposite of this idea so it is un-American as well as unjust. His efforts on behalf of social justice for black people have been fruitful, with many beneficial results, particularly in the southern states, but also elsewhere in the country. So he did not languish in the Birmingham jail in vain.

> **Source:** Martin Luther King's "Letter from Birmingham Jail" from *A Testament of Hope*, ed. J. M. Washington, pp. 289-302. (San Francisco: Harper & Row, 1986)

LETTER FROM BIRMINGHAM CITY JAIL

My dear Fellow Clergymen,

While confined here in the Birmingham city jail, I came across your recent statement calling our present activities "unwise and untimely." Seldom, if ever, do I pause to answer criticism of my work and ideas. If I sought to answer all of the criticisms that cross my desk, my secretaries would be engaged in little else in the course of the day, and I would have no time for constructive work. But since I feel that you are men of genuine good will and your criticisms are sincerely set forth, I would like to answer your statement in what I hope will be patient and reasonable terms.

I think I should give the reason for my being in Birmingham, since you have been influenced by the argument of "outsiders coming in." I have the honor of serving as president of the Southern Christian Leadership Conference, an organization operating in every southern state, with headquarters in Atlanta, Georgia. We have some eighty-five affiliate organizations all across the South-one being the Alabama Christian Movement for Human Rights. Whenever necessary and possible we share staff, educational and financial resources with our affiliates. Several months ago our local affiliate here in Birmingham invited us to be on call to engage in a nonviolent direct-action program if such were deemed necessary. We readily consented and when the hour came we lived up to our promises. So I am here, along with several members of my staff, because we were invited here. I am here because I have basic organizational ties here.

Beyond this, I am in Birmingham because injustice is here. Just as the eighth century prophets left their little villages and carried their "thus saith the Lord" far beyond the boundaries of their hometowns; and just as the Apostle Paul left his little village of Tarsus and carried the gospel of Jesus Christ to practically every hamlet and city of the Graeco-Roman world, I too am compelled to carry the gospel of freedom beyond my particular hometown. Like Paul, I must constantly respond to the Macedonian call for aid.

Moreover, I am cognizant of the interrelatedness of all communities and states. I cannot sit idly by in Atlanta and not be concerned about what happens in Birmingham. Injustice anywhere is a threat to justice everywhere. We are caught in an inescapable network of mutuality, tied in a single garment of destiny. Whatever affects one directly affects all indirectly. Never again can we afford to live with the narrow, provincial "outside agitator" idea. Anyone who lives in the United States can never be considered an outsider anywhere in this country.

You deplore the demonstrations that are presently taking place in Birmingham. But I am sorry that your statement did not express a similar concern for the conditions that brought the demonstrations into being. I am sure that each of you would want to go beyond the superficial social analyst who looks merely at effects, and does not grapple with underlying causes. I would not hesitate to say that it is unfortunate that so-called demonstrations are taking place in Birmingham at this time, but I would say in more emphatic terms that it is even more unfortunate that the white power structure of this city left the Negro community with no other alternative.

In any nonviolent campaign there are four basic steps: (1) collection of the facts to determine whether injustices are alive, (2) negotiation, (3) self-purification, and (4) direct action. We have gone through all of these steps in Birmingham. There can be no gainsaying of the fact that racial injustice engulfs this community.

Birmingham is probably the most thoroughly segregated city in the United States. Its ugly record of police brutality is known in every section of this country. Its injust treatment of Negroes in the courts is a notorious reality. There have been more unsolved bombings of Negro homes and churches in Birmingham than any city in this nation. These are the hard, brutal and unbelievable facts. On the basis of these conditions Negro leaders sought to negotiate with the city fathers. But the political leaders consistently refused to engage in good faith negotiation.

Then came the opportunity last September to talk with some of the leaders of the economic community. In these negotiating sessions certain promises were made by the merchants-such as the promise to remove the humiliating racial signs from the stores. On the basis of these promises Rev. Shuttlesworth and the leaders of the Alabama Christian Movement for Human Rights agreed to call a moratorium on any type of demonstrations. As the weeks and months unfolded we realized that we were the victims of a broken promise. The signs remained. Like so many experiences of the past we were confronted with blasted hopes, and the dark shadow of a deep disappointment settled upon us. So we had no alternative except that of preparing for direct action, whereby we would present our very bodies as a means of laying our case before the conscience of the local and national community. We were not unmindful of the difficulties involved. So we decided to go through a process of self-purification. We started having workshops on nonviolence and repeatedly asked ourselves the questions, "Are you able to accept blows without retaliating?" "Are you able to endure the ordeals of jail?" We decided to set our direct-action program around the Easter season, realizing that with the exception of Christmas, this was the largest shopping period of the year. Knowing that a strong economic withdrawal program would be the byproduct of direct action, we felt that this was the best time to bring pressure on the merchants for the needed changes. Then it occurred to us that the March election was ahead and so we speedily decided to postpone action until after election day. When we discovered that Mr. Connor was in the run-off, we decided again to postpone action so that the demonstrations could not be used to cloud the issues. At this time we agreed to begin our nonviolent witness the day after the run-off.

This reveals that we did not move irresponsibly into direct action. We too wanted to see Mr. Connor defeated; so we went through postponement after postponement to aid in this community need. After this we felt that direct action could be delayed no longer.

You may well ask, "Why direct action? Why sit-ins, marches, etc.? Isn't negotiation a better path?" You are exactly right in your call for negotiation. Indeed, this is the purpose of direct action. Nonviolent direct action seeks to create such a crisis and establish such creative tension that a community that has constantly refused to negotiate is forced to con-

521

front the issue. It seeks so to dramatize the issue that it can no longer be ignored. I just referred to the creation of tension as a part of the work of the nonviolent resister. This may sound rather shocking. But I must confess that I am not afraid of the word tension. I have earnestly worked and preached against violent tension, but there is a type of constructive non-violent tension that is necessary for growth. Just as Socrates felt that it was necessary to create a tension in the mind so that individuals could rise from the bondage of myths and half-truths to the unfettered realm of creative analysis and objective appraisal, we must see the need of having nonviolent gadflies to create the kind of tension in society that will help men to rise from the dark depths of prejudice and racism to the majestic heights of understanding and brotherhood. So the purpose of the direct action is to create a situation so crisis-packed that it will inevitably open the door to negotiation. We, there-fore, concur with you in your call for negotiation. Too long has our beloved Southland been bogged down in the tragic attempt to live in monologue rather than dialogue.

One of the basic points in your statement is that our acts are untimely. Some have asked, "Why didn't you give the new administration time to act?" The only answer that I can give to this inquiry is that the new administration must be prodded about as much as the outgoing one before it acts. We will be sadly mistaken if we feel that the election of Mr. Boutwell will bring the millennium to Birmingham. While Mr. Boutwell is much more articulate and gentle than Mr. Connor, they are both segregationists, dedicated to the task of maintaining the status quo. The hope I see in Mr. Boutwell is that he will be reasonable enough to see the futility of massive resistance to desegregation. But he will not see this without pressure from the devotees of civil rights. My friends, I must say to you that we have not made a single gain in civil rights without determined legal and nonviolent pressure. History is the long and tragic story of the fact that privileged groups seldom give up their privileges voluntarily. Individuals may see the moral light and voluntarily give up their unjust posture; but as Reinhold Niebuhr has reminded us, groups are more immoral than individuals.

We know through painful experience that freedom is never voluntarily given by the oppressor; it must be demanded by the oppressed. Frankly, I have never yet engaged in a direct action movement that was "well-timed," accord-ing to the timetable of those who have not suffered unduly from the disease of segregation. For years now I have heard the words "Wait!" It rings in the ear of every Negro with a piercing familiarity. This "Wait" has almost always meant "Never." It has been a tranquilizing thalidomide, relieving the emotional stress for a moment, only to give birth to an ill-formed infant of frustration. We must come to see with the distinguished jurist of yesterday that "justice too long delayed is justice denied." We have waited for more than 340 years for our constitutional and God-given rights. The nations of Asia and Africa are moving with jet-like speed toward the goal of political independence, and we still creep at horse and buggy pace toward the gaining of a cup of coffee at a lunch counter. I guess it is easy for those who have never felt the stinging darts of segregation to say, "Wait." But when you have seen vicious mobs lynch your mothers and fathers at will and drown your sisters and brothers at whim; when you have seen hate-filled policemen curse, kick, brutalize and even kill your black broth-ers and sisters with impunity; when you see the vast majority of your twenty million Negro brothers smothering in an air-tight cage of poverty in the midst of an affluent society; when you suddenly find your tongue twisted and your speech stammering as you seek to explain to your six-year-old daughter why she can't go to the public amusement park that has just been advertised on television, and see tears welling up in her little eyes when she is told that Funtown is closed to col-ored children, and see the depressing clouds of inferiority begin to form in her little mental sky, and see her begin to dis-tort her little personality by unconsciously developing a bitterness toward white people; when you have to concoct an answer for a five-year-old son asking in agonizing pathos: "Daddy, why do white people treat colored people so mean?"; when you take a cross-country drive and find it necessary to sleep night after night in the uncomfortable corners of your automobile because no motel will accept you; when you are humiliated day in and day out by nagging signs reading "white" and "colored"; when your first name becomes "nigger" and your middle name becomes "boy" (however old you are) and your last name becomes 'John," and when your wife and mother are never given the respected title "Mrs."; when you are harried by day and haunted by night by the fact that you are a Negro, living constantly at tiptoe stance never quite knowing what to expect next, and plagued with inner fears and outer resentments; when you are forever fighting a degen-erating sense of "nobodiness"; then you will understand why we find it difficult to wait. There comes a time when the cup of endurance runs over, and men are no longer willing to be plunged into an abyss of injustice where they experience the blackness of corroding despair. I hope, sirs, you can understand our legitimate and unavoidable impatience.

You express a great deal of anxiety over our willingness to break laws. This is certainly a legitimate concern. Since we so diligently urge people to obey the Supreme Court's decision of 1954 outlawing segregation in the public schools, it is rather strange and paradoxical to find us consciously breaking laws. One may well ask, "How can you advocate break-ing some laws and obeying others?" The answer is found in the fact that there are two types of laws: there are just and there are unjust laws. I would agree with Saint Augustine that "An unjust law is no law at all."

Now what is the difference between the two? How does one determine when a law is just or unjust? A just law is a man-made code that squares with the moral law or the law of God. An unjust law is a code that is out of harmony with the moral law. To put it in the terms of Saint Thomas Aquinas, an unjust law is a human law that is not rooted in eternal and natural law. Any law that uplifts human personality is just. Any law that degrades human personality is unjust. All seg-regation statutes are unjust because segregation distorts the soul and damages the personality. It gives the segregator a false sense of superiority, and the segregated a false sense of inferiority. To use the words of Martin Buber, the great Jewish philosopher, segregation substitutes an "I-it" relationship for the "I-thou" relationship, and ends up relegating persons to the status of things. So segregation is not only politically, economically and sociologically unsound, but it is morally wrong and sinful. Paul Tillich has said that sin is separation. Isn't segregation an existential expression of man's tragic separation, an expression of his awful estrangement, his terrible sinfulness? So I can urge men to disobey segregation ordinances because they are morally wrong.

Let us turn to a more concrete example of just and unjust laws. An unjust law is a code that a majority inflicts on a minority that is not binding on itself. This is difference made legal. On the other hand a just law is a code that a majority compels a minority to follow that it is willing to follow itself. This is sameness made legal.

Let me give another explanation. An unjust law is a code inflicted upon a minority which that minority had no part in enacting or creating because they did not have the unhampered right to vote. Who can say that the legislature of Alabama which set up the segregation laws was democratically elected? Throughout the state of Alabama all types of conniving methods are used to prevent Negroes from becoming registered voters and there are some counties without a single Negro registered to vote despite the fact that the Negro constitutes a majority of the population. Can any law set up in such a state be considered democratically structured?

These are just a few examples of unjust and just laws. There are some instances when a law is just on its face and unjust in its application. For instance, I was arrested Friday on a charge of parading without a permit. Now there is nothing wrong with an ordinance which requires a permit for a parade, but when the ordinance is used to preserve segregation and to deny citizens the First Amendment privilege of peaceful assembly and peaceful protest, then it becomes unjust.

I hope you can see the distinction I am trying to point out. In no sense do I advocate evading or defying the law as the rabid segregationist would do. This would lead to anarchy. One who breaks an unjust law must do it *openly, lovingly* (not hatefully as the white mothers did in New Orleans when they were seen on television screaming, "nigger, nigger, nigger"), and with a willingness to accept the penalty. I submit that an individual who breaks a law that conscience tells him is unjust, and willingly accepts the penalty by staying in jail to arouse the conscience of the community over its injustice, is in reality expressing the very highest respect for law.

Of course, there is nothing new about this kind of civil disobedience. It was seen sublimely in the refusal of Shadrach, Meshach, and Abednego to obey the laws of Nebuchadnezzar because a higher moral law was involved. It was practiced superbly by the early Christians who were willing to face hungry lions and the excruciating pain of chopping blocks, before submitting to certain unjust laws of the Roman Empire. To a degree academic freedom is a reality today because Socrates practiced civil disobedience.

We can never forget that everything Hitler did in Germany was "legal" and everything the Hungarian freedom fighters did in Hungary was "illegal." It was "illegal" to aid and comfort a Jew in Hitler's Germany. But I am sure that if I had lived in Germany during that time I would have aided and comforted my Jewish brothers even though it was illegal. If I lived in a Communist country today where certain principles dear to the Christian faith are suppressed, I believe I would openly advocate disobeying these anti-religious laws. I must make two honest confessions to you, my Christian and Jewish brothers. First, I must confess that over the last few years I have been gravely disappointed with the white moderate. I have almost reached the regrettable conclusion that the Negro's great stumbling block in the stride toward freedom is not the White Citizen's Counciler or the Ku Klux Klanner, but the white moderate who is more devoted to "order" than to justice; who prefers a negative peace which is the absence of tension to a positive peace which is the presence of justice; who constantly says, "I agree with you in the goal you seek, but I can't agree with your methods of direct action"; who paternalistically feels that he can set the timetable for another man's freedom; who lives by the myth of time and who constantly advises the Negro to wait until a "more convenient season." Shallow understanding from people of good will is more frustrating than absolute misunderstanding from people of ill will. Lukewarm acceptance is much more bewildering than outright rejection.

I had hoped that the white moderate would understand that law and order exist for the purpose of establishing justice, and that when they fail to do this they become dangerously structured dams that block the flow of social progress. I had hoped that the white moderate would understand that the present tension of the South is merely a necessary phase of the transition from an obnoxious negative peace, where the Negro passively accepted his unjust plight, to a substance-filled positive peace, where all men will respect the dignity and worth of human personality. Actually, we who engage in nonviolent direct action are not the creators of tension. We merely bring to the surface the hidden tension that is already alive. We bring it out in the open where it can be seen and dealt with. Like a boil that can never be cured as long as it is covered up but must be opened with all its pus-flowing ugliness to the natural medicines of air and light, injustice must likewise be exposed, with all of the tension its exposing creates, to the light of human conscience and the air of national opinion before it can be cured.

In your statement you asserted that our actions, even though peaceful, must be condemned because they precipitate violence. But can this assertion be logically made? Isn't this like condemning the robbed man because his possession of money precipitated the evil act of robbery? Isn't this like condemning Socrates because his unswerving commitment to truth and his philosophical delvings precipitated the misguided popular mind to make him drink the hemlock? Isn't this like condemning Jesus because His unique God-consciousness and never-ceasing devotion to his will precipitated the evil act of crucifixion? We must come to see, as federal courts have consistently affirmed, that it is immoral to urge an individual to withdraw his efforts to gain his basic constitutional rights because the quest precipitates violence. Society must protect the robbed and punish the robber.

I had also hoped that the white moderate would reject the myth of time. I received a letter this morning from a white brother in Texas which said: "All Christians know that the colored people will receive equal rights eventually, but it is possible that you are in too great of a religious hurry. It has taken Christianity almost two thousand years to accomplish what it has. The teachings of Christ take time to come to earth." All that is said here grows out of a tragic misconception of time. It is the strangely irrational notion that there is something in the very flow of time that will inevitably cure all ills. Actually time is neutral. It can be used either destructively or constructively. I am coming to feel that the people of ill will have used time much more effectively than the people of good will. We will have to repent in this generation not merely for the vitriolic words and actions of the bad people, but for the appalling silence of the good people. We must come to see that human progress never rolls in on wheels of inevitability. It comes through the tireless efforts and persistent work of men willing to be co-workers with God, and without this hard word time itself becomes an ally of the forces of social stagnation. We must use time creatively, and forever realize that the time is always ripe to do right. Now is the time to make real the promise of democracy, and transform our pending national elegy into a creative psalm of brotherhood. Now is the time to lift our national policy from the quicksand of racial injustice to the solid rock of human dignity.

You spoke of our activity in Birmingham as extreme. At first I was rather disappointed that fellow clergymen would see my nonviolent efforts as those of the extremist. I started thinking about the fact that I stand in the middle of two opposing forces in the Negro community. One is a force of complacency made up of Negroes who, as a result of long years of oppression, have been so completely drained of self-respect and a sense of "somebodiness" that they have adjusted to segregation, and, of a few Negroes in the middle class who, because of a degree of academic and economic security, and because at points they profit by segregation, have unconsciously become insensitive to the problems of the masses. The other force is one of bitterness and hatred, and comes perilously close to advocating violence. It is expressed in the various black nationalist groups that are springing up over the nation, the largest and best known being Elijah Muhammad's Muslim movement. This movement is nourished by the contemporary frustration over the continued existence of racial discrimination. It is made up of people who have lost faith in America, who have absolutely repudiated Christianity, and who have concluded that the white man is an incurable "devil." I have tried to stand between these two forces, saying that we need not follow the "do-nothingism" of the complacent or the hatred and despair of the black nationalist. There is the more excellent way of love and nonviolent protest. I'm grateful to God that, through the Negro church, the dimension of nonviolence entered our struggle. If this philosophy had not emerged, I am convinced that by now many streets of the South would be flowing with floods of blood. And I am further convinced that if our white brothers dismiss us as "rabble-rousers" and "outside agitators" those of us who are working through the channels of nonviolent direct action and refuse to support our nonviolent efforts, millions of Negroes, out of frustration and despair, will seek solace and security in black nationalist ideologies, a development that will lead inevitably to a frightening racial nightmare.

Oppressed people cannot remain oppressed forever. The urge for freedom will eventually come. This is what happened to the American Negro. Something within has reminded him of his birthright of freedom; something without has reminded him that he can gain it. Consciously and unconsciously, he has been swept in by what the Germans call the Zeitgeist, and with his black brothers of Africa, and his brown and yellow brothers of Asia, South America and the Caribbean, he is moving with a sense of cosmic urgency toward the promised land of racial justice. Recognizing this vital urge that has engulfed the Negro community, one should readily understand public demonstrations. The Negro has many pent-up resentments and latent frustrations. He has to get them out. So let him march sometime; let him have his prayer pilgrimages to the city hall; understand why he must have sit-ins and freedom rides. If his repressed emotions do not come out in these nonviolent ways, they will come out in ominous expressions of violence. This is not a threat; it is a fact of history. So I have not said to my people "get rid of your discontent." But I have tried to say that this normal and healthy discontent can be channelized through the creative outlet of nonviolent direct action. Now this approach is being dismissed as extremist. I must admit that I was initially disappointed in being so categorized.

But as I continued to think about the matter I gradually gained a bit of satisfaction from being considered an extremist. Was not Jesus an extremist in love—"Love your enemies, bless them that curse you, pray for them that despitefully use you." Was not Amos an extremist for justice—"Let justice roll down like waters and righteousness like a mighty stream." Was not Paul an extremist for the gospel of Jesus Christ—"I bear in my body the marks of the Lord Jesus." Was not Martin Luther an extremist—"Here I stand; I can do none other so help me God." Was not John Bunyan an extremist—"I will stay in jail to the end of my days before I make a butchery of my conscience." Was not Abraham Lincoln an extremist—"This nation cannot survive half slave and half free." Was not Thomas Jefferson an extremist—"We hold these truths to be self—evident, that all men are created equal." So the question is not whether we will be extremist but what kind of extremist will we be. Will we be extremists for hate or will we be extremists for love? Will we be extremists for the preservation of injustice—or will we be extremists for the cause of justice? In that dramatic scene on Calvary's hill, three men were crucified. We must not forget that all three were crucified for the same crime—the crime of extremism. Two were extremists for immorality, and thusly fell below their environment. The other, Jesus Christ, was an extremist for love, truth and goodness, and thereby rose above his environment. So, after all, maybe the South, the nation and the world are in dire need of creative extremists.

I had hoped that the white moderate would see this. Maybe I was too optimistic. Maybe I expected too much. I guess I should have realized that few members of a race that has oppressed another race can understand or appreciate the deep groans and passionate yearnings of those that have been oppressed and still fewer have the vision to see that injustice must be rooted out by strong, persistent and determined action. I am thankful, however, that some of our white brothers have grasped the meaning of this social revolution and committed themselves to it. They are still all too small in quantity, but they are big in quality. Some like Ralph McGill, Lillian Smith, Harry Golden, and James Dabbs have written about our struggle in eloquent, prophetic and understanding terms. Others have marched with us down nameless streets of the South. They have languished in filthy roach—infested jails, suffering the abuse and brutality of angry policemen who see them as "dirty nigger—lovers." They, unlike so many of their moderate brothers and sisters, have recognized the urgency of the moment and sensed the need for powerful "action" antidotes to combat the disease of segregation.

Let me rush on to mention my other disappointment. I have been so greatly disappointed with the white church and its leadership. Of course, there are some notable exceptions. I am not unmindful of the fact that each of you has taken some significant stands on this issue. I commend you, Rev. Stallings, for your Christian stance on this past Sunday, in welcoming Negroes to your worship service on a non—segregated basis. I commend the Catholic leaders of this state for integrating Springhill College several years ago.

But despite these notable exceptions I must honestly reiterate that I have been disappointed with the church. I do not say that as one of the negative critics who can always find something wrong with the church. I say it as a minister of the gospel, who loves the church; who was nurtured in its bosom; who has been sustained by its spiritual blessings and who will remain true to it as long as the cord of life shall lengthen.

I had the strange feeling when I was suddenly catapulted into the leadership of the bus protest in Montgomery several years ago that we would have the support of the white church. I felt that the white ministers, priests and rabbis of the South would be some of our strongest allies. Instead, some have been outright opponents, refusing to understand the freedom movement and misrepresenting its leaders; all too many others have been more cautious than courageous and have remained silent behind the anesthetizing security of the stained—glass windows.

In spite of my shattered dreams of the past, I came to Birmingham with the hope that the white religious leadership of this community would see the justice of our cause, and with deep moral concern, serve as the channel through which our just grievances would get to the power structure. I had hoped that each of you would understand. But again I have been disappointed. I have heard numerous religious leaders of the South call upon their worshippers to comply with a desegregation decision because it is the *law,* but I have longed to hear white ministers say, "Follow this decree because integration is morally *right* and the Negro is your brother." In the midst of blatant injustices inflicted upon the Negro, I have watched white churches stand on the sideline and merely mouth pious irrelevancies and sanctimonious trivialities. In the midst of a mighty struggle to rid our nation of racial and economic injustice, I have heard so many ministers say, "Those are social issues with which the gospel has no real concern," and I have watched so many churches commit themselves to a completely otherworldly religion which made a strange distinction between body and soul, the sacred and the secular.

So here we are moving toward the exit of the twentieth century with a religious community largely adjusted to the status quo, standing as a tail—light behind other community agencies rather than a headlight leading men to higher levels of justice.

I have traveled the length and breadth of Alabama, Mississippi, and all the other southern states. On sweltering summer days and crisp autumn mornings I have looked at her beautiful churches with their lofty spires pointing heavenward. I have beheld the impressive outlay of her massive religious education buildings. Over and over again I have found myself asking: "What kind of people worship here? Who is their God? Where were their voices when the lips of Governor Barnett dripped with words of interposition and nullification? Where were they when Governor Wallace gave the clarion call for defiance and hatred? Where were their voices of support when tired, bruised, and weary Negro men and women decided to rise from the dark dungeons of complacency to the bright hills of creative protest?"

Yes, these questions are still in my mind. In deep disappointment, I have wept over the laxity of the church. But be assured that my tears have been tears of love. There can be no deep disappointment where there is not deep love. Yes, I love the church; I love her sacred walls. How could I do otherwise? I am in the rather unique position of being the son, the grandson, and the great—grandson of preachers. Yes, I see the church as the body of Christ. But, oh! How we have blemished and scarred that body through social neglect and fear of being nonconformists.

There was a time when the church was very powerful. It was during that period when the early Christians rejoiced when they were deemed worthy to suffer for what they believed. In those days the church was not merely a thermometer that recorded the ideas and principles of popular opinion; it was a thermostat that transformed the mores of society. Wherever the early Christians entered a town the power structure got disturbed and immediately sought to convict them for being "disturbers of the peace" and "outside agitators." But they went on with the conviction that they were "a colony of heaven," and had to obey God rather than man. They were small in number but big in commitment. They were too God—intoxicated to be "astronomically intimidated." They brought an end to such ancient evils as infanticide and gladiatorial contest.

Things are different now. The contemporary church is often a weak, ineffectual voice with an uncertain sound. It is so often the arch—supporter of the status quo. Far from being disturbed by the presence of the church, the power structure of the average community is consoled by the church's silent and often vocal sanction of things as they are.

But the judgment of God is upon the church as never before. If the church of today does not recapture the sacrificial spirit of the early church, it will lose its authentic ring, forfeit the loyalty of millions, and be dismissed as an irrelevant social club with no meaning for the twentieth century. I am meeting young people every day whose disappointment with the church has risen to outright disgust.

Maybe again, I have been too optimistic. Is organized religion too inextricably bound to the status quo to save our nation and the world? Maybe I must turn my faith to the inner spiritual church, the church within the church, as the true ecclesia and the hope of the world. But again I am thankful to God that some noble souls from the ranks of organized religion have broken loose from the paralyzing chains of conformity and joined us as active partners in the struggle for freedom. They have left their secure congregations and walked the streets of Albany, Georgia, with us. They have gone through the highways of the South on tortuous rides for freedom. Yes, they have gone to jail with us. Some have been kicked out of their churches, and lost support of their bishops and fellow ministers. But they have gone with the faith that right defeated is stronger than evil triumphant. These men have been the leaven in the lump of the race. Their witness has been the spiritual salt that has preserved the true meaning of the gospel in these troubled times. They have carved a tunnel of hope through the dark mountain of disappointment.

I hope the church as a whole will meet the challenge of this decisive hour. But even if the church does not come to the aid of justice, I have no despair about the future. I have no fear about the outcome of our struggle in Birmingham, even if our motives are presently misunderstood. We will reach the goal of freedom in Birmingham and all over the nation, because the goal of America is freedom. Abused and scorned though we may be, our destiny is tied up with the destiny of America. Before the Pilgrims landed at Plymouth we were here. Before the pen of Jefferson etched across the pages of history the majestic words of the Declaration of Independence, we were here. For more than two centuries our foreparents labored in this country without wages; they made cotton king; and they built the homes of their masters in the midst of brutal injustice and shameful humiliation—and yet out of a bottomless vitality they continued to thrive and develop. If the inexpressible cruelties of slavery could not stop us, the opposition we now face will surely fail. We will win our freedom because the sacred heritage of our nation and the eternal will of God are embodied in our echoing demands.

I must close now. But before closing I am impelled to mention one other point in your statement that troubled me profoundly. You warmly commended the Birmingham police force for keeping "order" and "preventing violence." I don't believe you would have so warmly commended the police force if you had seen its angry violent dogs literally biting six unarmed, nonviolent Negroes. I don't believe you would so quickly commend the policemen if you would observe their ugly and inhuman treatment of Negroes here in the city jail; if you would watch them push and curse old Negro women and young Negro girls; if you would see them slap and kick old Negro men and young boys; if you will observe them, as they did on two occasions, refuse to give us food because we wanted to sing our grace together. I'm sorry that I can't join you in your praise for the police department.

It is true that they have been rather disciplined in their public handling of the demonstrators. In this sense they have been rather publicly "nonviolent." But for what purpose? To preserve the evil system of segregation. Over the last few years I have consistently preached that nonviolence demands that the means we use must be as pure as the ends we seek. So I have tried to make it clear that it is wrong to use immoral means to attain moral ends. But now I must affirm that it is just as wrong, or even more so, to use moral means to preserve immoral ends. Maybe Mr. Connor and his policemen have been rather publicly nonviolent, as Chief Pritchett was in Albany, Georgia, but they have used the moral means of nonviolence to maintain the immoral end of flagrant racial injustice. T. S. Eliot has said that there is no greater treason than to do the right deed for the wrong reason.

I wish you had commended the Negro sit—inners and demonstrators of Birmingham for their sublime courage, their willingness to suffer and their amazing discipline in the midst of the most inhuman provocation. One day the South will recognize its real heroes. They will be the James Merediths, courageously and with a majestic sense of purpose facing jeering and hostile mobs and the agonizing loneliness that characterizes the life of the pioneer. They will be old, oppressed, battered Negro women, symbolized in a seventy—two—year—old woman of Montgomery, Alabama, who rose up with a sense of dignity and with her people decided not to ride the segregated buses, and responded to one who inquired about her tiredness with ungrammatical profundity: "My feet is tired, but my soul is rested." They will be the young high school and college students, young ministers of the gospel and a host of their elders courageously and nonviolently sitting—in at lunch counters and willingly going to jail for conscience's sake. One day the South will know that when these disinherited children of God sat down at lunch counters they were in reality standing up for the best in the American dream and the most sacred values in our Judeo—Christian heritage, and thusly, carrying our whole nation back to those great wells of democracy which were dug deep by the Founding Fathers in the formulation of the Constitution and the Declaration of Independence.

Never before have I written a letter this long (or should I say a book?). I'm afraid that it is much too long to take your precious time. I can assure you that it would have been much shorter if I had been writing from a comfortable desk, but what else is there to do when you are alone for days in the dull monotony of a narrow jail cell other than write long letters, think strange thoughts, and pray long prayers?

If I have said anything in this letter that is an overstatement of the truth and is indicative of an unreasonable impatience, I beg you to forgive me. If I have said anything in this letter that is an understatement of the truth and is indicative of my having a patience that makes me patient with anything less than brotherhood, I beg God to forgive me.

I hope this letter finds you strong in the faith. I also hope that circumstances will soon make it possible for me to meet each of you, not as an integrationist or a civil rights leader, but as a fellow clergyman and a Christian brother. Let us all hope that the dark clouds of racial prejudice will soon pass away and the deep fog of misunderstanding will be lifted from our fear—drenched communities and in some not too distant tomorrow the radiant stars of love and brotherhood will shine over our great nation with all of their scintillating beauty. Yours for the cause of Peace and Brotherhood,

Martin Luther King, Jr.

Questions:
1. Why is King protesting? How does he justify breaking the law?
2. Compare King's notion of nonviolent resistance with Gandhi's notion of love-force.

28.4   Keith B. Richburg, A Black Man Confronts Africa

Keith B. Richburg was born in Detroit in 1958, graduated from the University of Michigan in 1980, and completed a master's degree in international relations at the London School of Economics in 1983. He then began a career in journalism with the Washington Post and from 1991 to 1994 was based in Nairobi as the paper's African bureau chief. Richburg won the National Association of Black Journalists' foreign reporting award in 1993 for his coverage of the civil war and famine in Somalia and has received other awards for his coverage of African affairs. Whereas some black Americans in search of their roots and ethnic and cultural identity turn to Africa, Richburg, who was black, found little to identify with while living there. In the following selection, he provides an interesting perspective on the turbulent continent.

Source: From Keith B. Richburg, *Out of America: A Black Man Confronts Africa* (New York: Basic Books, 1997), pp. 225–29. Reprinted by permission.

It's been a long journey now, and I'll be leaving Africa soon. I'm beaten down, weary, ready to leave all of these lurid images behind me, ready to go home. I've seen too much death, too much misery, too much hatred, and I find I no longer care.

Africa. Birthplace of civilization. My ancestral homeland. I came here thinking I might find a little bit of that missing piece of myself. But Africa chewed me up and spit me back out again. It took out a machete and slashed into my brain the images that have become my nightmares. I close my eyes now and I am staring at a young woman atop a pile of corpses. I see an old man on the side of the road imploring me for a last drop of water before he dies in the dirt. I see my friends surrounded by an angry mob as they try to fend off the stones that rain down to crush their skulls. I see the grotesquely charred body of a young man set on fire. I see a church altar desecrated by the blood of the dead, and bullet holes forming a halo around Christ's likeness on the cross. Then I see Ilaria, beautiful Ilaria, bleeding to death in her car on the side of the road. There is an old man, broken and bent, who still limps from the pain of the torture that destroyed his limbs. There are the limbless beggars pressing their bloodied stumps against a car window. There is a child, smiling at me, while he aims his loaded grenade launcher at my passing car.

My eyes snap open, but I remain frightened of these ghosts that I know are out there, in the darkness, in Africa. I tried my best to get to know this place, to know the people. But instead I am sitting here alone in my house in Nairobi, frightened, staring into the blackness of the African night. It's quiet outside and I'm feeling scared and lonely. I am surrounded by a high fence and protected by two large dogs. I have a paid security guard patrolling the perimeter, a silent alarm system, and a large metal door with a sliding bolt that I keep firmly closed, all to prevent Africa from sneaking across my front yard and bashing into my brains with a panga knife for the two hundred dollars and change I keep in my top desk drawer.

527

It wasn't supposed to turn out this way. I really did come here with an open mind, wanting to love the place, love the people. I would love to end this journey now on a high note, to see hope amid the chaos. I'd love to talk about the smiles of the African people, their generosity and perseverance, their love of life, their music and dance, their respect for elders, their sense of family and community. I could point out the seeds of democracy, the formation of a "civil society," the emergence of an urban middle class, the establishment of independent institutions, and the rule of law. I wish I could end my story this way, but it would all be a lie.

How can anyone talk about democracy and constitutions and the rule of law in places where paramilitary security forces firebomb the offices of opposition newspapers? Where entire villages get burned down and thousands of people made homeless because of competing political loyalties? Where whole chunks of countries are under the sway of armed guerrillas? And where traditional belief runs so deep that a politician can be arrested and charged with casting magic spells over poor villagers to force them to vote for him?

My language may seem dark and disturbing, but that's what the reality was for me—almost all dark and disturbing. More than three years here have left me bitter and largely devoid of hope, and largely drained of compassion.

Now when I hear the latest reports of the latest African tragedy—a tribal slaughter in Burundi, perhaps, a riot in a refugee camp in a remote corner of Zaire, maybe a new flood of refugees streaming across a border in Uganda or Sierra Leone—I can watch with more than casual interest because I have been there. I feel sorrow for the victims. I shake my head in frustration at the continent's continuing anguish. I might even rush off a contribution to the Red Cross or one of the other aid agencies struggling to help. But I feel nothing more.

Maybe I would care more if I had not been here myself, if I had not seen the suffering up close, if I hadn't watched the bodies tumbling over the waterfall, smelled the rotting flesh. Yes, perhaps from a different vantage point, I would still have the luxury of falling back on the old platitudes. Maybe if I had never set foot here, I could celebrate my own blackness, my "African-ness." Then I might feel a part of this place, and Africa's pain might be my own. But while I know that "Afrocentrism" has become fashionable for many black Americans searching for identity, I know it cannot work for me. I have been here, I have lived here and seen Africa in all its horror. I am an American, a black American, and I feel no connection to this strange and violent place.

You see? I just wrote "black American." I couldn't even bring myself to write "African American." It's a phrase that, for me, doesn't roll naturally off the tongue: "African American." Is that what we really are? Is there anything really "African" left in the descendants of those original slaves who made the torturous journey across the Atlantic? Are white Americans whose ancestors sailed west across the same ocean as long ago as the slaves still considered "English Americans" or "Dutch Americans"? And haven't the centuries on America's shores erased all those ancient connections, so that we descendants of Africa and England and Holland and Ireland and China are now simply "Americans"?

If you want to establish some kind of ethnic pecking order, based on the number of years in the New World, then blacks would be at the top of the list; the first slaves from Africa arrived in Virginia before the Mayflower even set sail. Black influence today is visible in so many aspects of American culture, from jazz to basketball to slang time to poetry. Spaghetti and dim sum and sushi have all become part of the American culinary scene, but what can be more American than down-home southern cooking—fried chicken and biscuits, barbecued spare ribs, grits and greens—and in the big houses of the old South, there was invariably a black face in the back, preparing the meals.

Yet despite our "American-ness," despite the black contributions to the culture America claims as its own, black Americans have consistently been made to feel like strangers in our own land, the land where we have lived for some four hundred years. I know, because I have felt that way too. It's subtle sometimes, that sense of not belonging. But in ways large and small, most black people in America would probably say they feel it every day.

I myself feel it whenever I'm "dressed down," not wearing a suit and tie, in a well-worn pair of old jeans and a T-shirt perhaps, and I walk into a department store or a corner shop. I can feel the store detective's eyes following me through the aisles, making sure I'm not there to shoplift the merchandise. And if I have a newspaper under my arm when I enter the store, I make a point of waving it openly to the sales clerk, just so she doesn't think later that I'm trying to pilfer it off the rack.

I feel it when I'm standing on a street corner in Washington or New York, trying to hail a taxi. If I'm on the way home from work, I remember to open my overcoat so the cab driver can see my dress shirt and necktie, so he will think: This is not some street thug who might rob me; this is a respectable black man on the way home from the office. And if I am in Washington and it's night, and I'm going west of Rock Creek Park, to Georgetown or one of the city's more affluent "white" neighborhoods, I make sure to stand on the correct side of the street so I am not mistaken for a black man heading east, to the black neighborhoods, to the areas where I know taxi drivers, even black ones, fear to tread.

I feel it, too, when I'm driving a car in America, anywhere in America. If I am pulled over by the police, I keep my hands clearly visible on the steering wheel; if I am wearing sunglasses, I remove them. Because I know I am a black man in America and I might be seen as a threat, a danger.

Questions:

1. *In addition to his job of reporting, the author writes that he was also searching for his "ancestral homeland." What caused him to declare, "I am an American, a black American, and I feel no connection to this strange and violent place"?*

2. *Richburg also lived in Washington, D.C., and New York City, and after residing in both cities, he claims that he and many other black Americans have consistently been made to "feel like strangers in our own land." What caused him to develop these feelings?*

3. *Compare and contrast Richburg's account of living in Africa with the views expressed by Theresa Andrews.*

28.5 Alain Destexhe, Rwanda and Genocide in the Twentieth Century

In the spring of 1994, the Western media reported "tribal warfare" of unusual ferocity in Rwanda, a small central African country with Zaire on its west, Uganda on its north, and Kenya on its east. Together with its southern neighbor, Burundi, Rwanda had been a German colony from 1885 to World War I and a Belgian mandate from 1925 to 1962. In 1994, the majority Hutus seemed intent on killing as many of the minority Tutsis, who had formerly enjoyed something of an elite status, as they could. In the summer months of the same year, the Rwandan Patriotic Front (RPF), a group composed largely of Tutsis in exile in Uganda, with some Hutus hostile to the regime, led an invasion that succeeded in toppling almost the entire Hutu government. The leadership of the fallen regime encouraged Hutus to flee the country, and hundreds of thousands did so, huge numbers ending up in a sprawling refugee camp in Goma, just across the Zairian border.

Alain Destexhe is an experienced observer of African affairs and the former secretary general of Médecins sans Frontières (Doctors Without Borders), a worldwide relief and health organization very active in Africa. In his work, excerpted here, he traces how the Tutsis, who raised cattle and acquired wealth and status separating them from the Hutus, who were mostly crop farmers and laborers, became the objects of murderous resentment.

> **Source:** From Alain Destexhe, *Rwanda and Genocide in the Twentieth Century*, trans. by Alison Marschner (New York: New York University Press, 1995), pp. 28, 30, 31–32, 33, 37–38, 43, 47, 49, 61–62, 70, passim. Used by permission.

HUTU RACIST IDEOLOGY

It took exactly fifty years . . . it or something very like it has indeed happened again. Just as Hitler's grand plan was founded on an ingrained European anti-Semitism which he played on by singling out the Jews as the source of all Germany's ills, the Hutu radicals are inheritors of the colonial lunacy of classifying and grading different ethnic groups in a racial hierarchy. While the Jews were described by Nazis as "vermin," the Tutsis were called *invenzi* ("the cockroaches that have to be crushed"). Anti-Tutsi propaganda presented them as a "minority, well-off and foreign"—so similar to the image developed to stigmatize the Jews—and thus an ideal scapegoat for all Rwanda's problems.

In a country which receives virtually no information from the outside world, local media, particularly the radio, play an essential role. For a large part of the population, a transistor radio is the only source for information and therefore has the potential for exerting a powerful influence. Rwandan radio broadcasts are in two languages, French and the national language, Kinyarwanda, which is spoken by all Rwandans. Less than a year before the genocide began, two close associates of President Habyarimana set up the "private" radio station, known as Radio *Mille Collines* (Thousand Hills). Assured of a large audience thanks to regular programs of popular music, the programs in Kinyarwanda broadcast unceasing messages of hate, such as "The grave is only half full. Who will help us fill it?" Christened "the radio that kills" by its opponents, it was the basic instrument of propaganda for the Hutu extremists, and the militias rallied in support of its slogans.

On 6 April 1994 the plane carrying President Habyarimana and President Cyprien Ntariyamira of Burundi was shot down by rocket fire. Although it is not yet known who was behind this assassination, it is clear that it acted as the fuse for the eruption of violence which led to the greatest tragedy in the history of the country.

As the stereotypes of physical characteristics do not always provide sufficient identification—and can even be totally misleading—it was the identity cards demanded at the roadblocks set up by the militias that acted as the signature of a death warrant for the Tutsis. As control of the road could not alone ensure that no Tutsi escaped, the militia leaders divided up the territory under their control so that one man was allocated for every ten households in order to systematically search for Tutsis in their immediate localities. In this way every Tutsi family could be denounced by somebody who knew the members personally: pupils were killed by their teachers, shop owners by their customers, neighbor killed neighbor and husbands killed wives in order to save them from a more terrible death. Churches where Tutsis sought sanctuary were particular targets and the scene of some of the worst massacres: 2,800 people in Kibungo, 6,000 in Cyahinda, 4,000 in Kibeho, to give just a few examples. In Rwanda, the children of mixed marriages take the ethnic group of the father and, although many of the Hutu killers—including some militia leaders—had Tutsi mothers, so effective was the indoctrination program, that even this apparently counted for nothing. Radio *Mille Collines* encouraged the violence with statements such as that made at the end of April 1994, "By 5 May, the country must be completely cleansed of Tutsis." Even the children were targeted: "We will not repeat the mistake of 1959. The children must be killed too." The media directly influenced Hutu peasants, convincing them that they were under threat and encouraging them to "make the Tutsis smaller" by decapitating them. In the northern areas occupied by the RPF, the peasants were astonished that the Tutsi soldiers did not have horns, tails and eyes that shone in the dark as they had been described in radio programs.

The genocide spread rapidly to cover the whole country under the control of the government army. By the end of April, it was estimated that 100,000 people had been killed. There are aspects of this genocide which are new and contemporary; others we have seen before. The use of propaganda, the way control was exercised over the administration: these are all reflections of the modern era. So too are the extreme racist ideology and the radical determination to exterminate all Tutsis in one all-encompassing blow. It would be a mistake to think that the killings were carried out in an archaic manner: the reality is that they were meticulously well organized. However, the means used to accomplish them were primitive in the extreme: for example, the use of machetes and *unfunis* (wooden clubs studded with metal spikes). Unfortunately, the media eclipsed the first aspect of its preoccupation with the second.

Nobody really knows the exact origin of the Hutu, Tutsi and Twa peoples (the Twa represent only one percent of the population and have never played a significant role in the region). The three groups speak the same language, share the same territory and follow the same traditions. By all definitions, this should qualify Rwanda as a nation in the true sense.

The first Europeans to reach Rwandan territory described the people and their way of life in terms very much influenced by the scientific ideas of their time. Until the beginning of the nineteenth century, the origin of Africa's many peoples was regarded by Europeans as rooted in the biblical story of Ham, Noah's son. The book of Genesis tells how Ham and his descendants were cursed throughout all generations after he had seen his father naked. The "Blacks" were believed to be descendants of Ham, their color a result of that curse. At the beginning of the nineteenth century, linguistic studies, archaeological research and rational thinking led to a questioning of this theory, which was subsequently replaced with a system of classifying people according to their physical characteristics: skin color, type of hair, shape of the skull, etc. Those who were then classified as "blacks" were regarded as "another" kind of human being, not descended from Noah. Yet this classification did not cover the whole population of the African continent. Explorers in the region we now know as Niger and the areas of the Zambezi and the Upper Nile, came across people that did not correspond to the caricature of the negro.

So it was that German, and later Belgian, colonizers developed a system of categories for different "tribes" that was largely a function of aesthetic impressions. Individuals were categorized as Hutu or Tutsi according to their degree of beauty, their pride, intelligence and political organization. The colonizers established a distinction between those who did not correspond to the stereotype of a negro (the Tutsi) and those who did (the Hutu). The first group, "superior Africans," were designated Hamites or "white coloreds" who represented a "missing link" between the "whites" and the "blacks." Also included in this group were the Galla peoples of Ethiopia and Somalia. "Any quality attributed to an African group must be read as a sign of interbreeding with 'non-negro' cultures":[1] this "hamitic" ideology translates into the hypothesis, for which there is no serious proof, that a migration of the Galla took place in the seventeenth century, thus explaining the similarities between the Galla and the Tutsi.

The Belgians also favored the Tutsi students and the main priority of Rwanda's schools was their education. As this was, inevitably, also the policy at the tertiary level, the educated elite at the country's university, Astrida, the future administrative and technical backbone of the country, were very largely Tutsi. The colonizers blamed the imbalance in the schools and resulting low social standing of the Hutu on Hutu passivity, making no acknowledgement of their own role in the situation. The legacy of this theory continues even today. The missionaries also supported the Tutsi power structure, using it to evangelize from the top down. The Tutsi chiefs, once they had become Christian, then felt a moral obligation to convert the Hutu masses. The seminaries were more open to the Hutu than the schools. Although, after 1959, the educated Tutsi sometimes backed the theory of the mono-ethnic origins of the population following the removal from power of the Tutsi aristocracy . . . the myth of Egyptian origins and Hamitic superiority was supported by many among the Tutsi people. Some Hutu discovered the extent to which they, the "native" people of the region, had been "despoiled" and developed their own theory of the "Ethiopian invaders," categorizing the Tutsi as colonizers, the same as the Belgians. Rwandan Tutsis were from now on treated as immigrants and the 1959 "revolutionaries" called for "the return to Ethiopia of the Tutsi colonizers." The Hutu had begun to believe that they alone were the native people of Rwanda.

Belgium, criticized at the UN for a colonial policy that ensured that only a handful of the local population in their colonies received sufficient training for them to eventually be promoted to the higher levels of their national administrations—a policy aimed at ensuring that they would not think they were capable of running their own country—gradually ceded power to the small Hutu elite. The democratic principle of majority rule was cited as justification for the removal of the Tutsi from their previous positions of influence; a complete reversal of previous political policy. The Hutu became the "good guys" who "have been dominated for so long by the Tutsi" and the Belgians now expressed "sympathy for the cause of the suppressed masses."

In 1959, a series of riots directed against the authority of the Tutsi chiefs were allowed by the Belgians to escalate into a revolution accompanied by massacres which killed more than 20,000 Tutsi. What happened in Rwanda illustrates a situation where the coexistence of different social groups or castes metamorphosed into an ethnic problem with an overwhelmingly racist dimension. The caricature of physical stereotypes, although they did not always hold true and were probably due to the principle of endogamy practiced by each group despite the number of mixed marriages, was manipulated to provide proof of the racial superiority of one group over the other. Archaic political divisions were progressively transformed into racial ideologies and repeated outbreaks of violence resulting from the colonial heritage which was absorbed by local elites who then brought it into the political arena. The present generation has internalized this ethnological colonial model, with some groups deliberately choosing to play the tribal card. The regimes that have ruled Rwanda and Burundi since independence have shown that they actually need ethnic divisions in order both to reinforce and justify their positions. Finally, however, it was the ethnic classification registered on identity cards introduced by the Belgians that served as the basic instrument for the genocide of the Tutsi people who were "guilty" on three counts: they were a minority, they were a remainder of a feudal system and they were regarded as colonizers in their own country.

Day by day, as the death toll increased in the spring of 1994, the reality that a genocide was underway became clearer. By the end of April, it was estimated that 100,000 people had been killed, by mid-May 200,000, and by the end of May half a million. Although nobody really knew the actual death toll, the signs of massacres were everywhere and the River Nyaborongo carried thousands of corpses towards Lake Victoria along what Hutu propaganda described as "the shortest way back to Ethiopia."

Taking humanitarian, rather than political, action is one of the best ways for a developed country to avoid facing up to its responsibilities in the wake of a disaster such as Rwanda. Another way is language. Employing a particular vocabulary can cast doubt on the actual causes of the massacre and foster confused images of the guilty and the victims. "Warring parties," "belligerents" and "civil war" on one hand, and "aggression," "massacre" and "genocide" on the other, are all strong words—but they are not synonyms in meaning. Under the cover of a supposed objectivity, to suggest that "both parties" have committed atrocities can often be seen as an underhand way of giving them the same status. To speak of tribal disputes when an armed majority perpetrates a genocide against an unarmed minority is patronizing and meaningless. The aggression against the Bosnians and the genocide of the Tutsis both exceed civil war. In the case of Rwanda, to compare the RPF with the Rwandan Armed Forces (FAR) is at best a display of ignorance, at worst propaganda. The FAR have committed a genocide and the RPF have carried out exactions: the two things cannot be compared. If a distinction is not made, then genocide is reduced to the status of common murder—but murder is *not* the same as genocide. They differ both in nature and in degree, a fact that needs to be constantly emphasized if the crimes committed in Rwanda are not to be pushed to the back of international consciousness.

The racist philosophy of the previous Hutu government and the dangers of trivializing, and even forgetting, the events of last summer are summed up perfectly in a remarkable interview with François Karera, the former mayor of Kigali, now living comfortably with his family in Zaire, just a few miles from the misery of the refugee camps (one of which he is responsible for). According to Karera, "The Tutsis are originally bad. They are murderers. The Tutsis have given the white people their daughters. Physically they are weak—look at their arms and legs. No Tutsi can build: they are too weak . . . they just command. . . . The others work. If the reasons are just, the massacres are justified. In war you don't consider the consequences, you consider the causes."[2]

The perpetrators of genocide should permanently lose any legitimacy as rulers of their people. They should be outlawed by the international community and brought to trial for their crimes. In the case of Rwanda, no attempt should be made to negotiate with those responsible for the genocide of the Tutsis: they are not only directly responsible for this worst possible crime against humanity, but also for the exodus from Rwanda and the catastrophic events in Goma which followed. When the new Allied forces won victory in 1945, there was never any question of providing a role for the Nazi party in the new Germany, nor of considering just how small a fraction of the population it really represented. The Nazis were banned outright and the authors of genocide then, as should happen in Rwanda today, lost any right to participate in public life.

Questions:
1. *How would you define "genocide"? Do you think that Destexhe is correct in indicting the Hutu leadership for this crime?*
2. *In the refugee camp at Goma at least tens of thousands and possibly several hundred thousand Hutus died, largely from cholera, which swept the area in epidemic fashion. Several media sources*

applied the term "genocide" to the tragedy at Goma, but Destexhe finds it inappropriate. What do you think?

3. *Destexhe finds only three bona fide cases of genocide in the twentieth century. Apart from the Nazis killing Jews and Hutus killing Tutsis, discussed here, what do you suppose his third example is? Would you add a third one? Do you think there is a valid conceptual border between genocide and generic mass murder? Why or why not?*

28.6 Declaration of Human Rights

One of the early acts of the United Nations was to proclaim a Universal Declaration of Human Rights. Work on the document began soon after the international organization was established and continued for approximately three years before the Declaration was formally promulgated by the General Assembly in December, 1948. In the Assembly ballot forty-eight member states voted approval of the Declaration and eight abstained. There were no negative votes.

The sessions of the drafting committees, which all together held hundreds of meetings to prepare the document, were far from harmonious. The topic of human rights is one not just of fundamental concern but also one about which different nations of the world held (and still hold) quite divergent opinions. The aim throughout the drafting sessions was to formulate a document that, although it would not satisfy the wishes of every nation entirely, would still embrace enough of these to meet with general acceptance. That it was almost completely successful in doing so is revealed by the final vote. As the president of the General Assembly pointed out at the time: "It was the first occasion on which the organized community of nations had made a declaration of human rights and fundamental freedoms."

The Declaration is a compilation of political, social, and cultural ideals to which all nations can aspire. It should be clear from a close reading of its text that no country in the world today fully realizes these ideals and, indeed, that many fall far short of doing so. Yet, although the Articles of the Declaration are not legally binding on its signatories, it has, as many delegates to the United Nations emphasized at the time, a moral force that can lead the nations of the world away from oppression toward more humane and liberal forms of society.

UNIVERSAL DECLARATION OF HUMAN RIGHTS

PREAMBLE

Whereas recognition of the inherent dignity and of the equal and inalienable rights of all members of the human family is the foundation of freedom, justice and peace in the world,

Whereas disregard and contempt for human rights have resulted in barbarous acts which have outraged the conscience of mankind, and the advent of a world in which human beings shall enjoy freedom of speech and belief and freedom from fear and want has been proclaimed as the highest aspiration of the common people,

Whereas it is essential, if man is not to be compelled to have recourse, as a last resort, to rebellion against tyranny and oppression, that human rights should be protected by the rule of law,

Whereas it is essential to promote the development of friendly relations between nations,

Whereas the peoples of the United Nations have in the Charter reaffirmed their faith in fundamental human rights, in the dignity and worth of the human person and in the equal rights of men and women and have determined to promote social progress and better standards of life in larger freedom,

Whereas Member States have pledged themselves to achieve, in cooperation with the United Nations, the promotion of universal respect for and observance of human rights and fundamental freedoms,

Whereas a common understanding of these rights and freedoms is of the greatest importance for the full realization of this pledge,

Now, therefore, The General Assembly

Proclaims this Universal Declaration of Human Rights as a common standard of achievement for all peoples and all nations, to the end that every individual and every organ of society, keeping this Declaration constantly in mind, shall strive by teaching and education to promote respect for these rights and freedoms and by progressive measures, national and international, to secure their universal and effective recognition and observance, both among the peoples of Member States themselves and among the peoples of territories under their jurisdiction.

ARTICLE 1

All human beings are born free and equal in dignity and rights. They are endowed with reason and conscience and should act towards one another in a spirit of brotherhood.

ARTICLE 2

Everyone is entitled to all the rights and freedoms set forth in this Declaration, without distinction of any kind, such as race, colour, sex, language, religion, political or other opinion, national or social origin, property, birth, or other status.

Furthermore, no distinction shall be made on the basis of the political, jurisdictional or international status of the country or territory to which a person belongs, whether it be independent, trust, non-self-governing, or under any other limitation of sovereignty.

ARTICLE 3

Everyone has the right to life, liberty, and the security of person.

ARTICLE 4

No one shall be held in slavery or servitude; slavery and the slave trade shall be prohibited in all their forms.

ARTICLE 5

No one shall be subjected to torture or to cruel, inhuman, or degrading treatment or punishment.

ARTICLE 6

Everyone has the right to recognition everywhere as a person before the law.

ARTICLE 7

All are equal before the law and are entitled without any discrimination to equal protection of the law. All are entitled to equal protection against any discrimination in violation of this Declaration and against any incitement to such discrimination.

ARTICLE 8

Everyone has the right to an effective remedy by the competent national tribunals for acts violating the fundamental rights granted him by the constitution or by law.

ARTICLE 9

No one shall be subjected to arbitrary arrest, detention, or exile.

ARTICLE 10

Everyone is entitled in full equality to a fair, and public hearing by an independent and impartial tribunal, in the determination of his rights and obligations and of any criminal charge against him.

ARTICLE 11

1. Everyone charged with a penal offence has the right to be presumed innocent until proved guilty according to law in a public trial at which he has had all the guarantees necessary for his defence.
2. No one shall be held guilty of any penal offence on account of any act or omission which did not constitute a penal offence, under national or international law, at the time when it was committed. Nor shall a heavier penalty be imposed than the one that was applicable at the time the penal offence was committed.

ARTICLE 12

No one shall be subjected to arbitrary interference with his privacy, family, home, or correspondence, nor to attacks upon his honour and reputation. Everyone has the right to the protection of the law against such interference or attacks.

ARTICLE 13

1. Everyone has the right to freedom of movement and residence within the borders of each State.
2. Everyone has the right to leave any country, including his own, and to return to his country.

ARTICLE 14

1. Everyone has the right to seek and to enjoy in other countries asylum from persecution.
2. This right may not be invoked in the case of prosecutions genuinely arising from non-political crimes or from acts contrary to the purposes and principles of the United Nations.

ARTICLE 15

1. Everyone has the right to a nationality.
2. No one shall be arbitrarily deprived of his nationality nor denied the right to change his nationality.

ARTICLE 16

1. Men and women of full age, without any limitation due to race, nationality, or religion, have the right to marry and to found a family. They are entitled to equal rights as to marriage, during marriage, and at its dissolution.
2. Marriage shall be entered into only with the free and full consent of the intending spouses.
3. The family is the natural and fundamental group unit of society and is entitled to protection by society and the State.

ARTICLE 17

1. Everyone has the right to own property alone as well as in association with others.
2. No one shall be arbitrarily deprived of his property.

ARTICLE 18

Everyone has the right to freedom of thought, conscience and religion; this right includes freedom to change his religion or belief, and freedom, either alone or in community with others and in public or private, to manifest his religion or belief in teaching, practice, worship, and observance.

ARTICLE 19

Everyone has the right to freedom of opinion and expression; this right includes freedom to hold opinions without interference and to seek, receive and impart information and ideas through any media and regardless of frontiers.

ARTICLE 20

1. Everyone has the right to freedom of peaceful assembly and association.
2. No one may be compelled to belong to an association.

ARTICLE 21

1. Everyone has the right to take part in the government of his country, directly or through freely chosen representatives.
2. Everyone has the right of equal access to public service in his country.
3. The will of the people shall be the basis of the authority of government; this will shall be expressed in periodic and genuine elections which shall be by universal and equal suffrage and shall be held by secret vote or by equivalent free voting procedures.

ARTICLE 22

Everyone, as a member of society, has the right to social security and is entitled to realization, through national effort and international co-operation and in accordance with the organization and resources of each State, of the economic, social and cultural rights indispensable for his dignity and the free development of his personality.

ARTICLE 23

1. Everyone has the right to work, to free choice of employment, to just and favourable conditions of work and to protection against unemployment.
2. Everyone, without any discrimination, has the right to equal pay for equal work.
3. Everyone who works has the right to just and favourable remuneration ensuring for himself and his family an existence worthy of human dignity, and supplemented, if necessary, by other means of social protection.

Questions:
1. What rights are considered universal in the Declaration?
2. Do you think all of rights enumerated in the Declaration should be included? Do you think they left any important rights out?

PART 29
Contemporary Issues in World History

29.1   A United Germany in a United Europe (June 5, 1990): Helmut Kohl

Germany has occupied a central position in the history of the late nineteenth and twentieth centuries. After nearly forty-five years of division, the events of 1989 presented opportunities for reunification. But the new realities posed new problems for Europe: Would Germany once again threaten its neighbors militarily? Would the financial costs of reunification stall the process? Who would bear the economic burden? Would the new Germany be politically neutral or maintain its central position in the NATO alliance? In 1990, German Chancellor Helmut Kohl addressed several of these questions in his speech to the American Council on Germany in New York City.

Source: "A United Germany in a United Europe" is from Helmut Kohl, speech delivered to the American Council on Germany, New York City, New York, on June 5, 1990. Contained in *Vital Speeches of the Day,* July 1, 1990, pp. 546–548.

HELMUT KOHL

We Germans are not oblivious of the fact that here and in other countries we are being asked questions as we head for unity:

What kind of Germany will emerge?
What will German unity mean for peace and security in the heart of Europe?
Will this Germany revert to old patterns of behaviour, or has it learned the lessons of history?

I shall attempt to provide answers here for the future, bearing in mind that we Germans can build on proven foundations as we move towards unity. Moreover, we Germans are determined, as we prove by our actions, to heed the lessons of our and of European history.

My first answer is this: A future united Germany will remain linked to the United States in close friendship and responsible partnership. . . . We shall remain together! This responsible partnership entails a future united Germany being a full member of the North Atlantic defense alliance.

We are thus drawing the first and most important conclusion from history: Peace, stability and security in Europe were ensured whenever Germany, the country in the heart of Europe, maintained firm ties, a fair balance of interests and mutually beneficial interchange with all its neighbours. On the other hand, when the Germans chose to go it alone or follow a separate nationalistic path, whether out of blind arrogance or criminal hubris, or when they were forced into isolation after a lost war, this resulted in discord, instability and insecurity for the whole of Europe.

A future Germany cannot and will not, therefore, drift back and forth between two camps. We do not seek neutrality or demilitarization, and we reject a non-aligned status. We Germans want to exercise our sovereign right, as enshrined in the Charter of the United Nations. . . . We want to be a member of . . . the North Atlantic defense alliance. Our immediate neighbours in the East—the Poles, Czechs and Hungarians support this position.

Our commitment to the Western Alliance—and this is my second answer—implies above all our commitment to the Western community of shared values. A future Germany will be a free and democratic state based on social justice and the rule of law, on respect for human dignity and human rights. Right- or left-wing extremism does not, as more than forty years of domestic stability prove, stand a chance in our country in the future either.

A future Germany will also remain a federal state. . . . There is no better a means of preventing tyranny and totalitarianism than a constitution which not only provides for checks and balances, but also envisages a federal system. We in the Federal Republic of Germany have such a constitution: Our Basic Law has in more than forty years proved to be the most liberal constitution in German history. . . .

My third answer is this: A united Germany will be an economically sound and socially stable country. The unanimous opinion of international economic organizations is that German unification will significantly boost world economic growth. The pent-up demand in the GDR [formerly East Germany] and in the reformist countries of Central, Eastern and South-Eastern Europe affords substantial market opportunities for everyone. . . .

The Federal Republic of Germany will strongly support this new economic and social start in the GDR. We are well prepared for this. For eight years our economy has been expanding. Business earnings, investments and employment are at a high level. We want to pave the way for private enterprise and the influx of private capital into the GDR. . . . I would like to repeat my invitation to American business: Become actively involved in the GDR to the mutual benefit. We

Germans do not seek a monopoly; on the contrary, we seek competition and the common advantages of the international division of labour.

A future Germany—and this is my fourth answer—will from the very beginning be a member of the European Community. A united Germany will take part in 1992 when the large single market with 336 million people is completed. A united Germany will, together with France, be a driving force behind European unification. Before the end of this year two parallel intergovernmental conferences will be started to lay the contractual foundation not only for economic and monetary union, but also for political union.

Finally, our commitment to federalism does not end at our borders. Federalism is our real goal for Europe as a whole. A united Germany will therefore also espouse the ambitious goal of laying the groundwork for a United States of Europe before the end of this century. We are thus drawing a further conclusion from our history: German unity has a future only if it is achieved in harmony with our neighbours, and not through confrontation with them. . . .

A future Germany, firmly anchored in the West, will—and this is my fifth answer—in the future, too, live up to its share of responsibility for ensuring peaceful and stable reforms in the neighbouring Eastern and South-Eastern countries. In following our path to national unity, we Germans do not call borders into question. On the contrary, we want to make them more permeable. We are willing to achieve lasting understanding and comprehensive, forward-looking cooperation. Our goal is international reconciliation. In particular we are willing to take account of the legitimate security interests of all our neighbours, not the least the Soviet Union.

We are convinced that this recognition will soon prevail in the whole of Europe: A future united Germany as a member of the Western defense alliance will increase the security of everyone concerned and thus become a cornerstone of a stable, peaceful order in Europe.

Questions:
1. How did Chancellor Helmut Kohl view the impact of a "new" reunited Germany on Europe?
2. What did Kohl mean when noting that "federalism is our real goal for Europe as a whole"?

29.2   The Reconciliation of France and Germany (September 24, 1990): François Mitterrand

As Europe moved away from the wasteland of World War II and the intellectual confines of the Cold War, toward a new era of intranational economic cooperation, many variables exist that may radically alter its face. A tunnel under the English Channel was constructed (dubbed "the Chunnel"), that not only physically links Great Britain and France but "threatens" to meld the cultures as well. Britain has lost the island status that protected it and offered a unique identity for centuries, in exchange for a more intimate link with the economic destiny of continental Europe. So too will the great enemies of the first half of the twentieth century, France and Germany, lie down together and reconcile past offenses for future gains. With the reunification of Germany and the reintroduction of the Czech Republic, Slovakia, Hungary, and Poland into the heart of Europe, there are great financial opportunities and the very real potential for domestic strife. With the introduction of the Euro in January 2002, most of the European continent set a new course as trading partners with a common currency and mission to link fortunes in world economic competition. The following speeches by European leaders of the late twentieth century testify to the changing nature of Europe.

Source: "The Reconciliation of France and Germany" is from François Mitterrand, speech delivered to the 45th Session of the United Nations General Assembly, New York, New York, on September 24, 1990. Contained in *Vital Speeches of the Day*, October 15, 1990, pp. 5, 7–8.

Think of the events that have shaken up Europe and the World in 1939, the popular movements that have emerged from the depths which, like the French revolution of two hundred years ago, have triumphed over structures and systems, set ways of thinking and acting, powers and fears, because of the simple, irresistible need to live differently, in accordance with the requirements of the mind. When the walls separating peoples came down, walls built on the foolish assumption that the order they were protecting would never be untouched by the great winds of space, dreams and ideas, I remember saying to my compatriots in France . . . that the end of one order did not necessarily mean that another order would be born immediately thereafter, and that it would be a very difficult process. And I would ask you this: what are we to do with this era we are entering, so promising, so perilous? What shall we make of it? . . .

I think that an era of hope is opening up for mankind, if the peoples of the world accept to overcome what they take to be the fatality of history, and of their own interest. Believe me, such a goal is within our reach. After destroying each other in three wars in less than a century, France and Germany have sealed their reconciliation, a rare occurrence indeed: They belong to the same community, they meet together, they are forging a genuine friendship. While I speak, on the eve of German unity, instead of harping on the tragic events they experienced in the past because of each other, our two peoples are turned toward the same future. And so it is that here in New York, I can send the best wishes of France to the Germans, who are preparing to celebrate a great moment of their history. The deep understanding between France and Germany is a reality. As you know, it makes itself felt in the twelve-nation European Community. Can you imagine the trouble and strife, the conflicts of age-old ambitions that were overcome forty years ago by a bold, almost unbelievable undertaking engaged in first by six, nine, then ten, now twelve countries of Europe? . . .

We Europeans are looking beyond the Community, to the horizon of the continent of Europe, the Europe of geography and history. . . . Where would our old continent be now if audacity had not managed to overthrow well-established patterns of thought? And if peoples and their leaders had not accepted to build a future different from the past? In this Europe these are countries which yesterday were known as Eastern bloc countries and which belonged to a rival system. Now they control their own destiny, but with what means at their disposal? . . . We must think of them, they are our brethren and we will be by their side, until as I said in France, a more fixed relationship will bring together all the countries of Europe, those of the East, those of the Community, those of the Free Trade Area, those who are part of no system, in what I have called a Confederation. . . . Europe has been the first field of application thereof and a very real one. . . .

At the beginning of this century and at the end of the previous one, our forebears expressed their dreams of peace with these three words: disarmament, arbitration, collective security. Theirs came to be an era of unrest, dictatorship and war. Let us act in such a way, I beseech you, that through the United Nations, law, solidarity and peace may finally rule over a new era.

Questions:
1. *Begin headnote with "With the introduction of . . ."—change "speeches by European leaders" to "speech by Francois Mitterand"*
2. *Does Mitterand seem optimistic? Why or why not? What is the source of his optimism (or pessimism)?*

29.3   Ethnic Cleansing in Northwestern Bosnia: Three Witnesses

The dissolution of Yugoslavia, which began in 1991, resulted in great physical destruction. The once resplendent cities of Dubrovnik and Sarajevo are now battered, shell shocked, and strewn with rubble. By 1996 between 200,000 and 500,000 people were killed in the fighting, more than 3 million were refugees, and between 20,000 and 50,000 Bosnian Muslim women were raped.[1]

Ethnic, religious, and national rivalries in the Balkans run very deep. Certainly the animosity between the Muslim and the Christian populations in the Balkans stretches back over six hundred years of bloodied history. These ethnic and religious tensions came to a flash point in the years immediately following the death of Communist Party leader Marshal Tito, who had ruled Yugoslavia with considerable skill between 1945 and 1980. To assuage the ethnic rivalries after the death of Tito, the seat of government of Yugoslavia in the 1980s rotated among the six autonomous republics of Serbia, Croatia, Bosnia-Herzegovina, Macedonia, Slovenia, and Montenegro. But this system of rotation soon proved unworkable, and in 1991 Croatia and Slovenia declared their independence from Yugoslavia. Serbia, the largest of the republics, tried to forestall further dissolution, but the Republic of Bosnia-Herzegovina also declared its independence from Yugoslavia.

Of the six former Yugoslav republics, Bosnia is the most ethnically and religiously diverse. It is the only republic not established on a purely ethnic or religious basis. It was not until 1971 that the Muslims in Bosnia gained official separate recognition in the Yugoslav census. Prior to 1971, Muslims were identified as "Yugoslav" or "other." This distinction underscores the difficulty of defining precisely who and what a Bosnian is, because Muslims, Serbs, and Croats all lay claim to this designation. At the time of the 1992 referendum on independence, the 4 million Bosnians were divided approximately into a population that was 44 percent Muslim, 31 percent Serbian, 17 percent Croatian, with the remainder being Gypsies,

Albanians, and other Balkan or Western European people. This religious and ethnic division was further complicated by the fact that large concentrations of Serbs live in western Bosnia close to the Croatian border and large concentrations of Muslims live in eastern Bosnia close to the Serbian Republic. Begin-

ning in the spring of 1992, brutal internecine fighting broke out among the Muslim, Serbian, and Croatian populations in Bosnia. The practice of "ethnic cleansing," or the forced removal (or annihilation) of a targeted population from its homes, villages, and cities, has been used by all groups against their enemies throughout this war. The following accounts are the statements of three Muslim survivors of Serbian ethnic cleansing in former Muslim-occupied areas of northwestern Bosnia-Herzegovina who were later interrogated in Zagreb, Croatia, and Wifferfuerth, Germany.

Source: From Ante Beljo, ed., *Bosnia-Herzegovina: Genocide: Ethnic Cleansing in Northwestern Bosnia* (Zagreb: Croatian Information Centre, 1993), pp. 43–44, 77–79, 94–95. Reprinted by permission of the Croatian Information Centre.

A WITNESS FROM THE OMARSKA AND TRNOPOLJE CAMPS (NEAR PRIJEDOR); MUSLIM, BORN 1931, MALE

After the occupation of Kozarac, on May 27, 1992, I was imprisoned for the first time in Ciglane (the Brickyards) near Prijedor. I spent two days and three nights there. Then I was transferred to the "Keraterm" camp and after three days, I spent another six days in the Omarska camp. The last camp I was taken to was Trnopolje. The total number of days spent in various camps is one month and twenty days.

We heard that they took away children from their mothers and that the children were never returned. Women were separated from men. People slept on the concrete floor under the eaves of the brickyard. People would urinate at a spot ten meters away from the rest of the prisoners. The people imprisoned there were mostly from the village of Kozarac, the surrounding area of Prijedor and even from Bosanski Novi.

They caught us in such a manner that they used the Red Cross emblem and shouted into a megaphone: "Surrender, the Red Cross is waiting for you, you will be protected." There were twenty-one buses on the road and in front of them they separated women and children. We had to keep our heads lowered in the bus. Some buses drove straight through the woods and into Trnopolje, the others went to Ciglane (the Brickyards).

They would take people to Ciglane by night. Then machine-gun fire would be heard and that person never returned. I saw how they tortured a reserve policeman. First they broke his bones and then they put a piece of clothing into his mouth, drenched him in gas and set him on fire.

In Omarska they battered and interrogated people. I think that I saved myself by my persistent claim that I have no brothers or children. I did not betray anyone for being in battle or having arms. The camp was on the Banja Luka-Bosanski Novi railroad. There was also a mine with screening towers 20 meters high. Inside the towers there were bins (10 3 6 square meters) each containing some 300 people. These bins were used for screening ore. Each bin had four floors and there were 8,000 people in six rooms. We could not sleep but maybe doze on somebody's shoulder. There was no light. At last, after three days, we got one loaf of bread to share among six people. We urinated inside the same room we occupied. My two brothers were there and one of them died on the second floor. I did not dare look at him and I did not know that he died until I came to Trnopolje and was told so by some people. Approximately thirty-five or forty people died in six days. We got bread once every three days. Later we even got some beans. They would come to the door, and we would form a circle and take our food in a piece of cardboard or a milk pack that we found there. Every day they would give us as much water as we could catch in a piece of cardboard. On several occasions they put a hose through a steel mesh platform which separated each floor. The camp was divided into three sections: A, B and C. No one survived in the C section. I know that because later nobody from the C section came to Trnopolje. Three men from the village of Kozarac committed suicide. Two of them got out through the drain and the guards outside killed them. Besides the towers, there were also prisoners in the storage building. There were only thirty women in the camp. Interrogations were carried out every night. They put a gun barrel into my mouth and thus I lost seven teeth. Many did not return after the interrogation. Interrogators were educated Serbs. I know three of them. Two of them were Mladen Mitrovi´c, our neighbor, and Slobodan Kuruzović, a local teacher. They were both some sort of commanders in the camp. They wore caps with the Chetnik insignia.[1] They beat camp prisoners. They used to tell us that they would kill thirty Muslims for each Serb killed.

I was the only one from the C section to mount a bus with forty-five men, mostly older in age. Young men would come to the camp, and the older ones would leave. Boys and young men did not stand a chance.

We arrived in the Trnopolje camp at 5:00 p.m. It was as if we were free at last. We were happy for being able to lie on the concrete. Upon my arrival, there were some 4,500 people in the central fenced-in area surrounded by guards. However, the entire village of Trnopolje was a camp, and seen from this angle it contained 10,000 prisoners. Some women were allowed to go home escorted by Chetniks and prepare meals. On the one side of the camp there was a highway, and on the other side there was a railroad where people were hurled into cattle wagons for the purpose of ethnic cleansing. From

539

the cinema where I spent my first night, Bakir Mahić was taken out. They entered every night and took away people in succession, not according to any list or bill of indictment. They would take boys to a macadam road and tread on them. However, less people died here than in Omarska because there was some food. In the entire central camp area there was one school and one outdoor toilet. We got enough drinking water and A.V. would pass us a hose over the fence.

Once the camp commander gave me permission to go home for a visit and after 2.5 kilometers the guards caught us, forced us into a van (seven people on top of another seven people, etc., like logs), and then they returned us to the camp. They filed us in the clinic and there I saw captured Muslim doctors. In front of the clinic I saw how Chetniks carved the Chetnik insignia (four cyrillic S) into S.K.'s chest. He was a big thirty-one year old man. After that they cut the sinews on his legs. They threw another man on the ground and cut his spine in half with a knife so that his legs were instantly paralyzed. The Chetniks who call themselves Rambos did such things. Those particular members of irregular units had various details to their uniform such as reticular masks on their faces, black gloves, and black ribbons on their foreheads. They were not Bosnian Serbs because they talked in Ekavian dialect (used in Serbia) and they often used the word "bre" (Serbian dialect). Through an open window I could hear women crying from twenty meters away. One girl was saying through tears: "People, leave me alone, I was operated only a month ago." "Do you have a mama?," they asked her, and then they brought her parents to her. They raped her mother in front of her and her father. Once they took five thirteen-year-old girls to Mirsad's house and returned them the following day in such a state that S.P., a medic, managed to sew up two of them, while the other three had to be transferred to the Prijedor hospital. At least they said that they took them there. Ten women were raped under a poplar tree. Some thirty Chetniks were standing guard in shifts. Doctor P. told me how Zeljko Sikora from Prijedor, Czech by nationality, was mutilated. He also worked in the hospital as a medic. They chopped off his testicles and gouged out his eyes. He was falsely accused that he had castrated 300 Serbian children before the war.

After one month and twenty days spent in camps, I left Bosnia with a convoy of refugees.

Zagreb, July 31, 1992

A WITNESS TELLS OF THE INTERROGATION METHODS IN THE OMARSKA CONCENTRATION CAMP (NEAR PRIJEDOR); MUSLIM, BORN 1966, FEMALE

I finished electrotechnical school in 1985. Because of difficulties in finding employment, I was forced to work as a waitress for an entrepreneur in his restaurant. I worked there until September 1, 1991, when the restaurant was sold. I had to wait four months, until January 1, 1992, when I started working at a grill for the same owner. Our boss did not want to send us to the employment office to wait, because the restaurant was in the process of being built and he would need us at any time. I worked at the grill in shifts until April 30, 1992, when the government changed overnight. I was working the second shift and while walking through the city I saw armed persons in uniforms. I did not understand anything. At that point I was unaware of these events. At work I asked what was going on and they told me to be quiet and work. On the same day a curfew was proclaimed. Because of my grave financial situation I had to keep working. At work there were constant provocations, people would play around with weapons, but I put up with it thinking that it would pass. I heard them saying that all Croats and Muslims were going to be slaughtered and killed, but I never believed that would actually happen. They often asked me if I was a little "Ustasha," and gave me that nickname.2 All of this was more or less normal for me until they came to my place. First they told me that they would set all of my things on fire, that it all had to burn because it was Muslim, and after all of these provocations they took me to jail. At the Internal Affairs Office they hit me and yelled at me and looked for a Serbian flag to nail it on my head. They even said that they would carve it in my forehead. I spent the night in jail and in the morning I was taken to the Omarska camp. The drive to Omarska was horrible. They taunted me and hit me sometimes, and told me that I would never again return to Prijedor, and that they wanted an ethnically clean Greater Serbia. They drove me through Kozarac. At every one of their checkpoints they stopped and took me out with the intention of shooting me right on the spot. They told me to take a good look at Kozarac, which no longer existed and never again would. I could only see destroyed and burned houses. They told me that this was no longer Kozarac, that it was now Radmilovo. There were two militiamen with me in the car, Bato Kovačević and a certain Jančević. Both of them took some writing pads on this trip. When I arrived in Omarska, they said that I was an extreme case and that I had to be watched closely. First they took all my money and turned my pockets inside out. Several times they hit me over the back with automatic guns and they struck me with a cane twice. Then they took me to the interrogation room. While they were questioning me, they extinguished cigarettes on my legs because I could not answer their questions. I ended up with two open wounds. After the interrogation they locked me up with the other women. Here I was able to see the elite of Prijedor society. These people had had it all, and now they were poor and pathetic. Every day we watched what they did to our men. Prisoners had to lie out in the sun on their stomachs all day, while the guards danced on them. The worst was night time. They often came and took me out somewhere and raped me. In the morning Commander Zeljko Mejakić would call me and ask me how I had spent the night and if I had slept well. I could not say anything because they hit me a few more times with their fists or rifle-butts with the warning to shut up. This same commander knew what was happening because he was one of them. Every day I counted and looked to see where the men were taken after interrogation, either to another room or out in the field. When they took a man out we knew that there was one person less. Every morning and evening a truck came by and took all of those that were out in the field. They even came with a dredger to pick them up. In the course of the day they often took me to their office to clean up the blood. When I came in they would tell me whose blood it was and how they were beaten.

One day I was cleaning Asaf Kapetanović's blood and on the way back to my room I saw that they were taking Idriz Jakupović in for questioning. They were hitting him and yelling at him, and they threw him against the wall so that he broke his arm. This whole scene and all of these images are always in my head. These two are no longer alive, but they are not the only ones. Muhamed Cehaić, Abdulah Puškar, Nedžad Serić, Ziko and Osman Mahmuljin, Ado Begić and many others were killed in front of me. The way they killed men was to beat them to the point when they could no longer get up, so that they would lie there and rot. They would just throw them outside and let them die. This is very hard for me to write, because every moment that I spent in that camp is like an open wound. My writing about it only scratches the surface. I spent fifty-six days in this camp. Every night I listened to the people crying and moaning, begging and pleading for their torturers to stop, trying to convince them of their innocence. They were guilty on only one charge: for being Croatian or Muslim. Then the Serbs brought in the people from my hill (Bišćani). They beat and killed them. At the same time, members of the Serbian Red Cross arrived, and among them was a Mića from the medical center. He did not have a hand, but he was able to beat and kill people. Then they beat up and killed Ratih Kadirić, who worked as a driver at the medical center. There was a Zoran, called Zoka, who distributed the sour and moldy food, who was also one of the killers, and Kole, who carried an extension cord, Krle, Dražen Kačavenda, Mite, Drago, Živko who would not let us have our bread, Ckalja, who watched these scenes with pleasure, and many others whose names I do not know. After fifty-six days I was taken to Trnopolje with twenty-eight other women. I stayed there for three days and then I was released. I remained in the city, because I could not get to my house in the village. I knew nothing of my family. The people in my village were either forced out or killed. I stayed in the city for two weeks and then I left with a convoy for Travnik. Just as we departed, after a few kilometers, they began with the looting. Every few kilometers they stopped and looked for money, German Marks, jewelry and other things. They also took various pendants, nail-clippers, pencils, lighters, etc. Sometimes they took someone's child and said that they would kill him/her if they did not get a set amount of German Marks.

Subsequently they even stripped us of our clothes and shook us to make sure we hid nothing. In this way they stripped us of all we had, and in the end, on Vlašić Mountain, they took out 250 young and strong men and killed them. They took fifteen men out of the truck that I was in. In Travnik, after three months, I finally met up with my parents. They told me everything that had happened to them. I do not know anything about my brother. After several days I received an affidavit of support from Germany so I left for Zagreb with my parents. I stayed there a few days and had a medical check-up. This was a gynecological check-up. A friend of mine who had also been in the camp and was the only person who knew what I had been through got a telephone number that I could refer to. The wounds on my legs had gotten worse. Because of a lack of any kind of hygiene they got infected and I had to see a doctor about this as well. Because of fear I did not tell the doctor what had happened. After a month and a half the wounds healed, but still I have two scars. After a few days in Zagreb my uncle came for me and my family. Immediately after we exchanged greetings, he said he was inclined to kill me. Because of this vile treatment from him and his wife, I did not tell them any of the things I had experienced. Surely more provocations would have followed. After twenty days they threw my parents and me out. While I was going through all of these medical procedures I applied for a room from social services. This room was 13 square meters, but my uncle did not even like that, and he wanted to have me taken out of there as well. My aunt is German, so that the people from social services believed her more than me, but after all of these problems I am still here. I now have psychological problems and sometimes I ask myself what to do. I have not found work yet, and I do not know what to do because I am still afraid of any contact with men. Sometimes I wish I could work at anything just so that I do not have time to think about it all. This is about everything, in summary. I survived all of this and I have to keep on living.

Wipperfuerth, December 1992

A VICTIM OF RAPE IN THE VILLAGE OF RIZVANOVI´CI (PRIJEDOR COUNTY); MUSLIM, BORN 1977, FEMALE

After the attack on my village, I witnessed the massacre of civilians as the worst tragedy. At that point I did not know that something much worse than death was yet to come. My sister gave birth to a child in the basement where we hid, during the mortar attacks on the village. After the village of Rizvanovi´ci fell, and after the Chetniks came, I saw dead children, three to eight years of age near my house. I saw the destroyed mosque, and men who were taken away. Some more prominent men were singled out from the column and taken away. They shot them in the head. They fell down and remained lying there in grotesque positions. There was chaos, panic and death. My grandfather was accused of killing a Serb, and they executed him on the threshold of his house. A certain number of women and children remained in the village. We hid

541

in the basements of the destroyed houses. Our house was intact. That day, several Chetniks arrived. They searched for valuable things and men who hid in the nearby forest. One of the Chetniks, thirty years of age, ordered me to accompany him into the house. I had to go. I was terrified, but I did not comprehend what was going to happen to me. I knew that I would endanger the lives of the members of my family if I resisted.

When we entered the house, he searched for money, jewelry and other valuable objects. He could take everything he wanted. He ordered me to confess where the men were hidden. I did not answer. Then he ordered me to take off my clothes. I was horrified. I took off my clothes silently, and everything fell apart in me. Under my naked skin I felt I was dying. I closed my eyes. I could not bear look at him. He hit me with his fist and I fell down on the floor. Then he jumped on the top of me. He raped me. I cried, and squirmed, and bled a lot. I was a virgin. He ordered me to get up. I wanted to pick up my clothes and cover my naked and disfigured body, but he told me not to touch them. He ordered me to stand still and wait. He said I better be careful of what I did, because I am responsible for the fate of my family. He went out, turned around to make sure nobody saw him and then invited another two Chetniks to come in. I felt lost. I did not feel anything when they left. I do not know how long I was lying on the floor. My mother came in and found me lying there. And her seeing me in such a humiliating state was even worse than everything that had happened to me. I suddenly realized what had happened. I realized that I had been depraved, raped, deformed forever. My mother knew what was happening inside of me. That was the saddest moment in our lives. We both cried, screamed. She covered me. Together, we went back to the basement. I remember all that was happening to me later on through some sort of mist, some distorted dream. We were transported to Trnopolje, and then went on foot to Travnik over the Vlašiс́ Mountain, some thirty kilometers away. It was in Travnik that I emerged from this dreamy, confused state. Now, I sometimes find myself wondering if all this ever happened to me. To me of all people. My mother helped me tremendously. I want to become a mother one day. Only how? For me, men represent a horrible picture of violence and pain. I know that not all of them are like that, but this feeling of horror is stronger than my sense of reason. I cannot help myself.

In Zagreb, July 1992

Questions:
1. *How do you account for the brutality suggested in these statements, particularly since in many cases the oppressor and victim had, until recently, been neighbors and whose people had lived in the same community for hundreds of years?*
2. *It has been estimated that between 20,000 and 50,000 Bosnian Muslim women have been raped in this ethnic conflict. Why would rape become one of the preferred tactics of ethnic cleansing? Why would the woman in the second account admit that after seeing her uncle in Zagreb, "Immediately after we exchanged greetings, he said he was inclined to kill me"?*
3. *Do you see any connections between the Serbian "Program of the Society of National Defense" and these accounts of Serbian ethnic cleansing?*
4. *How would these readings compare to the other accounts of genocide in this section?*

29.4 Deng Xiaoping, A Market Economy for Socialist Goals

China is entitled to a special place in discussions of problems and challenges at the beginning of the twenty-first century. With well over a billion inhabitants and consequently a fifth of the world's population, China is struggling with the challenge of continuing a commitment to Communist Party leadership in an age in which Marxism in all its forms has suffered defeats. At the same time, the potential military and industrial strength of China, which has been notably lacking in strength of any sort for the last two hundred years, presents a challenge to China's neighbors and, in fact, the rest of the world.

After the death of Mao Tse-tung [Mao Zedong] in 1976, his successor, Deng Xiaoping [Teng Hsiao-p'ing], steered the country sharply away from the Maoist road to communism. Mao had tried to save China from poverty and "imperialism" with his brand of socialism but failed after nearly thirty stormy years of revolutionary frenzy. Boldly dismantling Mao's institutions, one by one, including the collective farms, Deng Xiaoping forcefully put forth his vision for China, a modern industrial and prosperous socialist nation. He felt confident that socialism in China could be saved by capitalistic means. The command economy, a principal feature of any socialist system, has steadily been replaced by the principles of market-oriented economy, and privatization of state-controlled enterprises has been greatly expanded. Material and profit incentives, which were despised for reflecting a decadent bourgeois mentality during the Mao era, have been reinstated to rekindle people's work enthusiasm. Deng also ended thirty years of isolation of the country from the West: He opened the door to foreign capital and technologies, luring them to China by creating so-called "special economic zones," where foreign investors enjoy tax breaks and low labor costs among other incentives. In 1992, Beijing openly declared the building of a "socialist market economy" as the central task of the government. The economic outcome of Deng's policies has so far been phenomenal. China's overall industrial and agricultural productivities have soared sharply. China's annual rate of economic growth since 1980 has been close to double digits. The standard of living of the Chinese people has risen sharply. In 1993, there were reportedly at least 40,000 millionaires in the Canton region alone. The following excerpts show Deng Xiaoping's rationale for introducing capitalistic principles to socialist China and his thoughts on the leadership succession.

Deng died in February 1997, but his bold vision for a prosperous China continues to live on in the policies of his successors.

Source: From Deng Xiaoping, *Selected Works of Deng Xiaoping*, 3 (1982–1992) (Beijing: Foreign Language Press, 1994), pp. 151–52. 360–61, 368–70, passim. Reported by permission of China Books and Periodicals.

There is no fundamental contradiction between socialism and a market economy. The problem is how to develop the productive forces more effectively. We used to have a planned economy, but our experience over the years has proved that having a totally planned economy hampers the development of productive forces to a certain extent. If we combine a planned economy with a market economy, we shall be in a better position to liberate the productive forces and speed up economic growth.

Since the Third Plenary Session of our Party's Eleventh Central Committee,[1] we have consistently stressed the importance of upholding the Four Cardinal Principles,[2] especially the principle of keeping to the socialist system. If we are to keep to the socialist system, it is essential for us to develop the productive forces. For a long time we failed to handle this question satisfactorily. In the final analysis, the superiority of socialism should be demonstrated in a greater development of the productive forces. The experience we have gained over the years shows that with the former economic structure we cannot develop the productive forces. That is why we have been drawing on some useful capitalist methods.

It is clear now that the right approach is to open to the outside world, combine a planned economy with a market economy and introduce structural reforms. Does this run counter to the principles of socialism? No, because in the course of reform we shall make sure of two things: one is that the public sector of the economy is always predominant; the other is that in developing the economy we seek common prosperity, always trying to avoid polarization. The policies of using foreign funds and allowing the private sector to expand will not weaken the predominant position of the public sector, which is a basic feature of the economy as a whole. On the contrary, those policies are intended, in the last analysis, to develop the productive forces more vigorously and to strengthen the public sector. So long as the public sector plays a predominant role in China's economy, polarization can be avoided. Of course, some regions and some people may prosper before others do, and then they can help other regions and people to gradually do the same. I am convinced that the negative phenomena that can now be found in society will gradually decrease and eventually disappear as the economy grows, as our scientific, cultural and educational levels rise and as democracy and the legal system are strengthened.

In short, the overriding task in China today is to throw ourselves heart and soul into the modernization drive. While giving play to the advantages inherent in socialism, we are also employing some capitalist methods—but only as methods of accelerating the growth of the productive forces. It is true that some negative things have appeared in the process, but what is more important is the gratifying progress we have been able to achieve by initiating these reforms and following this road. China has no alternative but to follow this road. It is the only road to prosperity.

The reason some people hesitate to carry out the reform and the open policy and dare not break new ground is, in essence, that they're afraid it would mean introducing too many elements of capitalism and, indeed, taking the capitalist road. The crux of the matter is whether the road is capitalist or socialist. The chief criterion for making that judgement should be whether it promotes the growth of the productive forces in a socialist society, increases the overall strength of the socialist state and raises living standards. As for building special economic zones, some people disagreed with the idea right from the start, wondering whether it would not mean introducing capitalism. The achievements in the construction of Shenzhen have given these people a definite answer: special economic zones are socialist, not capitalist. In the case of Shenzhen, the publicly owned sector is the mainstay of the economy, while the foreign-invested sector accounts for only a quarter. And even in that sector, we benefit from taxes and employment opportunities. We should have more of the three kinds of foreign-invested ventures [joint, cooperative and foreign-owned]. There is no reason to be afraid of them. So long as we keep level-headed, there is no cause for alarm. We have our advantages: we have the large and medium-sized state-owned enterprises and the rural enterprises. More important, political power is in our hands.

Some people argue that the more foreign investment flows in and the more ventures of the three kinds are established, the more elements of capitalism will be introduced and the more capitalism will expand in China. These people lack basic knowledge. At the current stage, foreign-funded enterprises in China are allowed to make some money in accordance with existing laws and policies. But the government levies taxes on those enterprises, workers get wages from them, and we learn technology and managerial skills. In addition, we can get information from them that will help us open more markets. Therefore, subject to the constraints of China's overall political and economic conditions, foreign-funded enterprises are useful supplements to the socialist economy, and in the final analysis they are good for socialism. . . .

The imperialists are pushing for peaceful evolution towards capitalism in China, placing their hopes on the generations that will come after us. Comrade Jiang Zemin and his peers can be regarded as the third generation, and there will be a fourth and a fifth. Hostile forces realize that so long as we of the older generation are still alive and carry weight, no change is possible. But after we are dead and gone, who will ensure that there is no peaceful evolution? So we must educate the army, persons working in the organs of dictatorship, the Communist Party members and the people, including the youth. If any problem arises in China, it will arise from inside the Communist Party. We must keep clear heads. We must pay attention to training people, selecting and promoting to positions of leadership persons who have both ability and political integrity, in accordance with the principle that they should be revolutionary, young, well educated and professionally competent. This is of vital importance to ensure that the Party's basic line is followed for a hundred years and to maintain long-term peace and stability. It is crucial for the future of China.

More young people should be promoted to positions of leadership. The present central leaders are rather advanced in years. Those who are a little over 60 are counted as young. They may be able to work for another 10 years, but 20 years from now they will be in their 80s, like me. They may be able to chat with people, as I'm doing today, but they won't have the energy to do much work. The current central leaders have been doing a good job. Of course, there are still quite a few problems in their work, but there are always problems in one's work. It is essential for old people like us to stand aside, give newcomers a free hand and watch them mature. Old people should voluntarily offer younger ones their places and give them help from the sidelines, but never stand in their way. Out of goodwill, they should help them when things are not being handled properly. They must pay attention to training successors of the next generation. The reason I insisted on retiring was that I didn't want to make mistakes in my old age. Old people have strengths but also great weaknesses—they tend to be stubborn, for example—and they should be aware of that. The older they are, the more modest they should be and the more careful not to make mistakes in their later years. We should go on selecting younger comrades for promotion and helping train them. Don't put your trust only in old age. I was already in a high position when I was in my 20s. I didn't know as much as you do now, but I managed. More young people must be chosen, helped, trained and allowed to grow. When they reach maturity, we shall rest easy. Right now we are still worried. In the final analysis, we must manage Party affairs in such a way as to prevent trouble. Then we can sleep soundly. Whether the line for China's development that was laid down at the Third Plenary Session of the Eleventh Central Committee will continue to be followed depends on the efforts of everyone, and especially on the education of future generations. . . .

We shall push ahead along the road to Chinese-style socialism. Capitalism has been developing for several hundred years. How long have we been building socialism? Besides, we wasted twenty years. If we can make China a moderately developed country within a hundred years from the founding of the People's Republic, that will be an extraordinary achievement. The period from now to the middle of the next century will be crucial. We must immerse ourselves in hard work: we have difficult tasks to accomplish and bear a heavy responsibility.

Questions:
1. What are Deng's justifications for injecting capitalistic principles into China's socialistic economic setting? Can socialism survive as a form of national ideology under the market-oriented economic reform?
2. What are the prospects for China's becoming a democratic nation? What problems do you see in a state where people experience an economic liberalization without political freedom?
3. Could the former Soviet Union have been saved had it adopted the reforms similar to those of Deng Xiaoping?
4. Deng talks about the leadership role of the Communist Party of China and about the need to combine socialism with a market economy. What do you think he means by "communist," as opposed to "socialist"? Or does he let these terms run together? Do you think there is a difference?

29.5 Pope John Paul II, Centesimus Annus

For two thousand years, popes have been writing "world letters" (encyclicals) to the faithful about the pressing theological, social, and moral problems of the day. On May 15, 1891, Leo XIII (Pope 1878–1903) published a revolutionary encyclical on the condition of labor and the need for social reform in the industrialized countries. Titled Rerum Novarum (Of New Things), the encyclical was a powerful defense of the rights of workers to organize and to form labor unions, to own private property, and to raise their families in dignity free from poverty and deprivation. Rerum Novarum attacked unregulated competition of free market capitalism and condemned the shallow materialism of Karl Marx's prescription of class revolution. To mark the centennial of Rerum Novarum and to reaffirm the Roman Catholic Church's commitment to speak out on matters of social justice, on May 1, 1991, John Paul II (Pope 1978–   ), issued a new encyclical titled Centisimus Annus, updating for the post–cold war world the Church's teaching on social justice.

Source: From Pope John Paul II, *On the Hundredth Anniversary of Rerum Novarum: Centesimus Annus.* Encyclical Letter of May 1, 1991 (Washington, DC: Office for Publishing and Promotion Services, United States Catholic Conference, 1991), pp. 66–97, *passim.*

It would appear that, on the level of individual nations and of international relations, *the free market* is the most efficient instrument for utilizing resources and effectively responding to needs.

But there are many human needs which find no place on the market. It is a strict duty of justice and truth not to allow fundamental human needs to remain unsatisfied, and not to allow those burdened by such needs to perish. It is also necessary to help these needy people to acquire expertise, to enter the circle of exchange, and to develop their skills in order to make the best use of their capacities and resources. Even prior to the logic of a fair exchange of goods and the forms of justice appropriate to it, there exists *something which is due to man because he is man,* by reason of his lofty dignity. Inseparable from that required "something" is the possibility to survive and, at the same time, to make an active contribution to the common good of humanity.

In Third World contexts, certain objectives stated by *Rerum Novarum* remain valid, and, in some cases, still constitute a goal yet to be reached, if man's work and his very being are not to be reduced to the level of a mere commodity. These objectives include a sufficient wage for the support of the family, social insurance for old age and unemployment, and adequate protection for the conditions of employment.

It would now be helpful to direct our attention to the specific problems and threats emerging within the more advanced economies and which are related to their particular characteristics. In earlier stages of development, man always lived under the weight of necessity. His needs were few and were determined, to a degree, by the objective structures of his physical make-up. Economic activity was directed towards satisfying these needs. It is clear that today the problem is not only one of supplying people with a sufficient quantity of goods, but also of responding to a *demand for quality:* the quality of the goods to be produced and consumed, the quality of the services to be enjoyed, the quality of the environment and of life in general.

To call for an existence which is qualitatively more satisfying is of itself legitimate, but one cannot fail to draw attention to the new responsibilities and dangers connected with this phase of history. The manner in which new needs arise and are defined is always marked by a more or less appropriate concept of man and of his true good. A given culture reveals its overall understanding of life through the choices it makes in production and consumption. It is here that *the phenomenon of consumerism* arises. In singling out new needs and new means to meet them, one must be guided by a comprehensive picture of man which respects all the dimensions of his being and which subordinates his material and instinctive dimensions to his interior and spiritual ones. If, on the contrary, a direct appeal is made to his instincts—while ignoring in various ways the reality of the person as intelligent and free—then *consumer attitudes and life-styles* can be created which are objectively improper and often damaging to his physical and spiritual health.

Widespread drug use is a sign of a serious malfunction in the social system; it also implies a materialistic and, in a certain sense, destructive "reading" of human needs. In this way the innovative capacity of a free economy is brought to a one-sided and inadequate conclusion. Drugs, as well as pornography and other forms of consumerism which exploit the frailty of the weak, tend to fill the resulting spiritual void.

It is not wrong to want to live better; what is wrong is a style of life which is presumed to be better when it is directed towards "having" rather than "being," and which wants to have more, not in order to be more but in order to spend life in enjoyment as an end in itself. It is therefore necessary to create life-styles in which the quest for truth, beauty, goodness and communion with others for the sake of common growth are the factors which determine consumer choices, savings and investments. Given the utter necessity of certain economic conditions and of political stability, the decision to invest, that is, to offer people an opportunity to make good use of their own labour, is also determined by an attitude of human sympathy and trust in Providence, which reveal the human quality of the person making such decisions.

It is the task of the State to provide for the defense and preservation of common goods such as the natural and human environments, which cannot be safeguarded simply by market forces. Just as in the time of primitive capitalism the State had the duty of defending the basic rights of workers, so now, with the new capitalism, the State and all of society have the duty of *defending those collective goods* which, among others, constitute the essential framework for the legitimate pursuit of personal goals on the part of each individual.

Here we find a new limit on the market: there are collective and qualitative needs which cannot be satisfied by market mechanisms.

Certainly the mechanisms of the market offer secure advantages: they help to utilize resources better; they promote the exchange of products; above all they give central place to the person's desires and preferences, which, in a contract, meet the desires and preferences of another person. Nevertheless, these mechanisms carry the risk of an "idolatry" of the market, an idolatry which ignores the existence of goods which by their nature are not and cannot be mere commodities.

Marxism criticized capitalist bourgeois societies, blaming them for the commercialization and alienation of human existence. This rebuke is of course based on a mistaken and inadequate idea of alienation, derived solely from the sphere of relationships of production and ownership, that is, giving them a materialistic foundation and moreover denying the legitimacy and positive value of market relationships even in their own sphere. Marxism thus ends up by affirming that only in a collective society can alienation be eliminated. However, the historical experience of socialist countries has sadly demonstrated that collectivism does not do away with alienation but rather increases it, adding to it a lack of basic necessities and economic inefficiency.

The historical experience of the West, for its part, shows that even if the Marxist analysis and its foundation of alienation are false, nevertheless alienation—and the loss of the authentic meaning of life—is a reality in Western societies too. This happens in consumerism, when people are ensnared in a web of false and superficial gratifications rather than being helped to experience their personhood in an authentic and concrete way. Alienation is found also in work, when it is organized so as to ensure maximum returns and profits with no concern whether the worker, through his own labour, grows or diminishes as a person, either through increased sharing in a genuinely supportive community or through increased isolation in a maze of relationships marked by destructive competitiveness and estrangement, in which he is considered only a means and not an end.

The concept of alienation needs to be led back to the Christian vision of reality, by recognizing in alienation a reversal of means and ends. When man does not recognize in himself and in others the value and grandeur of the human person, he effectively deprives himself of the possibility of benefiting from his humanity and of entering into that relationship of solidarity and communion with others for which God created him.

Man cannot give himself to a purely human plan for reality, to an abstract ideal or to a false utopia. As a person, he can give himself to another person or to other persons, and ultimately to God, who is the author of his being and who alone can fully accept his gift. A man is alienated if he refuses to transcend himself and to live the experience of self-giving and of the formation of an authentic human community oriented towards his final destiny, which is God. A society is alienated if its forms of social organization, production and consumption make it more difficult to offer this gift of self and to establish this solidarity between people.

Returning now to the initial question: can it perhaps be said that, after the failure of Communism, capitalism is the victorious social system, and that capitalism should be the goal of the countries now making efforts to rebuild their economy and society? Is this the model which ought to be proposed to the countries of the Third World which are searching for the path to true economic and civil progress?

The answer is obviously complex. If by "capitalism" is meant an economic system which recognizes the fundamental and positive role of business, the market, private property and the resulting responsibility for the means of production, as well as free human creativity in the economic sector, then the answer is certainly in the affirmative, even though it would perhaps be more appropriate to speak of a "business economy," "market economy" or simply "free economy." But if by "capitalism" is meant a system in which freedom in the economic sector is not circumscribed within a strong juridical framework which places it at the service of human freedom in its totality, and which sees it as a particular aspect of that freedom, the core of which is ethical and religious, then the reply is certainly negative.

The Marxist solution has failed, but the realities of marginalization and exploitation remain in the world, especially the Third World, as does the reality of human alienation, especially in the more advanced countries. Against these phenomena the Church strongly raises her voice. Vast multitudes are still living in conditions of great material and moral poverty. The collapse of the Communist system in so many countries certainly removes an obstacle to facing these problems in an appropriate and realistic way, but it is not enough to bring about their solution. Indeed, there is a risk that a radical capitalistic ideology could spread which refuses even to consider these problems, in the *a priori* belief that any attempt to solve them is doomed to failure, and which blindly entrusts their solution to the free development of market forces.

These general observations also apply to the *role of the State in the economic sector.* Economic activity, especially the activity of a market economy, cannot be conducted in an institutional, juridical or political vacuum. On the contrary, it presupposes sure guarantees of individual freedom and private property, as well as a stable currency and efficient public services. Hence the principal task of the State is to guarantee this security, so that those who work and produce can enjoy the fruits of their labours and thus feel encouraged to work efficiently and honestly. The absence of stability, together with the corruption of public officials and the spread of improper sources of growing rich and of easy profits deriving from illegal or purely speculative activities, constitutes one of the chief obstacles to development and to the economic order.

Another task of the State is that of overseeing and directing the exercise of human rights in the economic sector. However, primary responsibility in this area belongs not to the State but to individuals and to the various groups and associations which make up society. The State could not directly ensure the right to work for all its citizens unless it controlled every aspect of economic life and restricted the free initiative of individuals. This does not mean, however, that the State has no competence in this domain, as was claimed by those who argued against any rules in the economic sphere. Rather, the State has a duty to sustain business activities by creating conditions which will ensure job opportunities, by stimulating those activities where they are lacking or by supporting them in moments of crisis.

In recent years the range of such intervention has vastly expanded, to the point of creating a new type of State, the so-called "Welfare State." This has happened in some countries in order to respond better to many needs and demands, by remedying forms of poverty and deprivation unworthy of the human person. However, excesses and abuses, especially in recent years, have provoked very harsh criticisms of the Welfare State, dubbed the "Social Assistance State."

By intervening directly and depriving society of its responsibility, the Social Assistance State leads to a loss of human energies and an inordinate increase of public agencies, which are dominated more by bureaucratic ways of thinking than by concern for serving their clients, and which are accompanied by an enormous increase in spending. In fact, it would appear that needs are best understood and satisfied by people who are closest to them and who act as neighbours to those in need.

Faithful to the mission received from Christ her Founder, the Church has always been present and active among the needy, offering them material assistance in ways that neither humiliate nor reduce them to mere objects of assistance, but which help them to escape their precarious situation by promoting their dignity as persons. With heartfelt gratitude to God it must be pointed out that active charity has never ceased to be practised in the Church; indeed, today it is showing a manifold and gratifying increase. In this regard, special mention must be made of *volunteer work,* which the Church favours and promotes by urging everyone to cooperate in supporting and encouraging its undertakings.

In order to overcome today's widespread individualistic mentality, what is required is *a concrete commitment to solidarity and charity,* beginning in the family with the mutual support of husband and wife and the care which the different generations give to one another. In this sense the family too can be called a community of work and solidarity.

Apart from the family, other intermediate communities exercise primary functions and give life to specific networks of solidarity. These develop as real communities of persons and strengthen the social fabric, preventing society from becoming an anonymous and impersonal mass, as unfortunately often happens today. It is in interrelationships on many levels that a person lives, and that society becomes more "personalized." The individual today is often suffocated between two poles represented by the State and the marketplace. At times it seems as though he exists only as a producer and consumer of goods, or as an object of State administration. People lose sight of the fact that life in society has neither the market nor the State as its final purpose, since life itself has a unique value which the State and the market must serve. Man remains above all a being who seeks the truth and strives to live in that truth, deepening his understanding of it through a dialogue which involves past and future generations.

Questions:

1. *Pope John Paul II, in speaking of the "idolatry" of market economy, argues that "there are collective and qualitative needs which cannot be satisfied by market mechanisms." Can this view be reconciled with free market capitalism?*
2. *What does the pope mean when he insists that Karl Marx's concept of "exploitation" has been overcome in Western society but the problems of alienation and consumerism remain inherent in Western-style capitalism?*
3. *How would you compare the pope's view of economics with that of Adam Smith, Friedrich List, and Karl Marx?*
4. *According to Pope John Paul, what is the proper role of the state in a capitalist society? Do you agree or disagree? Why?*

29.6 Saddam's Invasion of Kuwait: Two Rationales

Saddam Hussein's military expedition to Kuwait speedily resulted in the subjugation of that oil-rich Emirate, and precipitated a lengthy crisis which was only (and then perhaps only temporarily) ended with Iraq's defeat by Allied forces in the 1991 Desert Storm War. As in other crises that have historically escalated into warfare, the question of "why?" is complex and multi-faceted. Saddam, in a "Victory Day" speech to his people (A), and the scholar Bishara Bahbah (B) offer their explanations.

Sources: Ofra Bengio, ed., *Saddam Speaks on the Gulf Crisis: A Collection of Documents* (Tel Aviv, The Moshe Dayan Center for Middle Eastern and African Studies, The Shiloam Institute, Tel Aviv University, 1992), pp. 110–116.

Bishara A. Bahbah, "The Crisis in the Gulf—Why Iran invaded Kuwait" in Phyllis Bennis and Michael Moushabeck, *Beyond the Storm: A Gulf Crisis Reader* (N.Y.: Olive Branch Press, 1991), pp. 50–54.

A

Message from President Saddam Husayn "on the occasion of the great victory day on 8 August 1988"—read by announcer. *Baghdad Domestic Service in Arabic 1700 GMT, 7 August 1990.*

In the name of God, the merciful, the compassionate.

O great Iraqi people, O sons of the glorious Arab nation, on 8 August 1988 matters were settled after eight years of dueling. That day was the day of days, and the communiqué that was issued on that day was the communiqué of communiqués. That day was truly the day of days because every day, beginning with the first day in the book of the second al-Qadisiyya that began on 4 September 1980 and ending with the last day of that eternal and great book of our people's life that preceded the day of days on 7 August 1988 has a share in the day of 8 August 1988. The communiqué broadcast on 8 August was the communiqué of communiqués because every communiqué issued from 4 September 1980 to 7 August 1988 is a vital part of the fruits of the record from which the banner of victory was raised high on 8 August 1988. From this we can see the peoples' record, and history cannot exist without the accumulation of repeated sacrifices, wisdom, bravery, patient work, and true struggle to God's satisfaction. By this we can see that the day of days began from the first day of the record and that the communiqué of communiqués was written in the first communiqué of the second al-Qadisiyya.

The day of days gives lessons to those who heed them, lessons whose meanings and dimensions go beyond the national borders to affect the entire nation and humanity at large. There are people who do not benefit from other people's lessons and there are those who do benefit. All this is determined by the fact that some leaders draw lessons in accordance with the patriotic and national aspects of human wisdom and some others learn the lessons they wish—but not the truth as it is.

We do not like lessons outside the course of life, except those affiliated with God. We do not give reason the full right to interpret things independently from the eye or give the eye the full right apart from reason. The two should cooperate in concrete and abstract matters. The blood of our martyrs has turned into a permanent torch along our people's path toward progress and a better life. The edifice of progress is rising with the passing of every day since 8 August 1988, and its foundation is becoming stronger on the basis of righteousness and justice. Mistakes in its course are being dealt with on the basis of the insistence of the people, who have defended rights and justice and offered sacrifices for them. Thus, the people deserve a life that is not disturbed by evil intentions, and the torch lit by the martyrs' blood that represents virtue and national and pan-Arab dignity should not be extinguished by the attempts of non-patriots, non-nationalists, and non-humanitarians.

Therefore, the day of days and the communiqué of communiqués became not the end of a stage in the life of the Iraqis and the nation, but the serious beginning of a life of honor and triumph in all walks of life—in theory and practice—as well as in the arena of the battlefield whenever the heat rises.

Therefore, we have the right and it is our duty to say that the day of the call, the second of this month, August, in this year, is the legitimate newborn child of 8 August 1988. in fact, this is the only way to deal with these despicable Croesuses* who relished stealing the part to harm the whole, who relished possession to destroy devotion, and who were guided by the foreigner instead of being guided by virtuous standards, principles of pan-Arabism, and the creed of humanitarianism in relations between the sons of the same people and nation. The second of August was a day bursting with these meanings. In the same way it is the legitimate newborn child of the struggle, patience, and perseverance of the Kuwaiti people, which was crowned by revolutionary action on that immortal day.

The newborn child was born of a legitimate father and an immaculate mother. It will be a loyal son to the Kuwaitis, Iraqis, and all the Arabs. Greetings to the makers of the second of August, whose efforts God has blessed. They have achieved one of the brightest, most promising, and most principled national and pan-Arab acts.

At a time when the second of August arrived to be the legitimate newborn son of the second Qadisiyya and its people—and with God's help, it will also be a loyal son—it and its consequences shall be the beginning of a new, lofty, and rising stage in which virtue will spread throughout the Arab homeland in the coming days and profanity, treachery, betrayal, meanness, and subservience to the foreigner will retreat from it. Many of the goals of the Arabs will move closer after some believed they were moving away from their places in the horizon. New suns and moons will shine, stars will glitter, light will expel darkness, and lunar and solar eclipses will withdraw from the skies of Iraq and the Arab world.

How can that be?

When the sun of the Arabs set in its faraway horizon, after Baghdad's eye was put out and its mind was ruined by the actions and rule of the foreigner, a pitch-black darkness prevailed throughout the Arab world, with the exception of local cases that used to emerge here and there and every now and then under certain symptoms and whose indications were not wholly pan-Arab. The Arabs had no sun, moon or stars to guide them to any road with a glimmer of hope.

When they saw before them the opportunity to be liberated from the darkness of the Ottoman era, and the virtuous and patriotic Arabs determined to change the image of the state of the Arabs, they fell into the claws of the forces of the age as soon as they took their first step. At a time when some foreign rulers were overthrown by Arab rulers to start with, and liberation revolutions and movements took place after the first Arab revolution to replace what was left with local, national, or pan-Arab alternatives, the partition and dispersion of the factors of power and capability throughout various regions retained a weak Arab homeland—weak individuals, actions, and aspirations. In this condition, every time the Arab took a step forward, he took two steps back, or a bit more or a bit less than that step, and was moved further away from the position he was supposed to be in.

The malicious Westerners, while partitioning the Arab homeland, intentionally multiplied the number of countries with the result that the Arab nation could not achieve the integration needed to realize its full capability. In this way, they also fragmented capabilities. While fragmenting the Arab homeland, they intentionally distanced the majority of the population density and areas of cultural depth from riches and their sources, something new to the life of Arabs. This became one of the most dangerous results of partition and a fatal wedge in Arab relations.

The wealth centered in one place, in the hands of a minority lacking in cultural depth or, more accurately, having no record of cultural depth. On the other hand, cultural depth and population density centered in a place remote from the sources of the new wealth, as I said. This malicious act resulted in the minority becoming so corrupt that it was cut off from its nation. It stopped mentioning this nation, except in lip service and on some ceremonial occasions. The wealth in the hands of this minority did not come as a result of legitimate hard work. The overwhelming majority of the nation, which was living away from the sources of wealth and enduring a major part of its negative impact on its life in the social, psychological, cultural, military, and political spheres, suffered a weakness that, if not overcome, could not allow this majority to play a vital and effective role in the life of the nation.

The authority of the honorable national and pan-Arab majority and its leading influence on the Arab life was absent and was replaced by the authority of the corrupt minority, which is connected with the foreigner. As a result, the nation was hit right between the eyes, and the damage it suffered was no less in its consequences than direct foreign rule. Indeed, at some stages of the nation's life direct foreign rule awakened—through reaction—the national and pan-Arab awareness and crystallized the factors of spiritual upsurge in which the nation invoked its genuine values from the depths of its culture.

But the nation's situation before 2 August this year was fatal to its soul and body. One could not but feel its descent into the abyss. This situation would rob rulers and people of their courage, whether among the corrupt wealthy minority or among the overwhelming majority of the poor Arabs. It would also block the capable collective efforts in the two places, make the people in both places dependent on foreigners in one way or another, and seriously upset the social life in both places. Moreover, efforts toward true interaction with the laws of the age would become absent or weak, and, consequently, the process of formulating these laws in a national and pan-Arab manner would be hindered in both places. Furthermore, the nation—in its cultural sense, collective capability, and joint action—would become lacking in both areas. The nation will return to its rightful position only through real struggle and jihad to place the wealth of the nation in the service of its noble objectives so that the opinion of the majority would become prevalent, capable, and honest, and the opinion of the minority will be respected when it is honest. Its conduct, then, will be remote from decay and corruption.

Two August has come as a very violent response to the harm that the foreigner has wanted to perpetrate against Iraq and the nation. The Croesus of Kuwait and his aides became the obedient, humiliated, and treacherous dependents of that foreigner. Instead of honoring its commitments toward the stem, the dead branch began stabbing the stem with a poisonous dagger in the back so that it might fall dead beside the dead branch and so that the living stem would not try to awaken the dead branch (sentence as heard). What took place on 2 August was inevitable so that death might not prevail over life, so that those who were capable of ascending to the peak would not be brought down to the abysmal precipice, so that corruption and remoteness from God would not spread to the majority as a result of need and poverty after the corrupt minority had distanced itself from God, values, books, and disciples. Honor will be kept in Mesopotamia so that Iraq will continue to be the pride of the Arabs, their protector, and their model of noble values, and so that Kuwait will join the march of its nation.

The lowly wallted and planned to harm the free women of Iraq, as they had done to free Arab women in other places. But their calculations went wrong because they did not know that we prefer death to this and that we cannot sleep without putting out the eyes of those who encroach upon Iraqi and Arab and Islamic values. Death is better than humiliation and subordination to the foreigner.

This was the 8th of August 1988, the day of days, in which the communiqué of communiqués was issued, declaring the great victory. It will be the fountainhead of all the sweet days in the life of the Arabs, and their compassionate mother, as was the day of 2 August this year.

Glory to the martyrs; glory to the free, living people; God is great; and accursed be the lowly.

(Signed) Saddam Husayn, 16 Muharram, 1411 Hegira, corresponding to 7 August 1990.

B

Saddam Hussein's decision to invade Kuwait on August 2, 1990 took friend and foe by surprise. One can explain Iraq's decision to invade Kuwait by outlining and reviewing the list of grievances Iraq had against Kuwait. These included: historical and territorial claims that Iraq had over Kuwait; Kuwait's refusal to lease two strategic islands to Iraq; Iraq's anger over Kuwait's pumping of huge quantities of oil from the Rumaila field which lies underneath both countries; Kuwait's refusal to forgive Iraq's debt incurred during the Iran-Iraq war; and Iraq's accusations that Kuwait had waged economic warfare against it.

Nevertheless, it can be argued that Saddam Hussein's personality played a key role in his decision to embark on such a disastrous venture. Moreover, Saddam Hussein seriously and persistently miscalculated and failed to predict other countries' reaction to his invasion of Kuwait. And, when the invasion did occur, he failed to realize that file coalition of forces amassed against him would soundly defeat his forces in a very short period of time.

Historical and Territorial Claims

The borders of present day Iraq and Kuwait are the product of the colonial powers. Under the terms of the San Remo conference in 1920, most of the territories of the Arab Middle East, formerly part of file Ottoman Empire, were divided between Britain and France, which received mandates from the League of Nations to establish and supervise national governments in these territories. In 1921, Britain established the kingdom of Iraq made up of the three former provinces of Mosul, Baghdad, and Basra (which had included the Ottoman district of Kuwait).

In 1922, the British High Commissioner for Iraq, Sir Percy Cox, delineated the modern borders of Iraq, Kuwait and Saudi Arabia. He gave Kuwait a coastline of 310 miles, leaving Iraq a mere 36 miles. Although this angered the Iraqis, they did little to alter that reality because Iraq was under varying degrees of British influence.

However, two developments led to a drastic change in Iraq's relative silence. In 1958, the pro-Western monarch in Iraq was overthrown in a military coup led by Major General Abdul-Karim Qasim. And, in 1961, Britain and Kuwait terminated the 1899 agreement which had allowed the Sabah family to run internal affairs in Kuwait but made Britain responsible for Kuwait's defense and external relations.

When, in June 1961, Kuwait declared its independence, General Qasim laid claim to Kuwait and threatened to annex it by force. British forces rushed to Kuwait deterred an Iraqi invasion. On February 8, 1963, Qasim was overthrown and the Ba'ath party, Iraq's current ruling party, subsequently recognized Kuwait's independence on October 4, 1963 in exchange for a large payment from Kuwait.

Notwithstanding this agreement, Iraqi regimes continued to raise questions over border issues. In 1973, a contingent of Iraqi troops briefly occupied a Kuwaiti border post.

In a somewhat unusual but interesting twist, and on the eve of Iraq's invasion of Kuwait, Iraq accused Kuwait of violating its territorial integrity. In a letter sent to the Secretary General of the League of Arab States dated July 16, 1990, Iraqi Foreign Minister Tariq Aziz complained that the Kuwaiti government had "...implemented a plot to escalate the pace of the gradual, systematic advance toward Iraqi territory. The Kuwaiti government set up military establishments, police posts, oil installations, and farms on Iraqi territory."

Access to the Gulf: Kuwait's Refusal to Lease Two Islands to Iraq

In its quest for a deep sea port in the Gulf, Iraq requested from Kuwait, in the early 1970s, control over the two islands of Warbah and Bubiyan. These islands overlook the approaches to Umm Qasr, one of Iraq's two ports on the Gulf. In 1975, Kuwait rejected an Iraqi proposal to cede Warbah island and lease half of Bubiyan island to Iraq for 99 years. Shortly after the outbreak of the Iran-Iraq war in 1980, Kuwait refused a similar Iraqi request. And, in 1989, after the end of the Iran-Iraq war, Kuwait refused another request to lease the two islands.

Given that one of the main reasons for the Iran-Iraq war was the issue ot who controls the Shatt al-Arab water-way which separates Iran and Iraq and which provides Iraq with its only access to the Gulf, Iraq viewed Kuwait's refusal to accommodate its needs with regard to a deep sea port as unfriendly. Thus, the issue of the two islands has been a major irritant in Iraqi-Kuwaiti ties.

The Dispute over the Rumalia Oilfield

Despite Iraq's recognition of Kuwait's independence in October 1963, the two governments did not settle their dispute over ownership of the huge 50-mile-long Rumaila oilfield, which lies beneath the Iraq-Kuwait border. About 90% of the banana-shaped field, which is estimated to contain 30 billion barrels of oil, is in Iraq. Nevertheless, Iraq claimed that during the 1980s Kuwait pumped over $10 billion worth of oil from the field that should have gone to Iraq, without any agreement between the two countries.

The significance of this Iraqi gripe against Kuwait becomes even more serious when considering the huge debt that Iraq found itself saddled with as a result of the Iran-Iraq war. More importantly, a significant portion of Iraq's debt was owed to Kuwait.

Kuwait's Refusal to Forgive Iraq's Debt

Saddam Hussein viewed Iraq's war with Iran as having been fought on behalf of all Arabs, helping to protect them from Khomeini's Islamic revolution. He, therefore, expected Arab countries, particularly those in the Gulf region, to be grate-ful for his role in checking the spread of Khomeini's Islamic revolution.

Iraq's war with Iran, by most estimates, cost Iraq about $500 billion. Iraq emerged from the conflict with debts exceeding $80 billion—about one and a half times its gross national product—including at least $30 billion in short-term debt that had to be repaid to Europe, Japan, and the United States in dollars or other hard currencies. About half of Iraq's debt was owed to Saudi Arabia, Kuwait, and the United Arab Emirates.

In February and July 1990, Iraq demanded money from the Arab states in the Gulf, and both times, it was turned down.

Economic Warfare

Kuwait not only refused to forgive the debt, it deliberately, according to Iraq, flooded the oil market in violation of OPEC production quotas agreed to by the major oil producers. This Kuwaiti overproduction depressed the price of oil and, in turn, hurt Iraq, which was already short on funds.

During the Baghdad Arab summit which was held at the end of May 1990, Iraqi President Saddam Hussein claimed that every one dollar drop in the price of a barrel of oil meant a loss of $1 billion a year for Iraq. He then added, in no uncertain terms, that in Iraq's present economic state of affairs, this overproduction amounted to "an act of war."

Iraq badly needed funds to rebuild its shattered economy, devastated by years of war with Iran. One of the ways that Saddam Hussein had maintained internal support for his policies was by spending generously on goods and services even through the bleakest moments of the war. Now that the war with Iran had ended, the Iraqi population's expectations for a better standard of living were on the rise. The rulers of Iraq were aware of that and strived to cope with these rising expectations. This created tremendous pressures to try and get Iraq's debt forgiven and to increase the income generated from the sale of oil.

In a memorandum dated July 15, 1990, addressed to the Secretary General of the United Nations, Iraqi Foreign Minister Tariq Aziz explicitly named Kuwait and the United Arab Emirates as the two "culprits" in overproduction.

Hussein's Personality and Miscalculations

Saddam Hussein's personality, compounded by the fact that he exercised absolute control in Iraq, played a key role in the unfolding of events in the Gulf. He views himself as one of the great leaders of history, ranking himself with Nasser, Castro, Tito, Ho Chi Minh, and Mao Zcdong. He has been consumed by dreams of glory, and he identifies himself with Nebuchad-nezzar, the King of Babylonia who conquered Jerusalem in 586 B.C., and Salah ad-Din who regained Jerusalem in 1187 by defeating the Crusaders. He believed (it is not clear if he persists in those beliefs) that there could be only one supreme Arab nationalist leader, and he was the one. He was driven by what he perceived as his mission to lead the Arab world.

Nevertheless, based on his actions and statements, Saddam Hussein is a pragmatic man. When he deemed certain "unthinkable" actions to have been in his favor or better than the existing alternatives, he carried out the "unthinkable."

In March 1975, he signed an agreement with the Shah of Iran, stipulating joint sovereignty with Iran over the disputed Shatt al-Arab waterway in return for Iran ceasing to supply aid to the Kurdish rebellion. Then, in June 1982, Hussein reversed his earlier militant attitude toward Iran and Khomeini and attempted to terminate hostilities by offering a unilateral ceasefire. And, on August 15, 1990, Hussein agreed to meet Iranian conditions for a permanent ceasefire by promising to withdraw from Iranian territory, agreeing to an exchange of prisoners, and, most importantly, agreeing to share the disputed Shatt al-Arab waterway—one of the main reasons for initiating the Iran-Iraq war in 1980—all because he desperately needed the 500,000 Iraqi troops who were tied up along the Iran-Iraq border.

Given his pragmatism, why then did Saddam Hussein occupy Kuwait and refuse to withdraw when it was obvious that a majority of the world community led by the United States supported UN Security Council reolutions that condenmcd Iraq's invasion of Kuwait, and subsequently authorized the use of force to evict Iraqi troops and liberate Kuwait?

Saddam Hussein's actions were based on serious miscalculations and misperceptions.

First, given Saudi Arabia's long-standing sensitivity to the presence of foreign troops on its soil, Saddam Hussein assumed that the Saudis would not ask, or be convinced, to accept U.S. and other foreign, particularly non-Muslim, troops to help defend their country and liberate Kuwait. He was wrong.

Second, Saddam Hussein overestimated the level of support he would have in the Arab world. He assumed that the have-nots in the Arab world would be happy with the demise of oil-rich Kuwait. He was surprised by the opposition to his occupation of Kuwait by even those who were closest to him, such as Jordan and the Palestine Liberation Organization.

Third, Saddam Husscin believed that the United States would not interfete militarily if he were to occupy Kuwait. When the United States decided to send troops to defend Saudi Arabia and liberate Kuwait, he thought that the U.S. was bluffing and would not wage a war against Iraq because of the former's Vietnam complex—the fear of being entangled in a long drawn-out war in a distant land. He felt that, even if the United States did attack Iraqi troops, the low tolerance of the American public to U.S. casualties would force the United States to end the war and negotiate an acccptable agreement with Iraq.

Fourth, Saddam Hussein was determined to attack Israel if a war erupted. He believed that Israel would then retaliate, leading to the collapse of the Arab, and hence, the international alliance against Iraq. When attacked, Israel opted not to retaliate and reaped enormous benefits for its restraint.

Fifth, Iraq's victory over Iran, albeit at an outrageous cost, and the end of the Iran-Iraq war, unleashed an unrealistic level of confidence in the Iraqi military's capabilities. Iraq emerged as the fourth largest army in the world—an army that was well-equipped, and battle-hardened. Where Saddam Hussein miscalculated was by assuming that this army would or could put up a fight against the U.S. and other Western armies. More importantly, the Iraqi leader miscalculated when he assumed that his troops were committed to fighting for the sake of retaining Kuwait.

Conclusion

Iraq's invasion of Kuwait will go down in history as one of those tragic events that precipitated as a result of one man's miscalculations. Whether Iraq had justifiable grievances against Kuwait no longer is the issue. These grievances were quickly overshadowed by the tremendous destruction caused by Kuwait's invasion, and during the battle for its subsequent liberation.

Many have argued that Saddam Hussein could have settled his grievances with Kuwait without having to physically occupy the country. Nonetheless what Saddam Hussein could or could not have done is in the realm of speculation. What is unshakably clear is that Iraq's invasion of Kuwait led to a chain of events which threaten not only Saddam Hussein's career, but also Iraq's ambition to be the dominant power in the Gulf and the Arab world.

Questions:
1. *Of what shortcomings does Saddam accuse the Kuwaiti leadership? To what historically anti-Arab elements does he attempt to link them? What part do jihad and pan-Arabism play in his arguments?*
2. *According to Bahbah, what part did the oilfields and oil production controversies play in Iraqi-Kuwaiti relations?*
3. *How does Bahbah assess Saddam's personality and the role it played in the unfolding of Gulf Crisis events? What miscalculations does he set forward as being crucial?*
4. *Compare and contrast the two documents; what is your assessment as to points of agreement, or divergence?*

29.7 "We Wage a War to Save Civilization Itself" (2001): George W. Bush

Basking in the faint glow of Cold War victory and somewhat adrift in foreign affairs during the 1990s, the United States, its image as a bastion of security and freedom now tarnished, had entered a new era. No longer the invulnerable "superpower," the United States once again was given purpose and direction—an evil to confront. The war against terrorism provided a new forum for the confirmation of its values as a nation and for its leadership in the Western world as these excerpts from President Bush's speeches following the disaster indicate.

Source: "'We Wage a War to Save Civilization Itself'" is from George W. Bush, speeches delivered to the people of the United States and to the General Assembly of the United Nations on September 11, November 8 and 10, 2001. Contained in *Vital Speeches of the Day,* October 1, 2001, p. 738 and December 1, 2001, pp. 98–99; 103–104.

Address Delivered to the Nation
(September 11, 2001)

Today, our fellow citizens, our way of life, our very freedom came under attack in a series of deliberate and deadly terrorist acts. The victims were in airplanes, or in their offices; secretaries, businessmen and women, military and federal workers; moms and dads, friends and neighbors. Thousands of lives were suddenly ended by evil, despicable acts of terror. The pictures of airplanes flying into buildings, fires burning, huge structures collapsing, have filled us with disbelief, terrible sadness and a quiet, unyielding anger. These acts of mass murder were intended to frighten our nation into chaos and retreat. but they have failed; our country is strong.

A great people has been moved to defend a great nation. Terrorist attacks can shake the foundations of our biggest buildings, but they cannot touch the foundation of America. These acts shattered steel, but they cannot dent the steel of American resolve. American was targeted for attack because we're the brightest beacon for freedom and opportunity in the world. and no one will keep that light from shining. . . .

Address to the Nation (November 8, 2001)

We are a different country than we were on September the 10th—sadder and less innocent; stronger and more united; and in the face of ongoing threats, determined and courageous. Our nation faces a threat to our freedoms, and the stakes could not be higher. We are the target of enemies who boast they want to kill—kill all Americans, kill all Jews, and kill all Christians. We've seen that type of hate before—and the only possible response is to confront it, and to defeat it.

This new enemy seeks to destroy our freedom and impose its views. We value life; the terrorists ruthlessly destroy it. We value education; the terrorists do not believe women should be educated or should have health care, or should leave their homes. We value the right to speak our minds; for the terrorists, free expression can be grounds for execution. We respect people of all faiths and welcome the free practice of religion; our enemy wants to dictate how to think and how to worship even to their fellow Muslims.

The enemy tries to hide behind a peaceful faith. But those who celebrate the murder of innocent men, women, and children have no religion, have no conscience, and have no mercy. We wage war to save civilization, itself. We did not seek it, but we must fight it—and we will prevail.

This is a different war from any our nation has ever faced, a war on many fronts, against terrorists who operate in more than 60 different countries. And this is a war that must be fought not only overseas, but also here at home. . . .

Address to the United Nations General Assembly (November 10, 2001)

We're asking for a comprehensive commitment to this fight. We must unite in opposing all terrorists, not just some of them. In this world there are good causes and bad causes, and we may disagree on where the line is drawn. Yet, there is no such thing as good terrorist. No national aspiration, no remembered wrong can ever justify the deliberate murder of the innocent. Any government that rejects this principle, trying to pick and choose its terrorist friends, will know the consequences.

We must speak the truth about terror. Let us never tolerate outrageous conspiracy theories concerning the attacks of September the 11th; malicious lies that attempt to shift the blame away from the terrorists, themselves, away from the guilty. To inflame ethnic hatred is to advance the cause of terror.

The war against terror must not serve as an excuse to persecute ethnic and religious minorities in any country. Innocent people must be allowed to live their own lives, by their own customs, under their own religion. and every nation must have avenues for the peaceful expression of opinion and dissent. When these avenues are closed, the temptation to speak through violence grows. . . .

As I've told the American people, freedom and fear are at war. we face enemies that hate not our policies, but our existence; the tolerance of openness and creative culture that defines us. But the outcome of this conflict is certain: There is a current in history and it runs toward freedom. Our enemies resent it and dismiss it, but the dreams of mankind are defined by liberty—the natural right to create and build and worship and live in dignity. When men and women are released from oppression and isolation, they find fulfillment and hope, and they leave poverty by the millions. These aspirations are lifting up the peoples of Europe, Asia, Africa, and the Americas, and they can lift up all of the Islamic world. We stand for the permanent hopes of humanity, and those hopes will not be denied. We're confident, too, that history has an author who fills time and eternity with His purpose. We know that evil is real, but good will prevail against it. This is the teaching of many faiths, and in that assurance we gain strength for a long journey. . . .

We did not ask for this mission, yet there is honor in history's call. We have a chance to write the story of our times, a story of courage defeating cruelty and light overcoming darkness. This calling is worthy of any life, and worthy of every nation. So let us go forward, confident, determined, and unafraid.

Questions:
1. *In his speech of September 11, Bush states that the U.S. was attacked "because we're the brightest beacon for freedom and opportunity in the world." Do you agree with this assessment? Why or why not?*
2. *Can you think of any instances in history where terrorism worked to achieve a political goal?*

29.8 Henry A. Myers, "Now, in the Twenty-First Century"

As the twenty-first century dawns, most age-old questions and issues are still with us. History certainly does not repeat itself in any mechanical way—technological inventions by themselves assure that—but history does give us an idea of the options available to humankind in coping with challenges. What follows is an attempt to identify some of the main challenges and review of the range of possible reactions to them.

CONFLICT AND CONFLICT RESOLUTION

As people centuries from now look back at the twentieth century, they may well give it the short name "Age of Social-Doctrine Conflict." Particularly in its core decades, roughly 1914–1990, no previous period in world history saw such continual struggle—coercive, psychological, and diplomatic—among protagonists of ideologies, with conflicts over nationalism, democracy, militarism, fascism, and communism, all in many variations, casting the longest shadows. Since the end of the cold war, the last four of these have faded somewhat as causes of conflict, whereas nationalism—in the sense of a force fueling struggles over ethnic claims—has assumed central importance.

As we have seen, nationalism is a powerful ideology, but it is more than a social doctrine: At the moment, it is a rationale for expansion and has had genocidal consequences; in fact, two of the most prolonged and wanton instances of mass killing since World War II, in the former Yugoslavia and in Rwanda, have taken place since the end of the cold war over "ethnic rivalries," which is a current media synonym for "nationalism." A third instance, in Cambodia had different, cold war–related roots. Although it is true that protagonists of "-isms" from Stalin and Hitler to Pol Pot hold an unchallenged world record for mass killings with tens of millions of victims in the twentieth century, it is also true that people seem able to recover more easily from even the rabid behavior induced by the worst of social doctrines than from ethnic hatreds. Identities based on "-isms" can be discarded. Most of the former believers in Italian Fascism or German Nazism abandoned their doctrinal persuasion with the defeat of their leaders—at least enough to blend in with the rest of their national populations. Former Communists in Russia are able to do the same thing; however, ethnic identities are nearly impossible to discard. There is no such thing as a former Bosnian Serb or former Hutu. The likelihood is that intense ethnic conflict will continue to plague the twenty-first century.

INTERNATIONAL LAW ENFORCEMENT

If ethnic conflict is a fact of world life, the only responses are either to let the conflicts burn themselves out, until victors have subdued weaker enemies at high human cost, or to intervene. Intervention here means the use of outside, international forces to establish and keep peace among the warring parties. This role was seen as a main one for the League of Nations after World War I. The United Nations' stronger structure than its predecessor's and an American commitment to it raised high hopes in 1945 after World War II for its future as international peacekeeper.

Actually, for the half century after World War II, the United Nations did not work significantly better than the League of Nations in its peacekeeping role. It did establish the uneasy peace that followed the war establishing Israel with the partition of Palestine, and it kept peace most of the time on Cyprus—a very meager record of efficacy from a global-peacekeeping standpoint. Some of its members contributed to the Korean War, but the Korean War was waged by the United Nations only because the Soviet Union was boycotting the organization during crucial proceedings while Chinese seats in the United Nations were held by the Nationalist government of Chiang Kai-shek on Taiwan rather than by that of Mao Tse-tung on the Chinese mainland. The power to veto Security Council actions, which was given to the former main allies from World War II as its permanent members, meant that a veto could be expected any time a cold war conflict called for UN intervention, and nearly all significant international hostilities after 1946 were cold war conflicts or became so with Third World countries in surrogate roles. This state of affairs called the North Atlantic Treaty Organization (NATO) into being. Its members were not all North Atlantic countries, which the name implies; rather, they were united by a determination to prevent further Soviet expansion in Europe. In this original role, NATO worked well: After its formation, the USSR did not expand any farther into Europe, although its detractors could claim that it was not NATO but the U.S. Strategic Air Command that was the real deterrent to Soviet expansion. Others minimized Soviet expansionist tendencies, but NATO appeared justified to its supporters largely because the United Nations was incapable of doing its peacekeeping job.

With the cold war over, NATO should theoretically be unnecessary. In the absence of expected vetoes, the United Nations can return to its original role, that of international peacekeeper. It is true that China is still a Communist country, but there are so few other Communist countries and causes that they should not keep the Security Council from working most of the time. It appears, however, that NATO members have not the slightest intention of disbanding; in fact, NATO forces have done far more fighting as NATO forces since the end of the cold war than during it. The simple fact appears to be that leaders of the NATO countries, with at least the passive support of the people who elected them, prefer NATO as an organization of countries more like their own—more stable, more democratic, and more predictable—than any random sampling of UN countries.

People in other parts of the world seem to feel the same way, preferring to have conflicts in their areas countered with forces from countries resembling their own. In West Africa, that force was the Economic Organization of West African States (ECOWAS), which began as a free-trade association but developed military forces in the Economic Organization [of West African States] Monitoring Observer Group (ECOMOG). Under the leadership of Nigeria, ECOMOG successfully intervened in the Sierra Leonean civil war and established much more peaceful conditions than any other force did after the May 1997 coup. Nigeria ran out of money to maintain its forces throughout the country, and so ECOMOG could not continue to enforce peace; but the point is that for more than a year this West African regional organization, rather than the United Nations, exercised peacekeeping functions in that country far better than the United Nations has been doing with its belated and less-than-focused effort there in 2000. The outlook, then, is for international but regional organizations to conduct peacekeeping operations, with the United Nations remaining mostly in the background.

GLOBALIZATION AND THE DIGITAL DIVIDE

With the rapid expansion of computer usage in the last two decades of the twentieth century, the gap in the standard of living between the developed North, with its increasingly digital economy and society, and the underdeveloped and distinctly less digital South has widened. The lines drawn are approximately those of the old First World (North) and Third World (South) of the cold war era, with the peoples of the Soviet bloc or Second World struggling with varying success to join the old First World in living standards. Almost no one opposes aid to alleviate poverty in the underdeveloped world; however, there is little current enthusiasm for how the World Bank or the International Monetary Fund has been tackling the problem with more loans, which often have not only failed to do much for progress in the underdeveloped countries but also left them with impossibly large sums to repay.

Immigration pressures on the developed world appear to be increasing. They keep the Mexican-American border porous in spite of U.S. efforts to control illegal entry and lead to tragedies such as that of the forty-seven Chinese who in June 2000 suffocated in a sealed truck at the port of Dover, in England. As the Digital Divide widens, people from the old Third World will desperately seek First-World jobs. This kind of pressure cannot be alleviated without making the old Third World considerably more like the First World economically. This means some—probably massive—displacement of local institutions and ways of life and, if past experience holds true, will lead to charges of imperialism, as if out of pure arrogance the new First Worlders wanted to refashion the poorer part of the globe into one that resembled their own. There will probably be increasing environmental concerns here as well. Cutting down rain forests may well continue to appeal to Brazilians as a means of gaining income and as a step toward developing Brazil's economy into one that provides well-paying jobs.

GLOBALIZATION AND NATIONAL INTERESTS

In the twentieth century, many countries, including the United States, saw internal political disagreement over how good an idea it was to strengthen international organizations and encourage global interaction, as opposed to focusing on domestic issues and aspirations. Protagonists of a more global outlook were the "internationalists" of the twentieth century, who were apt to term their opponents "isolationists." The 1990s saw a shift in enthusiasms and fears concerning globalization, and in the early twenty-first century the term centers most of all on international free trade or global capitalism. Large-scale business, which in the nineteenth century and first part of the twentieth century was inclined in most countries to favor tariffs and other restrictions on aspects of trade in which their countries could not compete well, adopted a much more international outlook. From the 1950s to the 1990s, politically conservative groups in the capitalistic countries increasingly favored free trade, whereas groups directed toward labor interests, human rights concerns, and environmental questions favored it less. There are exceptions, of course, but in general it is accurate to say that in the early twenty-first century, the right favors globalization with more fervor than the left.

Part of the reason for this is the growing association of globalization with the expanded role of multinational corporations. Democratic parties of the left had no problem with globalization in the twentieth century as long as it meant more cultural interchange and more authority for international organizations over national ones. However, if globalization today means increasing free trade with multinational corporations as the main players, this implies some restriction or stagnation of the public sphere at the expense of the private one.

Overall, the increasing public interest in economic developments—where private businesses, not governments, are the main players—is leaving government and politics in a less important role than before. Radio and television stations in the early twenty-first century report far more business and general economic news than they did a few decades earlier at the expense of governmental or political news. In doing so, they are appealing to what their publics consider to be important. Even public radio stations in the United States devote what thirty years ago would have seemed to be a disproportionate amount of time to reporting on "the marketplace." Globalization, the relatively good record of capitalism in the public mind in democratic countries, and the decreased interest in government and politics seem at least partly interrelated, with no change in that relationship in sight.

HUMAN RIGHTS

The failure of the United Nations to establish peace through its own interventions does not obscure the fact that the claims of human rights are taken more seriously in the early twenty-first century than before. NGOs and regional organizations are increasingly active and visible today. This raises the issue of national sovereignty and globalization from another perspective: How much sovereignty will nation-states have to give up to comply with the decisions of international bodies? After all, nation-states as we know them did not dominate the world map until the nineteenth century, and not completely until the twentieth century. Although more of them may emerge—a Palestinian one and one or more to establish more stable borders for peoples in the eastern Congo region and their neighbors—they appear to be subject to increasing influence by international, particularly regional, bodies.

As a sign of increased empowerment of women, the twentieth century saw four quite effective women prime ministers in different countries: Israel's Golda Meir, India's Indira Gandhi, Britain's Margaret Thatcher, and Pakistan's Benazir Bhutto, whereas Burma's Aung San Suu Kyi has been a leading and effective voice of the opposition to military dictatorship there for many years. There is enough consensus worldwide on the need to upgrade women's role in society to assure that the general trend toward treating women more as equals to men will continue, although the road in that direction is full of rough spots.

Internationally, the quest for women's rights runs into questions not only of national sovereignty but of different cultures' providing different standards of human rights. Are there really such things as "Asian rights" and "Muslim rights," for example, in which the group takes precedence over the individual, youth defers to age, and women defer to men, or do these attitudes and behaviors represent historical artifacts that might have claimed validity through the nineteenth and twentieth centuries but can no longer be defended in the twenty-first?

The evidence is overwhelming that the acceleration of economic, political, and social change in the twentieth century resulted in greater homogenization and less cultural diversity in the world. Against this background, China's special pleading for "Asian values" when accused of human rights abuses, such as harvesting kidneys and other human organs from prisoners, is a sham. Yet in Africa, the Middle East, East Asia, and other parts of the world, human rights activists are perceived as but another example of Western cultural imperialism. It seems possible that the seductive appeal of Western values, including human rights, will prove so strong that regional or cultural exceptionalism will not last to the twenty-second century. Nonetheless, the inherent tensions between the Western world's economic, political, and social values, including human rights, and the non-Western world's religious and cultural traditions will continue to collide and could well boil over into conflict. Thus, for example, a rich and powerful champion of non-Western values, such as Libya's Mu'ammar al-Gadhafi, could be tempted to order missiles to strike U.S. cities in retaliation for America's trampling of "Muslim values" in the name of human rights.

THE ASIAN CENTURY

While the United States dominated world events in the second half of the twentieth century and remains the sole super-power after the cold war ended, Asia was increasing in world importance as the century closed. Japan, South Korea, and Taiwan developed into stable and prosperous states with economies increasingly important for world trade. China was held back by drastic mismanagement under Mao Tse-tung, but beginning with the leadership of Deng Xiaoping and his system of combining collectivist control with capitalist incentives, China has played an increasingly large role on the global political and economic stage. China has the look of becoming a superpower within a matter of decades. As much as we may say that the cold war is over, it lingers on in Asia with the issue of China and Taiwan, as well as in relations between North and South Korea.

The "One China" policy came to mean something very different from the 1950s through the 1990s. Originally espoused by Chiang Kai-shek and the Kuomintang and endorsed by the United States, it held that the government of the Republic of China (on Taiwan) was the legitimate government of China and anticipated the day when it would return to remove the Communist usurpers from the mainland. Thus Taiwan's Republic of China successfully laid claim to China's seats in the United Nations through the 1960s. Then with the increasing legitimization of mainland China's People's Republic in the Nixon and Carter administrations, ending with the U.S. recognition of Communist China as the real China and relegating Taiwan to a hazy lesser status, "One China" for the mainland Chinese leadership quickly became the policy of treating Taiwan as a rebellious province of China.

Although it is true that far enough back Taiwan was ruled by China, it is equally true that China controlled Taiwan for only four years in the twentieth century: The Japanese took Taiwan in 1895 and held it until the end of World War II. Then from 1945 to 1949, Taiwan was indeed under (Kuomintang-run) China; since 1949 it has functioned as an independent state. There are several scenarios for the China-Taiwan issue in this century, with the extremes ranging from a mainland Chinese military conquest of the island to a discrediting and removal of communism in China along the lines of the upheavals that transformed the Soviet Empire into more agreeable successor states in 1989 and 1990. Taiwan could easily become a model for mainland China, having achieved economic wealth and stability along with a democracy strong enough that it enabled the first change of government in which an opposing faction replaced the previously ruling group as a result of free elections in four thousand years of Chinese history. China is still a country that people escape *from;* Taiwan has been a country people escaped *to* in its half century of independence. This speaks loudly for Taiwan as a model; the problem here is that the leaders of China are not looking for a model that will make them unnecessary. To be sure, the same thing could have been said regarding the Soviet Union in the mid-1980s: Soviet leaders were not looking for a model that would relegate them to irrelevance, but events resulting from *perestroika* overtook them.

The Korean case is altogether different. For starters, in Korea—unlike in the China-Taiwan confrontation—the free and prosperous protagonist is at least equal in power to its poor and totalitarian adversary. Famine and general economic deprivation seem to have reached extremes in North Korea sufficient to prod its leadership into accepting aid from South Korea. The recent meeting of the two heads of state seems promising in terms of diffusing tensions; however, there appear to be limits on how unified the country can become as a result of negotiated settlements alone. North Korean Kim Jong Il must know full well that German unification meant the end of East German leaders as anything more than likely defendants in human rights cases, and he can scarcely welcome a Korean unification that bodes the same sort of outcome. Of course, no one asked head of state and Socialist Unity (Communist) Party General Secretary Erich Honecker if he wanted to step down as leader and be considered for trial as a human rights violator. Events simply overtook him, and they may well do the same in Korea. A more realistic scenario is probably one in which Kim Jong Il attempts to use capitalism either as aid for development or to provide incentives for economic progress along the lines of Deng Xiaoping's program, although whether he could do so in the Korean context without drastically undermining his position and the system itself is doubtful.

Inter-Asian conflicts aside, Asia seems poised to take on a larger role on the world stage soon. The sheer size of Asia's population might not be much of a factor in determining Asian influence by itself; after all, India's very large population has done nothing for Indian influence on the global scene. Instead, it is the combination of large populations, economic development, and stable political systems in Japan, Taiwan, South Korea, and the smaller Pacific Rim states that should indeed make an increasing difference in the global balance of trade, cultural influence, military relations, and diplomatic power.

RELIGION AND TECHNOLOGY

Present-day religion tends to be sparingly dealt with in world history textbooks, but it remains a strong thread in the fabric of civilization. America with its stridently secular culture and fervently free market economy is also one of the most religiously vibrant countries in the world. This seeming contradiction raises the obvious question: Why is this the case? In the world at large, what is the appeal of traditional religion in an age so geared to life's material considerations?

Part of the answer to both questions may lie in the ever-growing bureaucratic and technological control of twenty-first–century life. Religion may serve as an antidote to this phenomenon. So, too, the atomization and sense of isolation that is at the center of twenty-first–century materialism may account for the growth in religious affiliation, especially in those religious traditions that offer believers simple answers—simplistic, of course, for critics—to life's problems in an increasingly complex, technological world.

Since the major world religions include a stress on compassion in their sacred books, their influence on world affairs should be benign, as it is in the case of religiously affiliated NGOs. There is a darker side to religious fervor, however, when it reinforces cultural rivalries, as in the case of the Ayatollah Khomeini's traditionalist Shiites in Iran against the West, or ethnic or national confrontations, as between Palestinians and Jews or between Hindus and Pakistanis. Protestant-Catholic tensions show only marginal signs of abating in Northern Ireland, and the atrocities in the Balkans reflect both intra-Christian hostilities between Catholic Croats and Eastern Orthodox Serbs and the even deeper conflicts between Christian populations and Muslims in Bosnia and Kosovo.

Beyond the effects of the Digital Divide, one sure thing about the twenty-first century is that its technology will make it different. Here the twentieth-century–record is impressive, and the continually accelerating march of technological progress through the past three centuries shows no sign of slowing down. Examples in two fields, communications and medicine, may serve to make this—in contrast with other conjectures about historical trends—an uncontroversial point.

In 1900, hard-rubber, one-sided phonograph records that played for a few minutes sold in the United States for $3.00 to $5.00 each, the weekly salary range for average workers. Think of it: three minutes of low-quality audio for your week's wages! Progress in the industry relegated even the greatly improved, double-sided, long-playing, high-fidelity, inexpensive records of the 1950s and 1960s to the status of historical curiosities as audiotape cassettes replaced both phonograph records and reel-to-reel audiotapes in the 1970s, only to be challenged by longer-lasting CDs with much better sound quality in the 1980s; these in turn have had to compete with new audio products of the computer age. Consumer interest and promising returns for investment in research combine to ensure that new items will fuel the communications revolution well into—perhaps throughout and beyond—the twenty-first century.

The medical picture also seems promising with some surety in the industrial world and at least hope in the developing world. In 1900, diabetes was a terrifying, fatal disease, thought to come "from a fall" and treated with state-of-the-art prescribed mild, and sometimes not so mild, doses of arsenic. In 2000, it is "under control" for most of those who have it. Tuberculosis claimed lives in epidemic proportions in 1900. In 2000, it is rare: The national U.S. organization devoted to combatting it has had to begin fighting other respiratory ailments in order to stay in business, although multi-drug-resistant strains of tuberculosis still present a challenge, particularly in Russia and China, to its complete eradication. Heart disease had no effective treatments in 1900, nor was the relationship of diet to heart problems understood. The discovery of cholesterol and its clogging effect on arteries, along with surgical techniques for heart transplants and coronary-artery by-passes, has added decades to the lives of heart patients, as has research that has developed plastic and metal heart components.

These are only the most obvious improvements in medicine and health care of the past century. They apply foremost to the industrial world, but considerable progress has been made in the developing world as well. Leprosy is still a fact of life in parts of Asia and Africa, but it has been arrested for most victims in most areas. Health problems in underdeveloped areas are often not so much the result of ignorance in medical science as of problems in implementations of programs: The prevention and treatment of malaria has been understood for a long time, but malaria still kills tens of thousands of people annually because political and economic factors keep delivery systems for the medicines from being implemented or sustained. Diarrhea kills countless thousands of African children every year, not because medical science fails to understand cause and effect concerning it, but because the educational effort necessary for its control has been sporadic.

The medical challenge for the twenty-first century will be to see the technology of the Western world implemented by developing countries while pursuing cures in research centers for the still-rampant plagues, particularly AIDS, and other killers and debilitators, notably cancer and spinal-cord injuries. It is estimated that more than 20 million people will have died of AIDS between 1980 and 2005, a number that is beginning to approach world-war–level casualty statistics. In several African countries, HIV-infected people exceed 10 percent of the population. The twentieth century was the first to make any headway against cancer, but even with success stories from early detection and combinations of radiation, surgery, and chemotherapy, much remains to be done. At the moment there is some faint hope—no more than that—for developing remedial, perhaps regeneration-inducing treatments for spinal-cord injuries.

Some technological problems seem to be beyond the mind of humans to solve. In the days of Moses, ax heads would sometimes fly off their handles, occasionally killing someone. In 2000, ax heads are still flying off their handles, even those of molded fiberglass. Persistent technology does, of course, have a proud record of coping with problems of the physical world, and, who knows, the year 2080 or so may even see that nut cracked with an affordable, all-metal but light-weight, one-piece ax.

Such problems as are posed by the ax head and handle are, fortunately, rare. The outlook is for technology to rise to the occasion most of the time in improving humankind's material standard of living, but this is only a part of the unfolding scenario for life in the twenty-first century. Whether the "Age of Social-Doctrine Conflict" can give rise to an age in which ethnic toleration and human rights come into their own and in which "developing countries" really do develop the capacity for improving their peoples' standards of living is still a very open question.

Questions:
1. *Assuming that present trends will continue can lead to bad predictions, such as one made in 1899— on the basis of the nineteenth-century trend in U.S.–Latin American relations—that by 1999 or 2000 what was then Buenos Aires would be called "McKinleyville." What present trends in global relations do you think will continue? Which are much less certain?*
2. *Are there problems with reasoning that (a) since the USSR freed itself from communism with relatively little violence, China can be expected to do the same thing, or (b) since East and West Germany were united quickly and peacefully after forty-five years of separation, the same should be possible soon for North and South Korea? Are these analogies valid?*